For Reference

Not to be taken from this room

THE NEW HISTORY
OF LITERATURE

ENGLISH POETRY
AND PROSE
1540–1674

THE NEW HISTORY
OF LITERATURE

1. THE MIDDLE AGES Edited by W. F. Bolton
2. ENGLISH POETRY AND PROSE, 1540–1674 Edited by Christopher Ricks
3. ENGLISH DRAMA TO 1710 Edited by Christopher Ricks
4. DRYDEN TO JOHNSON Edited by Roger Lonsdale
5. LITERATURE OF THE ROMANTIC PERIOD Edited by David B. Pirie
6. THE VICTORIANS Edited by Arthur Pollard
7. THE TWENTIETH CENTURY Edited by Martin Dodsworth
8. AMERICAN LITERATURE TO 1900 Edited by Marcus Cunliffe
9. AMERICAN LITERATURE SINCE 1900 Edited by Marcus Cunliffe
10. THE ENGLISH LANGUAGE Edited by W. F. Bolton

Volumes 3, 6, 9, and 10 will be published in 1987,
and volumes 5 and 7 in 1988.

ENGLISH POETRY AND PROSE 1540–1674

·

EDITED BY

CHRISTOPHER RICKS

Peter Bedrick Books
New York

First American edition published in 1987 by
Peter Bedrick Books
125 East 23 Street
New York, NY 10010

Library of Congress Cataloging-in-Publication Data

English poetry and prose, 1540–1674.
   (The New history of literature)
   Bibliography: p.
   Includes index.
   1. English poetry—Early modern, 1500–1700—History
and criticism.   2. English prose literature—Early
modern, 1500–1700—History and criticism.   I. Ricks,
Christopher B.   II. Series.
PR533.E5   1986   820'.9'003   86–14031
ISBN 0–87226–126–3

Printed in Great Britain

10 9 8 7 6 5 4 3 2 1

CONTENTS

INTRODUCTION

Literature is the texts. Literary history is the contexts. The essays commissioned to form Volume 2 of the *Sphere History of Literature* are intended to give a modern reader a sense of the many contexts within which literature exists. Without an understanding of context it is too easy to misunderstand or misjudge a work of sixteenth- or seventeenth-century poetry or prose. *Context*, rather than *background*, because the word context is more likely to remind us that we cannot so easily hive off the pure work of art itself from the circumstances and expectations within which it was created and which may often be truly said to form part of its meaning.

There is no rule which will tell in advance which of the various possible contexts is going to prove the most illuminating for any particular writer or work. The contributors to this volume have been free to select their own emphases. Sometimes the essential context has been seen to be that of the writer's life and times: Millar MacLure's essay on Spenser chooses this as the particular kind of knowledge and insight which the modern reader most needs. Sometimes the context is that of a literary kind or genre, as with Elizabeth Story Donno's study of the epyllion or minor epic, of which the best-known examples are Marlowe's *Hero and Leander* and Shakespeare's *Venus and Adonis*.

Sometimes the crucial context is the concurrence of a particular period and a particular circle of poets, and it is this concurrence which Maren-Sofie Røstvig investigates in the work of Andrew Marvell and the Caroline poets. A pervasive and flexible genre, the lyric, is here traced historically and critically by Alicia Ostriker; Leslie Dunn adduces the sister art, music, which provides part of the necessary context. J.C.A. Rathmell, on 'Ben Jonson and the Court', brings into focus the world of public praise and admonition. Or there are those genres which were transformed by a particular genius. Shakespeare transformed the sonnet sequence, and it is the critical argument about the nature of the sonnet sequence with which Thomas P. Roche's essay particularly concerns itself. Robert Ellrodt, in his study of George Herbert and the religious lyric, brings out the particular nature of Herbert's achievement by comparing it with the achievement of Crashaw, of Vaughan, and of Traherne.

T.S. Eliot pointed out that comparison and analysis are the tools of the critic. Both have to be used if we are to understand the living importance of 'translation' or 'imitation' in centuries when the word *novelty* was still hostile. So Patricia Thomson, in her essay on Wyatt and Surrey, shows how important it is to enter into the literary context of the Italian poems which the best Tudor poems made new and true for English literature. And Rachel Trickett, in her discussion of Restoration satire, leads us to the brink of another great age of 'imitation': the Augustan age.

With some writers, the essential context may be the other texts, the bringing to bear of the whole of an *oeuvre* upon successive parts of it. This is as true of an important minor writer like Sir Philip Sidney (here assessed by David Kalstone) as it is of the geniuses of the period: John Donne, whose *oeuvre* is illuminatingly synthesized by A.J. Smith, and John Milton. The relationship of *Paradise Lost* to the epic form, to ideas of the hero, and to Milton's own beliefs, is here explored by John M. Steadman. The editor of this volume examines, first, Milton's *Poems* (1645) in the context of their literary kinds (what exactly is a pastoral elegy or a masque engaged in doing?); and, next, *Paradise Regained* and *Samson Agonistes* within the context of ancient and essential critical arguments about style and structure. Finally, John Carey surveys – with sympathetic detail and yet with energy of judgement – the world of sixteenth- and seventeenth-century prose. It is a world which contains worlds. It stretches from Sir Thomas More and William Tyndale, through Thomas Nashe and John Donne, to Robert Burton, Sir Thomas Browne, John Milton, and John Dryden. Here too the aim of the critic–historian has been to provide a sense of the contexts within which a modern reader will be enabled to judge for himself, whether the relevant context is that of religious controversy, Biblical translation, Elizabethan prose-fiction, or political polemic.

One of the obvious advantages of a multiplicity of vantage-points is that more aspects of any particular work can be seen. So Andrew Marvell's satires are discussed primarily in the context of his other work by Miss Røstvig, and primarily in the context of Restoration satire by Miss Trickett. So Sidney's *Arcadia* is seen by Mr Kalstone primarily within the contexts of Sidney's works and of the heroic pastoral, whereas the *Arcadia* is seen by Mr Carey primarily within the context of Elizabethan prose. Another advantage of the multiplicity is that important critical disagreements are neither shirked nor factitiously ('stimulatingly') invented. Mr Carey thinks much less highly of the *Arcadia* than does Mr Kalstone, and we can understand why, not just from their frames of mind but from their frames of argument. The *Sphere History* is not committed to any single doctrine, though it prefers some doctrines to others because there is more to be said for them. It is committed to the belief that one of the critic–historian's duties may simply be to be informative, and that a literary history should therefore not be too afraid of deploying a good many out-of-the-way matters of fact if in any particular case such facts will help to make past literature accessible to a modern reader. Mrs Donno's essay on the epyllion is, for this reason, more manifestly factual than Mrs Ostriker's essay on the lyric – and this itself tells us something about the difference between the epyllion and the lyric. But a successful literary history will not *inform* its readers only in the sense of telling them things, but also in the sense 'to inspire or imbue somebody with feelings, principles, qualities'.

At the end is a table of dates, which will help to integrate one essay with another by presenting an outline of the main historical and literary-historical developments. Following the final essay is a series of bibliographies, listing the major editions and critical works. Editions from which quotations are made have been asterisked. When there is no standard edition, quotations are from the original editions unmodernized. But i/j and u/v, and than/then, are differentiated throughout according to modern practice.

A single volume on the present scale could not have coped with English drama as well as with the poetry and prose of the sixteenth and seventeenth centuries. Volume 3 of the *Sphere History* therefore deals with *English Drama to 1710.* The poems and prose of John Dryden form part of Volume 4 of the *Sphere History*, devoted to Augustan and eighteenth-century literature.

CR

1

WYATT AND SURREY

Patricia Thomson

The history of English poetry during the last two decades of Henry VIII's reign has as much to do with the past as with the future. In succession to John Skelton (1460–1529), that learned and humorous court retainer of the old school, arrive the 'new ... courtly makers', Sir Thomas Wyatt (1503–42), a gentleman and diplomatist, and Henry Howard, Earl of Surrey (1517–47), an aristocrat and soldier. But old is not to be distinguished from new in the comparison of Skelton's

> Twene hope and drede
> My lyfe I lede,
> But of my spede
>   Small sekernes;
> Howe be it I rede
> Both worde and dede
> Should be agrede
> In noblenes
> (*Garlande . . . of Laurell*, 1523, lines 1594–1601)

with Wyatt's

> At moost myschief
> I suffre greif
> For of relief
>   Syns I have none
> My lute and I
> Continuelly
> Shall us apply
>   To sigh and mone.
> (*Collected Poems*, ed. Muir and Thomson, no 51)

Both are complaints in the late medieval plain style, identical in form, in tone delicate, gracious and song-like, suited to the sophisticated, poetical, and musical circle of a king who even, and not without some reason, fancied himself as troubadour or minstrel.

Even Skelton's weightier lyrics are not without their counterparts in the work of his much younger contemporaries.

> Go, pytyous hart, rasyd with dedly wo,
>   Persyd with payn, bleding with wondes smart,
> Bewayle thy fortune, with vayvys wan and blo.
>   O Fortune unfrendly, Fortune unkynde thow art,
>   To be so cruell and so overthwart,
> To suffer me so carefull to endure,
> That wher I love best I dare not dyscure!

The rhyme royal stanza used by Skelton here, itself a legacy from Chaucer, is equally a favourite with Wyatt, who uses it in his fine sea-going address to Venus (no 78), as well as in the better known 'They fle from me' (no 37). The agonized intonation of the lover's lament is even better captured in Wyatt's 'O pitifull hert, with payn enlarged.' (no 5), and the urgency in his 'Goo burnyng sighes vnto the frosen hert.' (no 20). He, too, writes constantly of the heart 'That suffereth smert' (no 86), and of 'fortune overthwart' (no 52), while Surrey follows suit with an account of how 'love . . . shoteth eke, a hardy hart to wound' (*Poems*, ed. Jones, no 21), weeps and wails at 'fortunes wrath' (no 20), and, like Skelton, suffers the more because he has to bottle up his 'smart' in 'secret brest' (no 18). The shared lyric heritage, traditional ways of thinking about, and idioms for dealing with, such major topics as love and fortune, in addition to the common scene and setting of the court, account for much that these poets of different generations and different temperaments have in common.

On the other hand lyrics in the medieval aureate manner, the last and loftiest of their kind—

> O radiant Luminary of lyght intermynable,
> Celestial Father, potenciall God of myght—

have no counterparts in the work of Wyatt and Surrey, who, in strong contrast, uniformly cultivate an extreme verbal simplicity. This simplicity reaches its limits in certain monosyllabic passages which, according to context, will appear stark or sharp, colloquial or elegant, and which give substance to the claim that a major achievement of these younger poets lies in the carrying forward of all that was best in the medieval plain manner:

> It may be good, like it who list,
>   But I do dowbt: who can me blame?
> For oft assured yet have I myst,
>   And now again I fere the same.

(Wyatt, no 21)

> I fynde no peace and all my warr is done;
> I fere and hope, I burne and freise like yse.

(Wyatt, no 26)

> And last it may not long,
> The truest thing of all,
> And sure the greatest wrong
> That is within this thrall.

(Surrey, no 19)

> Such as I was such will I be,
> Your owne: what would ye more of me?

(Surrey, no 20)

A further part of this achievement consists in the muting of rhetorical extravagance and excess of the kind found, for example, in Skelton's early elegies:

> I wayle, I wepe, I sobbe, I sigh ful sore
> The dedely fate, the dolefulle destenny
> O hym that is gone, alas, without restore.
> . . . .
>
> O cruell Mars, thou dedly god of war!
> O dolorous Teusday, dedicate to thi name!
> . . . .
>
> O Atropos, of the fatall systers three!
> (*Upon the . . Dethe . . . of the . . . Erle of Northumberlande*,
> d. 1489, lines 1–3, 113–4, 120)

Contrast the absence of breast-beating, lugubrious adjectives, and apostrophes to supernatural powers, and, in consequence, the more subdued expression of grief, appropriate to the more private nature, of Wyatt's lament for Cromwell in 1540—

> The piller pearisht is whearto I Lent,
> The strongest staye of myne vnquyet mynde;
> The lyke of it no man agayne can fynde,
> From East to west, still seking though he went.
> To myne unhappe for happe away hath rent
> Of all my joye the vearye bark and rynde;

(no 236)

and of Surrey's for Wyatt in 1542:

> Dyvers thy death doo dyverslye bemone.
> Some that in presence of that livelye hedd
> Lurked, whose brestes envye with hate had sowne,
> Yeld Cesars teres uppon Pompeius hedd.
> . . . .

But I that knowe what harbourd in that hedd,
What vertues rare were tempred in that brest,
Honour the place that such a jewell bredd.

(no 29)

Only, however, when Skelton's work as a whole is compared with that of Wyatt and Surrey do those differences emerge that make it appropriate, as well as convenient, for the literary historian to distinguish old from new. It is not merely that Wyatt and Surrey, the former particularly, have left a far larger body of lyrics, in a far richer variety of forms, and of far greater versatility, than has Skelton, though that fact has importance. But they belong to the avant garde of the early Tudor period in a sense in which he does not. He clings to certain time-honoured forms, which they do not attempt, writing the best dream allegory, *The Bowge of Courte*, and the best morality play, *Magnyfycence*, of his time. The lively and original satires for which he is chiefly remembered are totally unlike Wyatt's. For though, in one place, he claims Juvenal as master, they are, in fact, closer to the medieval flyting than to the classical epistolary satire as imitated by Wyatt. A formidable classical scholar, he was at least as well versed in foreign literatures as were Wyatt and Surrey. Yet he did not look outside England for his literary models. Amongst the authors whose names drop so easily from his pen in *Garlande . . . of Laurell* are 'Plutarke and Petrarke, two famous clarkis'. But it is Wyatt who first reproduces in English prose a moral essay, *Quyete of Mynde*, by Plutarch, and in English verse the love sonnets of Petrarch. 'Virgill the Mantuan, with his Eneidos' is surveyed by Skelton in his turn. But Skelton leaves it to Surrey to imitate this literary model in the blank verse and epic manner of his translation of Books II and IV of the *Aeneid*. Similarly the other new forms imported by Wyatt, the French rondeau, the Italian strambotto and terza rima, pass him by. Quite what he would have thought of them remains unknown, though *Speke, Parrot* arouses the suspicion that he might have jeered at such new-fangled and foreign experiments. Though medieval poets do not eschew translation, their successors of the Renaissance attempt to copy the form as well as the substance of their originals. Imitation of classical and modern European forms becomes a valid creative activity. Wyatt and Surrey, unlike the author of *Speke, Parrot*, are to this extent touched by the spirit of the new Humanism.

To their immediate successors the difference appeared even sharper than it does to us, for it struck them in terms not only of relative modernity but of relative quality. 'Such', remarks George

Puttenham as he scornfully dismisses the jingles of 'common rimers', 'were the rimes of *Skelton*, usurping the name of Poet Laureat, being in deede but rude rayling rimer & in all his doings ridiculous' (*The Arte of English Poesie*, 1589). Very different are the reverential tones with which he brings in Wyatt and Surrey, 'the first reformers of our vulgar Poesie', 'the two chief lanternes of light to all others that have since employed their pennes upon English Poesie'. In his reading of literary history, these 'new . . . courtly makers' (for the familiar caption is his) were prompted by the 'sweete and stately measures and stile of the Italian Poesie' to polish 'our rude & homely maner of vulgar Poesie from that it had bene before'. Their first editor, Richard Tottel, had taken them as proof that English poets could do as well as the 'Latines, Italians and other' (Preface to *Songes and Sonettes*, 1557). Now the Elizabethans acknowledge them as pioneers in a Renaissance which was largely, though by no means exclusively, Latinate and Italianate. They bring English poetry into the European common market. Puttenham is not, of course, describing a revolution, but an evolution, or, rather, a reform by which the vernacular ('vulgar') English manner is refined, polished and improved. He commends Wyatt and Surrey as Dryden is to commend Waller and Denham, as the pioneers of a civilized, modern style.

To Wyatt, Surrey's senior by fourteen years, must go most of the credit for pioneering Italian Petrarchanism in England. Sweetness and stateliness are not uniformly apparent. In Wyatt's translation of Petrarch's canzone 'Quell' antiquo mio dolce empio signore', for example, the evident struggle to do justice to sound and sense simultaneously often produces failure in both. Thus the lucid and delicate

> Onde, s' i' non son giunto
> Anzi tempo da morte acerba e dura,
> Pietà celeste ha cura
> Di mia salute, non questo tiranno,

is rendered in garbled, obscure, unmusical phrases:

> That, as yet, it [i.e., death] hathe me not overtake;
> The hevynly goodenes of pitie do it slake
> And not this his [i.e., love's] cruell extreme tyranny.
>
> (no 8, lines 53–5)

With some help from Petrarch, the meaning emerges as 'If death has not yet overtaken me, it is because heavenly goodness out of pity prevents it, and not because the tyranny of love has abated'. But

there is no means of wringing rhythmic sense out of the first line:
the inversion of 'me' and 'overtake' is awkward, made simply for the
sake of the rhyme, and the number of stresses is an uncertain four
or five, falling indeterminately but apparently usually on unimportant words. Contrast the second line of the following translation
which avoids by a hair's breadth failure of the same kind:

> Amor, fortuna e la mia mente schiva
> Di quel che vede e nel passato volta.
>
> Love and fortune and my mynde, remembre
> Of that that is nowe, with that that hath ben.
>
> (no 31)

The strong central pause, the double epizeuxis ('that that' . . . 'that
that'), the favourite slogging monosyllables, are so arranged as to
enforce strongly the bleak antithesis between past and present.
Wyatt has capitalized words which could be unimportant, but are
not; and he has avoided clumsy inversion. It is evident, here, that he
is assimilating the substance of the Italian to his own plain English
manner. Elsewhere, however, he responds to fine phrases, if not,
with Keats, 'like a lover', yet with a due sense of the magnificence of
the Italian. Thus the first line of Sannazaro's sonnet 'Simile a questi
smisurati monti' achieves an equivalent splendour in Wyatt's 'Like
to these unmesurable montayns' (no 33), so that the reasons why
Puttenham spoke of a 'stately' Italian style become clearer.
Sweetness, a very common general term of approbation in the
sixteenth century, is less easily identified in Wyatt's versions of
Italian lyrics. But it would seem appropriate to the lightness and
brightness of his translation of Dragonetto Bonifacio's madrigal:

> Madonna non so dir tante parole;
> O voi volet' o no . . .
>
> Madame, withouten many wordes
> Ons I ame sure ye will or no.
>
> (no 34)

A final example of a translation from yet another Italian Petrarchan
will show that Wyatt takes considerable pains over his phrasing,
achieving in consequence both concentration of meaning and
vigour of rhythm. 'Se una bombarda è dal gran foco mossa', the
opening of a strambotto by Serafino, he firsts renders 'Like as the
canon in his rajing yre' (no 61). Then, with 'Like as the bombard',
he attempts to approximate more closely to the original (though
without deserting the English language, 'bombard' being our word

for the earliest type of cannon). Finally, he perfects the line as 'The furyous gonne in his rajing yre', at once getting rid of the colourless 'Like as', and, by the addition of 'furyous', giving appropriate force to the image of a gun in the moment of firing. In spite of some failures, there is, therefore, a creative spirit at work in these translations.

The same is true of Wyatt's attempts to render form, as distinct from phrase and rhythm. The effort to fit Sannazaro's sense exactly into the fourteen lines of the sonnet 'Like to these unmesurable montayns' proves, in the end, too much for him. The final comparison of birds' song to lover's lamentation forces him into a tautology ('tune and note'), before he collapses into inanity in the last half-line:

> Off the restles birdes they have the tune and note,
> And I alwayes plaintes that passe thorough my throte.
>
> (no 33)

That the effort was worth while is, however, shown in several attacks on the master sonneteer, Petrarch. 'The longe love, that in my thought doeth harbar' (no 4) and 'My galy charged with forgetfulnes' (no 28) are, like their originals, extremely concentrated. In the first Love emerges boldly to do battle in the lover's face, is morally defeated by his chaste and noble lady, and hence takes refuge, languishing, in the heart. In the second the lover suffers as a ship in a stormy sea, with rocks, wind, rain, clouds, etc., representing various aspects of his experience, until at last he is left 'dispering of the port'. The metaphors have had to be developed *pari passu* with the stories, experiences and ideas they embody, and the whole brought round to a conclusion. An alternative Petrarchan structure, illustrated in 'Caesar, when that the traytor of Egipt' (no 3), develops the relevant images or comparisons in the octave, leaving the sestet to apply the emergent ideas to the poet's own experience. All this calls for a structural tightness and control, a sense of direction, not found in many of the lyrics of purely English provenance, or in the rondeau, 'Yf it be so' (no 18), translated from the French. A comparable discipline is, however, imposed by the eight-line strambotto: Serafino's feelings run a course strictly parallel with that of his 'bombarda'.

With Wyatt's satires and Penitential Psalms, we come to poems which, unlike most of his lyrics, can be dated with fair precision, the former being composed some time after the publication of Alamanni's *Opere Toscane* in 1532, and the latter after the publication of Aretino's *Sette Salmi* in 1534. They are, in fact, mature works, belonging to the last decade of his life. They introduce into English a new Italian 'measure', the difficult terza rima, in which his master was the contemporary Florentine patriot Luigi Alamanni, whose satiric attack on the courts of sixteenth-century Europe is the source of 'Myne owne John Poynz'. This poem, for there is reason to suppose it the first of the satires, also launches a new satiric form in English. Wyatt's address to his friend Poins, following Alamanni's to Sertini, is in the classical epistolary form, as used originally by Horace, Juvenal and Persius. It is a confidential discourse, presenting the point of view of an individual, and expressive of his personality. Wyatt authenticates his self-portrait by boldly adapting Alamanni's references to his home life in Provence to his own in Kent. And with equal boldness he imitates Alamanni's exclusive and aristocratic tone, asserting, at the outset, that unlike 'the common sort' who judge by 'owtward thinges', he has regard to 'what dothe inwarde resort'. His regard for the truth, irrespective of appearances or conventional judgements, gives him authority, commanding respect for his moral indignation. Mounting steadily to controlled anger, this indignation is made emotionally convincing by the repetition, tercet by tercet, of 'I cannot' (rendering Alamanni's 'Non saprei' series):

> I cannot honour them that settes their part
> > With Venus and Baccus all theire lyf long,
> > Nor holld my pece of them allthoo I smart.
> I cannot crowche nor knelle to do so grete a wrong
> > To worship them, lyke God on erthe alone,
> > That ar as wollffes thes sely lambes among.
> I cannot with my wordes complayne and mone,
> > And suffer nought; nor smart wythout complaynt,
> > Nor torne the worde that from my mouthe is gone.
> . . . .
> I cannot, I; no, no, it will not be.
>
> > (no 105, lines 22–30, 76)

This tirade is more shapely than Skelton's, its emotion more disciplined, its expression more dignified. A contrast with one of Wyatt's Elizabethan successors also brings out its special virtues. John Marston honours him by a borrowing, but beyond the first line of one of his satires the resemblance ceases:

> I cannot hold, I cannot I indure
> To view a big womb'd foggie clowde immure
> The radiant tresses of the quickning sunne.
> Let Custards quake, my rage must freely runne.
> . . . .

My soule is vext, what power will'th desist?
Or dares to stop a sharpe fangd Satyrist?
Who'le coole my rage? who'le stay my itching fist
But I will plague and torture whom I list?

(The Scourge of Villanie, 1598, ii. 1–4, 7–10)

This is an effective realization of temper in disorder, but the cause of truth is damaged by the ridiculous excesses of Marston's language. Jonson, not without justice, makes mock of Marston. Tottel wins our assent when he calls Wyatt 'depewitted'.

Wyatt's Penitential Psalms, the first published of his poems, and, in the sixteenth century, amongst the most admired, do more even than the satires to correct the false impression that 'courtly' skills and tastes were exclusively light, lyrical and amorous. If, asks Surrey, Alexander enclosed his copy of Homer in a 'rich arke'.

> What holly grave, what wourthy sepulture
> To Wyates Psalmes shulde Christians then purchase?
> Wher he dothe paynte the lyvely faythe and pure,
> The stedfast hope, the swete returne to grace
> Of just Davyd by parfite penytence.

(no 31)

But while we join in his applause for these translations, we are also entitled to ask whether they are as remarkable as poetry as they are as evidence of piety. The Psalms provide a fair test: Sidney, a later translator, hails David as a poet. Does any of the poetry come through in Wyatt's rendering of his 'parfite penytence'? Why, first, does he choose, in addition to the Latin Vulgate Bible, a source apparently so unpromising as Pietro Aretino's long-winded, repetitious, and flowery prose paraphrase of the Penitential Psalms? All his prologues, even including the very free seventh one, are based on Aretino's, so that part of the answer is evidently that he likes the narrative framework they provide. His starting point and context are Aretino's: David's love for Uriah's wife Bathsheba, the warnings of the prophet Nathan, the consequent repentance, as told in II *Samuel*, xi-xii. The prologues depict David's solitary sojourn in the cave to which he withdraws, with his harp, to enact and sing this repentance before God alone. They bring constant reminders of his situation and state of mind, linking the seven penitential songs, dispersed in the psalter itself, in a single and continuous story. 'The swete returne to grace' is steady. By the second prologue 'Semyth horrible no more the dark Cave' (no 108, line 201), an appropriate preparation for the version of *Beati quorum remisse sunt*, 'Oh happy ar they that have forgiffnes gott' (no 108, line 217). Then, with the third prologue, a sunbeam 'Percyth the cave and on the harpe discendes' (no 108, line 311). David's eyes are dazzled, and he himself (in a curious anticipation of Wordsworth) is 'Surprised with joye, by penance off the hert' (line 16). At this point his love for God becomes more ardent than his love for Bathsheba has ever been, and he throws himself into the *Domine ne in furore tuo arguas me*, a plea as urgent, if uttered with more 'sobre voyce', as any Wyatt addressed to stony-hearted lady. Thereafter hope of forgiveness mounts, until in the seventh prologue David, at last assured of redemption, is rapt beyond this world, in a state of perfect grace:

> This word redeme, that in his mowght did sownd,
>   Did put David, it semyth unto me,
> As in a traunce to starre apon the grownd,
>   And with his thowght the heyght of hevin to se.
>   (no 108, lines 695–8)

The inwardness characteristic of this story of man's relationship with God is also reflected in the paraphrases of the Psalms themselves; and Wyatt, by skilful handling of Aretino, is frequently able to give it greater intensity. Compare, for example, the following versions of the verse *Domine ante te omne desyderium meum: et gemitus meus a te non est absconditus:*

Signore dinanzi a te, che ne le piu folte tenebre vedi ciò che ad altrui è impossibile di vedere, & ne profondi de i cori trapassa l'occhio tuo quasi sole in christallo, si è translato ogni mio desiderio, il qual per non havere altra voce che quella del pianto non puo esprimere in servigio de le mie colpe tutto quello che doveria, et che io vorria.
>   (The third Penitential Psalm, Psalm 38, vs 9)

> O Lord, thow knowst the inward contemplation
>   Off my desire; thow knowst my sighes and plaines;
>   Thow knowst the teres of my lamentation
> Can not expresse my hertes inward restraintes.
>   (no 108, lines 358–61)

On the Vulgate's statement, the revelation of David's feelings to God, Aretino builds his description of the heart's depths, seen by God's eye alone, piercing thick shadows as sun pierces crystal; and he then adds an observation to the effect that weeping is his only, though an inadequate, expression of the grief of sin. The gist of this is given by Wyatt, particularly in the stressed *inward* contemplation and *inward* restraints. But he is briefer. Consistent with his omission of all Aretino's visual imagery is his transmutation of

'vedi . . . vedere' into the triple 'knowst'. The forceful effect is
further enhanced by the succession of simple statements which
replace Aretino's smooth periodic sentence.

Repeated words, ideas, and sentence structures again charac-
terize the opening of his version of the well-loved sixth Penitential
Psalm, *De profundis clamavi ad te domine.* The cue is again given by
Aretino who, catching up the Vulgate's *profundis*, reiterates its
Italian equivalent in his descriptions both of the depths of David's
heart and sin and of the depths of the cave in which he dwells.
Wyatt distils the essence in a single tercet:

> Ffrom depth off sinn and from a diepe dispaire,
>> Ffrom depth off deth, from depth off hertes sorow,
>> From this diepe Cave off darknes diepe repayre,
> [The have I cald, o lord, to be my borow.]
>
> (no 108, lines 664–7)

The intention to sustain the 'of' structure and to emphasize 'diepe'
is thrown into relief by his correction of 'where darknes repayre' to
'off darknes diepe repayre'. And, in general, his poetic purpose is
particularly clear in this psalm. Though its prologue brings the
usual reminder that David is singing, lyricism is by no means a
motive as dominant as it is to be in the translation done by Sidney's
sister, the Countess of Pembroke:

> From depth of grief
>> Where droun'd I ly,
> Lord for relief
>> To thee I cry.

The writer of love songs could undoubtedly have constructed a
quatrain as elegant as this. But even apart from the fact that Wyatt is
committed to terza rima, he hardly conceives of his task in such
terms. His poetry is rather the vehicle for the expression of David's
personal struggle, acted out in the cave in a continuous crisis. It is
more dramatic than lyrical, more like a monologue by Browning,
especially in its vigour and occasional roughness, than a poem from
a Tudor song book.

Convenient as it may be to separate Wyatt's free compositions in
English forms from the Italianate imitations discussed above, the
same voice is frequently, in fact, heard in them. Though he often
writes conventionally (for example, of the lover's grievances) and in
a style hardly distinguishable from his predecessors', he definitely
emerges as the first English lyrist with a distinctive personality and
distinctive mannerisms. He is interested in 'inward' things: the

word occurs not only in the Psalms but in the comparatively light 'Alas the greiff' (no 5) and 'To wisshe and want' (no 58). 'What rage is this?', a carefully revised lyric, communicates as much intensity of feeling as the first satire or sixth Psalm, and does so by the same rhetorical means, the repeated word and structure:

> What rage is this? what furour of what kynd?
> What powre, what plage, doth wery thus my mynd?
> Within my bons to rancle is assind
>   What poyson, plesant swete?
>
> (no 101)

As his handling of Aretino suggests, Wyatt is not a highly visual poet. At least external appearances do not detain him long. His metaphors are serviceable:

> Me thought I swam and could not drowne.
>
> (no 53)

> In fortunes forge my Joye was wrought.
>
> (no 62)

On the other hand his sound effects are truly memorable, and not only for their sound but for their sense and emotional tone. Perturbation of mind is present in the intelligent quibbling on the meanings of 'file' (polish and deceive) in

> There was never ffile half so well filed,
>   To file a file for every smythes intent,
>   As I was made a filing instrument
> To frame othre, while I was begiled.
>
> (no 16)

Tension striving for release, the agitation of hope, renewed after three stanzas of lowering depression, is signified in the witty juggling with the word 'chaunce' in

> But yet perchaunce som chaunce
>   May chaunce to chaunge my tune;
> And when suche chaunce doeth chaunce,
>   Then shall I thanck fortune;
> And if I have suche chaunce,
>   Perchaunce ere it be long,
> For such a pleasaunt chaunce
>   To syng som plaisaunt song.
>
> (no 52)

Above all, Wyatt's refrains, more musical and more meaningful than any before Sidney, set him apart from predecessors, contemporaries, and immediate successors. Not for him the senseless or merely emotive 'hey nonny nonny' of Shakespeare or Dekker. Emotive the refrains 'In eternum' (no 71), 'I have done' (no 66), 'What may it availl me?' (no 58), and 'Spite of thy hap hap hath well hapt' (no 23) certainly are. In addition, they carry the main burden of Wyatt's meaning in the poems in which they occur, being also skilfully linked to the grammar of each successive stanza. This is, of course, only part of the evidence that shows his reputation to be founded not only in his gift for innovation, but in his poetic skills.

A similar combination of the innovative and the skilful makes Surrey too a poet both historically important and aesthetically pleasing. Circumstances have indeed combined to make comparisons between the two 'new . . . courtly makers' inevitable. And though Puttenham found 'very little difference' between them, critics from the eighteenth century on have tended to discriminate. In the first place, Wyatt's precedence as the elder, a fact simply not recognized by Puttenham, has earned him due credit for having been the first to Italianize English poetry, while Surrey's comparable contribution, which is to English classicism, has been properly acknowledged. Opinion as to their relative aesthetic value has, meanwhile, oscillated. In the eighteenth and nineteenth centuries Surrey's star outshone Wyatt's by virtue of his clearer sentences, more powerful visual imagination, and, above all, smoother and steadier rhythm. In the twentieth century Wyatt's greater intensity, inwardness and wit have won him admirers at Surrey's expense. From the sixteenth century's point of view the depreciation of one in contrast to the other would seem an absurdity. Wyatt and Surrey were (the latter claims) friends, not rivals. And even if some friendly literary rivalry between them be entertained as a possibility, Surrey's generous acknowledgement of Wyatt's 'heavenly giftes' would destroy any real sense of competition.

To Surrey, Wyatt's was 'A hand that taught what might be sayd in ryme' (no 28). His own willingness to learn, and even, with his period's characteristic lack of ceremony, to borrow, is shown more than once. Away from home on service in Boulogne (1545–6)

> Where I am now, as restlesse to remayn,
> Against my will, full pleased with my payn,
>
> (no 10)

he recalls Wyatt's mood when ambassador to the Imperial court (1537–9):

So hangith in balaunce
Off war, my pees, reward of all my payne;
At Mountzon thus I restles rest in Spayne.

(no 81)

Some of the resemblances between them are, of course, generic.
'Smart', 'pain', 'harm', 'wrong', 'rue', 'disdain', 'service', 'freedom',
'thraldom': the idiom of Surrey's love poetry is the same as Wyatt's
because both are traditional. Surrey's plain manner, already
touched on, may or may not have been influenced by Wyatt's. Nor is
it known whether or not his admiration for his friend's Penitential
Psalms accounts for his own translations from other of the *Psalms*
and from *Ecclesiastes*. On the other hand, Wyatt's example almost
certainly did inspire Surrey's few translations from Petrarch, as well
as his attempts at the new forms of sonnet and strambotto. And if,
on this Italianate ground, he is less obviously the experimenter, yet
his creation of the English sonnet form has at least as much to offer
to the future: of the Elizabethans, Sidney favours Wyatt's
Petrarchan form, while Daniel and Shakespeare invariably use
Surrey's easier English one.

Norfolk sprang thee, Lambeth holds thee dead,
Clere of the County of Cleremont though hight;
Within the wombe of Ormondes race thou bread,
And sawest thy cosine crowned in thy sight.
Shelton for love, Surrey for Lord thou chase:
Ay me, while life did last that league was tender;
Tracing whose steps thou sawest Kelsall blaze,
Laundersey burnt, and battered Bullen render.
At Muttrell gates, hopeless of all recure,
Thine Earle halfe dead gave in thy hand his Will;
Which cause did thee this pining death procure,
Ere Sommers four times seaven thou couldest fulfill.
    Ah Clere, if love had booted, care, or cost,
    Heaven had not wonn, nor Earth so timely lost.

(no 35)

The introduction of additional rhymes in the English sonnet
certainly eases matters: in Surrey's octave, for example, abab, cdcd
replaces Wyatt's usual abba, abba. But, rhyme scheme apart,
Surrey's 'easiness' is somewhat deceptive. His epitaph appears, at
first reading, merely a leisurely list of facts about his squire Thomas
Clere, who died in 1545 as a result of a wound received while saving
Surrey's life at the siege of Montreuil. Yet those facts are arranged,
with skilful unobtrusiveness, to fit the sonnet's shape and give its

climax strength. The octave is devoted largely to Clere's life, the first quatrain to his connections by birth, the second to the wife and, more particularly, to the master he chose for himself. With the sestet Surrey turns to the story of his death, deserting biography only in the final couplet, which not only voices his own loving tribute, but poignantly sets his earthly loss in the perspective of Heaven's gain. This perspective gives further distinctness and coherence to what has been said of Clere. For the solid factual statements about him are, collectively, symbolic of the chivalric life he shared with Surrey. They epitomize its special virtues, nobility of birth and hence of aspiration, love, friendship, loyalty, self-sacrifice, courage.

A similar symbolic picture, its vivid details observed from life, is painted in Surrey's famous description of his youth at Windsor in company with Henry Fitzroy, the king's illegitimate son: the stately halls and towers, the green courtyards and 'graveld ground', the young men at 'palme playe' missing the ball because distracted by the maidens on the roof tops, the story-telling, the jousting and other 'active games', the groves where one confides his love affair to another, the hunting of the hart in the forest, and, above all, the friendship, loyalty and honour. It is an image of a happiness seemingly the more bright and young because, in the perspective of time, it proves friable. For Surrey writes retrospectively and nostalgically. Henry Fitzroy died aged seventeen in 1536, and in 1537 Surrey found himself a prisoner in Windsor castle:

> So crewell prison how could betyde, alas,
> As prowde Wyndsour, where I in lust and joye
> With a kinges soon my childishe yeres did passe,
> In greater feast then Priams sonnes of Troye.
>
> (no 27)

That the writer of these two poems should reveal in his translations qualities sometimes missed by Wyatt comes as no surprise. In 'Alas, so all thinges nowe do holde their peace' (no 7), from Petrarch's 'Or che 'l ciel e la terra e' l vento tace', the opening description of nightfall is authentically rendered, with all the details subscribing to the idea of peace. The poems on Clere and Windsor show how willingly Surrey thinks in terms of such broad contrasts as Heaven and Earth, joy and sorrow, past and present; and he is therefore well able to cope with Petrarch's antithesis between the peace of bird and beast and the restless anguish of a wakeful lover.

Balance of opposites, the main structural feature of Petrarch's sonnet, gives shape, direction, and a simple logic to many of Surrey's shorter poems. In 'O happy dames', the majority are contrasted with the one who mourns her absent lord, leading her both to dread his dangerous travels and to hope for his safe return:

> And of ech thought a dout doth growe,
> Now he comes, will he come? alas, no, no!
>
> (no 23)

In 'Geve place, ye lovers' Surrey compliments his own lady by contrasting her with all others, beginning with a simple assertion of her superiority, and ending with the authority of Nature on his side:

> Sith Nature thus gave her the prayse
> To be the chiefest worke she wrought,
> In faith, me thinke some better waies
> On your behalf might well be sought,
> Then to compare, as ye have done,
> To matche the candle with the sonne.
>
> (no 12)

Here too the clear progression of the argument, the confident sense of going somewhere, is further assisted by the neatness with which Surrey fits a single sentence to his six-line stanza. Due emphasis falls on the main clause – 'In faith me thinke' – while the final contrast, of candle and sun, is delayed so as to enforce his conclusion.

Though the shorter poems provide some evidence of Surrey's 'epic' gifts – his dignity, control, lucidity, and even, as in the epitaph on Clere, his sense of narrative – the step from them to his major work is a long one. It is not necessarily a step forward in time, for the date of his *Aeneid* remains unknown. Those who suppose that his blank verse was influenced by that of contemporary Italian translations of Virgil would place it after the first of these, Liburnio's, appeared in 1534, when he was about eighteen. His most recent editor, Emrys Jones, regards it as early work. Nevertheless its modernity, in sixteenth-century terms, is sufficiently obvious. There is nothing quite like it in medieval or early Tudor poetry, not even in Wyatt's satires. Here our best early guide is not Puttenham but Roger Ascham (1515–68), the Humanist scholar and propagandist for the improvement of vernacular literature by imitation of the ancient classics. He has evidently read Surrey's Book IV, published in 1554, and, according to the title-page 'translated into English, and drawne into a straunge metre'. Accordingly he hails the author as 'first of all English men, in translating the fourth booke of *Virgill*', rejoicing in the strange metre because Surrey has 'avoyded the fault of Ryming' (*The Scholemaster*, 1570). Surrey, in other words, has found a true equivalent for the unrhymed verse of the classical poets, whose nobility Ascham constantly extols at the expense of the barbarousness of 'Gothic' rhymers. The attitude is similar to Puttenham's. Indeed, it is that of all would-be refiners of English poetry during what was already regarded as a period of renaissance.

In giving Surrey precedence, Ascham naturally takes no account either of William Caxton's prose *Aeneid*, translated from an intermediate French version and published in 1490, or of the Scottish poet Gavin Douglas's rendering of Virgil's text, done in 1513, in rhyming couplets. Surrey himself sits down with a copy of Douglas alongside his Virgil, so that, according to an authoritative reckoning, 40% of his lines show debts to Douglas's wording. This was a good choice of crib. Douglas aims at accuracy: he is quick, for example, to dissociate himself from Caxton, who 'Knew never thre wordis at all quat Virgill ment'. He also has some appreciation of Virgil's 'flude of eloquens', though himself more successful in rendering the narrative passages than the noble, oratorical, or meditative ones, or those containing epic similes. Nevertheless, there is no doubt that Surrey's primary source remains Virgil, and that he aims at imitation of his style as well as of his sense. He is quick to discard the obviously un-Virgilian in Douglas. There are Douglas's moralizing prologues: the one to *Book IV*, for example, takes the story of Dido and Aeneas as text for a sermon on unlawful love, and ends with the homely, practical warning, 'Be war with strangeris of onkouth natioun'. There are the terms which smack more of medieval chivalric romance than of Virgilian epic: the heroes are 'knychtis', Priam is addressed as 'Schir King' and assigned a 'gentill hart'. Above all, there is Douglas's expansiveness: his translation is about twice the length of the original.

In a piece of straightforward narrative, the Greek preparation of the wooden horse for the invasion of Troy, Surrey takes over Douglas's lively translation of *includunt* ('stuffit'/'enstuff'), while contriving, unlike him, a single unpadded sentence, no longer than Virgil's:

> huc delecta virum sortiti corpora furtim
> includunt caeco lateri penitusque cavernas
> ingentis uterumque armato milite complent.
>
> (*Aeneid*, ii. 18–20)

Of choyss men syne, walit by cut, thai tuke
A gret numbyr, and hyd in bilgis dern
Within that best, in mony huge cavern;
Schortly, the belly was stuffit euery deill
Full of knychtis armyt in plait of steill.

(Douglas, I, i,10–4)

In the dark bulk they closde bodies of men
Chosen by lot, and did enstuff by stealth
The hollow womb with armed soldiars.

(Surrey, no 41, lines 26–8)

Compare

saevit inops animi totamque incensa per urbem bacchatur.

(*Aeneid*, iv. 300–1)

Quharfor, inpacient, and myndles in hir rage,
Scho wyskis wild throu the town of Cartage,
Syk wyss as quhen thir nunnys of Bachus
Ruschis . . .

(Douglas, IV, vi, 39–42)

Then ill bested of counsell rageth she,
And whisketh through the town like Bachus nunne.

(Surrey, no 42, lines 388–9)

Surrey's description of Dido's feverish activities, when she suspects that
Aeneas means to leave her, is more compressed, and hence speedier in
effect than Douglas's. At the same time it would lose much of its vigour
without the words, 'whisketh' particularly, borrowed from him.

Surrey makes a similar adjustment in dealing with speech, as with
Sinon's plea to Priam:

quod te per superos et conscia numina veri,
per si qua est quae restat adhuc mortalibus usquam
intemerata fides, oro, miserere laborum
tantorum, miserere animi non digna ferentis.

(*Aeneid*, ii, 141–4)

Quharfor, Schir Kyng, be the hie goddis abufe,
And thar mychtis that trewth best knawis and lufe,
And by the faith onfylit and leil lawte,
(Gyf it with mortale folkis may fundyn be),
Have rewth and piete on sa feil harmys smart,
And talk compassioune in thi gentill hart;
Apon my wrechit sawle have sum mercy
That gyltles sufferis sic dyseyss wrangwisly.

(Douglas, II, ii,151–8)

Then, by the gods, to whom al truth is known,
By fayth unfiled, if any any where
Wyth mortal folk remaines, I thee beseche,
O king, thereby rue on my travail great:
Pitie a wretch that giltlesse suffreth wrong.

(Surrey, no 41, lines 178–82)

Though 'fayth unfiled', 'mortal folk', and 'giltlesse suffreth' obviously derive from Douglas, Surrey avoids his tiresome verbosity and redundancies such as 'leil lawte' and 'rewth and piete'. Douglas's movement, though too leisurely, is by no means turgid. But Surrey's blank verse pulses forward in a manner faithful both to the spirit of Virgil and to the demands of a heightened and persuasive English mode of speech. Momentum is produced by the delay of the main verb 'beseche' (compare Virgil's *oro*), flexibility by the variation in phrase length and the enjambement of the second and third lines, and emphasis by the inverted stresses at the beginning of the first and fifth lines.

As for the descriptive and elaborative passages, Surrey's phrasing sometimes matches Virgil's. If the sense of 'suadentque cadentia sidera somnos' (*Aeneid*, iv. 81) comes across well in Douglas's

And the declynyng of the starris brycht
To sleip and rest persuadis euery wicht,

(IV, ii, 61–2)

Surrey's compressed, alliterative rendering, 'And sliding starres provoked unto sleepe' (no 42, line 102), is also an imitation of its style. Again, when Aeneas, resisting Dido's entreaty, is compared to a wind-battered oak, Surrey succeeds better than Douglas in creating the sounds and images of buffeting:

ac velut annoso validam cum robore quercum
Alpini Boreae nunc hinc nunc flatibus illinc
eruere inter se certant.

(*Aeneid*, iv, 441–3)

And lyke as quhen the ancyant aik tre,
With hys byg schank, by north wynd oft we se
Is ombeset, to bet hym down and ourthraw,
Now heir, now thar, with the fell blastis blaw
The swouchand byr quhisland amang the granys.

(Douglas, IV, viii, 69–73)

> Like to the aged boysteous bodied oke,
> The which among the Alpes the northerne windes
> Blowyng now from this quarter now from that
> Betwixt them strive to overwhelme with blastes.
>
> (Surrey, no 42, lines 582–5)

It is not difficult therefore to share Ascham's enthusiasm for Surrey's *Aeneid*, however ridiculous, in the light of time, Ascham's prejudice against barbarous rhyme appears.

The enthusiasm for Wyatt and Surrey was fairly well-sustained and widespread in the sixteenth century. Like most courtier poets, they published very little during their lives: Wyatt's prose essay *Quyete of Mynde* appeared in 1528, and one of Surrey's elegies on Wyatt in 1542. For the rest, their work at first circulated in manuscript. After their deaths, however, it reached a wider audience through the medium of print. Wyatt's Penitential Psalms were published in 1549, some of Surrey's biblical translations *c.* 1550, his *Aeneid*, Book IV in 1554 and Book II in 1557, while a large number of shorter poems by both were included in Tottel's 'Miscellany', *Songes and Sonettes*, also of 1557. All earned rapid recognition. 'Tottel', constantly reprinted up to the year 1587, was particularly popular, and on all fronts. For it appealed not only to highbrows such as Puttenham, but to lowbrows such as Shakespeare's Slender, who considered it a vital adjunct of successful wooing: 'I had rather than forty shillings I had my Book of Songs and Sonnets here' (*The Merry Wives of Windsor*, I. I. 192–3). It even served as a model. George Turbervile drew heavily on Tottel's Wyatt section, his 'You hollow hilles and vallies wide', for example, being an adaptation of 'Resound my voyse ye wodes that here me plain' (no 22), and his 'You that in May have bathde in blis' of 'You that in love finde lucke and habundance' (no 92). Turbervile's poems were published in the 1560s and 1570s: and it is natural that Tottel's impressive collection should have exerted an influence during the two decades before the new lyric voices of Spenser and Sidney began to command attention.

2

SIR PHILIP SIDNEY

David Kalstone

Sidney's work – posthumously published – was part of the literary ferment of the 1590s; but his achievement properly belongs to a more barren decade. When he began writing in the late 1570s, he was to find little in contemporary English literature to admire; his *Defence of Poesie* names Spenser's *Shepheardes Calender*, but the other works praised – *Gorboduc*, *A Mirror for Magistrates*, and 'the Earle of Surreis Lirickes' – belong to the mid-century, all of them well-known when he was a boy. At his death in 1586, he himself had contributed to the renewal of English literary life the heroic romance and pastoral lyrics of the *Arcadia*, a pastoral entertainment (*The Lady of May*), a series of metrically inventive translations of the Psalms, the first and most energetic of the English sonnet sequences in *Astrophel and Stella*, and in *The Defence of Poesie* the noblest and most acute literary criticism of the age. In all his work the critic's prescriptive intelligence is close to the surface, almost as if to direct contemporary readers and writers to the nature of his accomplishment. For if he helped to domesticate European literary conventions in England – he was to Elizabethans the 'English Petrarke', and his *Arcadia* borrowed its title from the Italian begetter of the great Renaissance pastorals – he was also alive to the ways energetic writing might extend traditional meanings or call values into question.

So, in his *Arcadia*, when the noble princes and princesses set out to inspect a grove where shepherds are to perform pastoral eclogues, they find a scene as extravagantly appropriate as any in Sannazaro's *Arcadia*, the romance from which Sidney drew his title. It has its brook, its streams, its roses:

about it (as if it had bene to inclose a *Theater*) grew such a sort of trees, as eyther excellency of fruit, statelines of grouth, continuall greennes, or poeticall fancies have made at any time famous.[1]

---

[1] *The Complete Works of Sir Philip Sidney*, ed. Albert Feuillerat, Cambridge, 1912–26, i, 119. Hereafter cited as *Works*.

But the deliberate theatricality of the scene, first to be savoured for the delicacy and harmony of presentation, invites further questions about the nature of poetical fancies. The princes' identities are as yet unknown to the princesses they would like to woo; Musidorus is disguised as the shepherd, Dorus, and Pyrocles is dressed as an Amazon, Zelmane, but the courtly nature of their distressed gestures is unmistakable:

the Ladies sate them downe, inquiring many questions of the shepheard *Dorus*; who (keeping his eie still upon *Pamela*) answered with such a trembling voice, and abashed countenance, and oftentimes so far from the matter, that it was some sport to the young Ladies, thinking it want of education, which made him so discountenanced with unwoonted presence. But *Zelmane* that saw in him the glasse of her owne miserie, taking the hande of *Philoclea*, and with burning kisses setting it close to her lips (as if it should stand there like a hand in the margine of a Booke, to note some saying worthy to be marked) began to speake these wordes. O Love, since thou art so changeable in mens estates, how art thou so constant in their torments? when sodainly there came out of a wood a monstrous Lion, with a she Beare not far from him, of little lesse fiercenes . . .

The prince disguised as a shepherd answers questions in a trembling voice; the prince disguised as an Amazon recognizes in him a mirror of his own unhappiness. But Sidney underlines the very literary nature of their poses. With everyone frozen into position, the action becomes a tableau before our eyes. The hand being kissed becomes the pointing hand in the margin of a book. What it points to, and what Pyrocles' apostrophe to love invokes, is the appearance of a monstrous lion and bear – in this context a comic reminder that we may have been tempted to misinterpret this pastoral scene. It is almost as if we need the beasts to complete the picture, suggesting as they do the appetites being hidden under the guise of a golden setting and high rhetorical invocations to love.

The hand in the margin is a characteristically Sidneyan touch, the critic's prose pointer. It marks a connection between literary conventions and the emotions they are designed to represent, and suggests that any divorce between the two is a source of comedy. Sidney, discouraged with the state of English writing ('idle *England*, which now can scarce endure the pain of a pen') recommends the pursuit and understanding of classical and European literary models: 'as the fertilest ground must be manured, so must the highest flying wit have a *Dedalus* to guide him . . . that is, Art, Imitation and Exercise' (*Works*, iii, 37). But those three are not to be empty graces; the poet must sense the vitality of his literary guides. What

Sidney deplores in the *'Lyrical* kinde of Songs and Soncts' of his period, he takes care to avoid in his own *Astrophel and Stella*:

But truly many of such writings, as come under the banner of unresistable love, if I were a mistresse, would never perswade mee they were in love: so coldly they apply firie speeches as men that had rather redde lovers writings, and so caught up certaine swelling Phrases, which hang together like a man that once tolde me the winde was at Northwest, and by South, because he would be sure to name winds enough, than that in truth they feele those passions, which easily as I thinke, may be bewraied by the same for-ciblenesses or *Energia* (as the Greeks call it) of the writer.

(Works, iii,41)

The aim, then, is a truly animated use of conventions, not a random collection of devices. In most of his works Sidney makes the point explicitly, allowing, for example, a declaration of liveliness to launch his sonnet sequence ('Foole, said my Muse to me, looke in thy heart and write.') or a pointed metaphor in the *Arcadia* (the hand in the margin) to alert us to the dangers of stylized lament. In one sense, the *Arcadia, Astrophel and Stella,* and *The Lady of May* are literary manifestoes which complement *The Defence of Poesie*; they shape and attune a reader's response, and also represent Sidney's own developing effort to come to terms with the governing voices of literature.

The chief virtue of poetry, as Sidney sees it in the *Defence*, is that it delivers a golden world; 'since our erected wit maketh us know what perfection is, and yet our infected will keepeth us from reaching unto it' (*Works*, iii, 9). And the form that comes closest to fulfilling this mission is the heroic poem: 'the loftie image of such worthies, most inflameth the minde with desire to bee worthie'; epic poetry 'maketh magnanimitie and justice, shine through all mistie fearfulnesse and foggie desires' (*Works*, iii, 25). Heroic obligation and heroic education are never far from the centre of Sidney's work, though these concerns play against competing values in his pastoral masque, pastoral romance, and sonnet sequence, the genres in which he chose to write. The clear power of epic, voiced in the *Defence*, is in Sidney's verse and fiction more often poised against the lively presence of 'infected will' or the competing energies of love. One way of seeing his career – dangerous though it is to look for too much 'development' in so short a literary life – is in terms of the growing difficulty his protagonists have envisioning and attaining the perfection of the exemplary heroes mentioned in the *Defence*. The wit of Astrophel is at once more various and more clearly a 'fallen' power than the 'erected wit' of the visionary poet in Sidney's critical manifesto.

* * *

Questions of heroic energy are posed in what was probably Sidney's earliest work, the brief pastoral entertainment which came to be known in the eighteenth century as *The Lady of May*. Devised for one of Elizabeth I's visits to Sidney's uncle, the Earl of Leicester, at Wanstead (probably the visit of May 1578), the piece asks the Queen to make one of those choices so popular in Elizabethan and Jacobean masques. She is to award a husband to the young and beautiful May Lady, who has two suitors; in asking the Queen to choose, the Lady makes clear that 'in judging me, you judge more than me in it.' The rivals are Espilus, a rich shepherd with 'verie small deserts and no faults' and Therion, a forester with 'many deserts and many faults.' Like his comic ancestors, the bumptious Polyphemus of Theocritus and Corydon of Virgil's second eclogue, Espilus assumes that his weight in wool will recommend him. But as the debate moves to a more general level, to a choice of life, it is clear that the mere force of literary tradition will guarantee victory to the shepherd, whose supporters press his claim as representative of the contemplative life. The forester's followers present a more inclusive and original alternative:

I was saying the shepheards life had some goodnesse in it, because it borrowed of the country quietnesse something like ours, but that is not all, for ours besides that quiet part, doth both strengthen the body, and raise up the mind with this gallant sort of activity. O sweet contentation to see the long life of the hurtlesse trees, to see how in streight growing up, though never so high, they hinder not their fellowes, they only enviously trouble, which are crookedly bent. What life is to be compared with ours where the very growing things are ensamples of goodnesse?

(Works, ii, 336–7)

The appeal was lost on the Queen, who chose Espilus, perhaps not recognizing the unexpected turn the masque had taken, or perhaps seeing in it a covert appeal for the activist Protestant policies of Leicester.[1] It is, however, clear from the text that Sidney expected Therion to win and had composed for the conclusion a song consoling the shepherd's god Pan for his defeat at the hands of the forest god Silvanus:[2] 'Poore *Pan* (he sayd) although thou beaten be,/It is no shame, since *Hercules* was he.' The triumph of Hercules, archetypal man of action, in a pastoral masque suggests Sidney's

---

[1] Robert Kimbrough and Philip Murphy, 'The Helmingham Hall Manuscript of Sidney's *The Lady of May*', *Renaissance Drama*, ed. S. Schoenbaum, Evanston, Ill., New Series i (1968), pp 105, 107.

[2] For an extended discussion, see Stephen Orgel, *The Jonsonian Masque*, Cambridge, Mass., 1965, pp 44–57.

playful reinterpretation of bucolic virtue and retirement; in the image of the forester's life he takes a momentary pleasure in the vision of an undivided life, a free twinning of action and contemplation, of reason and an exemplary ease – conjunctions not so happily accomplished in the works to follow.

No reader of *The Lady of May* would then be surprised to find heroes introduced into the forest retreats of Sidney's *Arcadia*. Though it takes as a point of departure the entirely pastoral romance of Jacopo Sannazaro, and though much of the heroic material was added when Sidney came to revise the work sometime after 1580, a concern for heroic control dominates both the original and 'new' Arcadias. The later version (and the only one known until our century when the unrevised *Arcadia* was discovered and published)[1] opens with the entrance of the princes Pyrocles and Musidorus into that pastoral world where they are to test and be tested by love. But a great deal of energy and attention – almost all of Book II – is devoted to their heroic education and exploits, recounted by the disguised princes themselves as part of their wooing. Sannazaro provides a setting and his eclogues provide material for the pastoral games which serve as interludes between each 'act' of the romance, but the larger subject – the princes' wanderings – reflects Sidney's admiration for Greek and chivalric romance, for the *Aethiopica* of Heliodorus, the *Diana* of Montemayor, and the sprawling *Amadis de Gaula*.[2] Eclogues, performed by the 'real' shepherds of Arcadia, are carefully framed; when they are past, the narrative again places them and reflects upon the princes' joining in: 'In these pastorall pastimes a great number of dayes were sent to follow their flying predecessours, while the cup of poison (which was deeply tasted of this noble companie) had left no sinewe of theirs without mortally searching into it. . . .' (*Works*, i, 145). Though landscapes are described in terms of the traditional and golden pastoral world, Pyrocles and Musidorus, the heroic princes, cannot simply escape to Arcadia and pursue their loves with absolute immunity. The *Arcadia* brings forth

[1] The first publication of the *Arcadia* (1590) included the two and a half books which Sidney had revised before his death. Editions of 1593 and 1598 reprinted the revised books and completed the romance with the unrevised books of the Old Arcadia. The complete version of the Old Arcadia was not printed until Feuillerat's edition of 1926; a manuscript had been discovered and identified by Bertram Dobell in 1908.

[2] See Walter Davis, 'A Map of Arcadia', in Walter Davis and Richard A. Lanham, *Sidney's Arcadia*, New Haven, 1965, esp. pp 1–59.

the 'golden world' of poetry not simply by creating ideal settings, but by teaching its readers and characters *how* to see the pastoral world in relation to a whole range of earthly settings which encircle it.

An incident in Book II suggests Sidney's critical intention. The inhabitants of Arcadia have begun a mutiny. A painter is standing by – and, in introducing him, Sidney stresses that he is not a good one–

> This painter was to counterfette the skirmishing betweene the *Centaures* and *Lapithes*, and had bene very desirous to see some notable wounds, to be able the more lively to expresse them; and this morning (being carried by the streame of this companie) the foolish felow was even delighted to see the effect of blowes.
>
> (*Works*, i, 313)

The painter is so rapt in observing the wounds of others that he does not see a sword directed against himself and loses both hands. 'And so,' Sidney tells us, 'the painter returned, well skilled in wounds, but with never a hand to performe his skill.' This gruesome and pointed interruption reminds us not simply – as Ascham said – that experience is the worst teacher; it also suggests something about the superiority of stylized narrative and description to the crude use to which the copyist painter was about to put his artistic powers.

So, for example, when Sidney describes a disaster, the technique is less that of the photograph than of the foreshortened painting. The *Arcadia* opens with a shipwreck from which one of the heroes, Musidorus, is washed ashore and rescued. He persuades a fisherman to ferry him back to the wreckage in hope of catching sight of his comrade-in-arms Pyrocles:

> but when they came so neere as their eies were ful masters of the object, they saw a sight full of piteous strangenes: a ship, or rather the carkas of the shippe, or rather some few bones of the carkas, hulling there, part broken, part burned, part drowned: death having used more than one dart to that destruction. About it floted great store of very rich thinges, and many chestes which might promise no lesse. And amidst the precious things were a number of dead bodies, which likewise did not onely testifie both elements violence, but that the chief violence was growen of humane inhumanitie: for their bodies were ful of grisly wounds, and their bloud had (as were) filled the wrinckles of the seas visage: which it seemed the sea woulde not wash away, that it might witnes it is not alwaies his fault, when we condemne his crueltie: in summe, a defeate, where the conquered kept both field and spoile: a shipwrack without storme or ill footing: and a wast of fire in the midst of water.
>
> (*Works*, i, 9–10)

This moving and stylized description proclaims itself from the beginning as one observed by those whose eyes are 'ful masters of the object.' Our attention is directed inevitably to the way that mastery is performed: movement is almost suspended ('a ship, or rather the carkas of the shippe, or rather some few bones of the carkas'), and the increasing precision of Sidney's metaphor leaves us with a vision of the ship as if it had been picked dry by vultures. Then again, the blood from the wounds of the dead 'filled the wrinckles of the seas visage.' Far beyond the observed detail – waves appear furrowed – the intensity and horror depend upon our feeling that something human has been defiled, the sea personified as ancient and as victim.[1] In other words Sidney's descriptive powers force us again and again to remember that human beings in this shipwreck had been more death-dealing to one another than either fire or water had been. They had made themselves victims of their own panic and their own appetites. The eye becomes 'ful master of the object' when it grasps that essential point. Sidney's description is what he would call in *The Defence of Poesie* a 'speaking picture': what the educated eye ought to understand about what it sees.

There is a fuller, a more complex example in a later seascape. Book II is devoted to the adventures of Pyrocles and Musidorus, recounted against Arcadian settings as part of the wooing of the princesses Philoclea and Pamela. Musidorus is explaining how he and his cousin first set out on their exploits. The passage includes an elaborate description which begins with their calm embarkation and proceeds through a fierce storm, the ship driven upon the rocks, the crew panicked, only the princes emerging as survivors. The passage (*Works*, i, 191–4) is too long for quotation here, but the events may be told, as they just have been, in a single sentence. The impression one carries away is of an intense narration in which every stage of the adventure, every detail of the action, is ornamented and amplified by metaphors that touch other areas of the princes' experience. It is almost as if, as Musidorus retells his story, he is able to see the connections of this initial adventure to the high expectations and inevitable trials of love and politics in Arcadia. Setting sail, the ships 'kept together like a beautifull flocke, which so well could obey their maisters pipe.' Another comparison refers to expectations in love:

the seeming insensible Loadstone, with a secret beauty (holding the spirit

[1] John F. Danby, *Poets on Fortune's Hill*, London, 1952, pp 49–50.

of iron in it) can draw that hard-harted thing unto it, and (like a vertuous mistresse) not onely make it bow it selfe, but with it make it aspire to so high a Love, as of the heavenly Poles.

With that introduction the mood of the comparisons changes; the events which follow are narrated with constant reminders of their likeness to civil and personal treachery. The sea that receives the heroes has already been marked as having 'so smooth and smiling a face, as if *Neptune* had as then learned falsely to fawne on Princes.' The winds become 'fittest instruments of commaundement' in a 'tumultuous kingdome': night 'usurped the dayes right'. Such phrases contribute to an elaborate parallel between this scene and moments of public and private treachery. Above all, amid this concentration of analogies, Sidney introduces the theatrical metaphors which frame the action of the *Arcadia* at its critical moments: 'a mournefull stage for a Tragedie to be plaied on'; 'lest the conclusion should not aunswere to the rest of the play. . . .' At climactic moments we are reminded that we constitute an audience. Spectators are essential to the drama being played out: the princes who are characters undergoing the experience, one of whom is retelling it; and, of course, the reader of the romance. Our attention is focused on the *images* which remain from the adventure, images which convey its lasting effect and meaning:

Certainely there is no daunger carries with it more horror, than that which growes in those flowing kingdomes. For that dwelling place is unnaturall to mankind, and then the terriblenesse of the continuall motion, the dissolution of the fare being from comfort, the eye and the eare having ougly images ever before it, doth still vex the minde, even when it is best armed against it.

(Works, i,193)

The drama – and this is what makes it essentially Sidneyan – is finally and explicitly centred in the mind, in images which forever haunt it and in the effort of will to arm against them. It is no coincidence that Musidorus recounts this episode when he tells Pamela of the princes' education, and it is no surprise that his terms recall Sidney's language in the *Defence*: the princes received 'conceits not unworthy of the best speakers'; 'images . . . being then delivered to their memory, which after, their stronger judgements might dispens. . . .' What happens to them is what happens to the reader of literature described in the *Defence*: 'this purifying of wit, this enriching of memorie, enabling of judgement, and enlarging of conceit, which commonly we call learning' (*Works*, iii, 11). The categories are those of Musidorus: images delivered to memory and judgement. Sidney's emphasis is never on simple participation in the stream of events, or even simple delight in or fear of the images before one, but rather on control and mastery. His heroes become *readers* of their experience. Sidney's narrative is, in other words, the exact opposite of something like Miranda's wondering, uncomprehending description of the tempest in Shakespeare's last romance, or of the Clown's fragmented account of the storm in *The Winter's Tale*: 'now the ship boring the moon with her main-mast, and anon swallowed with yeast and froth, as you'ld thrust a cork into a hogshead.'

Sidney's description, while it registers the full horror and fear of the shipwreck, is governed by and comes to a full stop with the measured assurance of the prepared mind: 'a monstrous crie begotten of manie roaring vowes, was able to infect with feare a minde that had not prevented it with the power of reason.' The whole episode has been distanced, paced by the certainty of a mind prepared by reason, and witnessed by an eye which is 'ful master of the object'. Musidorus, all along, has been demonstrating in his way of telling the story a memory well-stored, rich in images, drawing likenesses to courts and pastures, stepping back theatrically to remind us that this is a stage for the education of princes. It is all much more explicit, much more self-consciously acted out for the reader than the adventures of Spenser's knights. Britomart and Redcrosse do not interpret themselves aloud for us; much more is discovered to the reader through their participation in the welter of experience. In the *Arcadia* the retrospective narratives of the princes and the highly directive prose of the third-person narrator are constantly demonstrating analytic powers, rich in images which 'enable the judgement.' For example, the memory of shipwreck crops up at important moments. Musidorus, discovering that his cousin Pyrocles is in love, registers this as a threat to their heroic ambitions:

What have I deserved of thee, to be thus banished of thy counsels? Heretofore I have accused the sea, condemned the Pyrats, and hated my evill fortune, that deprived me of thee; But now thy self is the sea, which drounes my comfort, thy selfe is the Pirat that robbes thy selfe of me: Thy owne will becomes my evill fortune.

(*Works*, i,61)

The true pitfalls and most potent dangers in Sidney's world are within. When Musidorus says 'thy self is the sea,' he means *self* in the strongest sense, one which he equates with *will*. Its failure is like the failure to stand against the fiercest natural powers; the forces released are as turbulent as those 'flowing kingdomes' whose images forever vex the mind. Musidorus, referring metaphorically to their own shipwreck, makes such connections explicitly and self-consciously. He brings into play images and associations alive in his memory, part of his heroic education. What is so special here is the degree to which described actions and landscapes so quickly become landscapes of the mind, and the extent to which heroes are both participants in and interpreters of their experience. When Musidorus enters Arcadia, he does not take on his shepherd's role with the easy wit of Marlowe's passionate shepherd in 'Come live with me and be my love,' nor with the initial relaxation of Spenser's Calidore in Book VI of *The Faerie Queene*. Rather he welcomes the disguise with a judicious appraisal of his fallen state: 'Come shepheard's weedes, become your master's mind.'[1] Pastoral details are almost immediately taken up as psychological markers, ways in which the heroes describe and test their own feelings.

It is in that light we can understand the essentially static poetry of the *Arcadia*.[2] The lyrics scattered through the text (this does not apply to the eclogues between the books, which belong principally to the Arcadian shepherds) have a choric function, the pursuits of love for a moment stilled in verse that bears the pressure of judgement: the princes lament their transformed state; the Queen Gynecia laments her lack of self-control (she is in love with Pyrocles, who in turn loves her daughter). To the shepherds Sidney gives more colloquial singing contests, an epithalamium, fabliaux taking comic delight in lust and adultery. But the norm for the aristocrats of the *Arcadia* – even when they join in pastoral dialogues or singing contests with the shepherds – is verse, self-conscious in its devotions, using the props of pastoral to express, understand, and, to some extent, control their feelings: 'My sheepe are thoughts, which I both guide and serve'; 'Transformd in shew, but more transformd in minde'; 'Over these brookes trusting to ease mine eyes.' The forms chosen are deliberately repetitive, the most extreme example being the beautiful double sestina 'Yee Gote-heard Gods, that love the grassie mountaines.' But even sonnets are

---

[1] *The Poems of Sir Philip Sidney*, ed. William A. Ringler, Oxford, 1962, p 13. Hereafter cited as *Poems*.

[2] See David Kalstone, *Sidney's Poetry*, Cambridge, Mass., 1965, esp. pp 71–101. Also Neil Rudenstine, *Sidney's Poetic Development*, Cambridge, Mass., 1967, pp 53–105.

divided into quatrains with strictly repeating verbal patterns, so as to reinforce the impression of plangent lament, of an unbreakable circle of desire and strong feeling. Only in Book III does Sidney start to use sonnets in which changes of tone transform the sestet and lead emotions in unexpected directions.

The emphasis on self-mastery and control should not, of course, suggest that Pyrocles and Musidorus are consistently perfect interpreters of their experience or their pastoral surroundings. The book's splendid comedy is often bound up with moments when the heroic eye is not entirely master of its object. The appearance of the lion and bear in Book I – an episode already discussed – is only one of many examples. At a turning point in the book, the princesses are taken off into captivity by their wicked aunt Cecropia because of just such a misreading of their surroundings. 'Devising how to give more feathers to the winges of Time,' they follow a troop of shepherdesses into the forest and at an innocent picnic are lulled by the 'pleasantest fruites, that Sun-burnd *Autumne* could deliver unto them' (*Works*, i,362). The scene is completed this time not by a lion and a bear, but by twenty armed men who carry them off to Cecropia's castle.

Sidney's princes, already alert interpreters of their martial adventures, must learn how to read these pastoral scenes, how to include love within the circle of their experience, making it compatible with the responsibilities of their active lives. Characteristically their days are full of conflict, their golden scenes often filled out by crouching attackers representing appetite.

O heaven and earth (said *Musidorus*) to what a passe are our mindes brought, that from the right line of vertue, are wryed to these crooked shifts? But o Love, it is thou that doost it: thou changest name upon name; thou disguisest our bodies, and disfigurest our mindes. But in deed thou hast reason, for though the wayes be foule, the journeys end is most faire and honourable.

(*Works*, i,117)

Oddly enough – and perhaps Sidney would have made it clearer if he had lived to revise the *Arcadia* beyond Book III – the princes are only freed from their predicament by a comic accident. The king, Basilius, supposedly dead but really only set asleep with a love potion, awakens just in time to save the princes from being punished for their 'lustful' attempts on the princesses. It is perhaps the only way out of a book where love is construed as a necessary lapse, one eventually leading to virtue, but where heroes self-consciously goe privately to seeke exercises of their vertue: thinking it not so worthy, to be brought to heroycall effects by fortune, or necessitie (like *Ulysses* and *Aeneas*) as by ones owne choice, and working.

(*Works*, i, 206)

No writer could set a higher standard for heroism, and none could have a sharper sense of our resources for self-bafflement.

In the *Arcadia* Sidney paid his strictest tribute to the heroic ideal and to the *Defence*'s epic vision of literature. Pyrocles and Musidorus win their princesses and return to their public responsibilities and the unrelenting demands of heroic vigilance, the 'journeys end . . . most faire and honourable.' *Astrophel and Stella*, beginning as well with a young hero's truancy to the world of love, never grants the rewards of the *Arcadia*. Astrophel continues his 'wailing eloquence,' neither winning Stella nor wishing to re-enter the hollow world of chivalry and 'great expectation.' Thomas Nashe's breezy summary – in a preface to the first (and unauthorized) edition of 1591 – tells only part of the story when he describes it as the 'tragicommody of love . . . the argument cruell chastitie, the Prologue hope, the Epilogue dispaire. . . .' The sequence indeed follows the plot line of the great tales of courtly love (*Troilus and Criseyde* was, reportedly, one of 'Astrophel's cordials'). And there are moments of dramatic confrontation in the interspersed songs when the voices of both lovers are heard, Astrophel facing Stella, entreating and ruefully refused. But in general the sequence of 108 sonnets directs us not to narrative excitements but to Astrophel's complicated and changing reactions, to an inner dialogue in the course of which we glimpse fragments of a familiar curve of events: Astrophel's falling in love, his expectations and victories and disappointments. Unlike the Arcadians, whose prose and verse demonstrate their awareness of heroic control and mastery, Astrophel in his poems conveys an incomplete and developing experience. He is a puzzled participant in his love for Stella and is engaged in a series of rich encounters with authority, testing the formulas with which others characterize experience. Assertions and distinctions of feeling challenge and qualify precept at every turn. Sometimes he encounters books: poets' phrases which do not seem adequate to the true voice of feeling (sonnets 1, 3, 6, 15, 74); the lessons of Reason, Virtue, and 'great expectation' (4, 10, 21) which trouble his growing allegiance to Stella; and finally Stella herself, 'fairest booke of Nature,' whose lessons are confusing and do not accommodate his strong desires

(62, 71). The sequence is filled with personifications from a textbook for lovers, figures whose importance Astrophel is continually challenging: Hope (67); Patience (56); 'traytour absence' (88); Doctor Cupid (61). His chafings and probings create the pattern of *Astrophel and Stella* – its definitions, its declarations against adversaries. Sidney, who helped domesticate the Petrarchan mode in England, also carried its habitual introspection to an extreme which helped undermine the tradition. The immediacy with which he follows the lover's turn of mind – from line to line or from sonnet to sonnet – draws us away from visions of the ideal mistress (like Petrarch's Laura) to an individualizing energy, impatient with the worshipful stance the lover finds himself assuming.[1] Where Petrarch's poet-lover, imagining his mistress, is drawn by the brilliance of her image, his turbulence balanced and transformed by intense lyric presentations of Laura, Astrophel can only fitfully, without strain, transport himself into these moods. By the end of the sequence, unlike Petrarch and unlike the idealized heroes at the end of the *Arcadia*, Astrophel is irrevocably, even joyfully, committed to the confusions of the fallen world. His understanding of love is not the purifying, gradual refinement of Petrarch's *Rime*, but rather an emerging clarification of and commitment to his own fallen nature as an earthly lover.

Charged with truancy to his heroic training, Astrophel moves from an opening series of harried defences against Reason and Virtue to redefine those words and claim their power for love. Sometimes jaunty, sometimes guilty and rueful, allowing full strength to 'Reason's audite,' he relies on energetic conversions:

> If that be sinne which doth the maners frame,
> Well staid with truth in word and faith of deed,
> Readie of wit and fearing nought but shame:
> If that be sinne which in fixt hearts doth breed
> A loathing of all loose unchastitie,
> Then Love is sinne, and let me sinfull be.
> (Sonnet 14; *Poems*, p 172)

Once committed to love, he alternately invokes the Petrarchan contraries ('Where *Love* is chastnesse, Paine doth learne delight' – Sonnet 48; *Poems*, p188) and bristles at the artificialities of courtship ('Alas, if Fancy drawne by imag'd things,/Though false, yet with free scope more grace doth breed/Than servant's wracke . . .' – Sonnet 45; *Poems*, p187). The pressures of desire

[1] Kalstone, pp 105–32.

challenge easy literary definitions of love: Stella imposes 'a Love not blind,' one anchored 'fast ... on *Vertue*'s shore,' so leading Astrophel to new discriminations:

> Alas, if this the only metall be
> Of *Love*, new-coind to helpe my beggery,
> Deare, love me not, that you may love me more.
>
> (Sonnet 62; *Poems*, p 196)

The sequence follows Astrophel from one crossroad to another, each of his bright distinctions proving not to be the irresistible gesture he had hoped it would be. New paths branch off constantly; new frustrations are discovered in his love until, wearily, he acknowledges the irreducible element of desire, by sonnet 72 greeted as his 'old companion': 'But thou Desire, because thou wouldst have all,/Now banisht art, but yet alas how shall?' Late in the series, sonnets give way to lyric confrontation in eleven songs, both characters now directly on stage, the impossibility of their love crystallized as Stella, regretfully, banishes him in honour's name. *Astrophel and Stella* ends with what amounts to a ceremony of grief; the last sonnets, more like songs than any others in the series, invoke personifications of Woe, Sighs, Thought, and Grief. After this clarification of feeling, the sequence can do nothing but end, with little truly resolved though emotions have been exhausted.

Astrophel's probing and puzzlement demand techniques which make these sonnets far different from the Arcadian poems.[1] Many of them are pitched toward an unexpected conclusion, the sonnet form filled out as if, while Astrophel speaks, his counter feelings are gathering and burst out in the final lines. Majestic praise of Stella as the 'fairest booke of Nature' drawing him forcibly to Virtue (71) is suddenly challenged:

> So while thy beautie drawes the heart to love,
> As fast thy Vertue bends that love to good:
> But ah, Desire still cries, give me some food.

Or the eloquent claims of the 'inward light' (5) – 'True, that on earth we are but pilgrims made,/And should in soule up to our countrey move' – crystallize a quiet countering resolve: 'True, and yet true that I must *Stella* love.'

But the true departure of *Astrophel and Stella* – what points ahead to Shakespeare and to Donne – is its more intense verbal activity: a

---

[1] Rudenstine, pp 172–96.

liberated control of sound, rhythm, and syntax which vividly transmits the sense of Astrophel as participant in rather than heroic
master of his experience. One can pose, for example, Pyrocles'
judicious lament, 'Transformd in shew, but more transformd in
minde,' against Astrophel's urgent discovery of what it is like to fall
in love:

> Flie, fly, my friends, I have my death wound; fly,
> See there that boy, that murthring boy I say,
> Who like a theefe, hid in darke bush doth ly,
> Til bloudie bullet get him wrongfull pray.
>
> (Sonnet 20; *Poems*, p 174)

Familiar as the scene of Cupid's ambush may be in Renaissance
poetry Astrophel's sonnet still manages to sound urgent and
irritated. He is experiencing in the present tense, what Pyrocles has
already weighed and assimilated before he begins his poem. A
traditional conceit is in the later sonnet animated by all the rhythms
of surprise, above all by the penetrating sounds (Flie, fly, my . . .
I . . . fly/See . . . say/ . . . like . . . theefe . . . ly . . . pray), the long *e*'s
and *i*'s and *a*'s, which keep these opening cries echoing through the
poem (in all the rhyme words of the octave, for example) until the
urgency is slowly damped down by the closed rhymes of the last
lines.

Syntax, too, follows the hesitations and pressures of feeling
rather than marking and controlling emotions as the Arcadian
sonnets do.

> Wo, having made with many fights his owne
> Each sence of mine, each gift, each power of mind
> Growne now his slaves, he forst them out to find
> The thorowest words, fit for woe's selfe to grone,
> Hoping that when they might find *Stella* alone,
> Before she could prepare to be unkind . . .
>
> (Sonnet 57; *Poems*, p 193)

These words have the quality of breathy yet considered speech. It is
possible to read the phrases of line 2 as intensified objects of
'made . . . his owne'; or, as spilling over into the following line, any
or all of them as the subject of 'growne now his slaves.' Such
deliberate fluidity makes it seem as if the battles and slavery to Woe
are now, wearily and firmly, a part of life, telescoped quickly behind
the redundant 'he' as if to put these experiences in place. The rapid
movement calls us back to the present, to new frustrations: as Stella
receives his 'plaints,' she sings his poem and so removes the sting of

his strong feelings. We must be alive to these syntactical pleasures which, slowing and quickening the flow of the sonnets, give privileged renditions of particular moments of feeling.

Astrophel and Stella often invites attention to such details; its resources, its more intense verbal activity allow a psychological subtlety which would have been inappropriate to the willed evaluations of the *Arcadia*. The movement of mind, so often praised in Donne, is already present in many of the sonnets of Sidney's sequence, though perhaps without so intricate a representation of the snares of thought. The pattern of *Astrophel and Stella* is one that both Donne and Shakespeare would have understood: exploring the possibilities of sustained praise and lyric vision leads to a shattered awakening and a recall to the desiring, unsatisfied self.

Auden has referred to Sidney as a poet's poet. Ambiguous praise, it highlights an important truth: that Sidney's range is not great and that many of his self-conscious efforts at formal effects are of interest only to those, like poets, whose concerns are highly technical. It was Auden and Empson who called attention to the wonderful double sestina, 'Yee Gote-heard Gods', reprinting it for an audience which might never have looked for it among the self-absorbed, sometimes drab lyrics of the *Arcadia*. Surely it suggested for their own poetry an example of the heightened effects of form divorced from the individualized, errant, probing voices of modern poetry. Yet Sidney himself was moving away from those patterened achievements. In *Astrophel and Stella* he discovered, triumphantly, that very different kind of voice which was to be fully at home in the spacious achievement of the Elizabethan stage: dramatic speech, committed to the wandering voices of the fallen world, the high road of English poetry ever since.

3

SPENSER

Millar MacLure

I[1]

He was the perfect Elizabethan. About six years old at the Queen's accession, he must always have kept as one of his first memories her great reception in the City. 'Time,' she said, 'Time hath brought me hither.' And he died four years before Time surprised her, in his friend Ralegh's great phrase, died before the absurd anticlimax of Essex's rebellion, the debate on monopolies, the impatient waiting of time-servers for a new ruler. Nowadays he would seem cut off in his prime, at the peak of his powers, in his late forties.

When a man writes as much poetry as he did, with such a correct and creative command of the genres as he exercised, it is natural to think of composition as the centre of his existence, with the secular career on the periphery, or as a kind of support for the imagination. But his public life – remembering that the distinction between public and private is hard to establish for any of the Elizabethan gentry – touched some of the most important locales and personalities of that extraordinary reign.

London first, his 'most kyndly Nurse', as he calls it in *Prothalamion*, with the Thames running softly between the Queen's houses of fame (Richmond, Greenwich), past the 'stately places' of the gentry, secularized ecclesiastical properties along the river from Westminster to the Temple. This is the London which Spenser celebrated in 1596, by way of digression as he sang the nuptials of the daughters of the Earl of Worcester at Essex House, where he had 'gayned giftes and goodly grace' from Leicester in times past. He was looking down a fairly successful career by then, he was established. But the beginnings had been obscure enough. Tradition says he was born in the City; when he wrote *Amoretti* LX

---

[1] The substance of this section, and other incidental sentences, are reproduced from my 'Edmund Spenser: An Introductory Essay', *Queen's Quarterly* lxxiii (1966), 550–8.

(1593?) he was forty, and his mother's name was (like his Queen's and his second wife's) Elizabeth. He was never a city man, as Ben Jonson was, or one of the wits of the Inns of Court, but he began his learning in a great school endowed by merchants; he had to wait for the perquisites and grants of the colonial civil service to become country gentry himself – in Ireland, but he claimed alliance with 'an house of ancient fame', the Spencers of Wormleighton and Althorp, who made their money, appropriately enough for Colin Clout, from sheep, and whose well-married daughters he celebrated in graceful dedications.

Jonson's master at Westminster was William Camden, whose antiquarian and historical works Spenser was to draw on for his *View* of Ireland and generally for his sense of British history; at Merchant Taylors School he had for headmaster Richard Mulcaster. Mulcaster was a birch and book man, but he was an enlightened schoolmaster too, and his textbooks (*Positions*, 1581; *First Part of the Elementary*, 1582) give the impression of a liberal and imaginative scholar, no pedant, but one who believed in the possibilities of the vernacular. Who can tell what a man learns or unlearns from a schoolmaster? Perhaps the 'good old shephearde, *Wrenock*' of the December eclogue of *The Shepheardes Calendar*, is Mulcaster. What those boys read in school, to which so much attention has been paid by T. W. Baldwin and others, the adages and sentences, the pieces of Roman authors, was not necessarily the most important element in the formation of their 'working wits', but it did train reason and memory, and made them inveterate rhetoricians. That training produced orators, not only in the sense of preparation for pleading at the bar, or lying abroad for one's country, but a habitual readiness of conference, amplification and flourishing of the commonplace, rotundity and formality, which informs alike love-letters, routine communications of county magnates to the Privy Council, scurrilous pamphlets – and courtly poetry.

Next, his 'mother Cambridge', adorned 'with many a gentle Muse, and many a learned wit'. Spenser went to Pembroke Hall as a 'sizar' or 'poor scholar' in 1569, took a good degree in 1573, and proceeded MA 1576. He went through the conservative, distinctively oral pattern of studies in rhetoric, logic and philosophy: lectures, disputations, declamations. His friend and colleague in Ireland, Lodowick Bryskett, in his colloquy preface to *A Discourse of Civill Life* (1606), speaks of him as being 'not only perfect in the Greek tongue but also very well read in philosophy, both moral and natural.' We find him rather stronger on the 'moral' side, e.g. in Aristotle's *Ethics* and Ficino's versions of Plato. His 'natural philosophy' is of that happily eclectic and mythological kind which C. S. Lewis has described in *The Discarded Image*, essential matter for a poet. His formative reading, in the Bible, Ovid, Natalis Comes, Ariosto, Chaucer, was mainly extra-curricular: a many-roomed mansion built on a foundation of Cicero and Virgil.

The connections of Cambridge with power in state and church were numerous and important, and in Spenser's time there the University was the most important debating forum for ecclesiastical dispute on its semi-academic side. Spencer was all his life an ardent Protestant nationalist, most explicitly in the *View of the Present State of Ireland* and *The Faerie Queene*, I and V; but there is no evidence to show that he espoused Thomas Cartwright's Presbyterian 'discipline', though *The Shepheardes Calender* offers some evidence for his sympathy with the moderate left-wing of Elizabeth's Establishment, and specifically with her sequestered Archbishop Grindal ('Algrind'). If some of his Cambridge associates, including John Young, Master of Pembroke, directed him to holy orders in a church to be further reformed, he did not respond.

How far he was influenced by the counsel, the coaxing, the salvos of ideas from Gabriel Harvey is an open question, though their friendship is commonly taken as the centre of Spenser's Cambridge experience. It is documented by Harvey in *Three Proper, and Witte, Familiar Letters: Lately Passed betwene Two Universitie Men* and *Two Other Very Commendable Letters, of the Same Mens Writing* [1580], a pompous and silly publication. The 'Hobbinol' of *The Shepheardes Calender* is chief among the circle of literary friends and promoters of Colin Clout, his personality distanced and muffled by the pastoral cipher; Spenser's fine sonnet to him dated from Dublin in July 1586, which describes that irritable and irritated don, that inveterate name-dropper (both of the living and the dead), that unsuccessful academic politician and would-be Machiavellian, as 'a great lord of peerelesse liberty' who sits 'like a looker-on/Of this worldes stage', tells us only how Cambridge must have looked from Dublin in 1586. Harvey pursued success in the margins of his books; Spenser in the world of affairs outside the University.

The future lay with the Leicester–Sidney connection, but we do not know just when that connection was established. If we are to believe the gloss to *The Shepheardes Calender* ('June'), Spenser had spent some time in 'the Northparts'; in 1578 he was secretary to John Young, now Bishop of Rochester; by mid-1579 he seems to have been attached to Leicester's household, and contemplating a continental trip in his service. He was also by then 'in some use of familiarity' with Sidney and Edward Dyer, discussing 'English [quantitative] versifying – and, probably, more important matters, including the (for that circle) suspect negotiations for a marriage of the Queen with Alençon. One may risk the conjecture that it was from the associations of this period that Spenser derived his un-sympathetic attitude to William Cecil, Lord Burghley, the Queen's right hand. So far as Spenser came to the attention of that busy and subtle statesman, the sentiment seems to have been reciprocated.

The break came in 1580: Spenser went to Ireland as secretary to Arthur Lord Grey of Wilton, the new governor of 'that wretched realm'. The appointment may have been secured through the Sidneys; the dedicatory sonnet to Leicester before *Virgils Gnat* (a translation of the pseudo-Virgilian *Culex* published in the *Complaints*, 1591) hints at some temporary estrangement. Parish registers of the period, for someone with a common name like 'Spenser', need some corroborative evidence, which in this case we do not have, but in 1931 Mark Eccles found that an 'Edmounde Spenser' was married in St Margaret's Westminster to one 'Machabyas Chylde' on 27 October 1579. The son of this marriage, Sylvanus, was given the name of a son of Richard Mulcaster.

Spenser's career in Ireland, punctuated periodically by visits to London, to the Court and his publishers, was the most important part of his life. He was not young, by the standards of the time, when he went there: getting on to thirty. But some poems were known to a circle of friends and *The Shepheardes Calender*, though published under a pseudonym, to a wider public, and he had had some experience in the circles of government. As a poet he was proved to have profited by his rhetorical training and could accordingly give tone and form to correspondence; as a university man, he had a training in generalization, very valuable in making opportunist actions look like adherence to principles. A humanist education was a preparation for affairs, and if all went well a man in Spenser's position could count on multiplying small offices and receiving estates.

All did go well, or as well as might be expected in Ireland. Spenser proved a loyal and competent servant to Grey until that unfortunate man's recall; he was successively Clerk of Faculties in the Irish Court of Chancery, a Commissioner for Musters in Kildare, and Deputy Clerk to the Council of Munster; when he died he was Sheriff-designate of Cork. Along the way he was rewarded with leases and manors: the last of these, Kilcolman, Co. Cork, was the prize. It was sacked in Tyrone's rebellion of 1598. Spenser became one of Yeats's people of the great house; the traveller, scholar, poet may still visit the ruins of Kilcolman, where Ralegh was a guest in 1590, and dedicate a moment's memory to that laurelled head. Spenser would have liked Lady Gregory too.

The friendship with Ralegh, commemorated intimately and gracefully in *Colin Clouts Come Home Again*, is matched in literary interest only by Spenser's marriage to Elizabeth Boyle on 11 June 1594(?), the occasion of *Epithalamion*. Spenser's chief contribution to the public life of Ireland in his time was *A View of the Present State of Ireland*, written in 1596 and circulated in manuscript copies, but not published until 1633, when it was dedicated to the then Lord Deputy, Wentworth.

Ireland was England's first and least successful colony, and a cemetery for political and military reputations; a land of cattle, Catholics, petty chieftains with their squads of guerillas, entrenched descendants of the Anglo-Norman landowners, and a peasantry wild (both in Yeats's romantic and the ordinary sense) from poverty and anarchy. The Tudor Protestant bureaucracy tried in vain to assimilate this chaos to something like the peace and prosperity of East Anglia. In retrospect, their policies seem myopic and brutal, and Spenser's proposals in the *View*, for 'pacifying' the country 'even by the sword', by strategically placed garrisons and re-settlement of the populace according to English usage, sound not unlike some twentieth-century methods of dealing with a poor and divided little country. But Spenser was not only an experienced official, but a humane and learned man, and his treatise sets the situation in the perspective of the land (which, it is clear, he had learned to love) and its history. The *View* is an often an undervalued companion to parts of *The Faerie Queene*, and provides some important insights into Spenser's mind and temper. The spirited defence of Grey, 'however envye list to blatter against him' (see the Blatant Beast of *The Faerie Queene* V & VI); the haunting picture of the desolation of Munster, where the people 'came crepinge forth upon theire handes, for theire legges could not bear them, they looked Anotomies of death'; the appreciative if rather condescending tribute to the Irish bards; the contempt for the wrong kind of 'gentleman'; and above all the fascination with Irish antiquities, of which he promises another book of his observations: all these testify to a catholic imagination undergirded by a strong moral sense that is only incidentally Anglo-righteous. Finally, Ireland, marked by the ruins, in stone and society, of former cultures, and the successive rise and fall of principalities and powers, gave to Spenser, as W. L. Renwick has observed, an outward and visible sign of that spirit which haunted his visions, mutability.

On 24 December 1598 Spenser delivered dispatches from Sir John Norris, governor of Munster, to the Privy Council. On 13 January he died at Westminster, 'a poore man' according to Camden's account and Ben Jonson's, and was buried in the south transept of the Abbey, Essex defraying the funeral expenses. Then Essex went to Ireland with great array and expectations, and returned the next year in failure and despair, his bubble reputation broken. In his dedicatory sonnet to Essex before *The Faerie Queene* Spenser had promised to 'make more famous memory / Of [his] Heroike parts'. Such are the 'cruel sports' of Mutability.

II

Spenser's education and career in the public service follow a pattern conventional for his time. His poetic progress is patterned too: it has the form which comes from early apprenticeship to a craft (his journeyman's 'masterwork' being *The Shepheardes Calender*) and a long determination to fulfil a grand design. An analogy has been noticed between Wordsworth's major works and the structure of a cathedral. Taking our cue from Hurd's characterization of *The Faerie Queene* as 'Gothick', we may apply the analogy more credibly to Spencer's *oeuvre*. The central fabric, at once cruciform (Book I) and insistent upon its direction to the secular shrine of Gloriana, distracting us continually by its incidental decoration, compelling us to interpret it as an allegory of the human condition as seen by a sixteenth-century Englishman – and unfinished, has many occasional attachments, little chapels, memorials, gargoyles, added from time to time. Such are the minor poems.

Spenser wrote no *Prelude*; in his time one has to look into the diaries of Puritan 'professors' to find accounts of the seedtime of the soul; but he seems to have preserved, in one form or another, some of the productions of 'the greener times of [his] youth'. The first of these is his anonymous contribution to *A Theatre wherein be represented as wel the miseries & calamities that follow the voluptuous Worldlings, As also the greate joyes and plesures which the faithful do enjoy* (1569), an anti-Catholic tract compiled by a Dutch Calvinist refugee, Jan van der Noodt. It consists of twenty-one 'visions' with wood-cuts (i.e. emblems) with prose commentary, from Marot's

French version of Petrarch's canzone 'Standomi un giorno solo a la fenestra', Du Bellay's *Songe* for *Les Antiquitiés de Rome*, and four visions based on images from the Apocalypse of St John. Taken as a sequence the visions complain of the impermanence of beauty and power and end with a sight of the New Jerusalem. (Spenser returns to this theme, finally, in the 'Cantos of Mutabilitie'.) The translator's signature is added in the *Complaints* volume of 1591, which includes 'The Vision of Petrarch, formerly translated', and 'The Visions of Bellay', all fifteen pieces of the *Songe*, now turned into sonnets. Other 'sundrie small Poemes of the Worlds Vanitie' in that collection, to which we shall return, may have been suggested by this early exercise.

From the Spenser–Harvey correspondence, the glosses to *The Shepheardes Calender*, and the publisher Ponsonby's preface to the *Complaints*, we learn that Spenser had written, in the decade between the *Theatre* and the appearance of the *Calender*, a number of poetical pieces. Some of these, on the evidence of their titles, were possibly incorporated into *The Faerie Queene*: e.g., the 'Pageants', the 'Epithalamion Thamesis' (*FQ*, IV, xi), the 'Court of Cupid' (*FQ*, III, xii), perhaps 'The hell of lovers'. Other 'Pamphlets looselie scattered abroad' seem to have been versifications of Scripture and religious allegories: 'Ecclesiastes' (which is concerned with the world's vanity), 'Canticum Canticorum' (one source for Spenser's guided tours of woman's beauties), 'Purgatorie' (?), 'The dying Pellican' (obviously an allegory of Christ), 'The Sacrifice of a Sinner', 'The howers of the Lord' and 'The seven Psalmes' (this could conceivably be a translation of Petrarch's seven penitential Psalms). 'Moschus his Idyllion of wandring love' was translated probably from the Latin of Politian; there was a Latin 'Stemmata Dudleiana' in praise of Leicester's house (the only extant Latin poem by Spenser is addressed to Harvey and is not distinguished); two lines from one of his 'sonnets' are quoted in the gloss to 'October'. We may lament the loss of a treatise (?) called 'The English Poet' and the 'Nine Comedies named for the nine Muses', which sounds characteristically ambitious, the 'Legends', and the 'Dreames', which Harvey liked 'passingly well . . . rare, queint, and odde in every pointe', with a commentary by E. K., the editor of the *Calender*.

An Elizabethan poet's decision to commit his work to the press, or not, is often mixed, and there is much double-talk in prefaces and dedications. But it is clear that the publication of *The Shepheardes Calender* in 1579, an event which most literary historians celebrate as a turning point in English letters, was very carefully prepared for by Spenser and his Cambridge friends. The dedication to Sidney, the incidental promotion of the anonymous author ('Immerito', the unworthy one), the extensive apparatus of epistle, argument and glosses appropriate to a scholarly edition of a classic, all point that way. At the same time the editor, who is probably Edward Kirke of Pembroke and certainly an intimate of Spenser and Harvey, is heavily coy about the little secrets of the coterie, though one gets the impression that he is not as much on the inside, or as learned either, as he would like his readers to think.

It needs to be emphasized that the editorial matter for this very well-received poem (four more quartos before the Folio of 1611) does not announce a revolution in genre or language: the intention is to place the new poet firmly in the accepted tradition of the pastoral, 'following the example of the best and most auncient Poetes,' E. K. writes, 'which devised this kind of wryting, being so base for the matter, and homely for the manner, at the first to trye theyr habilities.' (This commonplace is repeated in the proem to *FQ*, I.) So Virgil and the Italians and French, 'whose foting this Author every where followeth'. The loftier flight of the heroic poem is promised, and the Virgilian progress is eloquently stated in 'October'. The epistle to Harvey is largely an apologia for the language of the *Calender*, for its archaism and Doric rusticity, justified out of the tradition, and the glosses anxiously indicate the poet's expertise in rhetorical figures, his imitation of ancients and moderns in themes and expressions, and the complexity and decorum of his mythological allusions.

The true inventiveness of the work, then, is hardly to be found in the commentary, but in the poem itself. It announces one distinctive mark of Spenser's genius: the achievement of a unity out of diverse elements, externally by the imposition of a numerical or cyclical pattern, internally by the interrelation of themes and a dialectical balance of moods. The *Calender*, in spite of its debt to the *Kalendar & Compost of Shepherds*, a popular 'almanac' translated from a French original, seems at first what an Elizabethan would call a gallimaufry: it is by turns idyllic and satiric, mirthful and melancholy, a cabinet of genres (fable, ode, elegy, debate, complaint), of verse forms (thirteen of those), and of styles, from the 'old rustick language' which Sidney would not allow to the stately artifice of the Pléiade. It is a poetic testament of general significance and a *roman à clef*. But the shepherds' year begins ('January'), turns ('June') and ends ('December') with the poet-lover Colin Clout's complaint of his scornful love Rosalind. This is not to say that the *Calender* has a story; indeed the various conjectures about the identity of 'the Widdowes daughter of the glenne' seem to me largely irrelevant, for Rosalind is (in spite of E.K.'s sly digs in the ribs) little more, in the poem, than one image to focus the poet's feigned image of melancholy. The central motif of the *Calender* is not a broken love-affair but a broken pipe (see *FQ*, VI, x, 18). By a careful paradox, the triumphs of Colin the shepherd-poet are illustrated at appropriate places in the pattern: his ode to '*Eliza*, Queene of shepheardes all' in 'April'; his 'heavy laye' of Rosalind in 'August'; his elegy for Dido (whoever *she* was) in 'November'. These are what E.K. calls the 'Plaintive' and 'Recreative' (with 'March', the subject of which is Cupid, 'to springtime . . . most agreeable'); the 'Moral . . . mixed with some Satyrical bitternesse' are not apparently placed with reference to the seasons.

The shepherd is lover, poet, pastor. His world of artificial simplicity is at once self-contained (i.e., the poet may simply play with the idiom) and a mirror held up to the 'real' world outside. This may be a steel glass, like Gascoigne's, an instrument of satire, or a 'perspective' picture: look at its rude and homely surface from just the right angle, and you will see recognizable people. The poem moves insensibly from the openly didactic to the obliquely suggestive. In each of 'February', 'May' and 'July' a general moral lesson is taught, but there is a progressively explicit allusion to ecclesiastical affairs, until finally in 'September' we have a polemic against the wolves from Rome. The attacks on 'proude and ambitious Pastours', either by the feigning of fable or plain speech, are in the tradition of Langland, Latimer, and the Puritan attack on worldly bishops.

The poet also has his responsibilities, his 'pastoral' function, not to solace 'youthes fancie' with 'dapper ditties' but 'to restraine / The lust of lawlesse youth with good advise'. 'October' is Spenser's lost 'English Poet' in verse, and also carries us out of the *Calender* to the *Fowre Hymnes* and *The Faerie Queene*. In this dialogue of Piers and Cuddie, Cuddie stands in for Colin Clout, who is 'with love so ill bedight' that he cannot mount with the Muse. The fiction of Rosalind is preserved, but surely this tyrant love is not courtly infatuation but 'crabbed care' of lowly things (lines 100–2) or, simply, writing pastoral, the opposite of that love which erects the mind to transcendence over earthly matters (lines 91–6). In this eclogue, 'of contempt of Poetrie and plesaunt wits', another vision of glory is offered: Piers exhorts Cuddie to the heroic mode, to the celebration of Elizabeth and of Leicester; but the vision recedes, a Cuddie complains of the dearth of patronage, and summons the Bacchic images of inspiration only to turn wearily and modestly from that 'poetical fury'. For a moment, as E.K. notes, the poet abandons the decorum of the pastoral, as in the Sixth Book of *The Faerie Queene*, he transposes the heroic into a pastoral mode.

Colin in the *Calender* is subdued to the design; in *Colin Clouts Come Home Again* (1595; the dedicatory letter to Ralegh is dated from Kilcolman 27 December 1589; the poem was revised before publication) he appears as Edmund Spenser; the shepherds have been transferred to Ireland, and their comments and questions provoke Colin's account of his association with 'the shephearde of the Ocean' and their trip to Court (1589–90) when Spenser arranged for the publication of Books I–III of *The Faerie Queene*. The pastoral mirror is still held up, but it returns a personal and double image. Like the *Calender*, this rich and elegant work includes many things: autobiographical fragment in easy cipher, panegyric, satire, literary anecdote, catalogue of noble ladies, and a tractate of love. The decorous tentativeness of the *Calender* is now succeeded by an easy confidence, though barking Envy, anticipated in the prelude to an earlier poem, is recalled in 'the malice of evill mouthes, which are alwaies wide open to carpe at and misconstrue [his] simple meaning'; Spenser, like George Chapman, always felt the Blatant Beast breathing down his neck.

The poem is set in Colin's pastoral milieu: it begins with praise of his 'curious skill' on the pipe and ends with complaint and praise of Rosalind. But Rosalind is now transformed into a divine creature of 'heavenly hew', her thoughts as high 'as she her selfe have place': she is either an attribute of the Queen or an idea of heavenly beauty – or both. The narrative of the journey to Cynthia's court begins as a rural idyll, with Spenser and Ralegh reading each other their poems, Spenser's a little topographical myth of his Awbeg and Bregog rivers, Ralegh's something much more important, his 'lamentable lay' of 'the Ladie of the sea', and ends at her house of fame, where Colin 'found lyking in her royall mynd'.

But the Court is a house of pride too, no place for a shepherd, full of place-seekers, courtiers with filled tongues, pride, idleness; love is profaned there in 'courting vaine' (see *FQ*, III, x). Whereupon Colin assumes his function as priest of Love, sings the praises of Cupid as the most powerful of all the gods, and proceeds to an oracular hymn to Love as creator of the natural order.

The elegies on Sidney which make up the rest of the *Colin Clouts*

Come Home Again publication are of little interest. Spenser's *Astrophel* praises the accomplishments of the 'sclender swaine', celebrates his devotion to Stella, and transposes him into Adonis; it is a 'frame poem' for the other elegies to follow, and graciously impersonal. A better tribute to Sidney had already been paid, in *The Ruines of Time*. Spenser's other pastoral elegy, *Daphnaida* (1591), on the death of the wife of Sir Arthur Gorges, is an over-decorated imitation of Chaucer's *Book of the Duchess*, hyperbolic lamentation that goes on too long.

The *Complaints* (1591), collected by Ponsonby to ride the 'favourable passage' of the first part of *The Faerie Queene*, contains two important poems, 'The Ruines of Time' and 'Mother Hubberds Tale' and other miscellaneous 'parcels' of different times of composition, 'being all complaints and meditations of the worlds vanitie, verie grave and profitable'. We have noticed already the inclusion of the revised matter from the *Theatre*, here extended by 'the Ruines of Rome', a translation of Du Bellay's *Antiquitiés* and twelve sonnets of his own, 'Visions of the worlds vanitie', each emblematic of the power of the small and insignificant to help or destroy the great, the theme also of 'Virgils Gnat'. (We do not need to assume that any personal reference is intended.) 'The Teares of the Muses' may be early work too; it is a complaint of the general decay of culture in a materialistic and vulgar age, in which each of the Muses weeps over the decline of her own department. 'Muiopotmos, or The Fate of the Butterflie' does not seem to belong under the printer's rubric; the lovely dedication to Elizabeth Spencer, Lady Carey, suggests that it is a little presentation piece, a bit of graceful fun, and surely it is no treason to Spenser scholarship to take it that way, in spite of efforts to find a topical allegory on such heavy readings as that of Professor Nelson – 'delightful teaching of the tragic lesson that on earth happiness is its own destruction, &c.' This is a mock-heroic *jeu d'esprit*; in the sad fate of Clarion the butterfly, slain by Aragnoll the spider, the narrative flourished with Ovidian digressions and graceful parodies of heroic catalogues, Spenser's characteristic sense of mutability is subdued to a gentle smile.

Not so in 'The Ruines of Time', a grave meditation on the strife of time and art. Reproached on his return to England in 1590 that he had not commemorated the death of Sidney and the illustrious connections of his house, he 'conceived this small Poeme, intituled by a generall name of the *worlds Ruines*: yet specially intended to the renowming of that noble race'. The poem is composite, and it has been suggested that Spenser drew upon his 'Dreames', 'Pageants' and perhaps his 'Stemmate Dudleiana' to make it up: but it has a direction and a climax. Returning to an England changed much in a decade, his mind full of antiquities from Camden, he imagines the spirit of the Roman Verulamium lamenting over the 'vaine worlds glorie' and the mutability of the works of man; after an incidental tribute to Camden's eternizing labours, she passes to the detraction that has followed the death of Leicester, and adds, in a couplet recalled in bad times by another Anglo-Irish poet,

> He now is gone, the whiles the Foxe is crept
> Into the hole, the which the Badger swept.

There follows eulogies of other members of the Sidney–Dudley–Russell family, ending with a fine elegy for Sidney (lines 281–343), which leads into high praise of the eternizing power of poetry, concentrated in the memorable austerity of

> For not to have been dipt in *Lethe* lake
> Could save the sonne of Thetis from to die;
> But that blinde bard did him immortall make . . .

What seems like an overt attack on Burghley's scorn of poetry (lines 441–55) introduces two sets of 'tragicke Pageants', the first six of the fall of power and beauty, the second six of the resurrection and perfection of the images by which life, through art, achieves the ideal of a higher nature.

'The Ruines of Time' has a humanist perspective; 'Mother Hubberds Tale' re-enters the closed, almost domestic world of medieval satiric fable, with some contemporary intrusions which presumably do not all belong to that part 'composed in the raw conceipt of his youth'. The poem begins in the dog days, in a time of plague and death, the month when Astraea, goddess of Justice, left earth for the heavens (see *FQ*,V, i); the poet recalls, in an appropriately 'base' style, the time-passing tale of 'a good old woman', repository of the folk memory. The successive disguisings of the Fox and the Ape in the wide world provide the framework for a satire upon all estates in the manner of Gascoigne, or of the preaching friars and their successors in the public pulpits of Spenser's England. The beasts reject the ordered society; so they go through the 'yron world': the begging discharged soldier who proves an evil swain, the unlearned and worldly cleric (with the footnote that it is easy pleasant work being a Protestant, lines 446 ff.), the newfangled courtier (with a periphrasis of the *good* courtier and a savage description of what it is like to sue for favour at court: lines 892–914). When they come upon the sleeping Lion, and the Fox persuades the Ape to don his panoply, the general satire seems to shade into particular allusion, though the tyranny of these lords of misrule, their contempt of nobility, literature and the common people, and their punishment by divine intervention, are conventional enough.

When Spenser sent the manuscripts of his *Amoretti* and *Epithalamion* to Ponsonby late in 1594, there is no doubt that he intended the sonnets to be taken as the record of his courtship of Elizabeth Boyle and the great marriage hymn to serve as their inevitable sequel. Some of the sonnets, especially those which work out variations upon his mistress' pride, or her eyes, are conventional enough within what we loosely call the Petrarchan tradition; but this sequence *is* a sequence, arranged characteristically upon the cycle of the year. Sonnet IV begins a year, the cuckoo heralds spring in XIX, XXII belongs to Ash Wednesday, it is a new year again in LXII, Easter in LXVVIII, spring again in LXX. Spenser was married in June. The sequence also breaks from convention when the poet describes 'the happy shore' (LXIII), and the lady begins to consent and is (just before Easter) 'with her owne goodwill . . . fyrmely tyde' (LXVII). There follows (LXIX–LXXXV) a set of eloquent inventions on the theme of his happiness: she is his Elizabeth, he has finished half of *The Faerie Queene* and he can take time out to praise her too (LXXX); he will eternize her; her beauty ravishes him, but is in gentility and virtue 'divine and borne of heavenly seed (LXXIX); she is his Muse. But in the last four sonnets the tone changes: that old enemy a 'venemous toung' breaks his 'sweet peace', there is an absence in which he comforts himself with the 'Idea' of his love, and the sequence ends with the poet disconsolate. The fluidity of the mature Spenserian style at once diminishes the epigrammatic possibilities in the sonnet with its locking couplet, and gives an added richness and variety to the familiar comparisons: of his mistress to precious merchandise (XV), of his starless love to a wandering ship (XXXIV), and, finest of all, of the huntsman's capture of the 'beast so wyld' (LXVII).

The *Epithalamion* sets a crown on all the lesser poems and is a coronal for the poet's bride, a circlet of the hours of their wedding day. The rituals of marriage, pagan and Christian, in their stately ceremonial passage under the turning heavens, control and solemnize the passionate anticipation and fulfilment of the bridegroom, and turn a wedding in a little Irish town into a temple of fertility and sanctity. The long flowing stanzas play their varied melodies against the regular beat of the refrain. The poem is also an 'ornament', as Spenser calls it, and it makes a day stand still to compose a book of marriage hours, with the Muses as frontispiece, Cynthia–Lucina, Juno and finally the heavenly choir of saints as afterpiece, and between them pictures in which the poet's imagination fuses the natural setting (flowers, bells, bonfires, 'th'unpleasant Quyre of Frogs') with Renaissance decoration ('an hundred little winged loves' hovering over the marriage bed). Edmund and Elizabeth have been married 'in the fear of God' according to the Book of Common Prayer, but they are as gods too.

There is nothing particularly elusive or complicated about Spenser's 'doctrine of Love', though its sources, in the New Testament, in Plato as interpreted by Ficino, in the Italian theorists happily summarized by J. C. Nelson, in the tradition of *amour courtois*, and in the mythographers and emblematists, are diffuse and complex out of all reason. Spenser seems to have absorbed all this 'new theology', possessed it, and subdued it to his hand. He assumes that man dwells in distinguished if not divided worlds: in the world of nature we perceive and suffer Love as energy; in the world of grace we can contemplate Love's perfection and be 'transported' by the 'soueraine light' of its source. The pastoral world is confined in nature (see the celebration of Love in *Colin Clout*, lines 783–894), but the *Fowre Hymnes* (1596) take in both worlds, as Spenser's retraction in his dedication makes clear, and clearer than his critics. The two worlds are separated by the imperfect will of fallen man, for whom the creative power of Love may operate as tyranny and breed frustration and love-melancholy, and connected by the clearing of the vision which sees the Idea in the world of becoming ('Hymne of Heavenly Love', lines 283–4), and a *typology* of Love, in which Cupid's power prefigures the Incarnation, and Venus' 'informing' power, which we see here as in a mirror, looks forward to the absolute Sapience, the mirrorless beauty of the Divine Wisdom. This is the argument of the *Hymnes*, in which the poet begins as a courtly gentleman and ends as a seer.

III

The Faerie Queene was begun at least as early as 1579–80, when Spenser sent some of it to Harvey, and received the notorious comment, 'Hobgoblin runne away with the garland from Apollo'. Even taking into account Harvey's humanist prejudices, this could hardly be said of Books I and II as we have them, and it has been argued that Spenser began with an imitation of the narrative manner of Ariosto, we have it now in Books III and IV, with the intention of 'overgoing' *Orlando Furioso*, in the genre of the romantic epic. But about two years afterwards, according to Bryskett's *Discourse*, Spenser announced that he 'was well entered into' a poem 'in heroical verse, under the title of a Faerie Queene, to represent all the moral virtues, assigning to every virtue a knight to be the patron and defender of the same'. Some parts of the poem in something like its present organization were circulating in England by 1588, when Abraham Fraunce quoted II, iv, 35 in his *Arcadian Rhetorike*, and Marlowe borrowed a simile from I, vii, 32 in the second part of *Tamburlaine*. When Spenser published the first three books in 1590 he prefaced them with an explanatory letter to Ralegh, and added (apparently in successive stages during the binding) some seventeen dedicatory sonnets to highly placed persons, some of them tied to him by bonds of affection or esteem. Books IV–VI were finished by the time of writing *Amoretti* LXXX (1594?); in XXXIII, addressed to Bryskett, he complains of the 'taedious toyle' of the work. These were published in 1596 with a reprint of I–III from 1590. Matthew Lownes's folio of 1609 adds 'Two Cantos of Mutabilitie', which to the publisher appeared to be 'parcell of some following Booke' of 'Constancie'.

We should not be disturbed to find that the elaborate introductory apparatus which Spenser designed for his major work seems at odds with our experience of the poem itself. When Spenser read Homer or Virgil he found them brought into court with extensive rhetorical genuflections to patrons, prefaced by explanatory essays, and rich in commentary. He thought, quite properly, that a big poem needed as much of this as he could manage. Hence the dedication to the Queen, for which he received after some delay a pension of £50 (no small sum), and hence the promises of eternizing, if 'under a shady vele', to sundry noble persons. The sonnets to Grey and Burghley break through the façade of courtly compliment: Grey would understand that there was more than the topos of affected humility in the confession that this work was 'roughly wrought . . . In savadge soyle, far from Parnasso mount', and the poet tells the elder statesman that he should take the poem seriously (allegorically?), and so get at the 'fairer parts' of it. The 'Letter' to Ralegh had some diplomatic importance in 1590, but in substance is not so much addressed to the poet's well-placed friend as to an invisible committee of humanist readers, chaired perhaps by Gabriel Harvey, for it sets out what Thomas Warton called a 'grand, simple, and ultimate design' for a national epic. The 'Letter' pretends to be, and is in many respects an explanation, so that we may 'as in a handfull gripe al the discourse', but it is more a piece of general theory, and Nelson has pointed out its resemblance to such a document as Badius Ascensius' preface to the *Aeneid*. If we read it in that way we shall find what the poet means by calling *The Faerie Queene* 'a continued Allegory, or darke conceit', and his ideas about 'the Methode of a Poet historical'.

He begins by confessing that 'allegories', i.e., such pageants or shows as Warton and Lewis have emphasized as sources for Spenser's iconography, are open to 'gealous opinions and miscon-struction'. Therefore he explains that by the 'Faery Queene' he means glory 'in his generall intention'; by glory I take him to mean the total fulfilment or crown of his civilization. Here allegory, his *fiction*, directs the reader to an abstract ideal or quality. But in 'my particular' she 'is' Elizabeth: the fiction directs us to recognize a person, or rather two persons. *Politice* she is the Queene; *ethice*, as a 'vertuous and beautiful Lady', she is 'shadowed' in Belphoebe and others. By Prince Arthur 'before he was king' is 'sette forth magnificence in particular'. 'In particular' here does not equal 'my particular' just above, but something like 'generally' or 'above all'; Spenser does not suggest an Elizabethan 'particular' for Arthur; on the contrary he is 'furthest from the danger of envy, and suspition of present time'. In fact he is Britain, the realm, to which more than once on her public occasions Elizabeth professed herself married.

So much for vulgar misreadings. The piously learned, on the other hand, may object to wrapping up good doctrine in the clouds of 'Allegoricall devises'. To this the poet replies that to be an effective moralist these days one has to provide 'showes', teach by 'ensample' rather than by rule. Allegory in this context is the essential mark of 'an historicall fiction' according to the traditional modes; it is 'fashion-ing', i.e. exemplifying, 'coloring' a 'generall end' by delightful 'showes'. Readers are insinuated into excellence thus. So Homer, Virgil, Ariosto, Tasso have all 'ensampled' the good governor and the virtuous man. This vast design, to be completed in twenty-four books if the poet is 'encoraged', would for Spenser's readers complete the westward course of a heroic culture: from the first Troy to the second, through the cycle of Charlemagne and the counter-attack of Christendom in the Crusades, to Troynovant by the Thames.

As for the form of the poem, it is clear that if Spenser was concerned at all to balance the claims of the neo-Aristotelians and the liberals in the humanist descriptions of the heroic poem, he was on the side of Cinthio and of Tasso, who insisted on unity but admitted a 'natural' variety in the events and personages of epic. So he comes down firmly for a single hero, pattern of 'magnificence', according to Aristotle 'and the rest' the sum of all the virtues, imposed on a romantic cycle of exploits by twelve other 'patrons' of the twelve private moral virtues. To make a 'pleasing analysis' of time the poet begins, not in Gloriana's court at her twelve-day feast, but in 'the middest, euen where it most concerneth him'. Nothing could concern Spenser more than to begin with the knight of the Red Cross.

The Letter does not describe *The Faerie Queene* as we have it, or even the first three books with which it was first printed. It is rather a rationalization of a 'vision' or succession of 'pageants' much more complex, fluid, even intimate, the world in the mind of Edmund Spenser. Even if there were twelve private moral virtues 'devised' by Aristotle (and Spenser may have thought so), they could not include Holiness, Chastity, Courtesy – or Friendship and Justice as the poet understands them; Book II, of Temperance, is the only Aristotelian part of the poem, and then only if we approach it diagrammatically. And by 1596 Spenser seems to have abandoned even the distinction between private and public virtues, and to have consciously or unconsciously foreshortened his design. As Northrop Frye has observed, the poem is only in one sense a fragment, incomplete; in another, especially if we take the Cantos of Mutabilitie as a kind of mythological gloss upon it, it forms an imaginative whole. Nor does the Letter say anything at all about the most important quality of the poem, its *style*, by which time is continually being caught up in the dragging net of the stanza and space is perspectiveless, emblematic. The monstrous and the familiar, the sublime and the absurd, are all subdued to this rhythm, so that Sir Kenelm Digby was right when he wrote that we have to heed him with great attention to see his 'rare and wonderfull conceptions'. Of the three faculties of the mind figured by Spenser as the three 'sages' in the turret of Alma's house (II, ix), the third, memory, provided the matter of the poem; the second, reason, its doctrine; the first, a melancholy fantasist, wrote it.

The integrity of the poem, then, does not derive from Aristotle and the rest as Spenser contended, or from the intricacies of 'numerical composition', but from an 'in-forme' (George Chapman's word) of images which the poet created as his fairyland opened before him.

Fairyland is itself a mental landscape: though it has reminis-
cences of Ireland (the first of these, the Bog of Allen, is at II, ix, 16),
of the Court (V, ix), and other scattered vignettes of observation, it
is a characteristically syncretist world out of books and spectacles:
the Apocalypse, Ovid, Ariosto, Tasso, the mysteries, masks,
triumphs and entertainments, 'goodly arras of great majesty',
Hellenistic pastoral romance, the *loci amoeni* of the classical
rhetoricians, each shading into the other, a dream-cinema. It
cannot be mapped like Tolkien's Middle-earth; as in some
twentieth-century science fiction, the settings are either special
environments rigged to exemplify human capacity for good or evil,
or re-creations in a personal idiom of certain archetypal images,
such as the Underworld or the Earthly Paradise.

If we stop looking fretfully for Spenser's intentions, plans and
scenarios for his poem, wishing we had his 'foule papers', we shall
find that even the pattern of the virtues has a satisfying shape. In
terms of the 'historical fiction' Book I contains everything else that
happens or can happen in the poem: the victory of the English
Reformation is a manifestation of the fall and redemption under
grace of man and society, imaged in messianic and apocalyptic
Christian story. In the order that man creates, the complement of
the knight of the Red Cross is for Spenser the virtuous and
accomplished gentleman, the courtier, who cannot redeem the time
but only make it tolerable and beautiful by the arts of another kind
of grace. As Contemplation shows St George a vision of the New
Jerusalem, so Calidore is vouchsafed – but by accident – a vision of
the Graces, the teachers of civility. The heavenly city is 'high and
strong', eternal; the tableau of the Graces is as frail – and as eternal
(VI, x, 28) – as the poet's music. The books of Temperance and
Justice exhibit, within a fallen world, the disciplines of knowledge
and power. In the first, the little world of man is anatomized and
found to contain a legion of corrupt fantasies urging the will to
violence or seducing it to concupiscence. What Guyon learns and
acts upon is simply to distinguish the true dream which leads to
virtuous action in the pursuit of fame or to delighted contemplation
of beauty from these idle day-dreams, 'shows' of wealth or erotic
satisfaction. Guyon makes Hercules' choice of the hard way (a
commonplace of Renaissance mythography); Artegall is another
Hercules, wielding 'the club of Justice dread' (V, i, 3), trained for
his labours by Astraea (now stellified between Leo and Libra) upon
wild beasts, and his campaigns against anarchy in the body politic
and (with Arthur) against the bestial tyranny of Rome are reminis-

cent of the savagery of the Book of Judges. The sword in the hand of right corresponds in the state to the rationally-directed will in the individual.

At the centre of the poem as we have it are the books of Chastity and Concord, and this seems the right place in the design, for *The Faerie Queene* is a marriage poem. The sacred betrothal of St George and Una prefigures in Eden restored the promised union of Arthur and Gloriana in that other Eden; between these Britomart and Artegall carry the adventure and the prophecy. Venus is the presiding deity of these books; of generation in Book III, of the perfection of love and friendship in Book IV. But she is also invoked at the very beginning, in the proem to the first book, where, with a disarmed Cupid and a pacified Mars she makes up a trinity of beauty and harmony, and the veiled mystery of her idol (IV, x, 40–1), an image of the procreative, the *genial* principle, is a type of the veiled figure of Nature in the 'Cantos of Mutabilite', whose judgment (VII, vii, 58–9) sets time in the context of eternity. Wherever we go in Spenser's vision of the natural order, we find this 'moralized' Venus, who with her complement Diana figures (as in their alternates Amoret and Belphoebe: III, vi, 28) the play of freedom and restraint by which, as in a cosmic heartbeat, this mutable world is sustained. The woodgod Sylvanus can see Una only in these terms (I, vi, 16), and the vision of art, when the Graces dance to Colin's pipe, is on Venus' mount (VI, x, 8–9).

The Venus-figure is something we take in slowly from the poem, after we have read it more than once, and find its recurrences echoing in our minds. But the continued allegory of good and evil irresistibly controls the whole complex forward movement of the fiction, creating a pattern of opposites in which there is no moral neutrality. Cupid is a cruel tyrant in the House of Busirane (III, xi–xii); Venus' passion for Adonis an invitation to lust in Malecasta's house (III, i), and the 'bloody rage' of Mars is figured in the burning violence of Furor and Pyrochles (II, iv). The fundamental paradox of the whole superb encyclopaedic work is that the strife of light and dark, of Holiness with Antichrist, of Temperance with the perverted will, of Chastity with lust, of Friendship with strife and separation, of Justice with anarchy and tyranny, of Courtesy with baseness of heart and mind, is crossed by wonder at the diversity, the fecundity and the strangeness of the world created by the human imagination.

It follows that the delightful teaching of *The Faerie Queene*, for the twentieth-century reader at least, is an aesthetic rather than a moral discipline, and what it teaches is a lively response to the contexts of words and the content of images. The poem modulates, sometimes abruptly, sometimes imperceptibly, from explicit sign to implicit symbol, from exemplum to emblem, from naturalistic detail to the wildest fantasies of the unconscious, and the liveliness of mind and temper which it demands is good in itself. Spenser is, then, justified even in this generation, so far removed (perhaps) from his preoccupation with wars of religion, the achievement of nationality, the civilizing of the new rich, the didactic function of art, and the creation of a new idiom in poetry. For he was concerned to create a *style* of life, a secular ritual expressing the permanence and variety of the European inheritance.

4

THE EPYLLION

Elizabeth Story Donno

In hazarding his 'apprenteship in Poules' with the publication of *Scillaes Metamorphosis* in 1589, Thomas Lodge elected an auspicious moment to inaugurate a new genre, the epyllion or minor epic (minor in length, not necessarily in quality). In experimenting with a new form and in making the delight of the reader the chief concern of his matter and manner, he forecast poetic concerns typical of the 1590s. The moment was auspicious since the response elicited by the attacks on poetry in the preceding decades had provided critics and poets alike with both a defence and a programme. For poetry had been doubly impugned: the poet-whippers had attacked its *raison d'être* while the defenders, countering this attack, had proceeded to charge it with lack of excellence.

The redeploying of ancient charges against poetry (as Thomas Nashe declared in 1589 in his Preface to *Menaphon*) issued from 'the upstart discipline of our reformatorie Churchmen, who account wit vanitie, and poetrie impietie.' In part, the reformers were prompted by the anti-literary platonic and patristic tradition, but their more immediate reaction stemmed from an extreme Protestant bias which looked with distaste not only on the 'bold bawdry' of the writing of the Middle Ages but also on that of recent continental (especially Italian) authors. Although these attacks centred most frequently on plays and playhouses, the charges, as the apologists were quick to recognize in their rebuttals, were intrinsic to the undermining of imaginative literature. Consequently, they essayed a broad defence, stressing the antiquity and universality of poetry, its civilizing quality, its basis in *enthousiasmos*, in *mimesis* but above all stressing the notion that poetry was not only delightful but also profitable.[1]

---

[1] Their rationalizing moved from the assertion that poetry itself does not abuse but rather it is writers who abuse poetry (Sidney, Harington) to the notion that it is the readers who do the abusing. Defending even 'lascivious' poetry (*'Ovids* love

The pleasure–profit motive had been early enunciated by the humanists, and though they produced no criticism proper, their obiter dicta proved extremely influential in the Elizabethan period, affording the apologists a basis for their critical justification and for their programme. (This in despite of a Roger Ascham who could incorporate the humanistic concept of *eloquentia* and the literary attack of the staunch Protestant in one and the same work.) Picking up the humanistic justification, the apologists sprinkled their defences with the Horatian phrases they parroted so easily: the end of poetry is to mingle the *utile* with the *dulce* and *aut prodesse aut delectare* (though it should be noted that the latter phrase was most often rendered as if it were *et prodesse et delectare*). This pervasive critical doctrine (*both . . . and* instead of *either . . . or*) resulted in an overstating of the doctrine of profit;[1] critics and poets alike, in effect, erected a moral bulwark to defend their intention of delighting the reader.[2]

Concurrently, the apologists mounted their attack, and the taunts directed at the paper-blurrers, the poet-apes, the fry of wooden rimers reached a crescendo in the 1580s. The justice of their charges must, in general, be admitted, for following the appearance of the poetry of Wyatt, Surrey, and other courtly makers in the 1557 *Songes and Sonettes*, there was a distinct falling off: a poetical lag so far as publication is concerned of almost three decades. But what is to be admired is the way in which the Elizabethans set about to alter the situation and the amazing rapidity with which they were able to do so, thus fulfilling William Webbe's confident assertion – in 1586 – that English poetry would be held 'at a higher price in short space'.

Bookes and *Elegies, Tibullus, Catullus,* and *Martials workes*'), William Webbe affirmed 'that the workes themselves doo not corrupt, but the abuse of the users' ('A Discourse of English Poetrie,' 1586, in *Elizabethan Critical Essays*, ed. G. Gregory Smith, Oxford, 1904, i, 252).

1 Although acknowledgement of the pleasure motive seemed at times about to receive its due, the most direct avowal is to be found in that charming and sane, if somewhat gouty, critical work published in 1589 by George Puttenham, *The Arte of English Poesie*. In this treatise which counters the double attack, Puttenham openly affirms that the end of poetry is 'to refresh the mynde by the eares delight' (p 23) and 'to dispose the hearers to mirth and sollace by pleasant conveyance and efficacy of speach' (p 155). Ed. G. D. Willcock and A. Walker, Cambridge, 1936.

2 Underscoring the discrepancy between the purported and real intent was Nashe's query in 1589:
Are they not ashamed in their prefixed posies, to adorne a pretence of profit mixt with pleasure, when as in their bookes there is scarce to be found one precept pertaining to vertue . . .?
'The Anatomie of Absurditie' in *Works*, ed. R. B. McKerrow, Oxford, 1958, i, 10.

Though the apologists gave passing acknowledgement to the time-honoured phrase *orator fit, poeta nascitur* their dominant belief was that it was indeed possible 'to make of a rude rimer, a learned and courtly Poet'. In his *Defence of Poesie* (published in 1595 though written in the early 1580s), Sir Philip Sidney succinctly stated the means: Art, Imitation, Exercise.

To provide the Art there were the technical tools of the orator, the manuals of rhetoric. As an academic discipline, rhetoric had been a part of every schoolboy's experience; it remained for the literary critic to point out and illustrate its utility for developing a *poetical science* (Puttenham's phrase). To provide the Imitation, there were the esteemed models of the ancient and continental classics. Repeated emphasis on the principle of decorum in respect to the various genres led to a concern with the genres themselves, and this accounts in large part for the exploiting of the variety of literary forms and styles that mark the 1590s. For exercise the fledgling poet could experiment with literary kinds and with the manifold technical aspects of his art.[1]

This rallying of poetry's defenders determined the aesthetic of late Elizabethan poetry in general and of the epyllion or minor epic in particular. Although practising poets repeatedly invoked the pleasure–profit motive, their poetry often seems most concerned with the first half of the equation or with the second half interpreted either so broadly as to escape the limits of morality or so narrowly as to issue in a simplistic 'moral'. In their reliance on rhetoric as a means of achieving Art, the poets appropriated the humanist's method for the attainment of eloquence and his pragmatic recognition of the persuasive power of words. They tacitly affirmed their power to manipulate responses. If they achieved this end, their poems were efficient. Hence the ornamentation, the verbal flourishes, the wit and virtuosity should be recognized not as decorative but as functional. They are means to an end – to persuade by delighting. The humanistic concern with style as a means of attaining eloquence overshadows the (equally humanistic) justification of literature on the basis of profitable doctrine. Moral Ascham flatly asserts:

---

[1] Experimentation with a variety of lyrical forms and with techniques of versification had been ushered in with the publication of Spenser's *Shepheardes Calender* in 1579 (the work of a 'new Poete,' as E. K. pointed out in his dedicatory epistle, 'unknown to most men'), as well as with Sidney's varied metrical attempts in the *Arcadia* (i–iii, in part, pub. 1590; i–v, 1593), but its efflorescence was not to be seen until the 1590s.

Ye know not, what hurt ye do to learning, that care not for wordes, but for matter, and so make a devorse betwixt the tong and the hart.

(The Scholemaster, 1570)

In the course of the sixteenth century the concept of the eloquent humanist merges with that of the ideal courtier, himself a work of art; style becomes revelatory of personality. This notion is easily transferred from the courtier-poet to the rude rimer seeking to become a learned and courtly poet and filters into the literary world in general, reinforcing the concept of Art and the power of rhetoric. Originality is seen as the impress of personal style on well-worn topics and motifs. Manner is more important than matter. Hence the successive literary fashions of the 1590s which challenged the individual poet to put his mark on a variety of genres.

One such genre which was to intrigue youthful poets for some three decades was the epyllion or minor epic. No precise antecedents existed for the erotic-mythological verse narrative in sixteenth-century England,[1] and due credit for its introduction

---

[1] This is in direct contrast to its complementary genre, the tragical complaint, which, developing its own set of characteristics and conventions, also became popular in the 1590s. The basis of the latter lies in the medieval *de casibus* tradition brought up to date by the substitution of historical English figures, as exemplified in the many editions of the *Mirror for Magistrates*. When poets picked up this form in the 1590s, largely under the stimulus of Samuel Daniel's *Complaynt of Rosamund* (1592), they blended psychological and rhetorical elements deriving from Ovid's *Heroides* with those of the *Mirror* tradition; with the focus on a protagonist whose fall has been occasioned by passionate love, reciprocated or not, the moral implications of the tragical complaint are thus admonitory or hortatory. The internal limitations of the genre, resulting from its *ex post facto* narration, necessitated a dressing out of the ghost's recital with set speeches, *sententiae*, and apostrophes to Beauty, Fame, Fortune, etc. Rhetorical display became a substitute for dramatic tension. In his *Complaynt*, Daniel elected to use rhyme royal, tacitly acknowledging its suitability for 'grave discourses', as Gascoigne and other critics had pointed out, and this verse form remained standard although the influence of the epyllia is to be seen not only in matter but in the use of sixains adopted by some poets. Such cross fertilization of genres is further exemplified in the tragical legend poems (*e.g.*, Drayton's *Piers Gaveston*, registered 1593).
 Among examples of the tragical complaint are Thomas Churchyard's *Shores Wyfe*, first published in a 1563 edition of the *Mirror* but revised in 1593 to accord with the sweet new style; Thomas Lodge's *Elstred*, 1593; Anthony Chute's *Beawtie dishonoured written under the title of Shores Wife*, 1593; Drayton's *Matilda*, 1594; Richard Barnfield's *A Complaint of Chastitie* (on Matilda), 1594; Shakespeare's *Rape of Lucrece*, 1594 (modified both by a third-person narrative and by the selection of a protagonist from classical literature); John Trussel's *The First Rape of Faire Hellen*, 1595; and Thomas Middleton's *Ghost of Lucrece* (1600), which adjusts Shakespeare's narrative to the prevailing pattern. The profitable doctrine of the tragical complaint existed to please the wiser sort (as Gabriel Harvey had noted), but its pleasure, like that of the epyllion, derived from the rhetorical and verbal skill of the poet.

must be give to Thomas Lodge. However tentative his own notion of the form may have been, *Scillaes Metamorphosis*, looked at in retrospect, is seen to contain most of the elements which a number of poets utilized in producing similar compositions in the 1590s. As indicated by the original title (its reissue in 1610 was entitled *A moste pleasant historie of Glaucus and Scilla*) Lodge's poem, like later examples, has its source in a love episode taken from the rich reservoir of Ovid's *Metamorphoses*, the aetiological basis (concerned to demonstrate causes) of those varied amorous tales proving suggestive to poets both for conceits – expansible on occasion into myths – and for an easy means to conclude their poems.

Viewed by his defenders as a 'most learned and exquisite Poet' and by his detractors as the 'grand-maister of wantonnesse', Ovid was known to every schoolboy. While humanists and critics might voice some doubts about the *Amores* and 'that trumpet of Baudrie, the Craft of Love', the *Tristia*, the *Fasti*, the *Heroides* and, above all, the *Metamorphoses* were acknowledged as valuable aids to academic training in form and content. Of the translations of Ovid's works which proliferated in the 1560s, the most influential was that of the *Metamorphoses* by the Puritan Arthur Golding (i–iv, 1565; i–xv, 1567), who, apart from two justifying prefaces, recounts the tales for their narrative value alone and in as straightforward a fashion as his English fourteeners allow.[1] In his 'Preface too the Reader' Golding also emphasized the linking of tales ('as in a cheyne') so that each one seems to take its ground from that rehearsed before and relates to that which follows, but other translators of the 1560s elected to translate single tales.[2] Whatever their moral intent and

[1] In these two justifying epistles (one addressed to the Earl of Leicester, a patron with Puritan tendencies, and one addressed to the 'simple sort' of reader), Golding introduces almost every argument that later apologists were to employ, including the notion that misuse of matter derives not from the poet or translator but the reader himself. Of critics who would condemn both a book and its maker, he pointedly observes that 'These persons overshoote themselves', deceiving others by their inability to grasp the meaning of the author.

Inability to grasp the meaning of the author according to the simplistic 'morals' Golding sets forth would condemn a critic indeed. His interpretation of the story of Venus and Adonis, for example, is that the death of Adonis shows 'that manhod stryves/Against fore-warning though men see the perill of theyr lyves,' while Echo in the story of Narcissus represents 'the lewd behaviour of a bawd,' and Salmacis and Hermaphroditus show idleness to be the 'cheefest nurce and cherisher' of voluptuousness and voluptuousness 'breedes sin'.

[2] The anonymous translation of *The fable of Ovid treting of Narcissus* (1560); Thomas Peend's *Pleasant fable of Hermaphroditus and Salmacis* (1565); Thomas Underdowne's *Excellent historye of Theseus and Ariadne* (1566); and William Hubbard's *Tragicall and lamentable historie of Ceyx, kynge of Thrachine, and Alcione his wife* (1569).

however dismal their results, in their concern with individual episodes these translators forecast not only the recurring appeal of particular love stories for the writers of epyllia but also their practice in restricting the scope of their poems. The *Metamorphoses* remained their most frequently utilized source, though the *Heroides* (translated in 1567 by George Turbervile) as well as the epyllion of Musaeus contributed.

The account in *Metamorphoses* xiii. 900–68; xiv. 1–74 from which Lodge takes his point of departure is brief: Glaucus, newly transformed into a bushy seagod, sees Scylla, is smitten and, being rejected, seeks aid from Circe, who, in turn, is smitten and, in turn, rejected; in revenge she brings about the metamorphosis of Scylla. Taking over only the central fact of the myth, Lodge lets his inventive fancy shape and extend his matter to 786 lines. Other poets are to do the same; their concern with 'invention' relates, on the one hand, to the aetiological basis of Ovid's 'woorke of turned shapes', and, on the other, to the rhetorical theory of composition, a fine invention revealing (in Gascoigne's phrase) 'the quick capacitie of the writer'. The term thus comes to have a dual application, referring both to topic and to treatment. A 'fine invention' consists in selecting the kind of topic that the poet can treat inventively, that is, imaginatively, and in so doing make his poetic ability manifest.

The opening stanzas of *Scillaes Metamorphosis* establish a personalized and localized scene and situation. While wandering near the Isis sorrowing because of unrequited love, the poet encounters a grieving Glaucus, who reproves him for this grief only to ask for aid in moaning his own like state. As a melodious sound arises from the stream, Themis and her attendant nymphs appear. To this sympathetic audience Glaucus makes his complaint – an element which was to become standard in the genre. Recounting first the sorrows of love which he and the poet suffer, he extends their range by alluding to the wounded Adonis, to the passionate mishaps of the faire Lucina, to the Morne complaining of her Cephalus – allusions which become the fine inventions of later poets. He then particularizes the encounter with Scylla, which leads to his cataloguing the beauties of the beloved – an element which also becomes standard. Recital of her disdain leaves him alternately swooning and speaking, at which point Thetis arrives to chide her son. Since neither words nor tears can counsel a lover, the sympathetic company invoke the goddess of love herself. Straightway Venus arrives with Cupid, who shoots Glaucus with the arrow of disdain.

> Sodeinly the Sea-god started up:
> Revivde, relievd, and free from Fancies cup.

(st. 91)

Up to this point Lodge has presented the episode from the vantage point of the lover; but as the disdainful Scylla then floats into the company, Cupid shoots her with a golden arrow, and the situation is reversed. She becomes the wooer. Rejected, she speeds back to Sicily, followed by the rout of deities and nymphs, with the poet himself mounted on a dolphin. There Scylla utters *her* complaint to a sympathetic natural world, stirring Echo to respond in kind. This too becomes a popular motif, deriving ultimately from *Metamorphoses* iii. 495–8. In his major departure from Ovid, Lodge then relates how Scylla's distraught psyche (pictorially represented by the hellish figures Fury, Rage, Wan-hope, Despair, and Woe) brings about her monstrous transformation. Rejoicing in this metamorphosis, the rest of the company revel in Neptune's bower, paying tribute to 'lovely Venus and her conquering son'. The poet is then conveyed, again by dolphin, back to the Isis where, obeying the seagod's charge, he exhorts nymphs to yield 'when faithfull lovers straie not'.[1]

It should be clear from this summary that the poem is not designed to evoke an empathetic reaction. The love plaints, here and elsewhere in the genre, may harp on a universal string, but the fantasy of situation distances the form so that relevance to real-life emotions is at one remove aesthetically. The appeal lies in the inventive and verbal skill of the poet to delight his reader. In addition to the elements already mentioned as common to later epyllia (the mythological love episode, the personalizing and localizing of scene and situation, the lover's complaint, the catalogue of beauties, the vantage points of a male and a female wooer, the metamorphosis), Lodge employs the sixain form, which Gascoigne, Puttenham, and King James had declared best for matters of love and which was to be much used by other poets. In dedicating his volume to the 'Gentlemen of the Innes of Court and Chauncerie,' he anticipates other writers who directed their efforts

---

[1] The account of Anaxarete, metamorphosed into a statue for disdaining her lover, also appears in *Met.* xiv and may have given a hint to Lodge – if he needed one – in modifying the Scylla story. Golding moralized the example of Anaxarete as willing 'dames of hygh degree/To use their lovers courteously how meane so ere they bee.'

to the 'ingenious opinions' of a similarly sophisticated audience, and their efforts too, as they so frequently noted, were oftentimes the first heirs of their invention. Lastly, and importantly, he forecasts in the visual impact and haunting cadence of his verse the new persuasive power of Elizabethan poets.[1]

Marlowe's *Hero and Leander* was entered in the Stationers' Register 28 September 1593, but the earliest extant edition is dated 1598; since its influence is seen in epyllia published between 1593 and 1598, it must have circulated in manuscript or in an edition now lost. For his narrative he turned primarily to Musaeus' 'divine poem' (the epithet was later transferred to Marlowe), and secondly to the letters in *Heroides* xviii, xix; for Ovid himself, a later translator was to note, had deemed it an honour to become 'secretary' to the two lovers.[2] Musaeus' epyllion had already been translated or adapted into French, Italian, and Spanish, but the earliest version extant in English is that of George Chapman,[3] published in 1616 though it is likely that he had undertaken it in the late 1590s under the stimulus of Marlowe's 'excellent Poem'. But as Chapman acutely recognized both by his own ceremonious handling of the Continuation of *Hero and Leander* (1598) and by the comment in the dedication to his translation, Marlowe's work throughout was quite different from its major source in 'Stile, Matter, and invention'.

Its style is a superb medium for the poet's presentation of his matter and the revelation of his invention, reflecting what seems to be the informing principle of the poem: an energetic movement in one direction followed by an equally energetic countermovement. This pattern, a series of *contrapposti*, is exemplified in the metrical form, in the rhetorical techniques, and in the ideas. Movement followed by countermovement results, finally, in a sense of equipoise.

---

[1] As C. S. Lewis observed, 'Spenser had as yet published nothing that would give Lodge much help, and Sidney's verse (if we suppose Lodge to have seen manuscript copies of it) though far more serious and passionate has seldom this airy, seeming-artless grace' (*English Literature in the Sixteenth Century*, Oxford, 1954, p 489).

[2] Sir Robert Stapleton, who translated both Musaeus (1645) and the two books of Ovid (published together in 1647). Although Isaac Casaubon identified Musaeus as a late fifth-century grammarian, the habit of linking him with the legendary Greek poet of the time of Orpheus was a persistent tradition. Virgil, after all, had paid tribute by placing him in the Elysian Fields (*Aeneid* vi. 677) and Scaliger had declared him superior in style even to Homer (*Poetics*, Bk v. Ch. 5).

[3] Abraham Fleming remarked in 1589 that his Englishing of Musaeus 'a dozen yeares ago' was in print, but no copy of it is known (Douglas Bush, *Mythology and the Renaissance Tradition*, Minneapolis, 1932; reissued New York, 1957, p 305).

Marlowe's use of the couplet form permits his narrative to move along rapidly, but his predominant practice of stopping 'sentence and meaning . . . at the end of every two lines', as Gascoigne had enjoined, counters the headlong rush of the story. This alternation of speed and stasis is reinforced by a variety of rhetorical devices – *sententiae*, conceits, oxymorons, paradoxes, and hyperboles – often employed to strike either a realistic or an ironic note. The plentiful sprinkling of *sententiae*, which make neat observations on popular topics, are often placed so as to give a counter twist to the immediately preceding situation. For example, Leander, struck with Cupid's arrow shot from the modest eyes of Hero, becomes, in accord with convention, instantaneously enamoured, but for Hero it is the fiery gaze of Leander, already won, that causes her to relent: *'Such force and vertue hath an amorous looke.'*

The aetiological conceits, explaining within the compass of two lines why, for example, half the world is black or why the moon is pale, give a cosmic extension to the hyperbolic beauty of the protagonists. Extended, the myth-in-little becomes an inset 'narratio'. In his narration of Jove-born Mercury and the country maid Marlowe ironically handles the conventional form of the *pastourelle*, since the cunning god substitutes 'speeches of pleasure and delight' for 'brutish force', a device paralleling Leander's deceptive rhetoric with Hero. In turn, Hero enunciates the instinctive response of the girl when she queries Leander: 'Who taught thee Rhethoricke to deceive a maid?' The country maid, inwardly moved, remains outwardly mute except to pose an improper demand on her lover; Hero, outwardly moved, remains inwardly reluctant; her demand *'Come thither'* slips out 'unawares'. The consequences for this world of the maid's demand for a draught of heavenly nectar were dire: the abhorrence of love and learning by the everlasting fates, the inevitable link between learning and poverty, etc. The consequences of Hero's demand were left for Chapman to adumbrate. Marlowe again handles a conventional form ironically at the end of the second sestiad, where after the consummation Hero wishes the night were never done and grieves at the approaching day – a capsuled *aubade*. Overcome, suddenly, by modesty, she blushes; this 'false morne' brings forth the day 'before the day was borne'.

Numerous deities figure in the poem either explicitly or allusively. In each instance the immortals are projected in very mortal terms, sometimes to emphasize extremes of action in the cause of love ('Jove slylie stealing from his sisters bed/To dallie with Idalian Ganimed' or 'tumbling with the Rainbow in a cloud');

sometimes to heighten the alluring quality of the protagonists (Cupid, mistaking Hero for Venus, takes his rest, rocked on her ever-panting bosom, or Neptune, wooing Leander at the bottom of his watery domain, thinks him Ganymede until he discovers him to be nearly dead).

Neptune's counter wooing is also ironically handled. Not only does the seagod mistake Leander on two counts, as an immortal and as a maid – mistakes (as the poet has emphasized) not terribly important to deities under the compulsion of love – but he is also deluded in confounding love with pity. When Leander remains insistent on reaching Hero, Neptune hurls his mace only to recall it and wound himself; at this the countenance of Leander shows the pity proper to gentle hearts, whereupon the god concludes (like a courtly lover) that he is beloved. In contrast, the poet presents Leander's emotional reaction in realistic terms. Unlike a courtly lover, he does not conceal his love, crowning his bonnet with Cupid's myrtle, winding Hero's hair ribbon about his arm, and the impact of her beauty in her absence becomes vehement: 'Burnes where it cherisht, murders where it loved.' Again in the consummation passage where each kiss seems a charm to Hero and an alarm to Leander, the poet notes that 'Love is not ful of pittie (as men say)' – and gods believe – 'But deaffe and cruell, where he meanes to pray.' And he adds the poignant simile of Hero's response, comparing it to the fluttering and plunging of a bird whose neck is about to be wrung.

The protagonists, irresistible in their powers of attraction, are delineated by both contrasting and parallel devices. Hero is presented primarily in terms of her marvellous artificial attire, which in itself evokes wonder, and in terms of her effect on others – on gods (Apollo offers her his throne as a dower), on the world of nature (bees seek honey from her breath), and on men (who think on her and die). Leander, on the other hand, is presented primarily in terms of his physical beauties (insofar as the poet's 'slacke muse' can catalogue them) as well as in terms of their effect on gods and mortals.

His wooing of Hero is an alternate advancing and retreating. Initially, he woos like a bold, sharp sophister, piling argument on argument, the logical basis of each turning on a pragmatic conclusion.[1] That the poet is mocking the humanist approach

---

[1] The examples are taken from a wide range of topics – precious stones, navigation, music, usury, etc. Marlowe's facile handling of diverse topics would have won the approbation of Hoskins: 'Therefore, to delight generally, take those terms from

throughout Leander's *suasoria* is emphasized by the lines dealing with virginity as a virtue:

> Men foolishly doe call it vertuous,
> What vertue is it, that is borne with us?
> Much lesse can honour bee ascrib'd thereto;
> Honour is purchased by the deedes wee do.

(i, 277–80)

The witty audacity of Leander's relying on the pragmatic ends of the humanists as well as on their technique of persuasive oratory lies, of course, in the questionability of his cause – seduction. But being too much of a novice to understand Hero's intent in dropping her fan, he stays behind and (like the Ovidian Leander) writes a letter. Again, in his initial visit to her tower, Leander, in contrast to his earlier assured oratory, is tentative in action, and Hero 'with a kind of graunting put him by'.

For her part, Hero also alternately advances and retreats. Apart from its psychological realism, this pattern reflects her ambiguous position as 'Venus nun', a phrase which others beside Leander would have recognized as an oxymoron. Her yielding in the face of this central irony permits the poet to emphasize the cosmic power of love, which is reinforced by the accounts of and allusions to the passions of the immortals. It is this universal impulse which triumphs over the religious obstacle occasioned by Hero's unnatural role (a 'holy Idiot') and the geographic obstacle occasioned by Leander's abode across the Hellespont. And so the poet sets forth the consummation in terms of love and strife which, working on the four elements, had brought the world itself into existence, establishing thereby an inevitable process of attraction and repulsion. Trembling Hero strives against the advancing Leander and 'this strife of hers (like that/Which made the world) another world begat/Of unknowne joy'.

Marlowe's superb control of matter and manner creates the sense of intellectual verve which is such a dominant quality of the poem and explains its enormous influence on other writers of epyllia. His

---

ingenious and several professions; from ingenious arts to please the learned, and from several arts to please the learned of all sorts; as from the meteors, planets, and beasts in natural philosophy, from the stars, spheres, and their motions in astronomy, from the better part of husbandry, from the politic government of cities, from navigation, from military profession, from physic; but not out of the depth of these mysteries' (*Directions for Speech and Style*, ed. Hoyt H. Hudson, London, 1935, p 9).

allusive use of myth, including the disdainful Adonis, which Lodge
had also exploited, is picked up by other poets, as is the device of the
inset narrative (for example, Chapman and Beaumont). His witty
sententious style is imitated by almost all other poets, and many adopt
his verse form.

Shakespeare, however, in 1593 reverts to the sixains of Lodge for
Venus and Adonis, while blending elements that had appeared in both
poets to produce a distinctive example. The goddess herself is given
the *suasoria*, and she woos like a 'bold fac'd suitor', stressing the same
pragmatic ends as had Leander ('Gold that's put to use more gold
begets'). Though the figure of the forward female is Ovidian in
lineage, it seems to have been particularly appealing in the 1590s as a
reaction to the stance of the Petrarchan lover. In addition to whatever
psychological satisfaction a poet may have derived from redressing
the masochistic aspects of sonneteering, the strategy gave a tonic
variation to the composition of erotic poetry.

As a result, the pivotal irony of *Venus and Adonis* is that it is the poor
queen of love who is scorned in despite of her own law (line 250). Her
wooing, at times so ardent that it moves even Adonis to smile (as
Oenone's is to move Paris to 'chase a laughter'), at times frenetic,
makes for comedy. Yet the burden of her argument against 'fruitless
chastity', against 'love-lacking vestals' and 'self-loving nuns' is the
theme (familiar in the sonnets) that love is a means to arrest the
evanescence of beauty: 'And beauty dead, black Chaos comes again.'
Just as a serious overtone is added to this comic situation, so the
tragic note is undercut by elements of humour and fancy.
Stylistically, the poet uses an equally reductive technique: luxuriant
language, extravagant conceits, and extended *sententiae* are offset by
realistic passages of natural description (the shrinking snail, the
dew-bedabbled hare).

A new motif is the invitational element, adopted by other poets,
particularly Heywood and Drayton. And Venus, like a host of later
wooing beauties, delivers her own blazon. Her complaint (both a
'woeful ditty' and a 'heavy anthem'), though undelivered, is reported
as 'tedious', and its echoing sounds, in a realistic variation of the
sympathetic echo device, are those of 'shrill-tongu'd tapsters'. In
place of a set complaint, Venus declaims against death, and in lieu of
a mythological tale, Shakespeare provides the realistic account of the
jennet and the stallion. Yet he too, like Marlowe, accounts for the
sorrows that now attend love when Venus recites the dire consequences for the world of Adonis' death as she departs, cradling the
new-sprung purple flower.

The novel element in Thomas Heywood's[1] *Oenone and Paris* (1594), based primarily on *Heroides* xvi, xvii, is its pastoral locale, which provides the setting for Oenone's wooing and complaint. This element is most fully exploited in Michael Drayton's *Endimion and Phoebe: Ideas Latmus* (1595), where the splendid opening description confirms Sidney's assertion that 'Nature never set forth the earth in so rich tapestry as divers poets have done.' Drayton, it seems, invented the device of the goddess who disguises herself as a nymph in order to woo a reluctant mortal who is, in fact, her servant. Endymion, in turn, becomes the wooer (an inversion of the pattern found in *Scillaes Metamorphosis*). The wooing by the nymph-goddess affords opportunity for an extended blazon and invitation charmingly evocative of pastoral delights, an evocation which in the account of great Phoebe's appearance on Mt Latmus is intensified by an amalgam of poetic fancy and literary allusion. But before Endymion, already kindled 'with celestial fire', can be transported to the heavens, Drayton interrupts with a learned disquisition on the symbolic relation of the numbers nine and three; the result is that the poet's wearied muse stops short of recording Endymion's vision, clearly to be of neoplatonic import. Drayton's overlay of serious thought (Phoebe and mutability, the mystical numbers, the unrecorded heavenly vision) in turn proves suggestive to other poets, as do the allusions to contemporary poets in the concluding lines. Such allusions, together with comments on the state of patronage, appear in other examples of the genre and reflect the poets' restive attempts to extend its compass and significance.

The most radical attempt to give intellectual weight to the genre is that of Chapman in his *Ovids Banquet of Sence* (1595). Narrative is reduced to an account of Ovid's feasting his senses in Corinna's garden, Chapman, significantly, selecting here not a figure from mythology but a poet, the poet of love *par excellence*, whose rejection by Augustus implicitly relates to Chapman's own adverse comments on the state of contemporary poetry and patronage. A five-fold transformation takes place, for in the banqueting of each of his senses, Ovid experiences the metamorphosis of the potential of sense into spirit.

From the beginning, where in a one-stanza *reverdie* he describes the quickening power of the sun to animate the earth, the poet traces the quickening power of beauty, operating on the sensible

[1] For arguments supporting Heywood's authorship, see the edition of the text by J. Q. Adams, Washington, DC, 1943. Translations of the two Ovidian epistles are included in his *Troia Britanica* (1609), cantos 9, 10.

world, to animate man's soul. Vested in the figure of Corinna, beauty prompts love, and one of the themes of the poem is that such beauty-prompted love can produce a heavenly contentment, for there is 'More force and art in beautie joyned with love/Than thrones with wisdome' (st. 54). But – and Chapman repeatedly emphasizes the distinction between the potential and actual – if such love fails to inspire 'constant sympathy', beauty remains merely the witchcraft of nature, endlessly tempting. And Chapman is sufficiently of this world to admit that such contentment is seldom or never achieved.

Vested in the 'beauty-clad' naked figure of Corinna, beauty is the property of nature and should be adored, but in the first service of the banquet (*Auditus*) when Corinna takes up her lute and sings, beauty of nature conjoins with art. As the notes dance in his ears, Ovid feels his flesh fade and turn to spirit. He asserts that if only his soul could pass into those ravishing sounds, then the Chaos of his fleshly life would be digested into a Golden World. By listening to those notes, *he* can repair to heaven itself, but should he undertake to sing them, the gods themselves would then descend and listen (st. 28). Chapman adds, though, perhaps reflecting his doctrine of the poetical elect, that only Ovid can 'sound these sounds' which issue from the conjunction of love and poetry.

By sounds, as he makes clear in the gloss, he intends 'all utterance of knowledge, as well as musicall affections', and a second theme of this complex and tantalizing poem is that the conceptual can be made visible in art: *Intellectus in ipsa intellegibilia transit* (st. 24 and gloss). The poem is neoplatonic insofar as Chapman is concerned to show that heavenly beauty (like love) should become manifest in the world of sense. His sombre conclusion, however, is that sense in these days is degraded; and, as a result, the poets who have penetrated the contagion smothering the earth remain unknown and unprized (st. 114, 115).

In selecting the poet of sensual love to speak for the highest reaches of poetry and in selecting Ovid's wanton mistress of the *Amores* to embody the concepts of beauty, love, and art, Chapman ran the risk of obscuring his thematic ends. (He ran the same risk in addressing love sonnets to his mistress Philosophy.) The typical diction of erotic poetry, though redressed somewhat by the dehydrated terms of scholastic philosophy, sometimes jostles with the serious import of his poem, and the occasional comic insertions characteristic of the genre jar (st, 42, 57). But the symbolism and the recurring imagery, often of a sensory and cerebral beauty, provide the key to meaning.

John Marston's intent in the *Metamorphosis of Pigmalions Image* (1598) is also markedly obscured by his treatment, so much so that the author felt compelled to append a poem pointing out that his purpose was, in fact, to satirize the genre. In the story of Pygmalion's infatuation with the statue he has carved for himself, Marston unerringly chose an episode which permitted of parody. Though he compresses the blazon, invitation, complaint, and metamorphosis into little more than two hundred lines, he mocks both erotic situation and language, inserting touches of topical satire in the process. Yet he manages to titillate while he mocks.

John Weever's *Faunus and Melliflora* (1600) reflects the fashionable mode by extending a typical epyllion into an account of the origin of satire. *Salmacis and Hermaphroditus* (1602), ascribed to Francis Beaumont in the edition of 1640, in its ease and lightness and wit seems a return to a 'pure' example of the genre, but other writers tend to weight particular tonal elements. Since the diction of love poetry had become conventionalized to include either a physical or spiritual significance or both, the tonal emphasis depends on the poem as a unit rather than on any of its parts. Phineas Fletcher's *Venus and Anchises: Brittain's Ida* (ascribed to Spenser in the first edition of 1628), which uses a long stanza with linking rime, as had Chapman in his *Ovids Banquet*, reflects the Spenserian poetic: its delicate titillation is capable of a conceptual or sensuous extension.

Variations within the genre (which have caused some scholars to doubt that it exists) are to be explained, first of all, by its subject. As Puttenham had observed:

And because love is of all other humane affections the most puissant and passionate, and most generall to all sortes and ages of men and women, so as whether it be of the yong or old or wise or holy, or high estate or low, none ever could truly bragge of any exemption in that case: it requireth a forme of Poesie variable, inconstant, affected, curious and most witty of any others. (p 45)

Its subject then and, secondly, its length dictated the decorum of the epyllion: as a short epic, the high style, including rhetorical techniques of extended similes, amplification, etc., was proper; as a story of love, the middle style with its colloquial diction and discursive imagery was also appropriate; and, finally, as satire, which figured at first sporadically and then more prominently, the low style with its comic effects was suitable. Yet despite the latitude of treatment that decorum allowed, poets, it seems, were ever ready to exceed its limitations. (The genre of the tragical complaint did not admit of such latitude of treatment; thus its popularity was much shorter lived.)

As late as 1646 John Shirley published a characteristic epyllion, *Narcissus or the Self-Lover*, though it had probably been written earlier. Other writers of the seventeenth century, however, seemed attracted to the more shocking myths such as those of Myrrha and Cinyras (for example, William Barksted, H. A., James Gresham) or they diluted the genre by extension, appending mythologized or allegorized interpretations (as did Henry Reynolds, Shakerly Marmion). At mid-century, one direction remained to be exploited, that of travesty and burlesque.[1]

---

[1] The story of Hero and Leander, so much admired in the Renaissance, proved the most popular choice for parody: the anonymous *Loves of Hero and Leander* (1651) went through at least six editions, and in 1669 William Wycherley's *Hero and Leander in Burlesque* appeared. But even this approach had been anticipated by Thomas Nashe. See his prose parody of the story in the 'Prayse of the Red Herring' (1599), *Works*, iii, 195–201.

5

SHAKESPEARE AND THE SONNET SEQUENCE

Thomas P. Roche

'With this key, Shakespeare unlocked his heart', said Wordsworth, commenting on the sonnets, and thus provided one hundred and fifty-four skeleton keys for generations yet unborn to make off with the treasure of our greatest poet. The only trouble with these keys is that they do not work, and we are forced to agree with C. K. Pooler that 'No theory or discovery has increased our enjoyment of any line in the Sonnets or cleared up any difficulty.'[1] This essay will concern itself with problems of reading Shakespeare's sonnets both as sequence and as individual poems. It will not provide keys; it will not clear up difficulties; it will suggest ways in which I have come to enjoy reading Shakespeare's sonnets.

Shakespeare's sonnets are unique in the literature of the sonnet. They are great in so many ways that critics have found it difficult to restrain their sense of felt life from filling in the few facts we know about their composition. In 1609 Thomas Thorpe published one hundred and fifty-four sonnets followed by a narrative poem, *A Lover's Complaint*. We know also that garbled versions of Thorpe's 138 and 144 were published in 1599 in *The Passionate Pilgrim* and that Francis Meres says that the sonnets were circulating in manuscript.[2] At this point we leave fact to enter the realm of speculation. Indeed, we cannot be sure that the sonnets mentioned by Meres are the same ones published by Thorpe. Shakespeare had already published *Venus and Adonis* (1593) and *The Rape of Lucrece* (1594), and both of these poems as books differ in significant ways from the

---

[1] Quoted in *The Variorum Shakespeare: The Sonnets*, ed. Hyder Edward Rollins, 2 vols, Philadelphia and London, 1944, p xv. This edition is a splendid summary of criticism of the sonnets until 1942. References not cited in footnotes may be found by consulting the index of this edition, e.g., Wordsworth, vol. 2, p 142.

[2] Francis Meres, *Palladis Tamia*, London, 1598: 'As the soule of *Euphorbus* was thought to live in *Pythagoras*: so the sweete wittie soule of *Ovid* lives in mellifluous & hony-tongued *Shakespeare*, witnes his *Venus* and *Adonis*, his *Lucrece*, his sugred Sonnets among his private friends, &c.'

sonnets published by Thorpe. Both have dedications to Henry Wriothesley, Earl of Southampton, signed by Shakespeare. Both are relatively free from errors in printing, which would seem to indicate that Shakespeare had seen them through the press. Thorpe's edition of the sonnets is filled with errors that no author should have allowed to go unnoticed. In place of a dedication by Shakespeare is a much debated dedication by Thorpe: 'To the onlie begetter of/these insuing sonnets/Mr W. H. all happinesse/and that eternitie/promised/by/our ever-living poet/wisheth/the well-wishing/adventurer in/setting/forth/T. T.' Thousands of pages have been written about the identity of Mr W. H., and the phrase 'onlie begetter'. Since the first seventeen sonnets advise a young man to marry, many critics assume that the 'love' of Shakespeare's sonnets is a young man. Some go further and assume that the 'young man' of the sonnets is identical with 'the onlie begetter', whose initials are, of course, W.H., and the rush is on. One of the foremost contenders is that Henry Wriothesley, to whom Shakespeare dedicated his two earlier poems. One has only to reverse his initials and deprive him of his title. The other principal contender is William Herbert, Earl of Pembroke, to whom Hemming and Condell dedicated the First Folio in 1623. He has one advantage over Southampton in that his initials need not be reversed. There are many other contenders, but no new facts have appeared since Hyder Rollins (vol. 2, p 208) summarized the dispute in his Variorum edition of the sonnets: 'The world of Southampton–Pembroke theorizing is now all before the reader, where to choose his place of rest. Let us hope that providence will act as his guide; for, as the foregoing pages [twenty-three, in small print] have made evident, any verdict in the case of Pembroke versus Southampton is useless and supererogatory.' Rollins's monumental work makes it clear that for the first two hundred years of their existence Shakespeare's sonnets did not call forth the questions that most plague modern scholarship, clearly based on nineteenth-century assumptions about the relationship of a poet's life to his works. The Romantic poets created art out of their own lives, and the theory of creative imagination that evolved from their art we have transferred back to poets of an earlier age where theory distorts our reading. If Wordsworth wrote out of his own life, then Shakespeare too must have personally experienced what he wrote about in the sonnets. From this assumption evolved the story of the sonnets.

It tells of two people, a young man of high station and great beauty (sonnets 1–126) and a dark lady (sonnets 127–52). Shakespeare contrasts them as his good and bad angels (sonnet 144). He begins by telling the young man to marry in order to gain immortality through his children (sonnets 1–17) and continues with the promise of immortality through his poetry. His love for the young man's virtues continues to grow, and he becomes worried over the attentions to the young man from a rival poet (sonnets 78–86). At some point Shakespeare starts an affair with the dark lady, who is married to a man named William (sonnets 135–6) to whom she is apparently gladly unfaithful not only with Shakespeare but with the young man as well. Shakespeare is morally revolted but physically attracted (sonnets 127–52).

The story does not end, and even my inadequate summary shows it to be a pretty poor thing as story. It is somewhat surprising that a dramatist who relied so heavily on plot should make such a botch. It is even more surprising that he should have chosen the sonnet sequence to tell any story. Nevertheless one can construct such a story from a reading of the sonnets, and it remains one of the more useful fictions surrounding the sequence, even if we are not assigning the correct values to the people addressed. On the other hand, it leaves us with many uncertainties and not a few unpleasant problems. Disregarding the problem of the identities of these people, we are faced with the question of why Shakespeare should have written sonnets to any young man, a question that Shakespeare answered better than most of his critics in sonnet 20. I think that its sophisticated bawdry indicates quite clearly that Shakespeare realized he was violating the conventions by addressing a young man. But I do not wish to argue from internal evidence. The autobiographical fallacy clouds our reading too much for us to be able to read freshly.

Let us turn from autobiography to tradition, for Shakespeare's sonnets belong to a fully recognizable tradition of Renaissance poetry, that began with Dante and Petrarch. The formal excellence of their sonnets made it virtually impossible for later poets to ignore the conventions of the sonnet sequence, and Dante in *La Vita Nuova* and Petrarch in his *Canzoniere*, or *Rime*, established once and for all the conventions by which the sonnet sequence lived. There is first of all the poet-lover in virtuous and agonized pursuit of an elusive female figure, whose beauty to attract is matched by her virtue to repel the ardour of the poet-lover. Her beauty is usually associated with a blonde woman, and her virtue is so great that it continues to exercise influence on the poet-lover even after her death. The names of Dante's Beatrice and Petrarch's Laura have become the type of the unattainable loved one and have all but been absorbed in nineteenth-century theories of dark and smouldering unrequited passions. As in the case of Shakespeare historical researches have failed to turn up the real Beatrice and Laura, and neither Dante nor Petrarch is at all specific about the kind of reality enjoyed by their loved ones.[1] The fact that contemporaries of Petrarch could question the existence of Laura has not deterred the efforts of critics to continue their biographical researches and to attempt to restrict the meaning of these female figures to specific human beings. (In particular Giocomo di Colonna; see Morris Bishop, pp 68–9.) If these female figures are not at least partially allegorical, it would be hard to explain why so many poets in so many countries should have had such misfortunes in their love for ladies with the improbable names of Idea, Pandora, Diana, Cynthia, Fidessa, Castara.

The vitality of the sonnet sequence comes not from real life but from the multiple significances inherent in these female figures who symbolize all that is desirable and unobtainable in human life. We need not refer to outmoded theories of courtly love to explain the intensity and endurance of the tradition; we need only consider the later sequences, derived from Dante and Petrarch, to see that most of them emphasize only one half of the story these poets tell, and that half-story stresses again and again the unhappiness attendant on the poet's not obtaining his lady's love. In both Dante and Petrarch this unhappiness leads to the greater happiness of suffering – through to wisdom and virtue, but in all of the sonnet sequences I have read, with the exception of Spenser's *Amoretti*, the poet is enslaved by despair at the end, trapped by his unobtainable passion. There can be no doubt that the Renaissance reader would have felt some pity for the self-pity of the poet, but I do not think that he would have granted him its inevitability or his ensuing despair. Most of the sonnet sequences seem not merely to depict but to comment on the love: Go and do not likewise. The themes of devouring time and beauty destroyed, no matter how plangently expressed in the voice of the poet-lover, argue the same point of desires not to be fulfilled in this life.

[1] *Vide* 'Beatrice' in Giorgio Siebzehner-Vivanti, *Dizionario della Divina Commedia*, ed. Michele Messina, Florence, 1954. For more conventional views of Beatrice see Francis Fergusson, *Dante*, London, 1966, pp 14ff. and Michele Barbi, *Life of Dante*, trans. P. G. Ruggiers, Berkeley, California, 1954.

Seen in this light Shakespeare's sequence becomes a dramatic reversal of the conventional sequence. No other sonnet sequence gives marriage counsel, and Shakespeare's sequence opens with seventeen sonnets advising a young man to get married. The loved one becomes genuinely unobtainable because he is a man, and the dark lady, whose physical appearance is the reverse of the conventional lady, in becoming obtainable also becomes, if not undesirable, at least not satisfying. We do not burden Shakespeare with 'Platonic' overtones by insisting that the young man, his 'better angel', is his Beatrice, that the love is 'better' precisely because it does not depend on the flesh. That is why the sequence ends with the dark lady sonnets. We see Shakespeare not in the conventionalized despair of the poet-lover but, as one might expect, in the more realistic morass of a human involvement that will not satisfy all of him.

The tradition of the sonnet sequence will also help us in other ways to turn to more fruitful questions about Shakespeare's sequence. In the first place the sequences seem to be following a principle of ordering not based on the alleged narrative. The thirty-one poems in Dante's *La Vita Nuova* are arranged in an intricate pattern of threes, nines and ones that reflect the numerical symbolism associated with Beatrice and anticipate the numerical symbolism of the *Commedia* (Francis Fergusson, pp 20–3). We know from Petrarch's manuscript notations that he spent years putting poems and groups of poems 'in ordine'.[1] There is not time in an article of this length to describe the order, but order there is, and that order includes the placement of poems other than sonnets so that the sequences have not only a temporal but a spatial order as well. It has become increasingly clear to scholars that the interspersed songs in Sidney's *Astrophel and Stella* are grouped and placed in an order that gives meaning to the sonnets and to the sequence as a whole. The subject is complicated and, I believe, deeply involved in the theories of numerological composition recently advanced in studies of Spenser.[2]

We should also take into account those other poems, often narrative, that were published at the end of the sequence proper.

For Laura see E. H. Wilkins, *Life of Petrarch*, Chicago, 1961, p 8, and Morris Bishop, *Petrarch and His World*, Bloomington, 1963, pp 62–70.

[1] E. H. Wilkins, *The Making of the 'Canzoniere' and Other Petrarchan Studies*, Rome, 1951, pp 107ff.

[2] A. Kent Hieatt, *Short Time's Endless Monument*, New York, 1960; Alastair Fowler, *Spenser and the Numbers of Time*, London, 1964.

We have long been accustomed to accept Spenser's *Epithalamion* as the proper conclusion of the *Amoretti* sequence. It has been less common to think of Daniel's *Complaint of Rosamond* as a complementary poem to the *Delia* sequence, even though the sequence was always printed with the *Complaint*, which begins and ends with references to Delia. The poet-lover in despair at the loss of his Delia is paralleled by the complaint of a young woman who succumbed to the ardour of a lover. Delia, if she had any sense of life at all, would have been flattered by the poet-lover's attentions and been warned away by Rosamond's fate, which it must be remembered was also written by the same man. The tradition began with Petrarch's inclusion of the *Trionfi* with the *Canzoniere*, which must have led later writers to feel that the agonies of the *Canzoniere* were subsumed, or at least spiritually cauterized, in the progressive triumphs of love, chastity, death, fame, time and eternity, which provide a vast moral context in which to judge the poet-lover's agony.[1]

Another kind of proof that poets thought of sequences as something more than a collection of imploring sonnets is Barnabe Barnes's *Parthenophil and Parthenope, Sonnettes, Madrigals, Elegies and Odes*. The volume is divided into three parts: 104 sonnets, 21 elegies, and 20 odes. Each of these sections has other kinds of poems interspersed, and each of the first two sections ends with 'finis'. We might accept the work as three separate groups of poems except for the continuity of the subject matter and for the fact that all the various kinds of poems are numbered consecutively, with the result that ode 20 is followed by sonnet 105, which in turn is followed by sestina 5. Apparently Barnes thought of the three sections as comprising one whole work and numbered the poems accordingly. These are, of course, only tentative suggestions. I offer them to the reader only as possible new ways of considering Shakespeare's sequence as sequence.

The order in which the sonnets appear in Thorpe's edition has been subjected to much criticism, to much rearrangement, from Benson's edition of 1640 to the present day – as Rollins's edition makes clear. Most of these rearrangements have been carried out on the grounds of narrative clarity or thematic continuity. None of the rearrangements I have read gives the same sense of satisfying richness and diversity as Thorpe's. They seem merely to bring together all those poems that are alike in one way or another. They

---

[1] See Wilkins, *Making of the Canzoniere*, pp 379–406.

ignore the simple fact that one must have difference as well as similarity to make any pattern apparent to the reader. Thorpe's arrangement, if it is Thorpe's and not Shakespeare's, provides an amazingly large number of imagistic or thematic links between sonnets and sonnet groups. Where a sonnet does seem out of place, it may not be so much a case of intrusion or misplacement as an essential part of a pattern that we no longer recognize. With a poet as complex as Shakespeare it would be dangerous to suggest that there is no design in the sequence, for there are many indications that the order is less than accidental, even though a clear pattern does not emerge for us.

There are first of all the formal considerations. Shakespeare's sequence is different from the majority of sequences in its almost unswerving allegiance to the pentameter fourteen-line form of the sonnet. There are three deviations from this pattern. 99 is a fifteen-line sonnet. 126 is a poem of six couplets. 145 is an octosyllabic sonnet. The question is whether these formal differences are significant or accidental. I am not sure, but it seems more than accidental to end the major division of the sequence (1–126) with a poem that is not quite a sonnet. All references to time or the seasons or the months cease with 126, as do references to the muse and to the glass that the young man is for Shakespeare. This may account for the 'extra' line in 99, for with sonnet 100 Shakespeare reinvokes his muse and urges himself back to the task he had originally set for himself. It may also be significant that this exploded sonnet comes just before 100, the perfect number, for again in sonnets 100–5 all the major themes of the earlier sonnets are repeated and intensified. What I am suggesting, of course, is that the sonnets may be numerologically organized and that sonnet 100 is both conclusion and beginning.

Two other formal aspects of the sequence should be mentioned. Sonnets 153–4 have always given trouble to the critics. They are clearly set apart from the others in tone and quality. But these two elements relate them unmistakably to the sixteenth-century Greek Anthology and in particular to the kind of poem supposedly written by Anacreon, recently popularized by Ronsard, who is probably responsible for its entry into sonnet literature.[1] Shakespeare is not the only sonneteer to use 'Anacreontics'. Slipped unobtrusively between the last sonnet of the *Amoretti* and the *Epithalamion* are several short 'Anacreontic' verses. They too differ markedly in tone

[1] Isidore Silver, *Ronsard and the Hellenic Renaissance in France*, St Louis, 1961, pp 45, 46, 48, 133.

from Spenser's sonnets and marriage hymn and have similarly been dismissed from critical consideration. Nevertheless, if one is willing to give up a lugubriously sentimental approach to the reading of sonnets, one can see in these almost flippant Anacreontics a universalization of the love theme, a comic theogony, that tends to set the subject of love in a new perspective in much the same way that Marlowe's myth of Mercury redirects our moral apprehension of the love in *Hero and Leander*.

My second point is that *A Lover's Complaint* is an integral part of the sequence. Northrop Frye[1] has pointed out the rough parallel between the characters in the poem and in the sequence, but there is more to suggest that his poem, like the Anacreontics, is meant to give our moral apprehension another twist. The poem begins:

> From off a hill whose concave womb re-worded
> A plaintful story from a sist'ring vale,
> My spirits t'attend this double voice accorded,
> And down I laid to list the sad-tuned tale.

I do not think it too much to read these lines not only as a description of an echo but as a literal rewording of the 'story' that has already been told in the sonnets themselves. We should not look for direct correspondences, but the young seducer in the poem is described in terms that would suit the young man in the sonnets. The complaint of the young seduced woman bears the same relation to the sonnets that the *Complaint of Rosamond* bears to the *Delia* sonnets. It tells the story of love deceived:

> Ay me! I fell, and yet do question make
> What I should do again for such a sake.
>
> 'O, that infected moisture of his eye,
> O, that false fire which in his cheek so glowed,
> O, that forced thunder from his heart did fly,
> O, that sad breath his spongy lungs bestowed,
> O, all that borrowed motion seeming owed,
> Would yet again betray the fore-betrayed
> And new pervert a reconciled maid!'

It is the same old story, and 'all's to do again'. What the sonnets and *A Lover's Complaint* have in common is a highly realistic view of the torments produced by the passion of love, a view that exists

[1] 'How True a Twain' in *The Riddle of Shakespeare's Sonnets*, New York, 1962, p 36.

somewhere between the happy marriages of the comedies and the tragic apotheoses of *Romeo and Juliet* and *Antony and Cleopatra*. The sonnets, it seems to me, take a middle path between the joyously acceptable conventionality of the comedies and the dreamlike suppositiousness of the romantic tragedies. They seem closer to that most analytic of plays, *Troilus and Cressida*, and bear the impress of that play's irony-vivified poignancy. Love can be both a glory and a destruction, and the story that the sonnets tell is not so different from the jealousies and rivalries of Chaucer's *Knight's Tale* for us to eschew the providential moral of that tale as a likely comparison. As the sequence exists for us today, Shakespeare's poet-lover turns from the powerful and unfleshly love of the young man to the more immediate and ultimately unconsoling intimacies of the dark lady and ends his sequence with the contradictory clarities of sonnets 153 and 154, which tell us an even older version of Eliot's couplet:

> We only live, only suspire
> Consumed by either fire or fire.

These formal considerations of Shakespeare's sequence have not delivered any easy answers, nor were they meant to. They seem to me more fruitful than the biographical approach, for they enable us to see Shakespeare's sequence more clearly in the tradition of Western morality and poetic convention shared by Shakespeare and his contemporaries as well.

But we read sonnet sequences less often than we read sonnets, and we must now turn our attention to the particular excellences of particular sonnets. As the rhyme scheme (ababcdcdefefgg) would indicate, most of Shakespeare's sonnets fall into the pattern of three quatrains and a couplet, with a strong logical break between the second and third quatrains. This form of the sonnet offers innumerable possibilities of rhythm, syntax, and logic, a logic integrating form and the inexorable theme of time.

In turning from the idea of the sequence as a whole to the individual sonnets we find the remorseless logic of our own experience of love – its anxieties, frustrations, momentary anticipations and delights, which is why R. P. Blackmur called the sonnets a 'poetics for infatuation'.[1] His phrase is a deeply penetrating insight into the primary paradox of the sonneteer: love

---

[1] 'A Poetics for Infatuation' in *The Riddle of Shakespeare's Sonnets*, pp 129–61.

gives life to poetry and poetry will give eternal life to love. The paradox has been generally accepted as truth, but no poem is as warm as a woman, and no woman has so long a life as a poem. I think we find ourselves more often in agreement with Pound's youthful irony:

> When I behold how black, immortal ink
> Drips from my deathless pen, – ah, well-away!
> Why should we stop at all for what I think?
> There is enough in what I chance to say.
>
> It is enough that once we came together
> What is the use of setting it to rime?
> When it is autumn do we get spring weather,
> Or gather may of harsh northwindish time?
>
> It is enough that we once came together;
> What if the wind have turned against the rain?
> It is enough that we once came together;
> Time has seen this, and will not turn again;
> And who are we, who know that last intent,
> To plague tomorrow with a testament!

Our infatuation with our own experience makes us see 'beauty making beautiful old rime/In praise of ladies dead and lovely knights', but we do not believe it except as an act of reading, a prefiguration in poetry but without warmth. The issue is complex, but we should not fail to observe that the poet-lover in the throes of poetic creation is as much in love with the form of the sonnet as with his mistress, a point made by C. S. Lewis many years ago. What we respond to is art, our infatuation with poetics, and the only means we have to deliver us from infatuation is the observation of poetic form as it shapes and envelops our experience, without the selfishness of the purely private.

Critics of the sonnets have dealt well with the relation of poetry and love as theme, and I shall not burden the reader with a repetition of their work.[1] Fewer have dealt with the logic of the structure, and I shall now address myself to that problem in a few sonnets. One of the most common types is the when-when-then sonnet, a logical structure integrating verbal form and the theme of devouring time. We find it in sonnet 12 in which the octave is really

---

[1] J. W. Lever, *The Elizabethan Love Sonnet*, London, 1956; Edward Hubler, *The Sense of Shakespeare's Sonnets*, Princeton, 1952; J. B. Leishman, *Themes and Variations in Shakespeare's Sonnets*, London, 1963.

four two-line 'when' clauses, completed by the 'then' clause introducing the sestet. The division does not always coincide with the
break of octave and sestet. The 'then' can come early in the octave
(as in 30) or late in the sestet (as in 64). The extreme example of
this type is 138, which withholds the conclusion until the couplet
where the sudden turn of the pun on 'lies' and 'Lying' is strong
enough to reverse and rectify our reading of the first twelve lines:

> Therefore I lie with her, and she with me,
> And in our faults by lies we flattered be.

Even a cursory reading of this type of sonnet should make us aware
of the extreme dependence of Shakespeare's sonnets on logical
patterns and structure to determine the meaning of the poems.

We can do the same kind of analysis with the 'catalogue' poems: 18,
66, 129, 130. They follow the pattern of three connected quatrains
and a strong resolving couplet. Sonnet 18 is most interesting from this
point of view. It opens with a question about the propriety of the simile
that the poet has chosen: 'Shall I compare thee to a summer's day?'
the answer, 'Thou art more lovely and more temperate,' denies the
propriety and then proceeds to use the simile. If we pay attention to
the shifts in the relation of tenor (loved one) and vehicle (summer's
day), we shall see that the rest of the octave is a splendid expansion of
the vehicle, quite rightly admired. The third quatrain shifts to the
loved one, described in terms of summer, but emphasizing the
differences between tenor and vehicle. The artful opening question
sets up the logic by which the poem will develop. The simile works by
insisting on the dissimilarities in the similitude, while at the same time
transferring to the loved one all those lovely summer qualities the poet
is so busily disavowing.

The kinds of pattern I have been discussing can also be helpful in
solving one of the most vexing textual problems of the sonnets. The
first two lines of sonnet 146 read: 'Poor soul, the centre of my sinful
earth,/My sinful earth these rebel powers that thee array.' The
hypermetric twelve syllables of line two and the duplication of 'my
sinful earth' suggest that the compositor made a slip and thus lost
for posterity two syllables of Shakespeare's poetry. Clearly the line
needs to be emended, and over one hundred amateur Shakespeares
have made suggestions to win this do-it-yourself Shakespeare
game.[1] A study of the pattern of the poem will help us at least to the

---

[1] See the list in *Shakespeare's Sonnets*, ed. W. G. Ingram and Theodore Redpath,
London, 1964, pp 358–9.

meaning of those two syllables, if not to the precise word. The
sonnet breaks down into the octave, a quatrain and a couplet. The
octave can be divided into four two-line units, each of which uses a
dominant metaphor that unifies the disparate metaphorical
elements. The first two lines combine a cosmological image (centre
of my sinful earth) with war imagery (rebel powers) and clothing
imagery (array). Lines three and four pick up the clothing imagery
and transfer it to a building (Painting thy outward walls so costly
gay) and introduce words of deprivation (pine, dearth). In lines five
and six the metaphor continues the building imagery (walls, fading
mansion) and the financial imagery (costly, cost, lease, spend).
Lines seven and eight introduce the imagery of worms and eating. If
one now proceeds to the third quatrain, one will see that the
dominant image of each two-line unit is picked up in the
corresponding single line.[1] It will be easier to show this by
juxtaposing the appropriate lines.

> Poor soul the centre of my sinful earth,
> *** *** these rebel powers that thee array . . .
>
> Then soul live thou upon thy servant's loss . . .
> Why dost thou pine within and suffer dearth
> Painting thy outward walls so costly gay?
>
> And let that pine to aggravate thy store . . .
>
> Why so large cost having so short a lease,
> Dost thou upon thy fading mansion spend?
>
> Buy terms divine in selling hours of dross . . .
>
> Shall worms inheritors of this excess
> Eat up thy charge? Is this thy body's end?
>
> Within be fed, without be rich no more . . .

The relation of the two sets of lines would indicate a number of
possibilities for the missing syllables. If we want to emphasize the
primacy of the soul over the body, we may choose an image of
lordship (Lord of ?). If we want to emphasize the subjection of the
soul, we may choose an image of servitude (slave to, thrall to?). If we
want to emphasize the soul's deception, we may choose an image of
deception (Fool'd by?). The pattern of the sonnet has not brought
us to an answer, but it will allow us to disavow a number of

---

[1] I am indebted to Professor A. Walton Litz for drawing my attention to this
correspondence.

contending phrases that do not conform to the imagery of the sonnet as a whole.

One other sonnet deserves some comment to show the intricate balance between structure and imagery. It is the very famous 73.

> That time of year thou mayst in me behold,
> When yellow leaves, or none, or few, do hang
> Upon those boughs which shake against the cold,
> Bare ruined choirs, where late the sweet birds sang.
> In me thou see'st the twilight of such day,
> As after sunset fadeth in the west,
> Which by and by black night doth take away,
> Death's second self that seals up all in rest.
> In me thou seest the glowing of such fire,
> That on the ashes of his youth doth lie,
> As the death-bed, whereon it must expire,
> Consumed with that which it was nourished by.
>   This thou perceiv'st, which makes thy love more strong,
>   To love that well, which thou must leave ere long.

In many ways this is the quintessential Shakespearean sonnet. The structure is marked very clearly by the skilfully varied repetitions in lines 1, 5, 9, and 13, and each quatrain develops a new metaphor. The vehicles of the metaphors gradually tighten round the reader, moving from a season to a day to a fire, all unified by the element of fire that through the sun regulates the seasons and days.

In the first quatrain the speaker compares himself to a 'time of year', unspecified by name but vividly described in lines 2–3 by the autumnal attributes of the trees, which in turn become the tenor of a second metaphor: 'Bare ruined choirs', admirably analysed by Mr Empson in *Seven Types of Ambiguity* (1953 ed., pp 2–3). It should be pointed out, however, that this metaphor reverts to the first metaphor of trees in the conclusion of the line where we might expect 'boys' rather than 'birds'. The implications of Shakespeare's superb play of metaphor become clear only in the couplet, but he seems to be arresting the very seasonal process he is invoking.

The second quatrain is less complex, less energetic, in keeping with the decorum of the passage. Here again a second metaphor, 'Death's second self', is introduced, but the metaphorical linking of death and night is so common that we are hardly aware of it. The introduction of death and the word 'rest' in this last line of the quatrain cuts off any possibility of invoking the day–night process and ends the quatrain on a note of quiet finality.

The third quatrain compares the speaker's life to the glowing of embers, in which the physiology of fire determines both the meaning and the mood. To nourish fire, fuel must be consumed. In each of the first two quatrains Shakespeare has had to control his metaphor with great care so as not to suggest the cyclical processes of which autumn and night are a part; here the image of embers works admirably to suggest the finality he has been working for and the close link and interdependence of life and death. Some readers have seen in this fire metaphor a hint of the phoenix rising from its own ashes. For me this would destroy the mood of no-spring-after-autumn and no-dawn-after-night. The subtle arrangement of the words achieves a perfect balance between the ultimate finality of death and the subdued fire of the speaker's moribund mood. Ashes – deathbed – consumed are opposed to Lie – expire – nourished.

The three quatrains present an unusually poignant picture of man caught in annual, daily and physiological processes over which he has no control. Despite the poignancy it must be admitted that the first twelve lines of the poem are sentimental. They ask pity for a man who if he were writing from his own experience, could not have been forty-five. They are the *schmerz* of middle age. But the couplet puts all in perspective. The whole preceding twelve lines are reduced to the naked simplicity of the pronouns 'This', and the enigmatic 'that' of the last line, 'which THOU must leave ere long.'

> This thou perceiv'st, which makes thy love more strong,
> To love that well which thou must leave ere long.

I do not think that one should read 'leave' as 'forgo'. The brilliance of the shift from the speaker to the loved ones moves the poem from a particularized despair of an individual to a generalized statement about all of human life that includes the speaker and the loved one and the reader. The 'that' is both the speaker and life itself, and in the context of sonnets 71–4 it also means Shakespeare's poetry. Sonnet 71 sets up the situation: 'No longer mourn for me when I am dead . . ./Lest the wise world should look into your moan,/And mock you with me after I am gone.' Sonnet 72 develops the theme further, including the poetry as well as the person: 'For I am shamed by *that* which I bring forth,/And so should you, to love things nothing worth.' The irony of the situation is resolved by the couplet in 73 and all of 74, which insists 'but be contented when that fell arrest/Without all bail shall carry me away.' His body will be gone, but his spirit will remain, and

> The worth of that, is that which it contains,
> And that is this, and this with thee remains.

The rightness of the boast needs no further proof but redirects our understanding of that basic paradox, of which I spoke earlier.

Sonnet 73 seems to me the richest, the most evocative of one kind of Shakespearean sonnet, one kind of perfection. It elicits our emotional response before our intellectual. We are taken into the worlds of 'Bare ruined choirs', and night and embers long before we think about the problem of what *that* means. Others of the sonnets hit the intellect before they can become part of our literary lives. The particularized poignancy has been drained from them in the act of composition. Sonnet 94, one of the most perplexing of all the sonnets, is a good example. I have never found a satisfactory explanation of its meaning. Its intellectual abstraction makes it almost a paradigm devoid of meaning – except for the pattern its words make. One cannot refer with any certainty to moral or intellectual situations to which these words apply. One of its main difficulties is the abstractness of the diction, which does not specify its meaning precisely or draw the disparate elements of the poem together unless we resort to imposed ironies or tonal differences.[1] This may be either its glory or its fault. Sonnet 116 has the same kind of abstract diction but avoids the difficulties of 94. The first line and a half specifies the area within which the poem operates by picking up an associative word, 'impediments'.

> Let me not to the marriage of true minds
> Admit impediments . . .

Because of this word the poem must carry almost as an epigraph the line from the marriage service: 'If any of you know cause or just impediment why these persons should not be joined together . . .' The rest of the poem, except for the couplet, is a series of statements about love, which attempt to define it. The poem is justly celebrated but cannot compare with sonnet 129, one of the truly great poems, in which so much happens linguistically that we can hardly take it in.

---

[1] See Hubler, *Sense*, pp 102–6.

> Th' expense of spirit in a waste of shame
> Is lust in action, and till action, lust
> Is perjured, murd'rous, bloody full of blame,
> Savage, extreme, rude, cruel, not to trust,
> Enjoyed no sooner but despised straight,
> Past reason hunted, and no sooner had
> Past reason hated as a swallowed bait
> On purpose laid to make the taker mad.
> Mad in pursuit and in possession so,
> Had, having, and in quest, to have extreme,
> A bliss in proof and proved, a very woe,
> Before a joy proposed behind a dream.
>   All this the world well knows yet none knows well,
>   To shun the heaven that leads men to this hell.

This poem is really a syncopated catalogue in which the first two lines and the couplet make statements, and everything between is an intellectual analysis of lust, composed of adjectival forms completing the verb *is* in line 3. The usual form of the sonnet, so scrupulously observed, is neglected here. Syntax and alliterative patterns take over. The poem is a controlled series of balances that view lust grammatically through tenses (had, having and in quest to have) and the possible relationships of the words chosen. In this sonnet more than in any other Shakespeare seems to rely on the elements of language to sustain his fury. Line one seems to be a simple evocation of the old soul–body dichotomy in terms of an arid desert (waste of shame) – very much like the 'Poor soul' of 146, but the words are more incisive and bear the burden of the physiological meaning of spirit as seminal fluid, and we are given a very powerful statement and definition of the act of love, which is why Shakespeare adds 'in action'. The definition is concise and inclusive. Coupled to it is the other half of line 2 that suggests quite rightly that lust is prior to act. The list of adjectives in lines 3 and 4 is exquisite. From the legalism of 'Perjured' (lust has told something untrue and been convicted of it) we progress to 'murderous' (from act of mind to act) to 'bloody' (result of act) to the culpability of 'full of blame'. 'Extreme' in line 4 seems out of place but is picked up again in line 10 and acts as a link between the earlier and later series of adjectives. 'Not to trust' is superb because it introduces the whole world of social and personal backing off from the implications of the act. The rest of the poem should be clear; it justifies in terms of before and after an all too readily identifiable fact of life, which if you want goes back to the shame of line 1. The couplet rounds out the antithetical development of the first 12 lines with its opposition of heaven and hell and the inversion of 'well knows'.

These few observations on the logical patterns of the sonnets are not intended, as I suggested at the beginning of this essay, to be a key to unlock the heart of Shakespeare or even one of his sonnets. They are intended to direct attention to Shakespeare's art, which is logical, moral, impersonal, traditional, and indispensable for us no matter how we read it. The intensity of his sonnets does not invite comparison to our modern liberated fixations but to the deeply moral assurances of what human love can and cannot accomplish. Most important of all, his sonnets are indispensable for us in determining values, moral and aesthetic, that would abide our question, if we could only decide what questions to ask them.

6

THE LYRIC

(i)

THE POETRY

Alicia Ostriker

Lyric poetry exists between opposed poles of song and speech. Insofar as it approaches song, the lyric mode is graceful, impersonal, conventional: a communal rather than individual expression. Insofar as it approaches speech, lyric becomes our modern 'spontaneous overflow of powerful emotion', or 'true voice of feeling': an individual expression inclined to oppose conventional forms and conventional language. Renaissance England begat the finest body of lyric poetry in our language by a fruitful interplay between an established tradition of musical verse and a new, equally vital experimental spirit of individualistic verse. The decline of both principles by the close of the seventeenth century produced a decline in lyric. Chapter 8 will begin by outlining the curve of this process briefly, before considering the parts played by individual poets in driving that curve up, and following it down.

The commonplace, loose identification of lyric poetry and 'song', we must first realize, was literal fact for sixteenth- and seventeenth-century England, when 'music and sweet poetry' agreed in practice as well as theory. Tudor England already had a rich courtly and scholarly musical culture, fertilized from below by popular and folk song, carol, broadside ballad, and street cry, and fed from without by Continental forms. Music was a major social grace for Tudor and Elizabethan gentlemen, who were expected to perform in musical evenings much as eighteenth-century gentlemen were expected to play cards. Henry VIII and Elizabeth both wrote songs, as did their courtiers; Elizabeth played the virginals; and the nation produced, around the turn of the century, a galaxy of composers including Byrd, Willbye, Morley, Dowland, Weelkes, and Gibbons, equal to any in Europe.

Music in the sixteenth century could be all things to all temperaments. It was 'the food of love' because it stimulated the passions,
and it was a catalyst of virtue because its laws of harmony derived
from and imitated the divine music of the spheres:

> The man that hath no music in himself
> Nor is not moved with concourse of sweet sounds
> Is fit for treasons, stratagems, and spoils.

Above all, Renaissance music meant pattern, and the most constant
quality of Renaissance song is the cultivation of pattern in form and
language.

Formally, the sixteenth century was a period of extraordinary
development. Chaucer was an almost-forgotten ancient, but the
epigram, the satire, the elegy, the sonnet, various forms of pastoral,
and all the sub-classifications of song developed by classical poets,
French poets, and Italian poets, were brought home by Englishmen
eager to close the culture gap. There was also a new prosody, for
which all of Chaucer's accomplishments had to be re-
accomplished. Virtually the only lyric forms available to early Tudor
poets were short, simple iambic stanzas. Then came the first ottava
rima in English, the first terza rima, the first sonnets, the first
sonnet sequences. Accentual-syllabic metre became the permanent
basis of English verse, defeating both the confusing remnants of
alliterative 4-stress verse inherited from the fifteenth century, and
the ultimately barren experimentation with classical quantitative
verse attempted by Sidney, Spenser, Campion, and others.
Spenser's *The Shepheardes Calender* (1579) initiated the 'golden age'
of English lyric both in its pastoralism and in its metrical virtuosity,
ranging from ballad measure to the first English sestina; every
eclogue of the *Calender*, except its first and last, employs a different
form. After 1579, partly influenced by the rhythmic potential of
musical forms unconfined to a rigid beat, poets increasingly became virtuosi with stanza patterns, able to vary the standard iamb
with trochaic and anapaestic rhythms, and interested in producing
sophisticated new stanza forms of varying metres and line lengths.
This delight in complex lyric form continued in the seventeenth
century, simultaneously with the advance of verse in couplets which
ultimately would conquer the lyric.

For a modern reader, the most immediately striking aspect of
pattern in Elizabethan song is its cultivation of what we would call
stock responses. The conventional mines for the jewellery of conceit in lyric were Nature and Myth. The stock themes of lyric were

moral and amorous. Poets celebrated youth, love, and beauty bright
as the sun, or lamented the cruelty of fortune and the frailty of life
that withers as the primrose by the river.

Poets wrote, in brief, by the manipulation of accepted symbols.
The advantage of this method was that Elizabethan song did not
need to explain itself, because everything it 'said' was already
known. It needed only to array itself, like the lilies of the field which
outshone Solomon in his glory. As Agnes Latham says in her
introduction to Ralegh's poems: 'The typical Elizabethan [song]
contains no jot of personal emotion: as often as not it is translated
from a Frenchman, who had it from an Italian, who found it in
Plato; and the author is perhaps a literary hack, like Robert Greene,
living squalidly – and for all that the poem is as fresh as a flower. It
is baffling and beautiful: baffling because it is beautiful and nothing
else. Thought is not permitted to distort it nor feeling to betray it
into incoherencies.'

Traditions of course produce reactions. Not all poets are singers.
The idea of individualism, implicit in Christian doctrine and
already dividing feudal from modern Europe, was encouraged in
sixteenth- and early seventeenth-century England by the intellectual
shock waves of Reformation, Humanism, the beginnings of empire
and an open economy, and the beginnings of a scientific revolution
which exalted scepticism and empiricism over authority. For poets
as individuals, the distortions of thought and the incoherencies of
feeling are prime material. To explore what it means to be oneself
in particular rather than Anyman in general, poets sacrifice the
singing line, avoid or mock accepted commonplaces of language,
and develop new rhetorics. The beginnings of this reaction in
England occur as early as Wyatt. At the peak of the golden age, the
three giants – Sidney, Shakespeare, Spenser – all were touched by
it, as were many lesser poets. Then as the century turned, the
balance between communal song and individual speech shifted.
Instead of quasi-anonymous singers sharing conventional ideas and
techniques, we find a Jonson, a Donne, a Herbert, a Crashaw, a
Herrick, a Suckling, writing ostensibly not as personae but as
persons. Jonson and Donne were poetic rebels. With Donne in
particular, the private personality distinguished itself violently from
the rest of mankind, was pointedly anti-conventional, and made its
own experiences and thought processes the measure of all things.
Prosodically, the Donne revolution turned lyric metre over from the
'sweet line' typified by Spenser to 'strong lines' characterized by
unbalanced stanza forms and rugged rhythms, learned from dramatic

blank verse and following the twists of passion or dialectic, replacing
mental stasis by mental process.

As a corollary of the movement toward introspection,
seventeenth-century poets appropriated new territories for the lyric.
Speculation on abstract philosophical topics, and metaphors drawn
from science and technology, displaced the older language of moral
commonplace and of pastoral and mythic symbolism. Love poetry
cohabited with religious poetry to produce the new devotional lyric.
The private man's social interests entered lyric with Jonson. Politics
entered with Milton and Marvell. Vaughan and Traherne discovered the realms of childhood and nature — nature subjectively
experienced, as opposed to the conventional backdrop of pastoral
verse. Marvell made a Nature of divine paradox. Lyric poetry lost its
coherence in the seventeenth century as it branched in multiple
directions, and gained power, momentum, and variety.

Wyatt (1503–42) and Surrey (1517–47) inaugurate modern English
lyric not only because they imported the sonnet and sired
Petrarchanism for the sixteenth century, but because they illustrate
the two contrary inclinations which were to control future poetry.
Wyatt of course, in his lyrics as well as his sonnets, was a conventional courtly maker in the court of Henry VIII. Yet his best
poems seem anti-conventionally 'real'. He likes rhythmic
irregularity, colloquialism, and an air of conversation: 'Perdy, I
saide yt not'. 'It may be good, like it who list.' 'Now ha, ha, ha, full
well is me.' He likes a play of thought and argument, even in songs.
He is good at quick suggestion of dramatic situation. And instead of
languishing in love like a loyal Petrarchan, he commonly asserts his
refusal to play that game:

> Madame, withouten many wordes,
> Ons I ame sure ye will or no;
> And if ye will, then leve your bordes,
> And use your wit and shew it so.

Unlike Wyatt, as a love poet Surrey sings his lady's charms, is self-
effacing, and suffers gladly. Unlike Wyatt, he likes a slow, full,
balanced movement of verse without sharp edges. Unlike Wyatt, he
uses natural settings as a poignant background for human emotion:

> Alas, so all thinges now doe holde their peace,
> Heaven and earth disturbed in nothing;
> The beastes, the ayer, the birdes their song doe cease;
> The nightes chare the starres aboute dothe bring.

In Wyatt, formal organization is something to be tampered with, as a way of demonstrating peculiarities of private temperament. In Surrey it is something to be achieved, as a way of demonstrating rational and emotional order, control, and grace. If Wyatt reminds one of Donne, Surrey leads straight to Sidney and Spenser. Surrey's reputation has declined in the twentieth century, as Wyatt's has risen. But Surrey's metrical smoothness, his emotional sweetness, and his sense of formal decorum, were precisely what the sixteenth century needed. Thus the musical rather than the personal idea of poetry dominated lyric for fifty years of miscellanies, sonnets, romances, plays, and song books.

Tottel's *Miscellany (Songes and Sonettes*, 1557), which first printed the work of Wyatt and Surrey as well as other poets, leapt into immediate popularity and ran through nine editions by 1587. It set the vogue of miscellanies and more remotely of songbooks, as well as their prevailing themes of love and moral reflection. Among the later miscellanies were *A Paradise of Dainty Devices* (1576), *A Gorgeous Gallery of Gallant Inventions* (1578), and *A handful of Pleasant Delights* (1584). *The Phoenix Nest* (1593), includes work by Peele, Breton, Lodge, Ralegh, and Fulke Greville, has three fine elegies on Sidney, and a wide variety of lyrics in many forms and metres, especially the sonnet. *England's Helicon* (1600), a pastoral miscellany, has poems by Sidney, Spenser, Breton, Lodge, Peele, and Barnfield, and contains the quintessential pastoral of the age, Marlowe's 'Come live with me and be my love', as well as its quintessential anti-pastoral, Ralegh's 'The Nymph's Reply to the Shepherd'. *A Poetical Rhapsody* (1602) marks the conversion of miscellany to anthology, by reprinting successful poems, rather than publishing work from manuscripts.

Concurrent with the miscellanies was the development of lyric in drama and pastoral romance, and later the masque. From 'I mun be married a Sunday' in *Ralph Roister Doister* (1550) and 'Back and Sides go bare, go bare' in *Gammer Gurton's Needle* (1566), comes a flow of radiant lyrics by Lyly, Peele, Nashe, Lodge, Dekker, Sidney, Jonson, Beaumont and Fletcher, Ford, and others, which lasts well into the seventeenth century. Shakespeare's are the most famous. But it would be difficult to assert that 'Come away, come away death' is more sweetly melancholic than Beaumont and Fletcher's 'Take oh take those Lips away'; or 'Where the bee sucks there suck I' more sensuous than Lodge's 'Love in my bosom like a bee/Doth suck his sweet'; or 'Fear no more the heat o' the sun' more perfectly chilling than Nashe's 'Litany in Time of Plague':

> Beauty is but a flowre,
> Which wrinckles will devoure,
> Brightnesse falls from the ayre,
> Queenes have died yong and faire,
> Dust hath closed *Helens* eye.
> I am sick, I must dye:
>   Lord, have mercy on us.

Songs inserted in plays or tales bear little narrative burden and can afford to be purely ornamental. For this reason, perhaps, these songs, outside of Shakespeare's, commonly outlive their settings. Their crystalline tradition was so strong that it enabled Jonson to write neoplatonic lyrics without a trace of Jonsonian gruffness for his masques; caused Milton temporarily to cease Miltonizing for the translucent airs of 'Arcades' and *Comus*; and lent Dryden a delicacy in the songs for his plays which the plays themselves do not possess.

The songbook vogue, from 1588 (Nicolas Yonge's *Musica Trans-alpina*) to c. 1617 (Campion's *Third and Fourth Books of Airs*), provides a final source for the musical lyric. Both the polyphonic madrigal and the solo air lent themselves to short, metrically subtle stanzaic lyrics. Here the great master is Thomas Campion (1567–1620), who composed both words and music for his books of airs (1601 with Philip Rosseter, 1610, 1617), and wrote theory in both arts. Campion is one of the pure larks of the English tongue, whether mournfully courtly in 'Follow thy saint, follow with accents sweet', bawdy in 'It fell on a summer's day', moral (and very Jonsonian) in 'Though you are young and I am old', classical in his lovely adaptation of 'Vivamus mea Lesbia', devotional in 'Never weather-beaten sail', or artfully artless in 'I care not for these ladies' or 'There is a Garden in her Face':

> There is a Garden in her Face,
> Where Roses and white Lillies grow;
> A heav'nly paradice is that place,
> Wherein all pleasant fruits doe flow.
> There Cherries grow, which none may buy
> Till Cherry ripe themselves doe cry.

As a theorist (*Observations in the Art of English Poesie*, 1602), Campion defended rhymeless verse in quantitative metres, and was ably answered by Daniel's *Defence of Rime* (1603). His usual practice fortunately defied his theory, although his rhymeless 'Rose-cheekt Lawra' is the deservedly much-anthologized accomplishment of a perfect ear devoted to the Renaissance identification of physical and spiritual beauty, subsumed in a metaphor of musical harmony:

> Sing thou smoothly with thy beawties
> Silent musicke, either other
>   Sweetely gracing.

Meanwhile, however, while the art of song prospered, the more personal style of poetry we found nascent in Wyatt continued. During the fallow time between Surrey and Spenser, Thomas Lord Vaux, Nicholas Grimald (especially in the elegy on his mother), George Turbervile, Thomas Howell, and Thomas Tusser in the auto-biographical bits of his *Five Hundreth Points of Good Husbandry* (1573), all sustain some tinge of it. George Gascoigne (1542–77) is the best of these interim poets. His *Steel Glass* (1576) is a remarkably good-natured satire, and his amorous and reflective lyrics in *A Hundreth Sundry Flowers* (1573, pruned in 1575 as *The Posies*) often seem surprisingly spontaneous, direct, and natural. In his best work, a distinct personality applies its humour to itself – 'Gascoigne's Lullaby' affectionately sings to sleep the ageing poet's youthful years, gazing eyes, wanton will, and finally his comically impotent 'little Robyn'; and 'Gascoigne's Arraignment' delivers a mock-courtly allegory:

> At Beautty's bar as I did stand,
> When False Suspect accused me,
> George (quoth the judge), hold up thy hand,
> Thou art arraigned of flattery. . . .

> George (quoth the judge), now thou art cast,
> Thou must go hence to Heavy Hill
> And there be hanged, all but the head.
> God rest thy soul when thou art dead.

A finer poet in this tradition is Sir Walter Ralegh (1552–1618). Soldier, sailor, adventurer, favourite of Elizabeth and beheaded by James, paradigm of the Elizabethan aspiring mind – glamorous and doomed – most of his poetry was lost because he did not condescend to publish. What remains gives the taste of a keen and passionate intelligence. 'The Lie' is a poem like a knife. 'The Passionate Mans Pilgrimage' (1600) combines medievalisms – 'Give me my Scallop shell of quiet, My staff of Faith to walke upon' – with a foretaste of grisly Jacobean *discordia concors*:

> And this is my eternall plea
> To him that made Heaven, Earth and Sea,
> Seeing my flesh must die so soone,
> And want a head to dine next noone,
> Just at the stroke when my vaines start and spred
> Set on my soule an everlasting head.
> Then am I readie like a palmer fit,
> To tread those blest paths which before I writ.

In his 'Nymph's Reply', the opening reminds us immediately of Marvell: 'If all the world and love were young./And Truth in every shepherd's tongue'. The rest is typically complex, almost Shakespearean, in its tonal vibration between satisfaction and regret about the obvious truths:

> Thy gownes, thy shooes, thy beds of roses
> Thy cap, thy kirtle, and thy poesies
> Soone breake, sooner wither, soone forgotten,
> In follie ripe, in reason rotten.

Ralegh is tight, terse, brilliant. His diction is without fat; his prosodic turns often striking, never mellifluous. For a richer body of poetry, in which the singer-poet arranges formal delicacy while the speaker-poet arranges psychological complexity, one turns to the major sonnets and major sonneteers, Sidney, Shakespeare, Daniel, Drayton.

Sir Philip Sidney (1554–86) wrote 286 poems containing 143 different line and stanza patterns, 109 of which he used only once, and most of which were new to English. This argues a 'musician' in verse, as does the fact that he wrote samples of nearly every lyric 'kind' then existing in English. The poems of *Arcadia* and *Astrophel and Stella* are highly musical, conventional, artificial. Yet Sidney's language and rhythms strike far above the common level of the 1580s in scrupulous definition of mental, moral, and emotional states, and *Astrophel and Stella* tacitly depends upon a tension between Astrophel's sophisticated formal artifice as a sonneteer and the asserted 'pure simplicitie' of the lover who looks in his heart and writes of its private dilemmas.

Shakespeare, a pure musician in the songs from the plays and a pure metaphysician in 'The Phoenix and the Turtle', in the sonnets is both, and more. The sweetest singers of the century cannot match his 'sugared' imagery and intricate structures, the most fanatic hunters of an elaborate conceit cannot outrace him, and for dramatic representation of human consciousness, the voice of Shakespeare's sonnets is excelled only by those of the heroes and villains in Shakespeare's plays. Even more than Sidney, Shakespeare makes the form of conventional love poetry the pretext for anatomy of love as the marriage of true minds, lust as th' expense of spirit, Time in its malevolence, and Art in its triumph over Time.

Of the three giants, Edmund Spenser (1552–99) was the least touched by the impulse to individuality. Spenser was an almost totally musical poet, in the most expanded sense of that term, and the Spenserian persona is the embodiment of a type, the Orphic poet in various disguises, whose lofty, archaic, mythic diction, and luxurious formal structures, celebrate universal truth rather than private experience. The eclogues of *The Shepheardes Calender*, the *Amoretti* sonnets, the *Prothalamion* and *Epithalamion*, all have the formal polish which helped make Spenser not only 'the Prince of poets in his time' but the most widely imitated. His most personal poem is probably the *Epithalamion*, for which private bridegroom coincided with public poet to make the most splendid lyric of the early Renaissance.

Spenser's many disciples include Drayton in his pastorals and in the patriotism of 'To the Virginian Voyage' and the 'Ballad of Agincourt', although not in the realism of *Idea's Mirror*; Samuel Daniel for gentle moralizing in *Delia* and other lyrics; John Davies for the cosmic dance of *Orchestra*; William Browne; and George Wither for his pastorals, although Wither's one lyric triumph, 'Shall I wasting in despair', is distinctly un-Spenserian. In general, any seventeenth-century poetry which develops a pastoral vein, stresses moral purity, or employs a rich and fluent style, probably derives ultimately from Spenser. Most of this poetry, needless to say, is today unreadable. The exception, among Spenser's seventeenth-century heirs, was Milton, to whom we will return.

The two seminal lyricists for the opening of the seventeenth century were Ben Jonson (1572–1637) and John Donne (1572–1631), both anti-Spenserians. Jonson complained that the archaic Spenser 'writ no language'. Donne tacitly criticizes Spenser's Platonism and Puritanism in the rakish love poetry of *Songs and Sonets*, not published in his lifetime but widely circulated. Both poets might have complained of Spenser as T. S. Eliot complained of Tennyson and Browning, that he was a poet, and he thought, but did not feel his thought as immediately as the odour of a rose. Together they represent a revolution toward greater realism, concreteness, and individual self-exploration and self-assertion for the lyric.

Ben Jonson had a preacher for a father and a bricklayer for a stepfather. These two trades suggest something of his own craft: he is ethical, and architectural. Jonson, in his plays, masques, poems, criticism, and conversation, was a classicist. His teachers are Horace, Martial, Catullus. Opposed to the over-exuberance and strained artificial fancies he found effeminate in Elizabethan verse, he cultivates restraint and common sense, a diction 'pure and neat, yet plaine and customary', and above all, 'perspicuitie'. Thus instead of pastoral elegies, he masters the brief, understated Roman lament:

> Farewell, thou child of my right hand, and joy;
>   My sinne was too much hope of thee, lov'd boy . . .
> Rest in soft peace, and, ask'd, say here doth lie
> BEN. JONSON: his best piece of *poetrie*.

Instead of dressing his philosophy in fabulous language, he develops the rhymed couplet ('Inviting a Friend to Supper', 'To Penshurst', 'Epistle to One That Asked to be Sealed of the Tribe of Ben', etc.) in conversational language and syntax, out of which grew the smoother couplets of the Augustans. The bulk of Jonson's poetry is in a sense 'occasional' or familiar, but he wrote in many modes: epigrams complimentary or defamatory, moral odes, elegies, epistles, satires, songs, love poetry (not his forte), hymns, and unclassifiable pieces like the 'Fit of Rhyme against Rhyme' and the famous poem on Shakespeare. Jonson's social ideals were of a civilization, worldly, disciplined, intelligent, just; his aesthetic ideals were lucidity and decorum. Yet to say this is to miss the quality which makes him a seventeenth-century classicist, not an eighteenth-century neoclassicist. Jonson possessed a central devotion to an idea of Beauty, that '*Queene* and *Huntress*, chaste, and faire . . . Goddess, excellently bright', which he rarely made explicit, but which inspired both his ethics and his aesthetics, and made them one:

> It is not growing like a tree
> In bulke, doth make man better bee;
> Or standing long an Oake, three hundred yeare,
> To fall a logge at last, dry, bald, and seare:
> A Lillie of a Day
> Is fairer far in May,
> Although it fall, and die that night;
> It was the Plant, and flower of light.

Jonson's most fertile years in poetry, as well as drama and the masque, were 1598–1616. The 1616 folio of his works includes lyrics in two sections entitled *Epigrammes* and *The Forrest*; his later works, including the lyrics gathered together as *Under-Wood*, were posthumously published in 1640–1.

Among the Sons of Ben, the younger disciples who followed his tracks in the Roman snow, were Herrick, Carew, Randolph, Suckling, Godolphin, Cartwright, Davenport, Waller, Brome, and

Cowley. Of these, Robert Herrick (1591–1674) is the most important. Herrick, son of a goldsmith, divided his life between London and the 'dull Devonshire' where he was curate. His poetic personality is less robust, didactic, and severe than Jonson's, more easy and Epicurean. His creed – an engaging one – was 'To Live Merrily and to Trust to Good Verses'. In the over 1400, mostly brief, poems of *Hesperides* (1648), he excels at celebrating life's pleasures: pleasures of country life, for whose folk-rituals he has a near-Shakespearean sense; of girls with Cherrie-Ripe lips and sweet disorder in the dress; of 'Sack, thou more near than kindred, friend, man, wife'; of the life of wit, in the poems celebrating Ben Jonson; and of song itself. His Christianity is a calm affair, able to co-exist with playful devotions to Roman lars or English fairies. The themes of age and death bring Herrick to his depths, producing the most famous *carpe diem* poem in English, 'Gather ye rosebuds while ye may', and carrying the joyous ebullience of 'Corinna's Going a Maying' to its concluding

> So when or you or I are made
> A fable, song, or fleeting shade;
> All love, all liking, all delight
> Lies drown'd with us in endlesse night.
> Then while time serves, and we are but decaying;
> Come, my *Corinna*, come, let's goe a Maying.

Although on occasion Herrick composed complex stanza forms, most of his verse was in pentameter or shorter-line couplets and quatrains.

The Cavalier poets exhibit less learning than either Jonson or Herrick, and with the exception of Suckling, somewhat less metrical experimentation. Jonsonian decorum, which in Ben was a matter of intellectual passion, not inconsistent with rough assertiveness, in them became a purer smoothness, charm, and gaiety.

Carew (1594–1640), craftsman of 'Ask me no more' and 'Give me more love, or more disdain', produced his most interesting poem in his elegy on Donne, which partly imitates Donne's style to define it. Waller (1606–87), famous for 'Go, lovely Rose', wrote social, reflective, or elegantly amorous stanzaic verse, and helped 'refine' the balanced heroic couplet. Sir John Suckling (1609–42) – Millamant's 'natural, easy Suckling' – makes no pretence at seriousness, and thus emerges as a consistently lively and engaging sensibility, anti-romantic, anti-idealistic, but equally capable of pleasant irony about himself ('A Session of the Poets', 'Out upon it,

I have lov'd', etc.). Richard Lovelace (1618–57), a talent comparable to Daniel's, breathes perhaps the last breath of courtly idealism
in English poetry. 'I could not love thee (Deare) so much,/Loved I
not Honour more.' 'Stone walls do not a prison make,/Nor iron
bars a cage.' The hard-won discoveries of Renaissance Humanism
here find their serene ending.

The Donne revolution, parallel to the Jonsonian, was more
radical. Like Jonson, Donne drew 'a line of masculine expression'
against the 'soft melting Phrases' of Spenser and the Elizabethans.
Like Jonson a man of urbane learning, Donne kept the articulated
bone of thought visible under the skin of sentence and rhythm. Like
Jonson he spoke the language of prose; like Jonson (and unlike
Spenser) he had a sense of humour. Jonson and Donne are closest
when writing direct moral argument, with Roman elegy and satire
as the model. But where Jonson found his forms and ideals in an
established body of Latin writing, upon which he could rear temples
of self-assurance, Donne's affinities were on the one hand with the
crumbling world of medieval philosophy and theology, and on the
other with the dynamic world of new science and new philosophy
which 'calls all in doubt'. Doubt – not faith as in Spenser, nor
rectitude as in Jonson – is the characteristic stance of Donne's
mind:

> on a huge hill,
> Cragged, and steep, Truth stands, and hee that will
> Reach her, about must, and about must go,
> And what the hills suddennes resists, winne so.

The mind reveals itself in process of going about and about, in
tirelessly subtle self-awareness, playing or wrestling with uncertainties and distractions, trumpeting the challenge of its wit
equally in profane and sacred verse. The consequence for lyric
form was a relative neglect of Jonsonian decorum. Donne felt free,
apparently, to say any thing, in any style, on any occasion. Thus his
'songs' are never true songs but occasions for metrically irregular
conversation and introspective monologue. He can begin a love
poem ('The Canonization') with an oath – 'For Godsake hold your
tongue and let me love' – and conclude it with blasphemy. He can
pun and use explicitly erotic metaphors in sacred verse. He can
violate the decorum of love poetry, sacred poetry, and familiar verse
alike, by allusions to areas of recondite knowledge, as Jonson never
would: hence Jonson's remark to Drummond of Hawthornden that
'Donne for not being understood would perish'.

He did not perish immediately, for younger writers found much to imitate in both the devil-may-carelessness of 'Jack' Donne's secular verse and the complex ratiocination and spiritual struggles in the religious poetry of the Dean of St Paul's. The poets commonly grouped with Donne as 'metaphysicals' include George Herbert (1593–1633), his older brother Edward Lord Herbert of Cherbury (1583–1648), Henry King (1592–1669), Richard Crashaw (1612–49), John Cleveland (1613–58), Abraham Cowley (1618–67), Andrew Marvell (1621–78), Henry Vaughan (1622–95). Still, to speak of a 'school of Donne' or of 'metaphysical poetry' as if it were a standard programme based on Donne, is misleading.

George Herbert used Donne's conversational tone and rhythmical roughness, but less radically, and balanced them with variously patterned, coherent stanza forms which remind us that he was an accomplished amateur musician as well as a clergyman, and recall Sidney's or Campion's virtuosity. Herbert modifies his use of wit and paradox; and modifies his record of spiritual agonies and struggles by the sense he always retains of his God's ultimate kindness:

> How fresh, O Lord, how sweet and clean
> Are thy returns!

Herbert's posthumously published *The Temple* (1633) was immediately popular, and especially influential for Vaughan and Thomas Traherne (1637–74), both of whom resemble Herbert considerably more than Donne. Crashaw, on the other hand, in the violence and extravagance, and commonly the eroticism, of his religious rhapsodies, is more like Donne than like any other English poet. But his conceits on the Magdalen or St Teresa, in which as one scholar observes, 'over-ripeness is all', do not depend on intellect but on enthusiasm, and Crashaw's art probably was more influenced by the European Counter-Reformation than by any English movement. For this reason, Crashaw is usually classified as England's sole 'baroque' poet.

The Donnean stream in secular poetry flows partly through themes and attitudes he helped make popular. The 'cavalier' attitude toward love owes something to the rake of *Songs and Sonets*, and numerous seventeenth-century poems exist on the multiple-mistress theme of 'I can love both fair and brown' or on witty refutations of Petrarchanism and Platonism in love. Stylistically, the 'masculine expression' praised by Carew was imitated by many poets, major and minor. Its accepted traits were avoidance of ornament, cultivation of pointed paradox, startling conceits or obscurely learned allusions, and a difficult vocabulary. Not surprisingly, in many of the imitations, 'wit' keeps its name but descends to witticism.

Abraham Cowley, last of the 'metaphysicals' and a Spenserian and Jonsonian as well, is a case in point. Samuel Johnson, looking at metaphysical poetry from the wrong end of the telescope and seeing Cowley instead of Donne or Herbert, justly criticized such poetry for excess of learning and defect of passion. Cowley is interesting now, despite a prodigious output which ranged from the unfinished Biblical epic *Davideis* to the clever lyrics of *The Mistress*, and which made him the most popular poet of his day, chiefly as the mirror of an age which was occupied in tempering wit and enthusiasm to the regimen of good sense. His chief technical contribution to English verse was the 'Pindaric Ode', whose loose versification and 'soaring' tone became the only allowable vehicle for Augustan extravagance of fancy, and ultimately issued in the odes of Collins and Gray. Even at his most free, however, Cowley seems programmatic: he traces a graph of the pulse, not feeling its beat.

Most of the seventeenth-century poets mentioned here were Anglicans. John Milton, Nonconformist in literature as in doctrine, was a successor to Puritan Spenser. His poetry, like Spenser's, was an outgrowth of Christian Humanism seized by a myth-making imagination. However, where Spenser's style was musical and conventional, Milton, while fulfilling the demands of convention, also makes himself conspicuous as a personality in his poems. We may ascribe this fact to his rebellious temperament, or to the influence of the seventeenth-century urge toward individualism in lyric. Milton's style, in the major poems of his youth, 'On the Morning of Christ's Nativity', 'L'Allegro' and 'Il Penseroso', 'Lycidas', indicate that poetic works, for this aspirant, meant 'works' both in the broad Christian sense and in the narrower Puritan sense of 'labour'. His prosodic experiments were always energetic and vigorous. His sonnets typically concern not love but some moral problem of personality or politics, and their form, highly enjambed and irregular in rhythm, commonly violating in syntax the octet–sestet division of rhyme scheme, bespeaks no Spenserian harmony of smooth fluency, but a more rugged harmony whose signature is struggle. Of all Milton's lyric poetry, the only poems which retain the tone of semi-anonymous Elizabethan songster are the musical pieces, set by Lawes, in 'Arcades' and *Comus*.

The ageing Milton's young admirer and colleague, Andrew

Marvell, was another individualist. Marvell inherited portions of both Jonson and Donne, as well as the Elizabethans, yet he belongs to no school. His eye for natural detail and for the cosmic, social, and personal implications of natural setting are his own, not Spenser's. The praise of retired life in 'Upon Appleton House' mines a vein of social meditation opened by Jonson, but with greater scope and political sophistication and ambivalence. Like Donne, he has broad intellectual interests, but embodies them in a less impassioned, more reserved tone. His style is one of precise definition and visual imagery, and he can move from conceited compliment to irony in a moment. Yet in the greatest of seventeenth-century seduction lyrics, Marvell fuses Renaissance wit and passion, facetiousness and intensity, and issues one of the last challenges to that first dear enemy of the Renaissance imagination, Time:

> The Grave's a fine and private place,
> But none I think do there embrace . . .
> Let us roll all our Strength, and all
> Our sweetness, up into one Ball:
> And tear our Pleasures with rough strife,
> Thorough the Iron gates of Life.
> Thus, though we cannot make our Sun
> Stand still, yet we will make him run.

Most of Marvell's work after 1660 is in satire, not lyric. This change reflects his age, for the Restoration produced little lyric poetry of permanent value.

The decline of lyric poetry follows upon the divorce of lyric from its original communal sources, combined with a failure of the early exuberance associated with individualism in poetry. Restoration lyric, for all its charm or pomp, already operated under the limitation of a neoclassical criticism for which lyric was not a major form and which helped cut 'literary' poetry away from its old nourishment of song and folk poetry. It cannot use the old generalizing metaphors of myth and pastoral, courtly love, man as microcosm, except facetiously. And far from showing a compensatory interest in exploring the byways of individual consciousness, it foreshadows the Augustan age in which poets would not number the streaks on the tulip. Devotional enthusiasm and Cavalier charm had both been lopped by the Civil Wars. Thus the songs from Dryden's plays, for example, tend to be charming and cynical rehearsals of the vagaries of love. His odes on the power of music ('A Song for St Cecilia's Day', 1687, and 'Alexander's Feast', 1697), may be considered brilliant *tours de force* or schematic exercises, but they do not persuade emotionally in the old way of Spenser, Campion, Jonson, or Milton. A motto for the coming age was

> Here stop my Muse, here cease thy painful flight:
> No pinions can pursue immortal height.
>
> *(Absalom and Achitophel*, lines 854–5)

Social discourse was to become the staple of poetic language, and the neatly balanced couplet its standard vehicle. The Royal Society, one recalls, was established in 1660, when the immense intuitive and empirical accomplishments of Kepler, Galileo, Newton and Descartes were past history, and a task of consolidation remained. In political England, violent civil and religious strife had given way to an era of compromise. Correspondingly, the genius of Restoration literature was dramatic, didactic, critical, satiric; it was not lyric. The varied kingdoms explored by Renaissance lyric poetry were to become blank places on the eighteenth-century map, awaiting rediscovery by the Romantics.

POETRY AND SONG

Leslie Dunn

> If Musique and sweet Poetrie agree,
> As they must needes (the Sister and the Brother)
> Then must the Love be great, twixt thee and mee,
> Because thou lov'st the one, and I the other.[1]

When discussing the influence of music on Renaissance lyric poetry, critics often take their cue from the poets themselves, and speak in metaphors of kinship. Music and poetry become the 'sister arts', implying separate identities but a common ancestry, and a strong familial likeness – an implicit musico-poetic 'relationship' that was explored, and celebrated, throughout the Renaissance, not only by poets but by philosophers, critics, and theorists of both arts. In the explorations of song, however, music and poetry entered into relationships of another, more explicit and interactive kind, and the metaphor accordingly shifts from the fraternal to the sexual: one speaks of musico-poetic 'relations', of a 'marriage' between the arts. The general assumption, in either case, is that the relationship was a harmonious one, both literally and figuratively. Music and sweet poetry, like the fated lovers in the old romance, always agree.

Like the old romance, too, this vision of relationship is both an idealized and an essentially literary one, referring not so much to the actual meetings of music and poetry in the Renaissance, as to writings *about* them, and in particular to poetry written about music, or about itself in relation to music. Such texts were often more directly concerned with an idea, or imagery of music, than with music itself: they could define and celebrate the musico-poetic relationship without entering into any actual relations themselves. When the Renaissance poet, for example, conceived of his art as a kind of music, the 'harmonies' that resonated in his mind were more than likely not those of sensuous practical music, but 'music' of another, more abstract and intellectual kind. This definition of musico-poetic relationship was inherited from a tradition of ancient and medieval

---

[1] Richard Barnfield, Sonnet 1, 'To his friend Maister R. L. In praise of Musique and Poetrie', lines 1–4. From 'Poems: In divers humors', part of *The Encomium of Lady Pecunia* (1598). Reprinted in *The Anchor Anthology of Sixteenth-Century Verse*, edited by Richard S. Sylvester, New York, 1974, p 575.

musical thought, whose roots were in Pythagorean harmonics. *Musica*, in this tradition, was a kind of mathematics, a universal principle of number and proportion, subsuming both poetry and practical music as arts of proportionate relationship in time. The 'music' of poetry, thus defined, had less to do with its actual sound than with its construction – its *harmonia*, in Dante's sense – and was related to music itself through the common principle of Number. By embodying Number in the sound of words, of course, the poet, like the musician, did make an audible, sensuous harmony as well – 'word-music', to use a modern term. But these sounds, however well-according with actual music, however apt for setting and singing, were themselves 'musical' only in a metaphorical sense: the relationship was still one of analogy rather than of enactment.

At the same time, however, the Renaissance poet would be familiar with a tradition of practical musico-poetic relations, as enacted in contemporary modes of song: the formal and stylistic conventions, both literary and musical, associated with various song genres (ballad, broadside, courtly partsong, madrigal, consort song, ayre), as well as current theories of the 'proper' relationship between a text and its setting; the forms that words took, and the sounds they made, when sung. This knowledge of song-practice might help to shape the poet's general 'idea' of song, which might in turn help to shape a particular lyric composition, whether or not it was written for music in the literal sense. Drawing still closer to actual music, the poet might compose in the expectation of a particular kind of musical setting – a madrigal, for instance – with well-defined textual expectations of its own, or even write words for already-existing music. In such cases, music could be said to have had some practical influence on the poem.

There are many signs by which this kind of musical influence might be recognized: structural features, including certain stanzaic forms and rhyme schemes, and the use of a refrain; stylistic features, such as a predominance of end-stopped lines, relatively simple syntax, paratactic or cumulative logical structures, frequent verbal figures of repetition and parallelism; and the use of traditionally 'lyric' themes and imagery. In many cases, these conventions of song-verse could be traced back through several centuries of close interaction between poetic and musical forms, styles, and occasions, and represented a poetic accommodation to the limits imposed by musical performance. Close musico-poetic associations of this kind continued in sixteenth- and early seventeenth-century England, in widely varied contexts – sacred and secular, popular and 'serious'; songs for domestic enjoyment, for professional performance, and for grand public occasions – and in traditional styles, such as the ballad, as well as in innovative ones.

Yet even in a great age of songmaking, when poets were perhaps more directly conscious of the musical element in their own lyric conventions, the mere presence of songlike features in any given lyric does not in itself prove that it was conceived as a literal song. Poetic forms that were closely associated with music could be imitated in purely literary contexts, without direct reference to music; a poem could evoke song, or a sense of singing, entirely on its own. In fact, the lyric mode was defined as much in verbal as in musical terms, and the literary definitions had an independent life, no matter how close the practical association with music became. Even the word 'song' itself was used in poetic and musical senses interchangeably. When a poem was set to music, it took on a double lyric identity: it was both actual and metaphorical music, both literal and virtual song.

The sixteenth- and seventeenth-century sources of lyric poetry bear witness to these parallel lives, showing how frequently lyrics crossed, and recrossed, the boundaries between poem and song. Composers frequently drew their texts from contemporary poetical miscellanies, or from poetry in manuscript, framing their music to the life of the words.[1] In other instances the process was reversed, and words were fitted to an existing piece of music in order to convert it to a song. Some of Dowland's most famous ayres, including 'Can shee excuse my wrongs' and 'Flow my teares' – originally *The Earl of Essex's Galliard* and the pavan *Lachrymae* – were made this way; the tunes of these dances are of such an individual shape as to suggest that words were written especially for them, but for others of a more standard form the composer could easily find poetry ready-fitted by its own metrical structure. In a procedurally similar, though far less artful kind of songmaking, poems were set and sung to popular tunes. Secular lyrics of both courtly and popular origin were performed this way. So, too, were their sacred counterparts, the metrical psalms of the Protestant church, and the moral parodies of 'amorous' verse.

Some of these musico-poetic 'marriages' were so successful that they became lodged in the public memory as songs, words and music together; even today it is hard to think of *Greensleeves*, or the 100th Psalm, or 'Now is the month of Maying', without hearing the words shaped by their tunes. Yet what had been joined together could be put asunder. Song verses were frequently copied into manuscripts, or printed in later seventeenth-century collections, without their settings, just as song music was copied without its words, or recast in an instrumental version. This did not necessarily signify that the association between poem and

[1] The phrase 'fram'd to the life of the words' is William Byrd's, and occurs in the preface to his *Psalmes, Sonets, & Songs of sadnes and pietie* (1588).

setting had been broken; but it did indicate that they could, and did, lead separate lives. Then as now, an enthusiasm for lyric implied an ability to appreciate both words and music on their own.

It is best, then, to think of poem and song in the Renaissance as two distinct modes of lyric existence which, though they may have been more closely identified than they are now, both in imagination and in fact, were yet by no means identical. In theory, there was no distinction. Renaissance definitions of lyric looked back to the historical and etymological source, ancient Greek song, in which poetry and music had been fused, through rhythm, into a single melic utterance; the word *lyric* itself implicitly identified not only poem and song, but voice and instrument, composition and performance. Inspired by this ideal of musical speech, and by its legendary powers to stir the mind and soul, Renaissance musical humanists argued eloquently for a new 'union' of poetry and music in imitation of ancient models. In the same spirit, the Renaissance poet figured himself as a new Orpheus or David, and equated the sixteenth-century lute with the classical lyre. The act of singing became a central metaphor for the writing of poetry. One finds it evoked in English poems as various in their own lyricism as Wyatt's 'Blame not my lute', Spenser's *Epithalamion*, and Herbert's 'Easter'. The lyric 'marriage' was celebrated in poetry, too, most famously in Milton's 'At a Solemn Music' and Dryden's 'Alexander's Feast'.

Yet, though such poetical lyricism could be set to music, the adoption of the Orphic persona remained at heart a literary gesture, more related to Renaissance theories of poetic inspiration and power than to the practice of contemporary song. Some musicians embraced the Orphic ideal as well, but their methods of realizing it were necessarily different, as they conceived it in a different medium. Indeed, from the poet's perspective at least, the two modes of lyric could seem not only distinct but opposed, both in conception and in intent:

> I thought, if I could draw my paines
> Through Rimes vexation, I should them allay,
> Griefe brought to numbers cannot be so fierce,
> For, he tames it, that fetters it in verse.
>
> But when I have done so,
> Some man, his art and voice to show,
> Doth set and sing my paine,
> And, by delighting, frees againe
> Griefe, which verse did restraine.[1]

Donne's famous expostulation against songmakers may have been meant ironically, but it does point to a central fact of Renaissance

---

[1] Donne, 'The Triple Foole', lines 8–16.

musico-poetic relations, namely that actual songmaking, unlike the Orphic ideal, was a double process, to which poet and composer contributed separately. Moreover, for all the idealization of a 'perfect union' between poetry and music in song, in practice the setting and singing could significantly remake the poet's work, transforming it into something quite new. The prevailing aesthetic, reflecting both humanist and Reformation elevations of the Word, dictated that music should 'serve' the text, respecting both its form and its meaning. But musicians defined that service in various ways. The madrigalist, for example, felt free to alter the shape of his chosen text, sometimes almost beyond recognition, in order to create a suitable vehicle for his particular kind of musical expression; the lutenist composer, by contrast, might be similarly 'expressive' in his intent, but the conventions of his song-style usually ensured a greater 'respect' for poetic form, and a greater clarity of declamation. In sacred music there was a similar contrast between elaborate polyphonic settings and the 'plain style' of the Reformers, whose principal demand was that the words be clearly audible, and the music simple enough for congregational singing. Yet even the simplest setting is more than a mere carrier of the text. The most respectful composers inevitably refashioned their poems to some extent, just by translating them into song; the great songs of the period are also acts of interpretation.

Given all these intersections and divergences between ideal and actual, metaphorical and literal, poetic and musical perspectives on lyric, it can be as difficult to distinguish clearly between the various kinds of musical influence on poetry as it is to draw a clear line between poem and song. Renaissance poetry could be 'musical' in several senses simultaneously, with a single idea of lyric embracing them all. The definition of the poet, in Sidney's *Apology for Poetry*, is a fine example of such commingling:

He beginneth not with obscure definitions, which must blur the margent with interpretations, and load the memory with doubtfulness; but he cometh to you with words set in delightful proportion, either accompanied with, or prepared for, the well-enchanting skill of music.[1]

In one sense, this is an idealized vision of lyric composition – rich, like the *Apology* itself, in classical reference, evoking a lyric 'golden age' when music was an essential element of the poet's art. The definition of poetry itself as 'words set in delightful proportion' looks backward, too, not only to the actual form of ancient verse, with its system of proportionate temporal durations (quantities), but also the Platonic definition of song as an ordered movement of sound in time, words and

[1] *An Apology for Poetry*, edited by Geoffrey Shepherd, Manchester, 1973, p 113.

music governed by a single *rhythmos*, delighting both ear and mind with its sensuous image of the higher Pythagorean order.

At the same time, though, Sidney's definition looks to actual lyric, and the realities of contemporary musico-poetic relation. In the terms of the ideal it is a fallen world, where music and poetry are no longer inherently united, but must be brought deliberately together. Moreover, there are two distinct processes involved, one the poet's preparation, the other the musician's accompaniment; and, as the construction of the sentence implies, these no longer follow automatically from one another: it is 'either/or', not 'and'. Then, too, in the 'real' world of Renaissance lyric, words come first, and can be informed with their own internal 'music' – the 'delightful proportion' – without having been written either 'for' or 'with' musician's music. In effect, Sidney's own lyric imagination has silently conflated three different ways in which a Renaissance poem could make music: by structuring itself according to the laws of poetic number and proportion; by shaping its own structures to those of actual music; and by being incorporated into a musical structure, when 'set and sung'.

The *Apology for Poetry* gives no further explanation of these processes, but we may infer something from Sidney's own lyric practice. As for the internal 'music' of poetry, Sidney was one of the great composers of the Elizabethan period, bringing ancient theory into harmony with modern practice. Like many Elizabethan intellectuals, he was deeply influenced by his classical education, and viewed all questions of prosody through a Latin lens, defining 'delightful proportion' in quantitative terms. He also contributed to the effort to bring this *musica* into English verse by writing in classical metres. In doing so he joined the contemporary debate over the relative merits of quantitative and accentual verse – a debate in which music, both ideal and actual, played a defining role:

Now of versifying there are two sorts, the one ancient, the other modern: the ancient marked the quantity of each syllable, and according to that framed his verse; the modern observing only number (with some regard of the accent), the chief life of it standeth in that like sounding of the words, which we call rhyme. Whether or not these be the most excellent, would bear many speeches: the ancient (no doubt) more fit for music, both words and time observing quantity, and more fit lively to express divers passions, by the low and lofty sound of the well-weighed syllable. The latter likewise, with his rhyme, striketh a certain music to the ear; and, in fine, since it doth delight, though by another way, it obtains the same purpose, there being in either sweetness, and wanting in neither majesty.[1]

[1] *Apology*, p 140.

The more radical advocates of classical metre found no redeeming features in accentual verse: the very word 'rhyme' became for them synonymous with vulgarity, artlessness, disorder, a corruption of the true meaning of poetic *rhythmos* – which was, in the Pythagorean sense, a 'musicall numerositie in utterance'.[1] Yet others, like Sidney, were willing to see in English rhyme a 'music' of a different kind, coming from the order and agreement of sensuous sounds rather than of abstract proportions. And the most successful experiments with quantitative metre in English, including Sidney's own, were those that implicitly translated the ancient 'music' into the modern, weighing English syllables by the native measures of pronunciation, rather than by alien rules of orthography and position. In exploring these empirical, accentual equivalents for the classical 'longs' and 'shorts', poets learned to create patterns of English sound that had something like the ancient 'musicall numerositie' – a smooth flow of sound through time, a sense of duration within the accentual frame:

> Rose-cheekt *Lawra*, come,
> Sing thou smoothly with thy beawties
> Silent musick, either other
>   Sweetely gracing.
> Lovely formes do flowe
> From concent devinely framed;
> Heav'n is musick, and thy beawties
>   Birth is heavenly.
> These dull notes we sing
> Discords neede for helps to grace them;
> Only beawty purely loving
>   Knowes no discord;
> But still mooves delight,
> Like cleare springs renu'd by flowing,
> Even perfect, ever in them-
>   selves eternall.[2]

This poem, by Thomas Campion, is meant as an example of 'lyricall' verse in the ancient sense, but it makes a clear and audible poetic 'music' in modern terms as well. As such it participates in the wider Elizabethan search for new beauties in English sound – the 'slipper words and syllables, such as the toung readily utters, and the eare with pleasure receiveth' – which far transcended academic prosodical debate.[3] This new sound-aesthetic was also identified

1 George Puttenham, *The Arte of English Poesie* (1586) in *Elizabethan Critical Essays*, ed. G. Gregory Smith, London, 1904, vol. II, p 57.

2 'Rose-cheekt Lawra', from *Observations in the Art of English Poesie* (1602); reprinted in *The Works of Thomas Campion*, ed. Walter R. Davis, London, 1969, p 310.

3 Puttenham, *The Arte of English Poesie*; Smith, II, 63–4.

with music in the Elizabethan poetic imagination, through a separate process of metaphorical association with euphony, smoothness, beauty and pleasure – the ornaments of eloquence.

The second kind of poetic music-making involved a more literal association: words 'prepared for the well-enchanting skill of music'. Sidney doesn't actually say what this process entailed, but his references to 'proportion' and 'versifying' point in the right direction, for the most basic level on which poem and music interact is a structural one. Music is, as Ezra Pound said of rhythm, a form cut into time;[1] and any words sung to music will necessarily take on that form, as they are apprehended in musical time. The musical structure will determine the number and length of phrases, and the syntactic relationships between them – pairs or other groupings; patterns of repetition, variation, and contrast; the principal pauses, and the final close. On another level of organization, it will dictate the placement and degree of rhythmic emphases on individual syllables, and their relative duration and pitch – the basis of what we perceive as declamation in song. Indeed, a song-melody may be said to have an articulating function with respect to the text. The closer the correspondence between linguistic and musical structures, the more that articulation will seem to reflect, and reinforce, the contours of the words.

The Renaissance practice of writing and singing poetry 'to the tune' was essentially an art of recognizing and exploiting these correspondences, particularly on the level of versification. The tunes themselves came from various repertoires – traditional ballad and folksong, fashionable courtly ayres, popular dance tunes from England and abroad, the 'Church tunes' of the Protestant psalter – but they had some basic musical features in common, the most important, from the poet's point of view, being their great structural and rhythmic regularity. The most common shape was the tune of four phrases, each with four primary stresses, and a medial pause after the second phrase dividing the melody into balanced halves. The tunes usually had an emphatic metrical character as well, with regularly recurring strong beats, and a clear iambic or trochaic accentual pattern, in either duple or triple time.

What this sort of tune offered the poet was a metrical 'recipe', which might be used as the basis for any number of different poems, provided the principle of musical-metrical correspondence was respected. Conversely, a single tune could be made to accommodate a number of pre-existing poems, as long as there was a basic

---

[1] *ABC of Reading*, London, 1951, p 198.

structural 'fit'. Perhaps in part because of this practice, the degree of structural standardization, or generalization, in both poems and their tunes was high. The most popular Elizabethan metres, including ballad metre, poulter's measure, and fourteeners, can all be adapted easily to the standard 4-phrase melody, as can many of the more common stanzaic patterns. In fact, so close was the association between musical structure and versification that the word 'tune' itself was used to refer to both melody and metrical pattern.

This is not to say, however, that the association between music and metre was universal, or universally applauded: here, too, poetry could dissociate itself from song, even while exploiting one of its most literally 'songlike' features. The cruder forms of words 'to the tune', such as the broadside ballad, drew scorn from high-minded Elizabethan prosodists and critics. In their view it required no true 'arte' to

frame an Alehouse song of five or sixe score verses, hobbling upon some tune of a northern Jygge, or Robyn hoode, or La lubber, etc. And perhappes to observe just number of sillables, eyght in one line, five in an other, and there withall an A to make a iercke in the ende.[1]

It is true that some of these ballads depended upon their tunes to make metrical sense, and gave an impression of disorder on the printed page; while those that were metrically regular tended to reinforce their 'beat' in heavy-handed ways, with insistent alliteration and rhyming, strong caesuras, a regular correspondence between metrical and lexical stress, and a near-equality of stresses within a line – features which would only be further accentuated when the poem was sung to its emphatically metrical tune. The result was a relentless 'singsong' rhythm. The next generation of poets, who had learned to create subtle play between the metrical 'tune' and the rhythms of speech, found this style an easy target for parody:

> The raging rocks,
> And shivering shocks
> Shall break the locks
> Of prison gates;
> And Phibbus' car
> Shall shine from far,
> And make and mar
> The foolish Fates.[2]

Yet the same stylistic and metrical features were found in much 'serious' verse of the earlier Elizabethan period as well, particularly in

[1] William Webbe, *A Discourse on English Poesie* (1586) in *Elizabethan Critical Essays*, ed. G. G. Smith, vol. I, p 246.
[2] *A Midsummer Night's Dream*, I. ii. 32–7.

the poetical miscellanies such as Tottel's *Songes and Sonettes*, and *The Paradise of Dainty Devices*. This did make them ideally suited, in the structural sense, to singing 'to the tune', and many were published separately as broadsides. But Tottel's advertisement, in the preface to his Miscellany, of a 'stateliness of stile removed from the rude skill of common eares', suggests that the style was also cultivated for purely literary reasons, as part of the search for new eloquence in English verse, 'to the honor of the Englishe tong'.[1] The poets engaged in this great project may well have rejected writing 'to the tune' as an altogether lower form of poetic activity, despite the prominent 'tune' in their own verses.

Others, however, found metrical inspiration in music. Among Sidney's *Certain Sonnets* are eight headed 'To the tune of'; the tunes mentioned are Italian, Spanish, and Dutch as well as English. The imitation of these foreign musical models, which reflected the characteristic metres of poetry in their own languages, is credited with the introduction of both feminine rhyme and accentual trochaics into English. The 'Englishing' of Italian madrigal verse in the late 1580s and 1590s, which was another form of writing 'to the tune', had a similar effect. In order to match their words to the settings, the translators had to employ lines of varying length, unusual 'loose' or inverted syntax, and insistent feminine rhyme, all of which produced a peculiarly un-English poetic style. Yet expediency was converted to advantage in 'literary' madrigals that made effective use of the expanding and contracting rhythms, the short lines, and the 'kissing' rhymes of the Italianate forms. Thus the same musico-poetic practice that had apparently helped to lock Elizabethan poetry into a metrical straitjacket, and to give accentual rhyme a bad name, also became an agent of its rhythmic liberation. It was just one of many ironies in a period marked as much by the divergence, as by the convergence, of musical and poetic perspectives.

The mention of madrigals brings us to the last of Sidney's three kinds of lyric interrelation – the 'accompaniment' of words by music – and thus to the settings of sixteenth-century verse by contemporary composers which to many epitomize the kinship of music and poetry in the English Renaissance. The lives led by words in these 'marriages' were as various as the musical styles themselves. The consort-songs for solo voice and viols, popular in the earlier

---

[1] 'The Printer to the Reader', from *Tottel's Miscellany*, ed. Hyder E. Rollins, (rev. edn, Cambridge, MA, 1965) vol. I, p 2.

Elizabethan period, were the closest musical match for Tottel's 'stateliness of stile' in poetry, both historically and aesthetically. They were often structurally different from dance song and other strophic 'tunes', which were characterized by a dominant melody accompanied by simple chords; the polyphonic texture, and the use of imitative counterpoint, gave a different quality to the movement of words. Yet the composers of consort-songs followed the same form of metrical-musical correspondence, so that the 'singing-part' was a faithful image of the metrical pattern, and the poetic form was clearly perceptible, as the singing voice emerged from the integrated musical texture. Indeed, the consort-song was fundamentally a marriage of forms rather than of contents: the music was not designed to 'express' the text in a conceptual or affective sense, but rather to keep decorum with its own 'music'. Stylistically it was a suitable accompaniment to the solemn moral verse of the 1560s and 1570s, with which it was particularly associated.

In the madrigal, by contrast, the poem – often of no great substance in itself – became the groundplot for an exuberant musical invention. The original poetic shape was refracted into a brilliant mosaic of sound, the individual words and phrases repeating, crossing, chasing after one another through the different voices until the threads of metre and syntax virtually disappeared, only to re-emerge when the voices suddenly came together again at key points. The meaning, too, could be enhanced, and even transformed, by the use of an elaborate musical vocabulary, including 'expressive' harmony, rhetorical declamation, and rhythmic or melodic word-painting, to represent verbal content. It was in the madrigal style that composers learned to 'express divers passions', by exploring the associative and affective powers of their own sound-structures – music directly imitating poetry.

The solo lute ayre was the last of the three major song-forms to come into fashion, and it incorporated elements of both the consort-song and the madrigal, as well as of the ballad, dance song, and metrical psalm. Being part of the strophic song tradition, it gave prominence to the tune, in both the musical and the poetic senses: composers tended to set the text straightforwardly, line by line, with a minimum of verbal repetition or melisma, and a close correspondence between musical and poetic structures. In some cases, they made the correspondence even closer: Dowland and Campion, particularly, made effective use of the tendency towards rhetorical patterning in Elizabethan lyric, designing tunes whose own melodic and rhythmic patterns both parallelled and pointed the verbal design. In doing so they gave the traditional balance and repetitiveness of the strophic melody a new logic, and a new kind of relationship to the text. But their approach towards word-setting was not always so purely constructive: many lute ayres employ expressive musical 'figures' from the madrigal style, including word-painting, and musical declamation that is intended to represent the contours of impassioned speech. In some of the most passionate ayres, such as Dowland's 'Sorrow stay' and Daniel's 'Can dolefull Notes', this expressive musical language is so concentrated and intense that the song becomes the musical equivalent of a dramatic reading. These songs are very far from the lighter lyricism of the dance songs and 'tuneful' ayres. They point towards larger, more extended musical forms, and towards a kind of musico-poetic relationship in which the musical imagination clearly dominates.

Only in the songs of Thomas Campion, however, did the kinds of musico-poetic relationship with which we began – the poetic 'music', as well as the music for poetry – truly come into close relationship themselves. Of all the lutenist composers Campion was the only one who was a poet, rather than a musician, by profession, and hence the only one who viewed the process of musical composition from an essentially poetic perspective. In his ayres he brought the poetic and musical imaginations to bear upon one another, to explore both 'relationship' and 'relation' in a single lyric form. Like Sidney, he was influenced by the classical idea of poetic *musica*, and cultivated the inner harmonies of number and proportion in his quantitative verse. But he also realized that English word-sounds could be made to move 'musically' even within the familiar patterns of accentual rhymed verse, by adjusting the weight of individual syllables, and by interweaving sounds in a line so that the words moved through whole phrases, rather than in discrete metrical units punctuated by stress:

> When thou must home to shades of under ground,
> And there ariv'd, a newe admired guest,
> The beauteous spirits do ingirt thee round,
> White Iope, blith Hellen, and the rest,
> To heare the stories of thy finisht love,
> From that smoothe toong whose musicke hell can move:[1]

---

[1] 'When thou must home', from *A Booke of Ayres* (1601), no xx; Davis p 46.

He also understood that accentual 'tunes' could be at once metrically regular and rhythmically subtle:

> Follow your Saint, follow with accents sweet,
> Haste you, sad noates, fall at her flying feete;
> There, wrapt in cloud of sorrowe, pitie move,
> And tell the ravisher of my soule I perish for her love.
> But if she scorns my never-ceasing paine,
> Then burst with sighing in her sight, and nere returne againe.[1]

Of course Campion was not alone in this achievement. What set him apart from his contemporaries was the fact that he reached this poetic 'music' by a much more musical route, and related it directly to music in his songs. As a composer he understood how music literally in-forms words, how it gives to their sound a definite measure and weight; he learned to create the verbal equivalent of this movement in his poetry, and then to compose melodies that matched it. He had a deepened, because double, sense of the relationship between poetry and music as forms in time: the subtleties of rhythmic articulation, of melodic contour, of phrasing, of rhymes in both sound and syntax, through which each form could be made to articulate the other. The fruit of this special understanding is the especially close matching of poetic and musical sound-structures in his songs.

Campion has sometimes been criticized, on both sides, for the smallness of his lyric art. His poetry does not have the energy of thought or the intensity of feeling of Donne's or Shakespeare's; nor is his musical imagination as large and original as Dowland's or Byrd's. But to accuse him of lacking their expressive power is to miss the source of his own lyric strength: it lies in balance and containment, in the accommodation of poetic and musical energies within one frame. Campion was able to achieve this balance because he conceived of the ayre as an art of mutual articulation – not music imitating poetry, or poetry imitating music, but both imitating a common form. In that sense, he came closer than any Renaissance songmaker to realizing at least two of the period's greatest lyric ideals: the 'musicall numerositie in utterance', and the according of like with like.

---

[1] 'Follow your saint', no x. of *A Booke of Ayres*; Davis p 32.

7

BEN JONSON AND THE COURT

J. C. A. Rathmell

It was in 1616 that James I formally granted Jonson an annual pension in recognition of his 'good and acceptable service' to crown and court. By this time Jonson was over forty and the misdemeanours of his earlier years seem to have been forgotten or forgiven. The offences that had resulted between 1597 and 1605 in three prison sentences and a summons to appear before the Privy Council (to answer charges regarding allegedly subversive material in *Sejanus*) were largely a thing of the past. Jonson, for his part, declared his loyalty to the king in the most handsome terms. 'After God,' he wrote in *Discoveries*. 'nothing is to be loved of man like the Prince; he violates Nature that doth it not with his whole heart'.[1] There is no reason to believe that these patriotic sentiments were feigned, for he was essentially conservative by temperament. Jonson, however, was a far from conventional laureate. Although he was entrusted with a key rôle in devising masques and other royal entertainments throughout the reign of James I – a sure sign of his public standing – he remained a remarkably outspoken critic of the court. He deliberately cultivated a reputation for being his own man, and was evidently not displeased to be 'given out dangerous' (despite strenuous assertions to the contrary).[2] It is scarcely surprising that at the time of his death in 1637 – only a few years before the outbreak of civil war – he was praised by Lord Falkland, not as a celebrant of the court, but for having prophetically portrayed

> All the disorders of a tottering state,
> All the distempers which on kingdoms fall,
> When ease, and wealth, and vice are general.[3]

---

[1] *Ben Jonson*, ed. C. H. Herford and P. and E. Simpson, Oxford, 1925–52, I, 231; VIII, 594.

[2] Herford and Simpson, VIII, 117.

[3] Herford and Simpson, XI, 433.

Falkland was referring in particular to his tragedies, *Sejanus* and *Catiline*, but there can be no doubt that his praise of Jonson's diagnosis of the ills of his society was intended to have a more general application.

Jonson's was a highly contradictory personality. The self-doubts he expresses in his 'Expostulation with Inigo Jones' – doubts, above all, about his long-standing involvement in the production of lavish court masques ('O Shows! Shows! Mighty Shows!') – reflect a strain of uneasiness in his relations with the court that runs deep through all his works. This ambiguity of attitude is, paradoxically, the source of a highly fruitful tension in his poetry.

A small but significant indicator of the ambivalence of Jonson's stance is the fact that in 1616, when he was preparing the Folio edition of his works for the press, he added to *Cynthia's Revels* a prefatory dedication to the court, signing himself, with characteristic terseness, 'thy servant, but not slave'.[1] Much as he valued his association with the court (and James I's public recognition of his services), he valued his independence even more. Jonson was obliged to perform a delicate balancing act. On the one hand, too much court favour could put at risk the reputation for integrity by which he set such store (he took pride in declaring himself 'at feud/With sin and vice, though with a throne endued').[2] On the other, any too forthright shows of independence could alienate the court patrons on whom he relied for protection (among them, Lord Aubigny, brother of the Lord Steward of the Household, and the Earl of Pembroke, leader of the party at court that sought to moderate the influence of the royal favourite, Buckingham). Jonson's relations with the court were indeed far from simple. He regarded himself as no man's client, but the reality of his situation was that without the influential backing of highly placed patrons he could not have retained his position as a chief deviser of court masques (the fees for which formed a substantial part of his annual income), and in the absence of that support he would undoubtedly have suffered more severely than he did for his not infrequent indiscretions.

Jonson was of course anxious to keep open his lines of communication with the court for other less immediately practical reasons. His quasi-public position – one which he carefully consolidated

---

[1] Herford and Simpson, IV, 33. (This dedication does not appear in the quarto edition.)

[2] *Poems*, ed. Ian Donaldson, 111. All citations from Jonson's verse are from this excellent modern-spelling edition.

over the years – provided him with unique opportunities for addressing (and counselling) the court and its leading officers. This was a privilege and a responsibility to which he attached considerable importance. More than a hundred of his poems are written directly to particular, named, persons, the majority of them men and women holding high social or political rank in the state (including, for instance, privy councillors such as Salisbury, Suffolk, Ellesmere, Coke, Bacon, Pembroke and Portland). Most of these so-called 'complimentary' poems are concerned, directly or obliquely, with the social, political and moral obligations of public life.

Jonson was a past master of the art of combining compliment with counsel, and praise with tactful admonition. Bacon's view that 'the wisest princes need not think it any diminution to their greatness, or derogation to their sufficiency, to rely upon counsel' was one that he warmly endorsed: in his complimentary verse he simply extended that principle to include not only princes but all those members of society concerned with the government and welfare of the body politic. 'In sovereignty', he observed in *Discoveries*, 'it is a most happy thing not to be compelled; but it is the most miserable not to be counselled'.[1]

Although Jonson's poetry has received increasingly intelligent appreciation during the last twenty years, it has not yet wholly succeeded in ridding itself of the stigma that attaches to public verse. Much recent criticism has been concerned, indeed, to counter the accusation that his verse is too 'committed to compliment'[2] It is ironic that it should be found necessary to defend Jonson against this charge for not even the most hostile of his contemporaries – and he did not lack enemies – would have accused him of displaying undue deference to his superiors. His impatience with the bootlicking servility of the Jacobean court (as reflected in such memorable images as that of the sycophantic client

> ready to praise
> His Lordship if he spit, or but piss fair,
> Have an indifferent stool, or break wind well)[3]

---

[1] Bacon, *Works*, ed. J. Spedding, R. L. Ellis and D. D. Heath, 14 vols, 1857–74, VI, 423; Herford and Simpson, VIII, 601.

[2] Hugh Maclean, 'Ben Jonson's Poems: Notes on the Ordered Society' in *Essays in English Literature from the Renaissance to the Victorian Age*, ed. Miller MacLure and F. W. Watt, Toronto, 1964, 45.

[3] Herford and Simpson, IV, 356.

was legendary: he boasted to Drummond that he 'never esteemed a
man for the name of a lord', refused to defer to 'noble ignorants',
and loudly proclaimed his determination 'to write/Things manly,
and not smelling parasite'. That sense of his own worth, which, as
Clarendon dryly noted, rendered him 'superior to ordinary
obligations', was an essential component of his poetic personality.[1]

Pride, truculence, and thin-skinned resentment all contribute to
the distinctively uncompromising temper of his verse, so very
different from that of Donne's extravagantly flattering poetic
eulogies. Jonson could never have brought himself to assume the
self-abasing posture the latter adopts in addressing the young
Countess of Bedford:

> Nothings, as I am, may
> Pay all they have, and yet have all to pay . . .

More typical of Jonson's robust style is the 'Epistle to Sir Edward
Sackville' in which he rounds fiercely on the unnamed patron who
has committed the unforgivable sin of treating him negligently:

> Can I owe thanks for courtesies received
> Against his will that does 'em; that hath weaved
> Excuses or delays; or done 'em scant,
> That they have more oppressed me than my want?
> Or if he did it not to succour me
> But by mere chance, for interest, or to free
> Himself of farther trouble . . .?

As Aubrey observed, he 'ever scorned an unworthy Patrone'.[2] What
makes these lines so unmistakably Jonson's, however, is not just the
strong whiff of offended *amour propre*, but the tension between the
vernacular energy of the expostulating, speaking voice – Jonson's
anger is plainly not assumed – and the control exerted by the tightly
compacted latinate syntax. The extraordinarily close-knit texture of
Jonson's verse which results from this fusion of native and classical
elements is something that immediately sets it apart from that of all
his contemporaries, and not least from that of Donne (who, like
himself, was praised by contemporaries for his 'masculine expression').

It is here, in the texture of his verse rather than in its subject-
matter, that Jonson's originality lies. Clarendon (who, as a young
law student, came to know Jonson in the late 1620s and remained

---

[1] Clarendon, *Selections*, ed. G. Huehns, London, 1955, 64.
[2] Aubrey, *Brief Lives*, ed. Oliver Lawson Dick, London, 1950, 269.

an intimate member of his circle until he was called to the bar in 1633) speaks from first-hand experience of his distinctive qualities and limitations:

> Ben Jonson's name can never be forgotten, having by his very good learning and the severity of his nature and manners, very much reformed the stage; and indeed English poetry itself. His natural advantages were, judgement to order and govern fancy, rather than excess of fancy, his productions being slow and upon deliberation, yet then abounding with great wit and fancy, and will live accordingly . . .His conversation was very good, and with the men of most note.[1]

As Clarendon infers, Jonson's poetry, although by no means lacking in wit, is distinguished more by its incisive and deliberated judgements than by any very notable audacity of phrase or imaginativeness of conception. In this respect it has closer affinities with the relatively plain and sober verse of Greville and Daniel, poets considerably older than himself, than with that of Donne, his more or less exact contemporary. Jonson, like Greville and Daniel, prized 'perspicuity' as a stylistic virtue. All three shunned the elaborate hyperbole and baroque conceits of Donne's encomiastic verse (Jonson tartly remarked that the praise Donne lavished on his patron's daughter, Elizabeth Drury, in the *Anniversaries* would have been 'something' had it been applied to the Virgin Mary).[2] There are other similarities, too. Jonson insisted that his poetry was 'free/From servile flattery, common poets' shame'. Daniel, in much the same vein, claimed that he was no 'pensionary' poet and that his purpose was to preserve his verse 'free from that stain/Of flattering men in grace'.[3] As public poets concerned with public themes both were exceptionally sensitive to the danger of compromising their reputation and their art. Greville, whilst adopting an altogether more cautious and private stance, was equally resolute in his refusal to make accommodations and he frequently alludes in his verse to the beguiling 'sleights of grace and honour'.

Daniel, in his dignified but somewhat stilted epistles to his court patrons, and Greville in his sour reflections on the ignoble character of the Jacobean court, explore much that Jonson was to develop in his own more wittily astringent manner: the dangers of placing

---

[1] Herford and Simpson, XI, 512–3.
[2] Herford and Simpson, I, 133.
[3] J. Pitcher, *Samuel Daniel: The Brotherton Manuscript, A Study in Authorship*, Leeds, 1981, 139–40.

reliance on the prerogatives of power, fortune and place; the vulnerability of men in high office to the batteries of 'glory, honour, fame, renown, applause'; and the necessity to fortify oneself against the seducing baits of the court (not to mention the subtler 'ambushments' of flattery and self-regard). Most of these themes derive ultimately from classical and scriptural sources (mediated in some cases by authors such as Erasmus, Calvin, Montaigne, and Lipsius): a prime aim of both Greville and Daniel was to demonstrate their continuing relevance to contemporary social and political circumstances.

It would be wrong to make too much of Jonson's indebtedness to what has been called the 'native plain style'. Greville's verse, for instance, unlike Jonson's, is unashamedly didactic. He presents himself quite explicitly as a pilot to those who 'having lost sight of their gardens and groves, study to sail on a right course among rocks and quicksands'.[1] Jonson certainly knew Greville's verse (he possessed the posthumously published 1633 edition of his poems), but the temper and movement of Jonson's verse are utterly unlike Greville's. What the two poets do share is a searing contempt for the servility of the Jacobean court and a deep dismay at the unbridled power enjoyed by successive royal favourites:

> Slaves, and yet darlings of authority;
> Echoes of wrong; shadows of princes' might;
> Which glow-worm-like, by shining, shew 'tis night.

Greville's lines (from *Caelica* LXXVIII) reflect a weary acquiescence in the corrupt conditions of the contemporary political world: only in dark times could such obsequious creatures gain pre-eminence in the court. A similar disenchantment is registered in *Caelica* CI:

> But states grow old, when princes turn away
> From honour, to take pleasure for their ends;
> For that a large is, this a narrow way,
> That wins a world, and this a few dark friends . . .

Jonson's verse is always brisker and more urgent than this, but he is entirely in accord with Greville in his conviction that the health of a state is directly proportionate to the quality of the men who govern it. As he wrote in *Discoveries*, 'they are ever good men that must make good the times: if the men be naught, the times will be such'.[2]

---

[1] Fulke Greville, *Life of Sidney*, ed. Nowell Smith, Oxford, 1907, 224.
[2] Herford and Simpson, VIII, 571.

Jonson cannot have found much to admire technically in Greville's often laboured and maladroit verses and he was evidently unimpressed by the slack-jointed and essentially ruminative structure of Daniel's verse-epistles (he told Drummond that Daniel was 'a good honest man . . .but no poet'). There can be little doubt, however, that the sceptical attitudes embodied in their poems, and the generally bleak philosophical outlook they reflect, corresponded closely to his own.[1] A certain indifference to distinctions of rank and degree, a strong disposition to question the values of court society, and a dour emphasis on the necessity of cultivating the will to endure misfortune and resist oppression are shared by all these writers.

Jonson, L. C. Knights observes, 'defines his values by negatives, not only in the satiric epigrams but in poems that are not predominantly satirical'.[2] This too, is a tendency he shares with Daniel. In the verse of both poets the less admirable aspects of court life are never lost sight of, even in poems which are nominally celebratory in intention. In his 'Funeral Poem for the Earl of Devonshire', for instance, Daniel pays tribute to his former patron, but he praises his responsible and judicious exercise of power in such a way as to make the reader keenly aware of the fact that such power was commonly employed by courtiers in an altogether more capricious and arbitrary manner:

> the passage to his favours lay
> Not common to all comers, nor yet was
> So narrow, but it gave a gentle way
> To such as fitly might or ought to pass:
> Nor sold he smoke, nor took he up today
> Commodities of men's attendances,
> And of their hopes, to pay them with delay.[3]

The felt pressure of the suitors' importunities and of the frustrations generated by court magnates' habitual smoke-selling (i.e. offering of empty assurances) is a crucial part of the effect here for it is precisely this context that throws Devonshire's probity and honest dealing into relief. In much the same way, though more economically, Jonson praises his patron, the Earl of Pembroke, as a man

[1] Herford and Simpson, I, 132.
[2] L. C. Knights, *Explorations III*, London, 1976, 88.
[3] *Complete Works of Samuel Daniel*, ed. A. B. Grosart, 5 vols, I, 182–3.

> whose noblesse keeps one stature still,
> And one true posture, though besieged with ill
> Of what ambition, faction, pride can raise.

Pembroke's resolute conduct, in the self-seeking milieu of the court, is tacitly likened to that of the commander of a threatened outpost, courageously holding his ground in face of powerful opposition. Neither Daniel nor Jonson has recourse to striking conceits but a discreet and unobtrusive wit invites, and indeed obliges, the reader to visualize the material and political pressures of the court as formidable forces all too likely to carry the day unless resolutely confronted.

Jonson uses a not dissimilar strategy in the 'To Penshurst' (a poem otherwise quite unlike anything Daniel wrote) where the Sidney family's hospitable and unpresuming house is depicted as making a determined stand against the assaults of luxury and pride. This is one aspect of the familiar and oft-quoted opening lines that can easily be missed:

> Thou art not, Penshurst, built to envious show
> Of touch or marble, nor canst boast a row
> Of polished pillars, or a roof of gold;
> Thou has no lantern whereof tales are told,
> Or stair, or courts; but stand'st an ancient pile . . .

The very ungainliness of *stand'st* (and the difficulty the reader experiences in getting his tongue round it) creates a felicitous effect because it is so suggestive of the sturdiness of Penshurst's local resistance to the prevailing fashion for extravagant display. In the central sections of the poem the characteristic vices of the court (ambition, arrogance, envy, greed and so on) are felt as malign forces threatening to make their way into the poem but successfully held off. Jonson does not shut his eyes to the uglier political realities lying in wait outside Penshurst's sheltering walls. The humorous reference to the languid pikes in the Penshurst ponds 'now weary their own kind to eat' is an oblique reminder of the harshly competitive forces that the walls of the estate, 'rear'd with no man's ruin, no man's groan', only precariously keep at bay (court officers, he observes elsewhere, are the 'pikes in the pond, eat whom they list').[1] Again, we may recognize a kind of wit at work here, albeit quite different from that we associate with Donne. By a comic hyperbole the genial air of Penshurst is presented as imbuing all that come into its ambience with a spirit of self-sacrificing generosity.

---

[1] Herford and Simpson, VIII, 603.

'To Penshurst', nevertheless, is very far from being the benign praise of country life it is often taken to be. Sir Robert Sidney, as Jonson knew well, was harassed by debts and seeking desperately for means to recover his fortunes. 'If the house be in debt', Sidney wrote to his wife, 'I must pay it and will. But this we must at the last resolve: to keep such a house as we may, not as we would.'[1] 'To Penshurst' is in fact a poem which seeks to unite praise with tactful admonishment. Jonson's overriding design is not to celebrate country living, but to reconcile the hapless Sidney to living within his means and to impress on him that his true 'fortune' lies (as the closing lines suggest) in his possession of a harmonious close-knit family and a warmly loyal body of dependants. That, Jonson infers, is something that counts for more than any fortune that might accrue to him from court advancement. As so often is the case with Jonson's poems, counsel is offered under the cover of compliment.

The opening of 'To Sir Robert Wroth', another poem which hinges on a contrast between court and country values, has a similar edge to it:

> How blest art thou canst love the country, Wroth,
>   Whether by choice, or fate, or both;
> And, though so near the city and the court,
>   Art ta'en with neither's vice nor sport;
> That at great times art no ambitious guest
>   Of sheriff's dinner or mayor's feast;
> Nor com'st to view the better cloth of state,
>   The richer hangings, or crown-plate;
> Nor throng'st, when masquing is, to have a sight
>   Of the short bravery of the night . . .

What Jonson has in mind in stressing Wroth's nearness to the city and the court is not so much the geographical proximity of his Essex estate to London as the magnetic attraction exerted by the 'short bravery' of court masques and city feasts, and all that they represent. Wroth, like Sidney, elicits Jonson's approval to the extent that he demonstrates his immunity to such allurements:

> Let thousands more go flatter vice, and win
>   By being organs to great sin,
> Get place and honour, and be glad to keep
>   The secrets that shall break their sleep;
> And, so they ride in purple, eat in plate,

---

[1] *Historical Manuscripts Commission*, 77, IV, 162. See also J. C. A. Rathmell, 'Jonson, Lord Lisle and Penshurst', *English Literary Renaissance*, I, 1971, 250–60.

> Though poison, think it a great fate.
> But thou, my Wroth, if I can truth apply,
> Shall neither that nor this envy:
> Thy peace is made; and when man's state is well,
> 'Tis better if he there can dwell.

The intrusion of these potentially compromising forces into the protected world of Wroth's estate is an important aspect of the poem for it is precisely by the extent to which he reveals his power to withstand them that Wroth's integrity, like that of Pembroke and Robert Sidney, is defined.

Mr. J.B. Bamborough has claimed that Jonson's stylistic preferences for clarity and harmony 'virtually precluded a complex and plastic use of words'. In much the same vein, Professor Philip Edwards suggests that his complimentary poems – he refers in particular to his tributes to Pembroke and Cecil – are 'perfectly normal conventional exercises in well-established genres'.[1] Neither of these assertions can be accepted without qualification. Very often in Jonson's poetry an inflection of the voice, an unexpected emphasis, or the insertion of a parenthetic clause is sufficient to transform what might seem to be conventional praise into something considerably less straightforward.

The 'Epistle to Elizabeth, Countess of Rutland' provides an example of Jonson's habitual tendency to offer markedly uncomplimentary and even subversive reflections on the character of the court whilst ostensibly engaged in paying ceremonial tribute to his patron. Taking as his point of departure his inability to offer the seventeen-year-old Countess a New Year's Day gift comparable in size to those customarily offered to members of the court on this occasion (usually in order to further suits or cement alliances), Jonson contrasts his modest present of verse to the lavish donations of more ambitious clients. The Countess (Sir Philip Sidney's daughter) has, he implies, inherited enough of her father's good taste to rate his gift at its true value:

> With you, I know, my offering will find grace.
> For what a sin 'gainst your great father's spirit
> Were it to think that you should not inherit
> His love unto the muses . . .?

But the real force of the opening lines lies not in the tactful compliment to the Countess but in the indictment (packed away

[1] J. B. Bamborough, *Ben Jonson*, 1970, 161–2; P. Edwards, *Threshold of a Nation*, Cambridge, 1979, 152.

into what is nominally a subordinate clause) of ambitious suitors
who as a matter of routine political prudence press gifts into the
hands of

> every squire or groom that will report
> Well or ill, only, all the following year,
> Just to the weight their this day's presents bear.

Jonson's use of words here is, *pace* Mr Bamborough, remarkably
complex. 'Only' is ominously absolute, and 'just' punningly alludes
to the fact that the suitor's interests will be protected during the
ensuing twelve months with a degree of zeal directly proportionate
to the size of his gift ('*just* to the weight. . . .'), whilst simultaneously
pointing up the *in*justice of a system that sanctions, under the guise
of hallowed seasonal custom, what amounts to outright bribery. 'It',
in the ensuing lines, is the all-powerful gold that must – or so
conventional political wisdom decrees – be slipped into the palm of
every intermediary functionary of the court.

> While it makes ushers serviceable men,
>   And some one apteth to be trusted, then,
> Though never after; while it gains the voice
>   Of some grand peer, whose air doth make rejoice
> The fool that gave it, who will want and weep
>   When his proud patron's favours are asleep;
> While thus it buys great grace and hunts poor fame,
>   Runs between man and man, 'tween dame and dame;
> Solders cracked friendship, makes love last a day
>   Or perhaps less: whilst gold bears all this sway,
> I, that have none to send you, send you verse,
>   A present which, if elder writs rehearse
> The truth of times, was once of more esteem
>   Than this, our gilt, nor golden age can deem.

In insisting that gold will make ushers (and other minor court
officials) 'serviceable', Jonson has in mind principally the idiomatic
contemporary sense of the word: 'capable of being suborned,
readily manipulable'. But, typically, a faint echo of the older and
entirely honourable meaning, 'diligent in service', is allowed to be
heard, poignantly registering a recollection of ideals of duty and
fidelity no longer fashionable.

Jonson's satire is, however, only incidentally occasioned by the
pervasive corruption of the court. His scorn is directed chiefly at the
habit of mind that can conceive of fame and 'great grace' as being
purchasable commodities. The client who is so credulous as to

132   POETRY AND PROSE 1540–1674

believe that honour can be bought as easily as titles or offices, in
Jonson's view, deserves to be gulled: thus, the insidiously parenthetic 'then' ('apteth to be trusted, *then*') underlines the transitoriness
of such goodwill as bribery may temporarily secure. A similar irony
hovers around 'air' ('whose *air* doth make rejoice'), suggesting
simultaneously a patrician affectation of concern for the suitor's
interests and the illusoriness of the hopes the latter too precipitately
entertains (just as in *Volpone* the hopes of Mosca's clients 'turn air').
The whole passage is an extraordinary *tour de force*: its power is
partly a matter of the sheer density of meaning; but it also has to do
with the way in which Jonson's discreet wit, almost unnoticed,
invites the reader to distinguish between the fundamental meaning
of such words as 'grace', 'love', and 'friendship', and their debased
currency in contemporary court parlance where they have degenerated into euphemisms for the exercise of favour, and the ties
(and obligations) of factional alliance. ('Of the right and left hand of
me I hear no news but of grace and advancements', Greville bitterly
noted in 1603,' . . . Only my destiny is to wither in this excellent
clime').[1]

Very few of Jonson's complimentary poems are without their local
trenchancies. In many, for instance, Jonson explicitly dissociates
himself from the view that virtue is a natural adjunct of nobility and
that merit is 'entailed on title'. He consistently defies conventional
observance of degree and rank by presenting nobility and greatness
as qualities of spirit essentially detachable from their ancient
anchorage in pedigree. Thus, in a poem addressed to Sir Henry
Neville, he asserts, with a certain grim wit, that his title to honour
lies not in his ancestry but – unlike the majority of James I's
indiscriminate creations – in his active possession of the true
'elements of honour':

> Who now calls on thee, Neville, is a muse
> That serves nor fame nor titles, but doth choose
> Where virtue makes them both, and that's in thee,
> Where all is fair, beside thy pedigree.
> Thou art not one seek'st miseries with hope,
> Wrestlest with dignities, or feign'st a scope
> Of service to the public when the end
> Is private gain, which hath long guilt to friend.
> Thou rather striv'st the matter to possess,
> And elements of honour, than the dress.

[1] Ronald A. Rebholz, *The Life of Fulke Greville*, Oxford, 1971, 157.

Neville's worth is generously affirmed, but it is also defined negatively by reference to the many Jacobean placeseekers who, unlike Neville, have achieved their 'dignities' by persistent solicitation or unscrupulous opportunism. The poem, in short, is something more than a neatly turned compliment for in the act of praising Neville, Jonson also contrives to glance at the contemporary sale of honours (his title is merited, not bought) and at the notorious rapacity of Jacobean officeholders. 'Possess' carries a considerable freight of meaning in this context. It is not just a matter of Neville's being 'possessed' by virtue rather than by the *cachet* of title; the implication is also that Neville's responsible conception of public service precludes him from possessively exploiting his office for 'private gain'. Jonson's distinctiveness here, as elsewhere, lies in his ability to present Neville's 'virtue' not as some lofty abstract conception but as a very firmly realized capacity for acting honourably in face of not inconsiderable pressures to do otherwise. By reason of its etymological association with the Latin *vir* ('man'), the concept of virtue is inseparably linked in Jonson's mind with manliness and strength (hence his allusion, in another complimentary poem, to the 'Roman sound' of Sir Horace Vere's name).

Jonson's poems are primarily concerned with questions of responsibility, conduct, and, in the widest sense of the term, manners. But to consider him as (in John Hollander's phrase) 'a moralist with no pulpit' is to do less than justice to the strictly poetic means by which he secures his effects.[1] The power of the poet to 'reign in man's affections', Jonson recognized, lay not in the laudableness of his sentiments but in his mastery of his medium and his skill in exploiting its particular resources. In the 'Epistle to Katherine, Lady Aubigny', Jonson praises his patron's wife for keeping her distance from the fashionable world of the court with its mindless pursuit of spectacle and novelty:[2]

> . . . .wisely you decline your life
> Far from the maze of custom, error, strife,
> And keep an even and unaltered gait,
> Not looking by, or back (like those that wait
> Times and occasions, to start forth and seem);
> Which though the turning world may disesteem,
> Because that studies spectacles and shows,

[1] J. Hollander, ed., *Ben Jonson*, New York, 1961, 11.

[2] Lady Aubigny's non-participation in court entertainments may not have been entirely due to moral scruple. She married in 1609 and gave birth to eight children during the ensuing ten years.

> And after varied, as fresh, objects goes,
> Giddy with change, and therefore cannot see
> Right, the right way; yet must your comfort be
> Your conscience; and not wonder if none asks
> For truth's complexion, where they all wear masks.

What makes Jonson's praise count poetically is the way in which Lady Aubigny's steadfastness (her 'even and unaltered gait') and the 'giddy' restlessness of the pleasure-seekers with whom she is contrasted, are both faithfully registered in carefully calculated metrical and syntactical effects. The rhythmical movement of Jonson's verse is determined by his meaning: sense is never subordinated to the exigencies of metre or the constraints of rhyme. This is very strikingly the case here where the manner in which the prose sense thrusts its way through and past the potential impediment of rhyme (and in so doing prevents the reader from responding to the couplets as enclosed units) contributes powerfully to the impact. It is transparently the verse of a man who detested 'smooth and easy numbers' (for much the same reason, it might be added, that he distrusted the fluent courtier's 'smooth and comely' graces). Very often it is just those passages which to the unskilled reader may seem clumsy and ungainly (for instance: 'cannot see/ Right, the right way. . . ') that turn out, on closer inspection, to be the most artfully calculated.

Jonson's verse is not always as conspicuously muscular as this. On other occasions crucial emphases are secured not by masculine syntax but by an exceptionally poised cadencing. The 'Ode to Sir William Sidney', written in 1611 on the occasion of his twenty-first birthday, is in effect a reminder that Sir Robert Sidney's son must now take on adult responsibilities – he had the reputation of being a headstrong and impetuous youth – and not rest on the family laurels:

> Nor can a little of the common store
>   Of nobles' virtue show in you;
>   Your blood
>   So good
>   And great must seek for new,
> And study more;
>   Not, weary, rest
>   On what's deceased.
>   For they that swell
>   With dust of ancestors, in graves but dwell.

The subtle changes of rhythm, line-length, and pace play a vital rôle in giving what might otherwise be taken as presumptuous advice the air of courteous and kindly intentioned counsel. A similar finesse is frequently displayed in the choruses of the masques, as for instance, in the graceful tribute to Virtue in *Pleasure Reconciled to Virtue*:

> She, she it is, in darkness shines.
> 'Tis she that still herself refines,
>   By her own light, to every eye
> More seen, more known when Vice stands by.
> And though a stranger here on earth,
>   In heaven she hath her right of birth.
>   There, there is Virtue's seat,
>   Strive to keep her your own;
>   'Tis only she can make you great,
> Though place here make you known.

Here Jonson's idealism (his exalted sense of what the world might be) and his realism (his experience of the world as it is) come into unusually close conjunction, neither quite cancelling out the other. Despite the delicate celebration of Virtue's refining light, Jonson insists as dourly as ever that she will remain a stranger in the status-obsessed world of the court so long as greatness there continues to be equated not with qualities of mind or spirit but with the possession of power and place. It is that carefully withheld last clause, with its saddened acknowledgement of the values that prevail in the world, that carries the unmistakable stamp of Jonson's authorship. The effect is almost wholly due to musical phrasing, a skill in cadencing matched only, among Jonson's immediate successors, by George Herbert. Jonson's contributions to the masque are relatively slight works, but even in this area of his literary activity where the pressure to satisfy court taste was most acute, Jonson showed quite admirable resourcefulness in demonstrating that it was not necessary to be 'tied to rules/Of flattery'.[1]

By caring more that his services to the court should be just rather than 'acceptable' (as James I had described them in 1616) and by reserving his right to admonish as well as praise, even at the cost of causing offence, Jonson notably extended the range of court poetry and, indeed, the traditional conception of the court poet's function. 'If men may by no means write freely or speak truth but when it offends not,' Jonson observed in *Discoveries*, 'why do physicians cure

---

[1] Beaumont and Fletcher, *The Maid's Tragedy*, Act 1, scene 1.

with sharp medicines or corrosives? Is not the same equally lawful in the cure of the mind, that is in the cure of the body?[1] As a servant of three successive sovereigns, Jonson, throughout his long career, never deviated from his conviction that the court's best interests were served not by pandering to its own exalted image of itself, but by holding up to it a true and unflattering mirror.

[1] Herford and Simpson, VIII, 634.

8

THE POETRY OF JOHN DONNE

A. J. Smith

Donne's poems seem to give substance to the paradox of his career, that bizarre metamorphosis of libertine into saint, amorous adventurer into Anglican priest. The juxtaposition of love with piety, *Songs and Sonets* with *Divine Poems*, especially teases one in him because he is not an idealist but a cool sceptic who moves from the raciest delineation of amorous motives to a trenchant grasp of sin. His life, career, and personality have intrigued modern readers, at times to the detriment of his poetry. For his poems aren't casebook jottings or intimate confessions, and may elude us if we take them so. Indeed, we know too little of the circumstances of their composition even to dismiss Ben Jonson's unlikely assertion that Donne wrote 'all his best pieces err he was 25 years old'.[1] Donne's own drafts have not survived, and only seven of his poems were published in his lifetime; a few other pieces can be placed by a manuscript dating or by their reference to some contemporary circumstance. Otherwise the poems are at the mercy of personalizing preconception, which has ranged from the splendid hagiography of Izaac Walton, who at least knew Donne, to the speculations of modern commentators who have used his verse as evidence of psychic disorders supposedly like our own.

It seems appropriate to ask what the poems amount to in themselves. Donne's standing as an artist depends on the sense they make, and then on the coherence of his poetry altogether. One seeks what may not be there, a singleness of vision that would link the buccaneer of love with the Dean of St Paul's. If anything holds together so scattered a poetic activity it might be the constant element in Donne's poetry, his wit.

No poetry in English confronts one more self-confidently with its own vivid life, or has a like power to compel one's witness to a quick

[1] *Conversations with William Drummond of Hawthornden*, in *Ben Jonson*, ed. C. H. Herford and Percy Simpson, Oxford, 1925, i, 135.

variety of dramatic enactments. A few brusque lines snatch one into an action. Here the poet is harrying a woman to undress and get into bed with him; there he is cursing a former mistress who has betrayed him; elsewhere he turns back on the point of embarking for an expedition, to press a last present on a mistress –

'Here take my Picture'.

It's not just that Donne's poems tend to be theatrically conceived, and to succeed each other like concretely realized scenes whose very unlikeness sharpens their impact. The writing has substance, and the sense of a living context; it seems to come straight out of the local life of its time still pulsing with the turbulence of that. Donne's poetry shows us the grain of the times as no formal chronicler could, by its immediate enactment of a mind exuberantly caught up in the life of streets, courts, chambers:

> 'Tis ten a clock and past; All whom the Mues,
> Baloune, Tennis, Dyet, or the stewes,
> Had all the morning held, now the second
> Time made ready, that day, in flocks, are found
> In the Presence, and I, (God pardon mee.)
> As fresh, and sweet their Apparrells be, as bee
> The fields they sold to buy them; 'For a King
> Those hose are', cry the flatterers; And bring
> Them next weeke to the Theatre to sell;
> Wants reach all states; Me seemes they doe as well
> At stage, as court; All are players;

('Satyre iv')

This is art not casual observation, but Donne is an artist whose gift feeds on the life around it; his zest for experience mauls one with its aggressive vitality:

> Fond woman, which would'st have thy husband die,
> And yet complain'st of his great jealousie;
> If swolne with poyson, hee lay in' his last bed,
> His body with a sere-barke covered,
> Drawing his breath, as thick and short, as can
> The nimblest crocheting Musitian,
> Ready with loathsome vomiting to spue
> His Soule out of one hell, into a new,
> Made deafe with his poore kindreds howling cries,
> Begging with few feign'd teares, great legacies,
> Thou would'st not weepe, but jolly,' and frolicke bee,
> As a slave, which to morrow should be free;
> Yet weep'st thou, when thou seest him hungerly
> Swallow his owne death, hearts-bane jealousie.

('Jealousie')

Courtly poets sometimes showed their contempt and hatred for a
mistress's husband with ferocious gibes – 'Rich fooles there be.'[1]

But these lines catch something more detached and complex in
which cool appraisal of the gain to the lovers balances mocking
distaste and the relished expectation of the husband's fate. Their
very outrageousness imposes its own morality on a mercenary
world, putting wit and alert senses before bestial oblivion, the
perilous human engagement before a blind selflove:

> Nor when he swolne, and pamper'd with great fare,
> Sits downe, and snorts, cag'd in his basket chaire,
> Must wee usurpe his owne bed any more,

But this openness to life is no more an impulse to turn all experience into art than a random self-dramatization. Donne's central
preoccupations are strikingly few. His poetry characteristically presents the poet in relation to somebody else, or to a whole class of
people, and works to place or define the relationship. Its concerns
are a few fundamental aspects of human engagement – men's
relationship to women, to the public world of affairs, to God. For
the energy of Donne's world is really the vitality of his own mind;
what distinguishes him from artists with a comparable feeling for
life is his purposeful mental resource. His poetry isn't so much an
evocation of his world as a continual commentary on it, and not least
on the poet himself. One mark of this is that his love poems
themselves repeatedly take the style of tense argument or proof:

> Oh stay, three lives in one flea spare,
> Where wee almost, nay more than maryed are:
> This flea is you and I, and this
> Our marriage bed, and marriage temple is;

('The Flea')

The poet seeks in love an opportunity to manoeuvre himself into a
position where he can exercise his staggering dialectical skill:

> May he be scorn'd by one, whom all else scorne,
> Foresweare to others, what to her he' hath sworne,
> With feare of missing, shame of getting, torne:

('The Curse')

But such seeming-casuistry is only one cast of a radical play of
mind which constantly works to place an event or circumstance in a
wider context of men's motives and apprehension:

<hr>

[1] Sir Philip Sidney, *Astrophel and Stella* 24.

> Kinde pitty chokes my spleene; brave scorn forbids
> Those teares to issue which swell my eye-lids;
>
> ('Satyre iii')

The opening of 'Satyre iii' moves abruptly through a series of seemingly disparate considerations: the poet's satiric cross-purposes between rage and grief, the devotion we owe to religion, whether the pagan philosophers can be saved before Christians, the way fathers educate their children in religion; and then Englishmen's participation in the contemporary foreign wars, expeditions of discovery, the Spanish auto da fe, quarrels over women and honour in the London streets. The thread of Donne's argument holds all these together as they bear on men's practical unconcern with true Christianity. But it's his characteristic mode to call in a diversity of circumstances, weighing this area of concern against that, so as to see a claim or an experience relative to other human affairs:

> Is not this excuse for mere contraries,
> Equally strong: cannot both sides say so?

The movement of the poem amounts to a sceptical weighing of relative claims on one's devotion, in respect of the search for a possible truth.

The value of these writings isn't that they evoke particular occasions but that they embody argument in a searching activity of the mind. In the end their standing as autobiography is as little to the point as their debt to Ovid or their revolt against Petrarch. Our concern with them looks to their truth in themselves as models of placed experience. Thus a love poem takes a polemical form and moves by reference not to the poet's feelings but to contemporary politics:

> Till I have peace with thee, warre other men,
> And when I have peace, can I leave thee then?
>   . . . . In Flanders who can tell
> Whether the master presse, or men rebell? . . .
> France in her lunatique giddiness did hate
> Ever our men, yea and our God of late,
> Yet she relies upon our Angels well,
> Which ne'r retourne: no more than they which fell,
> Sick Ireland is with a strange warre possest,
> Like to'an Ague, now rageinge, now at rest. . . .
> And Midas joyes our Spanish journeys give,
> Wee touch all gold, but find no goode to live; . . .
> Here let mee warre; in these armes let mee lye;
> Here let mee parlee, batter, bleede, and dye.
>
> ('Loves Warre')

The constant stabbing and sifting of wit isn't random but expresses a settled attitude to our affairs. By thus calling in a world of external action to hold in balance with love Donne exposes the relativeness of the world's transactions altogether and questions its claims on us; his lines are a call to heed the doubtfulness of things, most of all where we normally take certainty as assured.

Part of the bite of the writing comes from the way it zestfully takes for granted a particular understanding of human conduct and of the way the world goes:

> Will no other vice content you?
> Will it not serve your turn to do, as did your mothers?
> Have you old vices spent, and now would finde out others?
> Or doth a feare, that men are true, torment you?
> Oh we are not, be not you so,
> Let mee and doe you, twenty know.
>
> ('The Indifferent')

Donne's poetry is as outrageous as it is unpredictable. One might suppose that it aims to scandalize or affront when it presents love as daring adultery or ingenious seduction; argues that sexual variety is a law of nature and the spice of life, or that being in bed with a woman is worth more than military glory; offers a praise of a woman's beauty which centres on her pudenda, or a comparison of women that exaggerates to nauseating grotesqueness the ill favour of some rival's mistress:

> Are not your kisses then as filthy, 'and more,
> As a worme sucking an invenom'd sore?
> Doth not thy fearefull hand in feeling quake,
> As one which gath'ring flowers, still fear'd a snake?
> Is not your last act harsh, and violent,
> As when a Plough a stony ground doth rent?
>
> ('The Comparison')

A mere wish to shock wouldn't count for much. But these extremes can be diverting if no more, and Donne contrives them in a variety of comic effects and kinds:

> Shee, whose face, like clouds, turns the day to night,
> Who, mightier than the sea, makes Moores seem white,
> Who, though seaven yeares, she in the Stews had laid,
> A Nunnery durst receive, and thinke a maid,
>
> ('The Anagram')

This time the monstrous hyperbole damns by praising, ironically following out Erasmus's old theme of the persuasion of a friend to marriage. In a tour de force of inventive sophistry Donne proves a woman excellently marriageable by demonstrating thus hyperbolically her extreme hideousness.

These intensifications are part of the comic world Donne projects and they are faithful to the motives of the poems. But they are of a piece with the radical mental life of the writing altogether. The outrageousness is the abrasive edge of a sceptical intelligence that constantly works to unsettle the accepted pieties in the interests of a harder truth:

> That loving wretch that sweares,
> 'Tis not the bodies marry, but the mindes,
>   Which he in her Angelique findes,
>   Would sweare as justly, that he heares,
> In that dayes rude hoarse minstralsey, the spheares.
>
> ('Loves Alchymie')

> Who ever loves, if hee doe not propose
> The right true end of love, hee's one which goes
> To sea for nothing but to make him sicke.
>
> ('Loves Progress')

> Now thou hast lov'd me one whole day,
> To morrow when thou leav'st, what wilt thou say? . . .
> Vaine lunatique, against these scapes I could
>   Dispute, and conquer, if I would,
>   Which I abstaine to doe,
> For by to morrow, I may thinke so too.
>
> ('Womans Constancy')

One constant office of wit in these poems is an uncommitted testing of the moral currency.

If there's any positive moral drift in so disruptive a poetic activity it draws from a steady vision of human conduct. One way of getting at that is to attend to the attitude Donne strikes, the tensions he set up between his protagonist and other people. Even in the Satires the moral alignment isn't straightforward:

> Away thou fondling motley humorist,
> Leave mee, and in this standing wooden chest,
> Consorted with these few bookes, let me lye
> In prison, and here be coffin'd, when I dye:
>
> ('Satyre i')

The poet writes as a solitary contemplative who is dragged from his books, partly by his own virile urge as it appears, to witness the active depravities of public life or of Court or the Law. But the

studies he leaves are no more exempt from human absurdity than
the life outside and have no more absolute claim on one:

> Here are Gods conduits, grave Divines; and here
> Natures Secretary, the Philosopher;
> And jolly Statesmen, which teach how to tie
> The sinewes of a cities mistique bodie;
> Here gathering Chroniclers, and by them stand
> Giddie fantastique Poets of each land.

Donne dramatizes a moral detachment which now prompts
amused derision at men's pretensions, and now a disturbed
diagnosis of corruptness:

> Th'iron Age *that* was, when justice was sold; now
> Injustice is sold dearer farre. . . .
> Why bar'st thou to yon Officer? Foole, Hath hee
> Got those goods, for which erst men bar'd to thee?
>
> ('Satyre v')

He offers us a vision of a civic jungle where our only weapon is a
wary guardedness, founded ultimately in a cool recognition of the
relativeness of human claims altogether in respect of the dust to
which we must all come:

> All men are dust; . . .
> O worse than dust, or wormes meat,
> For they do' eate you now, whose selves wormes shall eate.

In the amorous poetry the protagonist is a much more mercurial
figure. But essentially he enacts the amorous hero in a world of
half-men or lesser lovers – fat-living tycoons, jobbing merchants,
placeseekers and powermongers, sycophants and parasites:

> Take you a course, get you a place,
> Observe his honour, or his grace,
> And the Kings reall, or his stamped face
> Contemplate; what you will, approve,
> So you will let me love.
>
> ('The Canonization')

The poems repeatedly offer the prospect of love conducted in an
unsympathetic or hostile environment, which puts upon the poet
the need to justify his commitment in the face of the self-important
claims of the world at large:

> For Godsake hold your tongue, and let me love . . .
> Alas, alas, who's injur'd by my love?
>   What merchants ships have my sighs drown'd?
>   Who saies my teares have overflow'd his ground? . . .
> Soldiers finde warres, and Lawyers finde out still
>   Litigious men, which quarrels move,
>   Though she and I do love.

('The Canonization')

So the *Songs and Sonets* take a dialectical cast partly because they so often present themselves as urgent responses to implied disapproval or hostile credences, and as models for the true neophytes in love:

> To'our bodies turne wee then, that so
>   Weake men on love reveal'd may looke;

('The Exstasie')

Or they are attempts to celebrate a rare relationship in defiance of the world's misconstructions:

> I would that age were by this paper taught
> What miracles wee harmless lovers wrought.

('The Relique')

The celebration of love isn't remotely melodramatic, partly because it's done in a cool wary spirit which is much more concerned to define than to strike attitudes. Nor is it self-righteous. For the hero is marked off from the rest not by a conviction of right but by his different commitment which itself truly needs to be proved, his devotion to a person rather than his pursuit of an end:

> My love, though silly, is more brave,
> For may I misse, when ere I crave,
> If I know yet, what I would have.

('Negative Love')

> First, we lov'd well and faithfully,
> Yet knew not what wee lov'd, nor why,

('The Relique')

The poet is no more exempt from his own humanity than is a Mosca or a Face. The 'Elegies' in particular recall Jonson's comedies in the way they seize on a corrupt and corrupting energy, a driving obsessional life blinkered by monomaniacal devotion to wealth or prestige yet intensely (and justifiably) suspicious:

Though thy immortall mother which doth lye
Still buried in her bed, yet will not dye,
Take this advantage to sleepe out day-light,
And watch thy entries, and returnes all night,
And, when she takes thy hand, and would seeme kind,
Doth search what rings, and armelets she can finde,
And kissing notes the colour of thy face,
And fearing lest thou'art swolne, doth thee embrace;
And to trie if thou long, doth name strange meates,
And notes thy palenesse, blushings, sighs, and sweats;
And politiquely will to thee confesse
The sinnes of her owne youths ranke lustinesse;
Yet love those Sorceries did remove, and move
Thee to gull thine owne mother for my love.
Thy little brethren, which like Faiery Sprights
Oft skipt into our chamber, those sweet nights,
And, kist and ingled on thy fathers knee,
Were brib'd next day, to tell what they did see:

('The Perfume')

Mistrust is well grounded in the knowledge of one's own nature; and innocence, honour, kindness, candour, are mere politic shifts.

If this is a comic rather than a Swiftean vision it's because the world doesn't disgust the poet but delights him. The comedy arises from his hero's acceptance of the game and eagerness to engage in it on his own terms. His means is his wit, which here implies a suppleness of the mind, a freedom of resource, a grasp of all the moves:

Let mee thinke any rivalls letter mine,
    And at next nine
Keepe midnights promise; mistake by the way
The maid, and tell the Lady of that delay;
Onely let mee love none, no, not the sport;

('Loves Usury')

Above all he keeps a cool detachment even from the dominant passion itself which the tone of the address exactly fixes—

Come Madame, come,
('To his Mistris Going to Bed')

It's this tone and wit, so much more sane than mere nimble wits, that altogether distinguishes Donne's hero from the sexual picaro or the 'scholastic Don Juan'[1]. The measure of his poetry is the

[1] Pierre Legouis, *Donne the Craftsman*, Paris, 1928; New York, 1962, p 70.

quality of the experience, which has much to do with the poet's grasp of the real nature of this order of experience:

> Oh my America, my new found lande,
> My kingdome, safeliest when with one man man'd,
> My myne of precious stones, my Empiree,
> How blest am I this discovering thee.
>
> ('To his Mistris Going to Bed')

Navigators' feats, imperial dominion, diamond mines, aren't obvious or usual correlatives of love; though each has its point here. But overall this is a sharp delineation of an Antony-like impulse which makes piquant the abandon of amorous discovery with a pride of unique possession, and hence with the fear this entails – of the rest of the world, of her vulnerability, of one's own nature. The lines simultaneously set the larger world of arduous endeavour over against the intense local experience, and allow it in again as a heightening threat; the fear of the outside world is implicit in one's triumphing over it. Such writing has more to do with a keen self-candour than with thinking in the midst of feeling; the striking thing is that the poet should have seized thus dispassionately, and without belittling the impulse, the complex truth of the passion he imitates. What the lines do show us is how Donne's wit works to define and place even the most absolute of the heart's gestures.

One may speak of a sceptical detachment without devaluing the insight. Donne's realism doesn't entail an undue concern with low life, or for that matter with the seamy side of high life; though it may demand that 'low' or 'high' justify themselves as such:

> When, like a tyran King, that in his bed
> Smelt gunpowder, the pale wretch shivered.
>
> ('The Perfume')

A tyrant king is still but a man, shivering with ludicrous terror in his bed. There's a determination to be undeceived that reduces all our claims to the common human factor; that looks to motives rather than ends and anticipates an answer in terms of basic self-love – greed, or lust, or fear; that challenges us or experience itself to say that a placing isn't true, or above all, that it isn't truly human. The power of Donne's hero to preserve his independence and his detachment in a world of using, and being used, turns in the end on his knowing the world and the way it goes. That's more than a smooth worldly wiseness. It goes down to an engrained scepticism about human motives and human affairs altogether, which invites one to see life as it really is; to accept nothing untested in experience; and then perhaps to make of things what one honestly can.

*   *   *

There's no single account of love in the *Songs and Sonets* but a
variety of enactments of amorous encounters which does have a
pattern. How far this amounts to an original doctrine of love is in
question. But it's an academic issue whether Donne spurns the
accepted Petrarchan attitudes of love, or takes up ideas and distinctions from Renaissance discussions. In fact he does both. What
matters is that in these poems he seems truly to be discriminating
and resolving his own experience. They present him in the act of
finding his way towards an understanding, rejecting what doesn't
square with proved experience, seizing on and developing what
does. His originality stems from the singular positivism of his
concern with sex and love. It's crucial, for one thing, that love in the
Songs and Sonets is never a singleminded ardour, idealized in solitary
suffering, but a relationship that takes its chance with all the other
commitments of the world and has to be weighed in relation to
these.

Much of Donne's characteristic witty poise comes from his keen
grasp of the way of the world with sex. To say that 'No where/Lives
a woman true, and faire' isn't so much to denigrate women as to
characterize a corrupting world where only the ugly women can
possibly remain chaste. The whole end is to bring a powerful urge
into order without forfeiting one's masculine independence, to find
some accommodation between the demands of one's own nature
and the wills of others, that doesn't render one vulnerable or abject:

> Let me not know that others know
> That she knowes my paine, least that so
> A tender shame make me mine owne new woe.
>
> ('Loves Exchange')

Hence love becomes a sport of a man of the world, which proceeds
by tried laws and in which either party manoeuvres for advantage,
using the moral titles of fidelity, honour, revenge, as mere counters
in the game:

> womankinde,
> Who though from heart, and eyes,
> They exact great subsidies,
> Forsake him who on them relies,
> And for the cause, honour, or conscience give,
> Chimeraes, vaine as they, or their prerogative.
>
> ('A Valediction: of the Booke')

In the natural order of things the law of the game must be change
and variety, for apart from the imperative need to preserve one's

uncommitted independence the impulse itself is brief: 'For by to morrow, I may think so too'. It's the peculiar character of the passion that it dies with satisfaction, and turns to indifference or worse:

> Chang'd loves are but chang'd sorts of meat,
> And when hee hath the kernell eate,
> Who doth not fling away the shell?

('Communitie')

Yet the ritual is no more brutish than it's obsessive. The mark of the sport of sex, as these poems enact it, is its style, a cool ironic poise that above all disdains a slavery to an untried end.

Donne's case against idealizing attitudes of love is specifically their shrinking from experience, manifest in the way they fix love as a state of unrealizable devotion:

> Whilst yet to prove,
> I thought there was some Deitie in love,

('Farewell to Love')

Dante and Petrarch go rudely to the door, with four centuries of European tradition. All that deifying of women amounts to nothing more than a self-deception, a projection of unsatisfied desire:

> Thus when
> Things not yet knowne are coveted by men,
> Our desires give them fashion, and so
> As they waxe lesser, fall, as they sise, grow.

But in 'Farewell to Love' Donne's sceptical testing of love sharpens into a naturalistic dissection of sexual motives altogether. Here he brusquely characterizes love as a degrading self-enslavement, the urge to repeat an act that one knows in advance can't yield the satisfaction it promises but instead will humiliate and damage one, leaving only 'A kinde of sorrowing dulnesse to the minde'. The perverseness of the urge itself draws from our consciousness of the general perverseness of our condition, which impels us thus to seek to reproduce ourselves and lengthen our brief lives in our offspring. So strong is the fear of our own brevity that we would soon kill ourselves in a frenzy of attempted self-perpetuation did not nature impose her own check, the disillusionment of post-coital enervation. From this enslaving cycle our one way of escape and independence is to make the renunciation the title of the poem announces, ironically echoing a familiar Petrarchan motif, and bid farewell to love. Yet our dilemma here, too, must be kept in proportion; this is nothing in the end that an anaphrodisiac won't resolve:

> If all faile,
> 'Tis but applying worme-seed to the Taile.

Poems such as 'Woman's Constancy' or 'Loves Alchymie' aren't less sincere or serious because the truths they seize are harsh; but they don't put Donne's developed understanding of love. That presents itself as an achieved and rare assurance, not so much superseding the other accounts as exempting one singular condition of love from the general case. Indeed such poems as 'The Canonization', 'The Anniversarie', 'The Good-morrow' do something more positive, for they propose a human relationship which can stand against the way of the world altogether, and even remedy in that one area the inadequacies of our lives. These poems can be placed with a number of pieces scattered through the *Songs and Sonets* which seek by witty conceit to defend, define and celebrate this love. One cast of the wit of these poems is that it works continually to uphold a realized human regard in the teeth of what intrudes upon, threatens or denies it:

> Busie old foole, unruly Sunne,
> Why dost thou thus,
> Through windowes, and through curtaines call on us?
> ('The Sunne Rising')

> Alas, as well as other Princes, wee,
> (Who Prince enough in one another bee,)
> Must leave at least in death, these eyes, and eares,
> ('The Anniversarie')

The witty movement defines a mutualness which is not self-regarding but looks for fidelity, and which sets the two lovers together in that beyond the rest of the world, with its grandiose designs and self-absorbed lust for place, wealth, power:

> She'is all States, and all Princes, I,
> Nothing else is.
> Princes doe but play us; compar'd to this,
> All honor's mimique; All wealth alchimie.
> ('The Sunne Rising')

The conceited play becomes a matter of evaluating the established claims of the world in respect of this absolute attachment. The poems speak for our human possibility against the obsessive commitments that unman, dehumanize, desiccate, opposing mutual love to whatever cramps and inhibits the free play of mind and affections:

> Oh, let mee not serve so, as those men serve
> Whom honours smoakes at once fatten and sterve;
> Poorely enrich't with great mens words or lookes;
> Nor so write my name in thy loving bookes
> As those Idolatrous flatterers,
>
> ('Recusancy')

Love itself could be another such constraint if it became a slavery to sense. One mark of the mutual involvement Donne defines is that it isn't centred in physical contact and the senses:

> But we by'a love, so much refin'd,
>   That our selves know not what it is,
> Inter-assured of the mind,
>   Care lesse, eyes, lips, and hands to misse.
>
> ('A Valediction: forbidding Mourning')

But as the qualification indicates – 'Care *lesse*. . . .' – love isn't the prerogative of minds or souls alone either:

> But O alas, so long, so farre
>   Our bodies why doe wee forbeare?
>
> ('The Extasie')

The whole movement of 'The Extasie' works to define the interrelationship of souls and bodies in love which assures their unchanging stability:

> For, th'Atomies of which we grow,
>   Are soules, whom no change can invade

– and then to insist that though love doesn't depend upon physical union it doesn't reach its full expression without it:

> So must pure lovers soules descend
>   T'affections, and to faculties,
> That sense may reach and apprehend,
>   Else a great Prince in prison lies.

The play of an alert intelligence keeps this affirmation quite unsentimental. For the wit is always turning back in the midst of a celebration to locate or define the relationship itself:

> Where can we finde two better hemispheares
>   Without sharpe North, without declining West?
> What ever dyes, was not mixt equally;
>   If our two loves be one, or, thou and I
> Love so alike, that none doe slacken, none can die.
>
> ('The Good-morrow')

> Love is a growing, or full constant light;
> And his first minute, after noone, is night.
>
> ('A Lecture upon the Shadow')

The overt sophistry of the conceited argument is a way of getting at a delicate human truth; it prescribes the absolute condition for the continuance in mutual constancy of a relationship which 'though 'tis got by *chance*, 'tis kept by *art*' ('The Expostulation'). And if an unwavering firmness distinguishes it from all other human attachments, this love likewise stands against the frailty of everything else we know:

> Only our love hath no decay;
> This, no tomorrow hath, nor yesterday,
> Running it never runs from us away,
> But truly keepes his first, last, everlasting day.
>
> ('The Anniversarie')

So when Donne argues in 'The Canonization' that the two lovers give more wit to the riddle of the phoenix because they

> dye and rise the same, and prove
> Mysterious by this love

he implies something more than that this is a rare sexual relationship which coitus confirms rather than destroys. The witty figure discreetly allows us to understand that this is one small area of our lives in which we can rise above our own brief condition, and arrest the tendency of the whole mortal creation.

A survey of what these poems make of love can't convey their vivacious life. The continual play of intelligence in conceited dialectics and figurative ingenuity sets up an excitement in the witty movement overall that suggests, or stimulates, the dynamic life of the mind itself. For this is a pointed mental activity which gets its coherence from the formal pattern of the verse as it unfolds. The decisive factor here is the controlled movement forward, which allows a tense unpredictableness within the ordered development to a climax.

But an elaborate formal arrangement can work architecturally as well as dynamically, to fix a pattern in the way things relate to one another. The movement of 'Farewell to Love' shows how a formal scheme can itself hold together a structure of interrelationships which the looser sequence of prose could only falsify; the third stanza of the poem carries together the manifold disabilities that the Fall has put upon us, in the critical inter-connection they really keep. It's this simultaneity of complex sense that allows Donne to display the perverseness of our condition now, where our urge to repeat acts of coitus might itself accentuate the manifold shortness which we are frantically seeking to overcome thereby, not least, that of our own lives.

Writing in verse to a younger friend at an unknown date Donne spoke of himself as a lapsed poet whose Muse had 'because I'am cold,/Divorc'd her selfe: the cause being in me' ('To Mr B. B.'). Readers have generally felt that one large body of his verse does show a laboriousness that speaks of a loss of direction and of mental vivacity at some stage of his life. They have fairly judged him to be a poet whose imagination kindled only at a tangible stimulus, such as love or religion offered him, and supposed that in the area of his life where neither compulsion gripped him he fell back, when he was obliged to write verse at all, on rather desperately flogging his wits. His greatest admirers haven't felt obliged to get to grips with all those poems to and for patrons or friends, whose labyrinthine tortuousness of conceit one unravels to find some impossible hyperbole of praise, or incongruity of ingenious analogy amounting to wanton bad taste. He claims that a woman embodies all virtue in herself and sustains the world ('To the Countesse of Huntingdon'); or he argues that a mourning mother now incorporates her dead daughter too and will retain both their beings and qualities, preserved by their own virtue from decay and corruption:

> You that are she and you, that's double shee,
> In her dead face, halfe of your selfe shall see;
> ('To the Lady Bedford')

In his funeral poems he harps on decay and maggots, and can't even resist what stray satiric opportunities the reference opens to him:

> Thinke thee a Prince, who of themselves create
> Wormes which insensibly devoure their state.
> ('The Second Anniversary')

It all seems so uncharacteristically humourless and misproportioned that one naturally looks to the peculiar exigencies of Donne's situation. It's reasonable to think of these poems as bread and butter labour which exemplify all too clearly both his heavy dependence on patronage in the middle years of his life, and his own essential lack of interest in the performance.

One wouldn't deny the peculiarity or the peculiar difficulty of the

'Verse Letters' and the funeral poems. But the claim to be made
for them is that they are serious attempts to work out issues
central to Donne's vision and poetry.

   The paradox of what may seem the most farfetched of all
Donne's verse is that it starts in a sceptical determination to see
human affairs as they really are. The celebrated poetic letters
Donne wrote to a friend describing two incidents in the Azores
expedition of 1596 crackle with a wit which is steadily directed to
the taking down of the heroic pretensions of such enterprises, and
the flourishes of chivalry altogether:

> Whether a rotten state, and hope of gaine,
> Or to disuse mee from the queasie paine
> Of being belov'd, and loving, or the thirst
> Of honour, or faire death, out pusht mee first,
> I lose my end: for here as well as I
> A desperate may live,' and a coward die. . . .
>   How little more alas
> Is man now, than before he was? he was
> Nothing; for us, wee are for nothing fit;
> Chance, or our selves still disproportion it.
>
>   ('The Calme')

When some five years later he wrote 'The Progresse of the Soule',
possibly the oddest of his poems, the challenge had sharpened into
a ferocious exposure of the game of power altogether which shows
up men's lofty poses as the masks for cold self-interest:

> It mov'd with state, as if to looke upon
> Low things it scorn'd, and yet before that one
> Could thinke he sought it, he had swallow'd cleare
> This, and much such, and unblam'd devour'd there
>   All, but who too swift, too great, or well armed were.
>
> Exalted she'is, but to th'exalters good,
> As are by great ones, men which lowly stood.
>   It's rais'd, to be the Raisers instrument and food.
>
>   ('The Progresse of the Soule')

Commentators have justly spoken of a Machiavellian ruthlessness
in the vision of this work, which describes the transmigration of a
soul indifferently between human beings and beasts so as to trace
a harshly diverting picture of created existence as a predatory
jungle. But the argument tends a different way from Machiavelli's
lesson of expediency. Donne invites one to consider one's own
standing in a desperately dangerous world where, if men

> stand arm'd with seely honesty,
> With wishing prayers, and neat integritie,
> Like Indians 'gainst Spanish hosts they bee.
>
> ('To Sir Henry Wotton')

The sense of our vulnerability that runs through all these poems is also an awareness of how easily we are corrupted, and how every worldly impulse corrupts:

> Life is a voyage, and all our lifes wayes
> Countries, Courts, Towns are Rockes, or Remoraes;
> They breake or stop all ships, yet our state's such,
> That though than pitch they staine worse, wee must touch.
>
> ('To Sir Henry Wotton')

What the lines repeatedly bring home is the peril of acting at all in a world in which 'Utopian youth, growne old Italian' is the common experience; where either alternative may be disastrous and a relative grasp of affairs is the best we can hope for.

There's a moral uncompromisingness in the account of civil life that must bear on the way we take the lines with which 'The Progresse of the Soule' breaks off:

> Ther's nothing simply good, nor ill alone,
> Of every quality comparison,
> The onely measure is, and judge, opinion.

That outrageous relativism denies any absolute value to the world the poem has evoked.[1] But Donne's developed understanding isn't that there's no such thing as final truth. What he denies is that we are now capable of grasping it by our natural reason. Our knowledge is at best a relative evaluation of worldly affairs that isn't to be called truth. When we pretend to know more we fall into the contradictions and confusions that we see all round us in professed savants:

> And one soule thinkes one, and another way
> Another thinkes, and ty's an even lay.
>
> ('The Second Anniversary')

Moreover, far from getting nearer to truth as time runs on we are actually moving further from it, for the world itself is lapsing faster towards chaos and the latest dicta are only the most relative and highflown:

---

[1] See L. I. Bredvold, 'The Naturalism of Donne in Relation to Some Renaissance Traditions', *Journal of English and Germanic Philology* xxii (1923), 471–502.

> And new Philosophy cals all in doubt,
> The Element of fire is quite put out;
> The Sunne is lost, and th'earth, and no mans wit
> Can well direct him, where to looke for it.
>
> ('The First Anniversary')

Donne's radical sense of human relativity gives a settled direction to the movement of his poetry, which continually works to place our human circumstances relative to each other and relative to a final order of reality, or what assurance of it we can win in defiance of a world of uncertainty:

> But pause, My soule, and study ere thou fall
> On accidental joyes, th' essentiall. . . .
> And what essentiall joy canst thou expect
> Here upon earth? what permanent effect
> Of transitory causes? Dost thou love
> Beauty? (And Beauty worthyest is to move)
> Poore couse'ned cose'nor, that she, and that thou,
> Which did begin to love, are neither now.
> You are both fluid, chang'd since yesterday;
>
> ('The Second Anniversary')

But his relativism bears more intimately on the texture of his thought, in that it suggests a oneness in human experience which cuts across the categories and decorum of a world

> where some men play
> Princes, some slaves, all to one end, and of one clay.
>
> ('To Sir Henry Wotton')

The persuasion that none of our worldly claims is in the end worth more than any other reduces them all alike to a common order that negates the orders we conventionally impose. If one aspect of Donne's intelligence is a conspicuous openness to experience, this is partly shown in his refusal to compartmentalize the world in our ready-made and rigid-seeming categories.

The prospect of an impending dissolution haunts all these poems of Donne's middle years, of a lapse into nothingness such that our own physical decay only models the decline of creation altogether. This is no nihilism. One sees here how a sceptical grasp of worldly affairs has hardened into a sense of the inherent inadequacy of our state and of the general condition of created existence. If such poems as 'The First Anniversary' and 'To the Countesse of Salisbury' show him less keen to relish the depravities he seizes on it is because he has become oppressed, where he had been diverted,

by the difference between our human possibility and the squalid
actuality of our brief animal existence. This darkened moral engagement manifests itself in his poems as a preoccupation with a
twofold shortcoming. He looks at once to the disparity between our
condition as it is and as it ought to be, and to the distance between
our condition now and what it once was:

> Thus man, this worlds Vice-Emperor, in whom
> All faculties, all graces are at home; . . .
> This man, whom God did wooe, and loth t'attend
> Till man came up, did downe to man descend,
> This man, so great, that all that is, is his,
> Oh what a trifle, and poore thing he is!
>
> ('The First Anniversary')

The satiric fiction of 'The Progresse of the Soule' shows the
perspective that Donne continually worked to open to his wit in
these poems. He sought a way of holding our present condition
simultaneously against our first state, our ideal possibility, and the
final order of reality. The curious device of the transmigration of a
soul from the apple that Eve plucked, at the site of the future
Calvary, enables him to place us in several ways relative to the Fall,
to make a comparison and a contrast:

> In this worlds youth wise nature did make hast,
> Things ripen'd sooner, and did longer last;
> Already this hot cocke, in bush and tree,
> In field and tent, oreflutters his next hen;
> He asks her not, who did so last, nor when,
> Nor if his sister, or his neece shee be;
> Nor doth she pule for his inconstancie
> If in her sight he change, nor doth refuse
> The next that calls;

We see by ironic contrast with those early times how far we have
declined from their condition; but the comparison also shows us
what fallen creatures have in common.

In 'The First Anniversary' the witty advancement of the
celebratory hyperbole so as to show the dependence of all the
world's virtues on the personal qualities of the dead girl, is a way of
conceitedly analysing the decline of our world in every single one of
its aspects from the ideal conditions of innocence, and from the true
moral and metaphysical order:

> Then, as mankinde, so is the worlds whole frame
> Quite out of joynt, almost created lame:
> For, before God had made up all the rest,
> Corruption entred, and deprav'd the best:
> It seis'd the Angels, and then first of all
> The world did in her Cradle take a fall,
> And turn'd her braines, and tooke a generall maime
> Wronging each joynt of th'universall frame.

Donne's vision presupposes the aberration of our nature from an order it once had, the onset of corruption from a specific moment in time. The idea of a Fall is rooted in his understanding, but so is the persuasion of an accelerating decline of our part of creation from that event. The calamity which brought in time as well as sin and death makes urgent our consciousness of our own brevity, and gives us a peculiar concern with our standing now, at this precise moment in the decadence of the world when 'mankind decayes so soone,/We're scarse our Fathers shadowes cast at noone.'

But 'our businesse is, to rectifie/Nature, to what she was' ('To Sir Edward Herbert, at Julyers'), and the upshot cannot be despair. Donne's concern as a panegyric poet becomes the delineation of a character which can stand apart from, or against, the otherwise general lapse towards chaos:

> Be more than man, or thou'rt lesse than an Ant
> ('The First Anniversary')

Evidently this presented itself to him, at the soliciting of patrons, as a search for a quality in respect of which a person might be truly esteemed, may be celebrated absolutely and substantially and not by our relative and accidental worldly measure. Innocence must be one such quality, for the loss of it is precisely the issue of the Fall. As an innocent person is a type or model of the original state, still uncorrupted, so an innocent death is in one way no death at all, and in another way a re-enactment of the original calamity:

> When that Queene ended here her progresse time,
> And, as t'her standing house, to heaven did clymbe, . . .
> This world, in that great earth-quake languished; . . .
> Sicke world, yea dead, yea putrified, since shee
> Thy'ntrinsique Balme, and thy preservative,
> Can never be renew'd, thou never live,
> ('The First Anniversary')

Donne's boldness in the two 'Anniversary' poems for Elizabeth Drury is to press this complex sense through with his habitual rigour, disregarding the practical consequence that he is thus led to attribute a great deal to a young girl he hadn't even met. Ben Jonson 'told Mr Donne, if it had been written of ye Virgin Marie it had been something to which he answered that he described the idea of a Woman and not as she was'.[1]

Most of the people Donne celebrated, alive or dead, were past the age of innocence (Ben Jonson unkindly described one of them as the Court pucelle[2]). But the burden of the 'Anniversary' poems themselves is that we all have one way to resist the corrupting force of the world –

> And that thou hast but one way, not t' admit
> The worlds infection, to be none of it.
>
> ('The First Anniversary')

A tried election of virtue is possible, though rarely effected, that lifts a person beyond the common taint of the Fall. Donne's laudatory poems conceitedly develop the sense that this virtue not only converts what the world calls death into the entrance to life but sustains the world, which unknowingly owes what little vitality it still has to the charisma of a few moral heroes who model Christ:

> Hee was all gold when he lay downe, but rose
> All tincture, and doth not alone dispose
> Leaden and iron wills to good, but is
> Of power to make even sinful flesh like his.
>
> ('Resurrection, imperfect')

The terms in which Donne praises the people who thus in themselves resolve 'the issues of death' draw from his apprehension of a true order of reality and of qualities:

> Shee, of whose soule, if we may say, t'was Gold,
> Her body was th'Electrum, and did hold
> Many degrees of that; we understood
> Her by her sight, her pure and eloquent blood
> Spoke in her cheekes, and so distinckly wrought,
> That one might almost say, her bodie thought,
>
> ('The Second Anniversary')

But his analysis of the stages of the world's collapse no less supposes a proper relationship of things, which our arrogant self-sufficiency belies:

[1] *Conversations with Drummond*, p 133.
[2] Ibid. p 135.

'Tis all in pieces, all cohaerence gone;
All just supply, and all Relation:
Prince, Subject, Father, Sonne, are things forgot,
For every man alone thinkes he hath got
To be a Phoenix, and that there can bee
None of that kinde, of which he is, but hee.

('The First Anniversary')

The conceits of these poems build on a hierarchical order of being which is at the same time a network of interdependence. There is a right order of qualities from the lowest to the highest, with a proper order of relationships between them, and every created organism reproduces this order while it continues healthy. But such is the coherence of all being that a disorder anywhere affects the whole; as a true election of virtue anywhere helps preserve the whole structure from disintegration.

Donne's account of the effects of the Fall envisages a dynamic moral universe of qualities in inescapable flux, a pull of opposite tendencies with the world's being and our own eternal life at issue. The general movement now is the downward disintegration of any disordered organism towards chaos and dust. But thrusting counter to this is an upward force produced in the actions of the few true innocent or virtuous souls who are 'still/More Antidote, than all the world was ill,' ('The Second Anniversary'). In this life it is enough if one move up from earth to glass, from sense to a catalytic spirit that refines the impulse of sense to its own transparent purity:

Parents make us earth, and soules dignifie
Us to be glasse; here to grow gold we lie.

('Epitaph on Himselfe')

It is the paradox of a virtuous death that an apparent dissipation into earth is the occult process that finally transmutes the once base matter to gold.

One shouldn't in any case lose sight of the oddity of these poems or the intermittent stubbornness of their movement:

Looke to mee faith, and looke to my faith, God;
For both my centers feele this period.
Of waight one center, one of greatnesse is;
And reason is that center, Faith is this;

('Elegie upon the untimely death of the incomparable Prince Henry')

The lines make pointed sense; given the conceited premise they have logical rigour and a strict defining function. But the idiom shocks as it appears to have shocked some people in Donne's own day[1]:

> Immortal Mayd, who though thou wouldst refuse
> The name of Mother, be unto my Muse,
> A Father
>
> ('The Second Anniversary')

One could multiply instances of an incongruity which is woven into the texture of these panegyrics: the analogy of the beheaded man in 'The Second Anniversary', to show how our dead world still appears to have life and movement; the repulsive realism of the comparison, in the same poem, of the soul in the newborn infant body with a 'stubborne sullen Anchorit' who sits 'fixt to a Pillar, or a Grave. . . . Bedded and Bath'd in all his Ordures'; the elephantine gibes at the arrogant littleness of men who don't in fact live long enough now to be page to Methusaleh, but still claim to catch the heavens in their net and pull them down to us; the development in full mechanical circumstance of the conceit that virtuous men are clocks, and that the dead Lord Harrington was a public clock; above all, the constant interchange of unlike orders of reference, the domestic with the metaphysical, the physical with the moral:

> And color is decayd: summers robe growes
> Duskie, and like an oft dyed garment showes.
> Our blushing redde, which us'd in cheekes to spred,
> Is inward sunke, and onely our soules are redde.
>
> ('The First Anniversary')

Such engrained idiosyncrasy shows a persistence that goes beyond Donne's mere determination to sustain his character of original. One must take it as a function of the uncompromising effort to undo what we take for decorum, so as to open the way towards the true apprehension of reality.

The disquiet that drew Donne into Holy Orders is implicit in his mature verse, and it is in keeping that he wrote some of his best religious poetry well before he took that formal step, probably even before the 'Anniversaries'. 'A Litanie', one of the finest of all his

---

[1] See Donne's letter to George Garrard, 14 April, 1612. Ben Jonson spoke of the 'Anniversaries' as 'profane and full of Blasphemies' (*Conversations with Drummond*, p 133).

poems, may have been written in 1608. The sonnet sequence 'La Corona' was written before 1610 in a quasi-Spanish mode of ingenious meditation, which Donne never essayed again, on the Christian senses of a crown:

> But doe not, with a vile crowne of fraile bayes,
> Reward my muses white sincerity,
> But what thy thorny crowne gain'd, that give mee,
> A crowne of Glory, which doth flower alwayes;

> Ere by the spheares time was created, thou
> Wast in his minde, who is thy Sonne, and Brother,
> Whom thou conceiv'st, conceiv'd; yea thou art now
> Thy Makers maker, and thy Fathers mother,

The 'Holy Sonnets' themselves, the most celebrated of Donne's pious writings, were no more produced in a single impulse than were the *Songs and Sonets* but may represent his devotional exercises over a number of years. 'Goodfriday, 1613. Riding Westward', if the title of the early editions is accurate, was certainly written before Donne's ordination; whereas there is some evidence that the 'Hymne to God my God, in my sicknesse' was written in 1619 and 'A Hymne to God the Father' in 1623.

The odd notion of a witty piety, which is basic to Donne's religious verse, may strike one less at first than the sonorous address and sheer dramatic impact of some of the poems. A declamatory rhetoric isn't obviously a mark of inward sincerity and may disturb readers as much as the inwoven ingenuity:

> Death be not proud, though some have called thee
> Mighty and dreadfull, for, thou art not soe,

The hammering grandeur of such writing carries its own assumption of the momentousness of the issue. Whatever the perils thus dramatically encountered, it invests our human affairs with a dignity that befits man's standing, at the centre of a cosmic drama. There is no question here of an inward conflict or a personal anguish. The rhetoric itself is an affirmation; it proclaims the possibility of a heroic triumph snatched from likely defeat:

> At the round earth's imagin'd corners, blow
> Your trumpets, Angells, and arise, arise
> From death, you numberlesse infinities
> Of soules, and to your scattred bodies goe.

To rephrase that by the syntax alone would be to lose not only the vivid articulation Donne gains by running the sense across the lyric pattern, but the point of the lines:

> At the round earth's imagin'd corners,
> Blow your trumpets, Angells,
> And arise, arise from death, you numberlesse infinities of soules,
> And to your scattred bodies goe.

The slackened tension, like a paean on a damp string, takes with it the whole force of an assured resurrection which is the sense of the poem.

The tense urgency of the writing ultimately comes back to the understanding that the issues are fought out in every contingency. But in the 'Holy Sonnets' Donne takes care to fix the critical juncture as the moment of the poem itself:

> What if this present were the worlds last night?

To present oneself in mortal sickness or at the point of final judgment is a harsh way of making the issue imminent, bringing oneself up sharp against the reality that daily life dulls over:

> I runne to death, and death meets me as fast,
> And all my pleasures are like yesterday,
> I dare not move my dimme eyes any way,
> Despaire behind, and death before doth cast
> Such terrour,

The matter of the 'Holy Sonnets' is a man's struggle to recognize himself by first coming to terms with the way things inevitably are. The poems present themselves not as a mere record of the struggle but as dynamic enactments of it. This follows in itself from Donne's understanding of the real dilemma of our situation, which is that men must fall into sin and merit death, yet cannot avail themselves of Christ's love and atoning blood without God's grace:

> Yet, grace, if thou repent, thou canst not lacke;
> But who shall give thee that grace to beginne?

The resolution rests with God, but begins with the sinner himself in the submissive acceptance he displays to God. And in this sequence the poems themselves are the initiating instruments, in that they seek in the same impulse to involve God, and to work upon the poet himself:

> Batter my heart, three person'd God;

The violence of the means by which he disposes himself to submit to reality is also the evidence of the intensity of his wish to submit, in the teeth of the agents that pull the other way:

Least the World, fleshe, yea Devill putt thee out.

The dynamic assumption these poems make is that they stand between these vast conflicting forces and can decisively affect them.

Donne's pious poems are inherently dramatic because he sees the issue as a drama, and because he casts them as addresses to someone which invite immediate action and a self-recognition:

> Spit in my face yee Jewes, and pierce my side,
> Buffet, and scoffe, scourge, and crucifie mee,

But the terms of his concern aren't exclusive or even private. For while the critical matter for the poet is the disposition of his own soul, that consequence isn't peculiar to him or finally decided there. He takes station with us all on the universal stage, subject to the general circumstances that govern created nature since the Fall. In speaking out thus declamatorily at the centre of the action he looks to those universal conditions, and shows us too where we stand. That may not be our view of the character of a religious poet but it is implicit in Donne's understanding of religion itself as these poems show it.

The wit may be another matter:

> Father, part of his double interest
> Unto thy kingdome, thy Sonne gives to mee,
> His joynture in the knottie Trinitie,
> Hee keepes, and gives mee his deaths conquest.
> This Lambe, whose death, with life the world hath blest,
> Was from the worlds beginning slaine, and he
> Hath made two Wills, which with the Legacie
> Of his and thy kingdome, doe thy Sonnes invest,

It isn't obvious what these egregious quibbles and paradoxes have to do with sincere faith. To appeal to the convention of the Petrarchan lyric, or less intelligibly, to a 'baroque' sensibility, only cuts us off from the poems irrevocably. The question is how far the wit becomes its own end:

> When wee are mov'd to seeme religious
> Only to vent wit, Lord deliver us.

('A Litanie')

Donne himself was aware of the opening for showmanship that devout readers in particular have complained of in his own poems. But he also envisaged a right functioning of religious wit, or rather, a religion that is witty in itself – 'nor must wit/Be colleague to religion, but be it' ('To the Countesse of Bedford'). One can say at once that his wit is never an irresponsible ingenuity for the sake of the performance itself. It has a dramatic substance, a pungent life and force; and however dexterously, it does have point:

> Teares in his eyes quench the amasing light,
> Blood fills his frownes, which from his pierc'd head fell,

The little play of figure vividly enacts the issue of the crucifixion itself, the tempering of Christ's justice by His mercy.

The recurrent tendency of the wit in the movement of these poems is to generalize the reference and take it outward. A poem by George Herbert will evoke an external object, a posy of flowers or the monuments of a church, only to move inward by a sharply perceived likeness towards an intimate self-perception:

> My hand was next to them, and then my heart:
>
> ('Life')

But Donne's concern with an occasional event, such as sickness, is quite different:

> Oh my black Soule! now thou art summoned
> By sicknesse, deaths herald, and champion;
> Thou art like a pilgrim, which abroad hath done
> Treason, and durst not turne to whence hee is fled,
> Or like a thiefe, . . .

Far from looking to the local circumstances the poem at once moves wittily out to occupy one's mind with a diversity of vivid actions going on in the world at large. In a few lines we are presented with a challenge to a tournament, a self-exiled traitor, and the dilemma of a condemned thief between his wish for enlargement and his wish for life.

The 'Hymne to God my God, in my sicknesse' moves still more startlingly. The comically ingenious figure of the fevered poet as a flat map pored over by physician-cosmographers, takes us at once to a review of all the wished-for places in the world which are reached by straits:

> Is the Pacifique Sea my home? Or are
>   The Easterne riches? Is *Jerusalem*?
> *Anyan*, and *Magellan*, and *Gibraltare*,
>   All streights, and none but streights, are wayes to them,

This externality of the reference is the condition of what Donne is about here. When he uses his sickness to divert us with a series of brilliant external analogues, he affirms that what matters about a dangerous illness is the dilemma it finds one in, which these instances severally define and bring home to him. The topographical detail of the 'Hymne', hinging on the quibble on 'straits', bears back on his understanding of pain and sickness and their place in the whole natural economy now. It marks the coolly controlled effort of his mind to place his present straits in the context of a condition of the world where a desired bliss can be won only through well-endured hardship and suffering. Nor is the variety of this external life incidental. It's the means by which Donne brings home to himself the inevitable state of things, and the general laws that govern our fallen condition:

> And as a robb'd man, which by search doth finde
> His stolne stuffe sold, must lose or buy'it againe:
> The Sonne of glory came downe, and was slaine,
> Us whom he had made, and Satan stolne, to unbinde.
>
> ('Holy Sonnets' II)

It is a touchstone of the validity of his understanding that it should have the widest application wit can give it. So he is led to put even a personal and domestic event, such as the death of his wife, in the larger context of God's offer for his soul against the world, flesh, and devil:

> But why should I begg more love, when as thou
> Dost wooe my soule, for hers offring all thine:

Wit is a way of realizing a truth that is there but not otherwise accessible to us now, and which our conventional account of things only masks. It has an interest in disturbing our everyday understanding since it thus invites a wary appraisal of the limitations of our common knowledge, and of the mind itself. Donne is always sceptically aware of how little we know:

> At the round earth's imagin'd corners, blow
> Your trumpets, Angells,

'Imagin'd corners' pulls one up sharp, sending one's mind to the detail of the scene by recalling *Revelations* or old church representations of the Last Trump, and inviting one to ponder the discrepancy between what we once took for knowledge and what we think we know now. In the midst of the affirmation itself, the slight witty touch invites one's attention to the relativity of the mind's grasp.

In a fallen creation the search for reality must work against what our depraved understandings commonly take for granted. A continual effect of Donne's witty reference is to suggest the inadequacy of our complacent assumptions, to hold up to our notice the ironies and paradoxes implicit in our grasp of the world's traffic, or the identities we don't suspect:

> But, as oft Alchimists doe coyners prove,
> So may a self-dispising get selfe-love.
> And then as worst surfets, of best meates bee,
> Soe is pride, issued from humility,
> For, 'tis no child, but monster; therefore Crosse
> Your joy in crosses, else, 'tis double losse.
> And crosse thy senses, else, both they, and thou
> Must perish soone, and to destruction bowe.
>
> ('The Crosse')

To bring such human accidents into the witty order of the Christian truth he celebrates is to confirm the inherently paradoxical nature of truth itself, as we must see it. It points the paradox at the heart of our reality:

> Or wash thee in Christ's blood, which hath this might
> That being red, it dyes red soules to white.
>
> ('Holy Sonnets' 2)

But it also does something less readily acceptable:

> Take mee to you, imprison mee, for I
> Except you'enthrall mee, never shall be free,
> Nor ever chast, except you ravish mee.
>
> ('Holy Sonnets' 10)

The outrageousness of the sexual figure in a pious context parallels the effrontery with which he blatantly applies to Christ the casuistry he had once used to seduce women:

> No, no; but as in my idolatrie
> I said to all my profane mistresses,
> Beauty, of pitty, foulnesse onely is
> A signe of rigour:
>
> ('Holy Sonnets' 9)

More flagrantly shocking is the sexual paradox which emerges as the unlikely clinching stroke of the inquiry after the true Church:

> Who is most trew, and pleasing to thee, then
> When she'is embrac'd and open to most men.

The lines do sharply make the point that focuses the whole survey of the divisive claimants. But one's concern is why a perception about institutionalized Christianity should be cast in a figure which seems calculated to give offence; whose literal entailment, for one thing, would be that the true Church is a whore and Christ a wittol.

It's fair to say that only Donne would have pressed a figure thus far, as he presses every idea through to its rigorous limit. Yet the provocative witty life of the verse doesn't in effect remove the poems from common experience. On the contrary, it breaks down the remoteness of the metaphysical order to show the issues working tangibly in the texture of our daily lives. The attack arrests one into realization:

> Why are wee by all creatures waited on?

Bringing things home to ourselves thus is a way of relating our own concerns to the central issues of creation, but at the same time, of exposing the limitations of our experience and our grasp of reality. In the final regard our conventional niceties may become otiose. There is a calculated offence to decorum in the interests of a truth that has no truck with orders of decorum; which is itself to our eyes scandalous, and paradoxical, and ironic, and incongruous; and which admits no barrier between one order of experience and another.

Wit is inherent in the vision because poetic wit offers a human means of approaching reality. In 'Goodfriday, 1613. Riding Westward' the poet finds in an emergent event a moral character which itself reproduces an aberration of the metaphysical equilibrium:

> Let man's Soule be a Spheare, and then, in this,
> The intelligence that moves, devotion is,
> And as the other Spheares, by being growne
> Subject to forraigne motions, lose their owne,
> And being by others hurried every day,
> Scarce in a yeare their naturall forme obey:
> Pleasure or businesse, so, our Soules admit
> For their first mover, and are whirld by it.

His riding towards the west on Good Friday instances a distractedness common since the Fall to man's soul and the heavens, and directly relating to the circumstances of sin, atonement, and grace:

> O Saviour, as thou hang'st upon the tree;
> I turne my backe to thee, but to receive
> Corrections. . . .
> Restore thine Image, so much, by thy grace,
> That thou may'st know mee, and I'll turne my face.

In the same poem one of Donne's most arresting witty effects works by an opposite process, predicating the metaphysical order upon a physical event:

> Could I behold those hands which span the Poles,
> And tune all spheares at once, peirc'd with those holes?

The superimposing of an image of ultimate power and extent upon an image of total degradation is more than merely shocking. It seizes the radical truth of an event that focuses every order of existence and abolishes our conventional discriminations. The power of poetic wit is that it can enact such a simultaneity, which works to hold together the physical, moral, and metaphysical conditions in the relation they really have, and to overleap the limits we set between them.

Donne's wit in the end becomes a matter of seizing what is really there; of showing in the order of our human circumstances the moral and metaphysical order it truly holds, and approximating to the structure of reality as every order of existence displays it. In the 'Hymne to God my God, in my sicknesse' the physical details of the poet's illness enter only as they can relate his present state to his salvation:

> So, in his purple wrapp'd receive mee Lord,
> By these his thornes give me his other Crowne;

The prodigious metamorphosis of the flushed face of a fevered man into the purple mantle that Christ wraps round a saved sinner, his pangs of pain to the thorns of Christ's crown, gives the occasion its largest possible and final context. In superimposing Christ's blood, agony and saving dominion upon the local circumstance Donne identifies the sufferings by which we die a holy death, with Christ's sufferings on the cross that make such a death a means to glory. The witty stroke is a function of the vision itself, which seeks to see pain and mortal illness as the agent by which God raises a sinner. The wit that thus interweaves our human accident with final events is hardly a freak of sensibility. But it is more than a conspicuously bold way of saying something just. To make such a series of identities is to seize thus much of an order of reality in which every existential circumstance ultimately models the final truth.

The endeavour can take curious forms. Some notorious puns in 'A Hymne to God the Father' seem unapt to the beautiful lyric rhetoric that gives organic development to Donne's sense of sin:

> Sweare by thy selfe, that at my death thy Sunne
> Shall shine as it shines now, and heretofore;
> And, having done that, Thou hast done,
> I have no more.

Yet it is strictly to the point of the poem to relate the sources of life in our universe thus, the sun to the Son; and the play on Donne's name finally closes the gap between the poet and God, between Donne's progressive conviction of sin and mounting uncertainty of God's willingness to act. If we find such word-plays facetious or irreverent it is only secondarily because we don't now expect that a correspondence of sound may reveal an identity of sense and of nature. The essential reason is that we no longer anticipate such layers of meaning in the one event or idea, in virtue of the way the universe manifests in little, and at every level, the eternal condition of things.

In all, one sees no need to revise Ben Jonson's judgement that Donne is 'the first poet in the World in some things'[1] save to say that in everything he is like no one else, and that his distinguishing character is a radical play of intelligence. The least his poems offer is the life of an arresting mind with a sharp hold on men's motives and its own working. His dialectical wit operated to most subtle effect in his love poetry, whose naturalistic searching of amorous relationships seems specifically modern, and makes the esoteric ardours that sometimes pass for love look self-absorbed or unreal. Here Donne definitively maps an area of common human experience.

The tendency to seize on him for occasional marvels suggests that modern readers have sometimes valued his poems for their strange imaginative power without much regard to his steady discernment, or the radical apprehension of life that gave it direction. The neglect of his drift, as much as anything, has led to the undervaluing of his formal vitality and the prodigious complexities of organization which his disciplined grasp demanded.

If some part of his poetry moves by categories of thought now remote from us, it matters less than the quality of the mind which seeks this kind of sense or that in our existence. For his endeavour is in any case a central human concern. Donne sought for what little assurance he deemed possible to us by a coolly persistent determination to see things as they are, stripped of the imposture that our common use maintains. Comically or sombrely, his wit worked to pin down truth by placing what are only relative claims, bringing home the final certainties of our condition, seizing on the order of reality where the world's depravities or the limitations of our minds normally conceal it from us. It is the steady concern to get at the actuality of our human circumstances, and the search for ways of coming to terms with it, that holds all his poetry together in a coherent vision.

---

[1] *Conversations with Drummond*, p 135.

9

GEORGE HERBERT AND THE RELIGIOUS LYRIC

Robert Ellrodt

If we leave out some impersonal hymns and meditations – and among them Milton's 'Nativity Ode' – the best religious lyrics of the seventeenth century were written in 'the Donne tradition'. Their authors were all amateur poets who never attempted longer compositions in the nobler 'kinds'. They were all born within the pale of the Church of England, and, though Marvell strayed into the Puritan camp and Crashaw found full bliss in the bosom of the Roman Church, something of the Anglican spirit shines in all. All of them lived for a time in a sheltered social world, provincial and pastoral, homely and aristocratic. In the minds of all, the 'Elizabethan world picture' must have lingered: the sense of order and degree, form and design, sympathy and correspondence. Some of them, however, moved through a shattered world of civil war, cosmic change and cultural revolution into the Restoration world of infinite space, Hobbesian materialism or Cartesian dualism, and reasonable Christianity. The earlier poets – Herbert and Crashaw – wrote in the liturgical tradition of the Church: they lived in a sacramental world. Later poets – Vaughan and Traherne – chose to raise a freer world of spiritual meditation, Hermetic or Platonic, in Nature. Let them possess these worlds: 'each hath one, and is one'. They owe much to their age, but individual modes of apprehension, thought and feeling command their allegiance to the various doctrines and philosophies, their response to experience and their poetic utterance. A strong flavour of individuality is the distinguishing mark and excellence of the religious lyric in seventeenth-century England, as compared with earlier devotional verse or with the Baroque lyric of the Continent. This originality may be due to the example, though not to the influence, of Donne. Accordingly, rather than trace currents of thought or patterns of style and verse, this chapter will concentrate on 'the private world of imagination' (a phrase which has been used for Vaughan but applies to all), on the individual intuition of time and space and the personal modes of religious sensibility.

George Herbert (1593–1633) had a Welsh ancestry and a poetic lineage: his cousin, William Herbert, Earl of Pembroke, was the nephew of Sir Philip Sidney. 'If a literary genealogy must be traced for Herbert', Margaret Bottrall claimed, 'there is much to be said for affiliating him to Wyatt and Sidney as well as to Donne.' With Donne, however, Magdalen Herbert's younger son was intimately acquainted. Urged by an intelligent mother, the Cambridge student entered into a successful career. Public Orator from 1620, befriended by Bacon, he knew 'the ways of learning': scientific imagery, from 'the fleet Astronomer' and 'subtil Chymic' to medicine, metallurgy or navigation, is not absent in his poetry, though less obtrusive, more allusive than Donne's. But his youth and spirit 'also took/The way that takes the town' (Affliction I'). Enjoying powerful connections at Court and the King's favour, he could look for some 'great place'. Whether all hope of a public career did die with his 'friends' at Court and King James himself, or whether his youthful intention of dedicating his life to the service of God re-asserted itself decisively after the death of an ambitious and domineering mother, he resigned the Public Oratorship in 1626 and took Orders as deacon. His hopes of serving God were defeated for three years by ill health – a setback recorded in 'The Crosse' and other poems. In 1629, however, he married, was ordained and settled at Bemerton to lead the humble and active life Walton delightfully described and he himself suggested in his prose treatise, *A Priest to the Temple or, The Country Parson*. This halo of rustic piety, however, should not prove misleading. Though his translation of 'Outlandish Proverbs' shows a genuine taste for popular wisdom, reflected in his gnomic poetry, the chaplain of Lady Pembroke, the friend of Nicholas Ferrar, the divine who appended 'Brief Notes on Valdesso's Considerations', was a gentleman and a scholar. Homeliness and sophistication meet in his poems, enriched by his worldly experience. Besides, the English poet had served an apprenticeship to the Latin Muse in his polemical 'Musae Res-ponsoriae,' a defence of Anglican rite, and in his heart-felt elegies 'Memoriae Matris Sacrum.' He had courted wit and learned con-ciseness in the epigrams of 'Lucus' and 'Passio Discerpta'. Of the book of poems, 'which now bears the name of *The Temple* . . . Mr Farrer would say, "There was in it the picture of a divine soul in every page"' (Walton), but it also bore the mark of a conscious artist.

The Temple, however, can hardly be described as a fully organized whole, controlled by a dominant intention. Some kind of unity is no doubt conferred on the sequence by the architectonics of the Church, the liturgical year and Christian eschatalogy. From 'The Church-Porch' we proceed to 'The Altar' or leap to 'The Windows'; from 'Good Friday' we move to 'Easter', 'Whitsunday' and 'Trinity'; after 'Death', 'Doomsday' and 'Judgment', the reception of the soul in Heaven is beautifully dramatized in 'Love (III)'. One may agree that *The Temple* is at once 'The British Church', double-moated by God's grace, and a symbol for 'the life of man within that Church'; or even a hieroglyph for the body of the Christian as the living temple of the Holy Spirit, and yet fail to discover in the arrangement of the poems as clear a 'principle of organization' as J. H. Summers claimed. Others have argued that the Hebraic or even the classical temple for pagan worship were in the poet's mind, that he meant to suggest the substitution of the Covenant of Grace for the Covenant of Works (J. D. Walker), or to underline 'the contrast between the life of grace offered by the Church and the natural values of the ancients' (Mary Rickey). One may assent to the symbolic implications and reject the assumption of persistent or even consistent design.

To trace a clear spiritual pattern and progression in the sequence is no less hazardous, though ingenious minds may delight in reading the poems as an illustration of the three ways of the spiritual life or as a hieroglyph of time's passage: 'the soul moves in time from an earlier state of unpreparedness to a later one of preparedness'. Palmer's biographical heresy is revived when the poems are hypothetically rearranged to suggest a spiritual pilgrimage from affliction to joy in the acceptance of God's will and love.[1]

The subtitle still offers the safest description: 'Private Ejaculations'. Herbert's sense of form is obvious, but it is mainly displayed in the shapeliness of the isolated poem. His intuition of time is vivid but not expressed through continuance and progress.

With Herbert, as with Donne, 'Onelie the present is thy part and fee' ('The Discharge'). The moment of experience is recorded with dramatic immediacy in prayer, meditation or apostrophe. Brusque openings let us into particular situations:

> Busie enquiring heart, what wouldst thou know?
> ('The Discharge')
> What is this strange and uncouth thing? ('The Crosse')

[1] G. L. Gullickson, 'Order in George Herbert's *The Temple*', *D. A.* Nov. 1965.

Herbert's 'present', however, is more spacious than Donne's instant. It can espouse the continuity of music:

> Now I in you without a bodie move,
> Rising and falling with your wings:

('Church-musick')

In a poem by Donne the present leaps into being and may even rob the past of all reality, as in 'The Good-morrow'. In *The Temple* the moment gone may be the subject of the poem and a source of pathos, like a presence in absence:

> It cannot be. Where is that mightie joy
> Which just now took up all my heart?

('Temper II')

The Christian is eager to treasure or recapture gleams of spiritual joy: their very intermittence invites a brooding over the vanishing moment: 'Thou cam'st but now; wilt thou so soon depart . . .?' ('The Glimpse'). Herbert is the poet of return and rebirth in a different way from Vaughan's; not into a previous state but into the present:

> And now in age I bud again,
> After so many deaths I live and write;
> I once more smell the dew and rain,
> And relish versing: O my onely light,
>   It cannot be
>   That I am He
> On whom thy tempests fell all night.

His true bent is not restrospection, but recapitulation. A poem which opens as narrative will lead up to a present climax: 'I made a posie, while the day ran by . . . Farewell deare flowers, sweetly your time ye spent . . . I follow straight . . .' ('Life'). The self-enclosed narrative may also blur the distinction between the present and the future, which is apprehended as completion rather than grasped in anticipation (as in Donne's outcry: 'What if this present were the worlds last night?'). At the end of 'The Pilgrimage' the poet has firmly placed himself – that is, placed us – in present death – his own death: 'After so foul a journey death *is* fair,/And but a chair.' In his imagination past and future are rolled up into a ball – one of his favourite images. Distance, whether historical or eschatological, disappears: Christ is 'dying daily' ('Affliction III'). The drama of Redemption is told in the preterite as an apologue, but the words spoken on the Cross are intensely present:

> there I him espied,
> Who straight, *Your suit is granted*, said, & died.

Herbert's intuition of time, his mode of devotion and his sense of form are interrelated. A mind which takes in more than the present moment is capable of the concentration on religious experience which was denied to Donne's dispersed or pinpointed attention. 'All the day' may be filled with the ever-welling call of the loving heart: '*My joy, my life, my crown*' ('A true Hymne'). The poetry of ejaculation shows him at his most lyrical. Instantaneity and re-petition are combined in a space of time: 'this day' is a frequent phrase. More frequent still is the building up of the poem to an unexpected close, artfully contrived. Donne's agile mind could spring such surprises on us, but it tacked about from one argument to another. Through his piled-up statements or questionings, Herbert moves steadily towards a conclusion, which at once unifies and reverses the meaning:

> Then for thy passion – I will do for that –
> Alas, my God, I know not what.

or

> But as I rav'd and grew more fierce and wilde
>   At every word,
> Me thoughts I heard one calling, *Child!*
> And I reply'd, *My Lord*.

This premeditated composition turns the dramatic monologue into a single conceit instead of a succession of witty flashes. It is the triumph of form within the recorded moment of experience, within the self-enclosed lyric.

Emphasis on public worship rather than private devotion may be misleading. The reaction against romantic interpretations, though wholesome, has been carried too far by recent critics. In the age of Herbert, Summers reminds us, 'the expression of individual ex-perience was valued not for the sake of self-expression but for its didactic effectiveness; not because of its uniqueness but because of its universal applicability'. This approach may account for the com-position of obviously didactic poetry, like 'The Church-porch', or even for the faint effort at thrusting the lyrics into some sort of logical or theological order. It cannot account for the creative impulse. Self-expression need not be 'Romantic'. The religious lyric of the Middle Ages often was an Augustinian 'Soliloquy' – a colloquy between the soul and God as well as a self-communing. To Puttenham in his *Arte of English Poesie* (I.xxii–xxvii), to Sidney in his *Defence of Poesie*, to Donne in 'The Triple Foole', lyrical poetry was an outlet for human emotions. Though Walton's relation may not record Herbert's actual words, *The Temple* is, indeed, 'a picture of the many spiritual conflicts that have passed betwixt God and [the poet's] soul'.

Some of the pieces are even more clearly autobiographical than any of Donne's self-dramatizations, which only revealed or re-created a single experience. Not utterly fascinated by the present (which only joins the particular and the universal), Herbert can survey his whole life, enclose it in narrative ('Affliction I') or in drama ('The Collar'), gather in one past and present ('The Flower', 'The Glance'), retrace his steps to a distant point: 'And now, me thinks, I am where I began/Sev'n years ago' ('The Bunch of Grapes'). The poet, no doubt, is conscious of his sacerdotal office: unlike Donne, he does not confine his attention to his 'naked thinking heart'. The emphasis, however, is unchanged. The priest meditates on the perfection expected from Christ's minister, but he meditates in privacy: the poem comes to a close when the invitation is spoken: 'Come people; Aaron's drest' ('Aaron'). 'Miserie' defines the wearisome condition of humanity and the hero is Everyman. Yet, when the sick-tossed vessel is dashed on 'his own shelf', the personal meaning is flashed: 'My God, I mean my self'.

The common ideal of self-knowledge may be expressed in the Christian mode ('Church-porch', 'The H. Scripture', 'Even-song') or in Stoic phrase, as in the close of 'Content'. In his self-examination, however, Herbert hardly practises on his own heart, nerves and brain as keen a vivisection as Donne's. We miss the note of perplexity for his desire is not to seek himself but 'to seek God only' (as the Dean of St Paul's professed to do). His poetry is talk; and God, silent or speaking, is the poet's constant interlocutor. Donne only gave an illusion of dialogue: 'For Godsake hold your tongue, and let me [talk]' might have been spoken to his mistress. There is no give and take, even when he meets objections raised by his own mind. In his religious poetry the true centre of interest is the poet's self. Emotions of fear and love, acts of worship, egotistic petitions are directed to God as an object. The action of a Divine subject is never felt, with the single exception of a thrilling in-vocation: 'Heare thy selfe now, for thou in us dost pray' ('A litanie', xxiii). Only through his own prayer is Donne able to *realize* the Divine presence and the circle runs from self to self. Herbert's God will speak to his 'Child' ('Dialogue', 'The Collar', 'Artillerie'). Open dialogue is infrequent, but there is no interruption in the soul's intercourse with the divine lover, constantly addressed as 'my God', 'my Lord', 'my Master'.

Though his poetry is not always self-centred, Herbert discloses a
modern subjectivity of feeling and expression in such poems as
'Affliction (I)'. At other times self-examination may be veiled in
allegory or personification; it may thicken into emblem or
metaphor. Yet through such metaphors introspection will search
the closets of the heart and disclose an open breast, fit to challenge
the clearest diamond ('Confession'). This mode of self-awareness
may be responsible for flashes of irony or humour, unknown to the
religious poetry of Crashaw and Vaughan. The note of burlesque in
'Dooms-day' or 'Conscience' could be a simple illustration of holy
mirth. But the playful insight into the ruse of the human heart in
'Gratefulnesse' or 'Time' discloses a subtler form of irony directed
at oneself. There is sadness but also a touch of humorous
acceptance in the quiet admission of man's essential foolishness
('Miserie'). When a passionate outburst in 'The Thanksgiving',
'Affliction (I)', or 'The Collar' ends in the sudden recognition of its
futility, one feels the very surge of emotion was controlled from the
beginning by the poet's critical self-awareness.

This ironical detachment may account for Herbert's delight in
understatement. The constant expression of sacred truth in homely
language does not merely proceed from an ideal of Christian
simplicity. Such familiarity is not ingenuous but artful. This poetry
works like the glass described in 'The Elixir':

> A man that looks on glasse
> On it may stay his eye;
> Or if he pleaseth, through it passe,
> And then the heav'n espie.

A deeper complexity is achieved through the subdued expression
of feeling. When Herbert resorts to hyperbole, as in the super-
ficially Donne-like 'Church-monuments', he is least original. His
distinctive art and ambiguity are revealed in 'Death'. The poet's
apparently naïve gaze does not shrink from 'the uncouth hideous
thing', but there is a quiet irony and no horror in the contemplation:
'Thy mouth was open; but thou couldst not sing'. The Christian
knows that 'all [these] bones with beautie shall be clad'. There is no
shudder and no rapture, for the *simultaneous* awareness of the stark
reality of death and the glory of eternity tempers both fear and
exultation. The last stanza takes up the well-worn comparison of
death with sleep. Yet the sober assertion of immortality through the
stillness of sleep in an 'honest grave' rests on the fearless
acceptance of the gruesome image. Dissonance lurks under a

deceptive simplicity. The mention of the body as 'Half that we have' reminds us with Herbertian restraint that 'gluttonous death will instantly unjoynt' body and soul, as in Donne's sonnet 'This is my playes last scene . . .' The final balance between the symbols of downy sleep and dreadful dissolution expresses the poet's composure in front of life and death.

The colloquiality of language and rhythm, the even tone, the deliberate understatement are the stylistic expression of an intellectual control, all the more severe since Herbert was not even-tempered. There is a conscious avoidance of rude and strident emotion. It is through this self-consciousness and reticence that Herbert's poetry achieves obliquity or ambiguity. Empson's analysis of 'Hope' and 'The Pilgrimage' in *Seven Types* cannot be surpassed, but it should be related to the poet's cast of mind, which may give him a better title to 'metaphysical poetry' than many critics have acknowledged. 'His wit', Margaret Bottrall confessed, 'is one of his foremost qualities. But since this wit does not depend for its effect upon far-fetched conceits, recondite allusions or reasoned arguments, there seems to be no good reason for describing it as metaphysical, or for connecting it inseparably with the wit of Donne.' Yet, in Miss Rickey's words, there is no intimation that 'writing from the heart necessitates writing without the head'. The concentration and intellectual ingenuity of 'metaphysical poetry' is achieved by Herbert. It often lurks in his supposedly quaint titles: they all effect 'some special communication, either an enriching ambiguity, or the suggestion of a motif which qualifies the materials of the text itself' (Rickey).

It has been claimed that Herbert's wit was fired by the paradoxes of the Christian tradition rather than the example of Donne. Conceits based on the paradoxical nature of man's individual experience are bound to be fewer in *The Temple* than in the *Songs and Sonets*, but they are hardly less striking when they arise. 'Let me not love thee, if I love thee not' ('Affliction I'): man's love for God may be forgetful but its roots are so deep that the worst affliction that might be inflicted on the poet for this intermittence would be to root out his love altogether. Besides, even a traditional paradox can be modulated into something new, rich and strange. Thus, in 'The Reprisall', Herbert declares himself ready to die for Christ, yet owns his defeat: 'For by thy death I die for thee'. The paradox of 'Redemption' is refined when the Christian discovers that he only finds the strength of dying through the death of Christ.

In 'The Sacrifice', one of the longest and least personal poems,

'Metaphysical' ambiguity and richness have been traced to the liturgical tradition by Rosemond Tuve in *A Reading of George Herbert*. Without disclaiming the lineage one could show that neither the liturgy nor the mediaeval lyrics offer the same intellectual density, nor the same subtlety in dramatic irony.[1] One striking instance is this quiet proclamation of the awe-inspiring *Deus absconditus*:

> My face they cover, though it be divine.
> As *Moses* face was vailed, so is mine,
> Lest on their double-dark souls either shine.

Throughout the poem, indeed, attention is focused not on the sufferings of Christ nor even on the mystery of Redemption, but on man's blindness as discerned by the dreadful, yet loving omniscience of God. The sources of irony are more subjective here than in Greek tragedy: self-deceit, not deceitful fate, is exposed. Among innumerable poems on the Redemption, Herbert's 'Sacrifice' does not owe its distinctive excellence only to epigrammatic art, or dramatic vividness; its strength arises from the exclusion of easy pathos, from the intellectual control and terrifying lucidity.

A further distinction between a passive allegiance to some religious or literary tradition and the spontaneous workings of the individual imagination can be traced in the poet's awareness of the two natures in Christ or of man's amphibious nature. With Herbert as with Donne, the Incarnation is more than the centre of Christian faith: it commands their vision of the world and their inspiration as if it were a structure of their minds. In 'Affliction (IV)' the poet describes himself as 'A wonder tortur'd in the space/Betwixt this world and that of grace', but he always seeks to bring both worlds together and find the incarnation of spiritual reality in the grosser world, as in 'Sunday': 'The fruit of this; the next world's bud'. He delights in 'the bridall of the earth and skie' ('Vertue'). Man's middle nature between angel and beast is a Renaissance commonplace, but Herbert, unlike the Platonists or the satirists, is never tempted to consider either of them in isolation. In his intuition of the complexities of mire or blood, his soul will clap its hands and sing, for

> Whether I flie with angels, fall with dust,
> Thy hands made both, and I am there.

('Temper I')

---

[1] This has to be proved at length: see my *Poètes métaphysiques anglais*, i, 313–23.

Human experience is an experience of duality and union. As a Christian, Herbert cannot but believe in the Real Presence: the sacrament must be more than a figure of a purely spiritual reality. Yet the Anglican poet argued against transubstantiation with surprising scholastic acrimony in the MS poem on 'The H. Communion' excluded from *The Temple*. Though the ecstatic tone in 'The Invitation' and 'The Banquet' reveals a sacramental sensibility almost as keen as Crashaw's, the printed version of 'The H. Communion' still insists on 'the wall that parts/Our souls and fleshy hearts'. Yet it proclaims at the same time the influence of the Eucharist on the 'rebel-flesh', and the privilege of Grace, which alone can open 'the souls most subtile rooms' while the elements 'to spirits refin'd, at doore attend Dispatches from their friend'. This description of the Eucharist is more reminiscent of Donne's conception of love in 'The Exstasie' than of any theological doctrine. Both poets maintain between sense and soul a barrier which even the blood-begotten spirits cannot wholly overcome, yet they assert their close conjunction. Neither of them is satisfied by a merely spiritual ecstasy. In his rapture Herbert cries out: 'Give me my captive soul, or take/My bodie also thither'.

Through this sacramental approach one may trace a mode of thought and sensibility. More space than is available would be required to show how Herbert's mind apprehends the concomitance of two actions in divided or distinguished worlds; how his imagination grasps in a single flash the opposition and conjunction of two natures or realities, sensible and spiritual. Catholic doctrine, which the sensuous imagination of Crashaw will espouse of its own accord, blurs the distinction and relies on metamorphosis. Calvinistic and even Anglican doctrine asserted the simultaneity of a spiritual and a physical action, but their conjunction seemed gratuitous since the spiritual alone had efficacy and meaning. Herbert's mode of apprehension is truly original.

This mode governs his poetic inspiration as well as his religious emotions. His most deeply-felt paradoxes bring together but never confuse contrary notions, indissolubly connected in human experience: the finite and the infinite, time and eternity, life and death. Puritan writers, when they express spiritual truth, either keep the contrasting notions well apart or abolish the contrast in Neoplatonic idealism. With Catholics like Crashaw the sensible and the spiritual interfuse on the pattern of transubstantiation, and contraries, like pain and pleasure, melt into one another.

The same type of relationship obtains in Herbert's handling of the abstract and the concrete. Yet he seldom offers palpable abstractions, like Donne's 'dull privations and leane emptinesse'. He avoids scholastic quiddities. His mind seems to move in a purely material universe, clotted with objects. The contemporary vogue of emblems (see page 202) no doubt influenced his poetic inspiration, as Rosemary Freeman and others have shown. As Jean Hagstrum tersely points out in *The Sister Arts*: 'Herbert's poetry is not descriptive but emblematic . . . The iconic poetry of Drayton, like the tapestries it describes, contents the eye; Herbert's contents the mind.' However, one should make a further distinction. In the emblems of Quarles, image and idea are distinctly perceived. Many of Herbert's images are metaphors so condensed that the mind hardly forms a sensuous image in the quick apprehension of meaning:

> Thy clothes being fast, but thy soul loose about thee
>
> ('Church-porch')
>
> This is but tuning of my breast,
>   To make the musick better.
>
> ('Temper I')

When human dust and bones are described as 'The shells of fledge souls left behinde' ('Death'), this beautiful evocation should not call up a visual image of broken eggs and feathered souls, which would be even more grotesque than the winged hearts of the emblematists. The imagination is deeply stirred because the full significance is grasped through the lingering image of the actual bones, a faint and almost abstract impression of white brittleness and dereliction, together with the elation of a breaking out, a sense of flight and freedom.

Some poems, no doubt, call attention to an emblematic image, but one may wonder why 'Love Unknown' leaves us unmoved, whereas 'The Churche-floor' can evoke a poetic thrill. The heart's progress from font to cauldron or thorns is an unreal apologue, a mere fabrication. The 'square speckled stone' *is* an actual slab in the church-floor and *means* intensely ('is' and 'means' are interchangeable when we hear that the stone '*Is Patience*'). However this is not symbolism, for the sign and the thing signified are not truly one. Such images differ at once from symbols and from conventional emblems in the same way as Herbert's conception of the Eucharist differs from both Catholic and Calvinistic doctrine. In each case the poet's originality lies in a simultaneous apprehension. The stones are at once an object for the eye and for the mind.

Though the topics of *The Temple* 'can be accurately styled *metaphysical*', Miss Rickey observes, Herbert speaks of Heaven 'in terms remarkable only for their earthliness'. Yet, at his most sensuous, he will 'thrust' his mind into each experience, into the very sweetness and odour of the words *My Master*: 'This broth of smells, that feeds and fats my *minde* ('The Odour'). We do not breathe the freer air of Vaughan's or Traherne's spacious worlds of philosophic meditation. Herbert's world of devotion is a little stuffy, but intellect is ever watchful and never allows materiality to melt into mindlessness as in many of Crashaw's conceits.

This is not the poet of perspective and expansion. His imagination is circumscribed in space as in time. Its apprehension of the world is organic and kinesthetic. Images of muscular violence and contraction abound to suggest the inner wrestlings of the soul: 'Stretch or contract me, thy poor debter:/This is but tuning of my breast,/To make the musick better' ('Temper 1'). Sin is a 'press and vice' ('Agonie'), thoughts are 'a case of knives' ('Affliction IV'). Nor does the poet ever paint an effortless ascension, a smooth flight to Heaven: he will be 'toss'd from earth' ('Sunday'), 'tossed to God's breast' ('The Pulley').

Herbert's imagination may call for circumscription out of a yearning for security: 'O let me, when thy roof my soul hath hid,/O let me roost and nestle there' ('Temper 1').Space, distance, infinity only give pain and terror: 'O rack me not to such a vast extent;/Those distances belong to thee' ('Temper I'). The only world the poet gladly inhabits must be solid and full, like the boxes and chests, the cabinets 'packt' with sweets on which he dwells lovingly. He knows 'the soul doth span the world', but *his* will only 'hang content/From either pole unto the centre' when Heaven shrinks to a local habitation: 'Where in each room of the well-furnisht tent/He lies warm, and without adventure' ('Content'). This substitution of spiritual homeliness for cosmic amplitude or metaphysical profundity implies a limitation in imaginative range, a loss in poetic intensity. However, the dialectics of the finite and the infinite, immanence and transcendence, is ever present, though unobtrusive:

> Thy will such a strange distance is,
> As that to it
> East and West touch, the poles do kisse,
> And parallels meet.
>
> ('The Search')

No poet had a finer sense of the Divine presence and 'nearenesse'. 'Making two one' ('The Search'). And the God that will '[Him] self immure and close/In some one corner of a feeble heart' ('Decay') brings with Him infinite riches in a little room. When all differences are told, Herbert and Donne still have one common characteristic: their apprehension of the eternal and the infinite in a single point of space and time. 'Shine here to us, and thou art every where', the lover said to the 'Sunne Rising'. Herbert has the same metaphysical confidence when addressing his Sun and Son:

> Thy power and love, my love and trust
> Make one place ev'ry where.
>
> ('Temper')

Not with the Metaphysicals, but with the Baroque poets of the Continent is the inspiration of Richard Crashaw commonly linked. Born in London in 1612, the son of a Puritan preacher and polemicist, he died at Loretto, a Roman convert, in 1649. The conversion, however, had been no sudden change for the Charterhouse and Cambridge student who modelled his early verse on the Jesuit epigrammatists, for the fellow of Peterhouse, a hotbed of Laudian High Churchmanship, for the visitor at Little Gidding and the spiritual son of Mary Collet, for the exile in Leyden and Paris, the protégé of the Countess of Denby and Queen Henrietta Maria, the friend of Joseph Beaumont and Thomas Car, the flaming heart who yearned, when yet among the Protestants, for the mystical death of Saint Teresa.

Donne's devotion was self-centred. Herbert's attention centred on the intercourse between God and his own soul. Crashaw's ecstatic piety aims at self-annihilation. 'Leave nothing of my SELF in me', he cries out to the Foundress of the Carmelites: 'Let me so read thy life, that I/ Unto all life of mine may dy' ('The Flaming Heart'). Lyrical, intensely emotional, his poetry nevertheless proves impersonal. He is lost in the contemplation of some outer object: Christ, the Virgin or a Saint. Whereas the inner presence of God in the soul invited Herbert's self-questionings, Crashaw's faith and imagination are centrifugal: 'Goe, Soul out of thy Self . . .' ('To the Name Above Every Name').

An insight into the human heart can hardly be expected from such a poet, but he himself is a case for the psychologist. Ambiguity is displaced by the ambivalence that characterized Crashaw's sensibility long before he became acquainted with the Spanish mystics. In countless poems the same sharp confusion of pain and pleasure attends an ecstatic death, erotic in an 'Epithalamium', mystical in the Teresa hymns.

> O how oft shalt thou complain
> Of a sweet & subtle PAIN.
> Of intolerable JOYES;
> Of a DEATH, in which who dyes
> Loves his death, and dyes again.
> And would for ever so be slain.
> And lives, & dyes; and knowes not why
> To live, But that he thus may never leave to DY.
>
> ('A Hymn to the Name and Honor of the Admirable Sainte Teresa')

The metaphysical shudder, the anguish of the grave, therefore will be absent. The death of the body is but the ultimate ecstasy, 'When These thy DEATHS, so numerous,/Shall all at last dy into one,/ And melt thy Soul's sweet mansion' ('Teresa Hymn').

The influence of the erotic mysticism of the Counter-Reformation is undeniable, but Crashaw's own sensuality was revealed in his early poems, only published in 1646 as *The Delights of the Muses*. No chaster Muse can be found than 'That not impossible She' addressed in his 'Wishes To his (Supposed) Mistresse', yet more than sensuousness is betrayed by the Marlovian fascination for the 'crimson streame' of blood 'warme in its violet channel' (elegies on Mr Stanninow, on Lady Parker, 'On ye Gunpowder-Treason'). However, a merely erotic or a purely spiritual interpretation of the poet's sacred language should be rejected alike. An unconscious perversity may have been the starting-point, but a genuine sublimation was achieved. The *Epigrammata Sacra* and the other poems written before 1637 are filled with the imagery of blood and milk, wounds and breasts, and the psychoanalyst may gloat over the lines 'Hee'l have his Teat e're long (a bloody one)./The mother then must suck the Son'. The thirst for martyrdom is still morbid, not mystic. With the 'Nativity' and 'Assumption Hymns' or the lines 'On a prayer booke', we move away from blood to clearer themes, 'soft exhalations/Of soule; deare, and divine annihilations', but the 'rarifyed delights' called up in verse of Shelleyan lightness are not free from a cloying sweetness reminiscent of Salesian devotion.

'Lov's manly flame' first burned in the poems inspired by Saint Teresa, 'A Woman for Angelical height of speculation, for Masculine courage of performance more than a woman'. The poet himself for the first time struck the note of supreme intensity: 'Love thou art absolute, sole Lord/Of life and death'. He, too, had now in him all the eagle and all the dove, and quaffed 'large draughts of intellectual day'. The word 'intellectual', as Ruth Wallerstein observed, recurs in the poems from 1643 to 1652. Crashaw's insistent use does not denote a rejection of concreteness but the poet's images seem to lose their sensuous gloss. They are symbols used in ritualistic drama or discourse:

> O costly intercourse
> Of deaths, & worse,
> Divided loves. While son & mother
> Discourse alternate wounds to one another.
>
> ('Sancta Maria')

In the 'Stabat Mater' the wounds of Christ are no longer roses and rubies, or lips to be sensually kissed: their spiritual significance is

uppermost. The influence of the mediaeval liturgy on the poetic
imagination of the convert is suggested by his own free translation
of St Thomas's 'Adoro Te':

> Down down, proud sense! Discourses dy.
> Keep close, my soul's inquiring ey!
> Nor touch nor tast must look for more
> But each sitt still in his own Dore.

Crashaw had proclaimed himself Herbert's disciple in *Steps to the
Temple*, but those steps were mostly laid before 1634 and *The Temple*
was published in 1633. 'On Mr G. HERBERTS book . . . sent to a
Gentlewoman' was written in a key of devout gallantry and mystical
mawkishness alien to the spirit of Herbert. The influence of *The
Temple* is first felt in the second edition of 1648 and best traceable
in 'Charitas Nimia. Or the Dear Bargain':

> Lord, what is man? why should he coste thee
> So dear? what had his ruin lost thee?
> Lord what is man? that thou hast overbought
>   So much a thing of nought?
>
> Love is too kind, I see; & can
> Make but a simple merchant man.

One may choose to think that Crashaw changed his style as he
turned away from the Latin amorists, the Jesuit epigrammatists and
Marino to imitate George Herbert, translate the mediaeval liturgy
or read the Spanish mystics. The progress, however, is not merely
stylistic. Crashaw's taste matured and his sensibility was purified.
That the change proceeded from a spiritual evolution rather than
literary influence is confirmed by the very limitations of this poetic
development. The Teresian 'dowr of LIGHTS & FIRES' burned
away the sensual dross of the early poems, yet the fundamental
ambivalence persisted to the last. The poet may 'vow to make brave
way/Upwards, & presse on for the pure intelligentiall Prey'
('Epiphanie'), but his own splendid evocation of the 'mystic night' of
the Areopagite reveals the persistence and power of a visionary
imagination. It is felt even in the semi-abstract splendour of his
celebration of the 'frugall negative light':

> Now by abased liddes shall learn to be
> Eagles: and shutt our eyes that we may see.

The 'Epiphanie' Hymn is not an isolated poem in Crashaw's work,
as Warren and Watkin differently claimed. It shows the utmost

bound Crashaw's imagination could reach in one direction. The
true bent of his mind reasserts itself in the close, through the
sensuous and emblematic image of the visible Sun:

> Somthing a brighter SHADOW (sweet) of thee.
> Or on heavn's azure forhead high to stand
> Thy golden index; . . . .

However, the hard clarity and materiality of the emblem is un-
suited to the lyrical and musical inspiration of Crashaw. Donne's
and Herbert's imagination moved among fixities; their paradoxes
and ambiguities oppose or associate definite notions and emotions.
In the sensibility of Crashaw 'kind contrarietyes' ('The Weeper')
melt into each other and the result is transmutation rather than
paradox, confusion rather than complexity:

> No where but here did ever meet
> Sweetnesse so sad, sadnesse so sweet.

> ('The Weeper')

The characteristic ambivalence emerges when he calls to the 'soft
ministers of sweet sad mirth' (To the Name Above Every Name'),
yearns for 'all those stings/Of love, sweet bitter things' ('Sancta
Maria') or cries 'Welcome, my Griefe, my Joy' (Divine Epigrams).
Though its literary or liturgical descent is obvious, this rhetoric of
contraries has a personal significance. Joy and grief, day and night,
fire and water, were apprehended in static opposition by the
Petrarchans; they are now suggestive of change or exchange: 'A
commerce of contrary powres' ('Epiphanie'). We have entered a
world of movement and fluidity.

Donne's and Herbert's worlds of imagination, though dynamic,
were solid and dense; Crashaw's is a 'general flood'. Substances
like gold and silver, pearl and crystal only lend their lustre: their
hardness is dissolved in 'Thawing crystall', 'Warm sylver shoures'
('Weeper') or 'The water of a *Diamond*' ('Teare'). The prevailing
liquidity is not unlinked with the dominant thirst for feminine
tenderness, for the maternal milk. 'Sitiens laboro' (in the epigram
'Spes Diva') is the leit-motiv for 'this dry soul' who would be 'drunk
of the dear wounds' ('Adoro Te', 'Sancta Maria'). Streams and seas
are hyperboles for the outflow of milk or blood or tears, or the
'strong wine of love': fluids of human source. The deeper longings
of poets and mystics are expressed in their imagery. Traherne's
illuminations are conveyed in radiant symbols; Vaughan's yearning
for revelation and regeneration is expressed through gleaming light
and living waters. With other mystics fire is dominant. Crashaw's

sacred ebriety calls for 'brim-fill'd Bowles' and a 'draught of liquid fire' ('Flaming Heart'). Such fire will be a 'moist spark' ('Teare'), a flame 'quench't in a flood' (Epigram, 'Luc. 7'). Nor fire nor water attract the poet's imagination by themselves but only as they meet in 'sister-Seas of virgins Milke', in a woman's breast, 'the noblest nest/Both of love's fires and flouds'.

This watery and organic world is without space and perspective. Everything is in motion, but the sense of direction is lost. There is no Donne-like 'progress', no bullet-like trajectory: *vagus* is a favourite epithet in the Latin poems, but the wandering is felt from inside, not related to outer objects. Motion is a vagrancy or tremulousness at the heart of things – tears and stars and bubbles – or a streaming from nowhere, a swelling into a sea. When tears 'melt the yeare/Into a weeping motion' ('Weeper'), the conceit conveys an intuition of the very essence of time and movement, which finds its expression in liquidity.

Music is experienced and expressed in the same way. The soul will bathe 'in streames of liquid Melodie' – not in the airy sounds of an Ariel or Shelley. The 'sleeke' and 'lubricke' throat of the nightingale is an 'ever-bubling' spring: 'She opes the floodgate, and lets loose a Tide/Of streaming sweetnesse'. Following 'those little rills', the listener 'sinkes into a Sea of *Helicon*' ('Musicks Duell'). Liquidity once more has a milky substance: the 'creame of Morning *Helicon*' with which 'sweet-lipp'd Angell-Imps . . . swill their throats' ('Musicks Duell').

So unlike Herbert's moment, so like the poet's own description of the ever-renewed death of rapture, Crashaw's flowing and heaving time is a stream and swell of sensations, 'In many a sweet rise, many as sweet a fall' till 'A full-mouth *Diapason* swallowes all' ('Musicks Duell'). Each sensation spurts, climbs to the pitch of ecstasy and dies. Each musical resolution is a mystic dissolution. 'Young *Time* is taster to Eternity' but 'in the lap of Loves full noone/It falls, and dyes: oh no, it melts away/As doth the dawne into the day' ('On Hope'). Between the temporal and the eternal there is no discontinuity for the poet only seeks the endless extension of the pleasure felt in the very moment of death: erotic, musical or mystic. No intuition of transcendence is required when eternity is 'the long/And everlasting series of a deathless SONG' ('Name of Jesus').

These modes of imagination command the poet's apprehension of the Christian mysteries. Herbert's wonder, like Donne's, was truly metaphysical, nearer perplexity than admiration. Not because his Church distrusted miracles, but because of his concentration on spiritual experience the author of *The Temple*, though fascinated by the Incarnation and Passion, was never attracted to the miraculous. Crashaw was still in the fold of the Anglican Church when he wrote endless variations on the miracles of Christ. Even at his barest, in the Epiphany hymn, he still chooses to describe the eclipse of the sun with such precision that the symbolic significance is nearly lost in admiration of this 'new prodigious might'. The emphasis on the marvellous blurs the greater mysteries. The Nativity hymn seeks to unite 'all WONDERS in one sight' with no sense of the difference between the accidental – Summer in Winter, Day in Night – and the central paradox: 'Aeternity shutt in a span . . . Heaven in earth, & GOD in MAN'.

As the poet lived in a world of metamorphosis where tears turn into milk and dew, pearl and crystal, gold and silver, the Christian will incline of his own accord to the doctrine of transubstantiation. Herbert's interpretation of the Real Presence required a mysterious harmony between the world of nature and the world of grace. The mystery is explained away by post-Tridentine theology, but this explanation again implies a disruption of the natural order, a miracle. In the same way, Crashaw's central experience, the inversion of pain and pleasure, brings contradictory terms together in an oxymoron. But since there is a transfer of value and meaning, since pain *is* pleasure, transmutation again prevails over paradox. Even the death of ecstasy – a death 'in which who dyes/Loves his death, and dyes again' – is nothing but a succession of 'intollerable joys': pain in the mode of pleasure.

That is why Crashaw's conceits or paradoxes are pointless or superficial when you seek to grasp their meaning. But this intellectual approach is wrong. In *The Temple*, as in Donne's sacred poetry, attention was focused on the significance of the Christian mysteries and it was explored through the individual experience of the believer in some particular dramatic situation: 'For by thy death, I die for thee'. Crashaw does not explore or meditate. He contemplates scenes of the Passion of the Nativity (disregarded by Herbert) and, like a Baroque painter, seeks to excite our affections and his own through a violent display of images. The Ignatian technique known as the application of the senses becomes here a free surrender to the suggestiveness of each sensation. One feels that Crashaw might have been a greater poet if his imaginative associations had been dictated only by his deeper feelings and the major symbols. He often succumbed to an intellectual irritability which, in the literary atmosphere of the age, bubbled up in superfluous conceits. His true excellence lies in the lyrical afflatus, and the highest intensity is reached in strains of straightforward assertion and simple imagery. In such moments the figurative fancy displayed in 'The Weeper' no longer calls up visual images. Metaphors are 'felt': they spring from the poet's emotion and only bring us the same flush and glow. In the close of 'The Flaming Heart' lights and fires, the eagle and the dove, the thirsts and deaths of love and the soul's final kiss proceed from the symbolic imagination:

> O thou undanted daughter of desires!
> By all thy dowr of LIGHTS & FIRES;
> By all the eagle in thee, all the dove;
> By all thy lives & deaths of love;
> By thy larg draughts of intellectuall day,
> And by thy thirsts of love more large than they;
> By all thy brim-fill'd Bowles of feirce desire
> By thy last Morning's draught of liquid fire;
> By the full kingdome of that finall kisse
> That seiz'd thy parting Soul, & seal'd thee his . . .

Crashaw may be contrasted with Herbert for his reliance on the sheer emotional value rather than the meaning of such symbols. But with Vaughan and Traherne, as Louis Martz pointed out, we move away from 'the liturgical and eucharistic symbols' of both Herbert and Crashaw towards three 'dominant fields of reference'; 'the Bible, external Nature, and the interior motions of the Self' (*The Paradise Within*). One might be tempted to say, with due diffidence in the precision of literary terms, that we pass from the Metaphysical and the Baroque to the Pre-Romantic, or rather to the seventeenth-century Hermetic and Platonic Prelude of a later Romanticism.

Silurist and 'Swan of Usk', Henry Vaughan (1622–95) and his twin brother, the Hermetist Thomas, were born in Breconshire 'above the voiceful windings of a river'. Henry left Oxford without a degree to study law in London, but he took to literature among the wits, wrote his first poems and translated the 'Tenth Satyre' of Juvenal with his mind on Strafford. Always a staunch Royalist and a Churchman, he may have fought in the Civil War though he claimed he never shed innocent blood. His courtship and marriage inspired a trickle of love poems – the 1646 volume. A hardly thinner collection of commendatory and meditative verse, with translations from Ovid, Boethius and Casimire, appeared in 1651, though collected by 1647. 'To Amoret Walking in a Starry Evening' and

'Upon the Priorie Grove, His usual Retyrement' were already clear revelations of his poetic personality. More youthful verse and secular (though never profane) poetry made up a later collection, *Thalia Rediviva* (1678). But only with the two parts of *Silex Scintillans* (1650, 1655) will his name flow on for ever

> Through pastures of the spirit washed with dew
> And starlit with eternities unknown.
>   (Siegfried Sassoon, 'At the Grave of Henry Vaughan')

Whether inspired by the gloom of defeat in a Puritan commonwealth or grief at the death of a dearly loved younger brother, by the influence of George Herbert – acknowledged in the Preface – or a keener interest in the spiritual alchemy of Thomas Vaughan, a sense of conversion pervades the first part of *Silex Scintillans*. It is a record of private experience: secretive self-communings. The best poetry of Vaughan is subjective: 'A sweet *self-privacy* in a right soul' ('Rules and Lessons'). He addresses God – 'Thou that know'st for whom I mourne' – not the reader who will only discover incidentally that the loved one is now a brother, now a wife. The elegiac, *In Memoriam* note is insistent and 'unseen tears' blend with the theme of retirement and solitude – a retreat 'from the Sun into the *shade*' (advocated in the prose treatise *Flores Solitudinis*), a refuge in the Circle of the Cell ('Misery') or a deeper seclusion, the life 'hid above with Christ in God' or the 'Dear, secret Greenness' of the Seed growing secretly, 'unseen and dumb'.

Vaughan only meets himself in solitude, not in dialogue with a Mistress or his Master. His self-awareness is a self-expression in reverie and sympathy. Donne and Herbert focused their attention on a centre. Vaughan may long for the 'Centre and mid-day' but he can only 'see through a long night/Thy edges, and thy bordering light!' ('Childe-hood'). His diffusive imagination will 'Rove in that mighty, and eternal light' ('Resurrection and Immortality') or seek 'that night! where I in him/Might live invisible and dim!' ('Night').

Another expression of his subjectivity is his belief in Hermetic *sympathies*, proclaimed with a personal intensity of emotion in 'Sure, there's a tye of Bodyes'. The mysterious attraction which was still scientific truth to the seventeenth-century mind is much more than a source of conceits or intellectual perplexity to Vaughan: it is the nostalgic apprehension of a bond with 'Absents', an animistic experience of 'the strange resentment after death' of the 'Timber', wasting 'all senseless, cold and dark',

> Where not so much as dreams of light may shine,
> Nor any thought of greenness, leaf or bark.

Vaughan's intercourse with Nature has been aptly described by Elizabeth Holmes as 'a kind of interpenetration of himself with a spirit which his special philosophy taught him to find in the objects of Nature'. But, as the same critic pointed out, 'he not only believed with the Hermetists in the "tye of bodies", but he felt the tie; and the expression of his sense of kinship with the creatures of Nature leaves a curious impression in the reader's mind of a tie as strong as the physical or even the uterine link'.

In such projections, or in the dispersion of reverie, Vaughan, unlike Herbert, first goes out of himself; but unlike Crashaw, he returns to himself. In his self-diffusing he remains self-centred, but without a keen interest in his states of mind, without the feverish self-obsession of Donne or the self-probings of Herbert. He is apt to generalize his experience: 'Such is man's life, and such is mine' ('Miserie'). This oscillation from the universal to the individual occurred in *The Temple*, but the dramatic impact of personality was not so often diluted in impersonal reflection. Many of Vaughan's poems centre on a natural object ('The Waterfall', 'The Showre') or on a Biblical episode, a verse from Scripture, as if his meditation was provoked by some occasion from outside, whereas Donne's and Herbert's poems mostly sprang from the sudden awareness of an inner experience, a state of mind. Accordingly there will be little psychological complexity in *Silex Scintillans*. Similes do not aim at defining but intensifying the emotion, as in 'Unprofitableness':

> 'Twas but just now my bleak leaves hopeless hung
>   Sullyed with dust and mud;
> Each snarling blast shot through me, and did share
> Their Youth, and beauty, Cold showres nipt, and wrung
>   Their spiciness, and bloud . . .

Self-examination, when attempted, is conducted through allegory and the search is not ultimately directed to self-discovery. In 'Vanity of Spirit', an epitome of his mystic quest and favourite symbolism, the poet leaving his 'Cell' by 'dawn' lingered by a 'spring' (of living waters) and 'gron'd to know' the Author of Nature. The alchemist in vain 'summon'd nature' and rifled her 'wombe'. He 'came at last/To search [him] selfe'. Yet not after the manner of Donne seeking 'the *Ego*, the particular, the individuall, I' (*Sermons*, ed. G. R. Potter, v. 71). The 'traces' and 'Hyerogliphicks' he discovers in a 'nook' of his own soul, like the 'Ecchoes beaten from the eternall hills', are intimations of a Divine mystery and only build up another fantastic world of 'weake beames' and 'Moone-shine night'. Thus the poet's thought first turns to Nature, then from the contemplation of Nature moves to self-exploration, but with no Augustinian sense of opposition. In his comparison of Vaughan's quest with the questioning of Nature by Augustine in book X of the *Confessions*, Martz slurs over the movement of recoil, because it cannot be found in the poem: 'Interrogavi terram et dixit non sum'. Unlike Augustine, or Herbert at that, Vaughan leaves no clear boundary between the world of objects and the subjective experience; unlike Traherne he does not enclose the outer world in the sphere of soul. His longing for a fuller revelation in death, unlike Donne's, is not a search for his own identity but a yearning for the discovery of the Divine, were it 'but one half glaunce', through the rending of 'these veyls' ('Vanity of Spirit') or 'mists' ('They are all gone into the world of light') in either Nature or the soul. This is closer to the Hermetic approach than to Augustine's close analysis of memory in his journey of the mind towards God as a reality 'interior intimo meo'.

What Vaughan has in common with many Christian mystics is a yearning to recapture something lost. It may be connected with his particular intuition of time. Not for him the 'here and now' of Traherne, or, with a difference, Herbert. The present is always filled with the remembrance of things past or the expectation of future things. When momentary, the 'moment' is integrated to 'time's silent stealth' like the 'lingring' of the 'Waterfall'. The present is emotion recollected in tranquillity. Compare Donne's 'What if this present were the worlds last night?' and Vaughan's 'I saw Eternity the other night'. A sense of distance is forced upon us: 'Silence and stealth of dayes! 'tis now/Since thou art gone,/Twelve hundred hours . . .' There is no instant projection: the imagination seems to move up a continuous stream, in full awareness of duration: 'So o'er fled minutes I retreat/Unto that hour . . .' Indeed, 'The Retreate' and 'Looking back' are intimations of this fundamental mode which unifies the poet's essential longings for childhood, Eden and the Biblical ages.

Yet Vaughan does not 'long to travell back' merely to revive the past. Retrospection is inseparable from expectation, and the 'backward steps' towards Eden only supply an assurance that the 'forward motion' will ultimately take us to 'That shady City of Palme trees'. The distinctive note is the sense of delay and resistance: 'Tyme now/Is old and slow'. Therefore the intuition of the eternal cannot be a present apprehension: eternity is *beyond* time and *above* the World, as 'The Evening-watch', 'The Agreement' and 'The World' show. To Donne and Herbert eternity was a mode of being and a metaphysical concept. To Vaughan, as in the more naïve interpretations of Plato, it is the 'country beyond the stars', a world of light, calm and insubstantiality. The 'great Ring' gathers into itself all the impressions dear to the poet: 'Joys/Active as light, and calm without all noise' ('Mount of Olives').

'Beauteous shapes, we know not why,/Command and guide the eye' ('The Starre'). A feeling for sensuous beauty does command Vaughan's allegiance to Christian Platonism and his preference for natural theology. The aesthetic emotion in spiritual natures becomes an intuition of transcendence. The light of Creation is but the shadow of God, *umbra Dei*. The aesthetic contemplation of the created world only feeds the poet's dreams of Eden, his nostalgia for a diviner world, meditating 'what transcendent beauty shall be given to all things in that eternall World, seeing this transitory one is so full of Majesty and freshnesse' (*The World Contemned*). Hence the 'gazing soul' will dwell on 'the living works' of God

> And in those weaker glories spy
> Some shadows of eternity.

('The Retreate')

The mystic naturalism of the seventeenth-century Hermetists[1] suited this poet's sensibility. It implied an unbroken continuity in the material and spiritual world, not the abstract relation of form and matter in the contemplations of Marvell. 'Spirit' is the key word. It is more than 'that subtile knot, which makes us man', effecting the conjunction of body and soul as in Donne's 'Exstasie' or Herbert's 'The H. Communion'. It is the 'fire-spirit of life', the 'preserving spirit . . . Which doth resolve, produce, and ripen all' ('Resurrection') in the natural cycle, but is none other than 'the knowing, glorious spirit' ('The Book'), the Divine Intelligence 'whose spirit feeds/All things with life' ('The Stone'). The spirit that passes untainted through Nature still quickens, 'refines' and transmutes matter, raising it to immateriality, 'Till all becomes [God's] cloudless glass,/ . . . Fixt by [His] spirit to a state/For evermore immaculate' ('L'Envoy').

Vaughan, like the Hermetists, spurns the grossness of matter, yet obscures the distinction between 'spirit' as refined matter and the immaterial soul or mind. Accordingly his response to Christian

[1] Discussed also by Miss Røstvig in the following chapter.

dogma will be different from Donne's and Herbert's. He almost explains away the Resurrection when he discovers '*prolusions* and strong *proofs* of our *restoration* laid out in *Nature*, besides the promise of the *God* of nature' (*The Mount of Olives*; compare 'Resurrection and Immortality'). On the other hand, his exclamation 'O that I were all Soul!' contrasts with Donne's conviction that 'the body is not the man, nor the soul is not the man, but the union of these two make up the man'. He has therefore little interest in the paradox of the Incarnation as the meeting of two natures in Christ. The presence of the Redeemer in 'the fields of *Bethani* which shine/All now as fresh as *Eden*' ('Ascension-day') or his roaming at night 'where *trees* and *herbs* did watch and peep/And wonder' ('The Night') move him deeply through these associations with Nature and Paradise. His attention and hopes are not focused on the historical fulfilment of the Atonement, but on the 'mystic birth' of the Lord of Life in the individual soul ('Christ's Nativity'), on the process of regeneration described in the symbolism of the 'spiritual alchemists' ('Regeneration').

The religious poet at times imitates the conceited style of his predecessors, but a personal intensity is only felt in the mystical paradoxes that enlarge the imagination rather than perplex the mind:

> Most blest believer he!
> Who in that land of darkness and blinde eyes . . .
> Did at mid-night speak with the Sun!
>
> There is in God (some say)
> A deep but dazling darkness
>
> ('The Night')

The peculiar reverberation of Vaughan's poetry, when contrasted with Herbert's, its emotional impact and stronger appeal, at least for the Romantically inclined, proceed from a closer connection between his natural symbolism and the deeper layers of the archetypal imagination. From such hidden sources spring his dreams of Eden and Paradise, his yearning for a far-off 'country' or 'home' (a frequent word in *Silex*), his constant quest or 'search', ascent or 'Ascension', and the recurrent image of the archetypal Mount, the holy Hill and 'those *clear heights* which above tempests shine' ('Joy'). His light imagery is insistent and individual through the perception of light as substance – the 'firie-liquid light' of heaven ('Midnight') – as life or soul – the 'Sunnie seed' ('Cock-crowing') or Hermetic star-soul in each creature – and through the poet's sensitiveness to dawn as a new birth: 'mornings, new creations are' ('Day-spring';

compare 'Rules and Lessons'). The frequent association of light with
silence or the starry heavens rather than the radiance of noon is
remarkable. Hence the poet's ability to strike the deeper chords in his
celebration of 'Night'.

The pervasive water-symbolism suggests a longing for purity and
lustration, but is related to the feeling for life and growth expressed in
the symbols of vegetation. The reader of Vaughan 'shall feel/That
God is true, as herbs unseen/Put on their youth and green' ('Starre').
The analogical imagination alone was at work in the Biblical parable
which suggested 'The Seed growing secretly', but the poem achieves
the perfect fusion of the sensible and the spiritual through the
emotion awakened in the poet's soul by the actual life of the seed
underground: 'Dear, secret *Greenness*! nurst below/Tempests and
windes, and winter-nights . . .' Fancy plays with outward form.
Imagination here pierces at once to the heart of matter and the heart
of life: life, '*a quickness which my God hath kist*' ('Quickness'). This
realism of the symbolic imagination extends to all the recurrent
images and lends substance to spiritual emotions. Since 'not a wind
can stir' but straight the poet thinks of God ('Come, come . . .'), the
sensuous reality of breath and wind may be given to the Spirit who
first moved upon the face of the waters ('Midnight', 'Water-fall').

Neither the modes of sensibility nor the symbolic imagination
invite ambiguity or ambivalence in the poetry of Vaughan. His 'sad
delight' has nothing in common with Crashaw's. A unity of tone and
feeling prevails. Emotions freely mingle in a nostalgic pensiveness
without sharp contrasts or changes. Vaughan is the poet of osmosis
rather than transubstantiation. His debased use of 'mystical' in 'The
Water-fall' has been criticized by Empson, but it is the only apt word
to convey this emotional halo about things, this sense of their spiritual
depth, at once intense and vague, though more precise than the later
Romantic emotions because of its associations with a definite
theology or philosophy.

Therefore, Vaughan's greater moments are moments of balance
between mystery and clarity, symbolic suggestion and precise
allusion:

> God's silent, searching flight:
> When my Lords head is fill'd with dew, and all
> His locks are wet with the clear drops of night;
> His still, soft call;
> His knocking time; The souls dumb watch,
> When Spirits their fair kinred catch.
>
> ('The Night')

196 POETRY AND PROSE 1540-1674

With a few exceptions, isolated lines rather than poems have this haunting power, for the author of *Silex Scintillans* has neither the unerring artistry of Herbert nor the sustained intensity of Donne. Emotion cools and the style flags when vision or intuition fade into moral meditation. Despite a feeling for aural beauty – 'How shril are silent tears?' ('Admission') – the music of the verse is uneven. In the association of colloquiality and imaginative vision, Vaughan may reach heights unattained by the more conceited 'metaphysicals': 'I saw Eternity the other night' ('The World'). However, the lack of wit is felt when his plain utterance – in description or meditation – is no longer the language of the imagination. His literal conception of poetic sincerity, unlike the sophisticated simplicity of Herbert, looks towards the Romantic ideal; 'O! 'tis an easie thing/To write and sing;/ But to write true, unfeigned verse/Is very hard!' ('Anguish').

Yet this is how Thomas Traherne (1637–74), parson, poet, and mystic, wrote with ease among Restoration gentlemen:

> A simple Light, Transparent Words, a Strain
> That lowly creeps, yet maketh Mountains plain,
> Brings down the highest Mysteries to sense
> And Keeps them there, that is Our Excellence:
> At that we aim. . . .
>
> ('The Author to the Critical Peruser')

The true importance of Traherne, however, is not in the history of poetry, but in the history of thought and religious sensibility. Alone among the 'metaphysicals' he expounds a philosophy and delivers a message. Though influenced by the Hermetic writings, Plato and the long line of Platonists, from Alexandria to Florence and Cambridge, though well-read in the moralists of antiquity and probably acquainted with the more daring sects of the Puritan age, he only borrowed what responded to the needs of his mind and sensibility. He modified and made his own such ideas as entered into his Gospel of Felicity – including the Biblical texts he turned to his own ends.

His originality proceeds from a conjunction of self-centredness and expansiveness. The solipsistic absorption of the new-born child was the image of his own consciousness:

> Unfelt, unseen let those things be
> Which to thy Spirit were unknown,
> When to thy Blessed Infancy
> The World, thy Self, thy God was shewn.
>
> ('The Instruction')

Then indeed, 'The World was more in me, then I in it' ('Silence'). The child and the mystic, both inflamed 'With restlesse longing Heavenly Avarice' ('Desire') discover that 'self LOV is the Basis of all Lov' (*Centuries of Meditation*, iv. 55). But since the poet is 'a lover of company, a delighter in equals' whose Soul 'hateth Solitude' ('A Thanksgiving and Prayer for the Nation') – almost a Whitman figure – self-love overflows in a love directed to all men. A love still egocentric, for Traherne looks on his 'lovely companions' as his 'peculiar treasures' and seeks society in order that others may glorify him as he glorifies God.

Out of this intense awareness of his individual existence springs the poet's 'Insatiableness' (a revealing title): 'There's not a Man but covets and desires/A Kingdom, yea a World; nay, he aspires/To all the Regions he can see/Beyond the Hev'ns Infinity' ('Mis-apprehension'). However, man's desire is infinitely satisfied: 'all is yours', as Saint Paul and Seneca had proclaimed, for the world is seated in your soul. Distance is illusion; perception is spiritual possession since every object 'Was present in the Apple of my Eye' and 'in my Soul a Thought/Begot, or was' ('My Spirit'). Traherne anticipates Berkeley's theory of vision and the celebrated *esse est percipi*.

The poet, however, does not really call in question the reality of the outer world. His main point is that 'not to appear is not to be'. Thus his subjectivism supports the Christian and Hermetic notion that the prime function of man is to contemplate the Creation and glorify the Creator. But the mystic presses his claim further. A 'Mind exerted, will *see* infinity' ('My Spirit'), for 'We first by Nature all things boundless see' ('The City'). Though the astronomical discoveries and the theory of endless space fired his imagination, like Henry More's, Traherne's passion for the unbounded really proceeds from the dilation of an 'enlarged Soul', his vivid sense of the unlimited 'capacity' of the mind and his quenchless thirst for infinite treasures. The same instinct directs the contemplation of eternity by the soul 'whose Glory it is that it can see before and after its Existence into Endless Spaces' (*Centuries*, i. 55). At other times, however, Eternity is a more mystical experience, a vision of the world in glory, of the works of God in their changeless essence and beauty:

'The Corn was Orient and Immortal Wheat, which never should be reaped, nor was ever sown. I thought it had stood from everlasting to everlasting . . .'

(*Centuries*, iii. 3)

In the illumination of 'Innocence' (primal or recaptured) 'the ancient Light of *Eden*' shines over the present world and in the poet's soul. Paradise is here and now, not a distant dream. Even when the themes are alike, Traherne and Vaughan speak from a different point of view. Both poets herald the Romantic glorification of childhood, though Traherne's message alone is consistently based on the illumination of infancy and the conviction of original innocence. To both, however, childhood is essentially a symbol of a spiritual state. But Vaughan only longs to travel back: Traherne lives in a Paradise regained.

Religious contemplation in the Gospel of Felicity becomes a contemplation of the universe. Despite the idealistic transmutation of things into thoughts, attention is focused on what sense and the imagination can reach and apprehend. Though free from sensuality, the celebration of the senses in the 'Thanksgiving for the Body' strikes a note as yet unheard. The Christian mysteries are still an occasion for wonder, but the significance of the Redemption has suffered a sea-change when Christ is presented as the 'Heir of the whole world' who taught us 'how to possess all the things in Heaven and Earth after His similitude': 'To this poor Bleeding Naked Man did all the Corn and Wine and Oyl, and Gold and Silver in the World minister in an Invisible Manner, even as he was exposed Lying and Dying upon the Cross' (*Centuries*, i. 60).

In his absence of sin-consciousness, in his faith in the natural instincts, in his reliance on Reason and his conviction that 'Things pure and true are Obvious unto Sence' ('Ease') and irresistibly taught by Nature as long as it is uncorrupted by Custom, Traherne departs from the Christian tradition of Herbert, Crashaw and Vaughan. Despite his confidence in intuition (or because of it) he stands on the threshold of the age of *Christianity not Mysterious* and already looks in the direction of eighteenth-century primitivism. In his sense of wonder and illuminated vision he stands alone.

'Amazement was my Bliss' cried the mystic in 'Wonder', and the poet claimed, with Theophilus Gale, that 'Affections are the greatest Wits'[1] The purity of impression will shine through the transparency of the style:

> How like an Angel came I down!
>
> ('Wonder')

> Order the Beauty even of Beauty is
>
> ('The Vision')

---

[1] In *The Court of the Gentiles*: see Traherne's 'Commonplace Book', f 76 r°.

Lyrical ejaculation, though fitfully Blake-like in 'The Rapture', is usually artless to the point of formlessness. Rhapsodical accumulation, of Whitman-like amplitude in the 'Thanksgivings', proves wearisome in the shorter lyrics. Only the prose of the *Centuries of Meditation* reaches a higher excellence when it beats with rapture and burns with beauty, as in the record of the child's intimations of immortality.

The diversity disclosed by the divine poems of Herbert and Crashaw, Vaughan and Traherne shows that the distinguishing mark of the main 'metaphysical' poets is the individuality of their inspiration and style. It also suggests a historical evolution of wider significance in the modes of thought and sensibility and the forms of poetic expression. The literary historian could find confirmation of it in the lyrics of the minor poets though the various trends overlap chronologically.

One could speak perhaps with more propriety of a 'school of Herbert' than a 'school of Donne'. In tone and temper, sweetness and strength, subdued emphasis and deliberate understatement, in the homeliness of diction and imagery and their counterpointed rhythm, the religious lyrics of Thomas Beedome and Ralph Knevet, Edmund Elys and Nathaniel Wanley are obviously modelled on *The Temple*. The superiority of Herbert's approach and style in devotional poetry appears when the occasional felicity of these uninspired imitations is contrasted with the relative failure of a greater poet, Robert Herrick, when he affects a rustic yet elegant simplicity in his 'Thanksgiving to God, for his Home.' On the theme of Crucifixion the difference in intensity and thoughtfulness between the Vicar of Dean Prior and the parson of Bemerton is obvious. The baroque flame and luxuriance of Crashaw are trimmed and tempered in the poems on the Babe who lies 'the Lillie-banks among'. The vision of 'Eternitie' and 'The white Island: or place of the Blest' combines in a simple, 'romantic' mood Vaughan-like imagery and classical terseness.

While the strains of Donne and Herbert meet and mingle in the divine poems of John Collop and Thomas Philipott, William Strode and Patrick Carey are closer to Herrick and look forward to the Restoration. Saintsbury was attracted by Carey's absence of 'pose', but the 'Crashaw-like "Crucifixion"' is Crashaw diluted and sentimentalized, and 'the fine "Crux via Caelorum"' is no doubt fine, but with the straightforward, rhetorical impulse of Dryden's lyrics.

With the beautiful 'Nox nocti indicat Scientiam' of William Habington another trend had appeared: an already Vaughan-like contemplativeness in Nature, a philosophic meditativeness smoothly ranging from the personal to the great commonplaces. The line extends through John Hall and William Hammond to the lyrics of Thomas Flatman, who praised solitude and melancholy, exalted 'Thoughts' and the pleasures of the imagination in pre-Romantic fashion without the mysticism of Traherne. Eclecticism, however, prevailed before the Restoration. John Hall achieved a happy balance between the nearness of Herbert and the naïvety of Traherne in 'A Pastoral Hymn'. Hammond sweetly imitated 'The Forerunners' in 'Grey Hairs', yet he reminds us of Marvell and his urbane wit when he combines human and divine love, pastoralism and the Bible, an hedonistic awareness of the power of 'sense' and platonic philosophy, in 'A Dialogue upon Death' between Phillis and Damon. His obsession with the stars, his sense of secrecy and philosophic musings, recall the themes and inspiration of Vaughan in 'The World'. Yet his obtrusive scientific imagery and his abruptness are reminiscent of Donne in other poems. Douglas Bush declared Hammond's *Poems* (1647) 'not distinctive'. The critic may accept the aesthetic judgement but to the historian of literary taste there are few poets more 'characteristic' of their age. He offers in a few pieces a full though feeble illustration of the cross-currents in the religious lyric of the seventeenth century.

10

ANDREW MARVELL AND THE CAROLINE POETS

Maren-Sofie Røstvig

The Caroline poets are a mixed lot. When measured by the high standard of the generation that preceded them, some of them must be said to represent an attenuated and even a debased tradition. This is certainly true of John Cleveland and Abraham Cowley among the metaphysical poets, of Henry More among the Spenserians, and among the Cavaliers even Robert Herrick on occasion falls short of the standard of excellence usually associated with his name. On the other hand the verse of a typical second-generation metaphysical poet like Henry Vaughan carries the stamp of his own personality to such a degree that recognition is immediate; a poem by Vaughan is not easily confused with one by George Herbert, although theme and title may be the same. And once we come to Robert Herrick and Andrew Marvell, comparison with the preceding generation becomes invidious. These are poets who must be judged by standards they themselves created; both are perfectionists, and both combine the best of two traditions. Although a classicist, Herrick on occasion exploits techniques that are distinctly metaphysical, while Marvell's metaphysical subtlety is embodied in verse the formal elegance of which is outstanding.

Although the three traditions associated with the names of Edmund Spenser, John Donne, and Ben Jonson mark most of the poetry written during the second quarter of the seventeenth century, a distinct tendency may be observed to favour Horatian odes and epistles and themes associated with these forms. Among these themes none was more popular than the praise of the happiness of country life. *Castara* (1634, 1635, and 1640) by the Roman Catholic poet William Habington illustrates the change, in that most of the new poems added to the editions of 1635 and 1640 are Horatian odes and epistles, while the first edition consists largely of songs and sonnets in the Elizabethan manner. The sonnet, of course, was distinctly unfashionable by 1625, while songs and pastorals remained fairly popular. The poets did not always distinguish between pastorals on the one hand and, on the other, rural odes in the manner of Horace, but one may nevertheless submit as a reasonably valid generalization that rural odes and epistles became more popular than the pastoral, possibly because they were capable of presenting more complex arguments

The history of the epic in this period is a curious one; the heroic tradition was exploited by poets so intent on presenting religious or philosophical arguments that there is virtually no action. This is true of the epics written by Joseph Beaumont, Henry More, and Edward Benlowes. While Beaumont and More used the Spenserian stanza, Edward Benlowes (*Theophila*, 1652) created a stanza pattern of his own consisting of three lines, and into these he crammed so many conceits that the argument may be difficult to follow. Both Henry More (the Cambridge Neoplatonist) and Edward Benlowes, like Dante, based the structure of their epics on numbers possessed of a rich religious symbolism in keeping with the subject-matter. The popular pattern-poem, which we find in Robert Herrick's verse as well as in George Herbert's, is a simplified version of this tradition of so structuring a poem that its form becomes meaningful. If a poem is concerned with an altar, for example, then its printed outline should be that of an altar. This type of formal manipulation occurs more frequently in this period than in the poetry of the late sixteenth or the early seventeenth century, a circumstance which suggests that the desire must have been particularly strong, at this time, to compress as much meaning into a poem as possible. If the form, too, could be meaningful, so much the better.

The Renaissance fondness for emblem books continued well into the second half of the seventeenth century, but the genre underwent a process of popularization which inevitably entailed a loss of intellectual subtlety. An emblem consists of three parts that together constitute a whole: a motto, a symbolic picture, and an exposition. Such was the high reputation of emblems in the sixteenth century that they were recommended as part of the education of a prince; their appeal was aristocratic, and their content learned. By the 1630s however, emblems had become sufficiently simple to appeal to a wider audience, a development partly due to the fact that Protestants and Roman Catholics alike found the genre a useful vehicle for pious propaganda. The contrast between the early and the late phase is felt on comparing Geoffrey Whitney's statement (in *A Choice of Emblemes*, 1586) that he presented his book to 'the learned and those that are of good judgment', with the professed intention of George Wither (*A Collection of Emblemes*, 1635) to 'please/And profit vulgar Judgements (by the view/Of what they ought to follow or eschew.)'. And Quarles, like Wither, preferred what the latter called 'plaine and vulgar notions, season'd with a little *Pleasantnesse*, and relish'd with a moderate *Sharpnesse*.'

Francis Quarles (1592–1644) began his career as a poet with Biblical paraphrases, and these proved so popular that they appeared in a collected edition in 1632, and frequent reprints were called for in the years that followed. Even greater fame followed upon the publication, in 1635, of his *Emblemes, Divine and Morall*; a second volume appeared in 1638 (*Hieroglyphicks of the Life of Man*). Quarles fetched his emblems from two Continental collections, Herman Hugo's *Pia Desideria* (1624) and Phillippe de Mallery's *Typus Mundi* (1627), and their contents may be described as the Bible moralized. Quarles's vituperative passages on the world form a Caroline analogue to the impassioned rhetoric of Edmund Spenser. The *Emblemes* commence with the Satanic rhetoric of the Fall – we overhear the dialogue between Eve and the serpent – and then the reader is presented with various aspects of the lamentable state of the postlapsarian world whose very pleasures are tainted and indicative of decay. Man's fallen condition is best expressed in terms of paradox, as in Emblem I, 6:

> How is the anxious soul of man befool'd
>   In his desire,
> That thinks an hectic fever may be cool'd
>   In flames of fire?
>
> . . .
>
> Let wit, and all her study'd plots effect
>   The best they can;
> Let smiling fortune prosper and perfect
>   What wit began;
> Let earth advise with both, and so project
>   A happy man;
> Let wit and fawning fortune vie their best;
>   He may be blest
> With all the earth can give; but earth can give no rest.

It should be stressed, perhaps, that Quarles was a staunch Royalist and no Puritan; Phineas Fletcher and Edward Benlowes were among his best friends, and the quality of his verse is certainly far better than anything offered in the collections of pious verse published by the few Puritans who overcame their reluctance to employ verse in the service of God.

The gay worldliness of the Cavaliers is possibly responsible for the fact that a poet like Quarles tended to be placed among the Puritans by the nineteenth century, when Quarles's emblems were still cherished and reprinted for their sound moral and religious sentiments. Richard Lovelace (1618–57) and Sir John Suckling (1609–42) are splendid prototypes of the Cavalier poet – handsome men both, and men with a ready purse, a ready wit and a ready sword. John Aubrey, the Restoration biographer, calls Suckling an 'extraordinary accomplished Gent.' who 'grew famous at Court for his readie sparkling witt'. Suckling was the greatest gallant, too, of his time, 'and the greatest Gamester, both for Bowling and Cards', so that his sisters would come to the bowling-green, 'crying for feare he should loose all their Portions'. And Richard Lovelace was one of the handsomest men in England according to Aubrey, 'but proud'. Lovelace was thrown twice into prison, and it was while in prison in 1648 that he prepared his poems for the press.

The Cavalier mood is admirably expressed in Lovelace's 'To Lucasta, Going to the Warres', the last two lines of which have become proverbial: 'I could not love thee (Deare) so much,/Lov'd I not Honour more.' The combination of Epicurean sensuousness with Stoic fortitude in 'To Althea, From Prison' is equally typical:

> When thirsty griefe in Wine we steepe,
> When Healths and draughts go free,
> Fishes that tipple in the Deepe,
> Know no such Libertie.
>
> . . .
>
> Stone Walls doe not a Prison make,
> Nor Iron bars a Cage;
> Mindes innocent and quiet take
> That for an Hermitage;
> If I have freedome in my Love,
> And in my soule am free;
> Angels alone that sore above,
> Injoy such Liberty.

The image of the Stoic Wise Man, unperturbed by war and disastrous fortune, was one that served the defeated Royalists well in their hour of need. Lovelace's 'Orpheus to Beasts' reveals his ability to write pure poetry, and it is tempting to feel, behind this melodious lament for the slaying of Eurydice, a dirge for the passing of an age:

I

Here, here, oh here *Euridice*,
Here was she slaine;
Her soule 'still'd through a veine:
The Gods knew lesse
That time Divinitie,
Than ev'n, ev'n these
Of brutishnesse.

II

Oh could you view the Melodie
Of ev'ry grace,
And Musick of her face,
You'd drop a teare,
Seeing more Harmonie
In her bright eye,
Than now you heare.

The paradox presented in the third line is grasped on recalling that
the Renaissance believed that *spirits* were produced in the blood,
and that these spirits connect the soul with the body. Eurydice's
soul, then, is released from her body by the agency which usually
serves to connect the two. The fact that the first 'Here' is identical
in sound with the last 'hear' creates a circular effect so that the
poem enacts the circle of harmony so rudely broken with the slaying
of her who was harmony personified. As in tragedy, the effect is one
of catharsis; the loss of harmony is bewailed in a harmony so
exquisite that the death of Eurydice seems redeemed.

Sir John Suckling probably spent more time on gambling than on
the composition of poetry, but his output, although slender, places
him firmly among the better minor poets of his age. Despite the
greater popularity, at the time, of Abraham Cowley's love poems,
Suckling is still remembered with affection while Cowley is not. It is
often said that all the world loves a lover, but it ought to be added
that the preference is distinctly for a high-spirited lover of the kind
who can exclaim, with Suckling: 'Out upon it! I have lov'd/Three
whole days together'. And Suckling's advice to the unsuccessful
suitor is a fine example of Cavalier gaiety:

Why so pale and wan, fond lover?
Prithee, why so pale?
Will, when looking well can't move her,
Looking ill prevail?
Prithee, why so pale?

. . .
Quit, quit, for shame; this will not move,
    This cannot take her;
If of herself she will not love,
    Nothing can make her:
    The devil take her!

Suckling was a splendid pricker of balloons inflated with fashion-able pseudo-Platonic conceits. The tone of voice in the lines 'To Mistress Cicely Crofts' is distinctly ironical:

O that I were all soul, that I might prove
    For you as fit a love
As you are for an angel; for, I know,
None but pure spirits are fit loves for you.

Such is her skill in the philosophy of love that she can imagine 'a fire/Void of all heat, a love without desire', and the lady is equally learned in theology:

    You think, and you profess,
That souls may have a plenitude of joy
Although their bodies meet not to employ.

But I must needs confess, I do not find
    The motions of my mind
So purifi'd as yet, but at the best
My body claims in them an interest.

The satirical compromise suggested is to enjoy the body first and then the mind:

There rests but this, that whilst we sorrow here,
    Our bodies may draw near:
And when no more their joys they can extend,
Then let our souls begin where they did end.

Like Lovelace and Suckling, Thomas Carew (1594?–1640) died young. Carew, again like Lovelace and Suckling, favoured erotic themes, but, unlike them, his style often owes more to Donne than to Ben Jonson. The following 'Song', although prevailingly classical in the manner associated with Ben Jonson, contains a reference to scholastic thought (in line four) which strikes a distinctly metaphysical note:

Aske me no more where *Jove* bestowes,
When *June* is past, the fading rose:
For in your beauties orient deepe,
These flowers as in their causes, sleepe.

. . .
Aske me no more if East or West,
The Phenix builds her spicy nest:
For unto you at last shee flies,
And in your fragrant bosome dyes.

'Boldnesse in love' may have fetched its basic comparison from
emblem literature; the poem reads like versified comment on a
drawing of the marigold and the sun:

Marke how the bashfull morne, in vaine
Courts the amorous Marigold,
With sighing blasts, and weeping raine;
Yet she refuses to unfold.
But when the Planet of the day,
Approacheth with his powerfull ray,
Then she spreads, then she receives
His warmer beames into her virgin leaves.

This shows the purpose for which descriptions of nature were
usually introduced: they illustrate an argument or prove a point.
Running brooks and stones could be 'moralized' in a rather trite
and unimaginative manner, but the better poets used the technique to advantage.

Abraham Cowley (1618–67) and Thomas Stanley (1625–78) are
minor figures of considerable historical significance. Stanley
translated Pico della Mirandola's *Platonick Discourse on Love*, no
doubt because of the great popularity of the subject. Stanley's
version of Pico, though, is a summary rather than a translation. It
is interesting that he should have included it in his *Poems* of 1651,
many of which are distinctly Platonic. In 'The Dedication to Love'
Stanley describes Love as an omnipotent power capable of in-
verting the course of heaven and moving the firm earth. By its
'mysterious chains' it may even effect a union between the two
parts of the 'long-since torn Hermaphrodite'. This is an allusion
to the Platonic account of creation according to which man was
first created as an androgyne or bisexual being, the division into
two sexes representing a later development. Thomas Randolph
(1605–35) made fun of the whole idea in his lines 'Upon an
Hermaphrodite' (published in 1640). He was delighted by the
absurdity of the whole idea:

Sir or Madam, choose you whether!
Nature twists you both together
And makes thy soul two garbs confess.

. . .
Adam till his rib was lost,
Had both sexes thus engrossed.
When Providence our Sire did cleave,
And out of Adam carved Eve,
Then did man 'bout wedlock treat,
To make his body up complete.
Thus matrimony speaks but thee
In a grave solemnity.
For man and wife make but one right
Canonical hermaphrodite.

Abraham Cowley wrote love poems both for and against 'the
Platonicks', but none of them possesses much appeal today, extremely popular though they were at the time. Samuel Johnson
admitted that they might contain striking thoughts, but the poems
are not 'well wrought':

The compositions are such as might have been written for penance by a
hermit, or for hire by a philosophical rhymer who had only heard of another
sex; for they turn the mind only on the writer, whom . . . we sometimes
esteem as learned, and sometimes despise as trifling, always admire as
ingenious, and always condemn as unnatural.

(*Life of Cowley*)

Several of Cowley's love poems touch on themes subsequently
exploited by Andrew Marvell; thus Cowley's 'My Dyet', 'Love and
Life' and 'The Long Life' invite comparison with Marvell's 'To His
Coy Mistress'. On comparing the two poets, one sees at once how
lacking in semantic density Cowley's verse is, and how inferior in
formal elegance. As Dr Johnson put it, these love lyrics are not 'well
wrought'. Cowley's translations of classical poetry have more
literary value and greater historical significance. His translations of
the odes of Pindar and his original poems written in the irregular
Pindaric style helped to create the vogue for pseudo-Pindarics so
typical of the neoclassical period. Cowley's Pindaric ode on wit
gained universal fame, and even Dr Johnson remarked that it was
'almost without a rival'. Cowley's delightful *Essays and Discourses, In
Verse and Prose* (1668) are largely concerned with the idea of human
happiness as presented by poets like Horace and Virgil. The
felicitous combination of prose with verse, of a seriously held
philosophy of life with a witty and urbane prose style secured a
lasting reputation for Cowley's essays during the Restoration and
the eighteenth century.
    Robert Herrick (1591–1674) outranks the poets so far

mentioned, both in the quality and the quantity of his verse. His surprising longevity helps to explain the quantity. Suckling was approximately thirty-three when he died, Lovelace forty, while Herrick kept writing poetry up to the publication of his *Hesperides* (1648) when he was some fifty-seven years old.

The conflict, in Herrick's verse, between Herrick the pagan and Herrick the minister of God is easily exaggerated. Herrick decided in favour of an academic career rather late, after having served for some time as apprentice to his uncle, Sir William Herrick, who was a goldsmith. Herrick therefore obtained his first degree in 1617, his second in 1620. After this time he spent several years in London in the company of Ben Jonson and other wits about town, and he tended to think in terms of the Law as a career, rather than the Church. By 1627 he had become Chaplain to the Duke of Buckingham, and it was not till 1629 that he obtained the position for which he is remembered, when he was appointed Vicar of Dean Prior in Devonshire. Like Donne, therefore, Herrick was no longer a young man when he committed himself to the Church, so that many of his poems must have been written before he was ordained. Then, secondly, it is important to observe that Herrick often modifies the pagan character of a classical theme by adding Christian sentiments. Thus 'To the Virgins, to make much of Time' concludes by asking them to *marry*:

> Then be not coy, but use your time;
>   And while ye may, goe marry:
> For having lost but once your prime,
>   You may for ever tarry.

A third argument must also be advanced: like so many of his contemporaries, Herrick considered poetry as an art firmly based on classical traditions. This means that a poem is viewed as a conscious creation (as 'artificial' in the Renaissance sense, which was highly complimentary). However, since so much of Herrick's verse is occasional, or seems to be so, the temptation to identify the poetry with the poet is almost irresistible; the close connection, though, between many of Herrick's poems and specific classical themes and genres ought to warn against placing too much emphasis on the biographical element. It is hazardous, to say the least, to conclude that because 'His Return to London' – written after Herrick had been expelled from Dean Prior – refers to his years away from London as an *exile*, this is an indication that Herrick was dissatisfied with his vocation as a minister. The poem is simply written in the classical tradition of the praise of Rome, the terminology being so impeccably classical that Herrick refers to himself as 'a free-born *Roman*'.

'The Argument of his Book' is a summary of Herrick's favourite themes:

> I sing of *Brooks*, of *Blossomes*, *Birds*, and *Bowers*:
> Of *April*, *May*, of *June*, and *July*-Flowers.
> I sing of *May-poles*, *Hock-carts*, *Wassails*, *Wakes*,
> Of *Bride-grooms*, *Brides*, and of their *Bridall-cakes*.
> I write of *Youth*, of *Love*, and have Accesse
> By these, to sing of cleanly-*Wantonnesse*.
>
> . . .
>
> I write of *Hell*; I sing (and ever shall)
> Of *Heaven*, and hope to have it after all.

'I write of *Hell*' – is this an admission of guilt? Is Herrick saying that to write of all this is to write of Hell? Or is he, perhaps, being ironical at the expense of the Puritans to whom his 'cleanly-*Wantonnesse*' would indeed be proof of extreme sinfulness? Although the second alternative is plausible enough, a third interpretation is possible. Hell and Heaven may be metaphors for the parting and meeting of friends or lovers, since this is how Herrick himself defines parting: 'Deare, though to part it be a Hell, / Yet *Dianeme* now farewell' ('To Dianeme'). If this is so, then Herrick confesses freely that he sings of the Hell and the Heaven of lovers, but that he nevertheless hopes for Heaven in its religious sense. Such an interpretation is the more likely as Herrick's religious verse (his 'Noble Numbers') is concerned more with God's mercy than his wrath. Like John Milton and Henry More, Herrick seems to have considered the delights of the senses as neither good nor evil in themselves, and as supremely good when innocent. And, like some theologians and philosophers, Herrick defines evil as absence of being:

> Evill no Nature hath; the losse of good
> Is that which gives to sin a livelihood.

('Evill')

In 'To Daffadills' the sense of the tragic brevity of life – a theme often touched on by Horace in his odes – combines with a profoundly pious realization that if Time causes decay as well as growth,[1] it also permits us to exchange earth for heaven. Perhaps

---

[1] The idea that time causes both growth and decay was a frequently-discussed paradox. See p 241 for comments on Marvell's use of this paradox in 'To his Coy Mistress'.

the first impression created by this well-known lyric is of the strong
bond of love connecting all God's creatures; its concern with Time
is underlined by the circumstance that the printed outline resembles that of an hour-glass:

> Faire Daffadills, we weep to see
> You haste away so soone:
> As yet the early-rising Sun
> Has not attain'd his Noone.
> Stay, stay
> Untill the hasting day
> Has run
> But to the Even-song;
> And, having pray'd together, we
> Will goe with you along.
>
> We have short time to stay, as you,
> We have as short a Spring;
> As quick a growth to meet Decay,
> As you, or any thing.
> We die,
> As your hours doe, and drie
> Away,
> Like to the Summers raine;
> Or as the pearles of Mornings dew
> Ne'r to be found againe.

The comparison is no mere poetic exaggeration; Augustine had
compared the ages of man to the seasons or to the course of a single
day, the various cycles of the Sun being the symbol of a complete
cycle of life. In the eyes of God, a thousand years are as a day, and
the short 24-hour cycle not much different from the larger seasonal
cycle, or from the greatest cycle of all when the sphere of the whole
universe returns to the point where its movement first began.
Herrick's lyric conveys exactly the same feeling that one cycle of the
Sun equals another, since Time, whether long or short, is a mere
parenthesis in Eternity. Through the image of the pearls of dew,
however, the precious character of life is conveyed and its connection with Eternity. The image invokes the parable of the pearl
told by Christ according to Matthew, xiii. 45–6, where the pearl is
identified as the Kingdom of Heaven (i.e. Eternity), and many a
poet and preacher had used the drop of dew in the same manner as
a symbol of our immortal part which evaporates (dies) in order to
ascend to Heaven.

The tradition of so shaping a stanza that the outline represents an object related to the theme is of classical origin, and it experienced something of a revival in England during the first half of the seventeenth century. The last poem in *Hesperides*, 'The pillar of Fame', is an obvious instance of this technique, a more subtle one being provided by 'An Epithalamie to Sir Thomas Southwell and his Ladie':

> Now, now's the time; so oft by truth
> Promis'd sho'd come to crown your youth.
>> Then Faire ones, doe not wrong
>> Your joyes, by staying long:
>> Or let Love's fire goe out,
>> By lingring thus in doubt:
>> But learn, that Time once lost,
>> Is ne'r redeem'd by cost.
> Then away; come, *Hymen* guide
> To the bed, the bashfull Bride.
>
> . . .
>
> Night now hath watch'd her self half blind;
> Yet not a Maiden-head resign'd!
>> 'Tis strange, ye will not flie
>> To Love's sweet mysterie.
>> Might yon Full-Moon the sweets
>> Have, promis'd to your sheets;
>> She soon wo'd leave her spheare,
>> To be admitted there.
> Then away; come, *Hymen* guide
> To the bed, the bashfull Bride.

This type of stanza-pattern had been used in poems about altars, but here it may be intended to provoke associations also with the bed referred to so emphatically in the last two lines. If so, then the merging of the concepts could be taken to imply that marriage is a sacrament.

Herrick's treatment of the epithalamic tradition combines English and classical, pagan and Christian, and so does his adaptation of the themes derived from Horace's and Virgil's praise of the happiness of country life. This was a theme that Herrick returned to again and again – in 'The Country life, to the Honoured M. End. Porter', for example, or again 'The Hock-cart, or Harvest home: To the Right Honourable, Mildmay, Earle of Westmorland'. Closest to the classical tradition comes 'A Country life: To his Brother, M. Tho: Herrick', a worthy companion piece to the poems written in praise of country life by Ben Jonson, William Habington, or the Earl of Westmorland himself (*Otia Sacra*, 1648). Herrick, like Horace, associates country life with virtue and innocence; it teaches man how to confine his desires and to realize that 'Riches have their proper stint,/In the contented mind, not mint.' Those who always 'have the itch/Of craving more, are never rich.' Despite its simplicity, though, country life abounds with many blessings, chief of which is 'the function of a wife', as chaste as she is beautiful. The ideal Happy Man has a strong Stoic bias; he stands 'Centerlike, unmov'd,' and such is the man to whom these lines are addressed:

> . . . thou liv'st fearlesse; and thy face ne'r shewes
>   Fortune when she comes, or goes.
> But with thy equall thoughts, prepar'd dost stand,
>   To take her by the either hand:

Herrick praises his brother for having preferred 'The Countries sweet simplicity' to the corruption of the town, and identifies him with the Stoic Happy Man who is 'wisely true' to his own self 'and knowne to few'. The great cheerfulness of rural life is stressed even in the religious version presented in 'A Thanksgiving to God, for his House'. Everything about his house is small and unpretentious; the porch is low, his only guard is his harmless thoughts, and his very kitchen is small, yet such is God's mercy that no life could be richer:

> Lord, Thou hast given me a cell
>   Wherein to dwell;
> A little house, whose humble Roof
>   Is weather-proof;
>
>   . . .
>
> Some brittle sticks of Thorne or Briar
>   Make me a fire,
> Close by whose living coale I sit,
>   And glow like it.
>
>   . . .
>
> 'Tis thou that crown'st my glittering Hearth
>   With guiltlesse mirth;
> And giv'st me Wassaile Bowles to drink,
>   Spic'd to the brink.
>
>   . . .
>
> Thou mak'st my teeming Hen to lay
>   Her egg each day:
> Besides my healthfull Ewes to beare
>   Me twins each yeare . . .

However pleasing these poems on country life, Herrick's best known poems are his exquisite lyrics in praise of Julia. 'Upon Julia's Clothes' is rightly famous for its treatment of diction and rhythm; the rhythmical climax of the third line coincides with the semantic climax of the magnificently polysyllabic word, *liquefaction*:

> When as in silks my *Julia* goes,
> Then, then (me thinks) how sweetly flowes
> That liquefaction of her clothes.
>
> Next, when I cast mine eyes and see
> That brave Vibration each way free;
> O how that glittering taketh me!

By means of the one word, *liquefaction*, Julia is suddenly seen as a nymph covered only by the transparency of water. The comparison between one's mistress and the sun is one of the tritest of Renaissance themes, but here it is conveyed so delicately in the second stanza that it is realized only in the climactic phrase of the last line: 'O how that glittering taketh me!' Julia, then, is seen both as a nymph bathing in 'a well of living waters' to quote the *Song of Solomon*, and as a sun bathing in those fiery rays that cause the liquefaction of lovers and clothes alike. That the sun 'bathes' in the ocean may, perhaps, have been the association of ideas responsible for the imagery.

'To the Lark' merges the divine and the profane in a way that may seem utterly frivolous. Through its printed outline this poem raises an altar to the lark:

> Good speed, for I this day
> Betimes my Mattens say:
> Because I doe
> Begin to wooe:
> Sweet singing Lark,
> Be thou the Clark,
> And know thy when
> To say, *Amen.*
> And if I prove
> Blest in my love;
> Then thou shalt be
> High-Priest to me,
> At my returne,
> To Incense burne;
> And so to solemnize
> Love's, and my Sacrifice.

The robustness of Herrick's sense of humour is shown in his many two-line epigrams, one of which may be quoted here:

> *Batt* he gets children, not for love to reare 'em;
> But out of hope his wife might die to beare 'em.
>
> ('Upon Batt')

Different though they are, Andrew Marvell and Robert Herrick shared much the same fate in that their achievement as lyric poets went largely unnoticed by their own generation, and posthumous recognition arrived only towards the end of the nineteenth and the beginning of the twentieth century. It has been argued by Douglas Bush that Herrick's verse was 'too sensuously and smoothly Elizabethan' to become truly popular at the time when it was printed in 1648, when 'strong lines' in the metaphysical manner were fashionable. And during the Restoration period 'strong lines', too, became unfashionable, so that the neoclassical love lyric displays a simplicity which often borders on the inane.

Andrew Marvell (1621–78) was known to his contemporaries as the Member of Parliament for Hull who, after 1667, gained considerable notoriety as the supposed author of anonymous verse satires written against the Court. They had little or no knowledge of the body of poetry published posthumously in 1681, and Marvell therefore continued to be known largely as a patriot and a politician, the first decisive sign of an interest in his lyric verse being revealed by Charles Lamb in 1821 when he quoted five stanzas from 'The Garden' in one of his essays. The real break-through occurred exactly a hundred years later with T. S. Eliot's reassessment of metaphysical poetry in general and that of Andrew Marvell in particular.

During the first phase of the popularity, in this century, of the metaphysical school, the personality of John Donne tended to overshadow those of his followers, but of recent years scholars have distinguished more perceptively between the various metaphysical poets, at the same time that an increased knowledge of Renaissance traditions has revealed the surprising extent to which Marvell was capable of transforming familiar themes and techniques into poems that seem entirely fresh and original. Part of the secret of the attraction of Marvell's verse lies in a certain riddling quality which it possesses as a consequence of this process of transformation. The reader is exposed to a cat-and-mouse technique of such sly subtlety that he is sometimes left completely bewildered, and it is this element of the unresolved which has made the poetry of Andrew

Marvell the happy hunting-ground of critics bent on tearing out the heart of his mystery.

Andrew Marvell the man posits a similar puzzle; his friendship, during the 1640s, with Cavalier poets like Lovelace and Abraham Cowley is a matter of historical fact, but so is his friendship with John Milton and his allegiance to Oliver Cromwell. 'To His Noble Friend Mr Richard Lovelace, upon his Poems' (1649) deplores the degeneracy of the times in a manner typical of Royalist poets, but only a few years later Marvell wrote a panegyric on the occasion of the first anniversary of the government under Oliver Cromwell.

Did Marvell, then, change his mind or even turn his coat with the times, or is it possible to resolve these as it would seem conflicting attitudes into some sort of harmonious pattern? This particular problem is not merely a biographical one, since Charles as well as Cromwell figure in Marvell's verse, and so does the famous leader of the Parliamentary forces, Thomas, Lord Fairfax. It is as though Marvell, ironically aware of the intent scrutiny of posterity, perversely refused to be docketed and labelled, and so saw to it that he wrote on incompatible themes or subjects. Thus he paid homage to earthly as to heavenly love, he wrote poems praising and condemning gardens, and it is typical that each of the three poems acclaimed as masterpieces illustrates a different mode and a different area of human experience. 'An Horatian Ode upon Cromwel's Return from Ireland' deals with public issues, 'The Garden' praises complete withdrawal from the 'busie Companies of Men', while 'To his Coy Mistress' addresses the lady in a far from traditional manner but very much for the traditional reason. This great variety suggests a completely conscious attitude to the art of poetry, and a technique of writing which is basically dramatic. Indeed, several of Marvell's poems are dramatic dialogues or monologues, as, for example, 'A Dialogue between the Soul and Body' or 'The Mower's Song'. To add to the confusion, there is a sort of incompatibility embedded in the very web and woof of Marvell's verse, which combines a Cavalier flippancy with metaphysical profundity, sweetness and simplicity of form with great semantic density.

In reading Marvell, therefore, our expectation must be of the unexpected. If surprise is a major source of delight in poetry, then Marvell must be considered a past-master in the art of delighting his readers in this particular manner. More often than not, the element of surprise derives from a clever use of paradox, and to a casual reader Marvell's relentless pursuit of paradox may, perhaps, seem nothing but a clever mannerism. The rhetoric of paradox, though, may be a technique consciously chosen to do justice to the infinite complexity of life, and it has been so used by philosophers and poets alike since antiquity. The veritable epidemic of paradoxy which occurred during the Renaissance indicates complete familiarity with the classical tradition of the paradox, and proves that the age possessed sufficient intellectual and linguistic agility to exploit this tradition to advantage. As Rosalie L. Colie has put it,[1] paradox demands total control of thought and expression combined with an appearance of easy achievement – a statement which could be used to describe the peculiar quality of Andrew Marvell's verse.

One of the major problems in interpreting Marvell is resolved on considering the tradition of the paradoxical encomium, and this is the troublesome discrepancy so often felt between tone of voice and subject-matter. In 'The Garden', for example, the tone of voice is openly ironical except for one or two stanzas, but the subject is undoubtedly of serious religious import. This counterpointing of tone of voice and content is the chief technique employed in the paradoxical encomium, which praises what is usually not considered praiseworthy – folly, for example,[2] or complete inactivity. If the subject-matter is a serious one, the author must treat it in a deceptively facetious manner, and the other way round. It follows, therefore, that we must not be deceived by the quality which Pierre Legouis has described as Marvell's 'chatty' tone of voice; we must remember, instead, that the poetic *lusus* or jest, usually in the form of a paradox, has ancient roots in European literature. Indeed, to readers familiar with the Renaissance tradition of paradoxical writing, Marvell's ironical tone of voice combined with his frequent use of compressed verbal paradoxes is the plainest possible indication that his jests serve a serious purpose. From the Romantic period and until fairly recently the European mind has been largely out of sympathy with this tradition, and serious subjects have tended to be given a serious treatment. Earlier periods, however, were keenly aware of the danger of profaning the highest mysteries by presenting them directly, and this is a fear that Marvell himself gave direct expression to in the poem which he wrote 'On Mr Milton's Paradise lost'. No wonder, therefore, that Marvell

[1] 'Some Paradoxes in the Language of Things,' in *Reason and the Imagination*, ed. J. A. Mazzeo, New York and London, 1962, pp 93–128.
[2] The most famous example is the *Praise of Folly* by Erasmus, originally written in Latin (*Moriae Encomium*) and translated into English in 1549.

218 POETRY AND PROSE 1540-1674

preferred a joco-serious approach in so many of his poems and a
method involving a maximum of indirection.

Although Marvell uses simple words placed in a simple
syntactical pattern, his lines are usually so packed with meaning that
it is difficult to supply the necessary explanations without losing
sight of the poetry. In the case of a poet like John Donne, readers
are aware of the difficulty involved in understanding the text, and
the need for annotation is universally accepted and endured.
Marvell, however, wears his wisdom with such an air of gaiety that it
goes against the grain to submerge his lines in a flood of commentary. The solution adopted here is to select some poems for
relatively close study, while the rest will have to be treated in more
summary fashion. Some of the concepts referred to in the process
of explication will admittedly seem recondite rather than commonplace Renaissance lore, but we must not yield to the temptation
of using our own areas of ignorance to decide what may, or may not,
have been well known to the seventeenth century. It is, for example,
a Renaissance commonplace inherited from antiquity and the
Middle Ages that the universe is a finite sphere enclosing a system
of spheres, and that each is moved by a soul which inhabits it. The
circular shape, moreover, was taken to reflect the nature of the
Deity, both being without beginning or end, and the movement of
the spheres was attributed to love. All created things, and particularly the angelic spirits, circle around God, as Herrick explains in
the epigram defining Paradise ('Paradise is (as from the Learn'd I
gather)/*A quire of blest Soules circling in the Father.*'). When Marvell
wrote the poem which he entitled 'The Definition of Love', he
turned as a matter of course to the structure of the universe for the
terms in which he chose to convey his definition. He would also
have been bound to think in terms of the most famous definition of
love in the history of philosophy, the one given by Plato and so often
referred to by English poets from Spenser to Thomas Stanley and
Cowley. And according to Platonic thought love is the mutual
longing of the two separated halves of a circle; when the two meet,
they fall in love and thus the circle is again made complete. The
circle is an ancient symbol of perfection, and so is the concept of the
androgyne; to Marvell's generation both were familiar symbols of
prelapsarian perfection, and this state of perfection was marked by
complete union and rest (i.e. absence of striving, or movement),
while our fallen state is characterized by discord and division of
every kind, and by 'uncessant Labours'; Man is separated from
God, the creatures from Man, and male from female.

These concepts were sufficiently familiar to the age to be used by Herrick as well as Marvell; thus Herrick defines love as 'a circle that doth restlesse move/In the same sweet eternity of love,' ('Love what it is'), while another of Herrick's poems – 'His Age . . .' – defines the union of friends in terms of the circle, and yet another – 'The Eye' – compares the universe with its spheres and its straight and oblique lines to Corinna's eye ('Ah! what is then this curious skie, / But onely my *Corinna's* eye?').

It was therefore only to be expected that Marvell's 'The Definition of Love' should make use of much the same cosmic images; the element of surprise resides solely in the use that Marvell makes of them. The first puzzle is created by the title since a definition should be general, and Marvell seems concerned with a single lover's particular misfortune. The problem would be solved if his situation should reflect a universal predicament. That this may indeed be so, is suggested by the fact that it is Fate herself who has intervened between the lover and the achievement of his desire, the reason being that a fulfilment of the lover's wish would entail *her ruin*. To prevent this, Fate has placed the two so that they cannot possibly meet:

The Definition of Love

I

My Love is of a birth as rare
As 'tis for object strange and high:
It was begotten by despair
Upon Impossibility.

II

Magnanimous Despair alone
Could show me so divine a thing,
Where feeble Hope could ne'r have flown
But vainly flapt its Tinsel Wing.

III

And yet I quickly might arrive
Where my extended Soul is fixt,
But Fate does Iron wedges drive,
And alwaies crouds it self betwixt.

IV

For Fate with jealous Eye does see
Two perfect Loves; nor lets them close:
Their union would her ruine be,
And her Tyrannick pow'r depose.

V

And therefore her Decrees of Steel
Us as the distant Poles have plac'd,
(Though Loves whole World on us doth wheel)
Not by themselves to be embrac'd.

VI

Unless the giddy Heaven fall,
And Earth some new Convulsion tear;
And, us to joyn, the World should all
Be cramp'd into a *Planisphere*.

VII

As Lines so Loves *oblique* may well
Themselves in every Angle greet:
But ours so truly *Paralel*,
Though infinite can never meet.

VIII

Therefore the Love which us doth bind,
But Fate so enviously debarrs,
Is the Conjunction of the Mind,
And Opposition of the Stars.

In an age when astrology and astronomy were scarcely to be separated from each other or from religion, Fate was a synonym for the structure of the universe, and if this is the sense in which Marvell uses the word, he is saying that his love is such that its consummation would entail the ruin of the universe. This is a paradox indeed, since the universe is a manifestation and expression of love. The lovers have been placed by Fate as far apart 'as the distant Poles', and ruin would clearly ensue if the spherical universe, to permit a joining of the poles, were crushed flat. But why is fate so opposed to the lover's achievement of his impossible desire for an 'object strange and high'? And what is this object? And what are the curious iron wedges that prevent the poles from meeting, however fast the spherical universe keeps turning, prompted by love? Answers will be found on reading a few chapters in the popular handbook on the structure of the universe written by Sacrobosco or John Holywood, the *Tractatus de Sphaera*.[1] As this handbook explains, the universe is a round sphere and not a flat circle, and the poles of the world terminate the axis of the universe so that 'the world revolves on them', which is what Marvell states in stanza V. Since one of these poles is always visible to us and the other always invisible, nothing could possibly underline the separation of the lovers more strongly than the image which places them 'as the distant Poles'. The mysterious wedges are best explained in terms of one of Sacrobosco's definitions of a celestial sign or constellation; each sign may be viewed as a pyramid 'whose equilateral base is that surface which we call a "sign" whilst its apex is at the centre of the earth'. Since the signs follow the movement of the sphere it is obvious that they will always keep the poles apart, and it is equally obvious that unless they did this, the universe would be ruined. The poles are at the extreme points of the spherical universe, and it was axiomatic that extremes must pass through a mean before they are capable of meeting; in this case the Equator would be the mean, but here we find the meeting-point only of the Equinoctial line and the Ecliptic, the most famous of all oblique angles. The obliquity of this angle aptly symbolizes the hole-and-corner nature of 'oblique' or imperfect love. Since the 'iron wedges' of the celestial signs (the 'Opposition of the Stars' referred to in the last line) make a circling movement useless, what about a departure away from the poles in a straight line? According to the laws of perspective, parallel lines, when extended, are seen to meet, but this solution is excluded by the fact that their loves are 'so truly *Parallel*' (i.e. equal), that they 'Though infinite can never meet'; hence the lovers must remain content with a 'Conjunction of the Mind'.

The structure of the universe is relevant to that of man since the microcosmos of man reflects the structure of the macrocosmos, and the same is true of society. If one applies cosmic geometry to society, Marvell would seem to argue that the lovers are separated by social distance as effectively as by the extremes of cosmic distance, which explains why they can enjoy a conjunction only of the mind. Such a tame conclusion, however, is an absurd anti-climax after the splendid cosmic imagery, and it would also deny the implications of the title – that the predicament is a universal one. Moreover, it would align Marvell with that rather tiresome school of

---

[1] See the chapters included in English translation in J. J. Bagley and P. B. Rowley, *A Documentary History of England*, vol. I (1066–1540), Harmondsworth, 1966, pp 138–51.

Platonics mocked by Suckling as well as Abraham Cowley. As Cowley phrased it: 'So Angels love; so let them love for me;/ When I am *all Soul*, such shall *my Love* too be' ('Answer to the Platonicks'). A better solution is found on applying the cosmic images to man, and by positing that the closing of the circle referred to in Marvell's fourth stanza is an allusion to the well-known concept of the hermaphrodite. Edmund Spenser had re-buked lovers for entertaining the impossible notion of a perfect physical union; there can be no lasting union, in this life, be-tween male and female. Nature alone, so Spenser argues, is bi-sexual or capable of containing opposites; in the case of human lovers Concord or Love both joins and separates (*Faerie Queene*, IV, x, 34–5 and 41). Unless Concord contained 'heaven in his course', binding everything with 'inviolable bands', fire would mix with the air and land with water. It would indeed be a satisfying conclusion to a subtle poem, if Marvell's last stanza is a com-plaint that the physical union fails to satisfy because it is not complete and cannot ever hope to be complete; the 'iron wedges' of their separate personalities will always prevent the closing of the circle. The separation into male and female is as much a decree of steel as the separation of the poles of the universe, or of air from fire and land from water. Love may effect a temporary conjunction of opposites, but no lasting union. That perfect love should desire perfect union, as in the prelapsarian androgyne, is natural, but impossible. Francis I of France might have his portrait painted as an androgyne, half man and half woman[1], but the perfection symbolized by this union must remain an impossibility as it transcends the limits imposed by Nature, or Fate. Marvell's lover, then, realizes that his desire 'for object strange and high' – a desire rightly characterized as 'be-gotten by despair/Upon Impossibility' – is rendered impossible by the very terms of our existence, and so his final statement is an affirmation that a true union of lovers can be achieved only in the mind, which is a position as contrary to received opinion as at all possible.

'A Dialogue between the Soul and Body' presents a closely related aspect of our human predicament. Here the issue is the conflict in man himself of irreconcilable opposites:

---

[1] Edgar Wind reproduces this painting on plate 80 in his *Pagan Mysteries in the Renaissance*, London, 1958, 1967.

O who shall, from this Dungeon, raise
A Soul inslav'd so many wayes?
With bolts of Bones, that fetter'd stands
In Feet; and manacled in Hands.
Here blinded with an Eye; and there
Deaf with the drumming of an Ear.
A Soul hung up, as 'twere, in Chains
Of Nerves, and Arteries, and Veins.

Paradox alone can do justice to our fallen condition: our vision
blinds us, and our hearing makes us deaf. This argument presumes
that ultimate truth cannot be conveyed through the avenue of the
five senses; if the soul inclines too far towards sense perception, its
inner vision will be impaired, and it is the intuitive powers of the
mind (or pure intellect) that provide true knowledge. After the Fall,
however, this inner vision became largely obscured, as Milton
explains in *Paradise Lost* (ix. 1051–4, 1121–31; xi. 411–20).
Marvell's dialogue suggests that the division, in man, between mind
and body is as absolute as the division of man into male and female;
both as an individual and a lover man is at the mercy of a cosmic
joke or paradox imposing division and preventing union.

By stressing his despair at the separation in such a forcible
manner, Marvell compels us to realize the infinite sadness of our
fallen condition, thus indirectly drawing attention to the nature of
the perfection that was lost. It is interesting that Marvell should do
so in terms of the contrast between discord (or conflict, division)
and concord (or union). This way of thinking about the Fall is
typical of the syncretistic Neoplatonists of the Renaissance, but
Renaissance theologians, like some of the Fathers of our Church,
had assimilated so much of this philosophy that it would scarcely
have been felt as an alien element. Thus when Herrick defined the
number two as the 'lucklesse number of division' ('The Number of
two'), the authority which he invokes is, not Pythagoras, Plato, or
the Neoplatonists, but 'the Fathers'. Conversely Herrick (like
Milton in *Paradise Lost*, viii. 419–26) defines God as 'most One' (in
an epigram entitled 'God is One') or as above number: 'Jehovah, as
Boëtius saith,/No number of the *Plurall* hath.'

In *The Arte of English Poesie* (1589), Puttenham calls the paradox
the 'Wondrer', and Marvell certainly wonders ironically at the
condition of which he speaks. Although man has fallen away from
unity (or God) into multiplicity or discord, he still yearns for unity,
but it is his fate to suffer division. No solution is offered, but to a
Christian the answer is never in doubt: Christ is the healer of

discord, the restorer of our lost perfection as stated by Paul in his epistle to the Ephesians. Christ made 'in himself of twain one new man, so making peace' (*Ephesians*, ii. 15), and so, through Christ, man may partake of the same peace or union. 'A Dialogue between *Thyrsis* and *Dorinda*' states this argument directly, and it does so, appropriately enough, in language indebted to the Song of Solomon, a poem universally interpreted as a description of the union between Christ and the soul. 'Heaven's the Center of the Soul' to which the soul is irresistibly drawn, a point put even more clearly in the lines 'On a Drop of Dew'.

If the strength of this passionate concern with man's fallen condition seems surprising, we must remember the intensity of the religious mood which swept the English nation at this time when even the most moderate of men could be tempted to feel that the Kingdom of Christ was at hand. The Puritans by no means had a monopoly on religious sentiment; those who saw in Cromwell a scourge of God rather than a leader into the Promised Land, often found consolation in profound religious meditations tinged by Neoplatonic thought. It would have been hard to credit a man like Marvell with a share in the Millenarian enthusiasm which fired so many of his contemporaries, if he had not himself given expression to it in 'The First Anniversary of the Government under O.C.' The poet's hope is a tentative one, since the signs provided by the events of the day were capable of various interpretations; all he can say is that 'if these the Times, then this must be the Man'. Yet even this conditional clause today seems quite startling. To Marvell's generation, however, it did not seem at all absurd that England should have assumed the role of God's chosen people, and in innumerable pamphlets and sermons the great national events are persistently referred to in terms of the exodus from Egypt (i.e. the fallen state) and the entry into the Promised Land (i.e. the regenerated state). As Marvell states, if England were God's 'seasonable People' that would bend to Cromwell's as he to Heaven's will, then

> Sure, the mysterious Work, where none withstand,
> Would forthwith finish under such a Hand:
> Fore-shortned Time its useless Course would stay,
> And soon precipitate the latest Day.
>
> (lines 137–40)

Unhappily, though, most men 'Look on, all unconcern'd, or unprepar'd;/And Stars still fall, and still the Dragons Tail/Swinges the

Volumes of its horrid Flail.' The echo from Milton's 'On the Morning of Christ's Nativity' (published in Milton's *Poems*, 1645) is not only a compliment from one poet to another (Marvell's poem also contains two echoes from 'Lycidas'), it also serves to draw attention to the concept of the Last Day when Sin, through the final victory of Christ, shall be no more. But, to quote Milton, this 'must not yet be so'; the time is not ripe for the second coming. Marvell, as was to be expected, explains the situation in terms of a paradox: 'For the great Justice that did first suspend/The World by Sin, does by the same extend.' In other words, sin – which once caused the complete destruction of the earth through the Flood – now ensures the continuation of human existence in its fallen form because it prevents the regeneration that must precede the coming of Christ.

It is tempting to stress the doubt and despair which filled the English nation at this time at the expense of the high hopes for the regeneration of the individual and the state. But because we know that the end was disillusionment and the merry monarch rather than the *regnum Christi*, that the English, to quote Milton, chose 'a captain back for Egypt', we must not underestimate the effect of the hope, nor must we forget its close connection with Renaissance humanism. The strength of this hope is indicated by the large number of pamphlets, prose treatises and poems dealing with creation, the Fall, and the Scheme of Redemption, and many of these bear directly on the political scene since their concern is with the regeneration not only of the individual, but of the state as well. Ambiguous as man's nature is, he may sink to the level of a beast or rise to that of the second Adam (Christ), and while the Puritans attributed the work of regeneration entirely to the operation of divine grace, many humanists stressed the importance of a conscious choice. Marvell, therefore, is at one with his age in focussing on the conflict between guilt and innocence, the prelapsarian and the postlapsarian state. While 'The Garden' indicates that Paradise may be regained by the individual, 'Upon Appleton House' includes society in its perspective, which takes in the whole scope of the universal history of man through its many references to the chief phases in this history. Others of Marvell's poems merely describe the conflict between the state of innocence and the state of corruption or imperfection, but without resolving the tension. Whatever interpretation is adopted of the allegorical story narrated in 'The Nymph complaining for the death of her Faun', one point, at least, is clear: the lament is spoken by a creature who represents innocence, and the death of the faun is an act of wilful murder on the part of 'wanton Troopers'. The evocation of innocence, in the language and in the description of the delights of the garden, is so successful that readers cannot fail to be moved. It is, perhaps, because their style and manner are so different that the basic kinship between Marvell and Thomas Traherne has gone unnoticed.

If it is conceded that the larger part of the English nation was committed to a religious view of history, the curious passivity of many Royalists at the time of the execution of King Charles I is more easily understood. A religiously motivated loyalism to the man in power as the leader appointed by God, would explain the ambiguity in Marvell's attitude towards Charles and Cromwell in 'An Horatian Ode upon Cromwell's Return from Ireland'. As soon as their side was favoured by the events of the war, the Parliamentarians were quick to argue that a divine judgment had been passed through trial by battle, and many men of moderation must have shared the sentiments of Thomas, Lord Fairfax, when he wrote the following lines on the issue of the execution:

> But if the Power devine permited this
> His Will's the Law & ours must acquiesse.[1]

This is the tenor of many Civil War pamphlets, and this is what Marvell, too, states in his Horatian ode:

> 'Tis Madness to resist or blame
> The force of angry Heavens flame . . .

The very fact that victory 'his Crest does plume' proclaims Cromwell the divinely appointed ruler – whether as a scourge for sinners or saintly leader the future only would reveal. As John M. Wallace has argued, the delicate balance struck by Marvell in this ode is not unique, although the splendid phrasing may create this impression. Marvell's description of the execution suggests that he was a loyalist; Charles is presented as submitting meekly to the will of Heaven and freely giving up his power to God's chosen instrument:

---

[1] Quoted by John M. Wallace, *Destiny His Choice: The Loyalism of Andrew Marvell*, Cambridge, 1968, p 68.

> *He* nothing common did or mean
> Upon that memorable Scene:
> But with his keener Eye
> The Axes edge did try:
> Nor call'd the *Gods* with vulgar spight
> To vindicate his helpless Right,
> But bow'd his comely Head,
> Down as upon a Bed.
> This was that memorable Hour
> Which first assur'd the forced Pow'r.

The slowness of the rhythmical movement reinforces the impression that the poem is a deliberative oration where both sides are tried. The outcome, though, is not in doubt, since history already has provided the answer; Cromwell's victories are proof of his election as leader. Like Cincinnatus, Cromwell was called from his plough – or at least his garden – to serve the state:

> And, if we would speak true,
> Much to the Man is due.
> Who, from his private Gardens, where
> He liv'd reserved and austere,
> As if his highest plot
> To plant the Bergamot,
> Could by industrious Valour climbe
> To ruine the great Work of Time,
> And cast the Kingdome old
> Into another Mold.

As the context is one of classical allusions, the images, too, are necessarily classical, so that Cromwell is referred to as 'Wars and Fortunes Son'. In the two poems dedicated to Cromwell, however, the language is Biblical and Cromwell is presented as 'Heaven's Favorite':

> What man was ever so in Heav'n obey'd
> Since the commanded sun o're Gibeon stay'd?
> ('A Poem upon the Death of O.C.', lines 191–2)

'The First Anniversary of the Government under O.C.' presents Cromwell as Davidic King, that is, as a ruler appointed by God and an instrument of Providence. This is largely done through images presenting Cromwell as the Sun, the greatest cosmic power, or as the master 'musician' who imposes harmony on the state in the same manner that God imposed harmony on chaos through the act of creation. The 'wondrous Order and Consent' imposed by Cromwell implies regeneration of a spiritual kind, and in the personal passage where Marvell visualizes himself as a serious poet, he intimates that Cromwell hunts the beast of the Apocalypse:

> If gracious Heaven to my Life give length,
> Leisure to Time, and to my Weakness Strength,
> Then shall I once with graver Accents shake
> Your Regal sloth, and your long Slumbers wake:
> Like the shrill Hunstman that prevents the East,
> Winding his Horn to Kings that chase the Beast.
>   Till then my Muse shall hollow far behind
> Angelique *Cromwell* who outwings the wind;
> And in dark Nights, and in cold Dayes alone
> Pursues the Monster thorough every Throne . . .
>
>   (lines 119–28)

Although octosyllabic couplets were Marvell's favourite verse form, this poem proves his ability to write memorable heroic couplets and to balance his lines and half-lines with a skill that anticipates Dryden. The many references to patriarchs and prophets indicate that regeneration is again a main issue; thus Cromwell is compared to Noah's family of eight, 'Left by the Wars Flood on the Mountains crest', to Elisha and Gideon, and the circumstance that the timespan involved in these references extends from the first day to the last strengthens the impression that Cromwell is seen as an agent of God through whom the scheme of redemption is gradually extended through the world and all of time.

The secular and the religious aspects of government cannot always be kept distinct, and certainly not in the seventeenth century. Marvell's shift of allegiance, therefore, could also be taken to imply a recognition that a *de facto* government after a while tends to be accepted as a government *de jure*. Such a transition is clearly felt in Shakespeare's history plays, where Henry IV at first (in *Richard II*) is seen as being to some extent a usurper, but he appears much less so as he establishes himself as the accepted ruler in the two Parts of *Henry IV*.

Regeneration of the individual and of society is a major theme in the poems dedicated to Thomas, Lord Fairfax and presumably written while Marvell stayed on Fairfax's Yorkshire estate as a teacher of languages to his daughter. Comparatively little is known of Marvell's life and career before he became a Member of Parliament for Hull in 1659; we know that he grew up in Hull where his two sisters married into prominent families, and that he spent seven years at Trinity College, Cambridge, matriculating on 14 December 1633. A letter written by John Milton on 21 February

1653 contains the useful information that Marvell had just left the employ of the Lord General, and that Marvell, prior to his stay with Fairfax, had spent four years abroad in Holland, France, Italy, and Spain 'to very good purpose' and 'the gaining of these four languages'. The sequence, then, is one of seven years at Cambridge, four years abroad, possibly in the capacity of tutor, a few years in London before and after this grand tour, and an unspecified period in Fairfax's household after June 1650 (when Fairfax retired) up to the beginning of 1653. Before he became a Member for Hull in 1659, Marvell was the tutor of Cromwell's ward, William Dutton, and after 2 September 1657 he became Latin secretary, a post he had applied for in vain in 1653.

This brief sketch shows that Marvell was a competent classical scholar who had added modern languages to his stock of Latin and Greek, and his years at Cambridge would have exposed him to the double impact of its religious piety and its Platonism. The Cambridge Platonists, like Ficino and Pico della Mirandola, were syncretists in the sense that they believed that Plato and the other ancient philosophers had been given the same revelation as Moses, so that Plato was Moses Atticus. If Marvell did, in fact, share this syncretistic attitude, Fairfax would have found him a congenial companion, since the Lord General devoted much of his spare time during his retirement (and he retired at 38) to making an English translation of a French commentary on the Hermetic dialogues published by François de Foix in 1579. The reason why the dialogues attributed to Hermes Trismegistus enjoyed such a vogue during the Renaissance is stated by de Foix, who believed that Hermes, like Plato, revealed all the mysteries of our Christian faith concerning creation, the Fall, and the Scheme of Redemption.

Many of Marvell's images, like those of Spenser and Milton, assume familiarity with this syncretistic way of thinking about divine revelation, according to which the same truths may be discovered everywhere – in Nature (the Book of God's Works), in pagan myth and philosophy when properly interpreted, and in the Bible (the Book of God's Words). The interchangeability of the two Books is a basic assumption in Marvell's longest poem, 'Upon Appleton House, to my Lord Fairfax', while a study of syncretistic thought provides the best context for the images and paradoxes crammed into the nine short stanzas of 'The Garden'. But Marvell's praise of his 'delicious Solitude' must be connected with two powerful literary traditions as well, one stemming from the classical praise of the happiness of rural retirement, the other from the religious praise of the mystical or spiritual Garden of Eden reached through solitary contemplation. There is a large area of common ground between the two in that both attribute innocence to the rural scene, and theologians had underlined this similarity by introducing references to the Horatian and Virgilian praise of the husbandman in their comments on *Genesis*, ii. 8. There are many examples, in English literature, of poets and prose writers who combined the classical praise of country life with religious themes before Marvell did so in his poetic tributes to Lord Fairfax – Ben Jonson, William Habington, John Milton, and Robert Herrick come readily to mind.

Although 'The Garden' is not dedicated to Fairfax, it connects formally and thematically with those poems that are. The many bantering phrases used, and the ironical tone of voice, suggest that this poem may have been conceived as a paradoxical encomium of complete inactivity:

> How vainly men themselves amaze
> To win the Palm, the Oke, or Bayes;
> And their uncessant Labours see
> Crown'd from some single Herb or Tree.
> Whose short and narrow verged Shade
> Does prudently their Toyles upbraid;
> While all Flow'rs and all Trees do close
> To weave the Garlands of repose.
>
> Fair quiet, have I found thee here,
> And Innocence thy Sister dear!
> Mistaken long, I sought you then
> In busie Companies of Men.
> Your sacred Plants, if here below,
> Only among the Plants will grow.
> Society is all but rude,
> To this delicious Solitude.

Repose is a key concept, strongly contrasted with 'uncessant Labours' and 'busie Companies of Men'. Complete repose is praised at the expense of action, solitude is preferred to society, single life, even, to wedded bliss. And repose is praised because it represents the most intense creative activity, solitude because it is more refined than society, the single state because it fuses two paradises in one – whatever that may mean ('Two Paradises 'twere in one/To live in Paradise alone.'). The epithets *rude* and *delicious* have a paradoxical relationship to the nouns they qualify – Society and Solitude – and their effect is such that both seem ludicrous. And 'Garlands of repose' is a contradiction in terms, since repose scarcely can lead to any kind of victory. The air of mockery is intensified in the third stanza, where the beauty of women is slighted in favour of 'this lovely green'. Certainly the 'green' is lovely, as any garden enthusiast will readily affirm, but why should it be more *amorous* than women? This absurd proposition is then used to explain the hot pursuit of Daphne by Apollo and of Syrinx by Pan; the gods *desired* their metamorphosis. They wanted Syrinx to turn into a reed and Daphne into a laurel tree.

The statement, in stanza IV, that 'When we have run our Passions heat,/Love hither makes his best retreat', would seem to connect the garden with heavenly love in sharp contrast to mere earthly, sensual love. It is therefore confusing to discover, in the next stanza, that the amorousness of 'this lovely green' copies the erotic abandon of those 'Fond Lovers' so roundly denounced in the preceding stanza.

To understand this basic paradox it is useful again to remember the Renaissance tendency to reconcile the Platonic or Hermetic account of creation and the Fall with the Mosaic account, this reconciliation being the main purpose of the commentary on the Hermetic dialogues that Fairfax tried his best to translate. However, equally useful sources for this syncretistic vision are the prose and verse of Giordano Bruno, or Pico della Mirandola's famous *Oration on the Dignity of Man*. These and similar works describe the metamorphosis of man from his fallen state to a regenerated, higher state through a contemplative withdrawal from the sphere of matter (defined in terms of movement and number) into that of pure mind (defined as complete bodily repose and a return from multiplicity to unity through contemplation of the One). The theme of Marvell's poem, therefore, has the closest possible affinity with well-known concepts propounded by the syncretistic Neoplatonists of the Renaissance, and these are also the men who recommended a joco-serious approach in order to exclude readers incapable of a proper understanding. Fairfax, presumably, would be one of the few capable of penetrating to the core of the poetic fable by virtue of his professional concern with the Hermetic dialogues.

If we define the theme of 'The Garden' as metamorphosis achieved through repose, the metamorphosis being from a state of discord and division to one marked by harmony and union, then the fifth stanza must be taken to describe the loving union between man and all created things, a union which marked the prelapsarian state according to the Hermetic dialogues. The stanza, then, describes, not luxurious enjoyment of sensual pleasures, but a divine plenitude which implies unity through love.

Ben Jonson's 'To Penshurst' shows that a similar plenitude could be attributed to the rural scene in poems based on the classical theme of the happiness of country life. Ben Jonson describes an estate and a family where innocence prevails to such an extent that the effect of the Fall is virtually annulled, so that the creatures pay their homage to man as they once did to Adam; the very carp and pike 'leape on land,/Before the fisher, or into his hand.' The popular neo-Latin poet, Casimire Sarbiewski, similarly merged the concept of the Horatian Sabine farm with that of the Garden of Eden or the *hortus conclusus* (garden enclosed) of Solomon.[1]

The most important point made about the 'happy Garden-state' in stanza VIII is Adam's initial happy solitude. Paradise could be used in the Renaissance as a metaphor for the sexual organs,[2] and it is likely that this usage prompted Marvell's line about two paradises in one. The theory that man at first was an androgyne (i.e. a person with two 'paradises' in one) was so well known in the Renaissance that such an allusion would be no more learned than Marvell's references to classical myth. And, as we have seen, a number of poems were written at this time not only about Platonic love, but about hermaphrodites as well. The Hermetic context explains why Adam is referred to as an androgyne by Marvell; the Hermetic dialogues identify the Fall with the division into two sexes – an act which put man under the necessity of incessantly striving instead of enjoying complete repose, like God.

Stanzas VI and VII describe the union, not between man and the rest of creation, but between man and God. This union is achieved through a withdrawal from the lesser pleasures of the garden and by means of a concentration of the powers of the mind (the lines 'Mean while the Mind, from pleasure less,/Withdraws into its happiness' can be taken to convey both meanings). This withdrawal and concentration is the first stage towards the release of the soul from the body described in stanza VII. The mind is the image of God in man, since God is pure mind, and the mind is accommodated in the body by being joined to the soul, the soul in its turn being directly connected with the body through the avenues of the five senses, as the Hermetic dialogues explain. Marvell uses the two terms – soul and mind – with great precision. The mind can be

[1] Matthias Casimire Sarbiewski, *The Odes of Casimire (1646)*, Augustan Reprint Society Publication Number 44, Los Angeles, 1953. The following odes are based on the Song of Solomon: II, 19 and 25; IV, 19 and 21. Ode IV, 21 is particularly relevant.

[2] See, for example, John Ford, *'Tis Pity She's a Whore*, II, i, 42–9.

released only at death (the 'longer flight'); in this life, however, the soul may achieve a momentary release from the body, and since the soul was believed to have fire for its body (fire being the purest and most celestial of the elements), one understands why it 'Waves in its Plumes the various Light'. The fruit tree is a familiar symbol for Christ, the *nova poma* (new apple) hanging on the Tree of the Cross and freely offering himself to all who will accept the gift of redemption. Again it must be stressed that this juxtaposition of Christian with Platonic and Hermetic concepts should be viewed as evidence of a syncretistic bias of the kind that must be attributed to Marvell's patron, Lord Fairfax.

The concluding stanza returns the reader to the 'milder Sun' of the created universe, the Sun being the shadow of God according to Ficino and the Neoplatonists. The reference to the Sun and the zodiac forms a most appropriate conclusion, since the great circle of the Sun combines movement with repose, and since the movement of the stars enables us to compute time, and, as Plato tells us in the *Timaeus*, the computation of time is the beginning of wisdom. This is so because it enables man to reproduce in himself 'the perfectly unerring course of the sun' as Plato puts it, and so 'reduce to settled order the wandering motions in himself', and this is, of course, the purpose of the poet's retreat into his garden.

In 'The Mower against Gardens', '*Damon* the Mower', and the other poems where this fully dramatized character speaks, Marvell's attitude seems suddenly reversed in that it is now the garden which represents corruption. This is logical enough, however, as Marvell is intent on exploiting the paradox that now, after the Fall, gardens are a source of corruption because man has made them so. Only areas untouched by man have retained their innocence.

The praise of a patron's estate is a type of poem often based on the classical theme of the happiness of rural life; Ben Jonson's homage to Sir Robert Wroth, or Casimire Sarbiewski's to the Duke of Bracciano (Epode I) are good examples of the tradition within which Marvell worked when he wrote 'Upon Appleton House' and 'Upon the Hill and Grove at Bill-borow'. Fairfax himself is never treated ironically, but he is part of a world which is by definition paradoxical. Fairfax's command of this world seems absolute; thus he solves the most stubborn of all mathematical paradoxes, the squaring of the circle, by subjecting his bodily passions (symbolized by the square) to his immortal mind (symbolized by the circle), and on his entrance into his house the building imitates these 'holy Mathematicks': 'But where he comes the swelling Hall/Stirs, and the *Square* grows *Spherical*. This is more than a witty allusion to the fact that the square hall was topped by a cupola; what is involved, is man's mastery over matter, and the love which matter feels for man as the image of God – a basic point in those Hermetic dialogues that interested Fairfax so profoundly.

'Upon Appleton House' has been considered a rambling, loosely constructed poem, but this verdict must be reversed once we see through the surface veil of the wit. The familiar doctrine that poetry should teach and delight has been put to new and unsuspected use in this intriguing homage to Thomas, Lord Fairfax.

It is sufficiently plain that Marvell begins and concludes with praise respectively of Fairfax (stanzas 1–10) and his daughter Maria (86–97), but it must also be observed that the remaining 75 stanzas (11–85) are neatly divided into 25 stanzas (11–35) on 'The Progress of this Houses Fate' (stanza 11, line 84), and 50 on the estate (36–85). The family history is explicitly presented as part of God's providential plan for England, while many details in the description of the estate allude to major events in the universal history of man – creation, the Flood, the crossing of the Red Sea and other exodus events. Both histories, then, are providential, and the two are related also by means of the mathematical ratio which spells harmony: the 25 stanzas relate to the 50 as 1:2, the formula for the diapason or octave. Augustine repeatedly traced this ratio through God's works of creation and redemption (i.e. creation in space and time) as evidence of their harmony.[1] As used in the textual organization of this poem, the ratio states that the family history harmonizes with the history of the scheme of redemption.

The opening series of witty images and arguments toys with the relationship between the master and his house: the master delights in its 'straitness', but the house is distressed by his magnitude (7:53–4) and strives to adjust itself to him. In much the same way Nature accommodates itself to Maria who bestows upon the estate a 'more decent Order tame' (86:766), in strong contrast to the world which is a mere 'rude heap together hurl'd;/All negligently over-thrown' (86:762–3). With the request, in the penultimate line: 'Let's in', we are returned to the sober frame of the house where we first began. Additional links between the beginning and the end strengthen the circular pattern of the poem as a whole. The fishers

---

[1] See for example Augustine's treatise *Of the Trinity*, Book IV, chapters 3–6. Augustine's aesthetics are explained in M.-S. Røstvig, 'Ars Aeterna: Renaissance Poetics and Theories of Divine Creation,' *Mosaic* 3 (1970), 40–61; rpt in *Chaos and Form*, ed. Kenneth McRobbie (Winnipeg, Canada, 1972), pp 101–19.

who have 'shod their *Heads* in their *Canoos*' so that they move
'*Tortoise like*' (97:772–3) refer us back to Fairfax who is compared to
tortoises that dwell 'In cases fit of Tortoise-shell' (2:14). The topos
of the absence of decent proportions, in houses and the world at
large, links stanzas 2 and 96, while stanzas 3 and 95 denounce
hollow palaces. We observe, then, that not only is there linkage
between the beginning and the end, but that the images or topoi
that create the linkage are repeated in inverse order (abc . . . cba).
The main theme emerges when Fairfax's greatness is said to be
combined with humility: he is pleased to dwell within 'dwarfish
Confines' (5:38) so that 'Things greater are in less contain'd'
(6:44). This recalls the humility of Christ who accepted incarnation
under a lowly roof, while in the case of Maria the allusion is to the
Virgin: Maria precedes all virgins, just as the estate precedes all
other '*Woods, Streams, Gardens, Meads*' (94:752). Then, too, she
commands her natural environment as Fairfax does his house:
indeed, she bestows all her own qualities on them (beauty,
straightness, sweetness, and purity), and in return they serve her
(87–8). The four 'elements' of the estate – gardens, meadows,
woods, and river – are listed not only in stanza 94; in stanzas 87–8
they are enumerated no less than three times. This list in the first
stanzas on Maria takes us back to the last stanza in the opening
sequence on Fairfax where Nature, not Art, is seen as responsible
for shaping the 'fragrant Gardens, shaddy Woods,/Deep Meadows,
and transparent Floods' (10:79–80). But Nature is, of course, the
workmanship of God.

This frequent repetition of the list of the four 'elements' is the
clue we need in order to understand that these 'elements' structure
the 75 stanzas of the poem proper. After the history has been told
(25 stanzas) we are taken on a progress, beginning with the garden
and the meadows (25 stanzas divided into 11 and 14), and then
proceeding into the woods and to the river (25 stanzas sub-divided
into 18 and 7). The topos of retirement reinforces the balanced
pattern: As we enter the garden, Fairfax is said to have retired 'to
Peace' (36:283) and allusion is made to sunrise (37:289–90); at the
point of transition from the meadows into the woods the speaker
retires from a symbolic Flood into an equally symbolic Ark (61), and
he terminates his retirement 25 stanzas later with the setting of the
sun (83–5).

These retirements stand in stark contrast to the corrupt retirement of the nuns as described in the 25-stanza sequence on the
history of the house (11–35). The nuns retain the virgin Thwaites

within their walls, thus creating an 'unjust Divorce' (30:236) from her promised spouse, young Fairfax. Like Satan, they attempt 'the great Race [to] intercept' (31:248). The nunnery is a perverse garden of bliss, and the virgin Thwaites is induced to enter by a carefully prepared speech. The climactic conclusion of this speech of temptation (21–5) is at the textual centre of this segment, but the climactic action comes at the end when young Fairfax rescues his bride-to-be (29–35). The narrative ends as it began by referring to the demolishing of the convent: its ruins show 'The Quarries whence this dwelling rose' (11:88) and 'At the demolishing, this Seat/To *Fairfax* fell as by Escheat' (35:273–4). Fairfax is hailed apocalyptically as one of the 'Offspring fierce' who 'Shall fight through all the *Universe*' (31:241), but when we enter the garden his particular historical mission is achieved. What remains is to carry on the fight at a higher moral and spiritual level.

The eleven-stanza section on the garden has at its centre a lament for the loss of innocence. Heaven created England as a garden 'us to please', but to no avail: 'What luckless Apple did we tast,/To make us Mortal, and The Wast?' (41:327–8). This may perhaps be the explanation for Fairfax's retirement behind his flowery bastions in the first stanza (36), and the bastions are re-introduced in the last (46), thus closing the circle of this segment. On the last occasion they are directed, not against the temptation of the five senses (as in stanza 36), but against the more dangerous spiritual vices of pride and ambition as attributed to the '*Prelate* great' of Cawood Castle (the Archbishop of York). The apostrophe to England at the textual centre (41) is flanked by two five-stanza sequences. The first (36–40) playfully presents the flowers as a sweet militia intent on protecting its governor, while the second (42–6) laments the innocence that was lost. Homage to Fairfax is located halfway through each sequence. The flowers salute their Governor in stanza 38, while in stanza 44 the speaker pays tribute to the man who, 'had it pleased him and *God*./Might once have made our Gardens spring/Fresh as his own and flourishing'.

In the last stanza the 'invisible *Artillery*' of the garden plays 'ore the Meads below', 'Or innocently seems to gaze' (44:367–8), as a prelude to the moment when the speaker takes a decisive plunge: 'And now to the Abyss I pass/Of that unfathomable Grass . . .' (45:369–70). The phrases 'abyss' and 'unfathomable' tell us that the plunge is into the formless substance from which God created the world. Abyss, as Bartholomæus Anglicus explains in his treatise *On the Properties of Things*, means 'withoute foundement and grounde'.[1] Augustine connects it with incessant change: it is a 'formless fundamental [*informitas*] through which things are altered and changed from one form to another' (*The Confessions* XII. 11).[2] That life in the meadows mirrors the work of creation (in space and time) is suggested even more strongly when the cattle are said to resemble the 'Universal Heard' (i.e. all the creatures) as described by D'Avenant in his lines on the sixth day of creation (57:455–6). As in Augustine's *Confessions*, change is the main concept: 'No Scene that turns with Engines strange/Does oftner then these Meadows change' (49:385–6), and the changes include paradoxical inversions as in the first stanza (47) and the last (60). Also, we are in a world of *seeming*: the mowers 'seem like *Israalites* to be,/Walking on foot through a green Sea./To them the Grassy Deeps divide ,/ And crowd a Lane to either Side' (49:389–92). What we see seems partly good and partly evil. The crossing of the Red Sea fore-shadows redemption from sin through Christ,[3] but the bloody massacres (50–3) make us remember that shortly after the exodus, the Israelites turned their back on God because they trusted the false report of the spies sent into Canaan (Numbers 13:33 as echoed by Marvell at 47:371–2). As a consequence, God decreed that 'your carcases shall fall in this wilderness' where all must remain for 40 years (cf. Numbers 14:32–45). Marvell's pastoral version of the massacres and the triumph of the 'careless Victors' (53–4) has been given central placing within the segment, a point which emphasizes its importance. These lines may glance in the direction of the civil wars, but these were considered as part of England's re-enactment of redemption history. Moses/Fairfax (cf. stanza 78) may have been God's chosen leader, but the corruption caused by the 'luckless Apple' prohibits entry into the Promised Land until the end of time. (The entry into Canaan after 40 years in the wilderness foreshadows our entry from a state of sin into the new heaven and the new earth created after the destruction of the old.)

[1] Bartholomæus Anglicus, *On the Properties of Things*, tr. John Trevisa (Oxford University Press, 1975), I, 664 f. The chapter on the abyss is located in book 13, the section on water, since '*Abisus* is depnesse of water vnsey . . . For oute of Þe depnesse comen alle waters . . .'. The text is that of the first edition, in English translation, in 1495.

[2] Quotations from *The Confessions* are from the Penguin edition, tr. R. S. Pine-Coffin (Harmondsworth, 1964).

[3] On Biblical typology see Jean Daniélou, S. J., *From Shadows to Reality* (1960); the main types referred to by Marvell are identified by M.-S. Røstvig in *Marvell. Modern Judgements* ed. Michael Wilding (London: Macmillan, 1969), pp 215–32.

The retirement into the wood is a retirement from sin (i.e. the Flood, which is a type of sin) into a sanctuary; the wood is a 'yet green, yet growing Ark' (61:484), and the Ark of Noah is a familiar type or foreshadowing of redemption through the wood of the cross and hence, by extension, the church. The traditional character of Marvell's thought may be illustrated by a quotation from the medieval theologian, Hugh of St Victor: 'Turning, then, from the works of creation, as from a flood beneath us from which we have emerged, let us begin to treat of the works of restoration, and with them go, as it were, into the ark.'[1] The opposite of change is being fixed or unmoved (cf. Psalms 108:1 and Augustine's *Confessions* XI. 11), which is the state towards which we move as we read through the 25 stanzas on the woods and the river. Removal from the flood of sin into the Ark of salvation is the first phase, while the second phase on safe enclosure occupies the three last stanzas (76–8) in the segment on the woods. The segment on the river (79–85) presents perfect stasis: the river is a '*Chrystal Mirrour* slick' in the second stanza (80) and in the last two 'The gellying Stream compacts below' so as to *fix* the shadow of the 'modest *Halcyon*' (85:675–6) and 84:669). The very fishes are 'As *Flies* in *Chrystal* overt'ane', while men 'the silent *Scene* assist' (85:678–9). The combination of movement and rest in the description of the Halcyon is the attribute of God, as Augustine frequently states in his *Confessions* (cf. XIII. 37 'But you, O Lord, are eternally at work and eternally at rest.'). The same combination is found in the opening lines in the concluding passage on Maria: '*Maria* such, and so doth hush/'The *World*, and through the Ev'ning rush' (86:681–2). Indeed, 'by her *Flames*, in *Heaven* try'd,/*Nature* is wholly *vitrifi'd*' (86:687–8), a phrase which may allude to the crystallizing of the world at the last fire.

The history of the world, then, beginning with creation (47), proceeds from a state of constant change or flux (the meadows) to a state of being fixed. The conflagration or vitrification of the world marks the end of time, and does so in the stanza which occupies the fortieth position from the beginning – perhaps an allusion to the 40 years in the desert which was a type of all of time.

The desire to remain fixed although placed in a world governed by time and hence by change, permeates Augustine's *Confessions*. One quotation must suffice: 'But if only their minds could be seized and held steady, they would glimpse the splendour of eternity which

---

[1] Hugh of Saint-Victor, *Selected Spiritual Writings*, tr. by a Religious of C.S.M.V. (London, 1962), pp 146 f.

is for ever still' (*Confessions* XI. 11). Augustine uses the forest as a symbol of Holy Writ (leaves being the common denominator), 'nor is this forest without its deer' (XI. 2), which is an allusion to Psalms 29:9 where the deer penetrating the forest represents those who can understand the Scriptures.[1] Similarly Marvell's forest contains 'Sibyls Leaves' where all wisdom may be studied in a 'light *Mosaick*' (73); like Augustine (*Confessions*, XIII) Marvell fuses the Book of the Creatures with Holy Writ. God created a world dominated by time and hence by change, but we can avoid submersion by undergoing an inward change (Romans 12:2), and a soul transformed by spiritual gifts can 'scrutinize everything' (*Confessions* XIII. 22, quoting 1 Cor. 2:15) and so catch a 'glimpse of eternity *as it is known through your creatures*' (*Confessions* XIII. 21 quoting Romans 1:20). The desire to be safely enclosed and fixed begins and concludes the segment on the woods (61 and 78); the references to the Ark (61) and the crossing of the Red Sea (78) relate these stanzas to redemption history. The symmetrical arrangement of this segment is particularly emphatic:

Redemption (the Ark)	61–2	78–7	Redemption (Exodus and *imitatio Christi*)
Safe enclosure	63–4	76–5	Safe enclosure
Harmony of music in the 'Temple green'	65–6	74–3	Harmony of divine revelation; the forest as a church
Birds and trees	67–8	72–1	Man as bird and tree
	69: bird		
	70: tree		Judgment and Mercy

The last segment on the river (79–85) presents a world where 'all things are become new' (2 Cor. 5:17); the mirror of nature, and the mind which contemplates it, have achieved a new purity. The distinction between the sun and its reflection, for example, has been virtually obliterated. This is what we learn in the first two stanzas (79–80); in the last two stanzas (84–5) the *stasis* which binds even the river – that archetypal image of flux and transience – mirrors the abiding peace of the invisible world (cf. Romans 1:20). In the central stanza (82) the speaker recalls that '*young Maria* walks to

[1] See also Augustine's sermon on Psalms 29:9–10 (Vulg. 28:9–10). '*The Voice of the Lord perfecting the stags . . . And will reveal the woods.* And then will He reveal to them the darkness of the Divine books, and the shadowy depths of the mysteries, where they may feed with freedom . . . The Lord therefore first inhabiteth the deluge of this world in His Saints, kept safely in the Church, as in the ark.' Augustine, *Expositions on the Book of Psalms* vol. I (Oxford, 1847), pp 212 f.

night' so that he must forgo his 'Pleasures slight', but this is no
dismissal of the poem as a mere toy invented by a 'trifling Youth'.
Instead we should associate these phrases with the sentence which
precedes Paul's famous statement about seeing in a glass darkly:
'When I was a child, I spake as a child . . . but when I became a
man, I put away childish things' (I Cor. 13:11). When Maria comes,
the perfect comes, and the imperfect must pass away (I Cor. 13:10).
An apparently modest disclaimer, therefore, has been used to relate
Maria to the state of perfection, and as we read on – in Marvell's
poem and in chapter 14 of I Corinthians – Paul's concern with the
relationship between language and sense and with the importance
of knowing a language so as to understand what is being said, subtly
enhances the value of the compliment paid to Maria in stanza 89:

> *She* counts her Beauty to converse
> In all the Languages as *hers*;
> Nor yet in those *her self* imployes
> But for the *Wisdome* not the *Noyse*;
> Nor yet that *Wisdome* would affect,
> But as 'tis *Heavens Dialect*.

Such submerged allusions are found throughout, and with the
passing of time they have come to seem more obscure than they
were to Marvell's contemporaries. Take for example the lines on
the relationship between Fairfax and his house: 'Let others vainly
strive t'immure/The *Circle* in the *Quadrature*!/These *holy
Mathematicks* can/In ev'ry Figure equal Man' (6:45–8). This is an
allusion to the famous Vitruvian figure of universal man who stands
with arms and legs stretched within a square and a circle (whose
centre is his navel).[1] The square and the circle are the two most
perfect geometrical figures, and man is 'universal' in the sense that
his proportions reflect those of the universe; hence Vitruvius stated
that these proportions should be employed in the construction of
temples. In the Renaissance poets and architects like Leonardo da
Vinci, Palladio, and Leon Battista Alberti based their aesthetic
theories on this argument; Alberti, for example, recommended the
proportions that create the musical consonances (1:1, 1:2, 2:3 etc.).
The 'holy' *Mathematicks*, then, are the perfect geometrical forms
and ratios that pervade the universe, man, Fairfax's house and
estate, and the poem which praises them. The poem is a large circle

[1] Rudolf Wittkower, *Architectural Principles in the Age of Humanism* (London, 1967);
plate 4 reproduces an excellent drawing taken from an edition of Vitruvius
published in 1521. See also S. K. Heninger, Jr, *The Cosmographical Glass* (San
Marino, California, 1977), figures 85a and 85b.

enclosing circles within circles, while each part (i.e. each stanza) is a square consisting of 8 times 8 syllables.[1] However, the fusion between the circle and the square is given mathematical expression too in the structural number 25, which is the square of 5. And 5 is a circular number as well, since it reproduces itself in the last digit when multiplied with itself. The lines just quoted (6:45–8) may therefore be self-referring, that is, they may refer to the skilful arrangement whereby stanzas, segments and the poem as a whole are made to 'equal Man'.

A survey of Marvell's more traditional love poems would have to focus on 'To his Coy Mistress', a lyric based on the great paradox of Time. The problem is whether Time causes growth or decay, a point debated by philosophers and paradoxists with considerable fervour and ingenuity. Thus David Person stated, in his *Varieties* (1636), that if Time causes sublunary bodies to experience a 'rising, increase or growing', then love, too, when exposed to Time, would experience a similar growth. Marvell's poem, therefore, begins as a mock encomium of coyness, the argument being that since coyness means postponement, and since more time means more growth, then 'My vegetable Love should grow/Vaster than Empires, and more slow.' The time-span envisaged encompasses all of human history, as the lover would begin 'ten years before the Flood' (i.e. in the year 1646 Anno Mundi, the Flood having occurred 1656 years after time began) and the lady would be permitted to 'refuse/Till the Conversion of the *Jews*'. This takes us up to the very end of Time, the conversion of the Jews being one of the signs that the Kingdom of Christ is at hand.

The counter-argument, that Time causes decay rather than growth, begins with a heavily stressed *but*:

> But at my back I alwaies hear
> Times winged Chariot hurrying near:
> And yonder all before us lye
> Desarts of vast Eternity.

The Psalmist had asked, ironically, 'Shall the dust praise thee?' and 'in the grave who shall give thee thanks?'[2] Marvell's rhetoric is just as forceful:

[1] George Puttenham, *The Arte of English Poesie, 1589* (Scolar Press, Menston, 1968); p 83 defines the square poem and compares the figure to *hominem quadratum*, a 'constant minded man'.

[2] Psalm vi. 5 and xxx. 9. J. B. Leishman (in his British Academy lecture, 1961) invoked an epigram by Asclepiades in the Greek Anthology:
Hoarding your maidenhood – and why? For not when to Hades
   You've gone down shall you find, maiden, the lover you lack.
Only among the alive are the joys of Cypris, and only,
   Maiden, as bones and dust shall we in Acheron lie.

> Thy Beauty shall no more be found;
> Nor, in thy marble Vault, shall sound
> My ecchoing Song: then Worms shall try
> That long preserv'd Virginity:
> And your quaint Honour turn to dust;
> And into ashes all my Lust.
> The Grave's a fine and private place,
> But none I think do there embrace.

The solution is given in the third and last section, the swiftness and assurance of which is a matter partly of syntax and partly of imagery. All but the last couplet consist of a quickly-moving, long-sustained period presenting a string of images whose climax is reached with the following lines:

> Let us roll all our Strength, and all
> Our sweetness, up into one Ball:
> And tear our Pleasures with rough strife,
> Thorough the Iron gates of Life.

Despite the overtly sexual nature of the consummation described in this concluding section, the 'Ball' and the 'gates of Life' must not be taken to carry on the description of the amorous sport. The epithet 'iron' and the roughness of the sound pattern indicate that this cannot be an image of consummation. The exploding cannon-ball was a familiar Renaissance emblem illustrating the ancient paradox that we must learn to hurry slowly (*festina lente*). As Edgar Wind informs us, in his study of *Pagan Mysteries in the Renaissance*, the paradox had been invested with a profound significance because of a supposed connection with Platonic thought. Its true meaning was taken to be that man must learn to harness his own forces, or those of Nature, and then release them suddenly, in just the right place and moment. If he did this, miraculous effects could be achieved. Marvell's argument about Love and Time, therefore, concludes with a reconciliation between the seemingly irreconcilable aspects of Time. And a final turn of the ironical screw is achieved when it is remembered that the cannon-ball and its motto represented *prudence* or *wisdom* – which means that the advice to abandon coyness and instead behave with the utmost abandon, is couched in terms of an image usually taken to symbolize prudence in its most elevated aspect.

'Daphnis and Chloe' discusses love in terms that are distinctly cynical. Daphnis discovers, to his great mortification, that the moment he abandons the siege, the fair one is willing to yield. Such is his pride that he refuses to owe to his departure what his presence was unable to win:

> Rather I away will pine
> In a manly stubborness
> Than be fatted up express
> For the *Canibal* to dine.

The discovery has killed his love, so that a consummation 'But the ravishment would prove/Of a Body dead while warm.' The beauty of the lines almost hides the grossness they reveal, but the story ends in pure farce when Daphnis, out of peeved vanity rather than 'manly stubborness', every night sleeps with a different woman:

> Yet he does himself excuse;
> Nor indeed without a Cause.
> For, according to the Lawes,
> Why did *Chloe* once refuse?

What laws? Obviously of man, and equally obviously fallen man. The poem comments ironically not only on the fallen state of man, but on the pastoral genre indicated by the title. Here is a poem whose title suggests the innocence associated with pastoral, but whose contents reveal the very accents of corruption.

Interestingly enough one of Marvell's poems depicts or enacts the metamorphosis of the pastoral from a corrupt to an innocent genre. In 'Clorinda and Damon' Clorinda's attempted seduction of Damon is foiled and she is converted, instead, to his profoundly religious view of life. The poem ends by showing how the two join in offering praise to him whose words 'transcend poor Shepherds skill'.

The number of poems discussed here is sufficiently large to indicate that Marvell's achievement cannot be adequately explained in terms of the outstanding excellence of two or three poems. Marvell's prose and his verse satires belong to the Restoration period and represent a different type of achievement, yet these too must be included in an overall estimate. The satires that may be attributed to Marvell with reasonable confidence, such as 'The last Instructions to a Painter', focus on actual events often within a relatively short time-span. In the course of the 990 lines of the satire just referred to, no less than eighty-four contemporaries are included, many of whom cannot now be identified. Among the greatest of Marvell's victims are Charles II, the Duke of York, and Clarendon, the Chancellor, but the most interesting passages are perhaps those that describe events that take place in Parliament. The butt of Marvell's satire is always corruption – at Court, in Parliament, or the Church – and this constitutes a clear link with the themes that we find in the *Poems* of 1681. Thus the Speaker of the House of Commons is accused of betraying the House whose servant he is:

> The *Speaker*, Summon'd, to the *Lords* repairs,
> Nor gave the *Commons* leave to say their Pray'rs:
> But like his Pris'ners to the Bar them led,
> Where mute they stand to hear their Sentence read;
> Trembling with joy and fear, *Hyde* them Prorogues,
> And had almost mistook and call'd them Rogues.

(lines 857–62)

The fact that this chapter is headed 'Marvell and the Caroline Poets' is sufficient indication of the importance attached to Marvell's poetry today. As late as 1948 Marvell was classified as a minor poet in the *Literary History of England* edited by Albert C. Baugh, but this is a typical example of the way in which traditional value judgments tend to linger on in the pages of literary histories long after they have been abandoned by scholars and critics. Those who have classified Marvell as a minor poet have done so largely on the strength of the view expressed by T. S. Eliot in 1921 in his essay on Marvell, that to bring Marvell back to life is 'to squeeze the drops of the essence of two or three poems'. This was echoed by the *Pelican Guide to English Literature* (1956), which still maintains that Marvell's reputation 'depends on a few lyrics'. *The Concise Cambridge History of English Literature* (1946) by George Sampson states, more prophetically, that Marvell 'has yet to be seen in his true magnitude as one of the finest characters and noblest writers of his age'. Noble is an unexpected epithet; one would rather refer to Marvell as a supremely conscious artist possessed of such complete linguistic control that the seeming simplicity of his poetic texture has tended to hide the complexity which it encloses. Indeed, such is this complexity that we may, perhaps, be disputing the meaning of many of his poems 'Till the Conversion of the *Jews*'. If so, all we can do is to affirm our conviction that Marvell deserves 'this State', and that we would not 'love at lower rate'.

11

MILTON

(i)
POEMS (1645)

Christopher Ricks

It seems to have been in 1644 that John Milton first realized he was going blind. A year later there was registered for publication *Poems of Mr John Milton, Both English and Latin, Compos'd at several times.* The sense of encroaching blindness is sure to have played its part in prompting Milton to make himself manifest as a poet. By 1645 he was no longer a young man – thirty-six years old. He was not the kind of man ever to forget that 'There be of them, that have left a name behind them, to declare their praises. And some there be, which have no memorial'. In 1642 he had looked back, with a lucid confidence which is very different from vanity, upon his early conviction of his poetic destiny, a conviction strengthened by the praises which he had won during his Italian tour of 1638–9:

I must say therefore that after I had from my first yeeres by the ceaselesse diligence and care of my father, whom God recompence, bin exercis'd to the tongues, and some sciences, as my age would suffer, by sundry masters and teachers both at home and at the schools, it was found that whether ought was impos'd me by them that had the overlooking, or betak'n to of mine own choise in English, or other tongue, prosing or versing, but chiefly this latter, the stile by certain vital signes it had, was likely to live. But much latelier in the privat Academies of *Italy*, whither I was favor'd to resort, perceiving that some trifles which I had in memory, compos'd at under twenty or thereabout (for the manner is that every one must give some proof of his wit and reading there) met with acceptance above what was lookt for, and other things which I had shifted in scarsity of books and conveniences to patch up amongst them, were receiv'd with written Encomiums, which the Italian is not forward to bestow on men of this side the *Alps*, I began thus farre to assent both to them and divers of my friends here at home, and not lesse to an inward prompting which now grew daily upon me, that by labour and intent study (which I take to be my portion in this

life) joyn'd with the strong propensity of nature, I might perhaps leave
something so written to aftertimes, as they should not willingly let it die.
(*The Reason of Church-Government*)

At what point were the inward prompting and the strong propensity
of nature to become such as would precipitate Milton's poems from
privacy ('some trifles which I had in memory') to publication? He
had always been vividly aware both that he must bide his time and
also that time was not exactly his to bide. He had been grateful to
the friend who had urged him not to rust, and in reply he had at one
and the same time urged that his quiescence was not the same thing
as scholarly torpor and yet finally admitted that he too was uneasy
about time's thieving:

Yet that you may see that I am somtyme suspicious of my selfe, & doe take
notice of a certaine belatednesse in me, I am the bolder to send you some of
my nightward thoughts some while since since they come in fitly made up
in a Petrarchian stanza.

> How soone hath Time the suttle theefe of Youth
> Stolne on his wing my three & twentith yeere . . .

That had been in 1633. Ten years later his own wording may have
recurred to him, in the realization that time was now stealing his
three-and-thirtieth year. The poet who knew how easily a purposed
fame could be annulled by 'the blind Fury' who 'slits the thin spun
life' will have realized that blindness too could be the bitter enemy
of a fame still to come. Blindness was eventually to be defeated by
the blind poet. Yet in 1645 – at a moment when he was aware that
he had written little poetry for five years – there will have seemed
good reason to gather up all that he had hitherto achieved, so that
instead of John Milton known only for his tracts on divorce
(notorious rather than famous) there should be John Milton the
poet.

'Compos'd at several times': the 1645 *Poems* go as far back as
paraphrases from the Psalms written when he was fifteen. But
composition had not necessarily meant publication. It could even be
said that publication had not necessarily meant making Milton
himself public as a poet. The two most important works in the
volume, 'Lycidas' and *A Mask* [*Comus*], had indeed been published
before 1645, but neither of them would have done much to modify
the standing of Milton as a mere pamphleteer. For 'Lycidas' had
been signed merely 'J.M.' when it appeared in the volume of
obsequies for Edward King (1638), and *A Mask* had been altogether
silent as to authorship when published in 1637. Two smaller pieces

were reprinted rather than printed in 1645: 'On Shakespear' had appeared unsigned in Shakespeare's Second Folio (1632), and had unmasked itself only to the extent of being signed 'I.M.' in Shakespeare's *Poems* (1640); and Milton's second poem on the University Carrier, Hobson, had turned up, presumably unauthorized, in *A Banquet of Jests* (1640). So that although two of Milton's most important poems and two of his most ephemeral ones had already been published before 1645, *Poems of Mr John Milton* constituted his first bid.

Milton had been thinking of his own creativity when he praised Shakespeare's more fluent genius:

> For whilst to th' shame of slow-endeavouring art,
> Thy easie numbers flow . . .

Yet where was a 'great heir of Fame' to succeed Shakespeare? In 1633 there had appeared John Donne's *Poems* and George Herbert's *The Temple*, but both of these collections were posthumous – they were witnesses to what an earlier generation had achieved, rather than to what the present poetic generation was achieving. True, the infant prodigy Abraham Cowley had published in 1633 his *Poeticall Blossoms* at the age of fifteen, but the only other immediate predecessor of Milton who has much significance is Sir John Denham, who in 1642 had published *Cooper's Hill*, a topographical and didactic poem in heroic couplets which hindsight allows us to see as inaugurating Augustan poetry.

In 1645, two important poets were published by the same man, Humphrey Moseley. One was the talented and equable Edmund Waller, co-founder with Denham of Augustan poetry. Moseley, in his publisher's note to Milton's *Poems* ('The Stationer to the Reader'), invoked the good reception accorded to Waller in order to help Milton: 'that incouragement I have already received from the most ingenious men in their clear and courteous entertainment of Mr Wallers late choice Peeces, hath once more made me adventure into the World, presenting it with these ever-green, and not to be blasted Laurels'.

The difference between Milton and Waller is indeed the difference between choice pieces and evergreen laurels. But it was Waller who was acclaimed. His poems went through three editions in 1645, whereas Milton's original edition was still being offered for sale fifteen years later. 'Yet be it less or more, or soon or slow . . .' A 'great heir of Fame' may have to wait a long time before he comes into his inheritance.

*   *   *

By 1673 (the year before he died) Milton was at last entering on that inheritance. By 1673 he was the author of *Paradise Lost* (1667) and of *Paradise Regained* and *Samson Agonistes* (1671). So it was then, at the age of sixty-four, that Milton authorized the re-issue of his early poems. To the poems of 1645 he added others, some of which had already been written by 1645 (for example, 'On the Death of a fair Infant dying of a Cough'). Probably he had decided against including in the 1645 volume his 'At a Vacation Exercise in the College' (which he had written at Christ's College, Cambridge, in 1628) because to have done so would have smacked of egotism. By 1673 the youthful exuberance of this manifesto had been abundantly justified, and it was with legitimate pride that Milton could look back to his early hopes:

> Hail native Language, that by sinews weak
> Didst move my first endeavouring tongue to speak . . .
> I pray thee then deny me not thy aide
> For this same small neglect that I have made:
> But haste thee strait to do me once a Pleasure,
> And from thy wardrope bring thy chiefest treasure;
> Not those new fangled toys, and triming slight
> Which takes our late fantasticks with delight,
> But cull those richest Robes, and gay'st attire
> Which deepest Spirits, and choicest Wits desire:
> I have some naked thoughts that rove about
> And loudly knock to have their passage out;
> And wearie of their place do only stay
> Till thou hast deck't them in thy best aray;
> That so they may without suspect or fears
> Fly swiftly to this fair Assembly's ears . . .

In 1645 it would hardly have been clear by what right Milton was disparaging the poetic fashions of yesterday. By 1673 he had manifestly earned the right, by fulfilling in his own way the aspiration which he had buoyantly sketched while still a Cambridge undergraduate:

> Yet I had rather if I were to chuse,
> Thy service in some graver subject use,
> Such as may make thee search thy coffers round,
> Before thou cloath my fancy in fit sound:
> Such where the deep transported mind may soare
> Above the wheeling poles, and at Heav'ns dore
> Look in, and see each blissful Deitie
> How he before the thunderous throne doth lie . . .

Milton was indeed to make the English language search all its coffers on his behalf. 'Our Language sunk under him', said Milton's first important critic, Joseph Addison, with puzzled admiration, and went on: 'and was unequal to that greatness of Soul, which furnished him with such glorious Conceptions'.

Those glorious conceptions can be glimpsed in 'At a Vacation Exercise', which earned its publication in 1673. So did Milton's translation of Horace (the Fifth Ode of Book I): 'What slender Youth bedew'd with liquid odours', a poem which made clear – as had Thomas Campion's 'Rose-cheekt Lawra' – that in English lyric poetry a musical delicacy could be achieved without benefit of rhyme. Milton's other additions in 1673 were nine further sonnets, plus further translations from the Psalms. Walter Savage Landor was to insist that Milton 'was never half so wicked a regicide as when he lifted up his hand and smote King David'.

None of the later additions substantially changed the volume which Humphrey Moseley had offered to the public (an indifferent public, apparently) in 1645:

It's the worth of these both English and Latin *Poems*, not the flourish of any prefixed *encomions* that can invite thee to buy them, though these are not without the highest Commendations and Applause of the learnedst Academicks, both domestick and forrein.

Milton's Latin poems have their biographical interest – notably *Elegies I* and *VI*, addressed to Milton's friend Charles Diodati, the *Epitaphium Damonis* (a funeral elegy on the death of Diodati which asks comparison with 'Lycidas'), and *Ad Patrem* for its glimpse of Milton's relationship with his father. Poetic skill the Latin poems have, but not much poetic life, so that although Milton gains a place in *The Penguin Book of Latin Verse* it is in the knowledge that, in John Sparrow's words, when Milton wrote in Latin he 'ceased to be a poet and became an imitator.'

Yet is the distinction between a poet and an imitator one which would have meant much in 1645? When Moseley enlisted Milton among the 'learnedest men' and then enlisted Milton's admirers among 'the learnedst Academicks', was he not betraying the fact that the English as well as the Latin poems are more impressive as skilful and erudite re-workings of earlier poetic traditions than as poems in their own right?

A modern reader is always being warned by literary historians that the Renaissance placed quite a different estimate upon originality from ours. It is true that the emphasis of literary discussion was far

more upon the ways in which a writer could profit from his predecessors and far less upon the ways in which his predecessors might
threaten and constrict his writing. By 1886 Gerard Manley Hopkins
(who knew that poets are made as well as born) could complain that
the teachable skills had been neglected. He wrote to R. W. Dixon
about

the universal fault of our literature, its weakness in rhetoric. The strictly
poetical insight and inspiration of our poetry seems to me to be of the very
finest, finer perhaps than the Greek; but its rhetoric is inadequate – seldom
firstrate, mostly only just sufficient, sometimes even below par. By rhetoric
I mean all the common and teachable element in literature, what grammar
is to speech, what thoroughbass is to music, what theatrical experience
gives to playwrights.

In many respects the Renaissance poet was better served than his
Victorian counterpart. There are no Victorian equivalents to such
works as Abraham Fraunce's *The Arcadian Rhetorike* (1588), or
George Puttenham's *The Arte of English Poesie* (1589) – works which
combine the lucidity of handbooks with the charm of anthologies.
Through them, 'the teachable element' could be livingly taught.

We may get some idea of how far the emphasis has changed,
from the word *originality* itself. The literary world managed to get
on without the word until 1787, when Sir John Hawkins used it in
his life of Dr Johnson. For the adjective *original* in the sense 'such
as has not been done or produced before; novel or fresh in character or style', we have no example before 1756, when Joseph Warton
mentioned Dante's 'sublime and original poem'.

The dictionary draws attention to a major shift of emphasis,
visible in the progress of *original*. Instead of stressing, as it once did,
'*having* an origin', it comes to stress '*not* having an origin, but *being*
itself an origin'. There is a similar shift of stress in another word
dear to romanticism, *individual*, which once meant 'indivisible, not
separable' (Milton's 'With an individual kiss', 'On Time'), and only
since 1646 has meant 'distinguished from others by attributes of its
own'. *Novelty* was for a long time a disparaging word; James I wrote
against 'an inconsiderate and childish affectation of novelty' (1604).

'Originality' puts a premium on surprise, whereas the Renaissance poet thought that surprise had to be handled with care or
else it became cheap and empty. Jonathan Richardson in 1734 drew
the right distinction in praising the 'figures' of style in *Paradise Lost*:
'Milton's Boldest Borrow'd Figures, as his Own, when they Awaken
the Mind do it not with a Sudden Crash, but as with Musick; if they
Surprize, they don't Startle Us'.

Yet the difference between Renaissance and modern is far more one of emphasis than of principle. Intelligent thinkers about literature have always realized that the relationship of a poet to his predecessors is as equivocal as that of a man to his parents. 'As guides, not commanders': that was Ben Jonson's way of following the ancients. The humanist Roger Ascham, in *The Scholemaster* (1570), had been well aware that no poet would gain anything from a slavish adherence to that principle of 'Imitation' which he nevertheless so much believed in. Ascham knew that those who disagreed with him would probably travesty his position. 'They will say it were a plaine slaverie, and injurie too, to shakkle and tye a good witte, and hinder the course of a mans good nature, with such bondes of servitude, in folowying other'.

The Renaissance emphasis upon a proper 'Imitation' is clearest in their explicit doctrine of poetic kinds or genres. In fact, poets have always written with a consciousness of poetic kinds, and a Renaissance critic would have no difficulty in showing that nine-tenths of the poems in any modern volume fall naturally into poetic kinds with their conventions and expectations. The difference is that in the seventeenth or eighteenth century the poetic kinds were spoken of more explicitly, and less anxiously, than today. Jonathan Richardson insisted that Milton's '*Mask* and *Lycidas* are perhaps Superior to all in their Several Kinds', and after quoting Sir Henry Wotton's praise of *A Mask* he added: 'As great an Encomium have I heard of *Lycidas* as a Pastoral, and That when Theocritus was not forgot; Theocritus of whom Virgil was but an Imitator in his Pastorals'.

That Milton supported this emphasis is clear from the pamphlet *Of Education* which he published in 1644. He believed that there were levels of style, and he praised 'those organic arts which inable men to discourse and write perspicuously, elegantly, and according to the fitted stile of lofty, mean, or lowly'. We may not believe that levels of style can be as crisply differentiated as the three Renaissance labels suggest, but few would find a mistaken critical principle here, and we understand what Pope was later pointing towards when he offered the following advice:

After writing a poem one should correct it all over with one single view at a time. Thus for language, if an elegy; 'these lines are very good, but are not they of too heroical a strain?', and so vice versa. It appears very plainly from comparing parallel passages touched both in the *Iliad* and *Odyssey* that Homer did this, and 'tis yet plainer that Virgil did so, from the distinct styles he uses in his three sorts of poems.

(*Spence's Anecdotes*, ed. J. M. Osborn, Oxford, 1966, i, 171)

We may resist the confident tone, and we may be anxious about the tendency of useful classifications to become perfunctory slots, but we need not find anything academic or doctrinaire about Milton's respect for those who teach 'what the laws are of a true *Epic* Poem, what of a *Dramatic*, what of a *Lyric*, what Decorum is, which is the grand master-piece to observe'. Laws? Rules? But Milton knew that great poetry was created from the tension between what had been done and what had to be done. 'Whether the rules of *Aristotle* herein are strictly to be kept, or nature to be follow'd, which in them that know art, and use judgement is no transgression, but an inriching of art.'

'Not those new fangled toys . . .', Milton had urged. The modern reader finds it easy enough to see that 'Lycidas', say, is not newfangled, but not so easy to see that it is valuably new. If Milton's 1645 poems are true poems, then they will have been written to excite surprise as well as to gratify expectations. Assured that 'Lycidas' has important affinities with Theocritus, Bion, Moschus and Virgil, a reader may retort with the most basic and most searching question of all: So what? In effect, this was the question that Dr Johnson notoriously asked of 'Lycidas'.

'In this poem there is no nature, for there is no truth; there is no art, for there is nothing new'. Have Dr Johnson's accusations ever been satisfactorily met? The scholar is liable to amass literary parallels as a substitute for showing why such accusations are wrong. Five Classical Pastoral Elegies, Two Classical Consolations, Nine Renaissance Pastorals, The Theory of the Monody, Contemporary Elegies: these are the opening sections of Scott Elledge's volume on 'Lycidas', and though they are all relevant to 'Lycidas' none of them is a substitute for a refutation of the question 'So what?'

F. R. Leavis, it is true, has held that Johnson was wrong, but wrong because he asked 'Lycidas' to be something other than it is, asked it in fact to have poetic substance and not mere artistry:

But what does *Lycidas* yield if, as the duly responding reader does not, but Johnson must, we insist on reading it for its paraphrasable substance? . . . It is difficult to see how, granted the approach, Johnson's essential criticism can be disposed of. The answer, of course, is that the approach is inappropriate and the poem a different kind of thing from any appreciable by Johnsonian criticism. One may perhaps add, in fairness to Johnson whose approach does at any rate promote this recognition, that it is a lesser thing than post-Johnsonian taste has tended to make it.

('Johnson as Critic', 1944)

The trouble is that 'paraphrasable substance' slides into meaning substance pure and simple. It is a short step from this condescension to W. H. Auden's recommendation that 'Lycidas' should be read as if it were a poem by Edward Lear – otherwise 'it must be condemned, as Dr Johnson condemned it, for being unfeeling and frivolous, since one expects wisdom or revelation, and it provides neither'.

But is 'Lycidas' unfeeling and frivolous, does it provide no wisdom? The difficulty which the poem now presents is not a matter of details (a good annotated edition will sort those out) but of its whole proceeding. This difficulty, as Dr Johnson saw, is essentially a matter of conventions. Does anything here save the pastoral from being mere play-acting or (in Robert Graves's word) fancy-dress? 'Where there is leisure for fiction, there is little grief', insisted Johnson, repudiating the whole pastoral form: 'whatever images it can supply are long ago exhausted; and its inherent improbability always forces dissatisfaction on the mind.'

The critic's job, though, is to understand what poets understand: that no convention is in itself either good or bad, and that everything depends upon how it is used. Professor M. C. Bradbrook has defined a convention as 'an agreement between writers and readers, whereby the artist is allowed to limit and simplify his material in order to secure greater concentration through a control of the distribution of emphasis'. A convention is neutral. It is true that conventions usually grow up because of some basic truth or common attitude which they crystallize, but then it is also true that this makes them all too useful to anyone who wants to fake a basic truth or a common attitude. The literary critic must avoid the trap of supposing – as Dr Johnson does with the pastoral ('... *always* forces dissatisfaction ...') – that a convention is inherently unusable, inherently falsifying. The critic must avoid too the opposite trap, of supposing that a convention is inherently foolproof, inherently truth-telling. A literary convention well-used is like that useful convention, short-hand. Ill-used, it is forgery. The question remains: what is the human relevance of this pastoral? Or 'So what?'

One mistaken answer is to settle for a human relevance derived from Milton's biography. Mistaken, not because there is anything wrong with consciously using a poem as a biographical document, but because no biographical answer can meet the straight critical quesiton put by Dr Johnson. Mistaken, too, because 'Lycidas' is very unsatisfactory as a biographical document. Take the closing lines of the poem, which frame the elegy by showing us the shepherd who has been lamenting, and then conclude:

> At last he rose, and twitch'd his Mantle blew:
> To morrow to fresh Woods, and Pastures new.

The French critic Emile Saillens has said that these closing lines 'have not yet yielded up their secret'. But why should we suppose that they have a secret? To translate the fresh woods and pastures new into a personal announcement by Milton is to substitute a biographical explanation as to the lines' existence for an artistic and critical explanation. 'Mr Richardson conceives that by this last verse the poet says (pastorally) that he is hastening to, and eager on new works', observed the eighteenth-century editor Thomas Newton: 'but I rather believe that it was said in allusion to his travels into Italy, which he was now meditating, and on which he set out the spring following.' But the sentiment of Milton's closing line is so general as to be compatible with any of a million biographical speculations. Many of the original readers in 1638 are unlikely even to have known who 'J. M.' was, let alone to have been on the lookout for Personal Column announcements hidden in his poem.

The closing lines of 'Lycidas' do not constitute a code but a convention. A convention which, effectively used, crystallizes a valid human need: to return from death to life. Despite the fact that Shakespeare's Claudius is a hypocrite, there is something perennially true and not merely 'conventional' about his injunction:

> 'Tis sweet and commendable in your nature, Hamlet,
> To give these mourning duties to your father.
> But you must know, your father lost a father;
> That father lost, lost his; and the survivor bound
> In filial obligation for some term
> To do obsequious sorrow; but to persever
> In obstinate condolement, is a course
> Of impious stubbornness, 'tis unmanly grief.
>
> (*Hamlet*, 1.2.87–94)

'Obsequious sorrow': the burden laid on the writer of an obsequy is no different from that of the man who simply grieves: that he must bring grief to an end without curtly dismissing grief. The writer of a funeral elegy has the duty to grieve for some term, but he also has the duty not to persevere in obstinate condolement. 'Let the dead bury their dead'? At any rate the dead must be buried. Milton comes to bury Edward King and to praise him. So that 'Lycidas' bears out the truth of Puttenham's words on 'the forme of poeticall lamentations': 'Lamenting is altogether contrary to rejoising; every man saith so, and yet it is a peece of joy to be able to lament with ease, and freely to poure forth a mans inward sorrowes and the greefs wherewith his minde is surcharged'. What saves the convention from being perfunctory is the implication of '*At last* he rose, and *twitch'd* his Mantle blew'. *At last* conveys with tact and force that the funeral lament has not been brusque or brief, and *twitch'd* conveys a newly decisive movement, a sense that the speaker is, with firm decision, putting the past behind him, shouldering it rather than merely shrugging it off.

A similar convention is handled with no less skill in a modern pastoral poem whose naturalness might seem remote from the world of literary conventions: Robert Frost's 'Out, Out –'. A boy caught his arm in the saw:

> They listened at his heart.
> Little – less – nothing! – and that ended it.
> No more to build on there. And they, since they
> Were not the one dead, turned to their affairs.

Frost's ending carries conviction precisely because it risks the accusation of hard-heartedness, as do the people in the poem – and as do people in life, inevitably. Yet the poem is not cynical any more than are the people it describes, people shouldering the hard fact that they are not the one who is dead and that they still have their affairs. As with the close of 'Lycidas', the effectiveness of the convention – that funeral poems end by turning back towards life – is the effectiveness of its wording. The inevitability, the manly rightness (not the 'unmanly grief' mentioned by Shakespeare's Claudius), is finely captured by Frost by setting the singular (the dying boy) against the plural (those who are left). The sequence is *They . . . his . . . it . . . they . . . they . . . the one dead . . . their affairs*. So that 'the one dead' works far more powerfully, even while less sentimentally, than would, say, 'the dead boy', just as the plurality of 'their affairs' discreetly makes a point which, say, 'their work' would not.

'Pastures new': ever since Thomas Warton's edition at the end of the eighteenth-century, it has been known that 'pastures new' was not itself new. Phineas Fletcher had created a charming and slightly preposterous vignette in order to end Canto VI of *The Purple Island* (1633):

> Home then my lambes; the falling drops eschew:
> To morrow shall ye feast in pastures new,
> And with the rising Sunne banquet on pearled dew.

Milton releases different energies by moving the two words so that instead of forming the central rhyme of a triplet, they form the closing rhyme of a couplet – and of a poem and not just a canto. 'Lycidas' ends, as in some sense every funeral elegy ought to, with the word *new*. For a shepherd the new pastures represent something more than novelty or the wish for a change – they represent work and duty. He owes it to his sheep to move on to pastures new, and no more than the man who finally turns away from grief is the shepherd evading his responsibilities.

It is in such terms as these that the end of 'Lycidas' should be read, and not for biographical free-association. The risk with biographical readings is that they will ignore artistic aptness. If we foist into the poem Milton the man, then St Peter's lines on the bad priests will seem a 'digression', the expression of Milton's personal feelings rather than the creation of a poetic relevance. In this case Milton himself must bear some of the blame – not for any words which he wrote in the poem, but for some words which he subsequently wrote above it. When it was first published in the volume of obsequies for Edward King in 1638, 'Lycidas' had needed no headnote. Reprinting it in 1645, Milton explained its provenance: 'In this Monody the Author bewails a learned Friend, unfortunatly drown'd in his Passage from Chester on the Irish Seas, 1637'. A pity that Milton did not leave it at that. Between 1638 and 1645, Archbishop Laud had fallen from favour, and Milton could not resist giving himself a pat on the back: 'And by occasion foretels the ruine of our corrupted Clergy then in their height'. But though Milton's indictment of the bad priests is certainly relevant to Laud, it is not limited to any such instance. As readers our first duty is to the poem Milton wrote in 1637, not to the headnote which he added eight years later. Despite his grim glee in 1645, Milton had not included the attack on bad priests merely in order to give vent to his personal feelings, but because of its artistic relevance.

St Peter mourns angrily:

> How well could I have spar'd for thee, young swain,
> Anow of such as for their bellies sake,
> Creep and intrude, and climb into the fold?

A digression? Only to those who forget how instinctive it is to cry out 'Why did it have to be him and not one of the wasters?' 'Lycidas' is a poem about the outrage of death, and one of the most unforced questions is 'Why are the good taken and the evil spared?' Far from being a digression, the attack on the bad priests has immediate point. When King Lear cries out to the dead Cordelia.

> No, no, no life!
> Why should a dog, a horse, a rat have life,
> And thou no breath at all?
> (5.3.305–7)

we do not consider his cry to be a digression, an irrelevant attack on the animal kingdom. The cry of passionate outrage is the same – 'Why you, why not the lower forms of life?' In *King Lear*, lower in the scale of creation; in 'Lycidas', morally lower.

'Lycidas', like so much else in Milton, is an inquiry into justice and into 'the wayes of God to men'. It is one of our greatest poems on death, one problem which shatters into many bitter questions. Why does a man like Edward King, talented and devout, suddenly die?

'Lycidas' does justice to two different sets of beliefs. Milton the man possessed the belief in which the poem ends: Christian resurrection. But Milton the poet was willing to enter into and give consummate expression to beliefs other than his own. The distinction between the two beliefs should not be expressed simply as pagan versus Christian. For Milton, as for Spenser, the pagan and the Christian intermingled, and the pagan was often taken as a type of the Christian. Spenser, like many another Renaissance poet, could speak of Christ as Pan. The crucial distinction in the poem is between the belief in an after-life and no such belief. (This is not necessarily a pagan/Christian distinction, since although Christians accept the belief in an after-life, pagans don't necessarily reject it.) In other words, there is a change of premise in the poem. What might be called Part I of the poem (which doesn't imply that the poem splits apart, merely that it signals a clear shift of belief) consists of lines 1–164: 'Yet once more, O ye Laurels, and once more . . .' The premise is simply that 'Lycidas is dead'. Then Part II, based on a different premise, begins at line 165 with an echo of the opening line: 'Weep no more, woful Shepherds weep no more'. The premise of Part II is that Lycidas is not dead – he lives in Heaven.

The strength of the poem begins in the fact that it does not do what commentators so often praise it for doing: it does not make out that Part II follows from Part I. The Christian consolation is based on a different premise from that of mortality's stoicism. You can change the premise (and Milton indeed believes that men should accept the Christian faith), but only the glib will claim that the one will somehow evolve into the other. In brief, lines 1–164 are based on the assumption that Lycidas is dead, finished. The poem up to this point does justice both to our sense of outrage, *and* to the consolations (partial, it is true, but not nothing) which are available to those who do not believe in an after-life.

But with line 165 the poem denies the premise. Instead of the

assurance that 'Lycidas is dead', we are offered the opposite
assurance: 'Lycidas your sorrow is not dead'. By denying death, the
conclusion of the poem is able to offer a consolation different in
kind from the earlier consolations, a total consolation which can
absorb the partial consolations into itself but which stands upon a
different ground. The strength of the poem, a strength which
ensures that 'Lycidas' is not merely superfluous to the Christian
and irrelevant to those who believe in no after-life, lies in the fact
that lines 1–164 of the poem (three-quarters of the poem) do justice
to our sense of horror; do justice to the consolations available even
in the face of death; and do not claim that any larger consolation
must follow as the day the night.

The obvious contrast with 'Lycidas' would simply be most Christian elegies. Most Christian elegies bully those who disagree with
them, and insist on depicting the mortal condition in stark antitheses: either the Christian consolation is true, or there is nothing
whatsoever in this life which can provide any consolation to man
confronted by death. Milton may believe that those who believe in
no after-life are wrong, but he does not take the complacent view
that this life offers nothing to sustain them. His poem, of course, is
not concerned with the evidence for or against the existence of an
after-life, but it is concerned with an honest and heartfelt inquiry
into what this life offers to men. This life does not – as most
seventeenth-century Christian apologists often make out – offer
only Christian revelation.

In the volume for Edward King, one of the elegies was by King's
brother Henry King. It begins with sentiments which furnish the
perfect contrast to 'Lycidas':

> No Death! I'le not examine Gods decree,
> Nor question providence, in chiding thee:
> Discreet Religion binds us to admire
> The wayes of providence, and not enquire.

For Milton, as man and as poet, did examine God's decree, confident that God's decree would be vindicated by such examining,
and confident too that no Christian should avert his eyes from those
things in life which hardly seem to furnish evidence of an all-loving
all-powerful God. For Milton, Death could not so simply be dis-
sociated from God and Providence; Providence could not but be
questioned; and religion was more than 'discreet'. As a religious
poet, Milton belongs with a greater poet than Henry King: Gerard
Manley Hopkins, who could echo Jeremiah and say

> Thou art indeed just, Lord, if I contend
> With thee; but, sir, so what I plead is just.

But if the structure of 'Lycidas' is of one premise replaced by another distinct premise, there are clearly two places in the poem which would seem to threaten this structure, two places where it might be argued that the earlier part of the poem invokes an after-life. The first is Phoebus, who answers the cry 'What is the point of human endeavour?' ('Were it not better don as others use . . .'). Phoebus's answer is Fame – not Fame as a matter of being well known ('Fame is no plant that grows on mortal soil'), but a more impalpable and mystical notion of heavenly fame:

> As he [Jove] pronounces lastly on each deed,
> Of so much fame in Heav'n expect thy meed.

But it is important to know just what reward ('meed') Phoebus is promising Lycidas, and the last line is ambiguous. If we read it as if there were a comma after *fame*, then it suggests that Lycidas will go to Heaven: 'of so much fame, in Heav'n expect thy meed'. But if we accept Milton's impassive lack of punctuation, we may think of 'fame in Heav'n' as the sense-unit (as if it were hyphenated), in which case Phoebus would not be promising Lycidas an after-life in Heaven, he would be promising that Lycidas would be rewarded by being famous in Heaven. Milton is a poet well aware of the virtues of ambiguity – take the famous instance at the beginning of *Paradise Lost*, where 'And justifie the wayes of God to men' packs together 'justify to men the ways of God' and 'justify the-ways-of-God-to-men'.

The point of Phoebus's ambiguity would be that within the terms of the first part of the poem, within the premise that invokes no after-life, Phoebus's words promise no more – and no less – than a noble ideal of fame; but that from the vantage point of the end of the poem, when we look back as from a plateau over the ground we have crossed, then Phoebus's words can be seen to have contained the suggestion of an after-life, the suggestion of a promise punctuated as 'of so much fame, in Heav'n expect thy meed'.

The second difficulty that needs to be met is St Peter. Doesn't his presence in the first part of the poem inevitably bring with it the promise of an after-life? But the striking thing about St Peter's speech is the extent to which it does not invoke the after-life as an answer to his own lamentation. St Peter speaks as the voice of judgement. He has two keys, but only one of them receives an adverb, an adverb which ringingly rhymes:

> Two massy Keyes he bore of metals twain,
> (The Golden opes, the Iron shuts amain).

From that point, St Peter speaks in the iron accents of judgement upon the evil, not in the golden accents of reward for the good. To the question 'Why did it have to be Lycidas, and not one of the bad priests?', St Peter's answer is nothing about Lycidas's entering upon his reward, but is fiercely about the evil entering upon their punishment:

> But that two-handed engine at the door,
> Stands ready to smite once, and smite no more.

St Peter, to put it crudely, answers the indignant cry by insisting that the bad have it coming to them.

Neither Phoebus nor St Peter, then, explicitly offers an after-life for Lycidas. Implicitly their presence may suggest it. As a reader looks back over the whole poem, he can see that its first part says, or rather suggests, many things which will sit happily as part of the Christian consolation at the end of the poem. But as a reader goes forward through the poem, the terms are not blurred or manipulated. 'Lycidas' is simply more honest than most poems of its kind.

The hinge of the poem thus becomes line 164: 'And, O ye Dolphins, waft the haples youth'. Hinge, because although this line concludes the first part of the poem, it functions too as part of the consolation of immortality which immediately follows. Its double duty is manifest in the argument as to what it alludes to. Is it, as some commentators say, an allusion to Palaemon, whose dead body was brought ashore by the dolphins and who 'became a sea deity propitious to mariners' (Newton)? Or is it an allusion to the far more famous story of Arion carried ashore by the dolphins, alive and assisted by the power of his music? Both Palaemon and Arion seem to demand a place. Palaemon, dead like Lycidas. Arion, because like Lycidas he was a sacred singer. Since we see Palaemon in the allusion, line 164 ends the first part of the poem with tragic dignity. If we glimpse Arion in the allusion, then it hints at that salvation which immediately follows:

> Weep no more, woful Shepherds weep no more,
> For Lycidas your sorrow is not dead . . .

The allusion is, in truth, profoundly ambiguous.

'Lycidas' is fashioned in two blocks (three, if one differentiates the coda which ends it: 'Thus sang the uncouth Swain to th' Okes and rills . . .'). But within the first part, the construction is radiating, not linear. There is only one problem, death, though it precipitates many questions, and there is no such thing as a logical order for the questions which throng into the mind and heart at the coming of sudden death. Lines 1–14 present the premise: 'Lycidas is dead, dead ere his prime'. Lines 15–24 speak for piety, offer a dignified account of why it is we mourn the dead at all. Lines 25–36 present in emblematic form life itself, from morning to night, with companionship, work and play. Then: 'But O the heavy change, now thou art gon' – lines 37–49 present, again in emblematic form, death itself. Then, with line 50, 'Where were ye Nymphs . . .', the questions begin.

'Lycidas' does not claim to be an obituary of Edward King. Milton's headnote in 1645 does not even think it necessary to name the 'learned Friend', and 'Lycidas' is a poem about how the sudden death of somebody one knows raises once more the largest questions about life and death. 'Lycidas' does not claim to be a detailed and intimate portrait of King. True, its nature precludes it from achieving the personal tenderness which characterizes Henry King's 'The Exequy', but personal tenderness is not the only virtue possible to a funeral elegy. Although what 'Lycidas' achieves has its limits, we must not mistake its kind or suppose that it was Milton's egotism which stopped him from writing a poem like Cowper's 'On the Receipt of My Mother's Picture Out of Norfolk'. Milton attempted a poem more of that kind in his 'Epitaph on the Marchioness of Winchester' (written in 1631).

The questions which begin at line 50 all receive some sort of answer, some partial consolation, within the terms of mortality. The consolations are partial rather than total not because Milton was fudging the issue on behalf of Christianity, but because such consolations are indeed partial. Yet they are not nothing, and Milton does them justice. Each time a cry elicits some consoling answer. Lines 50–63: Why didn't anybody stop it? They couldn't stop it even for Orpheus, greatest of poet–priests (death, at least, is not invidious). Lines 64–84: What is the point of human endeavour? Fame, in some noble sense – call it, if you prefer, self-respect or what you owe to yourself.

Lines 89–102: Who did it? And here the partial consolation is superstition. If man insists on asking who causes such inexplicable tragedies (and if he will neither invoke Providence nor call them, as the insurance companies do, 'acts of God'), then the only answer left is superstition. Either the question 'Who did this to Lycidas?' is meaningless or it must be answered superstitiously. Milton himself

saw superstition as a bitter enemy of religious truth, and many
people do not find a superstitious view of life consolatory. But many
people do. Soldiers have long found some protection in the idea
that every bullet has its billet, or that a bullet may not have your
number on it. So that when the various suspects have been interro-
gated ('ask'd . . . ask'd . . . question'd'), a man who believes in no
after-life may find some consolation, some purposefulness at least
even if it is only an evil one, in superstition:

> It was that fatall and perfidious Bark
> Built in th' eclipse, and rigg'd with curses dark,
> That sunk so low that sacred head of thine.

Then comes Cambridge (lines 103–7): like all human institutions,
he can ask a question – 'Ah; Who hath reft (quoth he) my dearest
pledge?' More words are devoted to describing the ancient dignity
of Camus than Camus himself utters.

Lines 108–31: Why wasn't it one of the bad ones? The bad ones
will not escape. Then at line 132 begins the lovely flower passage,
lavish in its evocation of beauty. This passage embodies three kinds
of consolation available to those who believe in mortality (they are
available too to the Christian, but they are virtually all that mortality
has). The consolation of the natural world and its varied inexhausti-
ble beauty; the consolation of art itself, for the poem too is a funeral
wreath for Lycidas; and the consolation of ritual.

> Bid Amaranthus all his beauty shed,
> And Daffadillies fill their cups with tears,
> To strew the Laureat Herse where Lycid lies.
> For so to interpose a little ease,
> Let our frail thoughts dally with false surmise.

It is important to be clear just what Milton refers to as a 'false
surmise'. He does not say that the ease or the thoughts are false; the
'surmise' is the pretence that Lycidas lies here upon the hearse. For
Lycidas does not – the surmise is false. Lycidas is washed far away;
the idea or memory of Lycidas (here called Lycid for the only time
in the poem, as if to suggest some distinction) is present to be
honoured, but the body of Lycidas is not. 'For so to interpose a little
ease . . .': there is nothing ignoble about such ease, nothing false
about it. Milton does not make out that no consolations exist for the
man who thinks that death closes all. Yet he knows that any such
consolations have to face the brutal casualness of death, and the
poem at once evokes that casualness:

> Ay me! Whilst thee the shores, and sounding Seas
> Wash far away, where ere thy bones are hurld . . .

Then, after the mysterious dolphins, into the Christian consolation which denies death – 'For Lycidas your sorrow is not dead'.

Is all this the 'paraphrasable substance' which we ought not to bother with? Admirers of the poem will think rather of a fine phrase by Frank Kermode when he criticized some literary fictions for being 'too consolatory to console'. 'Lycidas' ends by offering what the Christian faith claims to offer: everything. But it begins, with unusual honesty, by offering something which is no less valuable, something of which we may wish to say that it is not nothing. The originality of 'Lycidas' is inseparable from its magnanimous honesty, and as Richard Hurd said in the eighteenth century, 'there is a very original air in it, although it be full of classical imitations'.

As original, and as full of imitations, is the earlier poem 'On the Morning of Christ's Nativity'. In December 1629 Milton wrote an elegy to his friend Charles Diodati. It was fervid, for the poem on which Milton was at work was not only longer and more ambitious than any he had yet attempted, it was also his first religious poem:

If you shall seek to learn what *I* am doing (if only you think it worth your while to seek to know what I am doing), I am hymning the King of Heavenly Seed, Bringer of Peace, and the blessed generations covenanted by the holy books, and the infant cry of God, and the stabling under a poor roof of Him who with His Father cherishes the realms on high, and of the star-begetting skies, of the companies attuning their strains in the high heavens, and of the [heathen] gods, of a sudden crushed, at their own fanes. This song I offered as gift on the birthday of Christ; the first light, as the dawn drew near, gave me this song.

(Translated from Milton's *Elegia Sexta*)

To this poem, 'On the Morning of Christ's Nativity', Milton was to give pride of place in 1645. At once supple and majestic, it stands as Milton's earliest major achievement – a poem combining amplitude and spontaneity, and offering up its Hymn in a stanza of Milton's own invention, swinging with confident grace in and out of varying line-lengths and then pausing upon the dignity of an alexandrine:

> Such Musick (as 'tis said)
> Before was never made,
>   But when of old the sons of morning sung,
> While the Creator Great
> His constellations set,
>   And the well-ballanc't world on hinges hung,
> And cast the dark foundations deep,
> And bid the weltring waves their oozy channel keep.

Such music is not merely mentioned but performed here. 'The end then of Learning', Milton had written in *Of Education*, 'is to repair the ruines of our first Parents by regaining to know God aright.' The poet too might for a moment recapture that music of the spheres which had once been accessible to human ears.

'On the Morning of Christ's Nativity' stands to Milton's work somewhat as 'The Wreck of the Deutschland' stands to Hopkins's. Each might be described as the first major work of maturity, and each takes pride of place in the respective volume. Each is a hymn to God, new in shape and fertile in praise. Each shows genius. Yet they present a similar problem when we try to estimate the nature of the respective genius. 'The Wreck of the Deutschland' succeeds more masterfully in its evocation of the storm, the cosmic power and the divine mystery than it does when it turns to the actual wreck itself, the human predicament of real living dying nuns, the human horror. Yet the whole point of the poem is that it must do justice simultaneously to the divine and the human – what can it come to, to accept with resignation and awe God's providence if the poem fails to convey with equal force the full human situation which constitutes the initial tragedy?

'On the Morning of Christ's Nativity' manifests something of the same imbalance of the cosmic to the human as 'The Wreck of the Deutschland'. For Milton's excited elegy to Diodati is not an accurate representation of the poem we now have. The angelic companies and the heathen gods are indeed triumphantly there, but what of everything which made the Nativity an inalienably human occasion as well as a cosmic one? 'Except that the "infant cry of God" and the "stabling under a poor roof" do not receive in the poem the fulness of treatment the account here leads us to expect, we can hardly ask better commentary than this upon the *Nativity Ode*.' But there is more to it than Mr Diekhoff's words would suggest – what is in question is not just a discrepancy between what Milton said he would do and what he actually did, but the significance of the discrepancy. For what Milton did was to minimize the baby, the mother, the stable. He did not of course remove them from his poem on the Nativity, but he consistently reduced them to the status of the merely mentioned, while allowing full scope for the cosmic significance of the occasion. J. B. Broadbent, in a closely argued and important essay in *The Living Milton*, has shown that whenever we compare Milton's poem on the Nativity with poems on the same subject by his predecessors or contemporaries (medieval carols, Southwell, Jonson, Herbert, Crashaw, Drummond,

Vaughan, Herrick), we find that Milton has consistently thrown the weight of his genius on to one arm of the greatly paradoxical event with which he has been dealing. Continually Milton minimizes the simply human (Mary as mother, Jesus as baby), and maximizes the divine.

It is not simply that Milton puts a different emphasis from that of other writers on the Nativity. The problem is that, as in 'The Wreck of the Deutschland', the poet has chosen a subject which by its very nature does not permit of *an* emphasis at all. 'The Wreck of the Deutschland' cannot be held to be emphasizing the divine significance of the tragedy rather than the tragedy itself, because the tragedy itself can be disjoined from its significance only at the cost of dehumanizing or falsifying the poem's whole enterprise. In the same way, the author of a poem on the Nativity cannot claim that he is writing about the divine aspects of the Nativity and not about the human aspects, since the Nativity is inseparably a poignantly human event and a magnificently cosmic one. 'Immensity cloysterd in thy deare wombe': Donne's great line reminds us that a full poem on the Nativity will have to do as much justice to the dear womb as to the immensity.

Mr Broadbent's subtle account of the poem is by no means dismissive of what Milton achieved in 'On the Morning of Christ's Nativity'. But he is right to argue that what Milton achieved is disconcerting in its imperiousness as well as thrilling in its might. The fact to which Mr Broadbent draws attention – that innumerable poems on the Nativity written by men of far smaller powers than Milton are yet able to sound as he could not a range of touchingly human notes for what was among other things a touchingly human occasion – this fact has its implications for all of Milton's mature art. Agreed, the Nativity should not be sentimentally reduced to a mother and a baby, but nor should the mother and the baby be slighted or reduced to the merely mentioned. There were dangers in Milton's magisterial powers, dangers which even his greatest work was not always to avoid.

The longest work in the 1645 volume, that which we now know as *Comus*, had not been acknowledged by Milton when it was originally published in 1637. *A Maske Presented at Ludlow Castle, 1634: On Michaelmasse night, before the Right Honorable, John Earle of Bridgewater, Vicount Brackly, Lord Praesident of Wales . . .*: the details of the occasion had been made clear enough, but not the authorship. But Milton's collaborator in the masque (and his senior), the musician

Henry Lawes, dealt with the point in his dedication of the masque to the Earl of Bridgewater's son, who had in 1634 played the part of the Elder Brother: 'Although not openly acknowledg'd by the Author, yet it is a legitimate off-spring, so lovely, and so much desired, that the often Copying of it hath tir'd my Pen to give my severall friends satisfaction, and brought me to a necessity of producing it to the publike view.'

It is now too late to do anything about the name *Comus*, though the original cumbrous title is to be preferred, and not only because it was Milton's title. Preferred, first, because Comus himself is neither the hero nor the cynosure of the piece. Next, because the original title insisted upon the most important single fact about the work: that it is a masque, not a poem. Third, that the long-winded title insists that like all masques this one was brought into existence for a particular occasion, in this case a night in 1634, and for a particular audience.

Is *Comus* a masque? Miss Enid Welsford went so far as to say that 'the masque is a dramatized dance, *Comus* is a dramatized debate'. But unless one considers the *raison d'être* rather than merely its usual form, the argument is fruitless. Masques, after all (as Eugene Haun has pointed out), could be very long or very short; they could contain much dancing, music, and spectacle, or not much; they could be didactic and dramatic in varying degrees. So that it is not the relative proportions of these various ingredients that will help to estimate the nature of Milton's enterprise here, but rather a fundamental inquiry as to what exactly the masque thought that it was doing. A masque may be a minor and ephemeral genre, but at its best it offers something different in kind from either a poem or a play, while still making some use of what poems and plays can do.

The best critic of the masque, Stephen Orgel, has pointed out that 'the text was only part of a masque, and not necessarily the most important part at that. The form was by nature a composite one, the joint creation of poet, designer, composer and choreographer; and in the seventeenth century it nearly always culminated in an hour or more of ballroom dancing in which both courtly masquers and spectators participated' (*Sphere History of Literature*, vol. 3).

Since a play may employ the services of a designer, composer and choreographer, the crucial distinction between a masque and a play becomes the relation of actors to audience. The medium of a poem is words. Ezra Pound remarked that 'The medium of drama is not words, but persons moving about on a stage using words.' What then is the medium of masque? Not just persons moving about on a stage using words, but persons some of whom are to be consciously regarded both as the characters whom they are playing and with a sense of their real-life selves. In a play the real-life self of the actor is to be utterly subordinated to his part – there would be something wrong with Laurence Olivier's playing of Othello if an audience were to find itself thinking about Olivier himself instead of or as well as about Othello. But a masque is a dual or bifocal form. Those taking part in it are not all professional actors (though some may be), and the story which they act out has to be seen in a dual light both by themselves and by the audience. From one aspect, the story exists in its own right and can have dramatic virtues. But if the audience has one eye upon the fictitious story, it has the other eye upon the real-life situation, the real-life selves of the crucial actors, and the real-life tributes which the masque is devised to pay.

So it will not sufficiently differentiate a play from a masque to say that a masque has lavish spectacle, dancing and music (there is no reason why a play should not have all of these), or even to say that a masque exists to celebrate a particular occasion. There is no reason why a play shouldn't do that too. What differentiates the masque is the way it celebrates: by making use of some of the people who come together for the celebration, so that their real selves are not forgotten but are one focus of this strangely bifocal genre. 'A unique kind of relationship between its action and its audience': Mr Orgel shows that the uniqueness of the masque was that

it appealed to its audience in a very special way. It attempted from the beginning to breach the barrier between spectators and actors, so that in effect the viewer became part of the spectacle. The end toward which the masque moved was to destroy any sense of theatre and to include the whole court in the mimesis – in a sense, what the spectator watched he ultimately became. (*The Jonsonian Masque*, pp 6–7)

The importance of Mr Orgel's analysis is that it lets us define the masque 'not only by what it looked like, but by what, as a form, it was trying to achieve'.

What then was this particular masque at Ludlow Castle in 1634 trying to achieve? What, first, was it celebrating? The Earl of Bridgewater had been named Lord President of Wales in 1631; this position as viceroy was officially confirmed in 1633. In 1634 the Earl's family were to join him at his official residence, Ludlow Castle, and the masque was to celebrate the family reunion and the Earl's investiture. The music would be the work of Henry Lawes, to whom Milton was to address a sonnet in 1646. It is clear from the manuscripts of the masque that there was more music than has survived. Lawes himself would play the part of the Attendant Spirit who introduces the masque, surveys its events with a beneficent eye, and takes the shape of one Thyrsis. So that when the Elder Brother hails Thyrsis, the audience will be considering his words not only within the fable itself but also in the recognition that they are spoken too of the real-life Lawes:

> Thyrsis? Whose artful strains have oft delaid
> The huddling brook to hear his madrigal,
> And sweeten'd every muskrose of the dale . . .
>
> (lines 494-6)

Lawes/Thyrsis is important to the story because of the watchful reassurance which his presence confers. But the Lady and her two Brothers are important because they are the Earl's children. Lady Alice Egerton was fifteen, and her brothers were eleven and nine. She had recently appeared in Aurelian Townshend's masque *Tempe Restored*, and her brothers had appeared in Thomas Carew's *Coelum Britanicum*. With the experience not only of Lawes but also of the Earl's children, Milton was able to fashion a masque which asked much of, and gave much to, its youthful actors. We do not know who played Comus himself, or the nymph Sabrina who rescues the Lady when she is imprisoned by Comus's spell; neither Comus nor Sabrina is created out of an interplay between their roles in the fable and their off-stage selves, since neither of them has an off-stage self.

The fable of the masque is simple enough. The Lady and her two Brothers are on their way to attend their father's ceremony. In the wood the Lady gets separated from her Brothers, and she comes upon Comus and his riotous revellers. Comus simulates virtue, pretends to be a shepherd, and leads her off. The Brothers are told of this by Thyrsis, who warns them against Comus's magic, and gives them the protection of the plant haemony. Comus urges the Lady to drink his potion, but she spiritedly rebuffs him. The Brothers enter and drive off Comus and his crew, but they are unable to release the Lady, magically imprisoned in her chair, until Thyrsis calls upon Sabrina, nymph of the river Severn, who frees the Lady. She and her Brothers are thus able to resume their journey, and the masque ends after they have been presented to their parents at Ludlow Castle.

Right from the start, though, this fable is presented to the audience along with reminders of the off-stage situation which it was devised to celebrate. In his opening speech, the Attendant Spirit speaks of Neptune and his tributary gods, and then turns to the relevant entrusting of power, that to the Earl of Bridgewater:

> And all this tract that fronts the falling Sun
> A noble Peer of mickle trust, and power
> Has in his charge, with temper'd awe to guide
> An old, and haughty Nation proud in Arms:
> Where his fair off-spring nurs't in Princely lore,
> Are coming to attend their Fathers state,
> And new-entrusted Scepter, but their way
> Lies through the perplex't paths of this drear Wood . . .
>
> (lines 30–7)

The best commentary on what Milton was doing is again by Mr Orgel:

Comus is frequently adduced as the death blow of the masque, yet in many respects it applied Jonson's technique with a success the earlier poet himself rarely attained. That Milton was constantly aware of his work as a real masque – as a symbolic representation of the milieu in and for which it was created, as a production wherein, when the lords and ladies became masquers, the real world became indistinguishable from the world of the masque – is obvious from the frequency and complexity with which references to his audience, the Earl of Bridgewater and his family and court, are woven into the fabric of the piece.

(The Jonsonian Masque, p 102)

But what truth can be expressed through this bifocal form? The modern reader is likely to remain sceptical, since the only comparable occasions which still exist are trivial ones. Parents who watch a school play watch not only the play itself but also their children acting it; the pleasant tension of the occasion demands that the children should act well enough for the play's fable to exist but yet not so well as to achieve the professional transparency by which we forget about the off-stage selves of actors altogether. The same might be said of a party-game like charades, or of an amateur cabaret within an institution like a college – both the actors and the audience take their pleasure in combining a response to the charade or cabaret in itself with a response to the knowledge that it is these particular people already known to us who are doing the acting. School plays, charades, and amateur cabarets offer something of the double feeling characteristic of the masque. But then what saves Milton's masque from triviality?

The answer is the true relation that can exist between one's acting and one's actions. Milton's masque celebrates the accession to power of the Earl of Bridgewater, and the sequence of Milton's words suggests a relationship between the Earl's future ability to guide an ancient nation and his past ability to guide his young children:

> . . . Has in his charge, with temper'd awe to guide
> An old, and haughty Nation proud in Arms:
> Where his fair off-spring nurs't in Princely lore,
> Are coming to attend their Fathers state,
> And new-entrusted Scepter. . . .

A man must first be able to rule himself before he can rule others; in the words of Christ in *Paradise Regained*,

> Yet he who reigns within himself, and rules
> Passions, Desires, and Fears, is more a King;
> Which every wise and vertuous man attains:
> And who attains not, ill aspires to rule
> Cities of men, or head-strong Multitudes . . .
>
> (ii.466–70)

The goodness and obedience of the Earl's children are relevant to that goodness and obedience which the Earl must inculcate, with a firm discretion, in his territories. What better earnest could there be of the Earl's pre-eminent fitness to rule Wales than to show us that miniature society over which he has already proved his kindly rule: his family? The Lord President of Wales has fatherly responsibilities, and Milton writes long before the objection to 'paternalistic rule'. By fashioning a story, then, in which the Earl's children are shown acting with courage and firmness in the face of trials and temptations, Milton was able to suggest good cause for his confidence that the Earl of Bridgewater was indeed 'a noble Peer of mickle trust, and power'. The climax of the masque is the presentation of the children to their parents, when the fable for a moment slips aside and all eyes are upon the children as their off-stage selves:

> Noble Lord, and Lady bright,
> I have brought ye new delight,
> Here behold so goodly grown
> Three fair branches of your own,
> Heav'n hath timely tri'd their youth,
> Their faith, their patience, and their truth.
> And sent them here through hard assays
> With a crown of deathless Praise,
>   To triumph in victorious dance
> O're sensual Folly, and Intemperance.
>
> (lines 966–75)

After which there remains only the epilogue.

Yet doesn't all this too raise its own problem, since the masque is so unabashedly a vehicle for showing how good the children are? What saves the fable from being mere unctuousness? Again the answer is a relationship of acting to action. The Earl's children have shown, at least in some degree, their courage, self-command and obedience not only in the fable but by participating in the masque itself. Even when we allow for the fact that the masque as performed in 1634 was shorter than the published 1637 text, it still remains true that the masque was not only about a challenge to the children but did itself constitute a challenge to them. Only children (aged fifteen, eleven, and nine) in whom were budding the virtues which the Earl's upbringing of them ought to have inculcated could have acted this masque with success – such at any rate is the aspiration or the augury of the piece. Milton, who wrote much about education, created a masque which is about education and upbringing ('Here behold so goodly grown . . .'). The Earl's children deserve to be complimented within the fable for defeating Comus; within the masque but outside the fable, they deserve to be complimented for their manifest and enacted obedience, propriety and self-command in homage to their father. The most often recited of all nineteenth-century party-pieces was Mrs Hemans's

> The boy stood on the burning deck
> Whence all but he had fled . . .

The nineteenth-century boy who had to stand there and recite it must often have felt as if he were on a burning deck, longing to flee.

As an educational principle, the idea that children achieve virtues in part by learning how to say the right thing about virtues has its limitations (though it is not simply false). But the idea on which Milton's masque rests is one which may seem less dated or less servile when we find something similar in W. B. Yeats:

I think that all happiness depends on the energy to assume the mask of some other self; that all joyous or creative life is a re-birth as something not oneself, something which has no memory and is created in a moment and perpetually renewed. . . .

There is a relation between discipline and the theatrical sense. If we cannot imagine ourselves as different from what we are and assume that second self, we cannot impose a discipline upon ourselves, though we may accept one from others. Active virtue as distinguished from the passive acceptance of a current code is therefore theatrical, consciously dramatic, the wearing of a mask. It is the condition of arduous full life.

(Autobiography)

A masque like *Comus* begins in the wearing of a mask; it ends in demonstrating a relation between discipline and the theatrical sense.

It is on some such lines that Milton's masque must be differentiated from a play or poem. If we wanted a poem for comparison, there is Marvell's 'Upon Appleton House', another work which pays tribute to a great public figure at his noble home and which does so by invoking as indispensably relevant to his public powers his virtuous and happy family. At the end of 'Upon Appleton House', Marvell praises Lord Fairfax and his wife by praising their daughter Maria. She is a nymph who has resisted the stratagems of love, tears, sighs, and flattery:

> But knowing where this Ambush lay,
> She scap'd the safe, but roughest Way.

> This 'tis to have been from the first
> In a Domestick Heaven nurst,
> Under the Discipline severe
> Of Fairfax and the starry Vere.

Milton's Lady, like Marvell's Maria, has escaped the ambush, and she has done so because a true father, himself a true public figure, had succeeded in creating a domestic Heaven which yet has, like Heaven, a discipline severe. The difference between Marvell's tribute and Milton's is one of medium: Marvell creates, solely from words, a tribute to Maria and through her to her family, a tribute which is also a good augury. Milton brings his Lady on to the stage to say his words and to hear them said, so that the medium for his tribute (an augury too) is not words alone but the-Earl's-children-and-words. The vitality of *Comus* in comparison with the mere elegance of his other courtly tribute 'Arcades' (1630, in honour of Alice, Countess Dowager of Derby) stems from the fact that *Comus* is committedly a masque, whereas 'Arcades' is that more half-hearted or aimless thing, 'Part of an Entertainment'.

In the 1645 volume Milton attempted many poetic kinds. His *Reason of Church-Government* (1642) had mentioned 'those magnifick Odes and Hymns wherein *Pindarus* and *Callimachus* are in most things worthy', and three of the 1645 poems have affinities with such odes and hymns: 'On Time', 'Upon the Circumcision', and 'At a Solemn Musick'. Written probably in 1630–31, they manifest some of Milton's abiding concerns (notably, 'the fair musick that all creatures made' before the Fall), and they have considerable tech-

nical interest. Milton's experiments here with a varying line-length
and with entwined rhyming are important not only to 'Lycidas'
(based like them on an adaptation of the Italian *canzone*, as Professor F. T. Prince has shown), but also as anticipations of the
choruses in *Samson Agonistes*. After the great middle period in which
he was to deplore 'the troublesom and modern bondage of
Rimeing', Milton would return in *Samson Agonistes* to a sense of
what flexible rhyming could achieve. His three early pieces had long
ago given him some idea.

Then there are the sonnets. Dr Johnson believed that 'of the best
it can only be said that they are not bad'. But without confusing
historical interest with intrinsic value, one may still believe that
Johnson does less than justice to a sonnet such as 'On the late
Massacher in Piemont'. The great age of the sonnet was past – a
fact which brought with it the advantage that no longer did all bad
poets feel obliged to issue vacuous sonnet sequences. Milton's
sonnets – the only ones written between Shakespeare and the
Romantics which are still much read – stay for the most part within
the terms of 'occasional' verse. Yet, as Wordsworth commanded,
'Scorn not the Sonnet', for Milton had shown what the sonnet
could do:

> in his hand
> The Thing became a trumpet, whence he blew
> Soul-animating strains – alas, too few!

But as a sonnet writer, Milton had a wider range of instruments
than just the trumpet. Though often soul-animating, the best of his
sonnets have a hard and sandy texture of personalities which protects them against the smooth-sliding vapidity of so much sonnet
writing.

Mark Pattison pointed out that 'the effectiveness of Milton's
sonnets is chiefly due to the real nature of the character, person, or
incident, of which each is the delineation. Each person, thing, or
fact, is a moment in Milton's life, on which he was stirred.' There is
an idealistic fervour in the sonnets, but not an idealizing away of
people and things. Perhaps the praise ought not to be that 'the
Thing became a trumpet', but that the sonnet became a thing –
instead of an essence or a shimmer. Not that there was any simple
originality in Milton's subject matter – sonnets of public life had
been commonplace, but what was new was Milton's authoritative
directness.

Some of the sonnets are the work of Milton the prose controversialist. Of sonnets like 'A Book was writ of late call'd Tetrachordon' and 'I did but prompt the age to quit their cloggs', it might be said, as of Milton's prose, that they give as good as they get. A great poet, though, ought perhaps to give better. It is only in 'On the late Massacher in Piemont' (written 1655, added in 1673) that Milton's passionately uncomplicated indignation issues in a great sonnet, one which cries for divine vengeance against the Papal massacre of the Protestant Waldensians: 'Avenge O Lord thy slaughter'd Saints . . .'

It is a poem which has the right kind of simplicity, of directness. But the sonnets show too how an oblique treatment could bring out the best in Milton's poetry. One of his final sonnets, written in 1654 or 1655, 'Methought I saw my late espoused Saint', does not have his blindness for its central subject, but for that very reason it is perhaps his most poignant poem on blindness. 'Methought I saw . . .' 'Her face was vail'd, yet to my fancied sight . . .' Veiled to be one day unveiled in Heaven? Veiled like Alcestis brought back from the grave? Veiled by Milton's blindness? The biographers continue to dispute as to which wife Milton here has a vision of, Katherine Woodcock or Mary Powell, but what matters is the crystal simplicity of the vision itself. It is the crown of Milton's sonnets, combining the impersonality of the old literature and 'the old Law' with a touching personal humility and pathos.

There remain 'L'Allegro' and 'Il Penseroso', poems which present the literary critic with the difficulty presented by all poems the main point of which is charm: that there is little to be said about charm. They belong to Milton's Cambridge days, and probably date from 1631 or 1632. Neither poem offers any sure foothold for biographical speculation; both offer a wealth of parallels to earlier light-hearted poetic exercises. (J. B. Leishman amassed a great many such parallels.) L'Allegro banishes Melancholy and calls upon Mirth; Il Penseroso banishes Mirth and calls upon Melancholy. Each poem makes a case with a good-humoured delicacy. Clearly such a pair of complementary poems has an affinity with the academic exercise of which Milton left us examples in his Cambridge 'Prolusions'; E. M. W. Tillyard, who suggested this, pressed it to the point of invoking the debate of Milton's First Prolusion, 'Whether Day or Night is the more excellent'. The success of the poems is a matter of their unpretentiousness, their technical facility (Milton nowhere else made such various and sensitive use of the octosyllabic couplet), and their descriptive vignettes:

> But let my due feet never fail,
> To walk the studious Cloysters pale,
> And love the high embowed Roof,
> With antick Pillars massy proof,
> And storied Windows richly dight,
> Casting a dimm religious light.
>
> ('Il Penseroso', lines 155–60)

But religion here has been softened and attenuated into a delightful stage set. Such a religious light does indeed seem dim if we think of Milton's great religious poetry, and both 'L'Allegro' and 'Il Penseroso' offer light without heat. The comparison, to Milton's disadvantage when it comes to substantiality, would be with his good friend Andrew Marvell, a poet in whom a gentle touch and a charming tone can be surprisingly combined with strong conviction. 'L'Allegro' and 'Il Penseroso' show that Milton could create the delicate and miniature, but they do not show that he could fashion the delicate and miniature into the substantial. In short, they are not – as 'Lycidas', 'On the Morning of Christ's Nativity', and *Comus* are – the works which vindicate the words of Humphrey Moseley when he offered the 1645 *Poems* to the world: 'Let the event guide it self which way it will, I shall deserve of the age, by bringing into the Light as true a Birth, as the Muses have brought forth since our famous Spenser wrote; whose Poems in these English ones are as rarely imitated, as sweetly excell'd. Reader, if thou art Eagle-eied to censure their worth, I am not fearful to expose them to thy exactest perusal.'

PARADISE LOST

John M. Steadman

I

The creation of Milton's old age, the production of a blind
scholar closely identified with a defeated cause and 'fall'n on evil
dayes', *Paradise Lost* is also the fruit of a lifetime's 'labour and
intent study'. To it Milton brought his profound knowledge of
Scripture and Biblical commentary, his theological and scientific
erudition, his wide reading in the classics and his familiarity with
Renaissance poetics, his experience as rhetorician and logician,
and (above all) 'that one Talent which is death to hide,' his
poetic genius. In it he fulfilled the Renaissance ideal of the *poeta
doctus*, the learned poet. Only a profoundly learned man could
have drawn so readily on so wide and varied a store of erudition.
Only an exceptionally gifted poet could have welded his erudition
into a closely-knit structure and endowed it with poetic form. His
epic is thus a literary victory won out of personal and political
defeats, private and public humiliations. But it is also the reflection of a moral triumph, the outcome of his hard-fought
struggle with himself. The necessary precondition of mastering
his materials and the form he sought to impose on them was (as
he himself realized) self-mastery: 'He who would not be frustrate
of his hope to write well hereafter in laudable things, ought him
selfe to bee a true Poem', a 'patterne of the best and hon-
ourablest things. . . .' (*An Apology for Smectymnuus*).

Like many other writers of his period, Milton regarded epic
and tragedy as the loftiest, but also the most difficult, of the
genres – twin peaks of Parnassus to be essayed only after long
practice on lesser eminences, the easier gradients of elegy and
pastoral. Like Dryden, he believed that 'heroic poetry . . . has
ever been esteemed . . . the greatest work of human nature.'
From an early age he had displayed a keen interest in this genre
– though he did not yet, apparently, consider the loss of Paradise
as an epic theme. His brief epyllion on the Gunpowder Plot ('In
Quintum Novembris', composed when he was seventeen) had

exploited conventional epic devices – divine and infernal machinery and allegorical personifications – as means of adorning and amplifying his subject. His Sixth Elegy (written in December, 1629) had stressed the sobriety and chastity essential for the poet who aspired to celebrate heroic materials – divine councils and infernal kingdoms, wars (a subject he would eventually reject), and the deeds of pious heroes and demigods. In *Mansus* (written during his Italian journey, 1638–9) he had considered subjects drawn from British history; native kings, Arthur's subterranean battles, the feats of 'magnanimous heroes' of the Round Table against the Saxon invader. In *Epitaphium Damonis* (1640) he had again contemplated British themes: the voyages of Brutus, the wars of Brennus and Belinus and Arviragus, the birth of Arthur. In the Cambridge Manuscript he had noted (between 1640 and 1642) the possibility of a heroic poem on a Saxon subject; Alfred's adventures among the Danes had seemed to him comparable to the exploits of Ulysses. As late as *The Reason of Church-Government* (1642) he had still considered the possibility of an epic based on British or early English history ('our own ancient stories') and embodying 'the pattern of a Christian Heroe' in some 'King or Knight before the conquest'. Finally, in the *Defensio Secunda* (1654) he had likened himself to the epic poet who celebrates a single action instead of describing the whole life of his hero: 'I have at least embellished one of the heroic actions of my countrymen. . . .'

He never wrote the national epic he had once contemplated – and how seriously he had considered it is open to question. The suggestion that he probably compiled a list of epic subjects to complement his list of tragic themes seems unconvincing; the fact that his notes for tragedies include one epic theme (the exploits of King Alfred) argues against the existence of a separate list, now lost. Likewise subject to doubt is the widespread notion that he actually decided on – and later abandoned – plans for an 'Arthuriad'. Although an Arthurian theme undoubtedly attracted him when he wrote *Mansus*, it is much less prominent in *Epitaphium Damonis*. (Here the alleged 'Arthuriad' is literally embryonic, for instead of a tale of Arthur's martial exploits, Milton promises an account of the hero's conception – a legend that closely parallels the story of Amphitryon and the conception of Hercules.)

On the whole, the projected 'Arthuriad' seems to be largely an invention of Milton's biographers.[1] Though he *was* at this time thinking seriously about a national epic,[2] he had not yet settled on a definite subject. His immediate plans centred on the drama rather than the epic, and it was in that medium (perhaps as early as 1642) that he first attempted a major poem.

Unlike his early schemes for an epic, his dramatic plans included Biblical subjects in addition to arguments based on British history. In heroic poetry he sought a national theme; in tragedy he considered sacred as well as patriotic subjects, and in the Cambridge Manuscript his most fully developed dramatic plans are drawn from sacred history. His first major enterprise – a tragedy on the fall of

[1] In *Mansus* Milton apparently suggests *two* alternative Arthurian themes as subjects for heroic poetry – Arthur's underground battles *or* ('aut') *the* knights of the Round Table. Though Arthur's court would probably have figured prominently in the latter narrative, there is no indication that it would have celebrated Arthur himself as its hero or selected his exploits as epic argument. In the *Epitaphium Damonis* Igraine's pregnancy (with Arthur) is merely one among many British legends he proposes to celebrate; the persons and events he mentions range in time from the arrival of the Britons to that of the Saxons. He could hardly have compressed all of these stories into a 'regular' epic (except, as in *Paradise Lost*, through interpolated historical or prophetic episodes); yet he gives no indication as to which, if any, of these tales would have constituted the principal argument. (Conceivably, he may have envisaged a narrative poem of the chronicle type, or even a series of short narrative poems on each of these themes.) This passage offers little warrant for inferring that the heroic poem he contemplates would have been an 'Arthuriad'. The fuller account of his poetic ambitions in *The Reason of Church-Government* casts further doubts on any serious plans for such a work. He has not yet determined the identity or even the nationality of his 'Christian hero'. (The king or knight before the Conquest may be either British or Anglo-Saxon.) Nor has he decided on the length or form of his epic. (It may be either diffuse or brief, composed according to 'the rules of Aristotle' or observing the natural order followed by romancers like Boiardo and Ariosto.) Indeed, he has not even decided on his genre – whether to demonstrate his powers in an epic, a drama, or 'magnific odes and hymns'. Milton's early statements of his epic ambitions provide little solid evidence, therefore, for inferring that he had decided on an 'Arthuriad'.
Nor do they indicate that he regarded a national epic as a project for the *immediate* future. (The ambitious schemes mentioned in his Latin poems on Mansus and on Diodati's death are scarcely indicative of his immediate plans, any more than the 'wars' and 'pious heroes' of his Sixth Elegy.) Apparently he did not yet consider his powers sufficiently mature for a heroic poem. For discussion of his plans for an 'Arthuriad' see Roberta F. Brinkley, *Arthurian Legend in the Seventeenth Century* (Baltimore, 1932) and E. M. W. Tillyard, *The Miltonic Setting* (London and New York, 1938).

[2] Various explanations have been advanced for Milton's 'abandoning' his plans for a national epic and turning instead to a subject he had hitherto considered as a dramatic theme: doubts as to the historicity of King Arthur and other British worthies whose exploits he had promised to celebrate; the royalist overtones of these themes and in particular their close association with the genealogical claims of the Tudors and Stuarts; growing disillusionment with his countrymen in the later years of the Commonwealth. The closing of the theatres in 1642 may also

man – was to be a divine poem, based on Scripture and celebrating the justice and mercy of God. It was as a divine poet that he began – abortively – his career as a dramatist; and it was as a divine poet that he would eventually – many years later – achieve his principal triumphs.

Heading his notes for dramatic subjects in the Cambridge Manuscript are three sketches for a drama on Adam's fall. The first two drafts (untitled and subsequently cancelled) merely list the characters in order of their appearance. The third (entitled 'Paradise Lost') divides the drama into a prologue and five acts, with brief notes as to their content. A fourth and fuller draft appears later in the manuscript under the title 'Adam Unparadiz'd' but with the cancelled title 'Adams Banishment'. Both of these later drafts call for choral songs, and the fourth includes 'a masque of all the evils of this life and world.' Milton originally conceived his poem, therefore, as a *sacra rappresentazione* or *dramma per musica*; and like his epic it combined classical form, Biblical history, and Christian doctrine. (Music and spectacle had been characteristic of Greek tragedy, and it was a deliberate attempt to imitate classical drama on these points that fostered the development of the Italian opera. There is unconscious irony in Dryden's attempt to reconstruct *Paradise Lost* as an opera, thus reconverting Milton's epic into a music-drama.) From these scattered notes eventually developed a heroic poem comprising – as Andrew Marvell said – 'Heav'n, Hell, Earth, Chaos, All', an epic that 'considered with respect to design, [might] claim the first place, and with respect to performance the second, among the productions of the human mind' (Dr Johnson).

How far Milton proceeded in his drama on the fall and how much of it he incorporated in his epic is unknown. His nephew Edward Phillips recalled seeing 'Ten Verses, which several Years before the Poem was begun, were shewn to me, and some others, as designed for the very beginning of the said Tragedy'; these were the opening lines of Satan's apostrophe to the sun (iv. 32–41). About

---

have caused him to modify his original plans for *Paradise Lost* as a drama. Milton's real motives must necessarily remain conjectural, but they may well have been his temperamental distaste for the theme of 'Warrs' (as he himself asserts in *Paradise Lost*), his recognition of the epic potentialities of the theme of the fall, his awareness of advancing age (he was fifty in 1658, and must establish himself now or never as a major poet), and his desire to enrich the tradition of divine poetry with a Biblical epic. In contrast to Milton's detailed plans for a drama on the fall, his ideas for a national epic had always been vague, general, and even conflicting. He can hardly be said to have 'abandoned' his plans for such a work, for he had never, apparently, formulated them with any clarity. The significant fact, accordingly, is not so much that the theme of the fall 'displaced' British and Anglo-Saxon themes in his epic plans as that he elected to imitate the fall of man in a heroic poem instead of in a drama.

two years before the Restoration, according to John Aubrey (i.e. around 1658), Milton began his epic and spent some four or five years in composing it. He completed it (Aubrey continues, on Phillips' authority) 'about 3 years after the K.'s restoration' (i.e., around 1663). The poem was published in 1667, in ten books. The second edition (1674) increased the number of books to twelve by dividing Books VII and X.[1]

'Biographically,' Professor Hanford suggests, '*Paradise Lost* is two poems.' Having originally conceived and actually begun the poem as a drama in the early 1640s, Milton subsequently redesigned and rewrote it as an epic in roughly five to seven years (*c*.1658–*c*.1663 or 1665). More than a decade, apparently, intervened between the two stages of its composition – crucial years in his private and public life and for the political and ecclesiastical causes with which he had identified himself. As Secretary for Foreign Tongues to the Council of State, he had reached the zenith of his public career. He had won international fame as a Latin controversialist; all three of his major *Defences* had appeared before the end of 1655. But he had sacrificed his own eyesight in his service to the state; he had buried two wives and a son and daughter; he had broken irretrievably with the Presbyterian party; and he felt increasing misgivings about his nation's future – growing doubts concerning his countrymen's willingness and ability to preserve their hard-won liberties. On the national stage – that 'tragic scaffold' – a king and an archbishop had been executed for high treason. In church and state, royal and

[1] The 1674 edition is now regarded by many scholars as the more authoritative of the two, though certain readings in the 1667 are still widely accepted. How far either edition, in spelling and punctuation, actually conformed to Milton's intentions must remain uncertain, since relatively little is known about the circumstances under which proofs were read and corrected. (Robert M. Adams, in *Milton and the Modern Critics*, Ithaca, 1966, suggests that 'Milton . . . left the details of his text to the printer' and that 'if he checked proof at all, he usually checked it, not against the MS, but against memory and his own ear,' p 75.) Among the *Errata* listed in the first edition, one in particular ('Lib. 2. V. 414, for *we* r[ead] *wee*') has aroused considerable discussion in recent years concerning the spelling of Milton's personal pronouns; many scholars regard these variations as stressed or unstressed, emphatic or unemphatic forms. Among recent attempts to reconstruct Milton's intentions in spelling and punctuation, see the editions of his poetry by Helen Darbishire, John Shawcross, and B. A. Wright. In dividing Book VII (1667) line 641 was suppressed and four new lines added at the beginning of Book VIII (1674). In dividing Book X (1667) five additional lines were added as a head-link to Book XII (1674). In 1668 the arguments and a note on the verse were added to the remaining copies of the first edition. The second edition retained these features, but distributed the arguments at the head of each book and added two encomiastic poems by Dr Samuel Barrow and Andrew Marvell.

episcopal government had been abolished; yet the establishment of the Commonwealth and the further reformation of the church had failed to guarantee domestic concord. Monarchical sentiments were still strong among the Presbyterians themselves – even among men who, like Prynne, had suffered ignominious penalties under Charles I and Archbishop Laud. The Reformed clergy had become, in Milton's eyes, as greedy and intolerant as the episcopacy: 'New Presbyter is but Old Priest writ Large.' Open hostility between Independent and Presbyterian, Army and Parliament, had rendered constitutional procedures virtually impossible; only a thinly disguised military dictatorship – Cromwell's Protectorate – maintained the continuity of responsible government. When Milton resumed his work on Paradise Lost, Cromwell himself was in failing health, dying in the autumn of 1658.

The period in which Milton dictated his epic was marked by other reversals equally dramatic. The Restoration naturally terminated his public duties, already reduced because of his blindness. Forced into hiding and temporarily imprisoned for his defence of the regicides, he completed his poem in retirement, afflicted by illness and financial losses, publicly abused by partisans of the new regime, yet still visited by discerning admirers from home and abroad. Beginning his epic on the eve of the Commonwealth's collapse, he completed it after the final débâcle of the church and state he had fought for. His political and ecclesiastical ideals now seemed farther from realization than they had ever been. Restoration of the Stuarts had not only revived episcopacy with the monarchy; it had also awakened fears of an eventual return to papal jurisdiction under a Roman Catholic monarch.

Milton made ample use of the epic poet's traditional licence to speak in his own person, interposing his own commentary on action and characters, and introducing fairly extended statements about himself. Rhetorically, such passages functioned as ethical proof; as in the Defensio Secunda, they served, in part at least, to counter the accusations of his enemies. As in the Defensio Secunda, he contrasts his physical blindness with the inner light of spiritual vision. He laments the 'evil dayes' on which he has fallen, only to express the inner consolation he derives from his Heavenly Muse and the pleasure he still finds in 'sacred song'. He professes his distaste for the martial subjects conventional in epic literature; he is 'Not sedulous by Nature to indite/Warrs', to 'dissect' fabulous knights in imaginary battles, to describe the paraphernalia of tournaments or the ceremonial of courtly feasts. From time to time, he pauses to

282 POETRY AND PROSE 1540–1674

deliver satiric thrusts against kings, courtiers, or the Roman church. Antimonarchical commonplaces reminiscent of his political treatises recur in his portrait of Satan. As Professor Merritt Hughes has observed, Satan resembles Nimrod (the legendary founder of Babylon) as the archetypal tyrant. Moreover, the language in which Milton portrays the devil's regal pretensions recalls the arguments that Salmasius, Hobbes, and other defenders of monarchy had advanced for the divine right of kings; they were not only vicegerents of God Himself, but terrestrial 'gods'. Attended with 'God-like imitated State', Satan is the 'Idol of Majestie divine'; and his followers accord him the reverence due a divinity – 'as a God/Extoll him equal to the highest in Heav'n'. Like a king in parliament, Satan delivers his speech from the throne – and, with the aid of his principal confidant (Beëlzebub) tricks them into accepting a preconceived strategy that will serve his own ends. Finally, it is in terms of the similarities between the British monarchy and the infernal kingdom that their most notable difference becomes significant. England had been torn by dissensions not only between king and parliament, but between rival factions in parliament itself. In Hell, on the other hand, parliament and king unite in a common resolution; 'Devil with Devil damn'd/Firm concord holds, men onely disagree. . . .'

Other characteristically Miltonic convictions recur throughout *Paradise Lost*. Like his prose, his epic emphasizes the spiritual preconditions of liberty and its ultimate dependence on divine law. True freedom is founded on obedience to right reason; external liberty is based on inner liberty, and this in turn is contingent on inward righteousness. Inasmuch as deliverance had been a conventional epic theme, the nature and foundation of 'real' freedom possesses heroic implications. The teacher of righteousness is thus potentially more heroic than the general; the martyr, who suffers reproach for his witness to divine truth, exemplifies a 'better fortitude' than the physical courage of the soldier. The supremely heroic 'deliverer,' however, is Christ Himself, who alone possesses the fullness of divine wisdom and who alone can restore man's internal freedom through regeneration.

In his epic as in his theological treatise, moreover, Milton presents a version of predestination that seems closer to Arminian than to strictly Calvinist doctrine. Emphasizing human freedom and universal grace, he makes predestination to salvation contingent rather than absolute; in his view, this decree applies properly and specifically to election only rather than to reprobation, and man is at liberty to accept or reject divine grace.

II

Biographically, then, *Paradise Lost* represented the fulfilment of
Milton's lifelong ambition to 'adorn' his native tongue and to leave
something 'so written to aftertimes, as they should not willingly let
it die'. Historically, it consolidated, reshaped, and (for better or
worse) dominated the English epic tradition. Composed on
Homeric and Virgilian models and constructed (in intent at least)
according to what Milton, in *Of Education*, called the 'laws ... of a
true Epic Poem' as set forth 'in Aristotle's Poetics, in Horace, and
the Italian Commentaries' it was the first major 'classical' epic in
the English language. (Spenser's epic belonged essentially to the
romantic rather than to the neoclassical tradition.) In spite of
dissenting voices, it soon established itself as a modern classic.
Continental and British critics alike turned to it for examples of
the 'grand style,' illustrations of the Longinian sublime, or proof
that the moderns might successfully compete with the ancients.
Literary theorists must henceforth add Milton to the small group
of moderns who might compare with the epic writers of antiquity.
England's place in the European heroic tradition was, in large
part, achieved and consolidated by *Paradise Lost*.

Equally important for many of its early readers was its bearing
on the long-standing dispute over the relative merits of secular
and sacred themes. With greater scope than Du Bartas' *Judith* and
greater fidelity to neoclassical standards than *La Sepmaine*, it
reinforced the claims other poets had advanced in favour of
Biblical arguments for heroic poetry. Demonstrating once and for
all that a modern poet, writing in the vernacular, could successfully impose classical form on Scriptural subject matter, that the
Heavenly Muse could soar as high as (or perhaps higher than) the
muses of Helicon, it had rendered distinguished service on behalf
of 'divine' poetry.

In utilizing the Christian marvellous, Milton committed himself
on yet another controversial issue – the nature and function of epic
machinery. Several critics had ruled out the supernatural element
altogether as defying verisimilitude. Some had sanctioned the
Christian marvellous, permitting or indeed urging the heroic poet to
imitate the Christian God and his angels. Others had insisted that
divine persons were entirely too sacred for direct representation,
even in heroic poetry. Tasso had introduced the Christian God
and angelic messengers into his epic on the First Crusade;
Camoens had incongruously retained the classical gods in his

heroic poem on Vasco da Gama's expedition to India – nominally at least a Christian enterprise. Trissino had assigned the names and functions of the classical divinities to Christian angels, yet disguised the deity himself as Jove and the Blessed Virgin as Juno. Dryden, in turn, would subsequently advise the heroic poet to employ guardian angels as 'machining persons'.

Milton took a decisive stand on this issue not so much in his criticism as through the testimony of his poetry. Though his divine and infernal 'machines' perform essentially the same functions as those of classical epic, he usually managed to give them an even firmer basis in Scripture. To be sure, he did invent several of his angelic characters (neither Zephon nor Ithuriel had occurred as angels in the Bible; Abdiel was his own invention, an exemplar of the patient martyr and 'Servant of God'), but the foremost angels in the poem – Uriel, Gabriel, Raphael, Michael – had Biblical or Apocryphal authority behind them. His catalogue of devils included the classical divinities, yet he placed his chief emphasis on heathen idols specifically denounced in Scripture. In imitating the divine councils of classical epic, he invested his principal speakers (the Father and Son) primarily with attributes based on Scriptural tradition and theological commentary – including his own *Christian Doctrine*. His use of the Christian marvellous in *Paradise Lost* not only represented his own answer to a Renaissance dispute of long standing, but also served to perpetuate the quarrel. That the issue is still alive today – albeit primarily among Miltonists – is attributable largely to the influence of *Paradise Lost*.

In one notable instance, moreover – his quasi-heroic portrait of the fallen Archangel – Milton's epic machinery helped to reshape an iconographical tradition. Early illustrators of *Paradise Lost* – Fuseli, Blake, Charles Burney, and others – followed Milton's text in portraying the fallen angels as 'Godlike shapes and forms/ Excelling human' rather than as the grotesque monsters of mediaeval convention. By the end of the nineteenth century the iconography of Hell had been transformed. Lucifer and his angels had by now become as habituated to the shapes of Greek demigods as to the masks of apocalyptic beasts, and they owed this change principally to the opening books of Milton's epic.

On another disputed point – the question of the proper verse form for heroic poetry – Milton gave substantial support to the advocates of blank verse. The fact that unrhymed lines managed to contend successfully with alternative forms (the heroic couplet, rhyme royal, the Spenserian stanza, and *ottava rima*) as the

appropriate vehicle for English epic is, in part at least, attributable
to Milton's demonstration of its potentialities. Its subtle exploitation of enjambment to achieve a succession of infinitely
variable, infinitely flexible verse paragraphs made the blank verse
of *Paradise Lost* a formidable rival to the end-stopped heroic
couplet. Nevertheless, it was not only his verse form that left an
indelible stamp on English epic style; the diction and syntax of his
poem were equally influential. With its echoes of older tongues, its
idioms derived from Latin, Greek or Hebrew, its frequent
variations on normal word order, and its conscious attempt to
achieve elevation through forms of discourse remote from common usage, *Paradise Lost* left to the British poetic tradition an
artificial language specifically designed for the epic, consciously
framed in order to sustain the weight of heroic themes. Only a
language tempered by reflection, reinforced by classical and
Biblical precedents, and strengthened by carefully calculated
torsions could support the gravity of the heroic theme or withstand
the inner tensions that threatened to shatter the Renaissance ideal
of heroic virtue. Such a language Milton bequeathed to his
successors to use or abuse, to exploit at their own advantage or
peril.

Classical in form, English in medium, Biblical in subject matter,
Christian in doctrine and spirit, *Paradise Lost* gave added authority
to three overlapping traditions – the English vernacular epic, the
neoclassical epic, and the Biblical or divine poem. Through its
stand on some of the major issues that had confronted heroic
poets and epic theorists of the sixteenth and seventeenth centuries,
it left its mark on poetry and literary criticism alike. Yet it is almost
as significant for the history of ideas as for literary history. 'Dead
ideas' they may seem to be, but in Milton's era they were still
living issues.

III

The product of an age of conflicting values, *Paradise Lost* gave
formal expression to that conflict; it reflected tensions characteristic
not only of Reformation and Renaissance, but of Christian
humanism since Petrarch. Indeed, the paradox upon which the
poem is built – literary norms derived from classical authors, ethical
and religious ideals derived from Scripture – is equally characteristic of late antiquity. St Augustine had wept over Dido's fate; St
Jerome had wrestled with conscience and literary taste, his dual

allegiance to Christ and Cicero. If sacred and secular values, Biblical and classical themes coexist in uneasy alliance in *Paradise Lost*, the opposition is equally apparent in the works of other Christian artists (from antiquity through the eighteenth century) who similarly found difficulty in reconciling their delight in the secular arts of the ancients with their commitment to an otherworldly and Biblical faith.

The stresses that result from Milton's effort to fit Christian ethical ideals into a literary mould inherited from classical pagans might have wrecked the design of a lesser poet; Milton, on the other hand, successfully converted them into literary assets. The tensions between pagan and Christian ideals of heroism, secular and celestial conceptions of glory and shame or happiness and misery, carnal and spiritual strength and wisdom, and human and divine standards of merit became organic in *Paradise Lost* (and indeed in his other major poems, *Samson Agonistes* and *Paradise Regained*), affecting structure as well as texture. They conditioned its argument and fable, its development of character and thought (*ethos* and *dianoia*), and even its subtle manipulation of contrasting styles. They were indirectly responsible for many of its fundamental ironies; and they reinforced its exploitation of familiar 'Christian paradoxes' – strength in frailty and weakness in strength, wisdom in apparent folly and ignorance in apparent wisdom,[4] victory through seeming defeat and exaltation through humiliation – the paradox of the Fortunate Fall, the anomaly of God Incarnate, and that historic *scandalon*, the Messiah crucified.

The argument of *Paradise Lost* (like that of *Paradise Regained*) is based on the Adam–Christ parallel – the contrast between the 'earthy' and the 'heavenly' man, and the antithesis between the former's disobedience and loss of Paradise and the latter's recovery of Paradise through obedience. The fable further develops this parallel – and with it the contrast between divine and human standards – by opposing false and true images of heroic charity, contrasting the 'exceeding love' whereby Adam elects to perish with Eve (and thereby condemns the entire human race) with the Son's heroic 'excess of love' in choosing to die on man's behalf and thereby redeem 'the whole Race lost'. Primarily, however, it is through the antithesis between Heaven and Hell – their moral as well as their spatial opposition, their contrasting councils and en-

---

[1] Milton took the text 'My strength is made perfect in weakness' (*en astheneiai teleioumai*, II *Corinthians*, xii. 9) as a personal motto.

terprises, and their contrary ideals of heroism – that Milton elaborates the conflict between mutually exclusive value-systems, sacred and profane. The relationships within that 'infernal Trinity' – Satan and his Viceregents Sin and Death – parody the relationships between the Father, his own Vicegerent the Son, and the Spirit. The building of Pandaemonium counterpoints the creation of the world; the bridge that the infernal powers erect over Chaos parallels the golden chain that links Heaven and earth. If the struggles of Abdiel and other faithful angels foreshadow the future combat of the church against the world, the rebels in turn provide an archetype for the future monarchies of the Gentiles under the dominion of the prince of this world. Whereas the Messiah achieves exaltation through humiliation, Satan is brought low through his ambitious attempt to exalt himself above his peers. Whereas Christ discards the 'form of God' for the 'form of a servant,' Satan aspires to deity and scorns the office of the ministering angel as 'servile'. Though Satan and the Messiah voluntarily become incarnate – the one in serpentine form, the other in human – Satan resents the necessity that compels him to 'incarnate and imbrute' his angelic essence. Whereas Christ, as the perfect image of the Father, provides the perfect 'pattern' of the true hero (the 'godlike man') Satan achieves only a specious resemblance to the divine; and his heroic pretensions are ultimately exposed as brutishness, the contrary of heroic virtue.

The antithetical patterns in *Paradise Lost* are, however, more significant as testimony of Milton's artistry than as evidence of his inner conflicts; one should observe caution in drawing personal inferences from them. A generation ago, many critics still conceived his personality and career in dualistic terms – stressing the dichotomy of 'Milton the Puritan' and 'Milton the Poet' and the opposition between Reformation and Renaissance elements in his sensibility. In actuality, however, instead of a 'schizoid' Milton – a divided personality torn by contrary loyalties to literature and religion – one encounters in his major work an artist keenly aware of the value of contrast, a logician fully cognizant of the value of definition by contraries. *Paradise Lost* exploits the spiritual antithesis between Jerusalem and Athens as effectively as does *Paradise Regained* – and in the interest (paradoxically) of aesthetic unity. For in the final analysis, tensions inherent in the poem's intellectual structure are not only responsible for some of its real or imaginary inconsistencies – flaws that critics ever since Dryden have discovered in the poem; they are also a source of strength. The epic's inner 'dynamic' – like that of an arch or a dome – springs, in large part, from its resolution of contrary forces. Intellectually as well as poetically, *Paradise Lost* is a *concordia discors* – a harmony of opposites; like the universe it portrays, it imposes formal unity on a 'siege of contraries' – and herein lies one source of its value both as cosmic epic and as vindication of Providence. In the poetic narrative as in the course of world history, good and evil, just and unjust are woven into a single coherent pattern and serve – willingly or unwillingly – a controlling design. The disposition of the fable reflects the 'economy' of divine government; in the development of the plot an 'uncontrollable intent' – the divine will – overrules the actions of conflicting antagonists, human or angelic, and shapes them to its own ends. As divine *poet* or 'maker', Milton has taken his task seriously and conscientiously followed the example of the divine Maker; his poetic fiction is not only the imitation of an action, but an imitation of the world. As a work of art (a 'poem' or 'thing made'), *Paradise Lost* imitates Nature in its diversity as well as in its formal unity; imposing order on contraries, its 'vast design' reproduces in miniature the unity of the created world and the coherent design underlying the vicissitudes of world history – the unified vision of Providence.

In relating Milton's poem to the history of his life and times, the reader must, in all justice, recognize the limitations of the biographical approach. More than a few scholars have treated his epic as spiritual autobiography, assiduously mining its subsoil for personal and historical information. In its tragic theme, its 'pessimistic' view of world history, and (above all) its assumption that the 'wayes of God' really require justification, they perceive a reflection of the poet's old age and the 'evil dayes' on which he has fallen. *Paradise Lost* is in their eyes the author's personal *consolatio*, his attempt to reconcile his religious trust in Providence with apparently meaningless realities – his blindness and public disgrace, and the failure of the Lord's own cause. In the story of Adam's fall they find a close analogy to the defection of the poet's countrymen; both had fallen through folly, betraying themselves, their maker, and their posterity; both had forfeited a divine trust; both had rashly thrown away an earthly Paradise. In Milton's apparent preference for vague, general imagery, instead of concrete, visual detail, other critics – among them, George Saintsbury and T. S. Eliot – have detected the literary symptoms of physical blindness. Others have perceived the lineaments of Mary Powell in Eve, and in Satan the arch-rebel a self-portrait of Milton himself, the defender of regicides.

Most of the 'tragic' features of Milton's epic had, however, been

implicit or explicit in his youthful plans for a tragic drama on the
same subject. A 'pessimistic' outlook for the world, complemented
by an 'optimistic' promise of salvation for the elect, had been set
forth in the New Testament and had generally been characteristic
of Christian historiography (or prophecy). The justification of
God's ways and assertion of eternal Providence had preoccupied
the author of Job (traditionally regarded not only as a 'divine' poem
but as possibly the world's oldest surviving epic or drama). Milton's
imagery, in turn, was conditioned by the requirements of the high
style; it can be parallelled in other Renaissance artists (painters as
well as poets), who consciously sought elevation in style and design
by subordinating particular details to general effects for the sake of
organic unity. (In such cases the image appears 'vague' only when
detached from the whole; examined in its context, as a *part* of the
whole, it usually adds to the clarity of the general idea.)

In spite of numerous personal references, *Paradise Lost* provides
rather slippery evidence for the biographer. Though the outer shell
of his universe may have been firm enough to support Satan's
inquiring footsteps, it will hardly support much conjecture as to
what sort of cosmos Milton really believed in. Though his epic
presents a reasonably coherent 'world-view', it is a world-view
conditioned by aesthetic factors – the demands of the epic fable and
the requirements of poetic imitation. The speaker in *Paradise Lost*
is a masque, and the universe he portrays is (in part at least) an
artificial 'construct', a poetic fiction. Behind the masque there was
once a man, and behind his fictive cosmos a world that he regarded
as real – but both of them elude us. Milton's personality and beliefs
dissolve into the texture of the poem; and it is difficult, as well as
dangerous, to attempt to separate him from his creation.

IV

If *Paradise Lost* has sometimes misled the historian and the
biographer, it has proved equally embarrassing for the critic.
Several of the earliest commentators deplored its alleged violations
of the 'rules' and conventions of its genre; since some of the issues
they raised are still current today, it is well to conclude with a few
caveats to the reader.

1. The subject or 'argument' of the poem has often been confused with its *total* subject-matter, on the one hand, and its defence
of divine Providence, on the other. In discussing this point,
moreover, critics have sometimes failed to distinguish clearly

between the central action in the fable and the past or future events recounted in historical or prophetic episodes. Milton's actual 'Subject for Heroic Song' is, of course, the fall of man. (As he explicitly informs his reader, 'the whole Subject' is 'Man's disobedience, and the loss thereupon of Paradise'.) This is the action that the poet announces in the proposition, reiterates at the beginning of Book IX, and develops in his poetic fable. Technically, it is the argument of the poem. Though Milton also declares his intent to assert 'eternal Providence' and demonstrate the justice of God's ways, these are 'arguments' in a logical or rhetorical rather than in the strictly poetic sense. Critics have gone astray on this point through confusing two different meanings of a Renaissance critical term.

2. The question of the 'hero' of Milton's epic has always been a subject of controversy; in the first century after its publication, commentators pressed the rival claims of Adam, Christ, and Satan; and scholars are still debating this issue today. In the strictest sense, Adam alone is the 'principal hero' or 'epic person' of *Paradise Lost*; it is his action (cited in the first line of the proposition) that constitutes the nominal argument of the epic. Nevertheless, though neither Christ nor Satan is the 'principal hero' of the poem, both embody heroic archetypes (true and false, divine and worldly patterns of heroic virtue), acting as divine and diabolical champions in a holy war. Developing his narrative through the interplay of the infernal and celestial strategies, Milton represents Satan's plot against man and Christ's resolution to save him as heroic enterprises. Furthermore, three of the episodes 'heroically celebrate' Christ's major exploits – defeat of the rebel angels, creation of the universe, salvation of the world.

In mistaking Christ or Satan for the 'principal hero' of the poem, scholars have usually ignored the Renaissance critical distinction between 'epic person' and 'machining persons'. Not only do the latter play exceptionally prominent roles in the action of *Paradise Lost*, but they actually serve as heroic exemplars. In thus converting his divine and infernal machines into pattern-heroes (image and idol of heroic virtue), Milton made a fresh and original contribution to the heroic tradition, but he is still paying the price of this innovation. It cost him the understanding of his earliest critics.

3. Milton has been severely criticized not only for making the devil too 'good', but for making the deity too 'bad'. Besides their general dissatisfaction with his direct, anthropomorphic representation of deity, readers have objected in particular to the harsh tone of the speeches in which God the Father shifts the responsibility for

the fall from Himself to man, and to their abstract terminology – the jejune idiom of scholastic theology. In these alleged defects critics have variously recognized a deficiency in piety or literary tact, the unamiable reflection of a Puritan sensibility or a bold attempt to demonstrate how 'wicked' and 'repellent' the deity of Christian theology really is. In actuality, however, most of these features result from the nature of the poem Milton is writing and from the re-quirements of his narrative. The direct representation of deity as a *persona* in the fable is an inheritance from the Renaissance epic tradition; like Milton, both Vida and Tasso had regarded it as an act of piety to eject the pagan Zeus from their divine councils in favour of the Christian God. Milton's anthropomorphic image of deity derives, however, from Biblical as well as poetic tradition. As he points out in the *Christian Doctrine*, God had accommodated Himself to human understanding. Scripture offered an anthropomorphic (and anthropopathic) portrait of God; and, in conformity with the principles of theological accommodation and poetic decorum, Milton bases his own portraits of divine persons on Scriptural authority. Thus the ironic derision that Father and Son direct against their foes – one of the unpleasanter features of the poem for some of its readers – derives directly from the Psalms.[1]

The Father's judicial rhetoric is not inappropriate in a poem whose avowed intent is to 'justifie the wayes of God to men'. His theological idiom is consonant with the theological nature and tenor of his discourse; this is the most appropriate language for pro-mulgating a divine decree. The entire celestial strategy, set forth in this scene, hinges on theological concepts – the decree of predes-tination and the ultimate salvation of man; to overlook this fact is to miss Milton's conception of the nature of divine 'counsel' (the wisdom of divine Providence) and its relevance for the divine 'council' of epic tradition.

4. *Paradise Lost* is not the history of an action, but the imitation of an action. For the Renaissance critic this distinction was fundamental inasmuch as it marked the difference between poetry and history. Unlike the historian, the poet 'imitates' through feigning and inventing 'probable circumstances'. By ignoring this distinction, several critics have read *Paradise Lost* as though Milton had intended it for history rather than poetry; and it has even been suggested that he believed himself (under divine inspiration) to be

---

[1] Compare *Psalms*, ii. 4; xxxvii. 13; lix. 8; and *Proverbs*, i. 26; also Milton's translation of the Second Psalm (8 August, 1653), 'he who in Heaven doth dwell/Shall laugh, the Lord shall scoff them.'

adding 'historic details' to the Biblical narrative. Nevertheless, Milton, like Hamlet, knew a hawk from a handsaw; he was quite capable of distinguishing between the 'historical' events he found in *Genesis* and the 'feigned' details that he himself was adding, in his capacity as poet, to the Biblical account. Though (like Tasso) he censured other epic poets for selecting fictional and fabulous events as their arguments ('fabl'd Knights/In Battels feign'd'), this condemnation of the feigned subject or argument did not deter him (or Tasso either) from approving the poet's conventional prerogative to invent details and circumstances that might render his 'imitation' of a historical event more plausible and more moving.

Like other epic writers before him, Milton elected an historical event as his argument, yet nevertheless felt free to add his own fictions. Following apparently the same line of thought as Tasso and Edward Phillips, he chose as his subject a history sufficiently obscure and remote to exercise his powers of invention. The Biblical account of Adam's fall was 'obscure' enough (and Paradise itself sufficiently 'remote' in space and time) to give the poet maximum freedom in amplifying and reorganizing his materials, in subjecting them to the formal requirements of the epic fable, and in investing them with verisimilitude and probability, passion and admiration.

PARADISE REGAINED AND SAMSON AGONISTES
Christopher Ricks

'That Epick form whereof the two poems of *Homer*, and those other two of *Virgil* and *Tasso* are a diffuse, and the book of *Job* a brief model . . .' It would be wrong to take Milton's words in 1642 as if he were virtually signing a contract to write *Paradise Regained*. Yet his words, casual though they are in *The Reason of Church-Government*, anticipate the brief epic in which Job was to be an important point of reference.

There is no knowing when Milton wrote *Paradise Regained*. William Riley Parker, Milton's most scrupulous biographer, suspects that Milton may have begun it in about 1656–8, and then worked on it from about 1665 to 1670. *Paradise Regain'd. A poem. In IV Books. To which is added Samson Agonistes* was published in 1671, having been licensed in the previous year.

Milton's friend Thomas Elwood gave an account of the poem's inception which has since become famous:

After some common Discourses had passed between us, he called for a Manuscript of his; which being brought he delivered it to me, bidding me take it home with me, and read it at my Leisure: and when I had so done, return it to him, with my Judgment thereupon.

When I came home, and had set myself to read it, I found it was that Excellent Poem, which he entituled *Paradise Lost*. After I had, with the best Attention, read it through, I made him another Visit, and returned him his Book, with due Acknowledgment of the Favour he had done me, in Communicating it to me. He asked me how I liked it, and what I thought of it; which I modestly, but freely told him: and after some further Discourse about it, I pleasantly said to him, Thou hast said much here of *Paradise lost*; but what hast thou to say on *Paradise found*? He made me no Answer, but sate some time in a Muse: then brake off that Discourse, and fell upon another Subject.

After the Sickness was over, and the City well cleansed and become safely habitable again, he returned thither. And when afterwards I went to wait on him there (which I seldom failed of doing, whenever my Occasions drew me to London) he shewed me his Second Poem, called *Paradise*

Regained; and in a pleasant Tone said to me, *This is owing to you: for you put it into my Head, by the Question you put to me at Chalfont; which before I had not thought of.*

(*The Early Lives of Milton*, ed. H. Darbishire, p lvi)

Most modern commentators take it that Elwood must have been credulous and Milton sarcastic. 'How can one doubt,' asked E. M. W. Tillyard, 'that he was making fun of Elwood when remarking "pleasantly" that Elwood had put *Paradise Regained* into his head?' To Dr Tillyard, 'poor Elwood' had 'blundered into the subject that had ranked second in importance in *Paradise Lost*, the subject fully discussed and settled by God the Father in heaven, and dominating the last two books.'

Nevertheless Milton's words could just as well have been straight, and Elwood was not necessarily a fool in suggesting that *Paradise Lost* had not treated the ultimate destinies of man with anything like the power and imagination with which it had treated the Fall of Man. *Paradise Lost* had complained, with majestic bitterness, of the way in which previous epics had glorified a certain kind of heroism while neglecting the greater kind:

> Since first this Subject for Heroic Song
> Pleas'd me long choosing, and beginning late
> Not sedulous by Nature to indite
> Warrs, hitherto the onely Argument
> Heroic deem'd, chief maistrie to dissect
> With long and tedious havoc fabl'd Knights
> In Battels feign'd; the better fortitude
> Of Patience and Heroic Martyrdom
> Unsung . . .

> (ix. 25–33)

Yet in the end *Paradise Lost* was hardly remarkable for singing the better fortitude of patience and heroic martyrdom. Christ's sacrifice was mentioned, of course, but surprisingly little of Milton's space and energy seems to have been lavished upon it. Since Milton was in earnest about his claim to sing of such fortitude, he may have been aware that in the end the claim had not altogether been justified. Though he had not ignored 'Paradise found', he might still have seen a shrewd candour in Elwood's question.

Milton's nephew, Edward Phillips, recorded another tradition about the poem:

It cannot certainly be concluded when he wrote his excellent Tragedy entitled *Samson Agonistes*, but sure enough it is that it came forth after his publication of *Paradice lost*, together with his other Poem call'd *Paradice regain'd*, which doubtless was begun and finisht and Printed after the other was publisht, and that in a wonderful short space considering the sublimeness of it; however it is generally censur'd to be much inferiour to the other, though he could not hear with patience any such thing when related to him.

(*Early Lives*, pp 75–6)

There is no evidence for the story that Milton actually preferred *Paradise Regained* to *Paradise Lost*, but he did not like his later poem to be invidiously disparaged. (William Empson: 'I'm afraid I like *Bacchus* best of my own poems, maybe as the traditional mother dotes on the imbecile.')

What kind of poem is *Paradise Regained*? The best answer in terms of literary history is to be found in Barbara Kiefer Lewalski's book, *Milton's Brief Epic: the genre, meaning, and art of Paradise Regained*. Mrs Lewalski shows that two traditions came together in the making of *Paradise Regained*: that of commentaries on the *Book of Job*, and that of the brief Biblical epic. Milton had ample precedent not only for thinking of *Job* as an epic, but also for using it as a model for an epic poem. 'The important literary ancestry for *Paradise Regained* is the considerable body of poetic narrative on biblical subjects which flourished in Europe from the fourth through the seventeenth centuries.' The most recent attempt at the Biblical epic had been Abraham Cowley's *Davideis* (1656, in four books, but unfinished), in the preface to which Cowley defended Biblical epics against the accusations recently made by Sir William D'Avenant that they merely demeaned their sacred subject-matter.

Milton, then, was working within a recognized but controversial genre – one which had not attracted the most talented of poets. Mrs Lewalski lists 'the best-known and most influential brief epics', and it is clear that the best-known are now virtually indistinguishable from the unknown. Nobody but a literary historian, and few literary historians but Mrs Lewalski, would be likely to have spent much time on these brief epics by Juvencus, Sedulius, Ramsay, Marino, Sylvester, Joseph Fletcher, Montchrestien, Aylett, and Giles Fletcher.

But the precedents did not bind Milton:

Milton's genius is especially apparent in his choice of the episode to constitute his subject. As has been seen, precedents for a brief epic on the subject of the temptation of Christ are almost nonexistent. The temptation episode suggests itself to Milton, obviously, as a complement to *Paradise Lost*, but beyond this it is peculiarly suited to presentation as a brief epic, in that it could be treated as a transmutation of the single combat of hero and antagonist, the event which is traditionally the epitome and climax of an epic. The subject of *Paradise Regained*, Christ's encounter with Satan in the temptation, is the epitome and the symbol of the perpetual battle of the Son and Satan throughout all time – the battle which is displayed in its full extent in *Paradise Lost* through the councils in hell and heaven, the battle in heaven, Adam's fall, and the final prophecy of Christ's redemption. Milton's choice and treatment of his subject in *Paradise Regained* indicates that for him, as for Sannazaro, the brief epic is not merely any narration told in briefer compass than the full-scale epic, but that it is rather a significant condensation and epitome of the vast span of history treated *in extenso* in the 'diffuse' epic.

(*Milton's Brief Epic*, p 104)

Such is the literary historian's answer to the question of what kind of poem this is. In the terms of literary criticism, the best answer is Coleridge's. He rightly insists that *Paradise Regained* must not be judged as if it were trying to be the same kind of poem as *Paradise Lost*. But he also rightly insists that the kind to which *Paradise Regained* belongs is a lesser kind:

Readers would not be disappointed in this latter poem, if they proceeded to a perusal of it with a proper preconception of the kind of interest intended to be excited in that admirable work. In its kind it is the most perfect poem extant, though its kind may be inferior in interest – being in essence didactic – to that other sort, in which instruction is conveyed more effectively, because less directly, in connection with stronger and more pleasurable emotions, and thereby in a closer affinity with action.

(Notes on Milton, 1807)

An inferior kind, a lesser kind than *Paradise Lost*, because *Paradise Regained* is didactic. Most acutely, Coleridge points out that the real limitation of the didactic is that it is *less* (not more) morally effective and vivid, precisely because its moral purpose is too direct.

Paradise Regained is more concerned to transmit beliefs and allegiances than to create them. It does not have that power, which *Paradise Lost* has, to impel a reader to care about Christian truths. Ultimately *Paradise Regained* takes more for granted than a great poem does – such is the limitation of its kind, though by the same token such would be the area within which it could achieve its success. It stands to *Paradise Lost* somewhat as a good eighteenth-century hymn by Charles Wesley or Isaac Watts stands to the great religious poetry of Donne or Herbert.

Yet that *Paradise Regained* is 'perfect' (Coleridge's word) is not beyond question. The style, for example, is usually praised as bare and austere, remarkable for its 'compression and economy' (W. R. Parker). Louis Martz's important discussion of the poem in *The Paradise Within* takes as its natural starting-point the poem's style. 'The Meditative Combat' which Mr Martz then traces is a plausible extension of the clash between the two styles in the poem, Christ's and Satan's. We see 'that middle, georgic style which represents the way of temperance struggling against the self-indulgence of an elaborate style'. Mr Martz is explicit about the properties of 'the muted, chastened style': 'The firm and quiet manner of these lines (i. 455–64), dignified, yet modest, is representative of the ground-style laid down in Book I'.

But although parts of *Paradise Regained* are written in a 'muted, chastened style' (the very fine close to Book I, for example), much of the poem is written in a curiously over-emphatic style. The damaging thing about the repetitious, over-emphatic style is that it is so often put into the mouth of God or of Christ. If Satan is over-emphatic, a defence is open on dramatic (and moral) grounds. But one of the main points of the poem is to contrast the restless temptation by Satan with the massive simplicity and singleness (integrity) of Christ. Satan's arguments may well depend for their power on nothing more than 'what I tell you three times is true' but the corollary is that Christ should say things only once. Yet the following instances are all taken from just one of his replies to Satan (i. 411–35).

First, Christ insists that Satan is 'a poor miserable captive thrall'. But how can a thrall be anything but captive, since that is what the word means? And though *poor* and *miserable* are not exact synonyms, that is mainly because there are not in the end any exact synonyms. Yet wasteful writing certainly exists, and it can be argued that *poor* and *miserable* – in a context offered as austerely economical – duplicate too much of each other. Christ then tells Satan that

> the happy place
> Imparts to thee no happiness, no joy.

But is any distinction being made between happiness and joy? If so, it is impossible to discover it, and even if one tried to elaborate some distinction, then any distinction would imply that Heaven, which is described as happy but not as joyful, lacked whatever the distinction postulated. But if there is no distinction being made between 'no happiness, no joy', the style hardly presents a mind (in Mr Martz's words) 'tense, alert, watching any tendency toward elaboration'. Later in the same speech Christ attacks Satan as a liar: 'For lying is thy sustenance, thy food'. But what is the difference here between sustenance and food? (Not what differences might be said to exist in the English language, but what difference is established here within the poem?) 'What have been thy answers', Christ asks,

> what but dark
> Ambiguous and with double sense deluding?

Yet if they were ambiguous, it is hardly necessary to tell us that they had a 'double sense'.

Many of these phrases are pointed enough, but they are rhetorical in the bad sense, where emphasis is called in to do work which should be done by precision. Satan indeed shows the 'self-indulgence of an elaborate style', but there is more than one way of being self-indulgent, and of being elaborate. Christ's speeches eschew some of the forms of self-indulgent elaboration, but not all. 'Tempt not the Lord thy God': that has the monolithic strength and simplicity which Milton sums up in the image of Satan against Christ as 'surging waves against a solid rock'. But such simplicity is only intermittent in the poem. More often the note is different:

> And what the people but a herd confus'd,
> A miscellaneous rabble . . .
>
> (iii. 49–50)

The usual objection to this, and it is a powerful one, is that the speech is harsh, intolerant, and unchristlike. One can arrive at the same objection by a different route by asking whether 'miscellaneous rabble' is doing anything other than thump again on the same note as 'herd confus'd'. Or take the lines in which Christ attacks those who do not thank God, but who render

> Contempt instead, dishonour, obloquy?
> Hard recompence, unsutable return
> For so much good, so much beneficence.
> But why should man seek glory? who of his own
> Hath nothing, and to whom nothing belongs
> But condemnation, ignominy, and shame?
>
> (iii.131–6)

But the 'hard recompence' is the 'unsutable return', just as the 'so much good' is the 'so much beneficence'. Far from getting, as we do when Milton's verse is really working, two for the price of one, we are being fobbed off with one for the price of two. Man 'of his own hath nothing', and so it is hardly a surprise to be told that 'nothing belongs' to him.

Such over-emphasis is not limited to Christ. God the Father praises Job,

> Whose constant perseverance overcame
> Whate're his cruel malice could invent.

(i. 148–9)

But perseverance virtually includes constant, just as malice virtually includes cruel. There is this circularity even in the narrative parts of the poem, so that when Satan speaks to Christ we are told that he 'with words thus utt'red spake' (i. 320). Whatever appeals may be made to classical formulae, it remains a fact that he could hardly have spoken without words, and he would not have spoken them if he had not uttered them. And what are we to make of the repetition when Satan says to Christ:

> Thy Counsel would be as the Oracle
> Urim and Thummim, those oraculous gems

(iii. 13–4)

But perhaps the least satisfactory of such passages are those when Milton is using this in order to see that Satan comes out badly. The third Book begins:

> So spake the Son of God, and Satan stood
> A while as mute confounded what to say,
> What to reply, confuted and convinc't
> Of his weak arguing, and fallacious drift.

'Confounded what to say' contains 'mute', and 'what to reply' adds nothing to 'what to say' except the utterly misleading impression that Satan might speak to someone other than Christ. The 'weak arguing' is the 'fallacious drift'. At least, it is impossible to see what distinctions are being made.

The style of the poem should not be altogether equated with such passages (though they are frequent), but nor should it be equated with the show-pieces which usually figure in discussions of the economy and the classical or Gospel simplicity of the poem.

Nor is the style the only difficulty with the poem. Does Milton succeed in the huge task of making the *temptation* of Christ real to us? Christ must be both above temptation (insofar as he is God), and yet subject to temptation (insofar as he is man). Otherwise, if Christ does not seem to have even the faintest potentiality for falling, his victory must seem a mechanical one and no true counterpart to the Fall of Man. Does Milton enliven this crucial paradox?

Again, is the Satan of *Paradise Regained* so much less of an antagonist, so shabby and transparent in comparison with the Satan who tempted Eve, that Christ's victory is too easy and so again no counterpart to the Fall? *Paradise Regained* had made its relationship to *Paradise Lost* clear enough:

> I who e're while the happy Garden sung,
> By one mans disobedience lost, now sing
> Recover'd Paradise to all mankind,
> By one mans firm obedience fully tri'd
> Through all temptation, and the Tempter foil'd
> In all his wiles, defeated and repuls't,
> And Eden rais'd in the wast Wilderness.

(i.1–7)

The correspondence between that obedience and that disobedience is so essential, and so insisted upon, that there is something strange about the impassiveness with which Mr Parker describes the temptation in *Paradise Regained*: 'The second Adam is never tempted as was the first; he is not deeply in love and asked to recognize a hierarchy of love . . . Marriage was not for Christ, and since Adam's and Samson's temptations could not be applied to the perfect Man, the problem became one of choosing some that could' (*Milton: A Biography*, i, 617). Yet the poem's whole argument (and it is very much an argumentative poem) demands that Christ should have conquered where Adam was defeated. But Satan has so diminished that none of his temptations of Christ has the cunning with which he worked upon Eve, and moreover Christ is exposed to temptations different from Adam's and a great deal easier to resist than that temptation to set human love above divine love. The parallel becomes disingenuous.

Again, does Milton sufficiently differentiate Christ's victory from Job's? Otherwise it will not be clear why Eden was not 'rais'd in the wast Wilderness' when Job resisted all that Satan could do – Job

> Whose constant perseverance overcame
> Whate're his cruel malice could invent.

It is notable that Mrs Lewalski contradicts herself on this question. By the end of her book, she is affirming that 'Christ has already overmatched Job in the storm episode, for Christ has not given vent to any of Job's complaints, laments, or declarations of God's desertion', a comment which she supports with a reference to 'Protestant interpretations of these laments as evidences of weakness and sin' (pp 308, 413). But she had earlier described 'the dominant tradition' of commentary on *Job* as that in which 'Job's later outcries are simply pious lamentations like those of Jeremiah and of Christ on the cross, or else they are prophetic and typological utterances. Some commentators will concede that Job commits slight venial sins of ignorance and rashness, but others deny that he exhibits any imperfections whatever' (p 21). She had unequivocally placed Milton himself within this tradition:

Milton could readily adopt the 'epic' view of the Book of Job since, as the Job references in his prose tracts indicate, he seems to have accepted the 'heroic' interpretation of Job as a sinless, perfect hero overcoming all temptation. Job is 'most modest and patient of men', his outcries are evidence that 'sensibility to pain, and even lamentations, are not inconsistent with true patience', and he is an example, with Christ and various Old Testament personages, of magnanimity or proper self-regard.

(p 103)

What matters is not that Mrs Lewalski contradicts herself, but the implications. It is essential to the poem that it differentiate Christ's achievement from Job's (to which it often refers), and so she is led momentarily to present as sinful the Job whom earlier she had seen as sinless in Milton's eyes. The critical point is not whether Job's achievement could be shown by a theologian to be importantly less than Christ's, but whether this particular poem succeeds in showing us so.

Paradise Regained, then, is by no means an indisputable success. Many of the essential modern studies of the poem – Frank Kermode on its heroic ideals, Northrop Frye on its typology – are concerned more with the poem that Milton intended than with the one he wrote. But for a larger view of the poem, Dr Johnson's judiciousness is best:

Of *Paradise Regained* the general judgement seems now to be right, that it is in many parts elegant, and everywhere instructive. It was not to be supposed that the writer of *Paradise Lost* could ever write without great effusions of fancy and exalted precepts of wisdom. The basis of *Paradise Regained* is narrow; a dialogue without action can never please like a union of the narrative and dramatic powers. Had this poem been written, not by Milton but by some imitator, it would have claimed and received universal praise.

'Or whether those Dramatick constitutions, wherein *Sophocles* and *Euripides* raigne shall be found more doctrinal and exemplary to a Nation . . .' It was in 1642 that Milton was pondering that question. But when was it that he composed his own example 'Of that sort of

Dramatic Poem which is call'd Tragedy'? *Samson Agonistes* was published with *Paradise Regained* in 1671, and the traditional assumption has been that Milton wrote it at the end of his life, in the years following the publication of *Paradise Lost* in 1667. But Mr Parker has shown that there is no documentary evidence whatsoever for such an assumption:

Late *publication* proves nothing, suggests nothing; other early works discussed in this chapter [on Milton's life 1645–8] – two histories, the *Grammar*, the *Artis Logicae* – were published late, and no one has argued that they were written late. After about 1734 (no earlier – not by any of the seven early biographers) it was generally and uncritically *assumed* that Milton's *Samson* was his last poem.

(*Milton*, ii, 904)

(It might be said, though, that Milton's late publication of his early prose would not necessarily have a parallel in his poetic practice.) Mr Parker argues that *Samson Agonistes* – in its inception at least – is more likely to date from about 1647, both because of Milton's preoccupation with drama at that time in his career and because of the intrinsic nature and qualities of *Samson Agonistes* itself. Perhaps the strongest of his arguments derives from Milton's statement, prefatory to *Paradise Lost* in 1668, rejecting rhyme: 'If he meant it (who will argue that he did not?), then the rimes in *Samson Agonistes* were composed at some other time, not in 1667–9.'

> O that torment should not be confin'd
> To the bodies wounds and sores
> With maladies innumerable
> In heart, head, brest, and reins;
> But must secret passage find
> To th' inmost mind,
> There exercise all his fierce accidents,
> And on her purest spirits prey,
> As on entrails, joints, and limbs,
> With answerable pains, but more intense,
> Though void of corporal sense.

(lines 606–16)

Nevertheless the evidence for an early date is hardly less tenuous than that for a late date, and a reader is finally left with little more than his own hunch as to where *Samson Agonistes* belongs in Milton's career. To me, *Samson Agonistes* seems in its power and obduracy to be the sort of work much more likely to belong to Milton's late years than to his middle ones. It has the awe-inspiring extremism, uncompromising to the point of hardness, of such a bitter final statement as *Lady Chatterley's Lover*. Bitter and metallic.

God of our Fathers, what is man!
That thou towards him with hand so various,
Or might I say contrarious,
Temperst thy providence through his short course,
Not evenly, as thou rul'st
The Angelic orders and inferiour creatures mute,
Irrational and brute.
Nor do I name of men the common rout,
That wandring loose about
Grow up and perish, as the summer flie,
Heads without name no more rememberd,
But such as thou hast solemnly elected . . .

(lines 667–78)

Such poetry has its own virtues (dignity and a refusal to be ing-
ratiating, among them), but is not remarkable for delicacy,
spontaneity or suppleness. It is possible, though dispiriting, to think
that the style of *Paradise Lost* might harden into this (the closing
books of the epic already show a stylistic sclerosis); whereas it is
improbable that the poet of *Samson Agonistes* could have subsequently moved from so dour a style into the limber magnanimity
of the best of *Paradise Lost*.

Milton prefaced his 'Dramatic Poem' with an account of tragedy:

Tragedy, as it was antiently compos'd, hath been ever held the gravest,
moralest, and most profitable of all other Poems: therefore said by Aristotle
to be of power by raising pity and fear, or terror, to purge the mind of those
and such like passions, that is to temper and reduce them to just measure
with a kind of delight, stirr'd up by reading or seeing those passions well
imitated.

After this succinct and excellent re-statement of Aristotle's theory
of catharsis, Milton cites authorities who seem to uphold the dignity
of tragedy, among them Cicero and St Paul. 'This is mentioned to
vindicate Tragedy from the small esteem, or rather infamy, which in
the account of many it undergoes at this day with other common
Interludes' – an infamy due to vulgarities such as the improper
mixing of the comic with the tragic. His use of the Chorus Milton
acknowledges as 'after the Greek model'. As for his handling of the
plot: 'they only will best judge who are not unacquainted with
Aeschylus, Sophocles, and Euripides, the three Tragic Poets un-
equall'd yet by any, and the best rule to all who endeavour to write
Tragedy'.

In *Milton's Debt to Greek Tragedy*, Mr Parker traced in detail the
influence of the three Greek tragedians on *Samson Agonistes*. From

Milton's previous publications, it is clear that Aeschylus figured less in his thoughts than did Sophocles, whereas Euripides was of special importance to him. Nevertheless Milton was not the kind of writer to equate a temperamental affinity or admiration with an artistic propriety, and in the event *Samson Agonistes* does not owe very much to Euripides:

The fact that the prologos of *Samson* is a soliloquy; the irregular structure of the kommos; perhaps the amount of space allotted the Chorus – these are 'debts' which we must record. The characterization of Harapha and Dalila – indeed, certain elements in the portrait of Samson himself – are essentially Euripidean; and Euripidean, too, is the rhetorical element in the dialogue. But when we have said this, we have said almost all.

(p 248)

Aeschylus is of more direct importance, and especially his *Prometheus Bound*:

There is no denying a debt to Aeschylus in the bare dramatic conflict, the freedom from elaboration, the comparative paucity of action, the use of two actors, the small number of characters, and the lengthy conversations between Samson and the Chorus.

Yet it is Sophocles to whom *Samson Agonistes* owed most. *Oedipus at Colonus* has notable affinities with Milton's study of the inner heroism of a blinded guilty man seeking a true resignation and that service which is perfect freedom.

The role of the Chorus, the nature of the denouement, the use of tragic irony, the characterization of Samson, the portrait and function of the Messenger, the preoccupation with human misery against a background of cosmic mystery – these are matters of major importance.

(p 249)

Thanks to Mr Parker, the context of *Samson Agonistes* in literary history has been clearly mapped. What of the critical context? The best starting point is still the fierce hostility of Dr Johnson. He summarized his position in his life of Milton:

It is only by a blind confidence in the reputation of Milton that a drama can be praised in which the intermediate parts have neither cause nor consequence, neither hasten nor retard the catastrophe. In this tragedy are however many particular beauties, many just sentiments and striking lines; but it wants that power of attracting attention which a well-connected plan produces.

Nearly thirty years earlier in *The Rambler* (16 July 1751), Johnson had shown in some detail just what he meant by 'a well connected plan'. Enquiring whether *Samson Agonistes* was composed 'according to the indispensable laws of Aristotelian criticism . . . whether it exhibits a beginning, a middle and an end', Johnson traced the course of the play, concentrating in particular upon what Johnsonian English might call the concatenation of events: the question of whether an event at any point in the play had any probable or necessary connection with subsequent events:

At the conclusion of the first act there is no design laid, no discovery made, nor any disposition formed towards the subsequent event.

Johnson's final judgement praises the conclusion but still finds the structure deficient:

This is undoubtedly a just and regular catastrophe, and the poem, there-fore, has a beginning and an end which Aristotle himself could not have disapproved; but it must be allowed to want a middle, since nothing passes between the first act and the last, that either hastens or delays the death of Samson.

Miltonists have been impatient with Johnson. Mr Parker accuses him of 'wilfully misreading' the play, and Miss Marjorie Nicolson affirms:

As so often when he wrote about Milton, Johnson seemed to go out of his way to be perversely wrong. He failed to see that *Samson Agonistes* is pre-eminently a psychological study of the development of a human being.

Yet Johnson, though he could be mistaken, was not an inattentive or stupid reader, and he saw perfectly well that *Samson Agonistes* offered 'a psychological study of the development of a human being'. Of the interchanges with Manoah he says: 'This part of the dialogue, as it might tend to animate or exasperate Samson, cannot, I think, be censured as wholly superfluous.' Of Dalila's visit he says: 'nor has her visit any effect but that of raising the character of Samson'. But Johnson thought that it was not a sufficient defence of the events of the play to say that they affected Samson's psycho-logical development. It is not the presence of psychological de-velopment that Johnson deplores – it is the absence of any other structural principle in the play, the absence of any reason *other* than the psychological development of Samson for the entrances and exits of characters. The disagreement between Johnson and the Miltonists is not as to whether *Samson Agonistes* is a study in psychological development, but whether such psychological de-velopment is a sufficient structural principle to unify or validate the events in a work on the scale of *Samson Agonistes*. In a similar way a critic might grant that a unifying principle in Wordsworth's *Prelude* is that it traces 'the growth of a poet's mind'; might grant too that such growth is a valuable thing to trace; and yet might still believe that Wordsworth failed to find in this principle a sufficient unification for his very long poem. Or again, mood or atmosphere may indeed be a unifying factor in a poem, and yet there would be something unconvincing about the defence of the unity of, say, *The Faerie Queene* on the grounds that it had unity of mood. What may be a sufficient structural principle for a lyric may not be sufficient for an epic romance. Johnson's criticisms of *Samson Agonistes*, as always with Johnson, raise fundamental points about the nature of literature.

But do they perhaps raise rather points of critical authority? 'The indispensable laws of Aristotelian criticism': do we agree that Aristotle's insistence on a beginning, a middle and an end is a justified one? Milton himself certainly seems to have acknowledged the authority of Aristotle – the very first sentence of his preface to *Samson Agonistes* invoked Aristotle, and elsewhere he had spoken respectfully of 'the rules of Aristotle'. But the crucial question is not so much whether Milton would have agreed that the Aristotelian laws are indispensable as whether they are indeed so. Anybody who rejects Johnson's strictures on *Samson Agonistes* needs to make clear whether he does so on the grounds that Johnson's and Aristotle's insistence on cause and consequence in the events is a mistaken insistence, or on the grounds that *Samson Agonistes* is mistakenly described by Johnson as lacking such concatenation of events. Is the answer to Johnson that *Samson Agonistes* does have a 'middle' or that it does not and does not need to have? It is naïve to think that Johnson's arguments collapse into dust at a frown, and it is worth remembering that Milton's only reference in the 'Argument' to *Samson Agonistes* to the visits of Dalila and Harapha is to say of Samson: 'who in the mean while is visited by other persons'.

The next focus for critical argument is the antithesis itself of events to psychology. Do not the greatest tragedies combine the Aristotelian demands (a plot where events do have both cause and consequence) with psychological study? Again the question about *Samson Agonistes* would not be about what it does but about what it does not do. So that there are difficulties about Mr Parker's summary:

Attic dramatists – and Milton – were interested in the spiritual rather than the physical aspects of the old stories; hence speech predominates over action; plot is subordinate to character and emotion.

(*Milton*, i, 320)

But what of the antitheses themselves? Spiritual rather than physical: but the greatest thing in *Samson Agonistes*, its evocation of the hideous deprivation which is blindness, is at once spiritual and physical, and a great tragedy would show how intimately and indissolubly the spiritual is often related to the physical, rather than crisply separate off the one from the other. It is the same with 'speech' as against 'action' – can we so summarily disjoin these two human manifestations, and say that our concern is going to be with one rather than the other? Yes, we *can* disjoin them, but what is the price which we pay for the violence which this does to their subtle interrelatedness? 'Plot' or 'character': is not this disjunction, too, one which seems meaningless and unreal (as would the disjunction of 'plot' from 'emotion') in the presence of *Oedipus Rex* or *King Lear*? If it is retorted that such tragedies are different in kind from Milton's, it could still be the case that Milton's kind is ultimately a lesser kind precisely because it depends on antitheses (doing this rather than that) which the greatest tragedies show to be falsifications or simplifications. As Henry James said, 'What is character but the determination of incident? What is incident but the illustration of character? What is either a picture or a novel that is *not* of character?' As soon as it can be said of a particular work of literature that it deals in 'character' rather than in 'plot', then such a work is implicitly and artificially limiting its scope. Such artificiality is not the same thing as the artifice of the greatest tragedies.

Moreover the concatenation of events which Johnson desiderates is one of the best checks upon a poet's responsibilities towards his materials. Without such concatenation, it is too easy for a writer to manipulate events in order to bring about the psychological development which he too patently wishes to establish. Naturally Milton wishes to show a particular development, from Samson's despairing unfitness for doing the will of God to an upright fitness. But Milton's wish will be the more effective for not being at work upon a soft medium, and if Samson's development is truly to tell upon us, it is essential that there be some reason other than just Milton's wish to have it so which ushers in the psychological development. What is it that saves such a work from being a high-minded and high-handed manipulation, a rigging of the story in order to manifest a moral or spiritual lesson? The regeneration of King Lear, a man marred and touching in his humanity, may owe its greater tragic power to the fact that in *King Lear* the events of the play do have cause and consequence, do hasten or retard the catastrophe. So that Lear's psychological development is not something being staged by the

dramatist: it is as truthful as it is powerful, and has not simply been
made up or willed into existence by Shakespeare. The con-
vincingness of the events of the play is inseparable from its psychological acumen. To separate events from psychological development is ultimately to enfeeble or impoverish psychological development itself. 'We hate poetry that has a palpable design upon us,'
said Keats. What protects a work of literature against the suspicion
that it may be manipulating things in the interests of its design upon
us is that the events take place because that is indeed how events
take place, rather than because such a sequence of events will suit
the author's book. Aristotle's respect for the 'probable' and the
'necessary' in tragic plots is itself a respect for 'psychological drama'
in the fullest sense.

Milton said that tragedy was not only the most grave but also the
most moral of poetic kinds. Clearly *Samson Agonistes* is a very moral
poem insofar as that word means 'concerned with moral questions
and choices'. But whether it is moral in the sense of responding to
these questions with a sensitive and scrupulous moral sense: that is
a different matter, and a trickier one than the clean sweep of some
Miltonists would suggest. In what does the moral superiority of
God over Dagon consist? Or of Samson over the Philistines? Why is
Samson's pulling down of the pillars not the sin of suicide, and why
is it not a merely brutal act of revenge? If *Samson Agonistes* is a great
tragedy, it will urge us to think the more, and not the less, about
such questions. But they are questions which prompt some uneasiness, and some people have wished that they would go away.

The magic word for making such questions vanish has been
donnée – a word that has been used more and more unscrupulously
or ingenuously in literary criticism. The things which are indeed
'given' in a work of literature, and which the reader must accept if
he is to get anything at all from the work, are not matters of
meaning, conscience, and profound belief, but matters of situation,
incident, and convention. Things have come to a strange pass when
a critic like Chauncey B. Tinker can describe as one of the 'given'
conditions of *Samson Agonistes* the fact that the reader must delight
in the destruction of the Philistines, men and women:

There is only one barbaric tradition left in Milton's drama, but it is a
necessary one without which the plot could not move on to its conclusion. It
is the will of Jehovah that the enemies of Israel should be wiped out, men,
women, servants, and cattle. In their destruction the reader must feel
nothing but satisfaction. This is the one concession which must be taken
over from the ancient legend, like the mythical elements common in the

plots of Greek tragedy. These are among the conditions 'given', under which the author must work and which the reader must accept.
(*'Samsom Agonistes'*, in *Tragic Themes in Western Literature*, ed. Cleanth Brooks, 1955, pp 64–5)

But elements of a plot are different in kind from moral judgements. There are limits to what a *donnée* in great literature can be asked to encompass, and genocide is beyond them. Perhaps *Samson Agonistes* does indeed persuade us that we are right to feel satisfaction – but that is different from not even being under any obligation to persuade us.

The tragic status of *Samson Agonistes*, then, is more problematic, less obligingly self-evident, than might seem from the formal awe which it is customarily accorded. The issues raised by Johnson, which are not just pertinent but crucial, may not be of a kind which can be 'settled' but they are definitely of a kind which must be directly met. *Samson Agonistes*, if it is treated with anything other than the polite admiration which is reserved for ancient monuments, is a very disconcerting work, and some of us who praise its greatness may find that we are doing so in the same spirit in which Professor Helen Gardner praised *Lady Chatterley's Lover*: that it moves us to profound dissent.

12

SAMUEL BUTLER AND THE
MINOR RESTORATION POETS

Rachel Trickett

Restoration minor poetry is predominantly satiric, discursive, epistolary and lyric. In contrast to the others, the lyric mode, though generally popular especially in its traditional guise as words for music, aroused little critical interest. Political and social circumstances had produced a situation in which poetry's immediate justification was its capacity to engage in topical issues either satirically or argumentatively; to epitomize essential aspects of contemporary matters. Poetry had assumed public office; poets ceased to be amateurs and began to make their art their profession. Many were commissioned by private patrons for whom they produced complimentary verses, dedicatory epistles and panegyrics, or by political groups who encouraged the satiric vein which attracted all the most talented and original poets of the age.

A clear distinction can be made between these professionals and the more influential though less productive coterie of court wits, of whom George Villiers, Duke of Buckingham, Charles Sackville, Earl of Dorset, John Wilmot, Earl of Rochester, Sir Charles Sedley and Sir George Etherege were the most important. These, from the security of their social position, could afford to experiment, to establish critical fashions and make or mar literary reputations. John Oldham in his 'Satyr concerning Poetry' shows how keenly the working poets felt the difference:

> *Sidly* indeed may be content with Fame
> Nor care should an ill-judging Audience damn,
> But *Settle*, and the rest, that write for Pence,
> Whose whole Estate's an ounce or two of Brains,
> Should a thin House on the third day appear,[1]
> Must Starve, or live in Tatters all the year.

[1] The third performance of a play was traditionally for the author's benefit.

But the relation between the two groups was not without mutual profit. Each influenced the other. The light cultivation of the wits, their interest in French modes and their admiration for certain native traditions, especially for the Cavalier poets who had already polished and pointed the metaphysical style of wit, and for the 'refiners' of couplet, Waller and Denham, affected the taste of the professionals. The directness and the new candid tone of the working poets encouraged greater freedom in court epistles and satires. The wits' favourite pose of critical arbiter also gave considerable impetus to arguments on style and language which Hobbes had already initiated, and which the Royal Society with its distrust of traditional rhetoric had made a matter of contemporary dispute. If the earlier seventeenth century had been obsessed by thought, the Restoration was obsessed by language, style and their relation to social and political order, to sense and enlightenment.

Restoration poets believed that they had freed themselves from the follies of thought and style of the past half century as completely as from its political tyrannies. Yet their work often bears traces of their predecessors. The Restoration itself was a period of experiment and confused allegiances; the verse of its minor poets is sometimes original, sometimes openly, sometimes covertly conservative; its allusions range from the admired ancients to the outmoded metaphysicals. The tastes of the time were never so uniform as literary historians have tended to assume. But most writers and thinkers agreed in a determination to avoid at all costs the anarchy, confusion and dangerous mêlée of ideas, institutions and language which they associated with the Protectorate. They aimed at public security, ease of communication and sound sense with freedom to pursue an unenthusiastic, rational but thorough exploration of art, society and nature.

A desire for order and clarity is common to their critical pronouncements. They shared Hobbes's dislike for

the ambitious obscurity of expressing more than is perfectly conceived or perfect conception in fewer words than it requires. Which Expressions, though they have had the honour to be called strong lines, are indeed no better than riddles.

(*Answer to D'Avenant*, 1650).

And, like Atterbury in his Preface to the 1690 edition of Waller's works, they admired this slight and superficial poet because he had introduced 'the harmony of measure, that dance of words which good ears are so much pleased with' by a careful use of polysyllables and the regular disposition of the caesura. But beyond this basic area of agreement the better Restoration poets exhibit a variety of attitudes and manners which reflect the transitional nature of their age. This is particularly true of the satirists, of whom the most considerable after Dryden were Andrew Marvell (1621–78), Samuel Butler (1612–80), the Earl of Rochester (1647–80) and John Oldham (1653–83).

Marvell, best remembered now for his lyrics, turned exclusively to political pamphleteering and satire during his years as MP for Hull after the Restoration. He was forced to print his satires surreptitiously or circulate them in manuscript, and they were collected and openly published only after his death in the *Poems on Affairs of State*. But they were so widely popular that Burnet can call him 'the liveliest droll of the age, who writ in a burlesque strain, but with so peculiar and so entertaining a conduct, that from the King down to the tradesman, his books were read with great pleasure.' Sometimes, the pleasure was tempered by a more sober response. Pepys records coming across the latest instalment of 'Last Instructions to a Painter', Marvell's longest and most powerful satire, with its description of the unpreparedness of the English navy in the Dutch war, and how 'it made my hearte ake to read, it being too sharp and so true'. Burlesque is hardly the word we would use now of Marvell's direct, strong and vigorous attack, but it looks back to earlier modes in its disorderly profusion and complex irony, qualities which the new age associated with comic wit rather than with argument.

The balance which Marvell had preserved during and after the Civil War, and which so distinguishes his 'Horatian Ode', turned after 1660 to angry and contemptuous indignation at the triviality and corruption of the court and its policies. Recollections of the powerful role England had played in foreign affairs under Cromwell roused Marvell to bitter anger at the conduct of his unheroic successors. 'Last Instructions to a Painter' takes Waller's panegyric 'Instructions to a Painter' and turns it upside down in a violent and ironic account of the confusion, disorder and dishonesty of the manipulators behind the scenes of the Dutch war. Passages of heroic compliment to the fighters are offset by savage sketches of caballing courtiers, intriguing politicians and royal mistresses, culminating in the theatrical vividness of the incident where Charles II, waking from an uneasy sleep, sees the vision of naked, bound and dishonoured England by his bed. For all its wit, Marvell's style conveys a feeling of actual evil and a sense of patriotic shame and passion which is unique in the period. Alone among Restoration writers he is *laudator temporis acti*, and his anger at the condition of his country touched a deeper and more unsophisticated response in general readers than the detached play of ideas and attitudes characteristic of his literary contemporaries. The roughness of his manner reflects the chaos and confusion of the evil he attacks, and presents the Restoration political world in strong, dark colours that, even in his shorter satires, were meant to arouse indignation more than laughter. But it is typical of the age that though he was respected, he was not feared. The king, the court, the new poets admired his wit and remained unmoved by his intention. Marvell's radical concern for more fundamental national and political issues looks back to an earlier period. His anger shows itself in his rejection of those virtues of poise, clarity and precision which characterizes his lyrics, but the satires remain powerful and unjustly neglected examples of his complexity of range, and his moral and intellectual integrity.

Butler's *Hudibras*, the most celebrated satire of its time, is more often read about than read. This extraordinary burlesque, written in octosyllabics, learned, formless, frequently tedious but brilliantly exact in some of its comments on fundamental follies of human thought and conduct, has survived as a curiosity rather than a great poem. Its author, Samuel Butler, an obscure and largely self-educated scholar, published the first part of *Hudibras* in 1662 when the poem became an immediate success. Its subject – the arguments and adventures of the Presbyterian Sir Hudibras and his Independent squire Ralph, and its style – an improvised travesty of heroic romance in the manner of Scarron – were equally sympathetic to the Restoration public. *Hudibras*'s timely appearance made it the most admired and talked-of work of the decade. A second part appeared in 1663 and was followed by numerous imitations, spurious continuations and parodies. Butler's reputation was by now so high that he had every reason to expect substantial recognition but he received neither pension nor post, and in 1680, three years after publishing a third part of the poem, he died in poverty to become a by-word among the Augustans for the brutal and indifferent neglect of a so-called cultivated society.

As an example of the conservatism of general taste at the time, it is useful to remember that Butler and Marvell were more commonly admired as satirists than Dryden, Rochester or Oldham. Yet both in spirit belonged to an earlier generation and were metaphysical rather than Augustan wits, though Butler was as critical of the excesses of that school as of pedantry and false learning in general. (Butler's Character 'A Small Poet' is an attack on Benlowes, a minor follower of the metaphysicals.) John Wilders has shown in the Introduction to his edition of *Hudibras* that we may assume from the evidence of his Notebooks that Butler was essentially Baconian in his views. In this he was at one with his age, as well as in his dual attack on rational theology and enthusiasm. His Presbyterian knight is a false pedant; his Independent squire a fraudulent devotee of the inner light, while the quack astrologer, Sidrophel, parodies their hypocrisy and their arrogant self-deception. If the farcical episodes of the poem delighted simpler readers – the encounter with the bear-ward, Hudibras in the stocks, his wooing of the widow and his brawl with Sidrophel, the real meat of the satire and the reason for its prolonged popularity lay in its intellectual attack on the obscurantism of the puritan sects.

But *Hudibras* is a work whose sources reach further back than Bacon. It is a satire on the abuse of learning in the Lucianic tradition of Erasmus's *Praise of Folly* and Rabelais's *Gargantua and Pantagruel*, and a forerunner of Swift's *Tale of a Tub*. Butler's witty ingenuities match the metaphysicals', but his deeper affinities lie with the humanist satirists in their attack on the arrogance of reason and philosophic pedantry. Like theirs his is a learned work (for which Johnson admired it), where the whole apparatus of wit, subtlety, intellectual, logical and rhetorical skill is ironically employed to undermine the false importance men attach to them. Butler stresses these affinities by adopting the rambling idiosyncratic style of Rabelaisian parody. His knight and squire recall chivalric romance – Hudibras takes his name from *The Faerie Queene* – and they inevitably suggest Cervantes who was interpreted by the seventeenth century as a savage scourger of the follies of enthusiastic imagination, and is directly referred to in the poem.

Butler's satire, like Rabelais's, is dominated by verbal irony. This aspect of the humanist tradition was particularly suited to an attack on puritanism as a religion of hypocritical jargon, for the sects had long been distinguished by their peculiar habits of speech. Hudibras knows his terms of rhetoric and speaks 'A Babylonish dialect/Which learned pedants much affect', while Ralph disguises his self-interest under the cloak of Hermetic mumbo-jumbo. Butler presents puritanism as a Babel of tongues, an abuse of human thought in jargon and obscurity, a distortion of language to betray its true purpose of clear and simple communication. His style brilliantly reflects this – the parody of learning, the burlesque rhetoric, the mock heroic play with figures is all contained within an improvised casual measure which represents the colloquial ease of common speech. Some of his most memorable epigrams

> Compound for Sins, they are inclin'd to;
> By damning those they have no mind to . . .

achieve their effects from this metrical jauntiness set in a ponderous rambling context. It is a device which contrasts interestingly with Dryden's more specific contrivances, his use of blasphemy, for instance, to satirize the canting style of Shimei in *Absalom and Achitophel*. Butler makes no use of construction or sequent argument; he does not vary his tone according to the purpose of different passages; he lacks Dryden's strategic artistry. Instead, he follows the older manner of the farrago, relishing his own wit, delighting in his own jog-trot, and rejecting form for a loose travesty of the anarchy of mind which is his subject. The shapelessness of *Hudibras* enhances its humour; its digressiveness extends the range from specific to general satire. As a poem – a work of art, *Hudibras* is deliberately self-defeating. As general satire it was powerful enough to influence Swift, himself more attached to older than newer ways of thought, and to delight Johnson who hankered after the subtleties of a more distant learned tradition.

Butler's other poems are less interesting. *The Elephant in the Moon*, a satire against the Royal Society, extends the attack on enthusiasm to the new learning. Though he took no open part in the argument between ancients and moderns, Butler, like the later Augustans, instinctively sided with the conservative sceptics who doubted the wonders of empiricism as shrewdly as the mysteries of scholasticism. His *Characters* in prose which contain the same sort of epigrammatic observations that enliven *Hudibras* again look back to an earlier form – the Theophrastian sketch. For all his sympathy with the new dislike of obscurity and excess, Butler never shared the new interest in clarity of form.[1] His perceptive comment on Donne may also be applied to his own natural tendency:

Dr Don's writings are like Voluntary or Prelude in which a man is not ty'd to any particular Design of Air; but may change his key or moode at pleasure; So his compositions seem to have been written without any particular Scope.

(Characters and Passages from Notebooks, p.402)

---

[1] Saintsbury makes this point well when writing of Cleveland, the metaphysical satirist who influenced Butler. 'Like Butler . . . he was what he satirized in the literary way, and he caricatures himself.' (*Caroline Poets*, iii, 7).

The 'Design of Air' which Butler himself never intended, can be compared to the clear, defined structure in verse that newer poets were attempting. They deliberately limited their scope to a specific argument or theme. The digressive mode of the earlier seventeenth century – and of *Hudibras* – was gradually being exchanged for a more incisive, shapely style. Epistolary verse, in spite of its freedom to ramble according to mood, was restricted in length, and by its assumption of direct address from one correspondent to another, encouraged point and perspicacity of argument. Imitations from the French or the ancients were themselves an attempt to refine and clarify the language through the discipline of translation, and to restore order to the Babel which had been created not only by sects and pedants, but by the verbal licence of learned poets and metaphysical wits. Purification was the aim at whatever sacrifice of strength or range. Poets as limited by position and intention as the Restoration court wits were well suited to popularize such a retrenchment. They wrote, patronized, criticized and maintained their standards by an appeal to their own exclusiveness and their style of living. This they presented in verse with polish and a certain hard logic that in the best of them, Rochester, is turned into poetry by the force of a peculiar genius.

Much of Rochester's satire was contributed to the interchange of bawdy epistles, literary and personal lampoons and witty lyrics circulated between writers like Dorset, Mulgrave and Etherege. There is little literary value in the others' satires except for an easy fluency of style, but Rochester's are wider in range and infinitely subtler in technique. His preference was for the epistolary mode, and his finest poem, 'Artemisia in the Town to Chloe in the Country', uses it for a Chinese box effect of tone within tone and irony. Its satiric indirectness reflects a sophisticated attitude that deliberately contracts and confuses the moral standpoint of the work.

Artemisia writes to her friend in a tone as evasive as Rochester's irony can make it. She complains at the state of love, but her complaint, far from expressing the moral norm of the poem as David M. Vieth has suggested, is a delicate parody of the romantic idealizations of a literary lady. She begins by assuming that country Chloe wants

>   at least to hear what loves have passed
> In this lewd town, since you and I met last;
> What change has happened of intrigues, and whether
> The old ones last, and who and who's together ...

a tone that conflicts violently with her succeeding panegyric on love. But this, which begins enthusiastically and moves by hyperbole to the conclusion:

> On which one only blessing, God might raise
> In lands of atheists, subsidies of praise,
> For none did e'er so dull and stupid prove
> But felt a god, and blessed his power in love . . .

exposes love's great blessing as self-deception. Artemisia's complaint is largely against her own 'silly sex' for lowering the tone of love by making it a trade. As an example of this she introduces a fine lady back in town from the country whose long monologue occupies most of the rest of the poem. This character is clearly defined by her speech – and Rochester shows a remarkably sensitive ear for slang and affectation here – her whimsical actions, and her cynically realistic attitude to the passion Artemisia approves only in its politer form. The fine lady prefers fools to men of wit, and wonders at the folly of those wits who would rather see the truth than be blindly happy:

> They little guess, who at our arts are grieved,
> The perfect joy of being well deceived . . .

This phrase is close to Swift's famous definition of happiness in the Digression on Madness in *The Tale of a Tub* –'a perpetual possession of being well deceiv'd', and indeed Rochester's sustained indirectness often anticipates Swift's irony.

To prove her point, the fine lady produces the example of Corinna, a woman of pleasure whose misfortune is that

> . . . fate, or her ill angel, thought it fit
> To make her dote upon a man of wit,
> Who found 'twas dull to love above a day;
> Made his ill-natur'd jest, and went away.

But Corinna, only temporarily reduced, finds a country fool to batten on and destroy, for Nature the fine lady concludes, 'contrived kind keeping fools, no doubt,/To patch up vices men of wit wear out.' Sound if ruthless natural instinct preserves Corinna; equally natural stupidity wrecks her victim. Corinna, then, is less a moral example than an illustration of the fine lady's maxim that 'A woman's ne'er so ruined but she can/Be still revenged on her undoer, man.' The fine lady herself, though satirized for affectation, is not without wit. Artemisia comments on her character – 'some grains of sense/Still mixed with volleys of impertinence', but it is left to the reader to sift the grains. For the whole poem is deliberately deceptive in its standards. Though Artemisia promises in her next letter more stories 'As true as heaven, more infamous than hell', the poem provides no grounds for judging infamy. Rochester rather exposes a conflict of wit and folly, of sense and affectation, of artifice and nature, than of vice and virtue. The poem displays his style at its most craftily enigmatic, refusing to adopt any accepted moral standards. But this Epicurean indifference is complicated by the intricacy of the technique, the continually shifting viewpoint, as destructive as it is sceptical, which obliquely hints at a deeper realization of the values the poem seems to reject. 'Artemisia to Chloe' is devious in tone and intention, but direct, clear and wittily incisive in style. In this it is superior to 'Timon', an imitation of Boileau's version of Horace's 'bore' epistle, and to 'Tunbridge Wells' a piece of straight social observation in which Rochester shows his skill in satirical vignette and characteristic dialogue. The 'Satyr against Mankind' is again indebted to Boileau and behind him to Montaigne, but its temper is harsher and gloomier than theirs. Rochester opens brilliantly with the traditional misanthropic view of man, the quintessence of dust, led by 'old age and experience' to death and realizing that 'all his life he has been in the wrong'. But the poem offers no suggestion of what being in the right might have meant. The rest of it is disappointing. It lacks the vitality of the dramatic social satires, and the swaggering force of the monologues of self-justification where Rochester explores the sceptic's position and drives the notion of excess to its extreme.[1]

Rochester's satirical techniques influenced Pope, but Pope consistently underplayed his genius, criticized his carelessness, and even, in his copy of *Poems on Affairs of State*, inserted 'not' before the attribution 'by Rochester' of 'Tunbridge Wells', a poem which he undoubtedly remembered in his description of Sir Plume in *The Rape of the Lock*. Pope's more sanguine temper and his belief in a moral norm were repelled by the disillusionment underlying Rochester's libertine pose. Rochester's pessimism is closer to Swift's, though the greater satirist worked out the tensions between vice and virtue, wit and folly, scepticism and belief through his art, and in his life kept an icy control which is the other side of the coin from Rochester's self-destructive excess.

The genuine poetic talent of Rochester is apparent in his lyrics as

[1] See 'A Satyr', 'A Very Historical Epistle', 'Epistolary Essay'. I disagree with Vieth's interpretation of these poems as satires on the libertine or Hobbesian attitude they appear to represent.

well as in his satires. But his follower John Oldham recognized that his natural bent was invective:

> Satyr's my only province, and delight
> For whose dear sake alone I've vow'd to write,
> For this I seek occasions, court Abuse,
> To shew my Parts, and signalize my Muse.

('Upon a Printer')

Oldham, from a very different background, the son of a Nonconformist minister and himself a schoolmaster, attracted the attention of the wits by his early verses. He was also known to Dryden whose moving lines 'To the Memory of Mr Oldham' celebrate his powerful satirical talent. Oldham's commonplace book in the Bodleian Library contains transcripts of Rochester's 'Artemisia' and Dryden's *MacFlecknoe*, and it was such works, circulated in manuscript, that helped him to find his own bent. Unlike Rochester and like Dryden, he was a professional poet. He died at the age of thirty of smallpox, still comparatively unknown.

Oldham has often been misjudged, largely because of the lack of any modern scholarly text of his work, and critics have tended to look only at his most ambitious and least successful poems, the *Satyrs upon the Jesuits* which, though powerful examples of Juvenalian invective, lack the distinction and originality of his satires on the subject of writing, the 'Satyr concerning Poetry', 'Letter from the Country to a Friend in Town', and 'Upon a Printer'. It is in these last, not in his Rochesterian 'Against Virtue' or his Pindaric efforts that Oldham shows a unique mode of vigorous self-expression and genuine indignation, different from Rochester's scepticism or Dryden's genial comic irony. Though Pope censured him for a Billingsgate style, he found much to imitate in Oldham, particularly his comments on the profession of poetry. For Oldham paints a striking picture of the rougher side of Restoration literary life. His anger is passionate and direct. He adapts Juvenal's justification in the *Satyrs upon the Jesuits*, 'Nor needs there *art* or *genius* here to use/Where indignation can create a *muse*', but at its best his poetry is scarcely artless. When he attacks sycophancy and the worship of wealth his anger sustains a powerful panegyric:

> He, that is rich, is everything, that is,
> Without one grain of Wisdom he is Wise,
> And knowing naught, knows all the Sciences:
> He's witty, gallant, virtuous, generous, stout,
> Well-born, well-bred, well-shap'd, well-drest, what not?
> Lov'd by the Great, and courted by the Fair,
> For none that e're had Riches found despair.

When he writes about his 'beloved mistress' poetry, personal sincerity animates the lines:

> Thou sweet beguiler of my lonely hours,
> Which thus glide unperceiv'd with silent course,
> Thou gentle Spell, which undisturb'd do'st keep
> My Breast, and charm intruding care asleep:
> They say thour't poor, and unendow'd, what tho?
> For thee I this vain worthless world forego. . . .

The positive standards of Oldham's satires are honesty, sincerity and independence; their chief concern is with writing. He speaks indignantly of the neglect of great poets: 'On Butler, who can think without just rage/The Glory and the Scandal of the age?' and in his 'Satyr Touching Nobility' in imitation of Boileau, he gives new force to the traditional arguments for independence and integrity. He followed Rochester in attempting the Horatian manner though his natural style was Juvenalian, and claimed in the Preface to his imitation of the *Ars Poetica* that he had introduced a new mode into poetry by putting Horace 'into a more modern dress, that is, by making him speak as if he were living and writing now'. Oldham's importance lies partly in his establishment with Rochester of the imitation as a satiric genre, a mode in which contemporary attack could be generalized by continual reference to the ancient or foreign original. But his real talent lay in intense self-expression, a sustained passionate monologue in which concern for the craft of letters adds weight to his own spontaneous vigour.

Rochester and Oldham are outstanding among the younger satirists of the time, but a glance through the volumes of *Poems on Affairs of State*, a miscellany of topical Restoration verse first published after the Revolution, shows the enormous range of satirical poetry written in this period. Some of it is in the popular anonymous style of ballad or lampoon, but much is in couplet form, argumentative, serious and often vivid in its description of social life and political character. The same anthology contains a sprinkling of lyric verses as well on amorous rather than political affairs. Along with contemporary lyrics were printed Elizabethan and seventeenth-century verses, a mixture which also occurs in Dryden's *Miscellany* where many of Marvell's lyrics and some of Donne's *Songs and Sonets* and *Elegies* are found together with the work of the court wits and verse treatises of a more sober informative kind, like the Earl of Roscommon's 'Essay of Translated Verse'.

Restoration lyric poetry is often neither original in inspiration nor particularly novel in style; it has the scantiness and sophistication of the end of an era. The reputation of the wits as lyric poets survived into the eighteenth century, but the thinness of their output baffled later editors. An anthology first published in 1749–50 bore the title *The Minor Poets,or the Works of the Most Celebrated Authors of Whose Writings there are but small Remains.* Their lyrics were amateur and literally ephemeral since they wrote for each other's entertainment and seldom troubled to print. In his Preface to *Examen Poeticum* (1693), Tonson the publisher wrote:

> I have known several Celebrated Pieces so utterly lost in three or four years time after they were written, as not to be recoverable by all the search I could make after 'em.

From the evidence of what remains it cannot be supposed that poetry has suffered severely by this loss. Nevertheless, there are interesting developments in the lyric in this period, and one or two examples are valuable in their own right.

The lyric poets of the seventeenth century had learned to centre their poems on an epigram, a terse and witty statement of theme which could be elaborated in stanzaic form. From them Restoration poets inherited simplicity of diction, a lapidary elegance of style and the neat turning of a commonplace theme. Two of their favourite authors, Waller and Suckling, are good examples of what they hoped to imitate and improve. In *The Way of the World* Mirabel and Millamant cap each other's quotations from Waller's poem, 'The Story of Phoebus and Daphne Apply'd:

> Like *Phoebus* sung the no less am'rous Boy,
> Like *Daphne* she, as Lovely and as Coy. . . .

The neat equivalence between the situation of the poet and his mistress and the mythological figures thus presented in the opening lines is epitomized in the pretty verbal turn of the final couplet:

> Like *Phoebus* thus, acquiring unsought Praise,
> He catcht at Love, and fill'd his Arms with Bays.

Suckling ('natural, easy Suckling,' Millamant calls him) failed to equal Waller's verbal neatness, but he practised a light dialectic on those traditional themes which continued to occupy the wits. That of inconstancy is a good example.

Inconstancy in its wider context of variety was a favourite topic of metaphysical wit. The 17th Elegy attributed to Donne deals with it. Johnson in his life of Cowley illustrated his metaphysical exaggeration with the poem 'Five years ago (says Story) I lov'd you,' of which he remarks 'the difficulties which have been raised about identity in philosophy, are by Cowley with still more perplexity, applied to Love.' This perplexity Suckling tries to tidy up. In 'Perjury Excused' he reduces argument to neat excuse: 'My Flora, 'tis my Fate, not I/And what you call contempt is destiny,' and claims that to pretend love would be a perjury she could not tolerate. The Restoration lyrists improved on this.

Sir George Etherege's 'To a Lady Asking Him How Long He Would Love Her' develops the argument in a tone suited to Dorset's curt reminder of the new mood – 'We live in an age that's more civil and wise/Than to follow the rules of romances.' Etherege repeats the old argument that change is the condition of life: to refuse to love for fear of it would be as mad as 'to deny to live because we're sure to die'. The light analogy is in the same vein as the final stanza of Rochester's 'Love and Life':

> Then talk not of inconstancy,
> False hearts, and broken vows;
> If I, by miracle, can be
> This livelong minute true to thee,
> 'Tis all that heaven allows.

Argument is reduced to repartee; the neatness of the measure, the diction and syntax reinforce the quick sophistical trick. But even in this slight instance Rochester's superiority is clear in a command of lyric form which shows an intricate sense of structure both in language and thought.

Within the same form there was often variety of mood and treatment of theme. Etherege and Rochester again contrast well in their Dialogues on Inconstancy. Etherege's lover in 'The Forsaken Mistress' pretends regret at the inevitable change because a second love is never so good, and claims that he 'would but can no longer love'. Rochester's 'Dialogue between Strephon and Daphne' is characteristically harsher – 'Prithee now, fond Fool, give o'er' – and its arguments more intricate. Strephon explains inconstancy simply: 'Love, like the other little boys,/Cries for hearts, as they for toys' and change is the law of Nature. But the poem concludes on an unexpectedly ironic note in the complaining nymph's last rejoinder:

> Silly swain, I'll have you know
> 'Twas my practice long ago.
> Whilst you vainly thought me true,
> I was false in scorn of you.

This changes the dialogue on betrayed love and constancy into a sceptical comment on the whole form: the nymph goes through the proper motions of complaint but concludes by herself proving the point of Strephon's argument. Rochester's irony recalls Marvell's 'Daphnis and Chloe' where the situation of the coy mistress is unusually treated from the moment when the shepherd has decided to give up and, refusing Chloe's last-minute capitulation, has left for more accessible mistresses. Marvell comments:

> Yet he does himself excuse,
> Nor indeed without a Cause,
> For, according to the Lawes,
> Why did Chloe first refuse?

It is these laws that the Restoration court lyric defines and discusses. At its slightest, as in Etherege, Caroline gallantry is sharpened by a new dialectic of self-justification and a pointed, simpler style. At its best in Rochester, it retains a metaphysical complexity under a deceptively lucid and elegant manner. In his satire 'Timon', the old-fashioned affected wife of the boring host compares modern poets unfavourably with the inoffensive Suckling, but Rochester has few affinities with the cavalier. He is nearer Marvell in his ironic grace.

Rochester's imagery, too, has the resonance of true poetry. The opening stanza of 'Love and Life' is a patch-work of Hobbesian commonplaces of Imagination and Memory, neatly applied to the theme of justified inconstancy:

> All my past life is mine no more;
>   The flying hours are gone,
> Like transitory dreams given o'er
> Whose images are kept in store,
>   By memory alone.

But in the context of the lyric they intimate subtler analogies between life, the past, dream, memory and love than the professed argument could ever sustain in the work of a simpler poet. As a lyric poet, Rochester is not equalled by most of his contemporaries. Some were capable of a bold baroque image like Aphra Behn's 'Love in fantastic triumph sate/While bleeding hearts around him flowed', or a striking opening like Sedley's 'Love still has something of the Sea/From whence his Mother rose', which has the grace of allusion rather than the force of wit. Etherege's 'Sweetest Bud of Beauty' in anacreontics improves on Waller's original by its measure and terseness. Dorset's best lyric builds up to a brilliant clinching image:

> Love is a calmer gentler joy,
>   Smooth are his looks and soft his pace;
> Her Cupid is a black-guard boy
>   That runs his link full in your face.

It is typical of the mood of the wits to turn the traditional Cupid into a stand-and-deliver link boy, a menace of the contemporary streets.

There are other strains in Restoration lyric than that of the court wits, but none of equal importance. At the beginning of the period Mrs Katharine Philips (1631–64) continued the Platonic cult of the earlier age in her poems to women friends, and recalls the metaphysicals in an image like that of the magnetic needle turning and trembling to the lodestone, as a type of love. Philip Ayres (1638–1712), an ardent literary archaist now forgotten, was almost alone in the period in practising the sonnet. In the Preface to his *Lyric Poems made in Imitation of the Italians* (1687) he recognizes the old-fashioned nature of his 'sonnets, canzons, madrigals' but bravely defends it by claiming that though Dryden, Waller and Cowley had 'not stoop'd to anything of the sort', he has precedents in 'Mr Spencer, Sir Philip Sidney, Sir Richard Fanshaw, Mr Milton and some few others'. Thomas Flatman (1637–88), eccentrically placed by Saintsbury among the minor Caroline poets, represents contemporary fashions in his poem 'Retirement', a theme which was to be worked to death in the next century, in his tedious heroic epistle, 'Laodomia to Protiselaus', but more in an unusual lyric tone of familiar gaiety which anticipates Prior:

> I did but crave that I might kiss
> If not her lips, at least her hand,
> The coolest Lover's frequent bliss,
> And rude is she that would withstand
>   That inoffensive liberty;
> She (would you think it?) in a fume
> Turn'd her about and left the room,
>   Not she, she vow'd, not she.

('The Slight')

By the last decade of the seventeenth century several of the newer tastes had become fully established. Translation and imitation were given fresh impetus by Dryden's later works when he turned from satire to these safer forms. Sir Samuel Garth (1661–1719) who in the last year of the century produced the next mock-heroic satire after *MacFlecknoe*, *The Dispensary*, a comic account of squabbles in the medical profession in imitation of Boileau's *Le Lutrin*, also compiled and edited contemporary translations of Ovid. William

Walsh (1663–1708), Pope's early adviser, practised a mild, lyric vein in a politer form than the wits, and recommended imitation and correctness. Matthew Prior (1664–1721), who before the turn of the century had followed the fashion for personal and literary satire in his attack on Dryden, *The Hind and The Panther Transvers'd* (written in collaboration with Charles Montagu, later Earl of Halifax), and in his 'Satyr on the Poets' and 'Satyr on the Modern Translators', relinquished satire after the Revolution as too dangerous and kept the serious business of life and letters well out of his later lyric poetry. The real preference of poets and readers in these last years of the century was for light discursive epistles on a variety of subjects, especially such Horatian topics as the superiority of the country over the town. John Pomfret (1667–1702) hit the tone precisely in his poem 'The Choice' of which Johnson wrote 'Perhaps no composition in our language has been oftener perused.' Johnson describes this popular work as exhibiting

a system of life adapted to common notions, and equal to common expectations; such a state as affords plenty and tranquillity without exclusion of intellectual pleasures.

(*Life of Pomfret*)

This is a very different ideal of life from the court wits'. 'The Choice' with its temperate theme and fluent couplet form advertises a new fashion for sense and moderation in a modest practical mode.

The lyricism of these later poets, such as it is, is more a matter of mood and description than of form. The close link with music still evident in earlier Restoration poetry has begun to slacken. Restoration lyric had retained its musical function, and most songs of the court wits were set by contemporary composers. Forms which had a literary origin like the pastoral dialogue had become predominantly musical during the seventeenth century – a duet sometimes concluding with a chorus which might illustrate contrasting moods by contrasting voices. Well into the Restoration books of Airs and Dialogues were published which preserved the older lyric and sustained the new. English opera under Purcell never lost its respect for words, and it is worth considering whether the high style of Restoration verse – the poetry of passion in the heroic epistle, for instance – may not owe something to the declamatory manner of arioso and recitative which English composers originally inherited from Henry Lawes, and then developed through the influence of French and Italian styles. Rhetorical pointing and formal diction have much in common with this operatic technique. But by the end of the period a more florid and spectacular style of opera and a more elaborate manner of singing had begun to develop which helped to estrange poetry and music. Sound and sense began to seem inevitably distinct, and writers turned in disgust on the pantomimic nonsense of the new form. External structure in poetry, which is always best sustained by the rhythmic and technical discipline of lyric verse, grew less important in the next age than the pattern of discourse, the shifting moods and temper which could be displayed by internal manipulations within the fixed unit of the couplet. Descriptive word-painting to provoke sentiment, and a taste for statement, eloquent or intimate, are among the predominant traits of eighteenth-century verse. The poets of the Restoration had been still concerned with the sound of language as well as its sense: Dryden is more 'musical' than Pope. Nevertheless, their argumentative wit, and their interest in declamatory or informal discourse and in the subjects, particularily satiric, which suited these modes, helped to prepare the styles of their successors.

Thus Restoration verse reflects especially the transitional nature of its time, in close links with the thought and style of the past and experiments in new ideas and techniques. The satirists, caught up in the events of their age, were often originators in verse, yet among these the most admired were often the most traditional. The lyric poets adopted old forms to flout old conventions of love which were still sufficiently alive to be worth refuting. Even at the end of the period, the richness and diversity of seventeenth-century literary traditions proved strong enough to nourish works whose influence extended into the eighteenth century, and writers whose reputations were not submerged until the beginning of the nineteenth.

13

SIXTEENTH- AND SEVENTEENTH-CENTURY PROSE

John Carey

(i)
PROSE BEFORE ELIZABETH

In the history of English prose before Elizabeth, More and Tyndale are the major figures.

Sir Thomas More (1478–1535) has been regarded by Protestant historians as an enlightened Utopian who degenerated into a heretic-burner. They may be wrong (the Catholics think so), but his writing, falling into three periods, seems to support the view.

The first period, lasting into the mid-1520s, contains More's two masterpieces, *Utopia* (1515–16, in Latin) and the *History of Richard III* (extant in English and Latin versions, *c.* 1513–18), the Latin epigrams and the translation (1504–5, published 1510) of Giovanni Pico's *Life of Pico Della Mirandola*. During these years More was associated with the European humanist movement. He translated (1501) epigrams from the Greek Anthology with Lily, and (1505–6) Lucian with Erasmus, who wrote the *Praise of Folly* (1509) in More's house.

Though it centred on the revival of Greek, the movement was essentially a return to Christianity. Colet, lecturing on St Paul's epistles, was stripping off centuries of scholastic grime to reveal the challenge of New Testament teaching. The *Celestial Hierarchies*, monkishly attributed to Dionysius the Areopagite, were discredited by Grocyn. Erasmus produced his edition (1516) of the New Testament.

More's Utopians, though lacking the gospel, have arrived at practical Christianity (communist, pacifist, egalitarian), by the light of reason. It has been alleged that they lack faith, hope, and charity, but this is untrue. They tolerate numerous religions, but faith in providence and immortality is common to all, and More uses the word *charitas* to describe their treatment of neighbouring nations. They exemplify the plain teaching of Jesus. Through them More exposes the greed of the European military aristocracy. *Richard III* is a part of the same Christian revival: an attack on the *Realpolitik* of More's day already formulated, unbeknown to him, by Machiavelli. The *Life of Pico*, which ends with Savonarola's vision of Pico roasting in Purgatory for not becoming a friar, makes a comparable point. More himself lived from 1499 to 1503 in the monastery of the Carthusians, and always wore a hair shirt under his clothes (his daughter Margaret washed it, to keep it from his wife). On his way to fortune in 1522, with his Under-Treasureship and knighthood, he wrote the (unfinished) meditation on *The Four Last Things*, contemning 'this prison of the yerth'.

But the upsurge of primitive Christianity brought with it Luther, as well as Erasmus and Savonarola, and at this point More turned back. King and Church requested him to abuse Protestantism, and in the years immediately before and after his succession to Wolsey as Chancellor (1529) he obliged copiously. Best (it is not saying much) of the controversial prose is the *Dialogue* (1528) against Luther and Tyndale. *The Supplication of Souls* (1529) meets Simon Fish's projected confiscation of church property with a simulated appeal from the souls in purgatory, who would be left with no one to pray for them. The *Confutation* (1532) trudges through 500 folio pages to rebut 20 of Tyndale's *Answers* (1531) to the *Dialogue*. In 1532 Henry VIII's relations with Rome reached breaking-point; More resigned, but his onslaught on the heretics spread into the following year with three works: the *Apology*, *The Debellation of Salem and Bizance* and *The Answer to the . . .book which a nameless heretic hath named the supper of the Lord*. In the first he denies charges of cruelty against heretics, but admits that he has flogged two and considers it better for a heretic to burn than corrupt others (three did, at Smithfield, during his Chancellorship).

The third group of works is devotional, and belongs to the months in the Tower (from 17 April 1534 to 6 July 1535, when he was executed). *A Dialogue of Comfort* takes place between two Hungarian Christians – Anthony, old and calm, and Vincent, young and terrified. The terrible Turk (alias Henry VIII) threatens invasion, and Vincent wants to be told how to die bravely for the faith (More stood to be disembowelled alive: beheading was a last-minute favour). *A Treatise to receive the Blessed Body of Our Lord* followed, then *A Treatise upon the Passion* – begun, before imprisonment, in English, and continued in Latin, but ink and paper were denied before he could finish.

More's earliest English prose, the *Life of Pico*, is more vivid when it retains its Latin word order ('Great libraries, it is incredible to considre, with how mervelouse celeritee he readde them over') than when it fusses itself into alliterative hooks-and-eyes ('the favour of the common people, and the commendacion of folies'), while Pico on his deathbed, 'frushed' with fever, in 'twitches and pangs', shows the force of English vocabulary pushing aside the colourless Latin (which has *contracta* for the first, *aculeos* for the second).

Richard III has Latin antecedents too. It and *Pico* use the classical *cursus* patterns more insistently than the two *Dialogues*. Its wily ogre, taken over by Shakespeare, More found half-made in Tacitus' Tiberius. Scraps from Suetonius' *Caesars* and Sallust's *Jugurtha* and *Catiline* helped. Jane Shore is, *mutatis mutandis*, Sallust's Sempronia. Of course Richard is not just a fiction. Bits of his character can be matched in More's putative sources – the *Vita Henrici VII* of Bernard André and John Rous's *Historia*. This does not guarantee veracity, since André and Rous were furiously partisan. But it does suggest that More's account, for all its inaccuracy (Edward IV 13 years too old; Hastings and Buckingham with the wrong Christian names, etc.), owes as much to stories about Richard current in Henry VII's court (relayed, no doubt, by Morton, in whose household More served *c.* 1490–2), as to stylish Roman history.

At all events, *Richard III* is one of the great works of sixteenth-century art, and does not need to answer only to historical criteria. Erasmus said that More 'exerted himself to acquire a flexible prose style, making experiments in every kind'. This was in Latin, of course. In English the sentences usually tip across the page, anything up to 500 words long, complacently acknowledging that some find them 'too tedious to read', and obliterating that acute mind we know More possessed. One fact that comes out of the briar-patch of *Richard III*'s textual history, though, is that here More cut and polished assiduously. What seems to have been the simultaneous composition of a Latin and English version provided a peculiar kind of stylistic control.

Though trying for the historian, More's reticence about informants (his 'men say' formula) is integral to his atmosphere of whispered rumour. Richard was born feet first 'and (as the fame runneth) also not untothed' – the double negative afraid, as it were, to be more specific. As in rumour, vagueness and circumstantiality interweave. More has it 'by credible information' (actually it was his father who told him) that the night Edward IV died 'one Mystlebrooke' came with 'hastye rappyng' to the house of 'one

Pottyer dwellyng in Reddecrosse Strete without Crepulgate', and when Pottyer heard the news he exclaimed, 'then wyll my mayster the Duke of Gloucester bee kynge'. More is quick to escape from constitutional issues into the streets. We watch with the crowd while Jane Shore does penance, taper in hand:

In which she went in countenance and pace demure so womanly, and albeit she were out of al array save her kyrtle only: yet went she so fair and lovely, namelye while the wondering of the people caste a comly rud in her chekes (of whiche she before had most misse) that her great shame wan her much praise, among those that were more amorous of her body than curious of her soule.

The historian himself has some ado, we feel, to regain his composure with that last, dry balance. When we switch to Jane as she looks nowadays, 'nothing left but ryvilde skin and hard bone', it has the wisdom of folk-history – More conspicuously refrains from any moral, in contrast to his procedure in the devotional works, where the flesh is reviled with unconvincing thoroughness. It is on Jane's gay kindness that he places his final emphasis. From the *Dialogue of Comfort*, to differentiate, comes an account of another girl, whom God mercifully saves from adultery by sending a fever that:

wasteth away her wanton flesh, and beautyfieth her faire fell wyth the coloure of a kite's clawe, and maketh her looke so lovely, that her lover would have little lust to looke upon her, and maketh her also so lusty, that if her lover lay in her lap, she shud so sore long to breake unto him the very botome of her stomake, that she should not be able to refraine it from him, but sodainly lay it all in hys necke.

Not only more brutal, but more mechanical. It is because More's prose in *Richard III* is constantly responding to situations, rather than fitting them into a moral grid, that it outdistances his other English works. The medium is pliant, fragmenting, at crises, into accusation and rejoinder with violence splashed between – the arrest of Hastings is a case in point (in Shakespeare it becomes 3. 4. 75–81) – or hugging close to its subject-matter in descriptive passages, as when a messenger finds Edward's widow packing up to go into sanctuary:

about whome he found muche heavinesse, rumble, haste and businesse, carriage and conveyance of her stuffe into sanctuary, chestes, coffers, packes, fardelles, trusses, all on mennes backes, no manne unoccupyed, somme lading, somme goynge, somme descharging, somme commynge for more, somme breakinge downe the walles to bring in the nexte waye, and somme yet drewe to them that holpe to carrye a wronge waye. The quene her self satte alone alowe on the rishes all desolate and dismayde.

The frustrated movements of the first sentence, its lists of words (the Latin version skimps them) stuffed into gaps between longer units, imitate the mess they describe. In contrast, the last ten words, like a snatch from a song, linger over the crouching woman.

Presumably it is the need to win which destroys More's sensibility in his controversial prose. We may observe in it at any rate the effects of a split between stubborn argument and the fine vulgar humanity of the Jane Shore episode. Naturally logic and humanity both suffer from the separation, so that what we get, more often than not, is stretches of casuistry interrupted by 'merry tales'.

In the *Dialogue against Tyndale* (some 170,000 words) the entire logical superstructure rests upon an assumption (that the Church cannot be wrong) which renders the superstructure superfluous. Logic is a pastime to divert commonsense from questioning the basic issue. When the interlocutor in the dialogue argues from the sufficiency of the Bible, More replies that the Bible cannot be sufficient, since the Church mixes wine and water in the chalice, where the Bible stipulates only wine. Similarly it is not wrong to worship images, in spite of what the Bible says, since if it were the Church would not teach that Christ has left his image on the Vernacle for us to worship. The untouchable premise continually prevents genuine argument. Meanwhile More's earthy commonsense is isolated in the interlocutor, the devil's advocate, who always in the end surrenders improbably to the high, dry logic performed for his benefit. It is this figure who tells about the chapel of St Walery in Picardy, where pilgrims seeking relief from gallstone hang up wax replicas of their sex organs, and are issued with gold threads to tie round them (one man causing an uproar by asking how he should tie it round his wife's). His, too, is the story about the girl who was kept in a cage at Leominster Priory, and adored as a saint because she needed no food, until she was found to be sleeping with the prior every night, and put in prison, where her hunger, 'with voidance of that she had eten (which had no saintly savoure)', indicated that she was human after all. More's rejoinder, 'it had ben great almes the priour and shee had ben burned togyther at one stake', jerks us back to the inhuman bigotry he has imposed on himself. He defends the practice of admitting 'infamed' or 'infidel' witnesses in cases of heresy (though in financial cases, where the penalties were much smaller, they would have been disqualified), on the grounds that otherwise heretics might go unpunished 'for lacke of profe'. In a particular case, that of Thomas Bilney, he decides that it was right that Bilney was not

allowed to call witnesses in his defence, because if they had disagreed with the witnesses testifying against him it might have
produced 'great confusion'.

In the devotional works collisions between logic and humanity, or
commonsense, are repeatedly felt. The tenor of old Anthony's
comfort in the *Dialogue of Comfort Against Tribulation* is perfectly
orthodox (and perfectly devoid of moral worth): we should not
worry about tribulation because there is a fat reward in heaven.
Young Vincent seeks to enliven the discussion by deducing that in
that case we should pray for tribulation, not prosperity. More, we
gather, is alive to the logical difficulties inherent in the Church's
teaching. But he is not prepared to risk resolving them: old Anthony
escapes over shaky ground by asserting that, in fact, 'no man
presisely meaneth to pray' for 'continual prosperity'. It is a feature
of this *Dialogue*, indeed, that the alliance between faith and logic
becomes almost unbearably strained, and commonsense keeps
raising its anxious voice. Old Anthony 'proves' that we should not
fear prison, because it merely restricts our movement, which is true
of the world itself, yet we do not fear being in the world. Com-
monsensical Vincent replies that, though he 'cannot fynd aunswers
convenient', his mind 'findeth not itself satisfyed'. It is a good
moment, and the *Dialogue*'s tension would seem more genuine if
Anthony got away with less sophistry. We keep remembering
More's profession. It takes a lawyer to argue that God's most
merciful creation is Hell since it scares people into doing good, or
that we should not worry where our next meal will come from, since
either God will provide it, 'or els his pleasure is that thou and thine
shal live no lenger but die and depart by famine'. Meanwhile the
commonsense view is driven to its own extreme. More quotes
Wisdom, iii. 7, prophesying that the righteous will shine like the sun
and run about like sparks among reeds, and adds the 'carnall
mynded' man's reply: that 'he careth not to have his flesh shyne, he,
nor like a sparke of fyre to skippe about in the skye'. The answer
appeals, and the prose of it is suddenly better too, more sensitive to
the inflexions of a voice, than when More is clambering along the
branches of casuistry. By contrast Anthony and Vincent have a long
argument about whether it is possible to prove one is not dreaming,
Anthony maintaining that Vincent may even at that moment be
asleep:

It maye be that you be so for anything that you can say or do, whereby you
may with any reason that you make, drive me to confesse that your self be
sure of the contrary, sith you can doe nor say nothyng nowe, whereby you

be sure to be wakyng, but that you have ere this, or hereafter may, thinke your selfe as surely to do the selfe same thinges in dede, while you be al the whyle a sleepe, and nothing do but lye dreaming.

Clearly we are with an author whose logic has outpaced his language.

William Tyndale (*c*. 1495–1536), More's main opponent, came of Gloucestershire farming stock and heard about the reformist doctrines at Oxford (*c*. 1506) and Cambridge (*c*. 1518). The new, realistic Christianity of Erasmus entirely won him over, and he translated the *Enchiridion Militis Christiani* while he was working as a private tutor back in Gloucestershire, much to the consternation of the fat prelates who were his employers' usual dinner-guests. He was denounced as a heretic, but nothing could be proved. Hoping that someone would finance him while he was making an English translation of the Bible, he went to London, but More's friend Cuthbert Tunstall, the Bishop, had no time for young idealists. Within a year Tyndale was off to Wittenberg with £20 to live on – a present from a cloth-merchant, Humphrey Monmouth, who had taken him under his wing. The rest of his life he spent on the continent, dodging the Catholic authorities and living from hand to mouth, greatly assisted by the inept Tunstall, who followed him across the Channel and bought up English New Testaments, as fast as he could have them printed, to burn at St Paul's Cross. More, interrogating one of Tyndale's collaborators, demanded where the money was coming from, and was met with the reply: 'It is the bishop of London that hath holpen us'.

Tyndale, working from Erasmus's Greek, had his translation ready by 1525, and a Cologne printer, Peter Quentel, had already run off the first eighty pages when the authorities intervened. Tyndale escaped with the printed sheets up the Rhine to Worms, and it was from Schoeffer's press there that English New Testaments started to be smuggled into England in February 1526. By 1530 he had translated from the Hebrew, and published, the first five books of the Old Testament; Jonah followed in 1531, and probably Tyndale is responsible for the translation of the historical books of the Old Testament (Jonah to 2 Chronicles) which appeared after his death in 'Matthew's Bible' (1537). In 1534 he brought out a thorough revision of the New Testament with a sharp prologue disowning tinkered versions that a former associate, George Joye, had been circulating, and in 1535 a further revision. On May 21 he was kidnapped in Antwerp by the Papal police, hurried to the fortress of Vilvorde, near Brussels, and, after a year's imprisonment, strangled and burned.

It is convenient but misleading to separate Tyndale's Bible

translation from his other prose. As he saw it, everything he wrote was part of one campaign. The polemical writing (the word is too violent for Tyndale's sober certainty of waking bliss) tirelessly pointed out what it saw as the plain sense of Scripture, while the translations were fitted out with propagandist prefaces and notes to guide the reader into the Lutheran fold, besides themselves committing such heresies as rendering the Greek word for 'elder' as 'elder' and the Greek word for 'repentance' as 'repentance', which made More wonder whether they were not the work of Antichrist.

Outside the Bible, Tyndale's main works are the *Prologue upon the Epistle to the Romans* (1526, mainly an Englishing of Luther), the *Parable of the Wicked Mammon* and the *Obedience of a Christian Man* (both 1528). Justification by faith, not works, is the message of all three: the last mounts an attack on Papal authority. After these came the *Practice of Prelates* (1530), advising Henry VIII against divorce (Tyndale's brother John had to process through London with the book round his neck to discourage any further advice); the *Answer unto Sir Thomas More's Dialogue* (written 1530, printed 1531); the *Exposition* (1532) of the sermon on the mount (drawing on Luther's sermons); and *The Supper of the Lord* (1533), seconding his young friend John Frith's doubts about transubstantiation. Frith was burned at Smithfield a few months later, but Tyndale continued to argue his case in a *Brief Declaration of Sacraments* (1533), while in 1535, in *The Testament of Master W. Tracy*, he defended a Gloucestershire gentleman who had had the temerity to die without leaving part of his property to the church, and had been dug up and burned as a punishment. Tyndale has only one thing to say, and the problem for the critic is how he manages to say it so often (three volumes in the Parker Society edition), yet still conduct us forward, alert, through page after page.

The answer, partly, is style. Gavin Bone's judgement, 'Tyndale hated literature', would be true only if literature meant ornament. The masterly thing about Tyndale's style is its not seeming to be there. We have to stop and shake it before we can see the working parts. The sentences are clear and short, the reasoning cool and trenchant. When Tyndale is wrong he cleverly admits it and publishes the correction. More had objected to 'senior' as a translation of Greek *presbyteros*, because the word carried a sneer in modern English. Tyndale agrees:

Of a truth *Senior* is no very good English, though *Senior* and *Junior* be used in the universities: but there came no better in my mynde at that tyme. Howbeit I spied my fault since.

He substitutes 'elder' (More wanted 'priest', of course).

With this openness goes intelligence, More believes the church must be right because God would not let so many people be wrong. 'The Turks', Tyndale observes, 'being in number five tymes moe than we are', believe the same. Again, some reformers had ventured to hope that if treasure were not lavished on images and relics the poor would benefit. More, hoping to look realistic, replied that this was naive. Even if subscriptions to the church were stopped, the moneyed classes would be unlikely to let the poor see much of the surplus. Tyndale gracefully turns the point:

Now I aske M. Mores conscience, seying they have no devotion unto the poore which are as Christes own person . . . with what minde do they offer so great treasure to the garnishyng of shrines images and reliques?

The holes and corners of Popish superstition are scraped out with a merciless smile. Why are communicants discouraged from handling the bread? They might find out it *was* bread:

and for that cause to strength their faythes, he [the Pope] hath imagined litle prety thinne manchetes that shine thorow, and seeme more lyke to be made of paper or fine parchement than of wheate floure.

This cool amusement is a deadly answer to More's ferocity. 'In the xiii [chapter] he rageth and fareth excedyng foule with him selfe': Tyndale makes it sound as if he is watching something at the zoo, and we hasten to join him on the right side of the bars.

Everything he touches, he touches frankly. He inspires confidence by not being pompous. Once you have faith, he says, anything you do pleases God, 'as when thou makest water. And trust me if either winde or water were stoppcd, thou shouldest feele what a preciouse thynge it were to do either.' More could only touch such matters in 'merry tales': his tendency to snigger does not escape Tyndale: 'Many there are which abstaine from the outward dedes of fornication and adulterie, nevertheless rejoyce to talke therof and laugh' – hypocritical, the inference is, as well as dirty-minded.

He is not a man for flourishes – the plain style makes him look reliable – but he varies the straightforwardness with occasional sarcasm, colouring and paradox. The sarcasm is dismissive mostly (on purgatory and pardons, for example, 'what greate feare can ther be of that terrible fire which thou mayest quench almost for three halfe pence?'). But because he is involved in terrible issues, it can be Swiftian and austere:

Let it not make thee dispayre, neither yet discourage thee (O reader) that it is forbidden thee on payne of life and goods, or that it is made breaking of the kinges peace, or treason unto his highnesse to read the worde of thy soules health.

The colouring usually consists of derisive lists. The church, Tyndale warns, cannot save you, 'though thou hast a thousand holy candels about thee, a hundred ton of holy water, a shipful of pardoners, a clothe sacke full of friers coates'. But occasionally he risks a poetic image. If we trust in Christ's blood, 'our sinnes vanish away as smoke in the winde, and as darknes at the commyng of light, or as thou cast a little bloud or milke into the mayne see'. This owes a lot to rhythm – the loosely dactylic roll sinking to rest on a spondee - but also 'smoke' comments quietly on what blood or milk looks like in water.

Tyndale's paradoxes are thinner on the ground than collecting some will suggest. They need dispersal for full impact: the reader is kept wary. 'Christ with all his workes did not deserve heaven': 'If thou geve me a thousand pound to pray for thee, I am no more bound than I was before': 'God is nothyng but hys law, and hys promises'; 'I am thou thy selfe'. The bill of heresies and errors charged against Tyndale is crammed with these flagrant snippets, patiently extracted by his accusers. So, of course, is the New Testament. When, in Tyndale, we come across 'The kingdom of heaven is within us' or 'Is not Christ then a minister of sin?', we hardly notice that he is quoting. Luther acquired the same habit. 'Where the spirite is, there it is always sommer' (in the *Prologue upon the Epistle to the Romans*), is Tyndale translating Luther imitating the New Testament.

But spasmodic livelinesses would not help much by themselves. Analyse, and you find that what keeps the style interesting even in run-of-the-mill stretches is the structure of the individual sentence, which repeatedly creates expectation in the first half and satisfies it in the second. Tyndale has unlimited ways of managing this: conditional clauses are placed first, to leave us in the air at mid-sentence ('Doe they never so evill, they must be reserved unto the wrath of God'); indirect questions come to the front for the same reason ('And what congregation is meant, thou shalt alway understand by the matter that is entreated of'); 'As . . ., even so . . .', 'Though . . ., yet . . .', 'Whereunto . . ., thereof . . .', and other two-handed engines, keep the expectation-count going up and down rhythmically.

If this makes Tyndale's prose sound like a box of syntactical tricks, we need to supplement it with factors that are not stylistic at all. Tyndale would not compel without something compelling to say. His message is that being good is not doing good but feeling good. It is like sunshine inside you, 'soul-health': organic, not outward. You do not have to try any longer. Morality, effort, laws, are things of the past. If good deeds do not come as naturally as leaves to a tree they had better not come at all. The tree-image is fundamental. The words 'tree' and 'fruit' fill his pages, along with other garden language: planting, weeding, ripeness; root, blossom, pith. The reason is doctrinal, not decorative. His basic manoeuvre is to capture the horticultural texts like 'a good tree bringeth forth good fruit' (*Matthew*, vii. 17) which had traditionally been in the justification-by-works camp. The fruit, Tyndale pointed out, does not make the tree good, but the tree the fruit. You have to be good before you can do good. The church, believing that good deeds make you good, 'turneth the rotes of the tree upward'. This simple argument struck at the whole economic fabric of the Catholic Church which rested on the assumption that spiritual assets were transferable: praying and penance could be done for you, for a consideration. But one tree cannot fruit for another. Tyndale rejected contemptuously, too, the calculating goodness advocated in More's *Dialogue of Comfort*. Goodness, like fruiting, is spontaneous, and does not have its eye on a heavenly bank balance.

Explaining away the reward-clause which certainly seems to be written into some Christian texts required a nimbleness that was bound to exasperate opponents. He tells us, for instance, that 'Many sins are forgiven her, for she loveth much' (*Luke* vii. 47) does not mean that she is forgiven because she loves, but that she loves because she is forgiven. It is like saying 'Sommer is nie, for the trees blossome'.

Tyndale brings religious thinking back from economics to biology. Being one of the elect is not earned, nor is it an abstract, speculative affair, but warmly conscious. You 'feel' the spirit in your 'heart' (the two words occur several times per page). You are 'swollen' and 'drunk' with love which 'springs' inside you and 'lusts' to do good. The concept is physiological. The wounded surgeon plies the steel: God 'launceth and cutteth out the dead flesh, searcheth the woundes, thrusteth in tentes, sereth, burneth, soweth or sticheth'. Similarly there are two kinds of belief in Christ, the one physiological, proved on the pulses, which issues immediately in love, obedience, lust for oneness; the other a correct opinion, which even the devils have. The distinction, like much of Tyndale's thinking, is found in Luther, and produces paradox: 'a man may have faith without faith'.

What about those whom God does not choose to save? They are damned, of course, for 'we are damned of nature; so conceaved, and borne, as a serpent is a serpent, and a tode a tode, and a snake a snake by nature'. There is no understanding why God chooses some and leaves others: 'Our darknes can not perceave his light'. It is easy to accept because it has the familiar unfairness of the distribution of good looks or robust health. Those without are not to blame, but we blame them:

> The crippled tree in the yard
> Accuses the poor soil, and yet
> Passers-by blame it for being a cripple and
> Rightly so.

Brecht cuts through to the same primitive reaction: the spiritual survival of the fittest.

It is an easy creed, too, because it is extreme. It makes an end of pretence. No one, says Tyndale, ever has obeyed or ever could obey the ten commandments. We do not get to heaven by being circumspect, killing only state-enemies, distinguishing mine from thine. When the spirit springs in our hearts we see at once that property is theft (Tyndale did not beat Proudhon to the phrase, but he did to the idea), that killing a Turk or a Jew is devilish, and that we had only thought otherwise because of the 'bloudy imaginations' which we had sucked 'into the bottome of our hearts, even with our mothers milke'. It is a creed to inspire martyrs, and did. John Tewkesbury, Richard Bayfield and James Bainham were burned by More and his friends rather than renounce what Tyndale had written.

It is one of the injustices of literature that when we think of the English Bible we think of the Authorized Version. This copies from Tyndale on a vast scale (nine-tenths of its New Testament is identical), and the same goes for the intervening versions. Miles Coverdale, a Yorkshireman and ex-Augustinian who had been Tyndale's proof-reader in Antwerp, produced the first complete printed English Bible in 1535 without going back to the Greek or Hebrew at all. In the Old Testament books which Tyndale had not translated, Coverdale depended on Latin versions and on Luther's German. 'Matthew's Bible' (1537) was substantially Tyndale, too, for books which Tyndale had translated, and Coverdale for those he had not. 'Thomas Matthew', the name on the front, was simply a cover for John Rogers, a former associate of Tyndale's, who put the volume together. The 'Great Bible' (1539), a copy of which had to be placed in every church by law, was 'Matthew's' revised by Coverdale who watered down the Protestantism of its notes to make it acceptable to the government. Later editions announced that it had been 'Oversene and perused' by 'Cuthbert Bysshop of Duresme', i.e. Tunstall, who fifteen years before had been buying up the New Testament part of it to burn. During Mary's reign a number of Protestant intellectuals escaped to Geneva and there, under the chairmanship of William Whittingham, produced a new version, the Geneva Bible (1560), which was to be Shakespeare's Bible (and also the *Soldier's Pocket Bible* issued to Oliver Cromwell's army). Coverdale was on the panel. The version followed Tyndale where possible, and was the first to translate direct from the Hebrew (or Aramaic) the Old Testament books Tyndale had not reached. The success of Geneva made the Great Bible obsolete, but the Elizabethan government could not stomach its Calvinist notes. Accordingly Archbishop Matthew Parker and a number of bishops or budding bishops were appointed to clean it up. The result was the 'Bishops' Bible' (1568), a failure, and rightly so, since its translators did not know enough Hebrew and had to use Latin cribs for the Old Testament. The Authorized Version (1611) was a second government attempt, this time successful, to capture the popular market. Forty-seven translators worked on it. In the preface Miles Smith, Canon of Hereford, congratulates himself and his colleagues on avoiding on the one side 'the scrupulosity of the Puritans', on the other 'the obscurity of the Papists'. For example, he explains, they have not bothered to translate any particular Hebrew or Greek word with the same English one each time it occurs.

Smith may, of course, merely be covering up for a failure of coordination among the members of the translating panel, but from what he says it seems likely that he really thought that a pleasant variation of roughly synonymous words was more important than strict accuracy, and the attitude is symptomatic of the literariness of the Authorized Version. When we compare it with Tyndale we frequently find that the directness of common speech in the earlier version has been replaced by a dignity which corresponds to no living medium. Tyndale's snake says to Eve, 'Tush ye shall not dye' (AV 'Ye shall not surely die'); Esau says to Jacob, 'Let me syppe of the redde potage, for I am fayntie' (AV 'Feed me, I pray thee, with that same red pottage; for I am faint'). 'The Lorde was with Joseph', in Tyndale, 'and he was a luckie felowe' (AV 'a prosperous man'); the Jews crow over Pharaoh's army, 'His jolye captaynes are drowned in the red see' (AV 'his chosen captains also'). The popular is made decorous in the later version, so that the sense of real life drops out of the narrative: 'And wone of the wenches/

behelde him as he sate by the fyer/and set good eyesight on him'
(Tyndale), as against, 'But a certaine maide beheld him as he sate
by the fire, and earnestly looked upon him' (AV). The Authorized
Version's fondness for the rotund sentiment, the polished rhythm,
fills it with phrases that have become clichés. Tyndale's more
jagged prose will not permit itself to be so easily disposed of.
Tyndale's 'for the daye present hath ever ynough of his awne
trouble' escapes the glibness of 'Sufficient unto the day is the evil
thereof'. The Latinate use of a participle where English requires a
subordinate clause is a fairly common expedient for this tidying up
of Tyndale in the Authorized Version. Its effect is particularly
unnatural in dialogue. The father of a demented boy, for instance,
in *Luke*, ix. 39, says that the spirit which possesses him 'with moche
payne departeth from him/when he hath rent him'. In the Authorized Version the spirit, 'bruising him, hardly departeth from him'.
    It is often asserted that Tyndale's homeliness lets him down in
'poetic' passages, and *Revelation* is particularly cited. Inspection
does not support the view.

And god shall wype awaye all teares from theyr eyes. And there shalbe
nomore deeth, nether sorow, nether cryinge, nether shall ther be eny more
payne, for the olde thinges are gone.

How inferior the last six words are, Gavin Bone comments, to 'for
the former things are passed away'. In the same context Mr Bone
claims that 'the word "fine" just keys up' Tyndale's 'Whose feet are
lyke brasse' in the Authorized Version of *Revelation*, ii. 18, 'And his
feet are like fine brass'. The taste which considers fine brass feet
more decorous than brass ones will always feel unhappy with
Tyndale, but it is his strength to avoid precisely that falsity which
such taste will be a constant prey to.
    Three figures smaller than Tyndale or More deserve mention in
an account of pre-Elizabethan prose: Elyot, Ascham and Latimer.
    Sir Thomas Elyot (1490?–1546), lawyer, diplomat, admirer of
Erasmus and friend of More, left off formal schooling at the age of
twelve and, later in life, became a popularizer. He annoyed the
doctors by bringing out a medical treatise which you did not need
Greek to read – this was the much reprinted *Castle of Health* (1534)
– but he persisted in his helpful career and completed in 1538 a
Latin-English Dictionary and in 1539 *The Banquet of Sapience*, a
collection of moral sayings. He also translated bits of Isocrates and
Plutarch. His earliest, and for most people only, work, *The Book
Named The Governor* (1531), the first English book on education,

tries like the writings which followed it to make available for English readers the accumulated wisdom of the classics (as well as of Erasmus, Petrarch and Castiglione, from whom he borrowed widely). The second-hand morality that inevitably results is at least seriously offered, and has not wilted into decoration as it does with the Elizabethans. There is more to be said for Elyot than this, and more, too, than that he was an officious neologist (though he was). He had theories about extra-literary expression and its possibilities for education. He advocates painting and carving in the classroom (following the fifteenth-century Italian humanist Francesco Patrizi, whose popular *De Regno et Regis Institutione* was among his sources), and spends several pages constructing an intimate connection between the movements of the body in a dance and the mind's conception of various moral qualities (following up an idea from Plato's *Laws*). Congruently he is unconcerned (compared with the Elizabethans) about the mere verbal surface of his prose, but dedicated to the imaginative possession, through the words, of what he takes in hand, whether he is describing an artist emerging from his studio, 'stained or embrued with sondry colours, or poudered with the duste of stones that he cutteth', or a girl on her wedding night blushing and 'halfe laughinge halfe mourninge' when her husband speaks to her (this is the in *novella* 'Titus and Gisippus' which Elyot adapts from Boccaccio and insets in *The Governor*, achieving a narrative pace and delicacy that make most Elizabethan fiction redundant). His imaginative vision is expressed, naturally, through fusion and interplay. When he writes:

And I verily do suppose that in the braynes and hertes of children, whiche be membres spirituall, whiles they be tender, and the little slippes of reason begynne in them to burgine, ther may happe by ivel custome some pestiferous dewe of vice to perse the sayde membres, and infecte and corrupt the softe and tender buddes, wherby the frute may grow wylde, and some tyme conteine in it fervent and mortal poyson, to the utter destruction of a realme.

– we recognize that his prose has achieved quite unponderously an integration of the natural, human and political which challenges comparison with, say, Marvell's 'Little T.C. in a Prospect of Flowers'.

Roger Ascham (1515–68) was a don at St John's, Cambridge, and University Reader in Greek. Briefly (1548–9) he tutored Princess Elizabeth, until he fell out with her household. Then he spent three years as secretary to the English ambassador at the court of Charles V. This led to *A Report of the Affairs of Germany* (unfinished, and published posthumously *c.* 1570). Charles' 'un-kindness', Ascham decides, is at the root of the Empire's troubles. Some would say history must be more complicated than that, but at least the *Report* strove to interpret events as well as narrating them, and this made it a step forward in English historiography. The models were Polybius and Machiavelli. Ascham is better known for *Toxophilus* (1545), a Ciceronian dialogue in praise of his favourite sport, archery (which Cambridge colleagues meanly hinted he spent too much time at), and *The Schoolmaster* (1570). The first builds on Elyot's genius for expository prose, and develops ideas from him too. Ascham was not a pure-English crank like his friend Sir John Cheke (1514–57), but he refrained from 'adminiculation', 'con-glutinate' and suchlike Elyotisms, in order to show that a native vocabulary could be used with flexibility (the classical superstition about style-level varying according to matter remained dear to Ascham, as to the other humanists), and with precision. For the ancestry of *Toxophilus* scholars point to a tradition of field-sport-treatise going back to Xenophon's *Cynegeticus* (on hunting hares) and to the six-part classical pattern for the deliberative oration. Familiarity, not rhetoric, is what Ascham seems to be evolving, though. Asides help: Erasmus, Ascham reports, used to go riding for exercise, '(as Garret our bookebynder hath verye ofte told me)'. But these occasional chats, endearing as they are, are less effective in authenticating the experiences behind the prose than is Ascham's natural drift into simile and metaphor. Bores and humble-bees, studying and raising wheat, tight bows and 'treble-minikin' lute strings come together and indicate the threads of association that make up Ascham's consciousness. We frequently see through to these threads past the solid materials he has in hand, the grain of the bow or the cut of the arrow, as, for example, when the effect of stress on wood with a knot in it is illustrated by the movement of wavelets across water in which there is a 'whirlynge plat'. The depth of Ascham's sympathy with arrow and bow – he imagines moisture seeping into the bow if it is propped against a stone wall, and the arrow, a 'little poore shafte, being sent alone, so high in the ayer, into a great rage of wether' – finds expression through resort to this inner associative network. The type of occasion on which major adjustments to the network are achieved is represented in *Toxophilus* by the astonishing description (it has been called unex-travagantly 'one of the first triumphs of modern English prose') of how Ascham suddenly came to understand the movement of wind when he was riding from Topcliffe to Boroughbridge on a winter's day and watched the surface-snow sliding about the frozen countryside. It is more important to recognize that we have here the same sensibility as detected the wave-patterns in wood under stress than to learn that the rhetorical theory Ascham was following condoned such illustrative excursions.

As a literary critic, Ascham shows enthusiasm in *Toxophilus* for Chaucer's *Pardoner's Tale*, but his discernment is more remarkable in *The Schoolmaster* where he dismisses the *Mort Darthur*, condemns paraphrase as a school-exercise because it distracts attention from the best words in the best order, and ridicules the inflation which the Elizabethan malady of superflous pattern is already occasioning in the prose of the historian Edward Hall (*c.* 1499–1547), 'where many sentences of one meaning be so clowted up together, as though M. Hall had bene not writing the storic of England, but varying a sentence in Hitching schole'. Not that Ascham is against a little carefully designed antithesis and parallel himself – their presence in *The Schoolmaster* suggests that he has shifted his eye from Cicero to Isocrates. What he objects to are the windy bulges that eagerness to house these effects will produce in prose. He argues that it is the critic's job to scrutinize every syllable. His ideal is the conjunction of colloquial force and elegance – 'the pure fine talk of Rome' which he thinks he hears in certain Terentian comedies, neither over-literary nor formless. The stylist must distinguish between *inaffectatum* and *neglectum*. Like *Toxophilus*, *The Schoolmaster* worms its way into its reader's confidence by transmitting Ascham's personal feel. It begins as a reminiscence: a dinner party at Cecil's at which there was an argument about corporal punishment because some boys had just run away from Eton for fear of a beating. Ascham suspects the floggers' motives as well as their methods. Other anecdotes follow – the famous visit to Lady Jane Grey, for instance – and digressions, including a diatribe against Italian fashions ('I was once in Italie my selfe: but I thanke God my abode there was but ix dayes'). Alongside this personal expansiveness the struts and compartments of the main design are laid out with perfect clarity. The educational programme itself is mainly borrowed from Sturm, and from Erasmus, Elyot and Vives, but the planning remains Ascham's, discreetly reconciling personality with diagram. From this model of expository prose Bacon and Sidney (whose *Defence* often borrows from *The Schoolmaster*) were the gainers.

Hugh Latimer (*c.* 1490–1555) is the greatest exponent of colloquial preaching style in our literature. From the standpoint of scriptural interpretation he offers plain fare, exchanging the wiredrawn allegorical glosses of the Catholics for simple paraphrase of Old Testament history, mindful of a laity new to its vernacular bible. His sermons are baggy and unkempt, primed with funny stories, the *facetiae* of the medieval preachers (like the one about the woman who could not sleep, and told her friend she was going to hear the sermon at St Thomas of Acres: 'I never failed of a good nap there'), and shot through with personal confidences advertising his own earthy origins; how his father was a tenant-farmer and taught him to pull a crossbow, how his mother milked thirty cows, how 'they say in my country when they call their hogs to the swine-trough, "Come to thy mingle-mangle, come pur, come pur"'. When he tells a joke he exploits it with sure oratorical touch, turning it against his enemies, or snapping short the titters: 'It is no laughing matter, my friends, it is a weeping matter, a heavy matter.' Derisive alliteration (Cardinal Beaufort should have had 'a Tyburn tippet, a halfpenny halter'), and abusive compounding ('these bladder-puffed-up wily men') are his common currency, and he supplies, too, medieval-comic glimpses into hell, with the devil explaining, 'On yonder side are punished unpreaching prelates.' He has an understanding of popular linguistics comparable with Skelton's ('What, ye brain-sick fools, ye hoddy-pecks, ye doddy-pouls, ye huddes, do you believe him?'), and this enabled him to create idiom: he called non-resident clergymen strawberries, because they came once a year, and 'strawberry-preachers' became proverbial.

But all this colloquial muscle would lack point, would be a popular coating rather than the outgrowth of a staunchly popular sensibility, if it were not for Latimer's seditious (it was the word his enemies used) insistence on the mismanagement of the realm. It is this particularizing social conscience that links him with Langland. In the middle of the *Sermon of the Plough* he turns aside to in-vestigate the Court of Wards. In other sermons he focuses attention on the raising of farm-rents and the consequent price-revolution, on enclosures, on the fact that Sir Thomas Smith holds four offices at the same time, on the creation of an ignorant clergy ('If ye do this, ye shall answer for it': it is King Edward VI whom Latimer is talking to), on delays in the judicature ('I hear of many matters before my lord Protector, and my lord Chancellor, that cannot be heard'), on clothiers who thicken up substandard cloth with flock-powder, on wicked (and dead) Lord Seymour, ex-Lord Admiral, on university-entrance, on 'the poor labourers, gun-makers, powdermen, bow-makers, arrow-makers, smiths, carpenters, soldiers' to whom the king owes wages. Like the medieval preachers, he employs visual aids, picking one of the new shillings dubiously out of his purse, 'I had put it away almost for an old groat'. This slight on the coinage was resented in official circles, as Latimer is pleased to record in an ensuing sermon. The creation of an atmosphere of scandal around himself was a major aim, and he openly dares the authorities to punish him. He alludes to particular crimes and criminals ('I am not afraid to name him; it was Master Sherington'), and to recent miscarriages of justice. When he is reproved for this he repeats the allusion, implicating his reprovers. He recounts how he himself secured a pardon from Henry VIII for a woman accused of murdering her child, and tells of his own examination for heresy before the bishops, and how he heard 'a pen walking in the chimney behind the cloth'.

Latimer exhibits a literary intelligence of wonderful address, and the phenomenon is not repeated. No such conjunction of fearless criticism and idiomatic assurance can be found among the Elizabethan preachers.

(ii)

ELIZABETHAN PROSE

Elizabethan prose takes two main forms; pamphlet and fiction. Generally, the same authors supplied both. The fiction is thoroughly and (with the exception of Nashe's *Unfortunate Traveller*) deservedly dead. This is not just because it has been superseded by the novel, but also because it was meticulously superficial. The variegation of the prose surface with stock rhetorical figures was, generally speaking, all it was seriously interested in. Meaning was secondary. In this sense it has more affinity with fabric-design or with dancing than with literature. Narrative was either reduced to incident or replaced by moral diatribe and debate. These, though, were not purposeful; simply the arrangement and rearrangement of schoolroom-platitudes.

The taste for a 'Euphuistic' style naturally drew the Elizabethans' attention to the Greek romances. The best of these, Longus's *Daphnis and Chloe*, was garbled by Angel Day, whose translation (1587) from Jacques Amyot's French (which left out the love-lesson scene) was snapped up by Greene for *Pandosto* (1588), and so helped to produce *The Winter's Tale*. Thomas Underdowne, on the other hand, injected some much-needed vividness into his source when he published *The Aethiopian History of Heliodorus* in 1569. Laurence Twine's *Pattern of Painful Adventures*, based on *Apollonius of Tyre*, came out in 1576. The most famous modern descendant of the Greek pastoral romance, Montemayor's *Diana*, was Englished by Bartholomew Young (1598). Nothing much could be expected from these models, apart from Longus. Of works which might have encouraged a more vital relationship with the actual, Petronius' *Satyricon* was not known in English translation till the end of the seventeenth century (the manuscript of Trimalchio's dinner was rediscovered only in 1650). Apuleius' *Golden Ass* was shorn of its dazzling vocabulary and filled with blunders by William Adlington (1566), and *Gargantua and Pantagruel* had to wait for the resourceful Sir Thomas Urquhart (greatly assisted by Randle Cotgrave's brilliant *French and English Dictionary*, 1611). Urquhart's first two books appeared in 1653. The anonymous Spanish picaresque masterpiece, *Lazarillo de Tormes* (1554), was competently translated by David Rouland in 1576, but only Nashe seems to have learned from it.

The growth of Euphuism in English prose before Lyly can be traced at least as far back as Geoffrey Fenton's *Tragical Discourses* (1567), which derive ultimately from the stories of Matteo Bandello. Bandello, who has been compared with Defoe, was the greatest of the sixteenth-century *novellieri*, and offered rough Lombard idiom, direct narrative, and accurate pictures of social life. These qualities were successfully obscured by the turgid embellishments of François de Belleforest. It was Belleforest's *Histoires Tragiques* that reached Fenton, and he added further moralistic stuffing of his own. Also indebted to Belleforest (though it goes direct to Bandello for nine tales) is William Painter's *Palace of Pleasure* (two volumes, 1566 and 1567), which has stories from Cinthio, Plutarch and Margaret of Navarre as well, and sixteen from the *Decameron* (which was not translated in anything approaching entirety till 1620).

A more promising direction was indicated by George Gascoigne with his psychological (and, it has been argued, autobiographical) study of thwarted love in an English country house, *The Adventures of Master F.J.* (1573; in the second edition, 1575, the English setting is cautiously Italianized and the eroticism toned down). Gascoigne provides authentic observation of social and almost of sexual intercourse (the latter averted when the heroine, after arousing F.J. 'with the whole weight of hir bodye, and byting of his lips with hir friendly teeth' cools off suddenly). The medium is controlled so carefully that Gascoigne can make F.J. deduce, from a stylistic comparison of two letters received from the girl he is chasing, that one was written by her secretary. The Euphuistic novel, applying 'style' like custard, could include no such refinement.

The main current of Euphuism meanders on, however, through George Pettie's *Petite Palace of Pettie his Pleasure* (1576), which dressed up classical myths as Renaissance *novelle*, and John Grange's *Golden Aphroditis* (1577, the year before *Euphues*). Meanwhile the pamphleteers continued to record their environment with realistic clumsiness. John Awdeley's *Fraternity of Vagabonds* (c. 1561) and the more anecdotal *Caveat for Common Cursetours* of Thomas Harman (first edition lost; second, 1567), take a look at some victims of Elizabethan economics. The wish to be polite, which Lyly feeds, was stimulated by the conditions

Awdeley and Harman describe, but also by admiration for Baldassare Castiglione's famous *Cortegiano* (1528), translated by Sir Thomas Hoby. Readers who have been told that Beatrice and Benedick have been drawn from Hoby's Lady Emilia Pia and Lord Gaspar Pallavincino will be disappointed. It is, less excitingly, probable that Bembo's speech on Platonic love (Book 4) begot Spenser's *Hymns*. What strikes one is the failure of Hoby's English to keep up to the social level (here Lyly represents a clear advance). The word 'trade' inappropriately replaces the Italian *stile* or *maniera* – 'the trade and maner of courtiers', the 'kind of trade' of Leonardo and Raphael – and Lady Emilia astonishingly accuses Lewis, Count of Canosse, of 'repeating everie thing arsiversie' (*dicendo ogni cosa al contrario*). *Statue antiche di marmo e di bronzo* in the ducal palace become warehouse stuff, 'auncient images of marble and metall'.

John Lyly (*c*. 1554–1606), who is usually blamed for Euphuism, but merely took it further than anyone else, was the son of a minor official in Canterbury and spent his time at Oxford 'horning, gaming, fooling and knaving' (according to Gabriel Harvey). Although he asked Burghley (a distant relative) to pull the necessary strings, he could not secure a fellowship. This seems to have turned him against Oxford, and he wags his head over the riotous living at the University in his bestseller, *Euphues, The Anatomy of Wit* (1578) published four years after he went down. It is a cautionary tale of the prodigal son variety about a student who leaves Athens (Oxford) for metropolitan life in Naples, falls in love, betrays his friend, is jilted and repents. The plot trickles to a halt some time before the end, and the morality is then handed out undiluted in a series of letters (cribbed from Plutarch and others) about love, the existence of God, education and the deportment of exiles. Even before this happens, though, didacticism has predominated, letters, debates, proverbs, citations of authorities, harangues, all contributing to the earnest vacuity. A sequel, *Euphues and his England*, came out in 1580.

The components of Euphuism are well enough known: it depends on breaking the prose into brief clauses, matching in length (*isocolon*), structure (*parison*), and sound-pattern (*paromoion*, which includes transverse alliteration and rhyme). In the interests of this fragmentation constant antithethis is introduced, each affirmative paired with the negation of its contrary. Lists of rhetorical questions, of proverbs and exempla, and of similes from medieval natural history are the other ways of keeping the sense-unit short and repetitive. Because *parison* and antithesis involve syntax, they are figures of thought, not sound, and this means that Lyly's mannerism stultifies his intelligence as well as his acoustics. A kinder way of saying this is that he had an analytic mind that had to decompose its material and distribute it in series, and that could apprehend the world only through the perception of opposites. But whether we look upon the grammatical mannerisms as dictating to or dictated by Lyly's intelligence, it will not allow us to rate his intelligence very high. His moral thinking is nugatory. We only have to bring a work of genuine moral insight into view – *Rasselas*, say – for him to vanish into thin air. Even his admirers claim only an analytic St Vitus's dance, not an analytic mind, for him, since they observe that under its influence he repeatedly forces words into syntactic relationships, antithetical or otherwise, which their meanings will not bear out.

To imbue it with any interest, Euphuism needs to be regarded as a symptom. The Elizabethans, living in the break-up of a culture, with a new religion, a new statecraft, a new social system and a new science at the door, naturally enjoyed fitting well-worn materials into neat patterns. It was a substitute for technology, and gave the same feeling of control. Experience is reduced to adage, thought to a familiar manipulation, knowledge to what the ancients said. Pope, with infinitely more confidence, domesticates the savage world on Belinda's dressing table: 'The Tortoise here and Elephant unite./Transform'd to Combs, the speckled and the white'. His greater success reflects a sounder situation: British commercial enterprise really had, by his time, brought the world to the drawing-room. The Euphuists are regressive, not celebrating a great economic advance as Pope was, so their achievement is thinner (perhaps it is not just chance that the collapse of the Euphuistic fashion coincided with the defeat of the Armada). Still, what looks like inflation to us is actually the constant application of power to control an exploding environment. The high-society setting of the Euphuistic romance, and the perfect contentment its characters exhibit with the unserviceable moral counters their author allows them, manifest the same frantic conservatism. Significance must at all costs be restricted to the patterned surface. Our impression that we are among the ruins of a tradition of knowledge is perfectly correct, but we are probably wrong to assume that this aspect of the affair was lost on the authors. The obsession with deceptive appearance in Euphuist plots (what purport to be erotic tales are really deceit-tales), reflects the unease which the style is engineered to allay. All this, of course, does not excuse Euphuism. We have

Donne's third satire or Jonson's 'To Penshurst' to remind us how major writers reacted to the new conditions: Euphuism was the recourse of minor figures.

The determination to control experience and be polite at the same time is clear in the following extract.

Then Madam (quoth Peratio) you will appoint Love to be some metaphysicall impression that exceedeth nature and that affection is not limited by the motions of the mind according to the complexions when it is incident, Aristotle in his physickes being of this minde, that the interiour senses are tyed to the elementarie constitution of the external temperature, whereof I remember that Epictetus merily jesteth in his workes with the Ladis of Messena, that therefore they were inconstant because phlegmaticke, in that that complexion resembleth the water, which of all elements is most movable.
Morando and the rest of the company smiled . . .

This is from *Morando. The Tritameron of Love* (1587), by Robert Greene (*c*. 1560–1592). The tight syntax of Euphuism has by this time, it will be observed, relaxed, though when Greene started out on his copious and unrewarding prose works with *Mamillia* (1583), he kept as close as he could to Lyly stylistically, while angling for female readers by countering Lyly's misogyny. In 1584 came *The Mirror of Modesty*, Susanna and the Elders translated into Euphuistic debates, *Arbasto* and *Greene's Card of Fancy*, partly borrowed from an Italian translation of Achilles Tatius's *Clitophon and Leucippe*. *Planetomachia* (1585) begins as a text-book on astrology, but soon drifts into love-deceit narratives, patchily Euphuistic. Besides *Morando*, 1587 produced *The Debate Between Folly and Love*, *Penelope's Web* (Greene, who hoped to capture the woman's magazine market, does not expect his readers to know Homer, and promises a paraphrase of the epics), and *Euphues his Censure to Philautus*, in which Greeks and Trojans swop stories during a truce. Although this purports to be 'some of Euphues loose papers' it is already shaking off the Lylyan habits. Helenus's tale of Cimbriana has more narrative suspense wound up in it than anything else of Greene's, and the knights' trappings are Arcadian. *Alcida*, a Euphuistic romance inspired by Ovid's *Metamorphoses*, was licensed in 1588, also *Perimedes the Blacksmith*. This has nothing to do with blacksmiths – the title was meant to attract the artisan readers that Deloney catered for. A large chunk (Alcimides's harangue to his troops and the description of the battle) is copied verbatim from Hector's tale in *Euphues his Censure*. Greene was out to cover paper. *Pandosto* (1588) marks a dramatic improvement in style. It has humour and naturalism. The baby, Fawnia, found by the shepherd, 'wrythed with the head, to seeke for the pap', and when he carries her home his wife is furious to think her husband 'should be so wanton abroad, sith he was so quiet at home'. Readers who complain that the result is still not very good should try the earlier work. *Menaphon* (1589) makes fun of Euphuism: the new model is the *Arcadia*. The ingredients are songs and singing matches, noble nobles, expendable subjects, and rustic lovers who mix their metaphors for the amusement of the 'gentlemen readers'. Classicized nature is everywhere: we come upon Menaphon 'resting himselfe on a hill that over-peered the great Mediterraneum, noting how Phoebus fetched his Lavaltos on the purple Plaines of Neptunus'. Plot mix-up is taken so far that the heroine is almost ravished both by her son and by her father. The aristocratic propaganda of the *Arcadia* is obsequiously endorsed: it is felt to be particularly winning in a little prince to condemn one of his playfellows to death for insubordination. After *Menaphon* Greene relapses into Euphuistic romance with *Orpharion* (licensed 1589) and *Philomela* (1592, but written, he protests, 'long agoe'), and with *Never Too Late* and its sequel *Francesco's Fortunes* (both 1590). The latter retains Arcadian prejudices in its portrait of a 'clown' who has the impertinence to fall in love, and who is evidently supposed to be uproarious because he eats cheese and refers to farmhouse utensils. His is the only living idiom in the book. There follow Greene's dreary advertisements of his 'repentance' for 'riot' and 'incontinence' (neither of which, unfortunately, gets into his prose): *Greene's Mourning Garment* (1590), *Greene's Farewell to Folly* (1591), both largely moralized romance, *Greene's Groatsworth of Wit* (1592), warning Marlowe, Nashe and Peele against 'such rude groomes' as Shakespeare. *The Repentance of Robert Greene* (1592), allegedly autobiographical, and *Greene's Vision* (1592), in which with his usual sagacity he decides that what is wrong with his work is that it is too like Chaucer. Interspersed with these are his pamphlets on thieves and confidence-tricksters, *A Notable Discovery of Cozenage* (1591),the *Second* (1591) and *Third and Last Part of Cony-Catching* (1592), *A Disputation between a He Cony-Catcher and a She Cony-Catcher* (1592) and *The Black Book's Messenger* (1592). Greene's remedies are short-term – heavier irons and more hanging – and the distinction between the criminal and the gentlemen who can be taken in because he happens to have immoral tendencies is one that he never feels any misgivings about making. His own confidence-tricks are much in evidence: 'I have seen the world . . . Fraunce,

Germanie, Poland, Denmarke, I knowe them all.' It is in the *Defence of Cony-Catching* and *Quip for an Upstart Courtier* (both 1592) that we find Greene's best writing. The first may not be his but Nashe's. The violence of the anecdotes, in which a usurer has his ears nailed to a window-frame by a client's wife and a polygamist is tied to a bed by a girl he has deceived and publicly gelded, is unparalleled anywhere else in Greene. The swashbuckler with his moustaches 'standing as stiffe as if he wore a Ruler in his mouth' looks distinctly Nashean, but then so does the smart young man in the *Quip* who has his hair 'frounst with the curling yrons, to make it looke like a half moone in a mist', and the pawnbroker's nose 'purpled preciously with pearle and stone, like a counterfeit worke', so it may simply be that Greene is firmly under Nashe's influence in this last year of his life.

Greene's accounts of sharp practice in the cloth and leather trades and fashionable barbers' salons, which contribute to the *Quip*'s factual air, are not strictly his either, but derived from Philip Stubbes's *Anatomy of Abuses* (1583). Stubbes (*c.* 1555–*c.* 1610) is remembered as an anti-theatre Puritan, which is what the University Wits would have wished: not a gentleman, and bad at Latin, was Nashe's verdict. As it happens he was not a Puritan: *The Second Part of the Anatomy* (1583) supports episcopacy. More important, he was superior to Greene as a writer in nearly every respect. He is a more incisive social critic, attacking the importation of foreign textiles because of the effect on the wool-trade, recording and illustrating price-rises over the previous twenty years, recommending that the export of grain should be controlled as a counter-measure, outlining systems of poor-relief, consumer-protection, and a national health scheme. Unlike Greene he has moral convictions. He has seen the poor lying 'upon pallets of straw' in the London streets, and how domestic servants, once they fall ill, are 'caried forth, either in carts or otherwyse' and left to die. These facts are needed to put the glamour of the Elizabethan court in its proper perspective. 'Do they think', asks Stubbes, 'that it is lawfull for them to have millions of sundry sorts of apparell lying rotting by them, whenas the poore members of Jesus Christe die at their doores for wante of clothing?' Stubbes's responses are complicated (another advantage over Greene). He wants to condemn luxury outright, but keeps feeling that the 'real' aristocrats have a right to it, as a sort of badge. So we can find him both preaching natural equality – 'Dame Nature bryngeth us all into the worlde after one sorte' – and complaining that nobodies dress so well nowadays 'that it is verie hard to knowe who is noble'. Elegant women infuriate and entrance him with their powders and perfumes which make 'the bed wherein they have lyed their delicate bodies . . . smell a weeke, a moneth, and more, after they be gon', and their masks and wired hair, like 'grime sterne monsters'. It hurts him when they make themselves ugly and when they make themselves beautiful. He hopes his criticisms will be 'a nippitatum to their tender breasts'. He is passionately involved in what he condemns: the embroidered boothose, 'clogged with silk of all colors', the huge ruffs which 'goe flip flap in the winde'. His violent repulsion (he watches dancing couples 'smouching and slabbering' and demands that fornicators should be hanged or branded), is clearly an index of un-acknowledged repressions, but these, along with his frantic rationalizations (dancing is a bad thing because people have been known to break their legs at it), reveal a personality desperately engaged, which no one could claim for Greene's writing. Besides the *Anatomies* Stubbes left a piece of journalism, *The Intended Treason of Doctor Parrie* (1585), a book of prayers called *A Perfect Pathway to Felicity* (1592), and an account of the short life and long death of his wife Katherine, *A Crystal Glass for Christian Women* (1591). The eighteen-year-old girl remains perfectly collected on her deathbed, preaching tirelessly to the bystanders, including Satan, whom she sees clearly. The effect is unlikely. Only the whisperings which she repeats 'a thousand times together . . . "Oh my good God, why not nowe?"' make us think that here was a creature in agony.

Another despised 'Puritan' who turns out to be of more account than the polite writers is Stephen Gosson (1554–1624). His sermon, the *Trumpet of War* (1598), which abuses the continental reformers, shows he was not a Puritan either. He seems to have been a quite successful dramatist, but lets fly at the stage (he was almost certainly hired by the city authorities to do so), in his *School of Abuse* and the *Apology* for it (both 1579), and in *Plays Confuted* (1582). His Nashean agility can give even the classical exemplum a burlesque feel: Plutarch, he says, would not let 'the little crackhalter that carrieth his maistres pantouffles' inside a theatre; Venus, though worshipped by poets, 'made her selfe as common as a Barbars chayre'. Like Donne in the *Elegies*, he puts Ovid into a modern setting: the scene at the chariot-race from the *Amores* is transferred to a London theatre: 'suche heaving and shooving, suche ytching and shouldring, to sitte by women', the young men offering the girls 'pippines' and 'on small acquaintance' starting to 'dally with their garments to passe the time'. None of the exponents of what is misleadingly referred to as 'Elizabethan criticism' (Puttenham, Sidney, Webbe and the rest) conveys, as Gosson does, what it is actually like to be in an Elizabethan theatre – how one may 'sit out of the raine to view, when many other pastimes are hindered by wether' – and none of them has his explicit reference to actual plays ('the *Jew* and *Ptolome*, showne at the *Bull*'; 'the *Playe of Playes* showen at the *Theater*, the three and twentieth of Februarie last'; '*Cupid and Psyche* plaid at Paules' and so on), or his quotation from and scrutiny of particular speeches and actions. The apologists' vague claims about the moral effects of drama are met with witty pragmatism by Gosson. Actors, he observes, are not outstandingly moral, yet 'if any goodness were to be learned at Playes it is likely that the Players themselves which committ every sillable to memory shoulde profitte most'. After this Gosson's Euphuistic debate-romance, *The Ephemerides of Phialo* (1579), is disappointing, though the prostitute Polyphile's defence of hedonism arranges the moral platitudes paradoxically for once.

Other efforts at fiction between *Euphues* and the *Arcadia* which just deserve mention are Barnaby Rich's *Farewell to Military Profession* (1581), which improves current prose fashions with jest-book idiom, and relays (from Bandello) the plot of *Twelfth Night*; George Whetstone's *An Heptameron of Civil Discourses* (1583), another collection of framed *novelle*, one (from Cinthio) later transmuted into *Measure for Measure*; and Brian Melbancke's heavily Lylyan *Philotimus* (1583). Marginally more considerable are Thomas Lodge (1558–1625) and Anthony Munday (1553–1633).

Lodge began with a *Reply* to Gosson's *School of Abuse* which the 'godly and reverent', he says, suppressed, because it took the side of plays. Gosson procured a copy though and replied, dismissively getting Lodge's name wrong (William). Suppression was the best thing for it. Appeals to 'authority' are all Lodge can muster: a good example of a classical education paralysing though. *An Alarm against Usurers* (1584) is at least more in touch with life, though Lodge's prose gets hopelessly muddled over the monetary and legal details involved and has to fall back on limp morality ('Obey your parents . . . trust not to straungers'). *The Delectable History of Forbonius and Prisceria* (1584) is vacuous eloquence, the action, such as it is, briefly indicated in the occasional pause for breath. Its one hope is to sound upper-class: 'she gave answere to his amorous intreaties with this gracious affabilitie'. *Rosalind* (1590) – *As You Like It* without Touchstone, without Audrey, without Jacques, and without

Shakespeare – never quite lives up to the prose of its Dedication: 'Having with Capt Clarke made a voyage to the Islands of Terceras and the Canaries, to beguile the time with labour, I writ this booke, rough, as hatcht in the stormes of the Ocean, and feathered in the surges of many perillous seas.' The narcissistic style, flourishing the usual Euphuistic non-animals, is tiresomely assertive about its useless bits of advice, *Satis est quod sufficit, Non sapit qui non sibi sapit*, and so forth. Its descriptive grip is negligible; 'a faire valley (compassed with mountains, whereon grewe many pleasant shrubbs)' is about the size of it. Much better is the relationship between the two girls, arch and intimate; Lodge, on a troopship, is in need of some fantasy; 'And I pray you (quoth Aliena) if your roabes were off, what metall are you made of that you are so satyricall against women? Is it not a foule bird defiles the owne nest?' (Shakespeare noticed this, 4.1.186). 'Leave off (quoth Aliena) to taunt thus bitterly, or else Ile pul off your pages apparell and whip you (as Venus doth her wantons) with nettles.' As usual in Elizabethan fiction, the poems are more accomplished than the prose; the mock-artlessness, for instance, of:

> Like to the cleere in highest sphere
> Where all imperiall glorie shines,
> Of selfe same colour is her haire
> Whether unfolded or in twines.

In the *Life of Robert Duke of Normandy* (1591), a reworking of a medieval story, the Euphuistic orations stand around the blood and miracle of the legend with a strange composure which is almost interesting. Robert starts well by biting off his nurse's nipples, and, grown to manhood, has a Mother Superior parade her younger nuns naked, selects and rapes the most beautiful one and rounds off the evening by amputating her breasts. Spectacularly converted, he vows to eat only food fed to dogs, and so takes up residence with one of the Emperor's pet greyhounds. *A Nettle for Nice Noses* (1591) prods at the evils of Elizabethan London by way of a series of animal fables derived from a fifteenth-century work, and ends with a harangue against sex (promiscuity, Lodge explains, 'infeebleth the member'). Lodge's next three works may also be passed over quickly; *Euphues' Shadow* (1592) is a Lylyan romance bursting at the seams with sententious rubbish, *The Life and Death of William Longbeard* (1593) recounts in jest-book episodes the exploits of a cross between Robin Hood and a Trades' Union Leader in the reign of Richard I, and *The Devil Conjured* (1596) lectures, at times in workmanlike prose, about natural and black magic and 'These late eclipses in the sun and moon'. Bigger claims have been advanced for *A Margarite of America* (1596), based, Lodge says, on a Spanish book he found in the library of the Jesuits at Santos and written in the Magellan Straits where 'many bitter and extreme frosts at midsummer continually clothe and clad the discomfortable mountaines'. Again, this locale is more intriguing than anything in the novel. The villain, Arsadachus, with whom Margarita is unaccountably smitten, rapes and murders with the best will in the world, without causing us the slightest qualm. Eventually he disposes of his wife; 'with the carving knife he slit up the poore innocent ladies bodie, spreading her entrailes about the pallace floore'. It is surprising that C. S. Lewis should find it 'a brighter, bitterer, more dangerous world than ours'; there is nothing to spill but red ink. The second element is Arcadian: regalia and novelty gardens, with the usual tasteful combination of ingenious mechanics and Latin tags, and no expense spared (the tags are worked in everywhere; Arsadachus quotes *Sic itur ad astra* while eating his late wife's heart). There is also a Lylyan element. The characters settle down improbably at one point to discuss the five senses. Alliteration is maintained at all costs ('look downe from your thrones, and behold my throbbes'). In the same spirit Lodge indicates proudly that the lines in one of the inset poems can be read backwards, forwards, or in any combination of the two. Also in 1596 Lodge published *The Tears of the Mother of God*, a devotional tract, and *Wit's Misery, and the World's Madness* which mixes invectives against current conditions with obeisances to the 'gratious Prince' and her 'grave counsailors' – as if the government were in no way to be connected with the state of the country. Finally came *A Treatise of the Plague* (1603), in its small way a monument to the misdirection of human energies. Lodge puts his readers right about the Arabic for 'antidote' and the Greek for 'unicorn', but when it comes to remedies relapses into witch-doctoring (cut a live pigeon in half and clap it to the swelling, etc.). He advises against the isolation of suspected cases – the only useful precaution he could, in his state of knowledge, have recommended.

There is not much to be said for Anthony Munday's morals. He was a government spy, employed to betray those who had confided in him. Later he would attend the execution to supply any last bit of evidence that might be needed, and note down signs of terror for his ensuing write-up. He is a fine example of a patriot, always putting his country first. His *English Roman Life* (1582), recounting a stay at the English College at Rome, has a gluey fascination. The prose is rapid and awkward, and combines the trivial and the sensational knowingly; an account of a Jesuit flogging himself, of a carnival, of the burning of Richard Atkins, legs first, of the menu at the College (Munday sneers at how well they do themselves, and him). *Zelauto . . . a Friendly Entertainment to Euphues* (1582) is hardly Euphuistic, though it retains the flood of noble sentiment which, coming from Munday, looks even more sham than usual. The 'plot' is contrived to fit in with a number of illustrations, left over from other books, which the printer happened to have on hand. It livens up at the end with a story about a Jew demanding his bond and a rigged trial which Shakespeare appropriated for the *Merchant.* Munday was presumably copying from the lost *Jew* play Gosson mentions. Hence the tighter style.

Sir Philip Sidney's *Arcadia* is, like *Euphues*, a major work, in that prose could not be the same after it. With Sidney it is difficult to separate man from myth, particularly as in the years following his death there were political motives for confusing the two. Looking past the dead hero at the live courtier, our impression is of un-employed talent, of an accomplished appendage. His father, Sir Henry, was directly implicated in the business of government (and ruined himself financially in the process), but Philip, kept at home by Elizabeth when he wanted to sail on an expedition with Drake, obliged to retire to Wilton under a cloud when he meddled in politics, appears as a member of the governing class, related to several of the greatest men of the realm, but with negligible political function, to be brought in as part of the decorations, as in the Whitehall tournament where, in blue and gilt armour, he laid siege to the Fortress of Perfect Beauty, occupied by the ageing queen. Writing his prose epic Sidney invents a political scene – with monarch, rebels and civil war – which is really a stage for the posturing of the aristocrats. Being a prince in Arcadia relates more to striking an attitude than to practical government. Basileus, the king, begins the story by retiring into the woods for a year, and the attitudes start to be struck in the first chapter when Pyrocles, one of the heroes, appears floating on a bit of driftwood. Though ship-wrecked, Pyrocles sits 'as on horseback', full of 'unmoved majestie', and brandishes a sword 'about his crowne' (meaning head, but the wordplay is purposeful). This passage introduces another constant feature: the fiction of the obsequious elements. The wind sports with Pyrocles's hair and the sea kisses his feet (the figure was called prosopopoeia). It is a country fit for aristocrats to live in. In the famous bathing scene the princesses strike the water with their hands and it seems 'to smile at such beating' and to weep when it drips from their bodies. Later Pamela embroiders a purse, the silk 'lovingly embracing the wounds she gave it'. That it is a purse she is disguising has its own significance. The young nobles are expensively accoutred even in nominal disaster (Pamela is in prison at the time), but the connection of this wealth with money, or with the labour of the boorish creatures whom they elsewhere hack to pieces for insubordination, is never enforced. In this atmosphere it is not surprising that the counterfeit takes on a special importance. Pyrocles spends most of the novel disguised as an Amazon, and it is a portrait of Philoclea that he falls in love with. The lovely fake is also prominent in the tournament scenes, where the knights' sumptuous furniture repeatedly imitates living creatures. One knight is disguised as an eagle, with wings which flap as his horse gallops; another as a garden full of orange trees. Artefacts are justified by their clever resemblance to the real. Basileus has an elaborate water-garden full of contrived rainbows and mechanical birds which 'deceive' sight and hearing.

Opulent counterfeit is also the determining principle of the style. The broad array of rhetorical figures (John Hoskins, in his *Directions for Speech and Style*, was able to illustrate every figure of *elocutio* with an excerpt from the *Arcadia*) does not answer to any natural stress, but seems to be applied afterwards, as, of course, it was – Sidney first wrote the book in a relatively plain style, then decorated it. Comparison of the two versions quickly reveals life (and death) being disguised as courtly gesticulation. For example, when one of Erona's disappointed suitors slaughters her subjects the original version has: 'hee spared not man, woman, nor chylde, but with miserable tortures slewe them', and the later: 'he spared not man, woman, and child, but (as though there could be found no foile to set foorth the extremetie of his love, but extremitie of hatred) wrote (as it were) the sonnets of his love, in the bloud, and tuned them in the cries of her subjects'. This rhetoric of the revised *Arcadia*, in all its sterile variety, is part of the book's aristocratic cachet, amounting to a system of etiquette, not coarsened by utility. What is wrong with the style's pretentious ceremonial, the syntactical genuflexions of epizeuxis, antimetabole and the rest, is not, certainly, its complexity, but its failure to bring that complexity up against problems of meaning that it could get its fine teeth into. It is kept in the tilt-yard, with hardly a real hair to split. The characters are drenched in words which leave them still uncomplicated. And behind the

civilized figuring no respectable human values are to be encountered, as we realize abruptly when we come to the slaughter of
the Arcadian rebels by the aristocrats:

Yet among the rebels there was a dapper fellow, a tayler by occupation,
who ... began to bow his knees, and very fencer-like to draw neere to
Zelmane. But as he came within her distance ... Basilius, with a side blow,
strake of his nose ... As his hand was on the grounde to bring his nose to
his head, Zelmane with a blow, sent his head to his nose. That saw a
butcher, a butcherlie chuffe indeed ... and lifted up a great leaver, calling
Zelmane all the vile names of butcherly eloquence. But she ... hitte him so
surely on the side of his face, that she lefte nothing but the nether jawe,
where the tongue still wagged, as willing to say more, if his masters
remembrance had served. O (said a miller that was halfe dronke) ...
and ... fell withall, just betwene the legs of Dorus; who setting his foote on
his necke (though he offered two milche kine, and foure fatte hogs for his
life) thrust his sword quite through, from one eare to the other; which toke
it very unkindlie, to feele such newes before they heard of them, in stead of
hearing, to be put to such feeling ...

And so on. The elegant barbarity is allowable because the victims
are tradesmen. It shows up the *Arcadia*'s function as class-warfare,
as well as its fake civilization.

The victims in the last quotation are Deloney's audience.
Thomas Deloney (*c.* 1560–1600) was a weaver and ballad-writer,
but educated – his first known work is a translation of some Latin
documents about a Catholic Archbishop who came over to Protestantism. He was a political journalist, and played a prominent
part in a trade-dispute in 1595. His fiction for the working classes
was immensely popular, supplying what its readers wished to believe: that foreigners are funny, that apprentices marry rich widows,
and serving-maids, courtiers, that nobles talk Euphuism, that
Henry VIII rubbed shoulders with artisans and 'laughed heartily'
when they smeared his jester with dog droppings. *Jack of Newbury*
(1597) is about weavers; *The Gentle Craft* (two parts, 1597 and *c.*
1598), about shoemakers (it supplied material for Dekker's
Shoemakers' Holiday); and *Thomas of Reading* (*c.* 1598), about
clothiers. Memory is not taxed: there are jest-book episodes instead
of plots. Long Meg of Westminster, heroine of the most famous
jest-book, the *Life and Pranks* (1582), actually appears in the *Gentle
Craft*. A favourite unifying motif, naturally, concerns spectacular
recovery of fortune.

Deloney is a dramatist. Page after page of the novels contain
only dramatic dialogue, conveying background, incident and

psychology entirely through speech. At one stroke he puts himself in touch, as no other Elizabethan fiction-writer, with the major literary form of the age. It is no surprise to find the murder of Old Cole from *Thomas of Reading* among Shakespeare's sources for *Macbeth*. The other tragic climax in this book, the judicial blinding of Duke Robert (his sweetheart Margaret accompanying him on the scaffold), is also realized through direct speech:

O stay master doctor, till I have conveyed my loves countenance downe into my heart . . . O that I might give thee a kiss of twenty yeares long, and to satisfie my greedie eies with thy faire sight: yet it doth somwhat content me, because thou art present at my punishment, that I may hold thee by the hand, to comfort my heart at the sodaine pricke of my eie.

It has more humanity, and consequently more power, than Sidney was equal to.

Humanity is what Thomas Nashe (1567–1601) has generally been denied, though that he was the most vital of the Elizabethan prose writers does not need demonstration. He was a professional writer, one of the new middle-class intelligentsia which the Elizabethan administration could not absorb. After writing his Euphuistic *Anatomy of Absurdity* (1589) he realized the deadening effect of the prefabricated styles, and in the preface to Greene's *Menaphon* (also 1589) is already advocating a more 'extemporall veine'. What stimulated his reintroduction of colloquial versatility into prose was the publication, between 1588 and 1589, of a series of Puritan pamphlets under the name of Martin Marprelate (probably Job Throckmorton, a Warwickshire gentleman and MP). Nashe, who had an anti-Puritan bias, and no doubt needed the money, was employed to answer in kind (four replies, the most likely *An Almond for a Parrot* [1590], have been ascribed to him). The effect on his style is seen in *Piers Penniless his Supplication to the Devil* (1592), which includes the start of a slanging-match with Gabriel Harvey to which his other contributions were *Strange News* (1592) and *Have with you to Saffron Walden* (1596). *Christ's Tears over Jerusalem* (1593), Nashe's attempt to reinvigorate the moralistic diatribe against metropolitan sin, and *The Terrors of the Night* (1594), a sceptical ramble through demonology, were followed by his best works, the picaresque *Unfortunate Traveller* (1594) and *Lenten Stuff* (1599), an advertisement for kippers in the tradition of the Renaissance mock encomium, recommending, among other things, their body-building qualities: 'The most intenerate Virgine wax phisnomy, that taints his throate with the least ribbe of it, it will embrawne and Iron crust his flesh, and harden his soft bleding vaines as stiffe and robustious as branches of Corrall.'

Gleeful appreciations of Nashe's 'clowning' are beside the point not only because they undervalue the evolution of a style that could contain more disruptive energies than any available when he started out, nor only because they ignore his beautifully inventive imagery, but chiefly because they belie the elasticity that could adapt itself to the varied moods of a recklessly profuse intelligence. A key passage in this respect is Nashe's retelling of the Hero and Leander story in *Lenten Stuff*. It is a reaction to Marlowe's arch idyll that had come out the previous year, and deliberately throws the story open to new sensations. It introduces coarse laughter and facetiousness with elaborately redundant word-play and asides about Hero's old nurse, and these unsettle sentimental expectations. It enforces its novelty with new words: 'romthsome' (from the dialect 'roomth'), 'chat-mate' (Hero's nurse), 'frampold' (invented by Shakespeare the year before in *Merry Wives* to mean 'sour-tempered'):

the churlish frampold waves gave him his bellyful of fish-broath, erc out of their laundry or washe-house they woulde graunt him his coquet or *transire*, and not onely that, but they sealde him his *quietus est* for curvetting any more to the mayden towere.

The images bring the reader up at every turn against an exuberantly documented reality, urban, domestic, commercial (coquets and *transires* were excise warrants and emigration permits). Bits of literary stereotype arc thrown into testing collision with this: the chivalric 'curvetting to the mayden towere' next door to a laundry. But the fixity of burlesque is quite absent. Nashe's loving cultivation of the commonplace renovates experience for us: Leander 'sprawled through the brackish suddes' to Hero's tower, and when he is drowned 'boystrous woolpacks of ridged tides came rowling in, and raught him from her'. And the style can encompass gentleness:

Were hee never so naked when he came to her, bicause he shuld not skare her, she found a meanes to cover him in her bed, and, for he might not take cold after his swimming, she lay close by him, to keepe him warme. This scuffling or bopeepe in the darke they had a while without weame or bracke . . .

The indulgent irony, with its tender suggestion of the girl's warmth, has resilience because of the alert surroundings. 'Bopeepe' bathes the lovers' hectic enjoyment in innocence: it was a nursery game in which the nurse alternately hid and uncovered her head, to the delight of the child. Its applicability to what Leander is doing to Hero is apparent enough. 'Weame' meant a scar, and 'bracke' a flaw in cloth, so the phrase which means at first 'without interruption' also displays the lovers' bodies, without a scar or a stitch of clothing. Later in the story, when Leander is drowned, the childhood evocations appear again, in Hero's dream: 'towards cocke-crowing she caught a little slumber, and then shee dreamed that Leander and shee were playing at checkestone with pearles in the bottome of the sea'. But typically this submarine magic is put next to Hero's cold in the nose, 'she was so troubled with the rheume', a prosaic comment on her attempt to warm Leander the week before. The chequered sensibility for which the whole passage speaks inevitably recalls Eliot's remarks on seventeenth-century wit, which 'may be confused with cynicism by the tender-minded' because it involves 'a recognition, implicit in the expression of every experience, of other kinds of experience which are possible'.

The emphasis needs shifting to Nashe's flexibility because there has been a tendency to write him off as a callous buffoon on the evidence of violent scenes like the execution of Zadoch in the *Unfortunate Traveller* where the comic energy has attracted more attention than the physical awareness which accompanies it. In the description of the battle between the Swiss and the French, for instance – 'here unweeldie Switzers wallowing in their gore, like an Oxe in his dung, there the sprightly French sprawling and turning on the stained grasse, like a Roach new taken out of the streame' – the fearful clarity with which the wounded men are observed makes G. R. Hibbard's conclusion that Nashe 'seems to have been singularly lacking in human feeling' plainly inadequate, though it is easy to see how it could be arrived at by a critic determined to wrench a uniform tone from every passage.

Even when the burlesque element seems to be predominant, and to be directed unmistakably at the opulent artificialities of the *Arcadia*, we can sense Nashe's ambivalence. The furniture of Sidney's knights, counterfeiting eagles and orange-trees, reappears absurdly in the *Unfortunate Traveller*'s tournament scene. Surrey's horse is disguised as an ostrich, stretching out its neck to eat the metal bit, and his armour is:

all intermixed with lillyes and roses, and the bases thereof bordered with nettles and weeds, . . . his helmet round proportioned lyke a gardners water-pot, from which seemed to issue forth small thrids of water like citterne strings.

The watering can punches a hole in the Arcadianism, but typically Nashe at once snatches a delicate simile from this world of everyday objects which restores the damage. (The cittern, a kind of guitar, was a particularly familiar musical instrument: it used to be left lying around barbers' shops for the amusement of customers.) The simile, by eliciting the poetry of the commonplace, suggests what Nashe finds alien in the Sidnean mode, but also deters a dismissal of the passage as mere burlesque. Nashe's activities, over any period of more than a line or two, will not easily submit to a single label. A similar experience is provided by what Nashe makes out of Sidney's artificial gardens with their groves of mechanical birds:

By the mathematicall experimentes of long silver pipes secretlye inrinded in the intrailes of the boughs whereon they sate, and undiscerneablie convaid under their bellies into their small throats sloaping, they whistled and freely carold theyr naturall field note. Neyther went those silver pipes straight, but, by many edged unsundred writhings and crankled wanderinges a side, strayed from bough to bough into an hundred throats. But into this silver pipe so writhed and wandering aside, if anie demand how the wind was breathed; Forsooth the tail of the silver pipe stretcht it selfe into the mouth of a great paire of belowes, where it was close soldered.

Certainly there is a derisive ingredient, and the bathos of 'tail' and 'belowes' is calculated, but it is equally plain that Nashe does not find the imaginative potential of the engineering entirely resistible. When we discover that he has made up the words 'crankled' and 'inrinded' for the passage, it reinforces our impression that he is engaged creatively as well as destructively. This appears as duplicity to some critics. 'In most of his writings', Mr Hibbard complains, Nashe 'is not wholly absorbed in what he is saying, not concerned solely with conveying the nature and significance of something he is deeply interested in.' But conveying natures and significances will, for any metaphor-making mentality, preclude being 'wholly absorbed' in Mr Hibbard's sense. It is in Nashe's resistance to 'absorption' that his flexibility of response resides. This prevents him delivering the doctrinal certainties that Mr Hibbard is in search of. His fidelity is to his own agile imagination rather than to any set of convictions. As a result, even when he is subscribing to a moral or religious position, pious readers feel uncomfortable. This is the case in *Christ's Tears over Jerusalem*, a sermonistic warning about the depravity of London, written for a 'holy' and 'vertuous' patroness, of which the early part is put into the mouth of Christ. It has been interpreted as ferocious bad taste or as an exhibition of baroque sensibility, the root of the matter being that Nashe refuses to make his voluble imagination decent.

I have sounded the utmost depth of dolour, and wasted myne eye-bals well-neere to pinnes-heads with weeping (as a Barber wasteth his Ball in the water) . . . Not the least hayre of my body, but may it be as a pegge in a vessell, to broche bloode with plucking out.

Nashe's Christ is speaking. The context forbids the solution possible in, say, the Hero and Leander story, that Nashe is being funny. The mundane images compel our participation, but the tone, shunning 'grosse-brained formallitie', stands between us and our usual responses to the matter in hand. This means that Nashe, in this most dog-eared region of Elizabethan consciousness, the religious harangue, is able persistently to unsettle his reader without for a moment sacrificing intensity. Not that *Christ's Tears* comes very high among Nashe's prose, but it is a test-case because the subject obliges us to take his style seriously.

Nashe had few imitators and no successors. Henry Chettle's novel *Piers Plainness' Seven Years Prenticeship* (1595) contrives something for everybody, having half its action in Thrace, which is Nashean, inhabited by black-comic moneylenders, and half in Crete, which is Arcadian except that lovers undertake Euphuistic debates with themselves. Chettle hops from one convention to the next, eschewing the critical interaction Nashe demands. In Crete the heroine's uncle is about to take advantage of her in a convenient grove when the hero emerges from the bushes exclaiming: 'Villaine attempt not to defloure the Nymph'. In Thrace the usurer, having been too handy with the whip, like Nashe's Zadoch, is double-crossed by his smarting daughter and hanged, 'cursing his daughter execrablie, and blessing the beholders with his goutie heeles'. Nothing is done to bring the two levels into a perspective. An honester attempt at the picaresque, Nicholas Breton's *Miseries of Mavillia* (1599), has serious merit. The speech-habits of various classes are plausibly mimicked. Actuality is respected: at one point a detail in the mechanism of a pistol determines the action; geriatric nursing is feelingly described. Suddenly, at the end, Mavillia has her nose bitten off by a disappointed suitor. The bathos is meant to look Nashean, but indecorum has not been woven into the novel's design enough for that. By 1604, when Thomas Middleton's *The Black Book* appeared, imitation of Nashe is coming to mean vehement syntax plus a few received properties like the usurer's cough – 'a quarter of an hour long', ending in 'a rotten hawk and a hem' (in Chettle it had been 'a score of rotten coughes'). Not but what Middleton is more rewarding, with even this amount of Nashe in his blood than, say, Sidney or Lyly, neither of whom wrote anything as creatively realistic as his scene in which the devil, disguised as a constable, raids a London brothel.

It is Thomas Dekker (*c.* 1572–1632) who manages Nashe-pastiche best in *The Wonderful Year* (1603). Generally Dekker is too solemn and tender to profit much from Nashe's personality. He sees life as class-conflict. In *Work for Armourers* (1609) he wanders into a bear-pit, and what he finds there reminds him of poor men trying conclusions with the 'rich and mightie'. The dogs:

> might now and then pinch the great ones, and perhaps vex them a little by drawing a few drops of blood from them: but in the end they commonly were crushed, and either were carried away with ribs broken, or their skins torne and hanging about their eares, or else (how great soever their hearts were at the first encounter) they stood at the last, whining and barking at their strong Adversaries, when they durst not, or could not bite them.

But Dekker's pity for the destitute is rendered ineffectual by traditional respect for authority. In *The Bellman of London* (1608), which recalls the agrarian riots in the midlands the year before, he cowers in a loft while a ferocious band of 'idle Vagabonds' curse Justices of the Peace below. The work instructs honest citizens how to detect thieves (silently extracting page after page of cony-lore from Harman and Greene). Caught between oppression and anarchy, Dekker solaced himself with religion. In *Dekker his Dream* (1620), written after seven years in prison, Bunyan and Traherne seem not far off:

> I climbed to the tops of all the trees in Paradise, and eate sweeter Apples than Adam ever tasted. I went into the Star-Chamber of Heaven, where Kings and Princes were set to the Barre, and when the Court arose, I fed upon manna, at a table with Angels. Jerusalem was the Pallace I lived in, and Mount Sion the hil, from whose top I was dazeld with glories brighter than Sun-beames.

The Wonderful Year is different because of Nashe and because of the plague. The plague, unlike an agrarian riot, was an act of God, so for once it was allowable to watch the rich being slaughtered with a clear conscience. At the same time, pity and terror were inescapable, and so a complex arose for which Nashe had perfected the medium. Even Dekker's account of the Queen's death sounds flippant: 'Upon thursday it was treason to cry God save king James of England, and upon Friday hye treason not to cry so'. And when among the skulls and carcases we come upon rich burghers 'miching and muffled up and downe with Rue and Wormewood stuft into their eares and nosthrils, looking like so many Bores heads stuck with branches of Rosemary, to be served in for Brawne at Christmas', we are plainly approaching Nashe-land. In *News from*

Hell (1606) Dekker expressly invokes 'ingenious, ingenuous, fluent, facetious T. Nash', but the attitudes are now too stiff (the patriotism over English heroes killed in the Low Countries, for example) for the imitation to succeed. From *The Gull's Horn Book* (1609), usually reckoned Dekker's best prose, Nashean traces have almost vanished, and though the London scenes are dynamically informative the targets for humour are quite normal and the disruptive element is lost. Dekker's imagination, finally, is less versatile than Nashe's. His images do one thing at a time. Nashe's can begin, say, satirically and end up lyrical. Nashe's courtier:

> so puft up with bladders of Taffatie and his back like biefe stuft with Parsly, so drawne out with Ribands and devises, and blistered with light sarcenet bastings, that you would thinke him nothing but a swarme of Butterflies, if you saw him farre off . . .

suffers a sea-change with the last image, whereas Dekker's pages (from his *Seven Deadly Sins of London*, 1606), 'in light coloured suites, embroidered full of Butterflies, with wings that flutter up with the winde', are pretty from the start.

Following Nashe has taken us outside Elizabeth's reign. We must return to look at the prose of religious controversy, and particularly at Richard Hooker (c. 1554–1600). On the Puritan side the Marprelate tracts have already been mentioned. The leading spokesman here was Thomas Cartwright (c. 1535–1603), who was deprived of the Lady Margaret professorship of divinity at Cambridge for his views, and whose *Reply* (c. 1573), *Second Reply* (1575) and *Rest of the Second Reply* (1577) were all directed against John Whitgift (c. 1530–1604), later Archbishop of Canterbury, who had been responsible for this deprivation. On the other side, besides Whitgift himself, who reacted promptly to the Puritan *Admonition to Parliament* of John Field and Thomas Wilcox with his *Answer to a Certain Libel entitled an Admonition* (both 1572), John Bridges became notorious for his mammoth *Defence of the Government Established* (1587), 'very briefly comprehended', as Martin Marprelate put it, 'in a portable book, if your horse be not too weake'. After Bridges a dignified defence of the bishops and the 1559 church settlement was much needed, and Hooker was picked for the job. He had become Master of the Temple in 1585, and had distinguished himself in his sermons against the Puritan Walter Travers who was the afternoon lecturer. In 1591 he was presented with the living of Boscombe and made Prebendary of Netheravon, not to perform the attendant duties but so that, enjoying the proceeds in absence, he could settle in London to his *Of the Laws of Ecclesiastical Polity* with the help of Edwin Sandys the Archbishop's son (a law-student with a sinecure prebend at York), George Cranmer another young lawyer, and the theologian Dr John Spenser.

Hooker's commission required delicate handling. He had to steer between Rome and Geneva, and arguments justifying Anglican denial of the Pope's authority might all too easily be turned to account by Puritans dissatisfied with the authority of the bishops. The Puritan disparagement of human reason, and reliance on 'inspiration', alarmed and repelled him, as did the accompanying insistence on the utter depravity of fallen man. What he wanted to establish was a compromise position: that man needed both his rational faculties and the word of God as revealed to him in Scripture in order to arrive at a rule of conduct. But since the interpretation of the word of God was always in dispute, and since the Puritans were apt to claim that Jack's interpretation was as good as his master's, Hooker found himself being drawn away from this middle position and from reliance on the Bible towards an affirmation that the dictates of reason were themselves to be re-garded as the direct commands of God. Another difficulty was that the pillars of the Tudor state, whom his temperamental con-servatism required him to respect, and under whom he had accepted employment, were anxious that their spokesman should promulgate the theory of a state-church in which heresy would be a political as well as an ecclesiastical offence, and could be punished as sedition. But this did not accord exactly with his own tolerant view of Catholic practices, towards which his conservatism was never more attracted than when his Puritan opponents were irrationally maintaining that all things Roman were evil simply because they were Roman. That pressure was put on him, whether successful or not, to waive his personal sympathies in this respect is suggested by the notes Sandys and Cranmer wrote on the manu-script of Book VI, which happens to survive: for example, 'that which followeth, because it is one of the most absurd disputes that ever I read, and because it favoureth the papists in some points, if it were clean left out I should never miss it'.

He argues his case from first principles, drawing on the philosophy of St Thomas Aquinas. The starting point is God, whom Hooker apprehends as reason rather than will. God's reason is the eternal law which he has set down for himself to follow, and is the source of all other law. Natural agents (sun, moon, stars etc.) observe the law laid down for them because they cannot do otherwise. Voluntary agents (men) observe it by free consent. This observation is called virtue; its omission, sin. There are two ways of discovering the law. First: God has endowed men with reason to work out for themselves the order they ought to follow. All laws thus made only appear to be made by men, ultimately they are made by God. Human laws (e.g. the ecclesiastical laws of England) are special rules derived from natural law. Second: there is a revealed law (God's word) which concerns only the supernatural, and cannot be found out by reason. This argument gains two important objectives. It makes the Puritan error appear as a simple failure to distinguish between the natural and the supernatural, and it associates the Elizabethan religious settlement and obedience to it with eternal movements of nature like the rising and setting of the sun and the rotation of the planets.

It seems likely that as the work proceeded Hooker found it increasingly difficult to square his own beliefs with the demands of the Tudor state. Books VI–VIII were apparently suppressed by Sandys, and did not see print until the mid-seventeenth century. Books I–IV were published at Sandys's expense in 1593 to coincide with the passing of the Conventicle Act through the House of Commons and the execution of the Puritan dissenters Penry, Barrow and Greenwood. Book V came out in 1597.

Hooker chose the magisterial Ciceronian style for his propaganda, and the result has been generally acclaimed as 'a monument of pure and splendid prose style and of lucid philosophic thought'. C. S. Lewis writes of it affectionately as 'a model for all who in any age have to answer ready-made recipes for setting the world right in five weeks'. Professor Lewis's periphrasis for 're-forms' is an example of one of Hooker's own dishonest techniques. He vividly travesties, for instance, Puritan claims for the authority of the individual conscience:

A man whose capacity will scarce serve him to utter five words in a sensible manner blusheth not in any doubt concerning matter of Scripture to think his own bare Yea as good as the Nay of all the wise, grave and learned judgments that are in the whole world: which insolency must be repressed, or it will be the very bane of Christian religion.

The caricature of the stammering ignoramus makes Hooker's final snarl look almost like a smile. False analogy and loaded metaphor are also of service. 'Dangerous it were', pleads Hooker, 'for the feeble brain of man to wade far into the doings of the Most High' – 'wade' (a favourite verb) evoking perils that a neutral word like

'investigate' would have to forgo. Similarly when Hooker is pro-
testing – it is one of his commonest devices – that the points at issue
are not really very vital or numerous, he writes:

in truth they are fewer when they come to be discussed by reason than
otherwise they seem when by heat of contention they are divided into many
slips, and of every branch an heap is made.

His opponents' determination to be scrupulous is beautifully discredited by the figure of the living branch reduced to a pile of
shavings.

For the writer concerned to appear above mere controversy the
Ciceronian period offers distinct advantages. Hooker's way of
reaping these can be illustrated from Book I where he advances
against the Puritan disparagement of human reason and natural law
the example of a universe in which everything obeys natural law. He
does not, of course, believe that the universe is composed of
voluntary agents, so it cannot obey natural law in quite the way he
wishes mankind to. He clouds this distinction by admitting that
natural phenomena have no volition, but talking about them as if
they had: how would we manage, he asks, if they were to 'forget
their wonted motions', or if the sun were to 'stand and rest himself'?

Although we are not of opinion, therefore, as some are, that nature in
working hath before her certain exemplary draughts or patterns, which
subsisting in the bosom of the Highest, and being thence discovered, she
fixeth her eye upon them, as travellers by sea upon the pole star of the
world, and that according thereunto she guideth her hand to work by
imitation: although we rather embrace the oracle of Hippocrates, that 'each
thing both in small and in great fulfilleth the task which destiny hath set
down;' and concerning the manner of executing and fulfilling the same,
'what they do they know not, yet is it in show and appearance as though
they did know what they do; and the truth is they do not discern the things
which they look on:' nevertheless, forasmuch as the works of nature are no
less exact, than if she did both behold and study how to express some
absolute shape or mirror always present before her; yea, such her dexterity
and skill appeareth, that no intellectual creature in the world were able by
capacity to do that which nature doth without capacity and knowledge; it
cannot be but nature hath some director of infinite knowledge to guide her
in all her ways.

The reassuring expansiveness sacrifices life to gain weight. It could
not be further from the excitability of a spoken language, but it is
monumentally reliable. The monster sentence with its lumbering
turn ('nevertheless, forasmuch as'), which is intended to suggest a
patient endeavour to get all the cards on the table, is Ciceronian

Latin half-translated into English (Walton reports that Dr Stapleton, who happened to be in Rome when the *Laws* came out, read the first book straight through to the Pope, translating it into Latin as he went along). Soothing cadences do their bit to inspire confidence: the *cursus planus* (long, three shorts, long, short), based on Cicero's cretic-trochee, terminates five clauses of the extract ('bosom of the Highest', 'work by imitation' etc.). The meaning is perhaps not quite as dependable as the style would have us believe. We cannot, to be sure, detect any contradiction: Hooker commits himself to the view of nature as a blind machine, and repeats this in the sentence which follows. What the elongated syntax manages to do, after this firm statement, is to come round again to talking about nature as if it were a voluntary agent. The main clause is deferred as long as possible ('nature hath some director of infinite knowledge to guide her in all her ways'), and by the time it appears the personal pronoun, renounced during the Hippocrates quotation, has crept back, and we seem to be talking again about a character who might go astray and need a helping hand. The prose adheres to one theory of nature but toys with another to enliven the correspondence between human law and the law of the universe. Professor Lewis writes of Hooker's style:

The Latin syntax is there for use not for ornament; it enables him, as English syntax would not, to keep many ideas, as it were, in the air, limiting, enriching, and guiding one another, but not fully affirmed or denied until at last, with the weight of all that thought behind him, he slowly descends to the matured conclusion.

This excellently describes how the style is meant to be thought to be operating, though our excerpt suggests that the weight of thought may not be consistently 'behind' Hooker so much as stowed away for the time being while he floats to earth. To have a style which can keep opposed theories 'in the air' simultaneously is obviously expedient when the destination is compromise. If we select specimens of Hooker's view of human nature from different parts of the *Laws* we shall find that two distinct pictures emerge. On the one hand we have a man who naturally aspires to conformity with God, and whose will has as its natural object the good which reason leads him to seek. Nature has 'imprinted' in this man's mind an 'infallible knowledge' of certain useful rules, as, for instance, that the higher should always command the lower. It might be thought that a belief in this superior prototype argues no very familiar acquaintance with the standard model, but elsewhere Hooker can be found describing a man who is by nature prone to 'imbecilities', self-love, sensuousness, and a 'general blindness' to the laws of reason. The discrepancy is not to be removed by assuming that Hooker has in mind in the one case unfallen and in the other fallen man. Rather he has a lively sense both of what fallen nature can still achieve and of what it can sink to. His thought here is richer and more open to lived experience than his opponents' narrow convictions of human depravity. But he takes advantage of his broader view by invoking either extreme of it as convenience determines. There is a 'ground of reason even in nature' for elaborate ceremonials, since mankind has always had them, and they are therefore good. Alternatively it is natural for man to be 'savage, wild, and cruel' if he is not strictly subjected to law. Man is Caliban when Hooker is occupied with the behaviour of the Puritans, and Prospero when he is occupied with their theories. Change is another subject upon which Hooker can be observed shifting his ground. When faced with ardent reformers he will explain that changing an established law, even for the better, 'must needs be troublesome and scandalous', because it makes subjects suspicious and disobedient. Contrariwise, to those who derive their system of church-government from the Bible Hooker replies:

that neither God's being author of laws for government of his Church, nor his committing them unto Scripture, is any reason sufficient wherefore all churches should for ever be bound to keep them without change.

Again it must be stressed that the two views are not so much opposed as parts of a larger whole. Hooker's conservatism calls for a cautious distinction between past change and future. The style's function is to make every qualification Hooker needs sound reasonable. Its vice is that it is able to do this. As:

These things therefore considered, we lastly require that it may not seem hard, if in cases of necessity, or for common utility's sake, certain profitable ordinances sometime be released, rather than all men always strictly bound to the general rigour thereof.

If we rephrase this as 'Good laws should not be enforced' we are surprised to see how indecent it looks. The style, in Hooker, as Professor Lewis puts it, is there for use.

SEVENTEENTH-CENTURY PROSE

Around the beginning of the seventeenth century we find styles
developing which are more compact than Hooker, more sharply
meaningful than Lyly or Sidney, and less imaginative than Nashe.
The movement has been connected with the advance of Puritanism
and of science (a plausible alliance if we recall the Catholic Church's
suppression of new thought: the Royal Society was to have a high
percentage of Puritans among its members). It has been argued,
too, that the breakdown of old complacencies rendered obsolete the
rounded Ciceronian mode and encouraged a Stoicism which found
its natural expression in the terse, asymmetrical, fractured style of
Seneca. Justus Lipsius (1547–1606), the Belgian editor of Seneca
and Tacitus, and Marc Muret (1526–85), the French humanist, are
customarily invoked in this context. The English movement is seen
as an extension of continental anti-Ciceronianism. There is no
harm in these theories, but we should remember that they do not fit
all the evidence. Milton, for example, a Puritan, and not complacent, appears to find Ciceronian oratory a suitable medium in the
mid-century, and jeers at Hall for writing abrupt sentences 'as if all
above three inches long were confiscat'. We must understand, also,
when we see the 'Senecan' label attached to writers as different as
Browne and Burton, that it is hopelessly elastic as a critical aid.
When scholars quarrel about whether Bacon's style is 'Ciceronian'
or 'Senecan', we must realize that it is not a real issue since they
have merely picked different aspects of the classical styles and of
Bacon's style to compare. More will be gained from description of
the various English styles themselves than from contentious
slogans. Typical seventeenth-century objections to both the
Ciceronian and the Senecan styles are found in Bacon, whose
Advancement of Learning (1605) recommends the communication of
knowledge in aphorisms which, unlike Ciceronian periods, contain
only the 'pith and heart of sciences' and stimulate further enquiry
because they avoid conclusive sculpturing. Reworking this passage
twenty years later for the *De Augmentis*, Bacon adds a condemnation

of the Senecan style as a trick for making each sentence seem 'more witty and weighty than indeed it is'.

The effect of Puritanism on the new prose is most easily seen in the plain-style sermon, constructed according to a bald system of logical exposition. Laurence Chaderton (1538–1640), later the first Master of the Puritan foundation, Emmanuel College, Cambridge, seems to have been the first to lay down this standard for pulpit style in his Paul's Cross sermon of 1578, quoting distrust of 'enticing words of man's wisdom' from *I Corinthians*, ii 4. The phrase is taken up and aptly applied to Hooker's *Laws* in the Puritan reply, *A Christian Letter of Certain English Protestants* (1599). There continue, of course, to be Puritan preachers who do not conform to the new principles, notably Thomas Adams (c. 1583–1655), 'the prose Shakespeare of Puritan theologians' as Southey rather limitingly called him, who by judicious quotation can be made to sound like Donne or Browne.

Another of the new forms, the prose character, was more likely to develop into literature. In a sense it was not new. *Prosopographia* (description of a person) had been part of the schoolboy's rhetorical filing-system for years before Casaubon's famous edition of the Theophrastan characters (with Latin translations) came out in 1592. The first English borrower from Theophrastus, predictably, was Ben Jonson (in the speeches of Sir Politick Would-Be), and three years later the first formal collection, *Characters of Virtues and Vices* (1608), was published by Joseph Hall (1574–1656). Hall, later Bishop of Norwich and Milton's opponent, includes good types as well as bad, unlike Theophrastus, and his character of 'A Good Magistrate' is an important innovation because it brings social as well as moral criteria into the form. Adapting Theophrastus, he tends to whittle away local colour and precision and direct speech. He needed the *Characters* as *exempla* for his sermons, so a tone of exhortation replaces Theophrastus's objectivity. His honest types are uncompromising Stoic extremes (morality as well as style made Fuller call him 'our English Seneca'), and the wit of his *Characters* is a rapid, intellectual quality, unrelated to laughter. Paradox, difficult metaphor, and zeugma ('he is wont both to hide himself in retiredness and his tongue in himself') make for a style that moves quicker than the reader's mind. This element was greatly increased in the characters by Sir Thomas Overbury and 'other learned Gentlemen' appended to the second impression of Overbury's *Wife* (1614). By this time, too, the categorization has become regularly social and political, and is hardly ever merely moral. Sir Thomas

(1581–1613) had the advantage, reputation-wise, of being the victim of a scandalous murder (involving the Earl of Somerset and the fiendish Frances Howard, Countess of Essex). His book was a huge success and by 1622, when the eleventh edition appeared, the original twenty-two characters had grown to eighty-three. Thirty-two, added in 1615, are by John Webster, the playwright, and six prison-characters ('A Prison', 'A Jaylour' etc.), added the next year, by Thomas Dekker. Overbury wrote probably the first eleven. They are pungent, elliptical, affectedly obscure: occupying ground between the neoclassical satire of Marston and Guilpin, and Donne's *Paradoxes and Problems*. Compared with Lyly, the result is at least intellectual, but something more like a human being writes Webster's characters, and moral authority can be heard for the first time (of a coward, for example, 'such is the nature of his fear that contrary to all other filthy qualities, it makes him think better of another man than himself'). Webster's 'Fair and Happy Milkmaid', half-borrowed from Sidney, is more realistic than Sidney because what the pastoral is not is kept critically in view ('never came almond glove or aromatic ointment on her palm to taint it', and so on). The milkmaid makes her own kind of contact with the red-toothed economy which Dekker, in the prison-characters, peoples with tigers, wolves and vultures, sharks and hogs. Compassion and penetration are developed further in the *Microcosmography* (1628) of John Earle (c. 1600–65). His coward, by contrast with Webster's, 'is the man who is commonly most fierce against the coward'. His 'Vulgar-Spirited Man' abuses men out of favour and is 'the first that says "away with the traitors"', but at executions he melts, 'and for pity to see a man die, could kill the hangman'. It is this disillusioned adult voice which keeps us from being immune when Earle sentimentalizes over his 'Child':

We laugh at his foolish sports, but his game is our earnest; and his drums, rattles and hobby-horses, but the emblems and mockings of man's business . . . Could he put off his body with his little coat, he had got eternity without a burden, and exchanged but one heaven for another.

The character-form maintained its popularity throughout the century, and began enrichingly to concern itself with individuls rather than types. The pages of Clarendon's *History* are full of prejudiced *prosopographiae*, and in the autobiography (c. 1680) of the first Earl of Shaftesbury (Dryden's Achitophel) we have a masterpiece of actuality, his portrait of a country squire, Henry Hastings (too long to quote but easily available in David Nichol Smith's *Characters from the Histories and Memoirs of the Seventeenth Century*).

Of the essay (a form that keeps shading into the character, the epigram and the paradox) there were a number of exponents in the early part of the century – Sir William Cornwallis, Daniel Tuvill and Robert Johnson among them. John Florio's embroidered translation (1603) of Montaigne's *Essais* provided impetus. The English essayists are all eclipsed by Francis Bacon (1561–1626) whose aphoristic *Essays* of 1597 were expanded and added to in 1612. The final, augmented edition came out in 1625. Bacon's other main works in English are the *Advancement of Learning* (1605), reworked and Latined as *De Augmentis Scientiarum* (1623); the *Wisdom of the Ancients* (1619), first published in Latin in 1609, which reinterprets the pagan myths in the belief that they preserve evidence of a period of high intellectual achievement in prehistoric times; the *History of Henry VII* (1622); and the *New Atlantis* (unfinished, 1626), an imaginary voyage to a Pacific island inhabited by Baconian experimentalists.

Stylistically Bacon's aim was to eliminate style, or so he made out. The idea was to let the subject shine through purely transparent words which neither refract nor distort. Knowledge he described, following Heraclitus, as *lumen siccum*, a dry light; dry because not 'steeped and infused in the humours of the affections'. The 'first distemper of learning' happens 'when men study words and not matter'. Words 'entangle and pervert the judgment', so it is necessary at the beginning of any dispute to 'imitate the wisdom of the mathematicians' and define our terms. The confident distinction between words and matter derives from Quintilian's instruction: 'Let care in words be solicitude for things. For generally the best word is closest to actual things, and they are seen by its light.' It becomes, under Bacon's influence, a standard component of seventeenth-century stylistic theory, along with the notion that 'things' are tangible objects, so that the best words are concrete nouns. Bacon, in the *Novum Organum* (the treatise which establishes induction as the key to truth), offers 'chalk' as a representative of the best part of language, and opinionative adjectives like 'heavy' and 'light' as examples of the worst.

In spite of this distrust of persuasive rhetoric, and his intermittent allegiance to aphorism, Bacon is a persuasive rhetorician. The point is easily substantiated by reference to the *Advancement of Learning*, where Bacon is out to argue that 'a laborious and sober inquiry of truth' will be justified in what it provides for 'the benefit and use of man'. It seems innocent enough, though what Bacon is doing, for all his assurances that knowledge of God will improve as well, is secularizing education. In an admired passage near the beginning he criticizes the schoolmen for breaking theology up into infinite tiny points and testing each with objections and counter-objections:

Whereas indeed the strength of all sciences is, as the strength of the old man's fagot, in the band. For the harmony of a science, supporting each part the other, is and ought to be the true and brief confutation of all the smaller sort of objections. But, on the other side, if you take out every axiom, as the sticks of the fagot, one by one, you may quarrel with them, and bend them, and break them at your pleasure: so that, as was said of Seneca, *Verborum minutiis rerum frangit pondera*; so a man may truly say of the schoolmen, *Quaestionum minutiis scientiarum frangunt soliditatem*. For were it not better for a man in a fair room to set up one great light or branching candlestick of lights, than to go about with a small watch candle into every corner?

The dependably proverbial analogy of the fagot, the exhibition of classical authority (Quintilian), the commonsense bareness ('fair room', 'great light'), combine to make the proposition plausible, yet a very small pressure will crack it. It is true that a fagot can be broken more easily if taken apart, but if the individual components of a scientific hypothesis can be refuted, how can the hypothesis survive: 'Harmony' is beside the point: what matters is the truth of each axiom, not its convenience as a prop for others. As for lighting a room from a central candelabra, this will reveal one aspect; examining architectural details singly will disclose different aspects. Complete knowledge can dispense with neither. Bacon's façade readily collapses. His objection to the schoolmen did not really centre on their scrupulousness at all. His impatience with 'the smaller sort of objections' appears particularly specious in the context of a later passage where he is arguing in favour of scrupulousness:

So it cometh often to pass, that mean and small things discover great, better than great can discover the small: and therefore Aristotle noteth well, *That the nature of everything is best seen in its smallest portions*. And for that cause he inquireth the nature of a commonwealth, first in a family, and the simple conjugations of man and wife, parent and child, master and servant, which are in every cottage. Even so likewise the nature of this great city of the world, and the policy thereof, must be first sought in mean concordances and small portions. So we see how that secret of nature, of the turning of iron touched with the loadstone towards the north, was found out in needles of iron, not bars of iron.

The speaker here is evidently in favour of taking fagots to pieces and places his view above suspicion, once again, with classical lore and household objects.

The appearance of logic and of intricate division and subdivision do not prevent Bacon's argumentative procedure from being often a conspiracy of brute assertion and false analogy. The *Advancement* is addressed to King James whose subjects, Bacon assures him, will not be made less obedient by education. To suggest such a thing is 'a mere depravation and calumny, without all shadow of truth' – so far, the assertion; then the analogy:

For to say that a blind custom of obedience should be a surer obligation than duty taught and understood, it is to affirm that a blind man may tread surer by a guide than a seeing man can by a light.

A sighted man, though, can select one path and refuse others: a blind man has no choice but to obey. His progress *is* 'surer' in the sense of the word that would interest an absolute monarch.

It is the job of Bacon's style to usher one across these looser planks. To help it, it has a number of structural figures – the *isocolon* and *parison* of Euphuism, charged with argumentative force, plus *anaphora* and *epistrophe* (clauses which begin or end with the same words), and *antimetabole* (a favourite Sidnean flourish, made weight-bearing by Bacon, as: 'whereas the meaning ought to govern the term, the term in effect governeth the meaning'). Half-dead, often Biblical, metaphors (following paths, laying foundations, the fountain of knowledge, the light of knowledge, the branches of knowledge, the fruit of knowledge) make the reader feel at home.

Bacon's lack of tenderness is sometimes lamented ('The stage', he commented drily, 'is more beholding to love than the life of man'), but this is merely to fail to respond to his tough reasonableness. 'Deformed persons, and eunuchs, and old men, and bastards, are envious. For he that cannot possibly mend his own case will do what he can to impair another's', or 'There is little friendship in the world, and least of all between equals' – sentences like these are designed to advance the cause of scientific realism, and keep their punch to the end to make it more thrilling. Besides, they are rescued from the tedium of misanthropy by Bacon's genial acquiescence:

There is no man doth a wrong for the wrong's sake: but thereby to purchase himself profit, or pleasure, or honour, or the like. Therefore why should I be angry with a man for loving himself better than me? And if any man should do wrong merely out of ill nature, why, yet it is but like the thorn or briar, which prick and scratch because they can do no other.

After the theologians and satirists it sounds like sanity at last. More disappointing is the stiffness of the emotional life compared with Nashe's. When Bacon strikes an attitude he gives his whole mind to it:

So certainly, if a man meditate much upon the universal frame of nature, the earth with men upon it (the divineness of souls except,) will not seem much other than an ant-hill, whereas some ants carry corn, and some carry their young, and some go empty, and all to-and-fro a little heap of dust.

Bacon is persuading the king that learning will make men more resigned, so more tractable. The weightiness is not of a kind consonant with subtlety, or even with meaning. Ants do only three things for no better reason than that Bacon has noticed triple division has a conclusive ring. Four pages later quite a different view of learning is being taken – excited, new-worldish. Again the stops are pulled out:

If the invention of the ship was thought so noble, which carrieth riches and commodities from place to place, and consociateth the most remote regions in participation of their fruits, how much more are letters to be magnified, which, as ships, pass through the vast seas of time, and make ages so distant to participate of the wisdom, illuminations and inventions the one of the other?

What wisdom, illuminations and inventions are doing at all on the anthill, we are not meant to ask. The two attitudes are isolated because Bacon has no style flexible enough to let them slip into or imply each other. Nashe had.

The compartmentalization of Bacon's sensibility is what Professor L. C. Knights fixes on. Bacon's images, Knights maintains, are forensic, intended to convince or confound. They contain no vivid feeling for both sides of the analogy such as we find in more representative Elizabethans. The point has been challenged by Dr Vickers, with no great success. His patient demonstration that classical theorists regarded the image as essentially forensic does him no service. Insofar as Bacon was affected by these theorists (and if he was not, their introduction is irrelevant), it strengthens Knights's case. More material is Dr Vicker's observation that Bacon was particularly attracted to organic images: branches, roots, soil, veins, growth, putrefaction. That these subjects did indeed fascinate Bacon we can substantiate by reference to the *New Atlantis*, where the scientists carry out experiments in, for example, controlled putrefaction, producing snakes, worms, flies and fishes. But to enjoy writing about organic processes, and to find their wholesome or unwholesome associations useful in polemic, must not be confused with having a vivid feeling for both sides of an analogy. The point is worth insisting on because Dr Vickers is under the impression that his discoveries prove Professor Knights's objections 'ill founded'. If we take what Dr Vickers considers a 'wonderfully imaginative analogy' from Bacon, 'worthy of Nashe', and compare it with Nashe, the dissimilarity will be apparent. Bacon likens the schoolmen's division of every subject into minute questions to the way in which 'substances in nature which are solid do putrify and corrupt into worms'. Nashe, we recall, compared a courtier, covered in ribbons, with 'a swarme of Butterflies'. Confronted with Bacon's analogy, we see the questions differently when we consider they are like worms, but we do not see the worms differently by associating them with questions. The analogy works one way. With Nashe, the ribbons are seen as butterflies, and the butterflies transformed, because like ribbons. There is 'a vivid feeling for both sides of an analogy'.

What little headway there is to be made against Knights depends on the perception that 'forensic' and 'imaginative' do not exhaust the possible functions of imagery. Bacon is particularly interested in the image's exhibitionist potential: the intriguing knot, which comes undone with a flick of the wrist. 'Money is like muck, not good except it be spread', or 'Constancy is like a surly porter; it drives much useful intelligence from the door.' It would be pedestrian to classify these as 'forensic': Bacon's concern is the flash, not the earth it shifts. The time-scheme can be reversed. The enigma, innocently prepared for, suddenly jumps out at us: 'A single life doth well with churchmen; for charity will hardly water the ground where it must first fill a pool.' The *Essays* are full of similar examples. As with Nashe it is agility, suppleness, that is primary here (imaginative in him, intelligential in Bacon). We are well away from 'forensic' single-mindedness.

Andrewes, Donne, Burton and Browne, the other pre-Restoration prose masters (if we leave Milton and Hobbes aside for the moment), belong in the Senecan bag with Bacon according to the popular account, and we need to examine them separately to see how tenuous the grouping is.

Lancelot Andrewes (1555–1626) and John Donne (1552–1631) were best known as preachers. Andrewes, one of the most learned and powerful of Jacobean prelates, successively bishop of Chichester, Ely and Winchester, and a Privy Councillor, was engaged by James to answer Cardinal Bellarmine (in Latin) in the controversy over the Oath of Allegiance, and later crossed swords with Cardinal Perron. Besides Anglican propaganda for the European market, and sermons, he left a book of private devotions, *Preces Privatae* (1647, translated 1648), still treasured by the devout. Donne's English prose outside the sermons is more extensive. After the

Paradoxes and Problems (not published till 1633) came *Biathanatos* (published by his son, 1646?), a casuistical defence of suicide to which Donne always had a 'sickely inclination', and *Pseudo-Martyr* (1610), condemning the kind of suicide that Catholic martyrs were prepared to commit by refusing the Oath of Allegiance to James (it was written at James's request). *Ignatius his Conclave* (in English and Latin editions, 1611) is a satire on the Jesuits, set in hell, and with some resemblance to the *Satyre Ménippée*. Loyola, who enjoys a high place, disputes with various claimants, including Copernicus who is rejected on the grounds that his theories have damaged no one's religious faith, and 'may very well be true'. The *Essays in Divinity* (1651), a book of private meditations and prayers on the creation and the exodus written between 1611 and 1615, represent Donne's self-questionings before entering holy orders. The *Devotions* (1624) are much more ostentatiously personal, though. Donne produced them during a dangerous illness the previous winter, plotting the course of the disease with minute and morbid analysis of his own reactions.

The first thing you notice about Andrewes's sermons is that they are very dull. Even his admirers admit it. For Eliot, who ranks them with the finest English prose of any time, the dullness is a positive merit. Andrewes is not entertaining, he argues, because he sticks closely to the point. Donne's sermons can be enjoyed by the irreligious, but Andrewes's cannot. Donne is vulgar, a spellbinder: Andrewes, pure, and dull. It did not seem like that to his contemporaries. Nashe was so intrigued by Lyly's extravagant praise of Andrewes's preaching that he went to hear for himself, and kept on going, held by the man's 'incomparable gifts'. Andrewes's close- cropped manner seemed to others not pure, but affectation. 'I had almost marr'd my own natural Trot by endeavouring to imitate his artificial Amble', said Bishop Felton, and Thomas Birch's *Life of Tillotson* (1753) picks on Andrewes as behind the 'great corruption' of pulpit oratory. His persistent scraps of Latin and Greek and his aping of patristic word-play seemed tasteless to Restoration ecclesiasts. 'It is not', sneered Robert South:

shreds of Latin or Greek, nor a *Deus dixit* and a *Deus benedixit*, not those little quirks or divisions into the *hoti*, the *dioti* and the *kathoti*, or the *egress*, *regress* and *progress*, and other such stuff (much like the style of a lease) that can properly be called wit.

Much of this is the normal Restoration blindness to Elizabethan and Jacobean achievement, but it reflects, too, a lighter attitude to Scripture. When Belinda in *The Provoked Wife* says 'Ah! But you know we must return good for evil' and the heroine replies 'That may be a mistake in the translation', she gets a laugh no one would have dared to get at the start of the century. To Andrewes, as to Donne, Scripture was the undoubted word of God, so every scruple of it held a fraction of God's breath. It was hardly a question of ignorant credulity. Andrewes knew more about the transmission of the Biblical books than most modern readers. Fuller says he was expert in fifteen languages (including Chaldee, Syriac and Arabic), and he supervised the translation of the historical books for the Authorized Version. When preaching he dissects his text into syllables, even letters: not so much a religious thinker as a religious philologist. He lets us watch as he presses the shy connotations into the open. Taking the words 'righteousness shall look down from heaven' (Psalm lxxxv), he fixes on the verb:

The Greeke word is to *look* (as we say) *wishly* at it, as if we would looke *dia*, even through it; the Hebrew word, (that) is, as if *Righteousnesse* did *beat out a window*: So desirous was she, to behold this *Sight*.

The process is surgical. We sense the expert knowledge gathered behind the point, lifting the film from the word's violent interior. At its most compelling, the method dramatizes whole situations. Andrewes takes John's account of how Mary Magdalen stood weeping by the sepulchre and saw the risen Christ and mistook him for a gardener, and he coaxes its most unassuming words into a richer life. 'But', the Latin *autem*, in the sentence 'But Mary stood', becomes one of the proofs of her love:

But Mary *stood* (that is as much to say, as) others did not, *But*, she did. *Peter* and *John* were there but even now. Thither they came, but not finding *Him*, away they went. They went: *But Marie* went not, she *stood still* . . . *To stay* while others doe so, while company stayes, that is the worlds love: But *Peter* is gone, and *John* too: all are gone, and we left alone; then to *stay*, is love, and constant love.

Meditation (Andrewes was said to spend five hours each day in prayer) turns inward and re-emerges dynamic, charged with understanding. Mary's words to the supposed gardener are squeezed with the same determination:

To one, a meere stranger to her, and shee to him, shee talks of one thrise under the terme of *Him. If thou hast taken Him, tel me where thou hast laid Him, and I will fetch Him; Him, Him,* and *Him,* and never names Him, or tels who He is.

Love's own dialect, Andrewes observes. Lovers always suppose everyone will know who they are talking about. And how could she fetch him: a woman carry a corpse? It is just love's unreasonableness: 'Never measures her owne forces, no burden too heavie, no assay too hard for love'. Rigorous attention to the words on the page has made Andrewes an acute dramatic critic. Explication is his natural element. Of the three divisions of the sermon – explication of the text, confirmation of its truth, and application of it to his listeners' lives – he typically engages in the first; Donne, in the third.

Textual scrutiny binds its own spells. The exhibition of getting down to brass tacks is not the same as getting down to them, and we can find Andrewes prodding hopefully at words which are already perfectly clear, and distinguishing them from alternatives which would never have occurred to anyone else. John Eachard, wittiest of the Restoration pulpit-critics, parodies the result:

I have also sometimes thought that their logical pains may be somewhat spared who, when there is no need of it, divide everything (be it what it will) into affirmative and negative: For instance; 'it is said in Job i There was a man in the land of Uz: *Homo non lapis*, a man not a stone: *Homo non lignum*, a man not a tree; *Homo non leo*, a man not a beast'.

'Relevant intensity' is Eliot's motto for Andrewes, but the intensity too often outstays the relevance. Besides, a style so addicted to antithesis can colour the theology purveyed. Typology (the correspondence between Old and New Testament figures), or the rift between the worshipper's soul and his body, or the separateness of Christ's divine and human natures, and other splittable subjects, take on a particular allure.

Antithesis, when it outlives genuine opposition, stays behind as a merely verbal event, and there is a tendency for Andrewes's other figures to impress a verbal cogency on the listener as distinct from a cogency of thought. *Anadiplosis* (the last word of one clause repeated as the first of the next), and its extended form, *climax*, will rivet the superstructure together while things remain not at all so compelling underneath. The repetition of a key word ('turn' and its derivatives 138 times in the Ash Wednesday sermon of 1619, for instance), is another way of establishing verbal intensity which is less genuinely intense than the dramatic insight in the Mary Magdalen sermon. Further, the concentration on verbal analysis looks less intelligent when it tries to cope with life outside the text. Preaching at Holyrood on the words 'he hath anointed me that I should preach the gospel to the poor', Andrewes decides to take a popular slap at the Puritans and argues that as 'anointed' implies oil those anointed to preach are learned academic divines like himself who have been obliged to use most lamp-oil sitting up late over their books. Possibly he was meaning to be funny, but even so the levity would not fit in with Eliot's picture of him 'wholly absorbed in the object'.

In distinguishing Donne from Andrewes it does not do to pretend that there are not affinities, or that these do not include similar traces of sterile verbalism. He knew less about languages, so some avenues were closed, but images from grammar and rhetorical nomenclature and enquiries into the etymology of Biblical names can easily be found in his sermons, and like Andrewes he will expatiate on the words of his text as if they made up an object not a meaning: a building or a garden or a map. His social opinions, when glimpsed, seem no more respectable than Andrewes's: worship of thrift and industry; praise for Sir William Cockayne, in his funeral sermon, on the grounds that though his parents had a great fortune it did not slacken his efforts to get more; abuse of beggars ('dogs') – 'how few of these, who make beggery an occupation from their infancy, were ever within Church, how few of them ever *Christned*, or ever *maried?*' – the voice of the Pharisee. The church receives an honour, Donne says, from the fact that 'Honourable and worshipfull Persons' of the city come and sit in St Paul's choir. The state has every right to compel a man to remain in the religion in which he has been baptized (so much for the poet of 'Satire III').

As for verbal repetition, Donne's texture is often more heavily repetitive than Andrewes's. But here a distinction occurs. Repetition in Andrewes signals insistence; in Donne, restlessness. *Anadiplosis*, clauses in chain-gang, each with its tail between the jaws of the next, is replaced by *anaphora*, clauses starting with the same words but each urgently slanting off by itself:

some remembrance of the wantonnesse of my youth, some mis-interpretation of a word in my prayer, that may beare an ill sense, some unclean spirit, some power or principality hath depraved my prayer, and slackned my zeale.

The sentences collect agitatedly, elbowing each other. Interpolations, parentheses, increase the nervousness, as Donne corrects, qualifies, snatches a look at the Bible, the Fathers. Coordination is the rule rather than subordination, so that the clauses seem about to fall apart, as in a baroque altarpiece the figures lean precariously to give an impression of movement momentarily arrested. When Donne says that God is 'a multiplied elephant, millions of elephants multiplied into one', we get the same sense of the halves of the metaphor wanting to spring away from each other. 'First and last are but ragges of time'; 'If every gnat that flies were an Archangell'; 'A Monarchy will ruine, as a haire will grow gray' – the halves are fleetingly held. Donne invents violent distortions of nature to carry his unrest. The angels, he says:

are Creatures, that have not so much of a Body as *flesh* is, as *froth* is, as a *vapor* is, as a *sigh* is, and yet with a touch they shall molder a rocke into lesse Atomes, than the sand that it stands upon; and a milstone into smaller flower, than it grinds.

The same rage for disproportion that in the poems makes a flea into a temple or eclipses the sun with a wink makes its way into the sermons disguised as a teaching-aid. Donne, for example, arrives to preach on the text 'Where your treasure is, there will your heart be also', and glances at the hour-glass fixed to the front of the pulpit as a guide to the preacher:

if I had a Secular Glass, a Glass that would run an age; if the two Hemi-spheres of the World were composed in the form of such a Glass, and all the World calcin'd and burnt to ashes and all the ashes, and sands, and atoms of the World put into that Glass, it would not be enough to tell the godly man what his Treasure, and the Object of his Heart is.

Holocaust and pulverization on a colossal scale are the essentials here, and their application to the godly man's treasure is quite arbitrary. The reader, though he will not forget them, will be hard put to it to recall what argument it was Donne fitted them into. The lack of cohesion is part of the result of a poet having to use sermons as (in Eliot's phrase) 'a means of self-expression'. No one forgets how the flea or the wink fit into the poems they belong to. In the sermons Donne's hunger for disproportion, because it cannot be made the central issue, as it can in a poem, has to hook on to any convenient twig of doctrine, and often eclipses it. Dr Webber has produced the term 'the manacled abstraction' to describe how Donne succeeds in trapping spiritual concepts within physical analogies. Our example would suggest, though, that the spiritual concept is superseded, not manacled. Effects of di-mension – the strength of angels, the length of eternity – can be suggested with these physical materials, but spiritual concepts are a more delicate matter. When Donne writes of the sinner: 'every sin casts another shovell of Brimstone upon him in Hell', we may appreciate that he is trying to express the spiritual through the physical, but the crudity of the result cannot escape us, particularly when we compare say, 'Air and Angels':

> Twice or thrice had I loved thee,
> Before I knew thy face or name;
> So in a voice, so in a shapeless flame,
> Angells affect us oft, and worship'd bee . . .

Here the analogy cherishes and transmits the spiritual apprehension; it does not supersede it. The effect is hard to match in the sermons. Instead we have Donne trying to goad himself into awe with large numbers – 'millions of millions of sins', 'legions of Angels, millions of Angels', 'a thousand millions of millions of generations' – and evolving visions of physical distortion so arresting that we have no inclination to look past them at any spiritual message they happen to be accompanying.

Not that one would have it any different, but when Donne admits that actuality really does interfere between him and spiritual experience, we respond with an intimacy which the wild physical analogies cannot arouse:

I throw my selfe downe in my Chamber, and I call in, and invite God, and his Angels thither, and when they are there, I neglect God and his Angels, for the noise of a Flie, for the ratling of a Coach, for the whining of a doore; I talke on, in the same posture of praying; Eyes lifted up; knees bowed downe; as though I prayed to God; and, if God, or his Angels should aske me, when I thought last of God in that prayer, I cannot tell: Sometimes I finde that I had forgot what I was about, but when I began to forget it, I cannot tell. A memory of yesterdays pleasures, a feare of to morrows dangers, a straw under my knee, a noise in mine eare, a light in mine eye, an any thing, a nothing, a fancy, a Chimera in my braine, troubles me in my prayer.

The passage offended Eliot. 'These are thoughts', he wrote, 'which would never have come to Andrewes. When Andrewes begins his sermon, from beginning to end you are sure that he is wholly in his subject.' But Donne's subject is his inattention. His success results from the confrontation of the bare facts of human behaviour, without the intervention of any bright simulacrum. The same realism keeps him on the watch for an opportunity to strike through his congregation's complacency with the macabre or the theatrical, whereas Andrewes's gaze is inoffensively fixed on his text, existing in the neutral space between himself and his auditors. When time is running out and the congregation is getting restless, Donne lets off paradoxes among them:

This minute that is left, is that eternitie which we speake of; upon this minute dependeth that eternity: And this minute, God is in this Congregation, and puts his eare to every one of your hearts, and hearkens what you will bid him say to your selves: whether he shall bless you for your acceptation, or curse you for your refusall of him this minute.

The tactics belong to a religious orator rather than a religious teacher. Donne's immediacy is self-defeating insofar as it concentrates attention on the sermon-experience. The performance moves and terrifies –

women fainted and men wept at his sermons – but religion may soon come to settle for an hour of emotionalism a week. A quite worldly social outlook could co-exist, as we have seen, with this brand of intensity. 'A plain convincing reason', wrote Swift, 'will edify a thousand times more than the art of wetting the hand-kerchiefs of a whole congregation.' Intimidation stands in for argument too often and too grossly in Donne for us not to acknowledge the relevance of Swift's criticism.

The next of our 'Senecan' stylists, Robert Burton (1577–1640), differs so radically from Donne that by turning to consider him we shall get an impression of the spaciousness of the category. Burton was an Oxford don, of comfortable means, who failed to get on in the church because of his refusal – it is his own explanation – to kow-tow to 'griping patrons'. He had written only some Latin verses and a Latin play when, in 1621, he brought out the *Anatomy of Melancholy* (enlarged 1624), which rocketed him to fame, but he wrote nothing else and, always a prey to melancholy, hanged himself in the end – or so it was rumoured. Criticism of the *Anatomy* has adhered to one of a few easy approaches. It has been admired as a repository, 'an amusing and instructive medley of quotations and classical anecdotes' (to quote Byron). Sterne, who stole whole pages from it, made the best use of this approach. Alternatively its 'quaintness' has been simpered over. Lamb is the classic case here. Then there are those, like the Rev T. E. Brown, who have regarded it as a 'rueful and most melancholy abuse' of scholarship, a 'labyrinthine joke' that Burton was wasting his time over in Christ Church Library when he should have been down at the river 'cheering the struggling crew'. Finally came the moderns, led by Sir William Osler in 1914, who demanded that it should be accepted as a great medical treatise, 'serious in purpose'. His successors have urged us to see Burton as a pioneer of modern psychiatry and a constructive sociologist.

The post-Ostler approach seems the only one worth attention, but it has serious drawbacks. Into whatever department we look we shall find Burton amassing opinion (about 1,250 authors are cited, 200 of them medical), but we shall find him indecisive, inconsistent or unoriginal. When he describes his Utopia the political angle is so little thought out that he does not even say whether there is to be a parliament. His judicial system reflects strong prejudices, but is backward and senseless. Debtors, for instance, are to be imprisoned for a year and, if they have not paid up by then, hanged. How prison will help them to settle debts, Burton does not say. As an economist he echoes contemporary mercantilists like Thomas Mun in recommending the expansion of manufacture and commerce, yet he condemns acquisitiveness and feels sure that the love of gold is the basis of debauchery and extravagance. He calls poverty 'the fountain of all other miseries', yet can be found preaching about it as 'a blessed estate, the way to Heaven'. He detests idleness, and imagines that it, rather than unemployment, is what creates swarms of beggars, but he detests, too, the results of industry, and is outraged when he sees 'an hirsute beggar's brat', who has been ready to run errands for 'an old jerkin', wearing 'silk and satin, bravely mounted, jovial and polite'. He will have enclosures in his Utopia, he says, but stipulates, that they will not cause depopulation. The point of enclosures, though, was that they substituted large-scale wool for open-field arable farming, so they necessarily interfered with food production and economized on labour. It remains for Burton to explain how his Utopian peasants are to eat and work. His idea of a balance of trade is that our exports of finished goods should exceed our imports, and that we should stop exporting raw materials. This simple scheme fails to take into account the reaction of overseas markets. In the early seventeenth century we were exporting large quantities of wool and unfinished cloth to the Low Countries. Eight years before Burton wrote, Cockayne had, in fact, persuaded the government to stop unfinished cloth leaving the country. The Dutch had immediately retaliated by banning the importation of all English cloth and stepping up their own industrial output. Germany also expanded her cloth industry. Thus between 1620 and 1624 our cloth export trade decreased by one third as a result of adopting the policy Burton recommends.

Burton's grasp of anatomy is not much more impressive than his politics and economics. He reproduces Galen's anatomical notions, but negligently and with several omissions. Like Galen he believes that the middle division of the heart is pierced with small holes through which blood passes from the right ventricle to the left. This account had been found not susceptible of experimental demonstration, and denied by Colombo (whose name Burton mentions) before the end of the sixteenth century. In 1628 Harvey's treatise on the circulation of the blood put an end to it. Yet in ensuing editions of the *Anatomy* Burton omits any allusion to the major anatomical discovery of his time, and retains the exploded theory. His original contribution to psychology, as to anatomy, is nil. He is incurious about the operation of the memory, though Vives had already theorized cogently in this area, and he does not seem to see the need for research into the problem of allocating mental faculties to different regions of the brain, though Bacon in the *Advancement* had singled this out as the 'most necessary' question. Burton can be found subscribing explicitly both to the theory of innate ideas, and to the opposed *tabula rasa* theory. He is quite content with the traditional answers about the interaction of mind and body, even when the traditional answers conflict, so alternates between the thesis which separates thought from organic life and the thesis which maintains the dependence of intellectual faculties on the balance of the humours.

If we turn from these subjects to religion we find ourselves forced to conclude that Burton is not only not a scientist but also not a thinker. His head-wagging about mankind's lack of charity and tolerance combines with prejudices against Catholicism and nonconformity so extreme as to be derisory even by seventeenth- century standards. 'The worst Christians of Italy are the Romans, of the Romans the Priests are wildest, the lewdest Priests are preferred to be Cardinals, and the baddest man among the Cardinals is chosen to be Pope.' The story about the 6,000 skeletons of new- born infants found near a convent represents the level of Burton's investigation into the religious life. The puritans, meanwhile, are nothing but 'a company of rude, illiterate, capricious base fellows', while the Church of England divines are 'a base, profane, Epicurean, hypocritical rout'. His allegiance to the Anglican Church seems quite unrelated to its actual condition, since he is as emphatic as its opponents that it is rife with 'imposture and knavery'. As with Swift, we sense a virulence against all kinds of religious conviction with nothing richer than a lip-service conformity behind it. This part of the *Anatomy* answers perfectly to Keats's description, 'snarl and countersnarl', and a corresponding negativeness permeates, as we have seen, more theoretic sections, where Burton either refuses to reach a conclusion or contradicts himself.

The dismissal of Burton as thinker plainly cannot be accompanied by his dismissal as writer, and it remains to ask where exactly, if not in the thought, the value of the *Anatomy* resides. Once formulated like this, the question is not difficult. The book is valuable as self-expression. Burton manages to radiate his own awkward personality out of a conglomeration of second-hand matter which one would have thought it impossible to unify. Indecision, prejudice, contradiction, now become crucial to the effect. We have forced upon us an impression of aggressive irresponsibility. Repeatedly we come to realize that Burton has collapsed the whole fabric of his argument and is sneering at us from behind the lines, but just at what point he lost confidence in it we are unable to decide. Lecturing on a man's duty to comfort his friend, he proposes driving out one grief with another: 'to pull out a tooth, or wound him, to geld him'. Or, at the end of a list of moral maxims he advises us to hunt for more in 'Isocrates, Seneca, Plutarch, Epictetus, &c., and for defect, consult with cheese trenchers and painted cloths'. We hear the chair on which Burton has invited us to sit being lifted away as we descend. In the same spirit, after filling pages with dietary advice, he switches to jeering at people who are prepared to take advice about their diet. More often we are nastily uncertain whether the chair is still there or not – as when Burton touches upon trepanning: ''tis not amiss to bore the skull with an instrument, to let out the fuliginous vapours'. Can he, in the circumstances, mean to sound so casual? In the same way the onslaught on Catholicism keeps making us wonder whether it has started to be comic. The reverence for scholarship that seemed to be basic to the enterprise vanishes when Burton turns on scholars. They know everything it is not useful to know, but are 'circumvented by every base tradesman'. He himself has 'read many books, but to little purpose', and is thinking of abandoning the academic life to become a miller, or sell ale. This scouting of pedestrian standards is echoed in the disorder and repetitions in the chapters on the symptoms of melancholy, as compared with the pretentious synoptic table at the start, and in the frequently inaccurate quotations – dredged up out of a huge memory, not painfully recorded.

What keeps Burton at his books is not the pursuit of truth but the fascination of excess. Immoderate pleasures, superfluous industry, spectacular perversions: 'Valerius makes mention of one that in a famine sold a mouse for two hundred pence', 'Caligula gave 100,000 sesterces to his courtesan at first word, to buy her pins':

Cornelius Gemma . . . related of a young maid, called Katherine Gualter, a cooper's daughter, *anno* 1571, that had such strange passions and convulsions, three men could not sometimes hold her; she purged a live eel, which he saw, a foot and a half long, and touched himself; but the eel afterwards vanished; she vomited some twenty-four pounds of fulsome stuff of all colours, twice a day for fourteen days; and after that she voided great balls of hair, pieces of wood, pigeon's dung, parchment, goose dung, coals; and after them two pounds of pure blood, and then again coals and stones, of which some had inscriptions, bigger than a walnut, some of them pieces of glass, brass etc. besides paroxysms of laughing, weeping and ecstasies etc. . . . . They could do no good on her by physic, but left her to the clergy.

Burton's style falls in with this apotheosis of excess by its hectic accumulation of lists and catalogues, and by its defter movements too, as when he is working himself into a state over the extravagance of women's clothes: 'an hundred yards I think in a gown, a sleeve' – the outrageous jump from gown to sleeve multiplying his thrill at the wastefulness of it all. The colossal vocabulary works in the same direction, ransacking scientific and technical terminologies as well as slang and inkhornism and the new word-hoards of Elizabethan and Jacobean literature. In theory excess is at the root of the melancholy disease, and Burton vociferates against it, but his own addiction is obvious. He alternately wallows in whatever pungent matter he can rake together, and lifts up his hands in pious exclaim. The two activites correspond to the voracious torrent of his prose and the skeleton of members, sections and subsections that pretends to regiment it. Even in drier, scientific stretches the impatient tug of his personality can be felt:

The gall, placed in the concave of the liver, extracts choler to it: the spleen, melancholy; which is situate on the left side, over against the liver, a spongy matter, that draws this black choler to it by a secret virtue, and feeds upon it, conveying the rest to the bottom of the stomach, to stir up appetite, or else to the guts as an excrement.

Rapid, graphic, lithe, careless of rhythm ('large tracts of the *Anatomy* can hardly be said to have any continuous rhythm at all', complained Saintsbury), the style gets its business done and keeps the familiarity of oral exposition at the same time. 'I had not time to lick it into form', Burton explained, 'and writ with as small deliberation as I do ordinarily speak.' The luggage of quotation does not, incidentally, conflict with this claim, since Anthony Wood records that 'no man in his time' could compete with Burton for 'dexterous interlarding' of his 'common discourses' with excerpts from classical authors.

But the compulsive collection of vivid material from the past distinguishes Burton clearly from the advancing thinkers of the century. Descartes, by contrast, starts the *Discourse on Method* with a modest and conclusive rejection of the whole of Renaissance culture. Burton's passion is not for truth but for knowledge at once sensational and codifiable. The abstract, the unimaginable, repel him. In spite of his excitement over excess he finds both current theories of the universe unacceptable: the Ptolemaic, because the sun would have to travel in 24 hours a distance it would take a horseman 2,904 years to cover; the Copernican, because the stars would have to be so far away that an observer on one of them would see the earth's orbit as no more than a point. These concepts defeat Burton's imagination, so he calls them 'opposite to reason', without proffering any alternative. The limitation this example suggests is matched by a limitation within Burton's personality. There is one set of experiences, the sexual, he cannot throw himself open to. His social and his sexual frustration interact since, as a don, he was not allowed to marry, and the sedentary life answered a need of his nature, as did the wish to escape from it. The aggressive academic, bewildering his audience with obscure tomes and scornful laughter, also, and for similar reasons, tells endless puerile stories about the filthiness of women, culled from medical treatises, the church fathers, and other likely sources. Picked out of the Latin in which they are often coyly left, they shed no very enticing light on Burton's sensibility. As a cure for love, he recommends catching the girl in various unbecoming postures:

as Brassavola the physician found Malatesta, his patient, after a potion of hellebore which he had prescribed, on all fours, hands on the floor, anus pointing skywards, squirting black bile against the white wall, making all the room and herself filthy.

We are expected, like Swift's feeble young man, to be shattered by the discovery that women excrete. Douglas Bush's complacencies about Burton's 'sanity of mind and largeness of heart, his love of life and of human beings', fall queerly into such contexts. Tell a bereaved husband, Burton recommends, quoting Seneca:

if such a woman at least ever was to be had, 'he did either so find or make her; if he found her, he may as happily find another'; if he made her . . . he may as good cheap inform another.

We may allow that this glib substitute for feeling is what Burton needs for hitting back at the world with, but that does not lessen the poverty of it. Comparisons with Rabelais, prompted by the style and the dirt, founder here. They also quickly expose the narrowness of Burton's abilities.

Sanity of mind and largeness of heart are more readily conceded to Sir Thomas Browne after reading his prose (even if he did believe in witches and give evidence which helped to hang two). Browne (1605–82) was a quiet Norwich doctor, and rather more than a dabbler in science. He never became a member of the Royal Society, but achieved European fame early with *Religio Medici*

(1643; written 1634–5; there were two pirated editions in 1642), a piece of ruminative self-exposure quickly attacked by heresy-hunters (notably Sir Kenelm Digby and Alexander Ross). *Pseudodoxia Epidemica* followed in 1646, a response to the Baconian plea for 'a Kalender of popular Errors' in natural history, and in 1658 *Hydriotaphia: Urn-Burial* and *The Garden of Cyrus*, Christian – Platonic meditations on mortality and what transcends it, the one sparked off by the discovery of some burial urns (Saxon, not Roman as Browne supposed) in a field at Old Walsingham in Norfolk, the other by the conviction that the number five can be discovered in the make-up of all created things. There were two posthumous works, *A Letter to a Friend* (1690) on the death of a patient (arguably written in 1656 about Robert Loveday's death), and *Christian Morals* (1716), which rewrites some of the moral advice from the *Letter*, and amounts to an older, less paradoxical *Religio Medici*. Browne's nonchalant, rhythmic talk in the *Religio* is quite distinct from Burtonian bustle:

For my Religion, though there be severall circumstances that might perswade the world I have none at all, as the generall scandall of my profession, the naturall course of my studies, the indifferency of my behaviour, and discourse in matters of Religion, neither violently defending one, nor with that common ardour and contention opposing another; yet in despight hereof I dare, without usurpation, assume the honorable stile of a Christian.

As Browne punctuates it the sentence does not end there, but saunters on for another fourteen lines. We are made aware of a mind sliding easily into concessions, qualifications, digressions; stacking thought against thought more or less as they occur (manuscript evidence of careful revision and expansion warns us against assuming that the effect was spontaneous). The preliminary announcement of the topic ('For my Religion'), like a chapter heading, is a common feature of Browne's sentences. Often it is an indirect question: 'What Song the Syrens sang, or what name Achilles assumed when he hid himself among women . . .'. This famous passage ends up, characteristically, in head-scratching: 'what bodies these ashes made up, were a question above Antiquarism'. In this way Browne is able to fit the acquired sentence-structure to his personality by making it eagerly enquiring at the start and eventually sceptical: 'That Miracles are ceased, I can neither prove, nor absolutely deny.'

The relaxed style intimately conveys Browne's tolerant cast of mind (the contrast with Burton's mind and style is instructive). 'I could never divide my selfe from any man upon the difference of an opinion.' He muses, with satisfaction, upon the distance between his own reasonableness and the prejudices he observes in other people: 'I could digest a Sallad gathered in a Church-yard, as well as in a Garden.' He is perfectly happy to eat frogs and snails and toadstools. At the sight of snakes or scorpions, 'I finde in me no desire to take up a stone to destroy them'.

Browne's open-mindedness is a part of his Platonic and deeply unscientific scepticism, which he combines unexpectedly with earnest biological research. 'No man can justly censure or condemne another, because indeed no man truely knowes another.' True knowledge is the prerogative of God alone. The experimental scientist contacts only shadows and appearances. Even when a physical object is destroyed, its essential being ('form') remains: the object has merely withdrawn into its 'indestructible part'. This feeling for the independence of the visible and invisible worlds lies near the root of the well-known 'contradictions' in Browne's character: the physician who had studied at the most advanced medical schools in Europe, but noted down magical amulets in his commonplace book. His estimate of reason is itself equivocal. The Church of England he finds 'consonant unto reason'; 'I borrow not the rules of my Religion from Rome or Geneva, but the dictates of my owne reason' – but mysteries like the Trinity and the Resurrection lure him precisely because they leave his reason floundering: 'I love to lose myselfe in a mystery, to pursue my reason to an *oh altitudo*'. Nor is reason regarded as constraining the mind to certain conclusions, but as letting it skate attractively among the systems: 'the libertie of an honest reason may play and expatiate with security'.

Structural principles in Browne's prose can be seen, with a little ingenuity, to spread out from his interest in generation and embryology. When he was at Padua, Fabricius, the effective founder of modern embryology, was still professor (later Browne recommended his books to his son), and it has been deduced from *Pseudodoxia* and Browne's commonplace book that it was in his house at Norwich that the first experiments in chemical embryology were undertaken. The enthusiasm shapes the prose in different ways. Professor Huntley discovers sentences which he calls 'metabolic' because they go from a low point in subject-matter, diction or rhythm to a high (imitating generation), or the opposite (decay). The choice of metaphor is plainly affected also – the Baconian advice in *Christian Morals*, for instance: 'Joyn Sense unto Reason, and Experiment unto speculation, and so give life unto

Embryon Truths'. The development of the embryo involved, for Browne, a passage from spirit to matter. At the heart of the seed lay not matter but a 'plastic principle'. As usual the theory is clothed in sensuous credentials: it may, he says, be:

attested by observation in the maturative progresse of Seeds, wherein at first may be discerned a flatuous distension of the husk, afterwards a thin liquor, which longer time digesteth into a pulp or kernell observable in Almonds and large Nuts.

Even when Brown is occupied with a subject quite remote from embryology, his prose can be caught dropping into this graduated concretion. Christ's resurrection becomes:

that rising power, able to break the fasciations and bands of death, to get clear out of the Cerecloth, and an hundred pounds of Oyntment, and out of the Sepulchre before the stone was rolled from it.

Cloth to ointment to stone: the professional interest reshapes an alien context. Browne's concern with the microcosm, the hugely inclusive miniature, clearly relates, too, to his embryology. His language fuses the two: 'the truest Microcosme' is 'the wombe of our mother', and the womb-shaped burial urns resemble the 'inward vault of our Microcosme'. The biology of minute creatures owes its appeal to the branching dimensions that lie folded within: 'in these narrow Engines there is more curious Mathematicks'. The same mind is intrigued to consider 'how many thousand severall words have beene carelessly and without study composed out of 24 Letters', and the exciting expandability transfers to morals: 'Pride, a vice whose name is comprehended in a Monosyllable, but in its nature not circumscribed with a world', and to evolution: 'the magicke of that sperme that hath dilated into so many millions'. Mystical numbers, hieroglyphs, and magically meaningful signs satisfy the same urge for seeing the world in a grain of sand, and Browne is permanently attached to them. He believed, like many contemporaries, that all the objects of the natural scientist's investigation were expandable hieroglyphs, on the other side of which sat God. God even seemed to have given up hieroglyphs at times and written Hebrew, Arabic and Greek characters in plants, producing words which must be vastly meaningful but looked frustratingly like nonsense. 'In a common [plant] among us we seem to read *Aiaia, Viviu, Lilil.*' He got a worried letter from a fellow scientist, Dr Henry Power, asking which plant it was. The hieroglyph-mentality stops Browne being a scientist because it makes him rummage under the surface of nature for what he expects to find:

Something we expected in the more discernible texture of the lungs of frogs, which notwithstanding being but two curious bladders not weighing above a grain, we found interwoven with veins, not observing any just order.

The care with which the tiny lungs are handled is suddenly squashed by the last phrase. 'Something' means a hieroglyph, a quincunx, and, not finding it, Browne discounts the organism's real pattern.

Complementary is the appeal of the contracted essence which contains all the past as the embryo contains all the future. Man will truly be a microcosm, Browne argues, when the last fire has devoured the world, because God will then contemplate creation 'in its epitome or contracted essence'. Hence Browne's obsession with ashes. Further, once you accept the resurrection of the body, ashes are both quintessence and embryo: they will flower again. The thing, Browne held, could be demonstrated in the laboratory:

This is made good by experience, which can from the ashes of a plant revive the plant, and from its cinders recall it into its stalk and leaves againe.

He was thinking of Quercetanus's experiment, where you put a solution of plant-ashes out in the frost and got what looked like leaves forming on the sides of the vessel. The fallacy is immaterial. What matters is that, for Browne, ash became sperm: cremation and conception united. The body, though he knows expertly its 'tender filaments', gets to be thought of as a 'mass', a clumsy accretion: 'that mass of flesh that circumscribes me'. From this nexus images of encumbrance or of embryonic survival within an environment of corruption permeate the prose.

These determine Browne's thought even in regions where they are quite inapplicable; notably, in ethics. The style images vice as physical involvement: a 'web' of sin from which we need to disentangle ourselves. Virtue, as a sort of seed surrounded by decay. The dubious commonplace about great virtues going with great vices gains a quite spurious weight from the application of this type of scientific analogy. 'Venemous dispositions', Browne affirms, contain 'certaine pieces that remaine untoucht', and these 'by an Antiperistasis become more excellent', just as 'the greatest Balsames doe lie enveloped in the Bodies of most powerful Corrosives'. This has all the force of Browne's imaginative habits behind it. The intimacy and unreliability of the statement are inextricable. The insidious power of 'scientific' method is constantly floating unseaworthy ideas in Browne's morality. He relates that he used to believe certain heresies, and refrained from discussing them with his friends, 'but suffering them to flame upon their owne substance, without addition of new fuell, they went out insensibly of themselves'. The implication that discussion is not a good way of correcting one's opinions comes out looking as incontrovertible as a law of combustion. The discovery of the microscope can also be seen affecting Browne's moral perspective. He talks, in the *Garden of Cyrus*, about observing 'the shop of a Bees mouth' through 'augmenting glasses', and the bee-and-microscope experience is evidently still inhabiting his thought when he writes in *Christian Morals*:

Look upon Vices and vicious Objects with Hyperbolical Eyes, and rather enlarge their dimensions, that their unseen Deformities may not escape thy sense, and their Poysonous parts and stings may appear massy and monstrous unto thee; for the undiscerned Particles and Atoms of Evil deceive us, and we are undone by the Invisibles of seeming Goodness.

That you can see a bee more accurately when enlarged, and a vice when exaggerated, are propositions that could slip by together only in a style where scientific analogy has begun to obscure thought. We think uncomfortably of the hanged witches.

An object of more general uneasiness is Browne's weakness for pretentious polysyllables. It is true that words which look as if they are Browne's often turn out to have been earning a decent living in the language for some time: 'antiperistasis', for instance, comes in Sylvester's Du Bartas, and 'amphibology' in Chaucer. Also it does not do to take too high a line with a writer who has contributed to the language words like electricity, hallucination, insecurity, precarious, medical and literary. But when Browne sets to to describe a pair of nutcrackers we may wonder whether language is being used as medium or obstacle:

the old Nucifragium or Nutcracker . . . consisting of two Vectes or armes, converted towards each other, the innitency and stresse being made upon the hypomochlion or fulciment in the decussation, the greater compression is made by the union of two impulsors.

Six words here had been in the language for ten years or less, of which two (vectis and fulciment) had been introduced by Wilkins, first secretary of the Royal Society, in a work on mechanical geometry. No doubt Browne felt he was being scientific, but the long words persist in quite unscientific contexts. Camps, for instance, become 'castrensial mansions', and the word 'burying' is bypassed by 'carnal interment', 'depositure', 'inhumation', 'sepulture', 'subterraneous deposition' and so on. The explanation usually advanced, rhythm, has the disadvantage of equating rhythm with mindless sonority. It seems more illuminating to view the polysyllables alongside Browne's other imaginative habits, his pleasure in hieroglyph and mystery, in the 'involved aenigmas and riddles' of the Trinity, Incarnation and Resurrection, in the 'cryptick and involved method' of God's providence. Relevant, too, is his attachment to the ceremonious, the vestment, the icon: 'I should violate my owne arme rather than a Church window.' The glinting syllabic clumps are verbal ceremonies, and when, as often, they are partnered by homely synonyms, Browne seems to be expressing through his vocabulary that contrast between the simple embryo and the massy carapace that overshadows it which is at the centre of his poetic vision and which appears more obviously in passages like that on the Norfolk urns:

these dead bones have already out-lasted the living ones of Methuselah, and in a yard under ground, and thin walls of clay, out-worn all the strong and specious buildings above it; and quietly rested under the drums and tramplings of three conquests.

We are likely to be more appreciative of the richness of Browne's vocabulary (and personality) when we compare him with Izaak Walton (1593–1683). Walton never went to grammar school or university so, on the analogy of Bunyan, we might expect a great deal. His father kept a pub in Stafford, and he was apprenticed to a London sempster and became a successful draper himself with literary friends including Drayton and Jonson and, casually, Donne. It is clear that he found writing difficult. Corrections and insertions clutter the one surviving manuscript. He revised his *Lives* assiduously in each new edition to proclaim with greater emphasis the dignity of his subject and his own modesty, and to plump his limp prose in the hope of making it elegant (for example, 'as dead bodies are usually fitted for the grave' in the 1658 *Life of Donne* becomes 'as dead bodies are usually fitted to be shrowded and put into the grave' in 1670 and 'as dead bodies are usually fitted to be shrowded and put into their Coffin, or grave' in 1675). The impression of incompetence, which academic critics have regularly found charming, is heightened by the dense population of basic conjunctions and by Walton's repeated assurances that everything is under control: 'I proceed to tell my reader', 'I must now again look back', and so on. The naïvety is false, however, and Wordsworth's 'Sage benign' has turned out, on inspection, to be an unscrupulous High Church propagandist, suppressing and distorting evidence at every turn in order to preserve his narrow, prejudiced view of the subject of his biography.

The *Life of Donne* (1640, revised 1658, 1670 and 1675) was written as an introduction to the sermons and this, coupled with Walton's usual determination to dignify the episcopal church, results in the eclipse of Donne the wit, poet, controversialist and theologian in favour of Donne the pietist. *Biathanatos* is glossed over; *Ignatius*, ignored. Intimate friends – the Countess of Bedford, Magdalen Herbert – disappear. So do Donne's bachelor-years with the Egertons, poetically crucial, and open to Walton because his informants included Henry King whose father was the Egerton chaplain. A holy deathbed, indispensable for Walton, is patched up from one of Donne's sermons. In revision some Donne letters are introduced, cleansed of mundane detail and reworded in the interests of piety; also, sneers at common people 'busie about what they understand not, and especially about Religion'. Sir Henry Wotton was a subject even more resistant to the saintlike mould. In his *Life* (1651, revised 1654, 1670, 1672, 1675) Walton concentrated on the final phase, the good Provost of Eton reading his bible and disliking controversy, and cleverly evaded any account of Wotton's religio-diplomatic manoeuvring during his Venetian ambassadorship, and of worldly ambitions after he had taken orders. The *Life of Hooker* (1665, revised 1666, 1670, 1675) was a political job commissioned by Archbishop Sheldon and rewarded with a house in Paternoster Row. In 1662 Bishop Gauden had unwisely published the last three books of the *Ecclesiastical Polity*, which can be quoted both for and against absolutism and the bishops' apostolic succession. It was expedient for the High Church party to discredit such two-edged opinions. Walton elaborates the story of shrewish Mrs Hooker and her connivance in the destruction of Hooker's papers after his death. The lies were fed to him by the Cranmer family, and no doubt he believed them, though he would certainly have discounted them if they had failed to suit his prejudices. The *Life* also includes an onslaught on nonconformity and an idealized portrait of Whitgift (with a quite fictitious scene in which Whitgift warns Elizabeth against appropriating church property), and these elements are apparently meant to blur into the picture of Hooker himself. The *Life of Herbert* (1670, revised 1675) has an ulterior motive too. Treating the poems and the *Country Parson* as autobiography, and adding oral material from Arthur Woodnoth, Nicholas Ferrar's cousin, who had known Herbert in the last seven years, Walton reconstructs a shining example for the Restoration clergy of a man who did not think great family and talent made him too good for the ministry. Humble Herbert obscures Herbert *agonistes*, and inconvenient details remembered by Ferrar and Barnabas Oley (Herbert's saying he would not part with one leaf of Scripture for the whole world, for example, which sounds contentious and Puritanical), are prudently expunged. Walton's last *Life*, of Sanderson (1678, revised 1681), continues the propaganda aims of the *Hooker*, and was probably written to please Walton's friend Bishop Morley. Sanderson's last three years, after he had been made a bishop, and his long-suffering mildness during the interregnum occupy the centre of the stage. Walton does not scruple to record that Sanderson was 'several times plundered, and once wounded in three places' in the face of Sanderson's own testimony that he never saw 'so much as a pistol discharged, or a sword drawn'. While blackening the 'Scruple-mongers' Walton has so little understanding himself of the doctrinal issues at stake that he prints Sanderson's *Pax Ecclesiae* (1625) without realizing that its modified Calvinism will be anything but welcome to the contemporary church, or that it does not represent Sanderson's final opinion.

Professor Novarr, who has written more exhaustingly than anyone else about this process of suppression and distortion, adduces it as evidence of Walton's 'art'. But there is something deeply trivial about a theory of art which sets so little store by accuracy and honesty, and, as biography, it is inconceivable that Walton's simplified picture of Donne, say, should be more interesting than Donne himself. The imposition of a uniform style and tone on the five distinct lives constitutes the root distortion. Walton, much given to advertising his own humility, cringes affectionately before the representatives of power and place – 'the learned and charitable bishop of Durham', 'the very prudent and very wise Lord Elsmere' – and takes it as a mark of 'great humility and condescension' that Sanderson should talk with him for an hour while sheltering from the rain. When Sanderson outlines his scheme for fifty-two government-approved sermons to be read every Sunday, year in year out, Walton goes into obedient rapture over this recipe for intellectual stagnation. He classes opposition to government with spiritual wickedness, found only among the 'very dregs and pest of mankind', and his portraiture is a matter of twisting the five men he celebrates into his own servile postures. Two of them are among the century's major poets: Wotton was a minor poet and an enthusiastic collector of paintings. Walton's response to their aesthetic and intellectual life is of the crudest. Herbert's music gets mentioned as a 'diversion', but the exact information – which composers, what kind of music, even what instrument – is missing. Wotton when in Italy:

Became acquainted with the most eminent men for Learning, and all manner of Arts; as Picture, Sculpture, Chymistry, Architecture, and other manual Arts, even Arts of Inferior nature; of all which, he was a most dear Lover, and a most excellent Judge.

The hollow assertiveness is put up by a mind not stirred enough by what is passing through it even to attempt discrimination.

Walton's personality is working to narrow ends in the *Lives* and a constrasting fullness is soon felt in the *Complete Angler* (1653, enlarged 1655). It is not the ersatz Arcadianism, so warming to the hearts of nineteenth-century readers, that warrants the book, but the sensuous practicality of its instructions for catching and cooking fish, often brutal (live frogs being sewn on to hooks), and once or twice lifted word for word from the anonymous *Art of Angling* of 1577. Take the recipe for roast pike:

First, open your Pike at the gills, and if need be, cut also a little slit towards the belly. Out of these, take his guts; and keep his liver, which you are to shred very small, with thyme, sweet marjoram, and a little winter-savoury; to these, you must add also a pound of sweet butter, which you are to mix with the herbs that are shred, and let them all be well salted. If the Pike be more than a yard long, then you may put into these herbs more than a pound, or if he be less, then less butter will suffice: These, being mixt, with a blade or two of mace, must be put into the Pike's belly; and then his belly so sewed up as to keep all the butter in his belly if it be possible; if not, then as much of it as you possibly can. But take not off the scales. Then you are to thrust the spit through his mouth, out at his tail. And then take four or five or six split sticks, or very thin laths, and a convenient quantity of tape or filleting; these laths are to be tied round about the Pike's body, from his head to his tail, and the tape tied somewhat thick, to prevent his breaking or falling off from the spit. Let him be roasted very leisurely; and often basted with claret wine, and anchovies, and butter, mixt together; and also with what moisture falls from him into the pan.

The genial intimacy, caressing the fish with personal pronouns, and the robust laboriousness of directive, make the prose of the *Lives* look sallow by comparison. And there could be nothing more damaging to put beside Browne's nutcrackers than Walton's pike.

Walton's prejudices are certainly no more warping than those of John Milton (1608–74), but even if we give up the pretence that Milton's prose would be read if he were not also the poet, we cannot miss the greater virility and animation in which his imagination cloaks his most sterile bigotry. Walton's venerable bishops:

after a shamefull end in this Life (which God grant them) shall be throwne downe eternally into the darkest and deepest Gulfe of Hell, where under the despightfull controule, the trample and spurne of all the other Damned, that in the anguish of their Torture shall have no other ease than to exercise a Raving and Bestiall Tyranny over them as their Slaves and Negroes, they shall remaine in that plight for ever, the basest, the lower-most, the most dejected, most underfoot and downe-trodden Vassals of Perdition.

This is from *Of Reformation* (1641), Milton's first protest against the authority of bishops like those he had unctuously commemorated in his undergraduate poems. *The Reason of Church-Government* and *An Apology for Smectymnuus* were contributed to the campaign the next year. He inflates his enemies into grotesques who lurch or swagger around their ringmaster: a prelate with his 'many-benefice-gaping mouth . . . his canary sucking, and swan-eating palat'; ecclesiastical dignitaries 'under Sayl in all their Lawn, and Sarcenet, their shrouds, and tackle' exhibiting themselves in 'a Surplice Brabble, a Tippet-scuffle', emitting a 'loud stench' from feet and mouths; Bishop Hall, covered with a skin eruption, and straining to void his bowels, invited to 'Wipe his fat corpulencies out of our light'. 'Belching the soure crudities of yesterdayes Poperie', caked with 'vitious and harden'd excrements' these sensuous creatures, like Sin in *Paradise Lost*, rise from the dark levels of Milton's consciousness and parade their rich deformity.

The demands for the abolition of bishops constituted, according to Milton's own classification of his prose, his effort for religious liberty. The divorce pamphlets (1643–5) and *Areopagitica* (1644) dealt with domestic liberty, while *The Tenure of Kings and Magistrates* (1649), vindicating Charles I's execution, and the republican *Ready and Easy Way to Establish a Free Commonwealth* (1660), covered civil liberty. Divorce suddenly became important to Milton when his wife deserted him, though he had been jotting down opinions on the subject for some years. His argument that mental incompatibility, not just adultery, should be accepted as grounds for separation, and his vilification of those who take cognizance only of what happens in bed, co-exists with outspoken physical repulsion which presumably reflects his recent experiences with a frightened and unresponsive bride. He talks of being bound fast 'to an image of earth and phlegm' and condemned to 'grind in the mill of an undelighted and servile copulation'. Satisfying a woman and toiling in a mill are still linked in his mind when he comes to write *Samson Agonistes*, lines 415–16.

Areopagitica was written because Milton had been refused a

POETRY AND PROSE 1540-1674

licence for his first divorce tract, and in its grandest moments the personal strain can still be heard. 'Give me the liberty to know, to utter, and to argue freely according to conscience, above all liberties.' Stress the 'me', and the grandeur fades; yet the stress does not misrepresent the pamphlet's interests. It is quite content that other authors should be suppressed. 'No law', it takes it for granted, 'can possibly permit' anything 'impious or evil absolutely either against faith or maners', and all Roman Catholic writing is included under this embargo. 'Sharpest justice', 'the fire and the executioner', is called down on 'scandalous, seditious and libellous Books'. 'They who most loudly clamour for liberty', Johnson oberves, 'do not most liberally grant it.'

In his disagreement with the bishops Milton felt that the Bible was plainly on his side. He accuses them of 'ridiculous wresting of Scripture', and rejects their emphasis on its obscurity as 'a mere suggestion of the Devil to disswade men from reading it'. But his views on divorce brought him sharply up against the usual interpretation of Christ's words in Matthew xix, and it is now his turn to plead that 'there is scarce any one saying in the Gospel but must be read with limitations and distinctions to be rightly understood'. Christ's words are 'as obscure as any clause fetcht out of Genesis'. From the time of the divorce tracts on, the term 'nature' plays an increasing part in his arguments. It is 'against nature' to make incompatible people cohabit; so if the Bible does not say they may separate, it must be forced to. He appeals against all laws to 'the blameless nature of man', 'the guiltles instinct of nature'. If another writer used these phrases we might suppose he had a high opinion of human nature. With Milton we know the contrary is true. He can be found gloomily seconding Genesis viii. 21 on the inevitable wickedness of the human heart and, in the same pamphlet, rhapsodizing about 'the faultless proprieties of nature' which no law, Biblical or otherwise, can be permitted to impair. 'Nature' becomes for Milton a personal convenience: a respectable front for what his instincts dictate. More and more it takes over as the sole criterion: 'I suppose no man of cleare judgement need goe furder to be guided than by the very principles of nature in him' (this from his argument that it is 'natural' to exterminate Charles I). In *Tetrachordon* (1645) he takes it as axiomatic that 'no ordinance human or from heav'n can binde against the good of man'. It is the voice of Eve just before she picks the apple.

We may value Milton's pamphlets for their vituperation, which clearly recalls Nashe, and taps veins of the language too seldom accessible to his poetry. But his positive proposals also command assent, irrespective of the prejudice and egotism that enfold them: that men who are supposed to represent Christ should imitate him in unworldliness; that they should not be in alliance with any state or government, since he was not; that couples who hate each other should not live together, and should be free to remarry; that people have a right to rise against a tyrannical regime; that it is foolish to allocate power according to the chance of birth. Equally refreshing is the vehemence with which he urges their implementation – his rejoinders to the familiar complacencies about not setting the world right in a day: 'We must not run they say into sudden extreams. This is a fallacious Rule'; 'They say ... the government of Episcopacy is now ... weav'd into the common Law. In God's name let it weave out again.'

The long, articulated periods and the foliage of metaphor made Milton's prose, like Browne's, suspect by mid-century standards (Ross was quick to sneer at Browne's 'Tropicall pigments'). The strong feeling that something should be done to simplify prose style can be variously assigned to Puritanism, science and fear. While memories of the civil war were still fresh, certainty acquired a special value, and the feeling lingered that it would somehow not have happened if only issues had been coolly clarified. When Thomas Sprat wrote his *History of the Royal Society* in 1667 he suggested that eloquence 'ought to be banish'd out of all civil Societies, as a thing fatal to Peace'. He felt particularly upset about figurative writing, which clouds knowledge with 'mists and uncertainties'. The Society's plans for prose included a rejection of 'all amplifications, digressions and swellings' and a return to a verbal Eden of 'primitive purity, and shortness, when men deliver'd so many things, almost in an equal number of words'. In this Eden 'Mathematical plainness' would in some way be combined with 'the language of Artisans, Countrymen, and Merchants'. The movement had its wholesome aspect. The plush preaching of Jeremy Taylor (1613–67), sharply taken up by South in a Christ Church sermon of 1668, rapidly went out of fashion. On the debit side we have the misunderstandings enshrined in John Wilkins's *Essay towards a Real Character and a Philosophical Language*, published by order of the Society in 1667. Wilkins (1614–72), Warden of Wadham, virtual founder of the Royal Society, and brother-in-law of Cromwell, was a man of vision, who wrote with equal confidence about moon-travel, submarines, flying-machines, and arrangements of cog-wheels that would allow you to haul oak-trees out of the ground simply by blowing. Communications particularly occupied him. In his *Secret and Swift Messenger* (1641), a handbook of cryptography, invisible inks, smoke signals and other useful ruses, he intimates that the quickest way to get your messages carried is to cultivate 'Familiarity' with an angel – 'it is not so easie', he admits, 'to employ a good Angel, nor safe dealing with a bad one'. His *Essay* represents a prodigious labour, consisting essentially of forty numbered and sub-divided lists which comprise 'all such things and notions to which names are to be assigned'. A dictionary is appended by way of index. Forty basic squiggles are invented which can be adjusted to signify any item on their respective lists. These are to replace words, and Wilkins allocates phonetic values to them and constructs a grammar. The result is beautifully methodical, and quite dead. The theory of language behind it supposes that if there are fewer words available they will be used more precisely. Whole cartloads of 'synonyms' are jettisoned during the evolution of the lists, and Wilkins is at pains to stifle the adaptability of common verbs like 'break, bring, cast, clear' which have at present 'thirty or forty' different meanings. He hopes to arrest linguistic growth, and eject idiom ('phrases . . . which, if they were to be translated *verbatim* into another Tongue, would seem wild and insignificant'). His language, besides being international, will, he trusts, 'contribute much to the clearing of some of our Modern differences in Religion, by unmasking many wild errors, that shelter themselves under the disguise of affected phrases'.

It may seem obvious to us that by making the medium of communication less rich and intricate Wilkins was decreasing not improving the chances of precision. Removing names from the ballot paper ensures frustration, not consensus. But one way of feeling more sympathy with his aims, and of bringing this chapter of prose-history to an end, is to give some attention to the style of Thomas Hobbes (1588–1679) and glance forward, by way of comparison, at that of John Dryden (1631–1700).

Hobbes, of course, was not a member of the Society. Making little secret of the fact that what most people meant by religion was as intellectually respectable as belief in fairies, he was an embarrassment to an association of Christian gentlemen. Luckily his grasp of mathematics and physics was more enthusiastic than accurate, and his claim that he had squared the circle, along with his mistaken notions about the vacuum, provided welcome targets for counter-attack. Dryden did join the Society in 1662, and was elected to the fortunately abortive committee for 'improving the

English language'. But Hobbes's style is nearer than Dryden's to the Society's requirements. It rests on definition:

in the right Definition of Names, lyes the first use of Speech; which is the Acquisition of Science: And in wrong, or no Definitions, lyes the first abuse; from which proceed all false and senseless Tenets.

The only branch of knowledge in which definition has been properly insisted on from the start is, says Hobbes, geometry. It was the discovery of geometry that diverted him from classical literature and music to philosophy and science. Aubrey tells the story:

He was . . . 40 yeares old before he looked on geometry; which happened accidentally. Being in a gentleman's library . . . Euclid's Elements lay open, and 'twas the 47 El. libri I. He read the proposition. 'By G——', sayd he, 'this is impossible!' So he reads the demonstration of it, which referred him back to such a proposition . . . *Et sic deinceps*, that at last he was demonstratively convinced of that trueth. This made him in love with geometry.

Political theory, as Hobbes understands it, has to be deduced from the invariable laws that he is convinced govern human conduct – that all men are selfish, diffident, fearful, and hungry for power. Constructing the Hobbesian state is like building a theorem in geometry rather than, he says, playing tennis, where the rules are arbitrary. *Leviathan*(1651) rises from first principles, each step determining the next: from sensation to communication to social behaviour to politics. Gradually and, it seems, irresistibly, the steely reasoning arches into the air, until the reader, looking back, catches his breath to see how far away the ground is. Dipping into Hobbes produces the same incredulous reaction that dipping into Euclid produced in Hobbes. When the innocent reader hits on a sentence like: 'Another doctrine repugnant to civil society is that whatsoever a man does against his conscience is sin', his incredulity bristles. But travelling back over the proof he finds the proposition inevitable. Civil society depends on civil authority, and if another authority (the conscience) intervenes, society will disintegrate. To be a good citizen you must ignore your conscience. This kind of intellectual somersault is an important part of the exhilaration Hobbes provides. The common notion that he was an unpoetical writer – 'he had not much poetry in him', announces A. D. Lindsay in the introduction to the Everyman *Leviathan* – seems to arise from a misdirected attention to his efforts in verse. When his prose takes words and strips off the scales of habit so that the bright new definition springs out, the reader's sense of stepping through a low door on to unsuspected vistas is deeply poetic, and to disqualify it because it excites the intelligence, not the senses, is to sell out to the Augustan view of poetry as a glossy rind stuck over the intellectual core. On the other side of his redefinitions lies a harsh but compelling world:

Joy, arising from imagination of a mans own power and ability, is that exultation of the mind which is called GLORYING . . . *Sudden Glory*, is the passion which maketh those *Grimaces* called LAUGHTER; and is caused either by some sudden act of their own, that pleaseth them; or by the apprehension of some deformed thing in another, by comparison whereof they suddenly applaud themselves. And it is incident most to them, that are conscious of the fewest abilities in themselves; who are forced to keep themselves in their own favour, by observing the imperfections of other men.

The words selected – laughter as grimace, funny people as deformed – take a bitter look at life, but the argumentative steps are so firm that instead of resisting it we grow conscious of our own weak smiles. In the Hobbesian wonderland things we can remember seeming solid and dignified collapse at a touch. The future becomes 'a fiction of the mind, applying the sequels of actions Past, to the actions that are Present'. Unselfishness, which had seemed at least a possibility, dissolves: if the motive for an apparently unselfish act is not to gain friendship, reputation, or a reward in heaven, then it is to deliver the mind of the person who acts from 'the pain of compassion'. Intrinsic value vanishes:

The value of all things contracted for, is measured by the Appetite of the Contractors: and therefore the just value, is that which they be contented to give.

'Contented' makes it all sound so peaceful that the reader feels ashamed of his antiquated belief that it was possible to charge extortionate prices. Hobbes proceeds by redefinition of key terms and a cleverly slanted use of supporting ones. He condemns metaphor, but in the same breath talks of words being 'snuffed and purged' of ambiguity, so as to make deprivation seem attractive. While exploiting it, he is aware of the dangers of this misuse, and of the fluid nature of our vocabulary of praise and blame. What one man calls wisdom, another calls fear; one man's magnanimity is another's prodigality. Because they are interchangeable, such terms 'can never be true grounds of any ratiocination'.

The new hard outline Hobbes gives to his key terms leaves it in no doubt whether it is possible to interlock particular specimens. Certain popular conjunctions of words, he demonstrates, are not merely untrue but impossible. 'For example, if it be a false affirmation to say a *quadrangle is round*, the word *round quadrangle* signifies nothing; but is a meere sound.' Similarly if it is false to say substances have no matter, *'Immaterial Substances'* is a meaningless noise (Wilkins and others define spirits and the soul as 'immaterial substances'). These combinations, being without meaning, cannot be understood, 'though many think they understand, then, when they do but repeat the words softly, or con them in their mind'.

Impatience with metaphor is among the fashionable opinions Dryden shares with Hobbes. Shakespeare's language he considered 'so pestered with figurative expressions that it is as affected as it is obscure', and in rewriting *Troilus and Cressida* he promised 'to remove that heap of rubbish under which many excellent thoughts lay wholly buried'. Like Wilkins, Dryden distrusts idiom, and smokes it out 'by translating my English into Latin, and thereby trying what sense the words will bear in a more stable language'. His complacency about correctness is not made easier to stomach by his obsessive inexactitude. We are often reminded that he introduced new terms – criticism, critique, biography, hero – but it was not terms that were needed. The Elizabethan critics had hundreds, and nothing else. Incisiveness of the kind Hobbes had brought to morals and politics was required, but Dryden's mind had no comparable pugnacity or edge. He seems almost wilfully to keep his central concepts nebulous. It must have been infuriating for his opponents, as we can appreciate if we watch his shifty behaviour in the dispute with Sir Robert Howard about whether rhyme should be used in drama. Dryden, defining a play as an 'imitation of nature', though never sorting out what that means, replies to Howard's insistence that rhyme is not natural, since people do not naturally speak in rhyme, by slipping one meaning of 'nature' out of sight and substituting a more convenient one:

It has been formerly urged by you, and confessed by me, that since no man spoke any kind of verse *ex tempore*, that which was nearest nature was to be preferred. I answer you, therefore, by distinguishing betwixt what is nearest to the nature of comedy, which is the imitation of common persons and ordinary speaking, and what is nearest the nature of a serious play: this last is indeed the representation of nature, but 'tis nature wrought up to an higher pitch.

'Nature' first means here (the passage is from the *Essay of Dramatic Poesy*, 1668), what Dryden says it means in the *Preface to an Evening's Love* (1671): what is 'found and met with in the world'. Plainly if this is 'wrought up to an higher pitch' it can no longer be called 'nature'. And 'nature' in the phrases 'the nature of comedy' and 'the nature of a serious play' means 'essential quality', and only pretends to have something to do with the other word. Howard replied in his preface to the *Duke of Lerma* that it was not a question of what was most natural for a serious play but what was nearest to human behaviour. Dryden concedes the point at once, in the *Defence Of 'An Essay of Dramatic Poesy'* (1668), and makes out that this is what he has been saying all along:

I still shall think I have gained my point if I can prove that rhyme is best or most natural for a serious subject. As for the question as he states it, whether rhyme be nearest the nature of what it represents, I wonder he should think me so ridiculous as to dispute whether prose or verse be nearest to ordinary conversation.

Apparently 'most natural' is now synonymous with 'best', and 'natural' in the sense 'found and met with in the world' has been dropped. Indeed, Dryden pretends that it is wisest to dispense with the term: 'To return to verse, whether it be natural or not in plays is a problem which is not demonstrable of either side.' But he soon begins to creep back into the surrendered ground. Jonson used verse in his tragedies: 'which shews he thought it not unnatural in serious plays', and by the end of the *Defence* Dryden is truculently repeating the definition he began with: 'I never heard of any other foundation of dramatic poesy than the imitation of nature'.

To come directly from Hobbes to these fumbling evasions is to grasp the inferiority of Dryden's mind. Like the theologians Hobbes ridicules, he repeats the terms he inherits frequently to himself and imagines this is the same as understanding. Repeatedly he draws himself up to enunciate a definition, but out trickles another platitude as unserviceable as the last:

From that which has been said, it may be collected that the definition of wit (which has been so often attempted, and ever unsuccessfully by many poets) is only this: that it is a propriety of thoughts and words; or, in other terms, thoughts and words elegantly adapted to the subject.

It gets us nowhere because 'propriety' and 'elegance' are what Hobbes called words of inconstant signification, adding that they could never be the grounds of any ratiocination. One man's propriety is another's tameness. Dryden's criticism has rubber bones. The industriously negligent prose he puts over them fails to match up to the 'defining' procedure. It works much better, when it is allowed to, through implication and innuendo. Not that there is any reason why Dryden should write like Hobbes, but he accepted the fashion for definition when his concern to sound gentlemanly and his 'natural diffidence' could only make the result irritatingly incompetent.

There are too many generalizations already about prose-style in this period. If we want a bird's-eye view, though, we may remind ourselves how the Reformation demand for controversy destroyed More's style and how its demand for a vernacular Bible created Tyndale's. How the humanist endeavour dwindled into nationalism and (comparative) solidarity under Elizabeth, during whose reign fiction writers competed with foreign models and decorated themselves from rhetorical stock. Advance was left to dissidents and pamphleteers, and to Nashe. The half-century of constitutional crises and civil war nurtured virtuoso styles (Burton, Browne) which seem to be indexes of personality (and personality which is already something more limitable than Nashe's suppleness). A clamour for standardization follows immediately, appealing for precedent to Bacon whose style, imaginatively inferior to Nashe's, happened to point in the right historical direction. Only Hobbes made a great prose-work out of this mid-century tendency.

BIBLIOGRAPHY

* Editions from which quotations are made have been asterisked.

1. *Wyatt and Surrey*

Editions

Sir Thomas Wyatt, *Collected Poems*, ed. Kenneth Muir and Patricia Thomson, Liverpool, 1969.
*Henry Howard, Earl of Surrey, *Poems*, ed. Emrys Jones, Oxford, 1964. This contains all but seven poems, for which see *Poems*, ed. F. M. Padelford, New York, 1920; rev. 1966.
Tottel's Miscellany, ed. Hyder Edward Rollins, Cambridge, Mass., 1928–9; rev. 1965.
*John Skelton, *The Complete English Poems*, ed. John Scattergood, London, 1983.
Selections from Gavin Douglas, ed. David F. C. Coldwell, Oxford, 1964.

Biography

Kenneth Muir, *Life and Letters of Sir Thomas Wyatt*, Liverpool, 1963.
Edwin Casady, *Henry Howard, Earl of Surrey*, New York, 1938.

Literary history and criticism

John M. Berdan, *Early Tudor Poetry* 1485–1547, New York, 1920; re-issued 1961.
Gordon Kipling, *The Triumph of Honour, Burgundian Origins of the Elizabethan Renaissance*, The Hague, 1977. Contains fresh insights into the background of Henry VIII's courtly makers, including Wyatt, in a study of the Flemish impact upon them.
C. S. Lewis. *English Literature in the Sixteenth Century excluding Drama*, Oxford, 1954.
H. A. Mason, *Humanism and Poetry in the Early Tudor Period*, London, 1959. Contains a spirited attack on Wyatt's lyrics, a study of his translations (of particular value for the Psalms), and a discussion of 'The Relation of Surrey to Wyatt'.
Douglas L. Peterson, *The English Lyric from Wyatt to Donne*,

Princeton, 1967. 'A History of the Plain and Eloquent Styles', with sections on the medieval lyric and Tottel's Miscellany.

Raymond Southall, *The Courtly Maker*, Oxford, 1964. 'On the poetry of Wyatt and his contemporaries.'

Patricia Thomson, *Sir Thomas Wyatt and his Background*, London, 1964. A study of the poems, excluding the Psalms, in relation to the social and literary background.

2. Sir Philip Sidney

Editions

The Complete Works of Sir Philip Sidney, ed. Albert Feuillerat, 4 vols, Cambridge, 1912–26.
The Poems of Sir Philip Sidney, ed. William A. Ringler, Oxford, 1962.
An Apology for Poetry, ed. Geoffrey Shepherd, London, 1965.
The Correspondence of Sir Philip Sidney and Hubert Languet, trans. S. A. Pears, London, 1845.

Criticism

John Buxton, *Sir Philip Sidney and the English Renaissance*, London, 1954.
Walter Davis and Richard A. Lanham. *Sidney's Arcadia*, New Haven, 1965. Two separate studies, one dealing with the *Arcadia*'s relation to the romance tradition, the other dealing with the literary technique of the 'Old' *Arcadia*.
William Empson, *Seven Types of Ambiguity*, London, 1930. Includes in its first chapter a brilliant discussion of the double sestina, 'Yee Gote-heard Gods'.
Fulke Greville, *Life of Sir Philip Sidney*, ed. Nowell Smith, Oxford, 1907. An account by Sidney's contemporary and literary executor.
David Kalstone, *Sidney's Poetry*, Cambridge, Mass., 1965. Includes an account of Sidney's relation to the Italian tradition.
J. W. Lever, *The Elizabethan Love Sonnet*, London, 1956.
Robert L. Montgomery, *Symmetry and Sense*, Austin, Texas, 1961.
Kennth O. Myrick, *Sir Philip Sidney as a Literary Craftsman*, Cambridge, Mass., 1935.
Neil Rudenstine, *Sidney's Poetic Development*, Cambridge, Mass., 1967.
Hallett Smith, *Elizabethan Poetry*, Cambridge, Mass., 1952. Chapter III (The Sonnets) includes an interesting discussion of the *persona* of Astrophel.
Theodore Spencer, 'The Poetry of Sir Philip Sidney', *English Literary History* xii (1945), 251–79.
Jack Stillinger, 'The Biographical Problem of *Astrophel and Stella*', *Journal of English and Germanic Philology* lix (1960), 617–39. A sane and scholarly statement of the problem.

John Thompson, *The Founding of English Metre*, London, 1961.

J. P. Thorne, 'A Ramistical Commentary on Sidney's *Apologie for Poetrie*', *Modern Philology* liv (1956), 158–64.

Rosemond Tuve, *Elizabethan and Metaphysical Imagery*, Chicago, 1947. Includes finest occasional discussions of passages from Sidney.

J. A. Van Dorsten, *Poets, Patrons, and Professors: Sir Philip Sidney, Daniel Rogers, and the Leiden Humanists*, Leiden, 1962.

M. W. Wallace, *The Life of Sir Philip Sidney*, London, 1915. The standard biography.

Richard B. Young, 'English Petrarke: A Study of Sidney's *Astrophel and Stella*', in *Three Studies in the Renaissance: Sidney, Jonson, Milton*, New Haven, 1958.

3. *Spenser*

Editions, etc.

W. F. McNeir and Foster Provost, *Annotated Bibliography of Edmund Spenser.* 1937–1960 Pittsburgh, 1962. Supplements, F. I. Carpenter's *Reference Guide* (1923), and Dorothy F. Atkinson's *Bibliographical Supplement* (1937).

Charles G. Osgood, *A Concordance to the Poems of Edmund Spenser*, Washington, 1915.

Edmund Spenser, *The Works of Edmund Spenser: A Variorum Edition*, ed. E. Greenlaw, C. G. Osgood, F. M. Padelford and others, 10 vols, Baltimore, 1932–4.

*—— *The Poetical Works*, ed. J. C. Smith and E. de Selincourt, 3 vols, Oxford, 1909–10.

—— *The Faerie Queene*, ed. A. C. Hamilton, Harlow, 1977; ed. Thomas P. Roche, Harmondsworth, 1978.

Spenser Selections with Essays by Hazlitt, Coleridge & Leigh Hunt, ed. W. L. Renwick, Oxford, 1923. An excellent selection, with memorable short critical comments from Sidney to Keats.

*—— *A View to the Present State of Ireland*, ed. W. L. Renwick, London, 1934. Reliable text and invaluable commentary.

Biography

Alexander C. Judson, *The Life of Edmund Spenser*, Baltimore, 1947. [Uniform with Variorum.]

Criticism

Paul Alpers, ed. *Elizabethan Poetry: Modern Essays in Criticism*, New York, 1967. Includes eight essays on Spenser, including A. S. P. Woodhouse's influential 'Nature and Grace in *The Faerie Queene*'.

—— *The Poetry of The Faerie Queene*, Princeton, 1957.

Josephine W. Bennett, *The Evolution of The Faerie Queene*, Chicago, 1942.

Alastair Fowler, *Spenser and the Numbers of Time*, New York and London, 1954. On 'numerical composition'.

Northrop Frye, *Fables of Identity*, New York, 1963. Includes his important article 'The Structure of Imagery in *The Faerie Queene*'.

A. C. Hamilton, *The Structure of Allegory in The Faerie Queen*, Oxford, 1961.

Graham Hough, *A Preface to The Faerie Queene*, London, 1962. Valuable for Spenser's debt to Italian romantic epic.

H. S. V. Jones, *A Spenser Handbook*, New York and London, 1930.

C. S. Lewis, *English Literature in the Sixteenth Century excluding Drama*, Oxford, 1954. Contains his best short comment on Spenser, especially valuable on *Fowre Hymnes*. But see also Lewis's *The Allegory of Love*, London, 1936.

—— *Spenser's Images of Life*, ed. Alastair Fowler, London, 1967.

W. R. Mueller and D. C. Allen, eds, *That Soueraine Light, Essays in Honor of Edmund Spenser, 1552–1952*, Baltimore, 1952.

William Nelson, *The Poetry of Edmund Spenser*, New York, 1963. Learned and amply documented.

Paul E. McLane, *Spenser's Shepheardes Calendar: A Study in Elizabethan Allegory*, Notre Dame, Indiana, 1961. Identifications (often suspect) of personages in the *Calendar*.

M. Pauline Parker, *The Allegory of The Faerie Queene*, Oxford, 1960.

W. L. Renwick, *Edmund Spenser: An Essay on Renaissance Poetry*, London, 1925, 1961. Still the best introduction to Spenser.

Hallett Smith, *Elizabethan Poetry*, Cambridge, Mass., 1952.

Harold Stein, *Studies in Spenser's Complaints*, New York, 1934.

Rosemond Tuve, *Allegorical Imagery: Some Medieval Books and Their Posterity*, Princeton, 1966. Illuminates the background of *The Faerie Queene*.

Enid Welsford, *Spenser: Fowre Hymnes Epithalamion: A Study of Spenser's Doctrine of Love*, Oxford, 1967. An edition with elaborate critical comment.

4. *The Epyllion*

Editions

Elizabethan Minor Epics, ed. Elizabeth Story, Donno, London, 1963. Except for *Venus and Adonis*, includes the major examples of the genre from 1589–1646.

Seven Minor Epics of the English Renaissance, ed. Paul W. Miller, Gainesville, Fla., 1967 [Scholars' Facsimiles & Reprints]. Includes late examples not readily accessible elsewhere.

Elizabethan Narrative Verse, ed. Nigel Alexander, London, 1967. In addition to four of the popular epyllia, includes 'The Fable . . . treting of Narcissus', Henry Petowe's continuation of 'Hero and Leander' and 'Willobie His Avisa'.

Elizabethan Verse Romances, ed. M. M. Reese, London, 1968. Includes five of the popular epyllia, intended 'for sixth-form pupils and undergraduates'.

On Elizabethan poetry

M. C. Bradbrook, *Shakespeare and Elizabethan Poetry*, London, 1951.

Douglas Bush, *Mythology and the Renaissance Tradition in English Poetry*, Minneapolis, 1932; reissued New York, 1957.

Maurice Evans, *English Poetry in the Sixteenth Century*, London, 1955.

Hallett Smith, *Elizabethan Poetry: A Study in Coventions, Meaning and Expression*, Cambridge, Mass., 1952.

On Ovid, the epyllion, and its authors

F. S. Boas, *Ovid and the Elizabethans*, London, 1947.

Douglas Bush, 'The Influence of Marlowe's *Hero and Leander* on Early Mythological Poems', *Modern Language Notes* xlii (1927), 211–17.

C. B. Cooper, *Some Elizabethan Opinions of the Poetry and Character of Ovid*, Chicago, 1914.

G. Cross, 'Marston's "Metamorphosis of Pigmalion's Image": A Mock-Epyllion', *Etudes Anglaises* xiii (1960), 331–6.

M. M. Crump, *The Epyllion from Theocritus to Ovid*, London, 1931.

Phineas Fletcher, *Venus and Anchises (Brittain's Ida) and Other Poems*, ed. Ethel Seaton, London, 1926.

D. J. Gordon, 'Chapman's "Hero and Leander"', *English Miscellany* v (1954), 41–94.

A. C. Hamilton, 'Venus and Adonis', *Studies in English Literature* i (1961), 1–15.

Thomas Heywood, *Oenone and Paris* by T. H., ed. J. Q. Adams, Washington, DC, 1943.

Clark Hulse, *Metamorphic Verse: the Elizabethan Minor Epic*, Princeton, 1981.

William Keach, 'Marlowe's Hero as "Venus' Nun"', *English Literary Renaissance* 2, (1972), 307–20.

—— *Elizabethan Erotic Narratives*, New Brunswick, NJ, 1977.

J. F. Kermode, 'The Banquet of Sense', *Bulletin of the John Rylands Library* xliv (1961), 68–99.

C. S. Lewis, 'Hero and Leander', *Proceedings of the British Academy* xxxviii (1952), 23–37.

P. W. Miller, 'The Elizabethan Minor Epic', *Studies in Philology* lv (1958), 31–5.

Ovid, *The Heroycall Epistles . . .*, ed. F. S. Boas, London, 1928 (tr. by George Turberville, 1567).

*—— *Shakespeare's Ovid*, ed. W. H. D. Rouse, London, 1904; repr. Centaur Classics, London, 1961 (Arthur Golding's translation of the *Metamorphoses*, 1565–7).

R. Putney, '*Venus and Adonis*: Amour with Humour', *Philological Quarterly* xx (1941), 533–48.

C. C. Stopes, 'Thomas Edwards, Author of "Cephalus and Procris" and "Narcissus"', *Modern Language Review* xvi (1921), 208–23.

W. B. C. Watkins, 'Shakespeare's Banquet of Sense', *Southern Review* vii (1941–2), 706–34.

L. P. Wilkinson, *Ovid Recalled*, Cambridge, 1955.

5. *Shakespeare and the Sonnet Sequence*

Editions

A New Variorum Edition of Shakespeare: the Sonnets, ed. Hyder Edward Rollins, 2 vols, Philadelphia and London, 1944. This may be considered the standard edition. It contains a good text of the sonnets and summaries of critical arguments to 1942.

Shakespeare's Sonnets, ed. W. G. Ingram and Theodore Redpath, London, 1964. Helpful critical notes.

Shakespeare's Sonnets, ed. Stephen Booth, New Haven and London, 1977.

*The New Shakespeare: The Sonnets, ed. J. Dover Wilson, second edition, Cambridge, 1967. Wilson's commentary is indispensable.

Many other of the Elizabethan sequences may be found in Martha Foote Crow, *Elizabethan Sonnet Cycles*, 4 vols, London, 1896–8, and Sir Sidney Lee, *Elizabethan Sonnets*, 2 vols, London, 1904.

Criticism

C. L. Barber, 'An Essay on the Sonnets' in *Elizabethan Poetry: Modern Essays in Criticism*, ed. Paul J. Alpers, New York, 1967, pp 299–320.

Stephen Booth, *An Essay on Shakespeare's Sonnets*, New Haven, 1969.

Edward Hubler, *The Sense of Shakespeare's Sonnets*, Princeton, 1952.

Lisle Cecil John, *The Elizabethan Sonnet Sequences*, New York, 1938.

G. Wilson Knight, *The Mutual Flame*, London, 1955.

L. C. Knights, 'Shakespeare's Sonnets', *Scrutiny* iii (1934), 133–60, (reprinted in *Explorations*, London, 1946).

Murray Krieger, *A Window to Criticism: Shakespeare's Sonnets and Modern Poetics*, Princeton, 1964.

Hilton Landry, *Interpretations in Shakespeare's Sonnets*, Berkeley, 1963.

J. B. Leishman, *Themes and Variations in Shakespeare's Sonnets*, London, 1961.

J. W. Lever, *The Elizabethan Love Sonnet*, London, 1956.

C. S. Lewis, *English Literature in the Sixteenth Century excluding Drama*, Oxford, 1954.

Edward Hubler, ed., *The Riddle of Shakespeare's Sonnets*, New York, 1962.

Thomas P. Roche, Jr., *Petrarch and the English Sonnet Sequences*, New York, 1986.

Janet G. Scott, *Les Sonnets élisabethains*, Paris, 1929.

E. H. Wilkins, 'A General Survey of Renaissance Petrarchism' in *Studies in the Life and Works of Petrarch*, Cambridge, Mass., 1955, pp 280–99.

—— *The making of the 'Canzoniere' and Other Studies*, Rome, 1951.

Dame Frances Yates, 'The Emblematic Conceit in Giordano Bruno's *De Gli Eroici Furore* and in the Elizabethan Sonnet Sequences', *Journal of the Warburg and Courtauld Institutes* x (1948), 27–82.

6. *The Lyric*

Editions

Thomas Campion, *Works*, ed. Percival Vivian, Oxford, 1909.
John Donne, *Poems*, ed. H. J. C. Grierson, Oxford, 1912.
George Gascoigne, *Complete Works*, ed. John Cunliffe, Cambridge, 1907–10.
George Herbert, *Works*, ed. F. E. Hutchinson, Oxford, 1941; rev. 1945.
Robert Herrick, *Poetical Works*, ed. L. C. Martin, Oxford, 1956.
Ben Jonson, *Poems*, ed. Ian Donaldson, London, 1975.
Richard Lovelace, *Poems*, ed. C. H. Wilkinson, Oxford, 1925; rev. 1930.
Andrew Marvell, *Poems and Letters*, ed. H. M. Margoliouth, 2 vols, Oxford, 1927; rev. 1952.
Thomas Nashe, *Works*, ed. R. B. McKerrow, Oxford, 1958.
Sir Walter Ralegh, *Poems*, ed. Agnes M. C. Latham, London, 1951.
Henry Howard, Earl of Surrey, *Poems*, ed. Emrys Jones, Oxford, 1964.
Sir Thomas Wyatt, *Collected Poems*, ed. Kenneth Muir, London, 1949.

Anthologies and commentary

Derek Attridge, *Well-Weighed Syllables: Elizabethan Verse in Classical Metres*, Cambridge, 1974.
Norman Ault, *Elizabethan Lyrics from the Original Texts*, London, 1925; rev. 1966.
—— *Seventeenth-Century Lyrics from the Original Texts*, London, 1928.
A. H. Bullen, *Lyrics from the Dramatists of the Elizabethan Age*, London, 1889.
—— *Lyrics from the Song-Books of the Elizabethan Age*, London, 1891.
—— *Poems, Chiefly Lyrical, from Romances and Prose Tracts of the Elizabethan Age*, London, 1890.
B. H. Bronson, *The Ballad as Song*, Los Angeles and Berkeley, 1969.
Gerald Bullett, *Silver Poets of the Sixteenth Century*, London, 1947. Wyatt, Surrey, Sidney, Ralegh, Davies – complete or near-complete.

Edward Doughtie, ed., *Lyrics from English Airs 1596–1622*, Cambridge, MA, 1970. Contains poems from all the songbooks except Campion's.

E. H. Fellowes, *The English School of Lutenist Song Writers, Transcribed, Scored, and Edited from the Original Editions*, London, 1920–30. Includes airs of Campion, Dowland, Thomas Ford, Rosseter, Frank Pilkington, Thomas Morley.

—— ed., *English Madrigal Verse 1588–1632*. Third edition, revised and enlarged by Frederick W. Sternfeld and David Greer. Oxford, 1967. Contains both madrigal and lute song verse.

J. William Hebel and Hoyt H. Hudson, *Poetry of the English Renaissance*, 1509–1660, New York, 1938.

John Hollander, *The Untuning of the Sky: Ideas of Music in English Poetry 1550–1700*, Princeton, 1961.

—— *Vision and Resonance: Two Senses of Poetic Form*, New York, 1985. Especially chapters 1–4.

—— and W. H. Auden, *Selected Songs of Thomas Campion*, Boston, 1973. Good introduction, and music for some of the songs.

R. G. Howarth, *Minor Poets of the Seventeenth Century*, London, 1931; rev. 1963.

Herbert of Cherbury, Carew, Suckling, Lovelace

Catherine Ing, *Elizabethan Lyrics: a study in the development of English metres and their relation to poetic effects*, London, 1951. Some interesting readings of particular poems.

Elise Jorgens, *The Well-Tun'd Word: Musical Interpretations of English Poetry 1597–1651*, Minneapolis, Minnesota, 1982.

Joseph Kerman, *The Elizabethan Madrigal*.

C. Day Lewis, *The Lyric Impulse*, Cambridge, Mass., and London, 1965.

Marjorie H. Nicolson, *The Breaking of the Circle*, New York, 1950; rev. 1962.

Bruce Pattison, *Music and Poetry in the English Renaissance*, London, 1948.

Hyder Edward Rollins, *Tottel's Miscellany*, Cambridge, Mass., 1928–9; rev. 1965.

Louise Schleiner, *The Living Lyre in English Verse*, Columbia, MO, 1984.

Claude V. Simpson, *The British Broadside Ballad and Its Music*, Cambridge, MA, 1970.

Hallett Smith, *Elizabethan Poetry*, Cambridge, Mass., 1952. Chapter 5, 'Poetry for Music', excellent brief introduction.

Ian Spink, *English Song: Dowland to Purcell*, New York, 1974.

John Stevens, *Music and Poetry in the Early Tudor Court*, London, 1961.

—— *The Old Sound and the New*, Cambridge, 1982.

John Thompson, *The Founding of English Metre*, London, 1961.

Willard Thorp, *Songs from the Restoration Theater*, Princeton, 1939. With scores.

James Winn, *Unsuspected Eloquence: A History of the Relations between Poetry and Music*, New Haven and London, 1981.

7. *Ben Jonson and the Court*

Editions

Ben Jonson, ed. C. H. Herford and P. and E. Simpson, Oxford, 11 vols, 1925–52.
Poems, ed. Ian Donaldson, London, 1975. Exceptionally well annotated.
Complete Poetry, ed. W. B. Hunter Jr, New York, 1963.
Complete Poems, ed. George Parfitt, Harmondsworth, 1975.
Complete Masques, ed. Stephen Orgel, New Haven, 1969.

Criticism

J. B. Bamborough, *Ben Jonson*, London, 1970.
Anne Barton, *Ben Jonson, dramatist*, Cambridge, 1984.
L. A. Beaurlin, 'The Selective Principle in Jonson's Shorter Poems', *Criticism* viii, (1966), 64–74.
Philip Edwards, *Threshold of a Nation*, Cambridge (1979), 131–73.
Alastair Fowler, 'The "better marks" of Jonson's *To Penshurst*', *Review of English Studies* xxiv, (1973), 266–82.
—— *Conceitful Thought: the interpretation of English Renaissance poems*, Edinburgh (1975), 114–34.
D. J. Gordon, *The Renaissance Imagination*, 1975. Pioneering essays on Jonson's masques.
Thomas M. Greene, 'Ben Jonson and the Centered Self', *Studies in English Literature* x, (1970), 325–48.
L. C. Knights, *Explorations III*, London (1976), 81–94. Suggestive short study of Jonson's poetry.
F. R. Leavis, *Revaluation*, London (1936), 17–24.
A. S. Leggatt, *Ben Jonson: His Vision and his Art*, London, 1981.
Hugh Maclean, 'Ben Jonson's Poems: Notes on the Ordered Society' in *Essays in English Literature from the Renaissance to the Victorian Age*, eds Miller MacLure and F. W. Watt, Toronto (1964), 43–68. A brilliant and indispensable essay.
Hugh Maclean, '"A more secret cause": the wit of Jonson's poetry' in *A Celebration of Ben Jonson*, ed. W. Blissett et al., Toronto (1973), 129–66.
Earl Miner, *The Cavalier Mode from Jonson to Cotton*, Princeton, 1971.
J. G. Nichols, *The Poetry of Ben Jonson*, London, 1969. A lively full-length study.

David Norbrook, *Poetry and Politics in the English Renaissance*, London, 1984.

Stephen Orgel, *The Jonsonian Masque*, Cambridge, Mass., 1965.

G. A. E. Parfitt, 'The Poetry of Ben Jonson', *Essays in Criticism* xviii, (1968), 18–31.

—— 'Ethical Thought and Ben Jonson's Poetry', *Studies in English Literature* ix, 1969.

—— *Ben Jonson: public poet and private man*, London, 1976.

R. S. Peterson, *Imitation and Praise in the Poems of Ben Jonson*, New Haven, 1981. An admirably scholarly and penetrating work.

J. C. A. Rathmell, 'Jonson, Lord Lisle and Penshurst', *English Literary Renaissance* i, (1971), 250–60.

Joseph Summers, *The Heirs of Donne and Jonson*, New York, 1970.

Wesley Trimpi, *Ben Jonson's Poems, A study of the Plain Style*, Stanford, 1962.

Geoffrey Walton, 'The Tone of Ben Jonson's Poetry' in *Metaphysical to Augustan*, London, 1955.

David Wykes, 'Ben Jonson's "Chast Booke" – the *Epigrammes*', *Renaissance and Modern Studies* xiii, (1969), 76–87.

8. *The Poetry of John Donne*

Editions

*The Elegies and the Songs and Sonnets of John Donne, ed. Helen Gardner, Oxford, 1965.
*The Satires, Epigrams and Verse Letters of John Donne, ed. W. Milgate, Oxford, 1967.
*John Donne: The Anniversaries, ed. Frank Manley, Baltimore, 1963.
*John Donne: The Divine Poems, ed. Helen Gardner, Oxford, 1952, 2nd edn, 1978.
John Donne: The Epithalamions, Anniversaries and Epicedes, ed. W. Milgate, Oxford, 1978.
The Poems of John Donne, ed. H. J. C. Grierson, 2 vols, Oxford, 1912.
The Complete English Poems, ed. A. J. Smith, Harmondsworth, 1971.

Criticism

A. Alvarez, *The School of Donne*, London, 1961.
R. C. Bald, *John Donne: A Life*, Oxford, 1970.
Joan Bennett, *Four Metaphysical Poets*, Cambridge, 1934, revised as *Five Metaphysical Poets*, Cambridge, 1964.
John Carey, *John Donne: Life, Mind and Art*, London, 1981.
Herbert Davis and Helen Gardner, eds, *Elizabethan and Jacobean Studies Presented to F. P. Wilson*, Oxford, 1959.
T. S. Eliot, '*The Metaphysical Poets*', *Selected Essays*, London, 1932.
R. Ellrodt, *Les Poètes Métaphysiques Anglais*, 3 vols, Paris, 1960.
Peter Amadeus Fiore, ed., *Just So Much Honor*, University Park, 1972. Includes an essay by William Empson.
Helen Gardner, *The Business of Criticism*, Oxford, 1959.
Helen Gardner, ed., *Twentieth Century Views: Donne*, Englewood Cliffs, 1962.
Merritt Y. Hughes, 'Kidnapping Donne', *Essays in Criticism, Second Series*, Berkeley, 1934.
Frank Kermode, *John Donne*, London, 1957.
—— *Shakespeare, Spenser, Donne*, 1971.
F. R. Leavis, 'The Line of Wit', *Revaluation*, London, 1936.
J. B. Leishman, *The Monarch of Wit*, London, 1951.
C. S. Lewis, 'Donne and Love Poetry in the Seventeenth Century', and Joan Bennett, 'The Love Poetry of John Donne',

Seventeenth Century Studies Presented to Sir Herbert Grierson, ed. J. Dover Wilson, Oxford, 1938.

Louis Martz, *The Poetry of Meditation*, New Haven, 1954.

Mario Praz, *Secentismo e Marinismo in Inghilterra*, Florence, 1925.

—— 'Donne's Relation to the Poetry of His Time', *The Flaming Heart*, New York, 1958.

J. R. Roberts, *John Donne: An Annotated Bibliography of Modern Criticism, 1912–1967*, Missouri, 1973.

—— *John Donne: An Annotated Bibliography of Modern Criticism 1968–1978*, Missouri, 1982.

Murray Roston, *The Soul of Wit*, Oxford, 1974.

Wilbur Sanders, *John Donne's Poetry*, 1971.

A. J. Smith, ed., *John Donne: The Critical Heritage*, London, 1975.

—— ed., *John Donne: Essays in Celebration*, 1972.

Theodore Spencer, ed., *A Garland for John Donne*, Cambridge, Mass. and London, 1931.

Arnold Stein, *John Donne's Lyrics*, Minneapolis, 1962.

Rosemond Tuve, *Elizabethan and Metaphysical Imagery*, Chicago, 1947.

9. *George Herbert and the Religious Lyric*

Editions

The Poems of Richard Crashaw, ed. L. C. Martin, 1926; rev. 1957.
The Complete Poetry of Richard Crashaw, ed. G. W. Williams, New York, 1970.
The Works of George Herbert, ed. F. E. Hutchinson, Oxford, 1941; rev. 1945.
The English Poems of George Herbert, ed. C. L. Patrides, London, 1974.
Thomas Traherne: Centuries, Poems, and Thanksgivings, ed. H. M. Margoliouth, 2 vols, Oxford, 1958.
The Works of Henry Vaughan, ed. L. C. Martin, Oxford, 1914; rev. 1957.
Henry Vaughan: The Complete Poems, ed. by A. Rudrum, Harmondsworth, 1976.

Criticism

A. Alvarez, *The School of Donne*, London, 1961.
Joan Bennett, *Five Metaphysical Poets*, Cambridge, 1964.
P. M. Daly, *Literature in the Light of the Emblem*, U. of Toronto Press, 1979.
R. Ellrodt, *Les Poètes Métaphysiques Anglais*, 3 vols, Paris, 1960; rev. vols 1 and 2, 1973.
Stanley Fish, *Self-Consuming Artifacts: The Experience of Seventeenth-Century Literature*, Los Angeles, 1970.
Rosemary Freeman, *English Emblem Books*, London, 1948.
P. Grant, *The Transformation of Sin: Studies in Donne, Herbert, Vaughan and Traherne*, Amherst/Montreal, 1974.
Barbara K. Lewalski, *Protestant Poetics and the Seventeenth-Century Religious Lyric*, Princeton, 1979 (paper, 1984).
Louis Martz, *The Poetry of Meditation*, New Haven, 1954.
—— *The Paradise Within*, (Vaughan, Traherne), New Haven, 1964.
—— *The Wit of Love* (Crashaw), U. of Notre-Dame Press, 1970.
Earl Miner, *The Metaphysical Mode from Donne to Cowley*, Princeton, 1969.
Mario Praz, *Studies in Seventeenth-Century Imagery*, London, 1939.
S. C. Seelig, *The Shadow of Eternity: Belief and Structure in Herbert, Vaughan, and Traherne*, Lexington, 1981.
J. R. Summers, *The Heirs of Donne and Jonson*, London, 1970.

H. R. Swardson, *Poetry and the Fountain of Light*, London, 1962.
Rosemond Tuve, *Elizabethan and Metaphysical Imagery*, Chicago, 1947.
Helen C. White, *The Metaphysical Poets*, New York, 1936.
George Williamson, *The Donne Tradition*, Cambridge, Mass., and London, 1930.
—— *A Reader's Guide to Metaphysical Poetry*, London, 1968.

Crashaw

R. M. Bertonasco, *Crashaw and the Baroque*, Alabama, UP, 1971.
R. M. Cooper, ed., *Richard Crashaw Reassessed*, Salzburg, 1979.
Mario Praz, *The Flaming Heart*, New York, 1938.
Mary E. Rickey, *Rhyme and Meaning in Richard Crashaw*, U. of Kentucky Press, 1961.
Austin Warren, *Richard Crashaw*, Baton Rouge, 1935.
G. W. Williams, *Image and Symbol in the Sacred Poetry of Richard Crashaw*, U. of South Carolina Press, 1963.
R. V. Young, *Richard Crashaw and the Spanish Golden Age*, Yale UP, 1982.

Herbert

Amy M. Charles, *A Life of George Herbert*, Cornell UP, 1977.
M. Di Cesare and R. Magnani, *A Concordance to the Complete Writings of George Herbert*, Cornell UP, 1977.
T. S. Eliot, *George Herbert*, London (for the British Council), 1962.
S. Fish, *The Living Temple: George Herbert and Catechizing*, Los Angeles, 1978.
Barbara, L. Harman, *Costly Monuments. Representations of the Self in George Herbert's Poetry*, Harvard, UP, 1982.
E. Miller, *Drudgerie Divine: The Rhetoric of God and Man in George Herbert*, Salzburg, 1979.
A. D. Nuttall, *Overheard by God: Fiction and Prayer in Herbert, Milton, Dante, and St John*, London, 1980.
C. L. Patrides, ed., *George Herbert. The Critical Heritage*, London, 1983.
Mary E. Rickey, *Utmost Art: Complexity in the Verse of George Herbert*, U. of Kentucky Press, 1966.
Arnold Stein, *George Herbert's Lyrics*, Johns Hopkins Press, 1968.
Joseph Summers, *George Herbert: His Religion and Art*, London, 1954.
—— ed., *Too Hard to Clothe the Sunne: Essays on George Herbert*, U. of Pittsburgh Press, 1980.

M. Taylor, *The Soul in Paraphrase: George Herbert's Poetics*, The Hague/Paris, 1974.
Rosemond Tuve, *A Reading of George Herbert*, Chicago, 1962 (paper, 1982).
—— *Essays by Rosemond Tuve. Spenser, Herbert, Milton*, Princeton, 1970.
Helen Vendler, *The Poetry of George Herbert*, Harvard UP, 1975.

Traherne

A. L. Clements, *The Mystical Poetry of Thomas Traherne*, Harvard UP, 1969.
M. M. Day, *Thomas Traherne*, Boston, 1982.
G. R. Guffey and V. A. Dearing, *A Concordance to the Poetry of Thomas Traherne*, U. of California Press, 1974.
R. D. Jordan, *The Temple of Eternity: Thomas Traherne's Philosophy of Time*, Port Washington, NY/London, 1972.
A. J. Sherrington, *Mystical Symbolism in the Poetry of Thomas Traherne*, St Lucia, Brisbane, 1971.
Stanley Stewart, *The Expanded Voice: The Art of Thomas Traherne*, San Marino, Calif., 1972.
Gladys Wade, *Thomas Traherne. A Critical Biography*, Princeton, 1944.

Vaughan

T. O. Calhoun, *Henry Vaughan: The Achievement of Silex Scintillans*, U. of Delaware Press, 1981.
R. A. Durr, *On the Mystical Poetry of Henry Vaughan*, Cambridge, Mass., 1963.
Ross Garner, *Henry Vaughan: Experience and the Tradition*, U. of Chicago Press, 1959.
Elizabeth Holmes, *Henry Vaughan and the Hermetic Philosophy*, Oxford, 1932.
F. E. Hutchinson, *Henry Vaughan: A Life and Interpretation*, Oxford, 1947.
E. C. Pettet, *Of Paradise and Light: A Study of Henry Vaughan's Silex Scintillans*, Cambridge, 1960.
J. Post, *Henry Vaughan – The Unfolding Vision*, Princeton, 1982.
J. D. Simmonds, *Masques of God: Form and Theme in the Poetry of Henry Vaughan*, U. of Pittsburgh Press, 1972.
Hilda Tuttle, *Concordance to Vaughan's Silex Scintillans*, Pennsylvania State U. Press, 1969.

Minor poets

Minor Poets of the Caroline Period, ed. George Saintsbury, 3 vols, Oxford, 1906–21.

D. Bush, *English Literature in the Earlier Seventeenth Century*, Oxford, 1945, rev. edn 1966.

There are extensive bibliographies of Metaphysical Poetry by L. E. Berry (U. of Wisconsin Press, 1964) and R. Ellrodt (*op. cit.*, ed. 1973, vol. 2), of Vaughan by E. L. Marilla (U. of Alabama, 1948, Supplement, 1963), and an excellent *Annotated Bibliography* of Herbert by J. R. Roberts (U. of Missouri, 1978).

10. *Andrew Marvell and the Caroline Poets*

Anthologies

Minor Poets of the Caroline Period, ed. George Saintsbury, 3 vols, Oxford, 1905–21.

Cavalier Poets: Selected Poems, ed. Thomas Clayton, Oxford University Press, 1978. Contains excellent notes, a glossary, 'A Note on Renaissance Cosmology', and a select bibliography.

Silver Poets of the Seventeenth Century, ed. G. A. E. Parfitt, London, Dent, 1970.

Seventeenth-Century Poetry. The Schools of Donne and Jonson, ed. Hugh Kenner, New York and London, 1966. Contains a brief introduction and some explanatory footnotes.

Criticism

Don Cameron Allen, *Image and Meaning. Metaphoric Traditions in Renaissance Poetry,* Baltimore, 1960. Chapter 5 discusses 'The Grasse-Hopper' by Lovelace, chapters 6 and 7 Marvell's 'The Nymph Complaining' and 'Upon Appleton House'.

Rosalie L. Colie, *Paradoxia Epidemica. The Renaissance Tradition of Paradox,* Princeton, 1966.

Rosemary Freeman, *English Emblem Book,* London, 1948.

Wm. R. Keast, ed., *Seventeenth-Century English Poetry: Modern Essays in Criticism,* New York, Oxford University Press, 1971. Includes essays on Carew, Waller, Suckling, Lovelace, Marvell.

Louis L. Martz, *The Wit of Love,* Notre Dame University Press, 1970. Considers Donne, Carew, Crashaw, and Marvell and relates their poetry to the visual arts.

Earl Miner, *The Metaphysical Mode from Donne to Cowley,* Princeton University Press, 1969.

—— *The Cavalier Mode from Jonson to Cotton,* Princeton University Press, 1971.

Maren-Sofie Røstvig, *The Happy Man: Studies in the Metamorphoses of a Classical Ideal,* Vol. I: 1600–1700, Oslo and Oxford, 1954. Second rev. edn, Oslo and London, 1962.

Joseph H. Summers, *The Heirs of Donne and Jonson,* London, 1970.

James Turner, *The Politics of Landscape,* Oxford, 1979.

C. V. Wedgwood, *Poetry and Politics under the Stuarts,* Cambridge, 1960.

Thomas Carew

The Poems of Thomas Carew, ed. Rhodes Dunlap, Oxford, 1957.
Lynn Sadler, *Thomas Carew*, Boston, Mass., 1979.
Edward L. Selig, *The Flourishing Wreath. A Study of Thomas Carew's Poetry*, New Haven, 1958.

John Cleveland

Poems, ed. Brian Morris and Eleanor Withington, Oxford, 1967. Extensively annotated.

Abraham Cowley

Poems, ed. A. R. Waller, Cambridge, 1905.
Essays, Plays, and Sundry Verses, ed. A. R. Waller, Cambridge, 1906.
Poetry and Prose, ed. L. C. Martin, Oxford, 1949.
The Civil War, ed. Allan Pritchard, Toronto, 1973. Contains a long introduction (four chapters) and copious notes.
R. B. Hinman, *Abraham Cowley's World of Order*, Cambridge, Mass., 1960.
A. H. Nethercot, *Cowley: The Muse's Hannibal*, Oxford, 1931.
David Trotter, *The Poetry of Abraham Cowley*, Macmillan, 1979.

Robert Herrick

Poems, ed. F. W. Moorman, Oxford, 1915.
Poetical Works, ed. L. C. Martin, Oxford, 1956.
Hesperides: Or, The Works Both Humane & Divine, 1648, Scolar Press Facsimile, Menston, 1969: 2nd edn 1973.
Robert H. Deming, *Ceremony and Art: Robert Herrick's Poetry*, The Hague and Paris, Mouton, 1974.
A. Leigh DeNeef, *'This Poetick Liturgie', Robert Herrick's Ceremonial Mode*, Durham, North Carolina, 1974.
Roger B. Rollin and J. Max Patrick, eds, *'Trust to Good Verses': Herrick Tercentenary Essays*, Pittsburgh, 1978.

Richard Lovelace

Poems, ed. C. H. Wilkinson, Oxford, 1925; rev. 1930.

Andrew Marvell

The Poems and Letters of Andrew Marvell, ed. H. M. Margoliouth, 2 vols, Oxford, 1927; rev. 1952. Third edn rev. by Pierre Legouis, 1971.

The Poems of Andrew Marvell, ed. Hugh Macdonald, London, 1952; 2nd edn, 1956. The satires are not included.

Selected Poetry, ed. Frank Kermode, New York and London, 1967. Introduction and Notes.

Complete Poetry, ed. George de F. Lord, London, 1968. Second rev. edn 1984. Introduction and Notes.

The Complete English Poems, ed. Elizabeth Story Donno, London, 1974. Annotated.

An Account of the Growth of Popery and Arbitrary Government in England (Amsterdam, 1672). Facs. edn with an introduction, Farnborough, 1971.

The Rehearsal Transpros'd. Parts 1 and 2 (1672 and 1673), facs. edn, Farnborough, 1971.

The Rehearsal Transpros'd, ed. D. J. B. Smith, London, 1971.

Thomas O. Calhoun and John M. Potter, eds, *Andrew Marvell. The Garden*, The Merrill Casebook Series, Columbus, Ohio, 1970.

John Carey, ed., *Andrew Marvell. A Critical Anthology*, Harmondsworth, 1969.

Rosalie L. Colie, *'My Ecchoing Song': Andrew Marvell's Poetry of Criticism*, Princeton, 1970.

T. S. Eliot, 'Andrew Marvell', *Selected Essays 1917–1932*, New York and London, 1932.

William Empson, 'Marvell's Garden', *Some Versions of Pastoral*, London, 1935.

Kenneth Friedenreich, ed., *Tercentenary Essays in Honor of Andrew Marvell*, Hamden, Conn., 1977.

Pierre Legouis, *André Marvell. Poète, Puritain, Patriote, 1621–1678*, Paris and London, 1928. The standard biography.

—— *Andrew Marvell. Poet, Puritan, Patriot*, Oxford, 1965. Second edn 1968. Abbreviated, English translation of the above; new material added in footnotes.

J. B. Leishman, *The Art of Marvell's Poetry*, London, 1966.

C. A. Patrides, ed., *Approaches to Marvell*. The York Tercentenary Lectures, London, 1978.

Arthur Pollard, ed., *Andrew Marvell. Poems. A Casebook*, London, 1980.

Elizabeth Story Donno, ed., *Andrew Marvell. The Critical Heritage*, London, 1978. Criticism from 1673 to 1923.

John M. Wallace, *Destiny His Choice: The Loyalism of Andrew Marvell*, Cambridge, 1968.

Michael Wilding, ed., *Marvell. Modern Judgments*, London, 1969.

Francis Quarles

Quarles' Emblems, London, 1861.
The Complete Works in Prose and Verse, ed. Alexander B. Grosart, 3 vols, Blackburn, 1880, facs. edn, Hildesheim, 1971.
Hosanna, or Divine Poems on the Passion of Christ, and Threnodes, ed. John Horden, Liverpool, 1960, facs edn.
Hieroglyphikes (London, 1638), Menston, 1969 (facs. edn).
Karl Josef Höltgen, *Francis Quarles, 1592–1644*, Tübingen, 1978. In German, and with an English summary.

Sir John Suckling

Works, ed. A. H. Thompson, London, 1910.
Poems and Letters from Manuscript, ed. Herbert Berry, Ontario, 1960.
The Non-Dramatic Works, ed. Thomas Clayton, Oxford, 1971. Authoritative text with detailed commentary.

11. *Milton*

Editions

*Poetical Works, ed. H. C. Beeching, Oxford, 1900.
*Works, ed. Frank Allen Patterson *et al.*, 18 vols, New York, 1931–8. The last two volumes of this Columbia edition comprise a superb index.
Complete Prose Works, gen. ed. Don M. Wolfe, New Haven, 1953– . Eight volumes to date. Very fully annotated, especially historically.
Complete Poems and Major Prose, ed. Merritt Y. Hughes, New York, 1957. Extensively annotated.
Complete Poetical Works, ed. Douglas Bush, Boston, 1965; London, 1966.
Samson Agonistes and the Shorter Poems, ed. Isabel MacCaffrey, New York, 1966.
Paradise Lost & Paradise Regained, ed. Christopher Ricks, New York, 1968.
The Poems, eds John Carey and Alastair Fowler, London, 1968. Has the fullest and most up-to-date notes of any single-volume edition.

Biographies

Helen Darbishire, ed., *The Early Lives of Milton*, London, 1932.
John Deckhoff, ed., *Milton on Himself*, New York and London, 1939.
Christopher Hill, *Milton and the English Revolution*, London, 1977.
William Riley Parker, *Milton: A Biography*, Oxford, 1968. The fullest and most scrupulous biography.
E. M. W. Tillyard, *Milton*, London, 1930.

On Poems (1645)

Cleanth Brooks and John Hardy, *Poems of Mr John Milton*, New York, 1951.
Archie Burnett, *Milton's Style: The Shorter Poems, Paradise Regained, and Samson Agonistes*, London, 1981.
Scott Elledge, *Milton's 'Lycidas'*, New York, 1966.
Eugene Haun, 'An Inquiry into the Genre of *Comus*', *Essays in Honor of Walter Clyde Curry*, Nashville, 1954.
J. B. Leishman, '"L'Allegro" and "Il Penseroso" in their Relation to Seventeenth-Century Poetry', reprinted in *Milton*, ed. Alan Rudrum, London, 1968.

Stephen Orgel, *The Jonsonian Masque*, Cambridge, Mass., 1965.

C. A. Patrides, ed., *Milton's 'Lycidas': The Tradition and the Poem*, New York, 1961.

Rosemond Tuve, *Images and Themes in Five Poems of Milton*, Cambridge, Mass., 1957.

Enid Welsford, *The Court Masque*, Cambridge, 1927.

Mainly on Paradise Lost

Francis C. Blessington, *'Paradise Lost' and the Classical Epic*, Boston and London, 1979.

J. B. Broadbent, *Some Graver Subject*, London, 1960.

Dennis H. Burden, *The Logical Epic*, Cambridge, Mass., and London, 1967.

Dennis Richard Danielson, *Milton's Good God*, Cambridge, 1982.

John Deckhoff, *Milton's 'Paradise Lost': A Commentary on the Argument*, New York, 1946.

T. S. Eliot, 'Milton I and II', in *On Poetry and Poets*, New York and London, 1957. 'Milton II' was cut by Eliot for this printing; for the full text, see his British Academy lecture, 1947.

William Empson, *Milton's God*, London, 2nd edn, 1965.

J. M. Evans, *'Paradise Lost' and the Genesis Tradition*, Oxford, 1968.

Anne Davidson Ferry, *Milton's Epic Voice*, Cambridge, Mass., 1963.

S. E. Fish, *Surprised by Sin*, London, 1967.

Northrop Frye, *The Return of Eden*, Toronto, 1965; London, 1966 (as *Five Essays on Milton's Epics*).

Helen Gardner, *A Reading of 'Paradise Lost'*, Oxford, 1965.

Samuel Johnson, 'Milton' in *The Lives of the Poets*, 1779.

Maurice Kelley, *This Great Argument: A Study of Milton's 'De Doctrina Christiana' as a Gloss upon 'Paradise Lost'*, Princeton, 1941.

Frank Kermode, ed., *The Living Milton*, London, 1960.

John R. Knott, *Milton's Pastoral Vision. An Approach to 'Paradise Lost'*, Chicago and London, 1971.

F. R. Leavis, 'Milton's Verse', *Revaluation*, London, 1936. 'Mr Eliot and Milton', *The Common Pursuit*, London, 1952.

Barbara Kiefer Lewalski, *'Paradise Lost' and the Rhetoric of Literary Forms*, Princeton, 1985.

C. S. Lewis, *A Preface to 'Paradise Lost'*, London, 1942.

Michael Lieb, *Poetics of the Holy: A Reading of 'Paradise Lost'*, Chapel Hill, 1981.

Isabel MacCaffrey, *'Paradise Lost' as 'Myth'*, Cambridge, Mass., 1959.

C. A. Patrides, *Milton and the Christian Tradition*, Oxford, 1966.

John Peter, *A Critique of 'Paradise Lost'*, London, 1960.

F. T. Prince, *The Italian Element in Milton's Verse*, Oxford, 1954.
Stella Purce Revard, *The War in Heaven: 'Paradise Lost' and the Tradition of Satan's Rebellion*, Ithaca and London, 1980.
Christopher Ricks, *Milton's Grand Style*, Oxford, 1963.
John M. Steadman, *Milton and the Renaissance Hero*, Oxford, 1967.
—— *Milton's Epic Characters*, Chapel Hill, 1968.
—— *Epic and Tragic Structure in 'Paradise Lost'*, Chicago, 1976.
Arnold Stein, *Answerable Style*, Minneapolis, 1953.
Joseph Summers, *The Muse's Method*, Cambridge, Mass., and London, 1962.
A. J. A. Waldock, *'Paradise Lost' and Its Critics*, Cambridge, 1947.
Joan Webber, *Milton and His Epic Tradition*, Seattle and London, 1979.

On Paradise Regained

Frank Kermode, 'Milton's Hero', *Review of English Studies*, ns iv (1953), 317–30.
Barbara Kiefer Lewalski, *Milton's Brief Epic*, Providence, RI, and London, 1966.
Louis Martz, The Paradise Within, New Haven, 1964.
Arnold Stein, *Heroic Knowledge*, Minneapolis, 1957.

On Samson Agonistes

Galbraith M. Crump, ed., *Twentieth Century Interpretations of Samson Agonistes*, Englewood Cliffs, 1968.
Samuel Johnson, *The Rambler*, 16 July 1751.
William Riley Parker, *Milton's Debt to Greek Tragedy*, Baltimore, 1937.
Mary Ann Radzinowicz, *Toward Samson Agonistes*, Princeton, 1978.
Chauncey B. Tinker, 'Samson Agonistes' in *Tragic Themes in Western Literature*, ed. Cleanth Brooks, New Haven, 1955.

Miscellaneous

John T. Shawcross, ed., *Milton: The Critical Heritage*, London, 2 vols, 1970 and 1972.
William B. Hunter *et al.*, eds, *A Milton Encyclopedia*, 8 vols, Lewisburg, 1978–80.
William Ingram and Kathleen Swaim, eds, *A Concordance to Milton's English Poetry*, Oxford, 1972.

12. Samuel Butler and the Minor Restoration Poets

Editions

*Samuel Butler, *Characters and Passages from Notebooks*, ed. A. R. Waller, Cambridge, 1908.
*—— *Hudibras*, ed. John Wilders, Oxford, 1967.
—— *Prose Observations*, ed. Hugh de Quehen, Oxford, 1979.
John Oldham, *Poems*, with an introduction by Bonamy Dobrée, London, 1960. A useful introduction, but not a critical or entirely reliable text. Quotations in this chapter are taken from the original editions.
—— *The Poems*, ed. Harold F. Brooks and Raman Selden, Oxford, 1985.
Paul Hammond, *John Oldham and the Renewal of Classical Culture*, Cambridge, 1983.
John Wilmot, Earl of Rochester, *The Complete Poems*, ed. David M. Vieth, New Haven, 1968.
—— *The Poems*, ed. Keith Walker, Oxford, 1984.
—— *The Letters*, ed. Jeremy Treglown, Oxford, 1980.
David Farley-Hills, ed., *Rochester: The Critical Heritage*, London, 1972.
Jeremy Treglown, ed., *Spirit of Wit*, Oxford, 1982.
*George Etherege, *Poems*, ed. James Thorpe, Princeton, 1963.

Collections and anthologies

The Gyldenstolp Manuscript Miscellany Poems by John Wilmot, Earl of Rochester, and other Restoration Authors, ed. Bror Danielsson and David M. Vieth, Stockholm, 1967. A facsimile of one of the many manuscript collections, with a critical introduction.
Musa Proterva, Love Poems of the Restoration, ed. A. H. Bullen, London, 1889.
The Oxford Book of Seventeenth-Century Verse, ed. H. J. C. Grierson and G. Bullough, Oxford, 1934.
Poems on Affairs of State, vols I–VII, ed. G. de F. Lord, E. F. Mengel, H. H. Schless, Galbraith M. Crump, W. J. Cameron and Frank H. Ellis. New Haven, 1963–75. Further volumes are projected. An annotated and largely comprehensive selection from the original collection.
The following, of which there are no modern editions available, should be consulted:

Miscellany Poems by the Most Eminent Hands, ed. John Dryden (the last edition in Dryden's lifetime, London, 1694).

The Minor Poets, or the Works of the Most Celebrated Authors of Whom there are but small Remains, London, 1749–50.

John Playford, *The Musical Companion*, 2 vols, London, 1673.

—— *Choice Ayres*, London, 1676.

Criticism

H. J. C. Grierson, *Cross Currents of Literature of the Seventeenth Century*, London, 1929.

K. G. Hamilton, *The Two Harmonies, Poetry and Prose in the Restoration*, Oxford, 1963.

John Harley, *Music in Purcell's London*, London, 1968. On the social background of music in the Restoration.

R. E. Moore, *Henry Purcell and the Restoration Theatre*, London, 1961. On the relationship of music and drama, and on the development of opera.

James Sutherland, *Literature of the Later Seventeenth Century*, Oxford, 1969.

Rachel Trickett, *The Honest Muse*, Oxford, 1967. Considers Rochester and Oldham, the conventions of satire, and common attitudes in Restoration verse.

David M. Vieth, *Attribution in Restoration Poetry: A Study of Rochester's Poems of 1680*, New Haven, 1963. Bibliographically very important, but the critical discussion of individual poems is less reliable.

C. V. Wedgwood, *Poetry and Politics Under the Stuarts*, Cambridge, 1960.

J. H. Wilson, *The Court Wits of the Restoration*, Princeton, 1948. Important, entertaining and scholarly.

13 (i) *Prose Before Elizabeth*

Sir Thomas More

Works [ed. William Rastell] London, 1557. The only complete edition of the English works.

The English Works, ed. W. E. Campbell and A. W. Reed, London, 1931. Two volumes only published, containing *Life of Pico, Richard III, Four Last Things and Dialogue Concerning Tyndale.*

The Complete Works of St Thomas More, ed. L. I. Martz, et al., New Haven, 1963. Nearing completion in 16 vols, edited by many hands; a modernized selection to be in 7 vols.

Utopia, ed. J. H. Lupton, Oxford, 1895. Contains both the 1518 Latin and Ralph Robinson's English translation, 1551.

Four Last Things, ed. D. O'Connor, 1935.

Apology, ed. A. I. Taft, London, 1930 [EETS].

Dialogue of Comfort, ed. M. Stevens, London, 1951.

Treatise Upon the Passion, ed. P. E. Hallett, London, 1941.

English Prayers, and Treatise on the Holy Eucharist, ed. P. E. Hallett, London, 1938.

Correspondence, ed. E. F. Rogers, Princeton, 1947.

J. Delcourt, *Essai sur la langue de Sir Thomas More*, paris, 1914.

R. W. Chambers, *Thomas More*, London, 1935.

J. H. Hexter, *More's Utopia: The Biography of an Idea*, Princeton, 1952.

E. E. Reynolds, *Thomas More and Erasmus*, New York, 1965.

William Tyndale

Whole Works, London, 1572. The only complete edition.

Doctrinal Treatises, ed. H. Walter, London, 1848 [Parker Society].

Expositions and Notes on Scripture, ed. H. Walter, London, 1849 [Parker Society].

The Works of William Tyndale (Selection), ed. S. L. Greenslade, London, 1938. Includes an essay on 'Tyndale and the English Language' by G. D. Bone.

J. F. Mozley, *William Tyndale*, London, 1937.

The English Bible

The English Hexapla, London, 1841. Prints the Greek NT and the Wycliffe, Tyndale, Cranmer, Geneva, Rheims and AV versions.

A. W. Pollard, *Records of the English Bible*, London, 1911.
F. F. Bruce, *The English Bible*, London, 1961.

Sir Thomas Elyot

*The Book Named The Governor, ed. S. E. Lehmberg, London, 1962 [Everyman's Library].
Of the Knowledge which Maketh a Wise Man, ed. E. J. Howard, Oxford, Ohio, 1946.
Four Political Treatises, ed. L. Gottesman, Gainesville, 1967.
The Castle of Health, ed. S. A. Tannenbaum, New York, 1937. Facsimile of the 1541 edition.
S. E. Lehmberg, *Sir Thomas Elyot Tudor Humanist*, Austin, Texas, 1960.
P. Hogrefe, *The Life and Times of Sir Thomas Elyot*, Ames, Iowa, 1967.

Roger Ascham

*English Works, ed. W. A. Wright, Cambridge, 1904.
The Schoolmaster, ed. L. V. Ryan, Ithaca, New York, 1967.
L. V. Ryan, *Roger Ascham*, Stanford, 1963.

Hugh Latimer

*Latimer's Sermons, ed. G. E. Corrie, London, 1844 [Parker Society].
*Sermons and Remains, ed. G. E. Corrie, London, 1845 [Parker Society].
H. S. Darby, *Hugh Latimer*, London, 1953.
A. G. Chester, *Hugh Latimer, Apostle to the English*, Philadelphia, 1954.

13 (ii) *Elizabethan Prose*

Translators

William Adlington, *The Golden Ass of Apuleius*, ed. C. Whibley, London, 1895 [Tudor Translations].

Angel Day, *Daphnis and Chloe*, ed. J. Jacobs, London, 1890.

Geoffrey Fenton, *Tragical Discourses*, ed. R. L. Douglas, London, 1898 [Tudor Translations].

*Sir Thomas Hoby, *The Courtier*, ed. D. Henderson, London, 1948 [Everyman's Library].

(F. O. Matthiessen, *Translation: An Elizabethan Art*, Cambridge, Mass., 1931, includes a chapter on Hoby.)

William Painter, *Palace of Pleasure*, ed. J. Jacobs, London, 1890.

George Pettie, *Petite Palace*, ed. I. Gollancz, London, 1908.

David Rouland, *Lazarillo de Tormes*, ed. J. E. V. Crofts, Oxford, 1924 [Percy Reprints].

Laurence Twine, *Pattern of Painful Adventures*, ed. J. P. Collier, London, 1875.

Thomas Underdown, *An Aethiopian History*, ed. C. Whibley, London, 1895 [Tudor Translations].

Sir Thomas Urquhart, *Gargantua and Pantagruel*, ed. C. Whibley, London, 1900 [Tudor Translations].

Bartholomew Young, *Montemayor's Diana*, ed. J. M. Kennedy, Oxford, 1968.

Fiction-writers and pamphleteers

John Awdeley, *Fraternity of Vagabonds*, eds E. Viles and F. J. Furnivall, London,1869 [EETS].

*Nicholas Breton, *Works in Verse and Prose*, ed., A. B. Grosart, London, 1879 [Chertsey Worthies' Library]. Reissued, New York, 1966.

Henry Chettle, *Piers Plainness*, ed. J. Winny, Cambridge, 1957.

*Thomas Dekker, *Non-Dramatic Works*, ed. A. B. Grosart, London, 1884. Reissued, New York, 1963.

Plague Pamphlets, ed. F. P. Wilson, Oxford, 1925.

K. L. Gregg, *Thomas Dekker: A Study in Economic and Social Backgrounds*, Seattle, 1924.

M. L. Hunt, *Thomas Dekker: A Study*, New York, 1911.

M. T. Jones-Davies, *Un peintre de la vie Londinienne. Thomas Dekker*, Paris, 1958.

*Thomas Deloney, *Novels*, ed. M. E. Lawlis, Bloomington, Indiana, 1961.

M. E. Lawlis, *Apology for the Middle Class. The Dramatic Novels of Thomas Deloney*, Bloomington, Indiana, 1960.

*George Gascoigne, *Complete Works*, ed. J. W. Cunliffe, Cambridge, 1907.

C. T. Prouty, *George Gascoigne: Elizabethan Courtier, Soldier, and Poet*, New York, 1942.

*Stephen Gosson, *School of Abuse and Apology*, ed. E. Arber, London, 1868.

W. Ringler, *Stephen Gosson*, Princeton, 1942.

A. F. Kinney, *Markets of Bawdrie: The Dramatic Criticism of Stephen Gosson*, Salzburg, 1974.

John Grange, *Golden Aphroditis*, (facs. of the 1577 edn), New York, 1936 [Scholars' Facsimiles and Reprints].

*Robert Greene, *Complete Works*, ed. A. B. Grosart, London, 1881-6 [Huth Library].

R. Pruvost, *Robert Greene et Ses Romans*, Paris, 1938.

Thomas Harman, *Caveat for Common Cursetours*, ed. E. Viles and F. J. Furnivall, London, 1868 [EETS].

*Thomas Lodge, *Complete Prose Works*, ed. Sir E. Gosse, Glasgow, 1883 [Hunterian Club]. Reissued, New York, 1963.

E. A. Tenney, *Thomas Lodge*, Ithaca, New York, 1935.

*John Lyly, *Euphues and his England*, ed. M. W. Croll and H. Clemons, London, 1916.

G. K. Hunter, *John Lyly: The Humanist as Courtier*, London, 1962.

*Thomas Middleton, *Works*, ed. A. H. Bullen, London, 1885.

Anthony Munday, *English Roman Life*, ed. G. B. Harrison, London, 1925 [Bodley Head Quartos].

—— *Zelauto*, ed. J. Stillinger, Carbondale, 1963.

C. Turner, *Anthony Mundy*, Berkeley, 1928.

*Thomas Nashe, *Works*, ed. R. B. McKerrow, with corrections and supplementary notes by F. P. Wilson, Oxford, 1966.

G. R. Hibbard, *Thomas Nashe: A Critical Introduction*, London, 1962.

N. P. P. Rhodes, *Elizabethan Grotesque*, London, 1980.

Barnaby Rich, *Farewell to Military Profession* [Reprint], London, 1846, [Shakespeare Society].

*Philip Stubbes, *Anatomy of Abuses* and *Crystal Glass*, ed. F. J. Furnivall, London, 1877-82 [New Shakespeare Society].

Controversialists

*Richard Hooker, *Of the Laws of Ecclesiastical Polity*, ed. J. Keble, revised R. W. Church and F. Paget, Oxford, 1888.

P. Munz, *The Place of Hooker in the History of Though*, London, 1952.

C. J. Sisson, *The Judicious Marriage of Mr Hooker*, Cambridge, 1940.

*'Martin Marprelate', *The Marprelate Tracts*, ed. W. Pierce, London, 1911.

W. Pierce, *A Historical Introduction to the Marprelate Tracts*, London, 1908.

D. J. McGinn, *John Penry and the Marprelate Controversy*, New Brunswick, 1966.

L. H. Carlson, *Martin Marprelate. Gentleman. Master Job Throckmorton Laid Open in His Colors*, San Marino, 1981.

General

H. B. Lathrop, *Translations from the Classics into English from Caxton to Chapman*, New York, 1967.

M. Schlauch, *Antecedents of the English Novel, 1400–1600*, Warsaw, 1963.

S. L. Wolff, *The Greek Romances in Elizabethan Prose Fiction*, New York, 1912.

13 (iii) *Seventeenth-Century Prose*

Character-writers

Joseph Hall, *Heaven Upon Earth and Characters of Virtues and Vices*, ed. R. Kirk, New Brunswick, New Jersey, 1948.
  Richard A. McCabe, *Joseph Hall: A Study in Satire and Meditation*, Oxford, 1982.
The Overburian Characters, ed. W. J. Paylor, Oxford, 1936 [Percy Reprints].
*John Earle, *Microcosmography*, ed. S. T. Irwin, Bristol, 1897. A reprint with preface and supplementary appendix of P. Bliss's edition 1811.
Characters from the Histories and Memoirs of the Seventeenth Century, ed. D. Nichol Smith, Oxford, 1918.
B. Boyce, *The Theophrastan Character in England*, Cambridge, Mass., 1947.

Francis Bacon

Works, ed. J. Spedding, R. L. Ellis and D. D. Heath, London, 1857–9.
The Advancement of Learning and New Atlantis, ed. Arthur Johnston, Oxford, 1974.
L. C. Knights, 'Bacon and the Seventeenth-Century Dissociation of Sensibility', *Explorations*, London, 1946.
Brian Vickers, *Francis Bacon and Renaissance Prose*, Cambridge, 1968.

Lancelot Andrewes

Sermons, ed. J. P. Wilson, London, 1841–3.
Sermons, selected and edited with an Introduction by G. M. Story, Oxford, 1967.
T. S. Eliot, 'Lancelot Andrewes', *Selected Essays*, London, 1951.

John Donne

Biathanatos, reproduced from the First Edition with a Bibliographical note by J. W. Hebel, New York, 1930.
Paradoxes and Problems, ed. Helen Peters, Oxford, 1980.
Ignatius His Conclave, reproduced in facsimile from the edition of 1611 with an Introduction by C. M. Coffin, New York, 1941.

Ignatius His Conclave, ed. Timothy Healy, Oxford, 1969.
Selected prose, eds Evelyn Simpson, Helen Gardner, and Timothy Healy, Oxford, 1967.
Essays in Divinity, ed. E. M. Simpson, Oxford, 1952.
Devotions upon Emergent Occasions, ed. E. Savage, 2 vols, Salzburg, 1975.
Sermons, ed. G. R. Potter and E. M. Simpson, Berkeley, 10 vols, 1953–62.
E. M. Simpson, *A Study of Prose Works of John Donne*, Oxford, 1948.
Joan Webber, *Contrary Music: The Prose Style of John Donne*, Madison, Wisconsin, 1963.
J. Carey, *John Donne: Life, Mind and Art*, London, 1981.

Robert Burton

The Antaomy of Melancholy, ed. H. Jackson, London, 1932 [Everyman's Library].
B. Evans and G. J. Mohr, *The Psychiatry of Robert Burton*, New York, 1944.
W. R. Mueller, *The Anatomy of Robert Burton's England*, Berkeley, 1952.
J. R. Simon, *Robert Burton et L'Anatomie de la Melancholie*, Paris, 1964.
R. A. Fox, *The Tangled Chain: The Structure of Disorder in the Anatomy of Melancholy*, Berkeley, 1976.

Sir Thomas Brown

Works, ed. G. Keynes, London, 1928–31.
Religio Medici and Other Works, ed. L. C. Martin, Oxford, 1964. Contains *Hydriotaphia, Garden of Cyrus, Letters to a Friend*, and *Christian Morals*.
Pseudodoxia Epidemica, ed. Robin Robbins, 2 vols, Oxford, 1981.
Joan Bennett, *Sir Thomas Browne*, Cambridge, 1962.
F. L. Huntley, *Sir Thomas Browne: A Biographical and Critical Study*, Ann Arbor, Michigan, 1962.

Izaak Walton

Lives, ed. G. Saintsbury, Oxford, 1927 [World's Classics]. The 1678 text of the *Life of Sanderson* and the 1675 text of the other four *Lives*.
Complete Angler, ed. M. Bottrall, London, 1962 [Evryman's Library]. The text of the fifth edition, 1676.

The Complete Angler, ed. Jonquil Bevan, Oxford, 1983.
D. Novarr, *The Making of Walton's 'Lives'*, Ithaca, New York, 1958.

John Milton

*Conplete Prose Works, eds D. Bush *et al.*, New Haven, 1953–82.

Thomas Sprat

*History of the Royal Society, eds J. I. Cope and H. W. Jones, London, 1959.

Thomas Hobbes

*English Works, ed. W. Molesworth, London, 1839.
Leviathan, ed. A. D. Lindsay, London, 1914 [Everyman's Library].
J. Laird, *Hobbes*, London, 1934.
R. Peters, *Hobbes*, London, 1956.

John Dryden

*Of Dramatic Poesy and Other Critical Essays, ed. G. Watson, London, 1962 [Everyman's Library].

General

George Williamson, *The Senecan Amble. A Study in Prose Form from Bacon to Collier*, London, 1951.
Style, Rhetoric, and Rhythm. Essays by Morris W. Croll, eds J. Max Patrick *et al*, Princeton, 1966.
J. Webber, *The Eloquent I. Style and Self in 17th-Century Prose*, Madison, 1968.
S. E. Fish, *Self-Consuming Artifacts*, Berkeley, 1972.

TABLE OF DATES

[Titles are modernized]

1503	Sir Thomas Wyatt b. (?).
1509	Accession of Henry VIII.
	Erasmus, *Moriae Encomium* [*The Praise of Folly*].
1516	Sir Thomas More, *Utopia* (Latin; English translation, 1551).
1517	Henry Howard, Earl of Surrey b.
1520	William Dunbar d. (?).
1523	John Skelton, *Goodly Garland or Chaplet of Laurel*.
1529	Skelton d.
1531	Sir Thomas Elyot, *The Governor*.
1533	Ariosto d.
	Montaigne b.
	More, *Apology*.
1535	More executed.
1536	Erasmus d. William Tyndale burnt.
1539	The Great Bible.
1542	Wyatt d.
1547	Henry VIII d. Accession of Edward VI.
	Earl of Surrey executed.
	Cervantes b.
1549	The Book of Common Prayer, largely the work of Cranmer.
1552	Sir Walter Ralegh b. Edmund Spenser b. (?).
1553	Edward VI d. Accession of Queen Mary.
	Rabelais d.
	Gavin Douglas (d. 1522), translation of *Aeneid* (written *c.* 1513).
1554	Sir Fulke Greville b. Richard Hooker b. Sir Philip Sidney b.
1555	Latimer and Ridley burnt.
1556	Cranmer burnt.
1557	Richard Tottel and Nicholas Grimold (eds.), *Songs and Sonnets* (*Tottel's Miscellany*, which included Wyatt and Surrey).
1558	Queen Mary d. Accession of Elizabeth I.
	Thomas Lodge b. (?).
1559	George Chapman b. (?).
	William Baldwin (ed.), *A Mirror for Magistrates*.

1561	Sir Francis Bacon b.
	Thomas Norton and Thomas Sackville, *Gorboduc*, acted at the Inner Temple.
	Sir Thomas Hoby, *The Courtier* (translation of Castiglione's *Il Cortegiano*).
1562	Samuel Daniel b.
1563	Michael Drayton b.
1564	Calvin d. Michelangelo d.
	Galileo b. Christopher Marlowe b. William Shakespeare b.
1565	Arthur Golding, translation of Ovid's *Metamorphoses* I–IV.
1567	Thomas Campion b. Thomas Nashe b.
1570	Roger Ascham, *The Schoolmaster*.
1572	Thomas Dekker b. (?). John Donne b. Ben Jonson b.
1575	Tasso, *Gerusalemme Liberata*.
1576	The Theater built, the first in London.
1577	Robert Burton b.
1579	Sir Thomas North, translation of *Plutarch's Lives;* Spenser, *The Shepherd's Calendar*.
1580	Montaigne, *Essais* I–II.
1582	Richard Hakluyt, *Diverse Voyages*.
1586	Sidney d.
1587	Mary, Queen of Scots executed.
	Marlowe, *Tamburlaine the Great* acted.
1588	The Spanish Armada defeated.
	Thomas Hobbes b.
1589	Lodge, *Scilla's Metamorphosis*; George Puttenham, *The Art of English Poesy*.
1590	Sidney (d. 1586), *The Countess of Pembroke's Arcadia*; Spenser, *The Faerie Queene* I–III.
1591	Robert Herrick b.
	Sir John Harington, translation of Ariosto's *Orlando Furioso*; Sidney (d. 1586), *Astrophel and Stella*.
1592	Daniel, *Delia*; Nashe, *Piers Penniless*; Joshua Sylvester, translation of *La Semaine* of Du Bartas.
1593	Marlowe d.
	George Herbert b. Izaak Walton b.
	Drayton, *Idea*; Shakespeare, *Venus and Adonis*.
1594	Thomas Carew b. (?).
	Drayton, *Idea's Mirror*; Hooker, *Of the Laws of Ecclesiastical Polity* I–IV; Nashe, *The Unfortunate Traveller*; Shakespeare, *The Rape of Lucrece*.

1595 Sidney (d. 1586), *Apology for Poetry* [*Defence of Poesy*]; Spenser, *Amoretti, Epithalamion,* and *Colin Clout's Come Home Again.*

1596 George Peele d.
Descartes b.
Spenser, *Prothalamion, Four Hymns,* and *The Faerie Queene* IV–VI, with a revision of I–III.

1597 Bacon, *Essays;* John Dowland, *First Book of Songs;* Shakespeare, *Richard II, Romeo and Juliet.*

1598 Chapman, first part of his translation of the *Iliad;* Marlowe (d. 1593), *Hero and Leander,* completed by Chapman; Shakespeare, *Henry IV, Part I.*

1599 Spenser d.
Oliver Cromwell b.

1600 Hooker d.
John Bodenham (ed.), *England's Helicon;* Dekker, *The Shoemakers' Holiday;* Edward Fairfax, *Jerusalem Delivered,* translation of Tasso; Jonson, *Every Man out of His Humour.*

1601 Nashe d.
Robert Chester (ed.), *Love's Martyr,* including Shakespeare's *The Phoenix and the Turtle;* Shakespeare, *Twelfth Night* acted.

1602 Campion, *Observations in the Art of English Poesy.*

1603 Elizabeth I d. Accession of James I (James VI of Scotland).
Daniel, *Defence of Rhyme;* John Florio, translation of Montaigne's *Essays;* Shakespeare, *Hamlet.*

1604 Marlowe (d. 1593), *Dr Faustus;* Shakespeare, *Othello* acted.

1605 The Gunpowder Plot.
Sir Thomas Browne b.
Bacon, *Advancement of Learning;* Drayton, *Poems;* Jonson, *Sejanus.*

1606 Corneille b. Edmund Waller b.

1607 Chapman, *Bussy D'Ambois;* Jonson, *Volpone.*

1608 Thomas Fuller b. John Milton b.
Joseph Hall, *Characters;* Shakespeare, *King Lear.*

1609 Edward Hyde, Earl of Clarendon b. Sir John Suckling b.
Shakespeare, *Sonnets.*

1610 Campion, *Two Books of Airs;* Shakespeare, *The Tempest, Cymbeline, The Winter's Tale* acted *c.* 1610.

1611   The Authorized Version of the Bible; Donne, *Anatomy of the World*.

1612   Samuel Butler b. Richard Crashaw b. (?).
Jonson, *The Alchemist*; Webster, *The White Devil*.

1613   Jeremy Taylor b.
Francis Beaumont and John Fletcher, *The Knight of the Burning Pestle*.

1614   Ralegh, *History of the World*.

1615   Sir John Denham b.

1616   Cervantes d. Beaumont d. Shakespeare d.
Jonson, the First Folio of his *Works*.

1617   Campion, *Third and Fourth Books of Airs*.

1618   Start of the Thirty Years War.
Ralegh executed.
Abraham Cowley b. Richard Lovelace b.

1619   Daniel d.

1620   The Pilgrim Fathers to America in the *Mayflower*.
Campion d.
Bacon, *Instauratio Magna*.

1621   La Fontaine b. Andrew Marvell b.
Burton, *Anatomy of Melancholy* (subsequently much revised).

1622   Molière b. Henry Vaughan b.

1623   Pascal b.
Shakespeare, the First Folio of his *Works*; Webster, *The Duchess of Malfi* (acted 1613?).

1625   James I d. Accession of Charles I.

1626   Bacon d.
John Aubrey b.
Donne, *Five Sermons*.

1628   Greville murdered.
John Bunyan b.
John Earle, *Microcosmography*.

1631   Donne d. Drayton d.
John Dryden b.

1632   Dekker d.
John Locke b. Spinoza b. Sir Christopher Wren b.

1633   Herbert d.
Samuel Pepys b.
Cowley, *Poetical Blossoms*; Donne (d. 1631), *Poems*; Herbert, *The Temple*.

1634   Chapman d.

1635   Founding of the Académie Française.
Francis Quarles, *Emblems*.

1636   Boileau b.
Corneille, *Le Cid*.

1637   Jonson d.
Thomas Traherne b.
Milton, *A Mask (Comus)*, which had been acted 1634.

1638   Milton, *Lycidas*.

1639   Racine b.

1640   Burton d. Carew d.
William Wycherley b. (?).
Carew, *Poems*; Walton, *Life of Donne*.

1642   Civil War.
Galileo d. Suckling d.
Isaac Newton b.
Denham, *Cooper's Hill*; Milton, *The Reason of Church-Government*.

1643   Browne, *Religio Medici* (first authorized ed.).

1644   Milton, *Areopagitica*.

1645   Milton, *Poems*; Waller, *Poems*.

1646   Virtual end of Civil War.
Browne, *Pseudodoxia Epidemica (Vulgar Errors)*; Crashaw, *Steps to the Temple*; Vaughan, *Poems*.

1647   John Wilmot, Earl of Rochester b.
Cowley, *The Mistress*.

1648   Second Civil War.
Herrick, *Hesperides* and *Noble Numbers*.

1649   Charles I executed. Commonwealth.
Crashaw d.
Dryden, *Upon the Death of the Lord Hastings*; Lovelace, *Lucasta*.

1650   Descartes d.
Anne Bradstreet, *The Tenth Muse, Lately Sprung up in America*; Vaughan, *Silex Scintillans*.

1651   Hobbes, *Leviathan*.

1653   Cromwell made Protector.
John Oldham b.
Sir Thomas Urquhart, translation of Rabelais I–II; Walton, *The Complete Angler*.

1655   Marvell, *The First Anniversary of the Government under O.C.*

1656   Cowley, *Davideis*.

1657	Lovelace d. (?).
	Henry King, *Poems*.
1658	Cromwell d.
	Browne, *Hydriotaphia: Urn Burial*.
1660	Parliament recalls Charles II: the Restoration. The Royal Society established.
	Daniel Defoe b.
	Dryden, *Astraea Redux*.
1662	Pascal d.
	Butler, *Hudibras*, Part I (II, 1663; III, 1677); Fuller, *Worthies of England*.
1664	Matthew Prior b. Sir John Vanbrugh b.
1665	The Great Plague.
	La Rochefoucauld, *Maximes*; Marvell, *The Character of Holland*.
1666	Fire of London.
	Boileau, *Satires*; Molière, *Le Misanthrope*.
1667	Cowley d.
	Jonathan Swift b.
	Dryden, *Annus Mirabilis*; Milton, *Paradise Lost*; Molière, *Tartuffe*; Racine, *Andromaque*.
1668	Dryden Poet Laureate.
	Denham, *Poems*; La Fontaine, *Fables* I.
1669	Denham d.
1670	William Congreve b.
	Pascal, *Pensées*; Walton, *Life of Herbert*.
1671	Milton, *Paradise Regained* and *Samson Agonistes*.
1672	Joseph Addison b. Richard Steele b.
1673	Molière d.
	Milton, *Poems* (enlarging the 1645 volume).
1674	Herrick d. Milton d. Traherne d.
	Milton, *Paradise Lost* (second ed.).
1676	Dryden, *Aurengzebe*; Sir George Etherege, *The Man of Mode*.
1677	Racine, *Phèdre*.
1678	The Popish Plot.
	Marvell d.
	Bunyan, *The Pilgrim's Progress* I; Dryden, *All for Love*.
1680	Butler d. Rochester d.
	Rochester, *Poems*.
1681	Dryden, *Absalom and Achitophel*; Marvell (d. 1678), *Poems*; Oldham, *Satires upon the Jesuits*.

1682	Browne d.
	Dryden, *MacFlecknoe*.
1683	Oldham d.
1685	Charles I d. Accession of James II.
1687	Waller d.
1688	James II fled the country.
	Bunyan d.
	Alexander Pope b.
1689	Accession of William III and Mary II.
1690	Locke, *Essay Concerning Human Understanding*.
1694	Mary II d. William reigns alone.
	Voltaire b.
	Congreve, *The Double Dealer*.
1695	Vaughan d.
1697	Vanbrugh, *The Relapse*.
1700	Dryden d.

INDEX